C000182813

EUROPEAN WRECKS & RELICS

Compiled by Mike Bursell

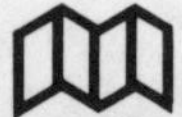

MIDLAND COUNTIES PUBLICATIONS

ISBN 0 904597 76 8

Published by
Midland Counties Publications (Aerophile) Limited
24 The Hollow, Earl Shilton, Leicester, LE9 7NA

Printed in England
by BL & U Printing Limited

Contents

Front cover photograph:
F-84F Thunderstreak 28879 (IRAN No.551) was installed on a plinth at Metz/Frescaty on 11.9 78 painted as "9-AU" in the colours of EC.1/9 'Limousin' 2.6.85, *Mike Bursell.*

Back cover photographs:
Tipsy S2 OO-TIP at the Brussels Museum. *Chris Michell*
Ex TAP L1049G Super Constellation "5T-TAF" (c/n 4618) has spent the last 15 years as a bar/restaurant at Safi, Malta, 8.88, *J. P. Newton.*

Introduction

Several years ago a certain Ken Ellis suggested to Dave Allport and myself (then jointly editing 'Humberside Air Review') that a need existed for a European version of the popular "Wrecks and Relics" and perhaps we might like to write it? Having some perception of the considerable work involved in such a task, we laughed off the suggestion and quickly changed the subject. This tactic worked very well for some time until one fateful day when I ordered a book from Midland Counties Publications. The book duly arrived, accompanied by a silver-tongued letter dated 25th October '86 once again floating the idea of a European version of "W&R". Perhaps I was caught in a weak moment but in any event the result, at long last, is the book you have before you. Looking back in the file it is amusing (to me anyway!) to see that a publication date of May '87 was suggested at the time!

This being the first edition of 'European Wrecks and Relics' a few introductory comments are in order. Firstly, some readers of this volume may wonder why a book purporting to cover European W&R omits the UK and Eire. The answer has already been hinted at in the first paragraph. This volume is intended to complement the original and long-standing 'Wrecks and Relics' (covering the UK and Eire) which has so far run to eleven volumes and has a well earned place as the standard bi-annual reference work on the subject. The other geographical omission is Eastern Europe, the reason here being that the museums of the European Communist countries are already well covered in Bob Ogden's 'European Aviation Museums' and outside of the museums there is precious little information available on the W&R scene in this part of the world. That little which is known has by and large already appeared in print in the enthusiast magazines. If however there is a sufficient influx of new information from readers of this volume then this omission may well be rectified in a subsequent edition.

'Why no maps?' the reader may enquire. The reason is that to be of much use as a navigational aid this book would need to be at least half as big again to accommodate the maps. It is felt that the book is already sufficiently weighty and expensive and instead directions, where available, have been included to the lesser known locations where a particular relic is still in residence. I have not attempted to give directions to large towns and aerodromes for which references are readily available elsewhere. Where directions are given they are intended to give the reader an idea of where to look on the map, rather than to provide comprehensive instructions on how to get there. There are many suitable maps on the market for potential 'tourists' and the compiler has found the Michelin series of particular help over the years. They do at least try to mark all the airfields!

Within each country the locations have been arranged in alphabetical order. This may not be the best arrangement for those of you visiting one particular region of a large country, but faced with different systems of geographical sub-division in each country this system seemed to be the best compromise. It does at least make it easier to refer to a particular location within the book. Your comments on the subject would be be welcome, for instance would you prefer to see France split into Departements?

The original 'Wrecks and Relics' follows the pattern of listing the current situation together with notes on those changes which have taken place since the previous edition. Due to the fact that this is the first 'Euro-Wrecks', I have obviously had to adopt a different format. You will find greater emphasis in this volume on aircraft which may no longer be extant. The purpose behind this is twofold. Firstly to point out those items which have recently departed in order to pre-empt a stream of letters advising me of relics which you have heard of and believe to have been erroneously omitted. Secondly, to bring to your attention relics which may still be extant despite not having been reported for some years. Bear in mind that some of the aircraft mentioned in this book are in particularly inaccessible spots and visits by wandering enthusiasts may be infrequent to say the least.

For this first edition, the criteria for inclusion have had to be varied between different countries. This takes account of variations in earlier coverage ranging from Holland and France with much previously published 'W&R' material whilst at the other end of the spectrum some countries have never (to my knowledge) been tackled at all. I have, broadly speaking, taken 1980 as a start date for coverage of this volume but have tried to avoid regurgitating all the previously published works on the subject. Considerations of available space also have to be borne in mind, so in the case of France for example you will find relatively little pre-1985 information. I trust you will find the balance about right. The reader seeking further, more dated, information on a particular country will find several excellent sources mentioned in the Acknowledgements and in the Introductions to individual countries.

Some comments with regard to the photographic coverage are appropriate. I have, with thanks to the numerous contributors for their suberb efforts, attempted to compile an interesting and varied photo section and I trust you will find the result interesting and informative. However, remember that photography of military and in some cases civil aircraft is frowned upon in some of the countries covered and access to some locations can be difficult. I would have liked to include some shots of Greek F-102 decoys, or range targets at Las Bardenas and Cazaux, but despite several enquiries these were not forthcoming (any offers?). By definition 'W&R' aeroplanes are often not in pristine condition and do not make a particularly photogenic subject but bear in mind that some pictures are included to illustrate unusual aircraft types or markings, to give a better idea of the location of a subject or just to show how much of it still survives. A picture is worth a thousand words, as they say.

A word of apology to those who are offended by the lack of accents throughout this book. My Word Processor lacks the technology to produce even an 'e' acute let alone the myriad other linguistic variations which I have come across in recent months. These are omitted on the grounds that as well as lacking the technology I am not fluent in all European languages and any attempt to add accents manually would inevitably be less than 100% accurate. Hopefully some of you may not notice the deficiency whilst the more cosmopolitan amongst you will instantly recognise where they should be.

The compiler is always delighted to receive any comments, corrections, updates, photographs or indeed anything which readers may have to contribute towards future editions of this volume. All correspondence via the publishers' address please.

Finally, a word of thanks to my wife Sylvia and daughters Carol and Fiona for their patience and support over the many months of preparation of 'Euro-Wrecks'. Without the 'assistance' of the latter (and incidentally I only had the one daughter when I started all this) no doubt you would have seen the finished product much earlier!

Mike Bursell
Hull, August 1989

Notes

SCOPE

The purpose of this volume is to record as far as possible the status and whereabouts of all aircraft known to be PRESERVED (ie in museum or other collections, under restoration for display etc); INSTRUCTIONAL (ie non-flying airframes in use for training); or DERELICT (ie non-flyable for a long period, fire dump aircraft, scrapped or damaged etc). In all cases the prime criterion for inclusion is that the aircraft no longer flies. The only flying aircraft listed are those which form part of a recognised museum or collection and which are therefore included for completeness. Similarly, gliders are only listed where they form part of a museum or collection. Airships, balloons, missiles and craft which do not provide for a human pilot are not included, but replicas are listed in order to avoid confusion with the real thing. Aircraft which fall into any of the above categories for only a short space of time are also excluded. In general, aircraft are only listed if they constitute at least a major fuselage section, though some sneak in by default as the compiler explains that a particular relic is too small for inclusion! As explained in the Introduction, the geographic scope of this book covers all of Western Europe excluding the UK and Eire.

ENTRIES

Where a particular entry requires a number of aircraft to be listed in tabular form, they are listed in order of manufacturer, though space constraints may dictate that the manufacturer is abbreviated or deleted altogether. Similarly the aircraft's designation may be abbreviated by the exclusion of full stops, hyphens etc for the same reasons. In general, the manufacturers used will be common sense. For instance, the Varsity is regarded as a Vickers product, not BAC or British Aerospace! All F-104 Starfighters are regarded as Lockheed products whether built by Lockheed, Canadair, Fiat, Fokker, Messerschmitt or whoever. Aircraft which were produced under another name by a company other than the original manufacturer are listed under the new manufacturer but with the original designation bracketed. For instance CASA built Junkers Ju 52s are listed as CASA 352L (Ju 52). Where possible, an aircraft will be identified by the markings actually worn whether they are correct (eg A123) or spurious (eg "A123"). Where appropriate and available, a permanent identity such as the constructor's number (c/n) or US serial will appear in the 'remarks' column with any subsequent identities being listed chronologically from left to right after the permanent identity. Abbreviations have been kept to a minimum but a decode is included in case any prove unfamiliar to the reader.

In a work of this type it is obviously of value to have an indication of the timeframe during which a particular relic has been in situ. With this in mind, where appropriate, an indication has been given of the dates between which a particular aircraft has been seen at a given location. These dates should not be taken as arrival and departure dates but reflect only the dates available to the compiler within which an aircraft has been confirmed. So an aircraft listed as "(noted '84-'87)" may well have been there from '79-'88 but I only have confirmation of the period shown. Some aircraft may for example be listed as "soc 30.1.78 (noted '88)" in which case it may be expected that the relic has been in situ some ten years but it is left to the reader to make that assumption. Some entries were last noted some years ago but may well still be current, it just needs someone to go and see!

LOCATIONS

Where possible brief directions are included to enable the reader to find a particular location on the map. Unless stated otherwise these directions are to the town or village mentioned and not necessarily to the actual location of the aircraft in question. Directions are not given where such information is not available to the compiler, where the location is a city, town or airfield.

ACCESS

Unless stated otherwise all locations listed are PRIVATE and access to them is strictly by prior permission only, if at all.

WARNING

In some of the countries covered by this book, photography, note taking and even just looking at civil or military aircraft may be frowned upon by the authorities. Readers are reminded of the advice contained in the official booklet 'Essential Information for British Passport Holders'; 'Hobbies like aircraft, train or ship spotting, and even bird watching, are liable to misinterpretation and may lead to your being arrested for spying in some countries abroad. If in doubt you should enquire from the local authorities or a British consular officer.'

Acknowledgements

This book would not have been possible without the assistance of many people. The compiler would like to express his sincere thanks for the contributions made by those listed below. Thanks are also due to those whose anonymous individuals whose assistance goes unrecorded, their snippets of information being passed on to the compiler over the years at numerous airfields and air displays, in the bar of a P&O ferry on a Summer night or via third parties. My apologies go to anyone whose name has been lost in the mass of papers which have deluged the editorial abode during the preparation of this book, your efforts are much appreciated.

Dave Allport, Michael Andersen, Darren Berry, Rod Burden, David Caris, Enrique Cortez, Steve Coulson, Dave Currie, John D Davis, Ken Ellis, Joe Evans, Mike Everton, Eric Gandet, Wal Gandy, John Grech, Mark Hall, Pete Hay, Dr Gottfried Holzschuh, Paul Jackson, Otger v/d Kooij, Stewart Lanham, Dave Lee, Barry Lewis, Neil Lewis, Rob MacNeil, Frank McMeiken, Chris Michell, Sid Nanson, John Newton, Jean Charles Oge, Lars Olausson, Bjorn Olsen, TW Owen, John Parish, Jeremy Parkin, Dave Peel, Per Thorup Pedersen, Patrick Vinot Prefontaine, Mark Reed, Eino Ritaranta, Lloyd P Robinson, Chris Salter, Jose Luis Gonzalez Serrano, Robbie Shaw, Ian D Smith, Peter Spooner, Phil Stevens, Roy Sturges, Andy Thompson, Colin Walford, Alan Warnes, Dave Weinrich, John Wegg, Peter George Wild, Dave Wilton, Andrew Yarwood.

Acknowledgement is also due to the following publications, both amateur and professional, whose pages have been perused for items of "Wrecks and Relics" news.
'Air' (West London Aviation Group), 'Air Fan' (French monthly magazine), 'Ali Antiche' (published by the Italian preservation group GAVS), 'British Aviation Review' (British Aviation Research Group), 'Flypast' (Key Publishing), 'Hawkeye' (Gatwick Aviation Society), 'Humberside Air Review' (Humberside Aviation Society), 'Scramble' (Aviation Society of the Netherlands), 'Strobe' (East of England Aviation Group), 'Trait d'Union' (Branche Francaise d'Air Britain).

Many other reference sources have been dipped into over the months of preparation of this book. Readers are referred to the following which have been of particular help.

Air Britain Civil Aircraft Registers (various).
Belgian Civil Register 88-89, Aviation Society of Antwerp 1988
Belgian Military Aviation, Paul A Jackson, MCP 1977
Civil Aircraft Registers of Europe, LAAS International 1987
DC-4, John & Maureen Woods, Airline Publications & Sales 1980
Dornier Do 27, P-M Gerhardt, Air Britain 1987
Douglas DC-6 Parts 1 & 2, Ian MacKintosh, Airline Publications & Sales 1978
Dutch Military Aviation, Paul A Jackson, MCP 1978
Dutch Wrecks and Relics, Wim Zwakhals, Airnieuws Nederland 1984
European Aviation Museums & Collections, Bob Ogden, Key Publishing 1985
French Military Aviation II, Paul A Jackson, MCP 1979
French Military Wrecks and Relics, Mike Bursell, BARG 1986
French Post War Transport Aircraft, J Chillon/J-P Dubois/J Wegg, Air Britain 1980
Guida Agli Aerei Storici Italiani, M Gueli/F D'Amico/R Rovere, Ateneo & Bizzarri 1978
Italian Military Aviation, Frank McMeiken, MCP 1984
KLu/MLD, JH Arends/H Cazemier/K van der Mark, APG/GEAS 1988
Spanish & Portugese Military Aviation, John Andrade, MCP 1977
US Military Designations & Serials since 1909, J Andrade, MCP 1979.
West German Military Aviation, Paul A Jackson, MCP 1976
West German Military Wrecks and Relics, GA Hiltermann, ASN 1983

Abbreviations

Many abbreviations are explained as they appear in the text, the rest are listed here.

A	AAC	Army Air Corps
	AB	Air Base
	AdlA	Armee de l'Air
	ADWC	Air Defense Weapons Center
	AES	Air Engineering School
	AEW&CS	Airborne Early Warning & Control Squadron
	AFB	Air Force Base
	AFS	Antony Fokker School
	AHU	Ana Hava Us
	AISA	Aeronautica Industrial SA
	Akg	Aufklarungsgeschwader
	ALAT	Aviation Legere de l'Armee de Terre
	ALE	Aviazione Leggera dell'Esercito Italiano
	AMD-BA	Avions Marcel Dassault - Breguet Aviation
	AMI	Aeronautica Militare Italiana
	ANG	Air National Guard
	arr	arrived
	AWA	Armstrong Whitworth Aircraft
	AWTI	Air Weapons Training Installation
B	BA	Base Aerea
	BA	Base Aerienne
	BAe	British Aerospace
	BCRE	Bureau Central des Relations Exterieures
	bdr	battle damage repair
	bdrt	battle damage repair training
	BEA	British European Airways
	BelgAF	Belgian Air Force
	Bu	Bureau Number (ie serial allocated by USN Bureau of Aeronautics)
C	CA	California
	CAA	Civil Aviation Authority
	CALE	Centro Aviazione Leggera dell'Esercito
	Cat	Category (accident damage assessment eg Cat.5 = write off)
	CATCS	Central Air Traffic Control School
	CDC	Centre de Detection et de Controle
	CEAM	Centre d'Experiences Aeriennes Militaires
	CELAG	Centre d'Etude et de Loisirs Aerospatieux de Grenoble
	CET	Centre Ecole Technique
	CEV	Centre d'Essais en Vol
	CEVSV	Centre d'Entrainement en Vol Sans Visibilite
	CIEH	Centre d'Instruction des Equipages d'Helicoptere
	CIET	Centre d'Instruction des Equipages de Transport
	CIFAS	Centre d'Instruction des Forces Aeriennes Strategiques
	CMP	Centro Manutenzione Principale
	CMVV	Centro Militare Volo a Vela
	c/n	constructor's number
	CNAF	Chinese Nationalist Air Force
	CofA	Certificate of Airworthiness
D	DCAN	Direction des Constructions et Armes Navales
	DCM	Direction Central du Materiel

D	DFVLR	Deutscher Forschungs und Versuchsanstalt fur Luft und Raumfahrt
	DLA	Defense Logistics Agency
	DVM	Depot Vliegtuig Materieel
E	EB	Escadre de Bombardement/Escadron de Bombardement
	EC	Escadre de Chasse/Escadron de Chasse
	ECM	Electronic Counter Measures
	ECT	Escadre de Chasse et de Transformation/Escadron de Chasse et de Transformation
	ECTT	Escadre de Chasse Tous Temps/Escadron de Chasse Tous Temps
	EdeC	Escadrille de Convoyage
	EdeR	Escadrille de Remorquage
	EE	Escadrille Electronique
	EFIPN	Escadron de Formation Initiale du Personnel Navigant
	EH	Escadre d'Helicopteres/Escadron d'Helicopteres
	ELA	Escadrille de Liason Aeriennes
	ELAS	Escadrille de Liason Aeriennes et le Sauvetage
	EPNER	Ecole du Personnel Navigant d'Essais et de Reception
	ER	Escadre de Reconnaisance/Escadron de Reconnaisance
	ERGM	Etablissement Regionale Generale du Materiel
	ESALAT	Ecole de Specialisation ALAT
	Esc	Escadre, Escadron, Escuadron etc
	Esk	Eskadrille
	Esq	Esquadron
	Est	Erprobungsstelle
	ET	Escadre de Transport/Escadron de Transport
	ET	Escadre de Transformation
	ETE	Escadron de Transport et Entrainement
	ETOM	Escadron de Transport d'Outre Mer
	EVO	Elementaire Vlieg Opleiding
	EVS	Elementaire Vliegschool
F	F	Flygflottilj
	FBS	Flugbereitschaftstaffel
	FC	Forsokscentralen
	FDG	Flugziel Darstellungs Gruppe
	FFS	Flugzeugfuhrerschule
	FHS	Flyvabnets Historiske Samling
	FIS	Fighter Interceptor Squadron
	FLKS	Flyvevabnets Konstabelskole
	FLSK	Flyveskolen
	FLSP	Flyvevabnets Specialskole
	Flt	Flight (organisational)
	FTS	Flying Training School
	FY	Fiscal Year
G	GAM	Groupe Aerien Mixte
	GAVS	Gruppo Amici Velivoli Storici
	GE	Groupement Ecole
	GI	Groupement Instruction
	gia	ground instructional airframe
	GLAM	Groupe des Liaisons Aeriennes Ministerielles
	GmbH	Gesellschaft mit beschrankter Haftung (Company)
	GMT	Groupe de Marche de Tchad
	GSERI	Gruppo Squadroni Elicotteri da Ricognizione
H	HAF	Hellenic AF
	HavLv	Havittajalaivue (fighter squadron)
	HFB	Heeresfliegerbattallion
	HFS	Heeresfliegerstaffeln
	HFVS	Heeresflieger Verbindungsstaffeln
	hrs	hours (ie flying hours)
	HQ	Head Quarters

	Htg	Hubschraubertransportgeschwader
I	IlmaSK	Ilmasotakoulu
	IRAN	Inspect and Repair As Necessary
	ItAF	Italian Air Force
J	Jbg	Jagdbombergeschwader
	Jg	Jagdgeschwader
K	KLu	Koninklijke Luchtmacht (Netherlands Air Force)
	KuljLLv	Kuljetuslaivue (transport squadron)
	KY	Kentucky
L	Lekg	Leichtenkampfgeschwader
	LETS	Luchtmacht Elektronische en Technische School
	l/f	last flown
	LTBS	Luftforsvarets Tekniske Bifols Skole
	Ltg	Lufttransportgeschwader
	LVA	Luchtvaart Afdeling
	LVR	Luftwaffenversorgungsregiment
M	MAS	Military Airlift Squadron
	MASDC	Military Aircraft Storage and Disposition Center (Davis Monthan, AZ - since renamed AMRC Aerospace Maintenance & Regeneration Center)
	Met	Meteorological
	Mfg	Marinefliegergeschwader
	MLD	Marine Luchtvaart Dienst
	MLG	MarinefliegerLehrGruppe
	MLM	Militaire Luchtvaart Museum
	MTU	Moteren-Turbinen-Union
	MU	Maintenance Unit
N	NAF	Naval Air Facility
	NASM	National Air & Space Museum
	NATO	North Atlantic Treaty Organisation
	NBC	Nuclear, Biological & Chemical
	NCO	Non-Commissioned Officer
	NLR	Stichting Nationaal Lucht en Ruimtevaart Laboratorium
	ntu	not taken up
O	OCU	Operational Conversion Unit
	OGMA	Oficinas Gerais de Material Aeronauticao
P	PortAF	Portugese AF
R	RAAF	Royal Australian Air Force
	RAE	Royal Aircraft Establishment
	RAF	Royal Air Force
	RCAF	Royal Canadian Air Force
	RCN	Royal Canadian Navy
	RDAF	Royal Danish Air Force
	RLS	Rijks Luchtvaart School
	RMV	Reparto Manutenzione Velivoli
	RNorAF	Royal Norwegian Air Force
	RRALE	Reparto Riparazione Aviazione Leggera dell'Esercito
	RSV	Reparto Sperimentale Volo
	RSwedAF	Royal Swedish Air Force
	RTA	Reparti Tecnico Aerea
	RVR	Reparto Volo Regionale
S	SAAF	South African Air Force
	SALE	Section Acceuil de Liaison et d'Entrainement
	SAR	Search and Rescue
	SAS	Scandinavian Airlines System
	SC	Squadriglia Collegamenti
	Skv	Skvadron
	SLVSV	Section de Liason et de Vol Sans Visibilite
	SNIAS	Societe Nationale des Industries Aeronautiques et Spatiales (Aerospatiale)

S	soc	Struck Off Charge
	Sqn	Squadron
	Stn Flt	Station Flight
	SVBAA	Scuola Volo Basico Avantato Aviogetti
	SVBAE	Scuola Volo Basico Avantato Elica
	SVBIA	Scuola Volo Basico Iniziale Aviogetti
	SVE	Scuola Volo Elicotteri
T	TAP	Transportes Aereos Portuguese
	TEA	Trans European Airways
	TFS	Tactical Fighter Squadron
	TFW	Tactical Fighter Wing
	TH	Technische Hoogschool
	THK	Turkish Air Force
	TRW	Tactical Reconnaisance Wing
	TsLw	Technischeschule der Luftwaffe
	TT	Total time (ie accumulated flying hours)
	TT	Target Towing
	TU	Technische University
	TVO	Transitie Vlieg Opleiding
	TWU	Tactical Weapons Unit
U	UFO	Uit Faserings Onderdeel
	UK	United Kingdom of Great Britain and Northern Ireland
	UNFIL	United Nations Forces In Lebanon
	USAF	United States Air Force
	USAFE	United States Air Forces Europe
	USAAF	United States Army Air Force
	USAREUR	United Staes Army in Europe
	USCG	United States Coast Guard
	USN	United States Navy
V	VUD	Vervroegde Uit Diensttrading
	VVO	Voortgezette Vlieg Opleiding
W	WA	Washington, USA
	wfu	Withdrawn from use
	WG	West Germany
	WGAF	West German Air Force
	Wg	Wing (organisational)
	WGN	West German Navy
	w/o	written off
	WS	Waffenschule
	WTD	Wehrtechnische Dienststelle fur Luftfahrzeuge

AUSTRIA

Austria's neutral position between East and West has enabled her post-war Air Force (founded in 1955) to obtain equipment from both sides of the Iron Curtain. This gives the various museums in the country a fascinating variety of ex military hardware which is occasionally supplemented by new exhibits from the Eastern bloc, for example the An-2 presented by Mikhail Gorbachov. Where else can you find preserved aircraft of British, American, Russian, Swedish and Italian origin which were all retired from the same Air Force?

DIETACHDORF

In 1976, a car breaker's yard here held SAAB J 29F Tunnan 29392/I (yellow). It was not heard of again until the wings were seen with Air Classik at Monchengladbach in the early eighties and the complete aircraft subsequently turned up with the museum at Sinsheim, WG. In 7.88 this "barrel" returned to Austria and is now displayed at Vienna airport.

GRAZ/THALERHOF

Preserved on the base (Fliegerhorst Nittner) in 9.84 was SAAB J 29F Tunnan 29588/D (red) whilst 29541/H (yellow) was displayed in a playground in nearby Feldkirchen. The former was still current during 1988 whilst the latter has joined the museum collection here (see below).

On the civil side of the field, the cockpit section of the Militky-Brditschka MB-E1 OE-9023 (c/n 51) was noted in a hangar 8.86. This was the first electrically powered aircraft and crashed on 13.10.77.

The Osterreichisches Luftfahrtmuseum (Austrian Air Museum) had been established on the civil side of the field by 9.84 and was first opened to the public on 28.5.87. Seven gliders are held in store whilst the following are on display.

Antonov An-2	2919	ex Polish AF (noted '84-88).
Cessna F150L	OE-ATP	(c/n 1093) (noted '88).
DH Venom FB.54	J-1733	ex Swiss AF (noted '84-'88).
Klemm L.20	-	part of fuselage (stored '88).
LIM-2 (MiG-15bis)	1B1326	ex Polish AF (noted '84-'88).
Luscombe	-	no further details.
Bf 110G-2	-	substantial wreckage recovered from lake, stored.
SAAB J 29F Tunnan	29541	'H' (yellow) ex Austrian AF & Feldkirchen (noted'88).
SA226TC Metro II	OE-LSA	(c/n TC-315) ex Austrian Air Services, crashed 17.9.84 (wings & fuselage shell stored '88).
TS-11 Iskra	1H0221	ex Polish AF (noted '84-'88).
Yakovlev Yak-11	4C-AH	(c/n 171229) (ex 4A-AH) ex Austrian AF, on loan from Austrian AF, stored.

HUBHOF

At the 'Marchenland' children's amusement park in Hubhof (near Aggsbach-Markt, halfway between Linz and Wien on the A1/E5 motorway) is SAAB J 29F Tunnan 29560/E (yellow) in fair condition (engine & cockpit interior missing) and painted in a white/blue scheme applied by its previous owner in Wiener Neudorf.

LEOPOLDSDORF

The private airfield at Leopoldsdorf-Im-Marchfeld (20 kms SW of Wien) is the base for Land und Forstflug GmbH who operate a fleet of Cubs and Super Cubs for agricultural use. Dumped outside their hangar in 4.88 were the following relics.

PZL-101A Gawron	OE-AFF	(c/n 52076) derelict and wingless.

PA18-150 Super Cub OE-AGI (c/n 18-7609058) derelict, for spares use.
PA18-150 Super Cub OE-BUP (c/n 18-8314) crashed, for spares use.

LINZ/HOERSCHING

During the open day in 9.78 a scrap compound on the base (Fliegerhorst Vogler) was seen to hold the following wrecks.

SAAB 105oe	105-413	'C' (green), crashed at Linz 14.5.77.
SAAB 105oe	105-415	'E' (green), crashed 1.12.76.
SAAB 105oe	105-418	'H' (green), crashed 9.1.77.
SAAB 105oe	105-438	'H' (blue), crashed near Zeltweg 11.10.77.
SAAB J 29F Tunnan	29582	'J' (red)
Cessna L-19A	3A-CV	(c/n 22830, ex 51-16958) also marked OE-CCV.

Preserved on a pole inside the base in 9.78 was SAAB J 29F Tunnan 29447/B (yellow) ex 1 Staffel. The a/c was still current during 1988 (but reported as 29443/M (yellow) 7.88 and confirmed as 'M' (yellow) 8.88!). My best guess at the moment is that both aircraft are preserved here somewhere, further information welcome.

Withdrawn in '82 and noted in long term store here during 1986 were Agusta-Bell AB204Bs 4D-BF (c/n 3072), 4D-BH (c/n 3107), 4D-BM (c/n 3155), 4D-BR (c/n 3190) and 4D-BV (c/n 3201). It is worth recording that the Austrian AF are also believed to have 4D-BA (c/n 3039), 4D-BE (c/n 3066), 4D-BI (c/n 3118), 4D-BJ (c/n 3139), 4D-BN (c/n 3156), 4D-BO (c/n 3157), 4D-BQ (c/n 3189), and 4D-BS (c/n 3191) in long term storage somewhere. They might be in another hangar here, or perhaps elsewhere.

For many years DH Vampire T.55 5C-VF (c/n 15694, ex XH320) has been on display in the town in front of the technical school at Paul Hahn Strasse 4 (noted '76-'88).

On the civil side of the field, the wreck of crashed Beech V35A OE-DFK (c/n D8862) was noted in 8.83.

SPIZERBERG

The Osterreichisches Segelflug Museum (Austrian Glider Museum) has several dismantled gliders in store at this airfield near Deutschaltenburg.

STOCKERAU

The wreck of crashed MS892A Rallye Commodore OE-DPZ (c/n 10468) was noted stored in a hangar here (20 kms North West of Wien) in '87.

TULLN/ LANGENLEBARN

Three DHC-2 Beavers were stored here at Fligerhorst Brumowski after their withdrawal in 1976. Following disposal in a US Defense Logistics Agency sale on 9.11.82. They went Stateside in 2.83 and followed the example of many other ex military Beavers in going civil:-

DHC-2 Beaver	3B-GB	(c/n 1412, ex 58-7020) to N3930B at Kenmore Air Harbor, WA.
DHC-2 Beaver	3B-GC	(c/n 1416, ex 58-7021) to N39302 at Kenmore Air Harbor, WA, not refurbished (also quoted as ex 58-7022).
DHC-2 Beaver	3B-GF	(c/n 1221, ex 57-6569) to N39303 at Kenmore Air Harbor, WA, to Alaska 12.83 (also quoted as ex 57-6525).

Reported here in 5.86 was the fuselage only of L-19E Bird Dog 3A-BF (c/n 23933).

The Technische Schule (Technical School) here holds Bell OH-13H 3B-HD (c/n 2482) as a ground instructional airframe (Noted 5.86).

WIEN (VIENNA)

The Heeresgeschichtliches Museum (Military History Museum) in Vienna possesses a number of aircraft though these are normally in store and not on display. The museum can be found at the Arsenal, Objekt 1, 1030 Wien, in the Eastern suburbs.

Albatros BI	20.01	(c/n 01, prototype) on display '87.
Bell OH-13H	3B-HA	(c/n 2479, w/o 21.2.66) ex Austrian AF, on display '87.
LT-6G Texan	4C-TE	(ex 49-3191) ex Austrian AF, stored '87.

SAAB J 29F Tunnan	29566	'0' (yellow) ex Austrian AF, stored 1971/72 then displayed in front of the museum (current '87).
Yakovlev Yak-11	4C-AF	(c/n 171227, ex 4A-AF) ex Austrian AF, on display '87.
Yakovlev Yak-18	3A-AA	(c/n 10113) ex Austrian AF, stored '87.

The Technisches Museum fur Industrie und Gewerbe (Technical Museum for Arts and Crafts) is to be found at Mariahilfer Strasse 212, A-1140 Wien. On display here are several gliders and the following aeroplanes/helicopters:-

Bell OH-13H	3B-HO	(c/n 2493) ex Austrian AF.
Berg D I	101.37	(license built Aviatik)
Berg Nurflugel	-	(1931 vintage glider with which ski equipped pilot holds on to a wing!).
DH Dove 5	OE-BVM	(c/n 04488)
Etrich Taube II	-	
Fi 156C-3 Storch	D-ENPE	(c/n 110253, ex OE-ADO)
Oberlechner Job 15-150/2	OE-BLF	(c/n 068)
Pischof Autoplan	-	(Gnome engined, f/f 1910)
Wickenhauser Sportflugzeug	-	(built 1935) stored.

WIENER NEUDORF

SAAB J 29F Tunnan 29560/E (yellow) was displayed at the premises of the local Ford agent, Herr P Hinteregger, in a blue and white colour scheme. The aircraft has since moved to an amusement park at Hubhof.

WIENER NEUSTADT OST

In store at this airfield in 4.88 were the following aircraft.

Antonov An-2	CCCP-44998	ex Aeroflot, flown in by Soviet crew 27.10.87 as a gift by Gorbachov to a museum project (open store).
MS894A Minerva	OE-DRY	(c/n 12016) wfu, hangar store with parts missing.
Cessna 172	OE-DBM	(c/n 28638) wfu, hangar store with parts missing.

WIEN/SCHWECHAT (VIENNA AIRPORT)

The German based collection Air Classik display some of their aircraft on the terraces at Vienna Airport. These are now leased by Vienna Airport which will eventually come into ownership of the aircraft.

Sycamore Mk.52	7809	(c/n 13461) ex Htg.64, WGAF (noted '84-'89).
Hunting Pembroke C.54	5427	(c/n 1019) ex WGAF, nose only, ex Stuttgart & Dusseldorf (noted '84-'89).
Nord 1002 Pingouin	"08-12"	(c/n 163 ex HB-AOR, D-EOAR) (noted '84-'89).
T-6G Texan	"Y-34"	(c/n 88-42005, ex ADLA 51-14696/DJ of EALA.19/72 and F-BMJO) (noted '84-'89).
SAAB J 29F Tunnan	29392	ex 'I' (yellow) & Sinsheim, WG (arr 5.7.88, current '89 painted in spurious marks as (yellow) 'H').
Vickers Viking 1A	G-AGRW	(c/n 115) (noted '84-'89).

The Tunnan 29392 returned to Austria from Sinsheim, WG, on 5.7.88 having apparently been exchanged for ex Polish AF Mig-15bis/LIM-2 1B01006 which had found its way to Austria.

The General Aviation area holds Shrike Commander YU-BGA (c/n 1874-47) ex Transadria which has been in store for several years (current 4.88).

On the dump sits Cessna 421B "OE-FWB" (c/n 421B-0650, really OE-FLI ex Austrian Airtransport). This machine crashed as long ago as 22.6.76 and was still current in '87. The spurious registration is derived from the initials of Flughafen Wien Betriebsgesellschaft.

ZELTWEG

Displayed on the base at Fliegerhorst Hinterstoisser is Fiat G-46-4B 3A-BB (c/n 157, ex ItAF MM53397) (noted '76-'88). During 1984, the dump held SAAB J 29F Tunnan 29582/J (red). This machine was previously recorded in a scrap compound at Linz in '78.

BELGIUM

For a small country, Belgium is packed full of W&R material. The military bases received a generous helping of Thunderstreak decoys in the early seventies and the country is littered with light civil wrecks some awaiting rebuild and some beyond hope. There are a few airliner relics of one form or another and at the Musee Royal de l'Armee (better known as the Brussels air museum) one of the finest museum collections in Europe, displayed in the most impressive surroundings. An enlightened preservation policy has seen the museum acquire the remaining Thunderstreak decoys, all the stored H-34s at Koksijde together with some of the F-104s, all of which are available for exchange to enable the national museum to enlarge its coverage of Belgian aviation.

In the absence of any well known reference to provide a starting point, I have for the sake of completeness included some items from the mid to late seventies when Koksijde was still covered with discarded C-119s, the Pembroke fleet was up for disposal and Britannias could still be found derelict at Oostende.

Not mentioned in the text are a Hunter, Magister and Mirage 5BA BA-35 which are all owned by private collectors somewhere in the country. I have no further details of them so anything you can add, identities, locations etc, would be of great interest.

AALST

By 4.87 the airfield here (about 10 kms West of Brussels) had been closed and completely demolished, though the wrecks of Wa41A Baladou OO-LIB (c/n 96, CofA expired 18.2.81) and Wa30 Bijave OO-ZWN (c/n 14) still remained.

Evans VP-2 Volksplane OO-83 is on display somewhere along the road from Aalst to Gent.

ANTWERPEN (ANTWERP)

In use as an instructional airframes at the SITO4 school (at Emile Verhaeren laan 24) are N1203 Norecrin OO-AJK (c/n 261) and AA-1B Trainer 2 OO-WIF (c/n 0264) which crashed at Texel (Neths) 24.7.83. They have recently acquired F-84F Thunderstreak FU-36 (ex 52-7157) from Brustem. It is positioned outside the school.

Stored at the owner's house, somewhere in the Antwerp area, is the fuselage of Stampe SV4C N1024N (c/n 478).

ANTWERPEN/DEURNE (ANTWERP AIRPORT)

C-47B Dakota KP-4/OT-CNB (c/n 20864, ex 43-16398, soc 26.4.68) arrived here during 1970, the fuselage being used as a changing room for the local football club (FC Pagy). The aircraft was reportedly broken up for scrap in 11.76.

Noted at the airport in 8.82 were the wrecks of MS893A Rallye OO-TAM (c/n 10621, crashed here 15.11.81, wreck still here 9.84 as a spares source) and SV4C OO-NDJ (c/n 644). The wreck of MS880B Rallye Club OO-GRT (c/n 223) should still be here following an accident here on 15.5.83.

The wreck of L-21B Super Cub OO-KFC (ex 51-15633) has been stored here, dismantled, since being blown over at Rotterdam during the hurricane on 16.10.87. Boisavia Mercurey OO-KLO (c/n 22) has not flown since CofA expiry on 6.11.80 and remains stored here. Similarly, the fuselage of Cessna F150K OO-MKD (c/n F0546) is stored here, the CofA having expired on 13.7.83 and MS880B Rallye Club OO-RAF (c/n 1195) has not moved since 30.10.80 for the same reason. Cherokee Arrow III OO-TRI (c/n 28R-7837299) has been stored here since 11.2.84, though her CofA remained current until 6.12.84). MS880B Rallye Club OO-VAB (c/n 879) has been in store since CofA expiry on 3.6.77.

BEAUVECHAIN/BEVEKOM

Most Belgian front line bases received a generous helping of F-84F Thunderstreaks upon the type's retirement in the late sixties/early seventies, Beauvechain being no exception. Recorded here have been the following.

F-84F Thunderstreak	FU-123	(ex 53-6768)ex Koksijde store,soc22.6.71(noted'82-'88).
F-84F Thunderstreak	FU-125	(ex 53-6760) ex Koksijde store, soc 12.1.65 (noted '80-'86, tail from FU-106, to Ailes Anciennes - Toulouse at Toulouse/Blagnac 9.3.88 by C-160.
F-84F Thunderstreak	FU-143	(ex 53-6791) soc 5.6.64 (noted '72-'83 - see below).
F-84F Thunderstreak	FU-158	(ex 53-6891) soc 26.5.72 (noted '79-'80, fate unknown).
F-84F Thunderstreak	FU-184	(ex 52-6430) ex Koksijde store, soc 7.4.66 (noted '79 - airlifted to Tongerlo 17.12.86 for Brussels museum store).
F-84F Thunderstreak	FU-186	(ex 52-6620) soc 20.1.68 (noted '80 - airlifted to Tongerlo 17.12.86 with FU-184).
F-84F Thunderstreak	FU-191	(ex 52-6374) soc 24.4.66 (noted '72-'88).
F-84F Thunderstreak	FU-192	(ex 52-6605) soc 25.10.65 (noted '72-'88).
F-84F Thunderstreak	FU-194	(ex 52-6378) soc 16.9.65 (noted '72-'88 - see below).

By 1986 FU-143 had reached the end of its usefulness as a decoy and was suffering a fiery fate on the fire dump. It had already suffered considerably and was described as 'burnt out', however the mortal remains were noted again at the 1988 open day by which time FU-194 was on the fire dump.

At the open day in 1988, wreckage from F-16As FA-42 (ex 1 Wg, crashed at Gedinne 10.10.86) and FA-59 (ex 10 Wg, crashed at Overpelt 20.9.83, wreck to Evere 25.9.83) was found to be dumped in the barn next to the maintenance hangar.

The Officers' Mess at Beauvechain is located a kilometre or so from the base and houses Spitfire F.XIVe SG-31 (noted '79-'89) (350 Esc codes "MN-A" on port side in 1981 photo, uncoded on starboard side in 1987 photo) which is mounted on a pole within the site. This machine is ex RAF RN201 and has carried the spurious BelgAF serial "SG-3" since at least 1979 and probably earlier.

BEERVELDE

F-104G Starfighter FX-79 (c/n 9137) is preserved at a haulage company along the A14/E3 Antwerpen-Gent motorway near the Beervelde exit and is visible from the motorway. This Star arrived from nearby Kalken (qv) in the mid eighties.

BEVINGEN

Only half a mile or so from Brustem this military camp serves as a support site for its neighbour. Hunter F.6 IF-65 (c/n 8815) is preserved on a pole within the base devoid of serial (noted '74-'89).

BIERSET

Liege/Bierset serves a dual role as Liege airport and the base of 3 Wing equipped with the Mirage 5. Preserved aircraft on the base have comprised the following.

F-84G Thunderjet	FZ-107	(ex 51-10667 with tail of FZ-71/51-10195) painted as "FZ-153/JE-C" in 26 Esc marks, arrived from Brussels Museum for the show in 1983 but has since returned.
F-84F Thunderstreak	FU-156	(ex 53-6834) ex Koksijde store, soc 17.11.71. Initially used as a decoy (noted 6.76), later preserved in the 1 Esc area wearing their thistle emblem (noted '83-'89).
RF-84F Thunderflash	FR-32	(ex 53-7646) ex 42 Esc, arrived from ground instructional use at Saffraanberg (noted '83-'89).
RF-84F Thunderflash	FR-34	(ex 53-7677) ex 42 Esc, stored here since 6.72, preserved by main gate since 6.76 (current '89).

The decoy population here has comprised the following airframes, all given local cosmetic treatment to resemble the based Mirage 5s and even painted up with Mirage serials.

F-84F Thunderstreak FU-10 (ex 52-7115) ex Koksijde store, soc 14.4.71 (noted '74-'89 as "BA-01").
F-84F Thunderstreak FU-26 (ex 52-7162) ex Koksijde store, soc 25.2.71 (noted '72-'89 as "BA-06").
F-84F Thunderstreak FU-29 (ex 52-7175) ex Koksijde store, soc 10.5.71 (noted '79-'89 as "BA-02").
F-84F Thunderstreak FU-31 (ex 52-7178) ex Koksijde store, soc 8.1.71 (noted '74-'89 as "BA-08").
F-84F Thunderstreak FU-74 (ex 53-6777) ex Koksijde store, soc 26.3.71 (noted '72-'89 as "BA-04").
F-84F Thunderstreak FU-93 (ex 53-6717) ex Koksijde store, soc 16.12.70 (noted '74-'89 as "BA-03").
F-84F Thunderstreak FU-97 (ex 53-6539) ex Koksijde store, soc 18.2.71 (noted '80-'89 as "BA-09").
F-84F Thunderstreak FU-106 (ex 53-6722) ex Koksijde store, soc 31.3.71 (noted '72-'89 as "BA-05").
F-84F Thunderstreak FU-116 (ex 53-6768) ex Koksijde store, soc 22.9.70 (noted '75-'89 as "BA-07").
F-84F Thunderstreak FU-159 (ex 53-6824) ex Koksijde store, soc 30.4.71 (noted '74-'89 as "BA-06/BA-066", tail-less).

The Thunderstreaks were assisted in their decoy task here by at least two F-104G mock ups marked as "FX-03" and "FX-69" (both noted 1980). These were smaller than the real thing and unconvincing to say the least.

All the 'streaks except FU-26 and FU-31 can be found near the Administration buildings which are in a separate area of the base across the road from the main airfield gate. FU-26 and FU-31 were noted in 1983 derelict on the old airfield to the East of the main base. FU-26 has been used by the fire service since 5.84 FU-31 is still complete and standing on its undercarriage. Dumped next to FU-26 is the wreckage of LTV A-7P Corsair II 5501 (ex PortAF, crashed near Bierset 10.7.85).

The wreck of Mirage 5BA BA-55 (ex 1 Esc/3 Wg, crashed here 7.10.82) was still to be found lingering in the Western shelter area during 6.85 in use for bdr training. It was still current during 4.88. Mirage 5BA BA-51 has been relegated to bdr use and was first noted as such during 4.88.

The concentration of Belgian Mirage operations at Bierset during 1988 has also brought about the transfer from Florennes for bdr purposes of Mirage 5BA BA-02 (crashed 29.9.83) and Mirage 5BD BD-06 (crashed 2.7.85)

The Officers' Mess is located a mile or so East of the base and is guarded by Hunter F.4 ID-16 (ex 7 Wg, 9 Wg and 1 Wg, soc 11.1.60). This aircraft was painted up as "IF-33" but now wears the markings "IF-83/JE-P" representing a Hunter F.6 of 26 Esc/9 Wg based at Bierset until 30.4.60. The aircraft was still current in these marks in 1989.

Stored on the civil side is Cherokee 140 OO-JPS (c/n 28-7225575) whose CofA expired 15.10.86 and the wreck of Cherokee Six OO-PIF (c/n 32-7440073) which crashed at Heleme, France, on 29.3.86.

BORGERHOUT

The TIB School is believed to be located in this Antwerp suburb with two instructional airframes, namely OO-SIY Cessna F150H (c/n 0266, registration cancelled between '81 and '84) and Siai Marchetti SF260 OO-SMF (c/n 118, registration cancelled pre '75).

BRASSCHAAT

Located on the Northern edge of Antwerp, Brasschaat is one of Europe's best concealed airfields unless you happen to pick the right road. Preserved on a pole outside the control tower at this Belgian Army airfield is Auster AOP.6 A-15 (ex VT995, soc 9.12.57, to OO-FDH) (noted '77-'89). Since 1982 it has been painted as "A-16", the work of some 16 Esc airmen armed with a pot of paint.

Also located on the base (in the military hangars and consequently not accessible to the casual visitor) is Eric Voormezeele's aircraft collection several of which are airworthy with others undergoing restoration. Mr Voormezeele also owns the superb Skyraider OO-FOR which is kept at Zoersel and several of those machines listed below may actually be located at the BLa base at Werl, WG.

Bolingbroke IVT	9947	ex RCAF (allocated OO-BLH, to Saffraanberg for rebuild by 5.88).
DH82A Tiger Moth	OO-BYL	(c/n 3882 ex G-AFNR, W7952, G-ANBU) CofA expired 24.3.86.
Fiat G-46-4A	OO-VOR	(c/n 199, ex MM53293, I-AEKI)
Fiat G-46-3A	I-AEHO	(c/n 143, ex MM53093) stored.
Hawker Sea Fury T.20	OO-SFY	(ex VZ351, G-9-53, ES9506, D-CEDO) to Jimmie Hunt, Memphis, Tennessee in 10.85.
Hawker Sea Fury T.20	D-CACA	(ex VZ365, G-9-61, ES3612, D-CACA) to Jimmie Hunt, Memphis, Tennessee, in 10.85 as spares for the above.
HA1112MIL Buchon	C.4K-201	(c/n 182) arr 3.10.85, stored.
MS505 Criquet	OO-STO	(c/n 269/6, ex F-BBUK)
MS733 Alcyon	OO-MSA	(c/n 178) ex Aeronavale & store at Brest/Guipavas.
N1002 Pingouin	F-BCAS	(c/n 175) stored '86.
N1101 Noralpha	34	ex 'DJ' CEV, AdlA, and Etampes, stored.
N1101 Noralpha	OO-VAF	(c/n 119, ex F-BHER) CofA expired 29.4.80.
Harvard T.2B	H-39	(c/n 88-9728, ex 41-33265, EX292) arrived from Brussels museum c.1987 in exchange for B-67.
Harvard T.2B	B-67	(c/n 14A-1462, ex 43-13163, FT422) ex KLu, to Brussels museum c.1987 in a straight swop with H-39.
Harvard T.2B	OO-DAF	(c/n 14A-1494, ex 43-13195, FT454, KLu B-84, MLD 098, kept at Werl, WG).
Pilatus P2-05	OO-PIL	(c/n 31, ex Swiss AF U-111, OO-PTO) CofA expired on 16.7.82, thought to be at Werl).
Stampe SV4C	1086	(c/n 1086, OO-SVC not yet taken up).
Westland Lysander	1589	ex RCAF

The Harvard OO-DAF is of particular interest. The Belgian civil register gives its c/n as 14A-1494 which makes it ex 43-13195 etc as listed above. However, according to MLD files, they sold their Harvard 098 to the museum at Sinsheim, WG. Sinsheim claim to have repainted the aircraft after much research in its original colours - as FT454! If that is correct then we still need the real previous identity for OO-DAF which is current here as is FT454 at Sinsheim. Answers on a postcard please!

Noted on the airfield in a dismantled condition in 8.82 was PA18-95 Super Cub OO-ACC (c/n 18-3230, ex 53-4830, L-156) whilst L-21B Super Cub OO-ATY (ex 53-4821, L-147) was under restoration here recently following CofA expiry on 11.12.86.

BRUXELLES/BRUSSELS

Located in a palace in the Parc du Cinquentenaire is the Musee Royal de l'Armee which covers the entire military history of Belgium and includes one of Europe's great aeronautical collections. Major expansion of the aircraft side of the collection has taken place over the last twenty years with the permanent display rising from some fifteen aircraft to nearly one hundred. Up to the late seventies many of the collection's 'spare' aircraft were to be found hidden under balconies and around the exhibition hall but since then storage and restoration facilities have been obtained at Tongerlo (F-84Fs etc) and Tielen (Austers, SV4s, Cubs etc) to which aircraft have gradually been moved. This list includes all those aircraft in the museum collection, they are not necessarily all to be found here but may well be held in storage. The dates noted refer to sightings in the museum building here.

The museum also keeps some airframes at Koksijde having acquired all the BelgAF's decoy Thunderstreaks, all the stored HSS-1s and a number of F-104s for use as 'currency' in obtaining further exhibits. Their Mystere IVA and Meteor NF.11 are also stored at Koksijde. Since being taken over by the museum some of the Thunderstreaks have already moved and others can be expected to do so.

Aermacchi AL.60B	-	arrived late '88 (see under Gosselies).
Aeronca 7AC	OO-SND	crashed 18.8.81, stored at Tielen for the museum.

Airspeed Oxford	O-16	(ex MP455) arr 22.8.60 (noted '79-'88). NB: Wears a Percival c/n plate PAC/W/936, MP455 was BelgAF but was built by Standard Motors. However, Ken Ellis points out that Percival was a sub-contractor for almost all Oxford production and Dutch sources confirm that this is the genuine MP455.
Auster J/1 Autocrat	OO-ABN	(c/n 2047)
Auster AOP.6	OO-FDA	(c/n 2818, ex VT979, A-3) (noted '79-'88).
Auster AOP.6	OO-FDB	(c/n 2820, ex VT981, A-7) (noted '79).
Auster AOP.6	OO-FDC	(c/n 2824, ex VT988, A-8) (noted '79).
Auster AOP.6	OO-FDD	(c/n 2817, ex VT978, A-9) (noted '79).
Auster AOP.6	A-11	(c/n 2826, ex VT990, A-11, OO-FDE) (noted '79-'88).
Auster AOP.6	A-16	(c/n 2835, ex VT996, A-16, OO-FDI) (noted '79-'88, see also Brasschaat).
Auster AOP.6	OO-FDJ	(c/n 2832, ex VT993, A-17) (noted '79-'80).
Aviatik C.1	C227/16	(c/n 832) (noted '82-'88).
Avro CF-100 Mk.5	18534	(c/n 434) ex RCAF (noted '79-'88).
Bataille Triplane	-	fuselage & tail only - under rebuild during '88 to make a complete aircraft.
Boeing 707-329	OO-SJA	(c/n 17623) ex Sabena, front fuselage (noted '88).
Breguet 905 Fauvette	OO-ZJN	(c/n 45, ex F-CCJO)
Bolingbroke IVT	9895	(ex RCAF) (noted '79-'80, to Saffraanberg '88 for rebuild).
BN2A-21 Defender	B-06	(c/n 510, ex G-BDPU) 'LF' (arr 4.89, wfu after a hangar fire at Butzweilerhof).
Bu 181B Bestmann	"TP+CP"	(c/n 021969, ex OO-RVD) Luftwaffe marks (noted '79-'88).
Bu 181B Bestmann	OO-BLJ	(c/n 0216168/FR14, ex F-BBLJ, OO-RVA)
Caudron G.3	2531	(noted '79-'88).
Caudron C.800	-	(c/n 156)
Cessna 310	OO-SEL	(c/n 35524, ex N5324A, OO-CUC, 9O-CUC, 9Q-CUC, OO-CUC)
Chandelon Helicopter	-	
Dassault Ouragan	320	ex 'UQ' GE.314, AdlA, & display at Tours (noted '79-'88).
Dasault Mystere IVA	191	ex '8-NK' ex ET.2/8 AdlA, Chateaudun & Savigny Les Beaune, delivered to Koksijde store 16.11.88.
DH Chipmunk T.20	P-130	(c/n C1/0109) ex RDanAF (swopped for SV4C V-62) (noted '79, to Geldernaken).
DHC-3 Otter	OO-SUD	(c/n 297, Bu144669) (noted '82-'88).
DH82A Tiger Moth	OO-EVA	(c/n 85873, ex DF124, T-1)
DH82A Tiger Moth	OO-EVD	(c/n 86517, ex NM209, T-22)
DH82A Tiger Moth	OO-EVG	(c/n 86334, ex NL981, T-15)
DH82A Tiger Moth	OO-EVH	(c/n 85832, ex DE972, T-27)
DH82A Tiger Moth	OO-EVM	(c/n 86507, ex NM199, T-19)
DH82A Tiger Moth	OO-EVS	(c/n 3272, ex K4276, G-AOJX)
DH82A Tiger Moth	OO-EVT	(c/n 84875, ex T6534, G-AMTP)
DH82A Tiger Moth	OO-SOE	(c/n 3858, ex N6545, G-AMTV)
DH82A Tiger Moth	OO-SOF	(c/n 82592, ex G-AFWF, W6420, G-AMTL)
DH82A Tiger Moth	"T-24"	(c/n 83728, ex T7238, G-AMJD, OO-SOI) 'UR-!' (noted '79-'88).
DH82A Tiger Moth	OO-SOM	(c/n 84569, ex T6102, G-ANNC)
DH82A Tiger Moth	OO-SOW	(c/n 84567, ex T6100; G-APPT)
DH82A Tiger Moth	OO-SOX	(c/n 83830, ex T7303)
DH89A Dragon Rapide	OO-CNP	(c/n 6458, ex RS922, G-AKNV, EI-AGK, G-AKNV, OO-AFG) (noted unmarked '86-'88).
DH Mosquito NF.30	MB-24	(ex RK952) 'ND-N', soc 17.10.56 (noted '79-'86).
DH Vampire T.11	XH292	(c/n 15160) ex Woodford storage, arr 1973 (noted '79-'88).

DFS108 Schulgleiter	PL-21	ex Lucht Cadetten.
Dornier Do 27J-1	D-04	(c/n 2101) (arr 19.8.77, current '88).
Douglas C-47B Dakota	K-16	(c/n 20823, ex 43-16357) ex 'OT-CWG' 21 Esc/15 Wg, soc 3.8.72, arr 12.1.73 (current '88).
Douglas A-26C Invader	N67160	(ex 44-34765) (noted under restoration '79-'88).
UC-61K Argus III	314987	(c/n 951, ex 43-14987, HB713, ZS-BWM, ZS-BYN, F-OADB, F-BAMB, OO-LUT) (noted '79-'88).
UC-61K Argus III	OO-LMV	(c/n 1069, ex 44-83108, KK451, F-OAAY, F-BDAL, N9759F) (noted '79-'88).
C-119G Packet	CP-46	(c/n 11254, ex 53-8151) ex 'OT-CEF' 15 Wg (noted '80-'88).
Farman-Voisin	-	
Farman F.11A-2	-	(noted '83-'88)
Fiat G-91R/3	3085	(c/n 348) ex Jbg.41, WGAF (noted '83-'88).
Fieseler Fi 156C-3	KR+QX	(c/n 5503) (ex KR+QX, 3822/RNorAF, OE-ADT) (noted '83-'88).
Focke-Wulf Weihe	PL-50	ex Lucht Cadetten.
Fokker DR.1	"425/17"	replica (noted '83-'88).
Fouga CM170 Magister	MT-24	(c/n 281) Cat.3 landing accident at Solenzara 27.11.78, to Museum 16.5.79 (noted '80-'88).
Gloster Meteor F.8	EG224	'K5-K' (arrived 20.3.64, current '88).
Gloster Meteor F.8	EG247	painted as "EG244/MN-A" (arr 26.4.72, current '88, to Kbely, Czechoslovakia, by early '89 in exchange for a MiG-15).
Goppingen Govier	OO-ZPJ	
Halberstadt C.V	"9471/18"	thought to be really 3471/18, but marked as "3441/18" with c/n "1041" when seen here in '83 (noted '79-'88).
Hanriot HD.1	HD-78	(c/n VII/5153) (noted '79-'88).
Hawker Hurricane IIc	LF658	painted as "LF345/ZA-P" (noted '79-'88).
Hawker Hunter F.4	ID-44	ex Wevelgem, arr 26.2.70, to Florennes 9.6.75 then Paris for Musee de l'Air.
Hawker Hunter F.4	"IF-70"	(really ID-46) ex '7J-F' 7 Esc/7 Wg, Cat.4 13.6.57 & to gia at Saffraanberg, to museum 25.3.60 (noted '79-'88).
Hawker Hunter F.4/F.6	-	(nose section, recorded '83-'88, c/n 41H/691136).
Hunting Pembroke C.51	RM-4	(c/n 21) ex 'OT-ZAD' 21 Esc/15 Wg, soc 31.8.76, arr 4.1.77 (current '88).
Jodel D.9	00-15	(noted unmarked '83-'86).
Jodel D.9	00-40	(noted '82).
Kassel 12	-	
Kreit & Lambrickx KL2	OO-ANP	(noted '86-'88).
Lockheed T-33A	FT-34	(ex 55-3043) to Koksijde store 24.7.78, then here (noted '83-'88).
F-104G Starfighter	FX-12	(c/n 9029) ex Saffraanberg (arr 4.5.83, current '88).
LVG C.VI	5141/18	(noted '79-'88).
Mignet HM290	-	
Mignet Pou du Ciel	00-11	(noted '86-'88).
Mignet Pou du Ciel	00-33	stored, painted as "OO-BAM".
MiG-15bis	3911	(c/n 623911) ex Czech AF (arrived 6.3.89 in a swop for Meteor EG247 which went to the museum at Kbely).
Miles M.14A Magister	T9800	(c/n 1992, composite, ex T9800, TMR-50, G-1, OO-NIC) (noted '76-'88, might not be the real T9800).
Miles Messenger 2A	G-AKIS	dismantled '86, may be exchanged for something else.
Morane MS230	1066	(c/n 1066, ex F-BEJO) (noted '83-'88).
Morane MS230	-	rebuild to airworthy condition by Jane Booten.
Morane MS315	F-BCNT	(c/n 350) (noted '80-'88).
Morane MS500	F-BFCD	(c/n 374) (noted '86-'88).
MS880B Rallye	F-BSAM	(c/n 1555)
Nieuport 17C1	N5024	(noted '79-'83).

Nord 1002 Pingouin	"184"	(c/n 184, ex F-BERF) painted in spurious Luftwaffe marks (noted '80-'88).
Harvard T.2B	H-39	(c/n 88-9728, ex 41-33265, EX292) (noted '79-'86, to Brasschaat in exchange for B-67). This a/c was painted as T-6G "210/G" in the early '70s.
Harvard T.2B	H-21	(c/n 88-15950, ex 42-84169, EZ256) (arr 12.59, current '88).
Harvard T.2B	B-67	(c/n 14A-1462, ex 43-13163, FT422) ex KLu & Brasschaat (obtained '88 in a swop for H-39 in anticipation of a swop with a Yugoslav museum which fell through. Currently stored at Tielen).
F-86F Sabre	5316	(ex 52-5242) ex PortAF (arr 5.81, current '88).
Percival Gull IV	G-ACGR	(c/n D29) (noted under restoration '86-'88).
Percival Proctor IV	P-4	(c/n H-578, ex NP171 assuming this is the real P-4 which was w/o on 10.5.49) (noted '79-'88).
Percival Proctor V	OO-ARM	(c/n Ae84, ex G-AHZY) (noted '80).
Percival Prentice T.1	OO-OPO	(ex VS613, G-AOPO) (noted '80-'86).
Piper L-4H Cub	OO-GEG	(c/n 11694, ex 43-30403)
Piper L-4H Cub	OO-RVA	(c/n 12221, ex 44-79925)
Piper L-4J Cub	OO-AVX	(c/n 13128, ex 44-80832)
Piper L-18C Super Cub	OL-L87	(c/n 18-3149, ex 53-4749) (noted '79-'88).
Piper L-18C Super Cub	OO-LGA	(c/n 18-1597, ex 51-15597, FMCAN, F-BLLM)
F-84F Thunderstreak	FU-30	(ex 52-7169) ex Koksijde store, soc 30.11.71 (noted '79-'88).
RF-84F Thunderflash	FR-28	(ex 51-1945) ex Bierset (noted '79-'88).
F-84G Thunderjet	"FZ-153"	(ex FZ-107/51-10667 with tail from FZ-71/51-10195) painted as "FZ-132" then "FZ153" with various codes (noted '79-'89).
RRG Zogling	-	
RAF RE.8	8	(c/n 326, possibly ex A4719) (noted '79-'88).
Rumpler C.IV	-	
SAAB J 35A Draken	35067	ex '34' F 16 RSwedAF, arr 20.11.78 (current '89).
SABCA Junior	-	(c/n 2)
SABCA Junior	-	(c/n 3)
SABCA Junior	-	(c/n 10)
SABCA Junior	-	(c/n 11)
SABCA Poncelet Vivette	O-BAFH	(c/n 2)
SAI KZ III	OO-MAA	(c/n 72) (noted '86-'88).
Ka-2 Rhonschwalbe	PL-13	(c/n 77/55) ex Lucht Cadetten.
Grunau Baby II	PL-33	(c/n 09) ex Lucht Cadetten (noted '88).
Grunau Baby II	PL-36	ex Lucht Cadetten (noted '88).
Grunau Baby II	OO-ZBA	
Grunau Baby III	PL-37	(c/n 82/55) ex Lucht Cadetten (noted '88).
Schreck FBA Type H	5.160	(c/n 55) (noted '80-'88).
CP301 Emeraude	-	partially complete a/c noted 5.86.
Sikorsky H-19D	MM57-5979	ex 'CS-10' ItAF (noted '79-'80), to PortAF Museum in exchange for F-86F Sabre 5316.
Sikorsky UH-34G	B-6	(c/n SA181) ex 'OT-ZKF' 40 Esc, arr 20.8.81 (noted '83-'88).
Sikorsky S-58C	B-13	(c/n 58-395) ex 'OT-ZKM' 40 Esc, crashed near Aachen 15.10.71 (noted '78-'80).
Sopwith Camel F.1	B5747	(noted '79-'88).
Sopwith 1 1/2 Strutter	S85	(noted '79-'88).
SPAD XIII C.1	SP-49	(noted '79-'88).
Stampe SV4B	V-21	(c/n 1163, ex EVS, Cat.3 20.3.68) arrived from Goetsenhoven early '80s, to UK '89 in exchange for 2 Tipsy Trainers.
Stampe SV4B	V-28	(c/n 1170) ex EVS, soc 1970, arr '71 (noted '79-'83).
Stampe SV4B	V-56	(c/n 1198)ex EVS,Cat.4 23.5.57,arr '71 (noted'57-'86).

Stampe SV4B	"OO-ATD"	(really V-57, c/n 1199) the real OO-ATD was the famous escapee from Occupied Belgium which became MX457 (noted '57-'88).
Stampe SV4B	V-62	(c/n 1204) ex EVS, arr '76, to Denmark 4.6.77 in a swop for ex RDAF Chipmunk T.20 P-130.
Stampe SV4B	V-64	(c/n 1206) ex EVS, arr '70 (noted '79-'88).
Stampe SV4C	"102"	(c/n 28, ex OO-CLH, F-BFZC) in spurious Aeronavale marks as "5.S.25" (noted '79-'88).
Stampe SV4D	OO-SRS	(c/n 1208) (noted '80-'88).
Stampe Renard SR.7B	OO-SRZ	(c/n 1003) CofA expired 21.4.78 (noted '86-'88).
Sud Alouette II	A-08	(c/n 1467) ex Butzweilerhof, WG (arrived 11.11.88).
SE210 Caravelle	OO-SRA	(c/n 64, ex F-WJAK) ex Sabena, wfu 8.8.74, TT 24244 (noted '79-'88).
Spitfire LF.IXc	"MJ360"	(c/n 1301, ex MJ783, SM-15) "GE-B", port wing from SM-13 (noted '79-'88).
Spitfire FR.XIVe	SG-55	(ex MV246) w/o 11.10.48, rebuilt with parts of SG-37 (noted '79-'88).
Tipsy S.2	OO-TIP	(c/n 29, ex G-AFVH, OO-ASB) (noted '86-'88).
Tipsy Trainer 1	G-AFJR	(c/n 2) obtained '89 in exchange for Stampe SV4B V-21, probably held in store.
Tipsy Trainer 1	G-AFRV	(c/n 10) obtained '89 in exchange for Stampe SV4B V-21, probably held in store.
Voisin LA5-B	-	pod only (noted '83-'88).

The exchange of Harvards with Eric Voormezeele's collection arose because a museum in Yugoslavia wanted a Harvard in exchange for a locally built aircraft (though the deal fell through). The swop with Brasschaat meant that a Belgian Harvard would have stayed in the country whilst a former Dutch example departed.

A Morane-Saulnier MS500 has arrived from France in exchange for an ex Beauvechain Thunderstreak. the wings of this MS500 will be used to repair the museum's Fi 156C Storch OE-ADT.

BRUSSELS/ZAVENTEM

Over the years a good many airliners have passed through Brussels Airport for storage and/or scrapping. The following list is surely not exhaustive.

Boeing 707-131	OO-TED	(c/n 17665) stored by TEA hangar '85-'87, scrapped 9.87.
Boeing 707-328B	4X-ATE	(c/n 18456) arr 10.84 for spares recovery (current '89).
Boeing 707-321B	HK-2070X	(c/n 19266) arr 3.2.85, stored by TEA hangar '85, became 9Q-CBL.
Boeing 707-328B	OO-TYC	(c/n 19291) stored by TEA hangar '85-'86.
Boeing 720-051B	OY-APV	(c/n 18793) stored '88.
Douglas DC-8-51	OH-KDM	(c/n 45628) arr from Helsinki 11.2.85, noted 5.86, scrapped.
Douglas DC-8-53	9Q-CBF	(c/n 45629) ex Aero Carribean, stored 10.84-12.86 at least, fuselage only still here '88.
Douglas DC-8-55	N915R	(c/n 45916) arr 4.5.86, stored '87.
Douglas DC-8-62	N4761G	(c/n 45917) arr 7.9.84, to N803AX '85.
Douglas DC-8-62	N924CL	(c/n 46134) stored '85, to N802AX.

Based in the Sabena maintenance area, Sabena Old Timers took on the Musee Royal de l'Armee's ex RCAF Westland Lysander III 2442/OO-SOT/"SO-T" which flew again during 8.88 following a painstaking restoration. This machine was built from the frames of 2341, 2360 and 2442. The organisation also received ex PortAF Junkers Ju 52/3mg-7e 6309 (c/n 5670) from storage at Alverca, arriving at the airport on 24.4.85 to become OO-AGU on completion. By 1987 serious spar corrosion became evident which resulted in spare parts being obtained from a second aircraft, 6310. This machine remains in store at Alverca.

Cessna 310 OO-SEB (c/n 35546) has been in open storage adjacent to the DHL hangar whilst Cessna 310B OO-SEI (c/n 35636) is stored in hangar 8 (both are ex Sabena).

DHL have been using Convair 580 N73165 (c/n 368) as a source of spares for their resident CV580 fleet. It was here by 2.88, still wearing its American Eagle colours.

BRUSTEM

Preserved by the main gate here is Meteor F.8 EG-79/S2-R in 9 Esc markings (noted '79-'88). Lockheed T-33A FT-24 (ex 52-9892) is preserved near the Alpha Jet hangars (soc 8.1.80, noted '81-'87) whilst F-84F Thunderstreak FU-51 (ex 52-7215, ex Koksijde store and decoy here, soc 28.1.71) is displayed by the Magister hangars on the other side of the field (noted '79-'87).

The decoy population has comprised the following F-84F Thunderstreaks:-

F-84F Thunderstreak	FU-21	(ex 52-7170) ex Koksijde store, soc 28.5.70 (noted '72-'87, to Savigny-Les-Beaune, France, '88).
F-84F Thunderstreak	FU-28	(ex 52-7166) ex Koksijde store, soc 21.10.70 (noted '77-'87).
F-84F Thunderstreak	FU-36	(ex 52-7157) ex Koksijde store, soc 4.11.70 (noted '77-'87, to SITO4 School, Antwerpen).
F-84F Thunderstreak	FU-66	(ex 53-6677) ex Koksijde store, soc 24.11.70 (noted '77-'87).
F-84F Thunderstreak	FU-82	(ex 53-6587) ex Koksijde store, soc 3.12.70 (noted '73-'87).
F-84F Thunderstreak	FU-92	(ex 53-6702) ex Koksijde store, soc 24.9.70 (noted '73-'87).
F-84F Thunderstreak	FU-105	(ex 53-6707) ex Koksijde store, soc 18.8.70 (noted '73-'87).
F-84F Thunderstreak	FU-134	(ex 53-6759) ex Koksijde store, soc 9.11.70 (noted '72, last recorded in 9.84 in a burnt out condition on the fire dump).

Following the replacement of the based T-33As by the Alpha Jet in 1978/79, several T-33As were stored on the base awaiting their fate. Those that lingered for a reasonable length of time comprised the following.

Lockheed T-33A	FT-09	(ex 51-6663) Cat.4 damage sustained 4.8.76 after losing a tip-tank in flight, to Seifertshofen, WG, by 4.80.
Lockheed T-33A	FT-26	(ex 53-5725) mid-air collision 27.4.77 with FT-04. A safe landing was effected but the a/c suffered Cat.5 damage and appeared at Seifortshofen, WG, by 4.80.
Lockheed T-33A	FT-37	(ex 55-3082) stored, soc 5.2.80, departed for Alconbury 4.3.80 for bdr.
Lockheed T-33A	FT-38	(ex 55-3044) wfu 11.12.78, stored, to Ramstein 6.2.80 for bdr.

Piper L-21B Super Cub LB-04 (ex 54-2443, ex KLu R-153) crashed here on 10.9.77, the wreck spending several years in store here as a source of spares for the remaining four aircraft which are still in service as tugs for Lucht Cadetten gliders.

As a matter of interest, it has been suggested that the T-33A simulator formerly in use here could well have utilised the wreck of FT-08 (ex 51-6662) as a basis whist the Magister simulators (four of them) were built from F-82 Twin Mustang cockpits. They wear the 'serials' "P-603", "P-609", "P-612" and "P-619". The Alpha Jet simulator is a more modern high-tech device and wears the joke serial "AT-34". The real aircraft are AT-01 to AT-33.

CHIEVRES

Guarding the gate here is Meteor F.4 EG-18/VT-R (noted '77-'89). On 10.6.86 F-84F Thunderstreak FU-33 (ex 52-7192, ex Koksijde store, soc 18.1.71) was airlifted in from Florennes where it had served as a decoy for the last fifteen years. This 'streak is now assured a better future preserved on the base and was positioned by the gate on 18.2.87 and officially unveiled in 1 Esc codes as "3R-B" on 23.3.87.

DIEST/SCHAFFEN

Diest is a military airfield (North of Diest town) used for para-dropping but which also houses an Aero Club. Stored here are Stampe SV4B V-23 (c/n 1165) (noted 6.85 & 5.86) with OO-KRL/V-54 (c/n 1196), Cessna 140 OO-REL (c/n 9067, covered in dust by 1986, not having moved since 1979), Tiger Moth OO-EVE (c/n 85953, ex EM722, stored since CofA expiry 26.6.79) and M.1C Sokols OO-JAW (c/n 113) with OO-MAX (c/n 110). The hulk of an unidentified Swiss Chipmunk 22 (HB-TUA or 'TUE) is used as a spares source here.

DINANT

Gloster Meteor F.8 EG-162/"K5-K" (c/n 6496, OO-ARU ntu) is preserved at the Citadel which overlooks the town (noted '75-'89).

ERPS-KWERPS

MS883 Rallye OO-JNH (c/n 1550) crashed at Molenstede on 16.8.86. The wreck is now displayed here (just East of Brussels Airport) as an 'eye-catcher'.

EVERE

The depot at Evere (near Brussels Airport) houses, amongst other units, the Belgian AF's accident investigation branch. All crashed aircraft requiring investigation are brought here and to detail those aircraft recorded here over the last ten years or so would be to run through BelgAF attrition during this period. This falls outside the scope of this tome, the more so because the majority of wrecks here are transient in nature.

Two more permanent relics have been F-84F FU-20 and RF-84F FR-29. FU-20 (ex 52-7151) was allocated to ground instructional use on 1.7.65 and was displayed outside the crash investigation hangar in the mid seventies. Sadly, it was scrapped during 1.78. RF-84F Thunderflash FR-29 (ex 51-11279) was preserved on the base here by 1976 and was still current during '88.

Evere is also the base for the BelgAF's fleet of mobile display airframes parented by 21 Logistieke Wing and roaded around for use at recruiting displays, airshows etc. These are often seen at BelgAF displays providing a backdrop for the for the usual 'photo in the cockpit' sessions.

CM170 Magister	MT-9	(c/n 266) Cat.4 accident at Brustem 26.2.70, fitted with tail from MT-17.
F-104G Starfighter	FX-04	(c/n 9019) ex 10 Wg, suffered a ground fire during refuelling at Kleine-Brogel 13.7.76 and wfu.
Stampe SV4B	V-33	(c/n 1175, Cat.5 23.6.60) rebuilt by 21 Logistieke Wing at Beauvechain.

FLORENNES

Preserved near the main gate at Florennes were F-84F Thunderstreak FU-108 (ex 53-6610, soc 15.4.70) and Spitfire FR.XIV SG-57/RL-D (ex RM921, first noted here 6.72), however in mid 1987 the Spitfire was moved into a hangar on the base for restoration work expected to last two years.

In the 42 Esc shelter area RF-84F FR-27 (ex 51-1922) serves as a reminder of that unit's Thunderflash era and F-84F Thunderstreak FU-103 (ex 53-6597, ex Koksijde store, soc 5.3.71) was preserved in flying attitude next to the control tower on the South side of the base. During the mid eighties she was repainted as "FU-66" and positioned near the Staff Buildings (current '89). As noted below, long serving decoy FU-154 is also now preserved here as "FU-66" whilst a third airframe wearing those marks is the original which can still be found at Brustem.

The decoy complement has comprised the following F-84F Thunderstreaks.

F-84F Thunderstreak	FU-33	(ex 52-7192) ex Koksijde store, soc 18.1.71 (noted '72-'79, to Chievres 10.6.86 for preservation).
F-84F Thunderstreak	FU-45	(ex 52-7210) ex Koksijde store, soc 8.12.70 (noted '72-'87). To Savigny-Les-Beaune, France, during '88 in exchange for a Flamant (yet to appear) for Brussels museum.

F-84F Thunderstreak	FU-50	(ex 52-7011) ex Koksijde store, soc 28.5.70 (noted '72-'86).
F-84F Thunderstreak	FU-76	(ex 53-6536) ex Koksijde store, soc 28.1.71 (noted '72-'79, almost certainly the aircraft seen at Nancy, France in '85 as "28946/3-IV").
F-84F Thunderstreak	FU-91	(ex 53-6693) ex Koksijde store, soc 27.1.71 (noted '72-'79).
F-84F Thunderstreak	FU-144	(ex 53-6783) ex Koksijde store, soc 9.2.71 (noted '72-'87).
F-84F Thunderstreak	FU-152	(ex 53-6764) ex Koksijde store, soc 17.10.70 (noted '79-'82, probably still current if not burnt on the fire dump - confirm?).
F-84F Thunderstreak	FU-154	(ex 53-6806) ex Koksijde store, soc 8.10.70 (noted '77-'80, painted as "FU-66" during the mid eighties and preserved near the 2 Esc buildings, noted '86-'89).
F-84F Thunderstreak	FU-179	(ex 53-6941) ex Koksijde store, soc 2.9.70 (noted '72-'87)

Two Mirage 5 hulks were present on the base in 12.86, near the 2 Esc flight line was Mirage 5BD BD-06 (ex 42 Esc, crashed at Philippeville 3.7.85) whilst in the 42 Esc area was Mirage 5BA BA-02 (Cat.4 ground fire here on 29.8.83). Both served here as bdr training airframes and moved to Bierset during 1988 with the concentration of the remaining Mirage 5 fleet at that base.

FROIDCHAPELLE

The cockpit section of Cessna U206 OO-TAV (c/n 05587) is stored outside near a hangar here (South East of Charleroi).

GELDERNAKEN

Former RDanAF Chipmunk T.20 P-130 (c/n C1/0109) is under restoration for the Brussels museum with the Luchtvaarttechniek section of the Koninklijk Atheneum.

GENT/GAND

Although the airfield was officially closed in 12.84 (to be the site of a new factory) a visit in 3.85 found the dismantled wrecks of Rallye OO-AHF, MS885 Super Rallye OO-AKA (c/n 145) and MS893A Rallye OO-AMA (c/n 2601) in a hangar here. Both 'AMA and 'AHF were still present 4.87. OO-AKA and 'AMA have now progressed to storage at the owner's house in Paal.

GITS

In late 1987 C-47B Dakota K-1/OT-CWA (c/n 26501, ex 43-49240) turned up here (off the N63 between Roeselare and Torhout) and was still current in '89. This aircraft was retired to Koksijde for storage and soc 11.12.73. The registration N99346 was allocated in 3.77 but was not taken up and she was dismantled at Koksijde in the Spring of 1979. Where she went after 5.79 remains a mystery until she was re-discovered at Gits in late 1987. Had she been here all the time?

GOETSENHOVEN

Preserved inside the base was Stampe SV4B V-21 (c/n 1163, ex EVS, Cat.3 20.3.68, here by 1970) rebuilt with a tail donated by V-49. It moved to the Brussels museum during the early eighties and went to the UK early in '89 having been involved in an exchange to bring a pair of Tipsy Trainers to the Brussels museum.

The Link Trainer building contains the cockpit and centre fuselage sections of three crashed Siai-Marchetti SF260MBs which were salvaged and converted to simulators by 21 Logistieke Wing.

SF260MB	ST-10	ex EPE/EVS, crashed in West Germany 14.6.76.
SF260MB	ST-13	ex EPE/EVS, crashed 25.7.72, delivered here 3.76.
SF260MB	ST-28	ex EPE/EVS, force-landed near Ronse 13.3.81, arrived here 28.1.83.

In use here as an instructional airframe in the late seventies was Stampe SV4B V-19 (c/n 1161, ex EPE/EVS, Cat.5 at Koksijde 11.7.70). The aircraft may still be present but has not been confirmed in recent years (last reported '79).

The wreckage of Morane Saulnier MS887 Rallye OO-AST (c/n 2174) is stored in a hangar here.

GOSSELIES

The airfield at Gosselies serves as an airport for the city of Charleroi and houses the SABCA aircraft factory which currently builds F-16s for the BelgAF and overhauls several other BelgAF types. Centre Air Afrique Britannia 9U-BAD (c/n 13454, ex XL657, impounded at Oostende 25.2.77) was stored here for some time prior to being broken up in 4.81. Its mortal remains lie in a scrapyard North of the field and can be seen from the A15 motorway.

Sabena Boeing 737-229C OO-SDH (c/n 20914) crashed here on 4.4.78 and was dumped on the field. The hulk was still current in 4.81 but has since been removed.

Two ex Svensk Flygjanst Gloster Meteor TT.20 target tugs arrived here on 11.5.69 whilst staging through to Biafra to join the rebel air force. In the event their delivery flight ended at Gosselies and the two airframes languished in the open here until acquisition by the Brussels museum in 1982. They were then transported to the museum store at Tongerlo, going to Savigny-Les-Beaune (France) during '88.

Gloster Meteor TT.20 SE-DCF (c/n 5562, WM395, ex RDAF 51-512, H-512, D-CAKY ntu)
Gloster Meteor TT.20 SE-DCH (c/n 5549, WM391, ex RDAF 51-508, H-508, D-CAKU ntu)

Outside a hangar here in 5.83 was the fuselage of Aermacchi AL.60B-2 I-MACL (c/n 6218/38). Would this be the one which turned up at Brussels museum late in '88?

Stored inside the Aspair hangar are the remains of Siai-Marchetti FN333 Riviera OO-HEB (c/n 010), dismantled Siai-Marchetti S205-22R OO-TER (c/n 4-256) with the fuselage of S205-20R OO-WII (c/n 220) whilst the wreck of Siai-Marchetti S202-15 OO-HIA (c/n 01) lies outside nearby.

In another hangar is the stored fuselage of Grinvalds G802 Orion c/n 118 (OO-MCR allocated but ntu). The wreck of Cessna F152-II OO-CNM (c/n 01438, crashed at St Montan, France, 31.5.83) is also stored here.

Aviation Spare Parts Europe SA store B55 Baron OO-GRK (c/n TC-677) in a dismantled state (CofA expired 25.12.80).

PZL.104 Wilga OO-SUD (c/n 129450) is stored here, engineless. The CofA expired 4.6.81.

GRIMBERGEN

Two Cub fuselages were noted in the Publi-Air hangar here in 9.86, one being J-3C OO-XYZ (c/n 12416, ex 44-80120, OO-REX). By 1988 Robin HR100/200B OO-VEM (c/n 120) was stored near the hangar in a dismantled condition.

In 12.86 the wrecks of PA32 Cherokee Six OO-JPC (c/n 32-7340123, CofA expired 7.4.86) and Enstrom F28A OO-PMA (c/n 263, ex OO-BAN ntu, crashed at Libramont 25.4.86) were lying alongside the club hangar.

MS892A Rallye Commodore 150 OO-TAO (c/n 10457) was withdrawn from use here by 5.88. L-21B Super Cub OO-ACG (ex 53-4816) crashed at Olmen 29.6.85 and is now on prolonged rebuild here. J-3C-65 Cub OO-AED (c/n 12379/12207, ex 44-80083, OO-LIL) has been stored here since CofA expiry on 17.11.82 and may be accompanied by Aeronca 7AC Champion OO-GIO (c/n 4458) whose CofA expired 1.7.82. GY-80 Horizon 160 OO-GOD (c/n 47, ex F-OCCV) made a wheels-up landing here on 20.6.87 and has not moved since. Jodel D112 Club OO-MOG (c/n 1293, ex F-BMOG) has been dismantled and stored here following CofA expiry on 11.2.78.

Stored at the airfield are the mortal remains of Cessna F152-II OO-CNO (c/n 01472, ex OO-HNO ntu) which was destroyed in a crash here on 21.3.85.

HAINE-SAINT-PIERRE

N1101 Noralpha OO-RLR (c/n 103) is thought to be here, stored at the 'Armerie du Centre'.

HAVERSIN

Schleicher KA.4 Rhonlerche II OO-ZPI is thought to be stored at the owner's house here (off the N4 about 35 kms South East of Namur) together with her sister aircraft OO-ZUG.

HELCHTEREN

By 1980 the ranges here had received three former Kleine Brogel decoy F-84F Thunderstreaks. These comprised FU-63 (ex 52-10519, marked as "BA-56"), FU-18? (ex 52-6371, marked as "BA-02") and FU-183 (ex 52-6403, marked as "BA-06") all of which had been modified to resemble Mirages for their decoy duties at Kleine Brogel. Despite their high risk existence on a live firing range all three appeared to be in respectable condition and still standing on their undercarriages when their continued existence was checked during 6.89.

HEULE

In use as 'attention getters' at the Curiosa Museum are Cessna FR172F OO-LGF (c/n 0121) and an unidentified ex French civil N1203 Norecrin whilst inside they store the cockpit section of Cessna F150K OO-RDB (c/n 0562). Heule is on the Northern edge of Kortrijk/Courtrai.

HOEVENEN

Piper J-3C Cub OO-RAZ (ex 44-79651) is under a (very!) prolonged restoration here (just North of Antwerp), its CofA having expired on 21.12.71. PA18 Super Cub OO-SPJ (c/n 18-1547, ex 51-15547) is also being nursed back to flying condition, her CofA expired 25.6.80.

KALKEN

A scrap and surplus dealer located on the North side of the town (itself South of the E3 motorway betweek Gent and Lokeren) has dealt with aircraft scrap. F-104G Starfighter FX-79 (c/n 9137) ex 1 Wg suffered a Cat.4 accident at Beauvechain 14.12.79 and was soc 3.9.80. The wreck appeared on the Evere dump by mid 1980 and turned up in Kalken by 8.81. It subsequently moved on to Beervelde during the mid eighties.

Noted here during 9.83 were a pair of T-33A wings carrying the c/n 7684. This would make them from FT-23 (ex 51-17539) which was written off at Oldenmark on 11.7.61. The fuselage of FT-23 used to be here as well but has moved to Zele.

RF-84F Thunderflash FR-26 (ex 51-1886) used to be stored in another yard on the opposite side of the road to the dealer with FX-79 and FT-23. The aircraft was w/o following a crash landing on 23.10.70. The 'flash was involved in an exchange with an F-84F owned by Brussels museum but somehow ended up moving to Savigny-Les-Beaune, France along with F-84F Thunderstreak FU-21.

KALMHOUT

Douglas C-47B Dakota K-40/OT-CWS (c/n 33244, ex 44-76912, KN601) was soc on 8.5.67 and gravitated to Kalmthout by 7.73. The aircraft appears to be hard to find as several searches of the area in 1978/79 proved fruitless although a pilot from nearby Brasschaat at this time stated that it was easy to see when on finals to his base! The Dak was unfortunately scrapped some years ago.

KEIHEUVEL

Preserved at this small gliding airfield/leisure centre (North East of Balen) is F-84F Thunderstreak FU-197 (ex 52-6584, soc 2.2.65) which arrived from Kleine Brogel in 5.83 by US Army Chinook following many years in the decoy role. The aircraft was still present in good condition in 1989.

Schneider Grunau Baby III OO-ZTO is under restoration here and KA.4 Rhonlerche II OO-KEI (ex OO-ZEA) is stored, dismantled.

KIEWIT

This small civil field (also known as Hasselt/Zonhoven) boasts several relics most of which are attributable to a Mr V Melotte. Derelict in 1980 were Dornier Do 27A-5 OO-LVH (c/n 443, ex Heer PP108, PX222, 5715 and D-ENAT) whose CofA had expired

3.1.79 with Do 27A-3 OO-LHM (c/n 417, ex WGAF GB384, CA047, 5700) whose CofA expired 26.2.76. Both were in hangar storage covered in a thick layer of dust. Also stored at this time was PA18-95 Super Cub PH-DKA (c/n 18-3854, ex 54-2454, KLu R-164), spares source L-21B MM54-2504/EI-210 (ex Italian Army) and Piaggio P.149D 9027 (c/n 040, ex WGAF). All were still current in 1985 when two ex Lucht Cadetten Grunau Babies were noted stored in the glider hangar (PL-31 and PL-38). In 5.86 only the two Do 27s and L-21B PH-DKA were noted.

Cessna F150H OO-LGD (c/n F.0351) has been in store with Mr Melotte since CofA expiry on 1.4.75

The fuselage of MS880B Rallye Club OO-CLS (c/n 1194) is stored in the M Smets hangar here together with the unmarked fuselage of Cessna F150J OO-TOM (c/n 0500). Also stored on the field is the fuselage of Wa40 Super IV OO-JIR (c/n 003) whose CofA expired as long ago as 20.9.80. MS892A Rallye Commodore 150 OO-LMB (c/n 10909, ex PH-VRM) has been stored here in a dismantled condition since an emergency landing at Genk on 22.6.86.

Somewhere along the road from Genk to Hasselt, Nord N1203 Norecrin OO-PIF (c/n 100) is used as an eye-catcher.

KLEINE-BROGEL

Home of 10 Wing's two squadrons of F-16s, the main gate here boasts classic fighters of an earlier era.

F-84E Thunderjet	"FS-2"	(ex FS-17/51-9599) ex '8S-W' 31 Esc/10 Wg (suffered accident at K-B 9.4.56 and to gia at Saffraanberg). The a/c is painted in spurious markings as "FS-2/KB-1" (noted '63-'88).
F-84F Thunderstreak	FU-145	(ex 53-6613) ex decoy, to the gate in 4.80.
F-104G Starfighter	FX-86	(c/n 9147) suffered Cat.3 damage here 26.6.81, to the gate by 8.87.

Three further aircraft are displayed within each squadron area. F-104G Starfighter FX-96 (c/n 9166) is in the 31 Esc area with FX-61 (c/n 9104, soc 26.9.83) in 23 Esc's area. 31 Esc also have F-84F Thunderstreak FU-188 (ex 52-6369) which served as a decoy until at least 1979 and was on display with 31 Esc by 1982. This aircraft is painted as "FU-131/8S-H" (which crashed on 21.8.57).

In use as decoys over the years have been the following Thunderstreaks.

F-84F Thunderstreak	FU-49	(ex 52-7008) ex Koksijde store, soc 23.2.65 (noted '72-'85 as "BA-05", probably the a/c on the fire dump in '86-'87).
F-84F Thunderstreak	FU-63	(ex 52-10519) soc 11.2.65, (noted '72-'79 as "BA-56", to Helchteren ranges by 1980).
F-84F Thunderstreak	FU-67	(ex 53-6681) ex Koksijde store, soc 19.1.65 (noted '72-'88 as "BA-03").
F-84F Thunderstreak	FU-145	(ex 53-6613) ex Koksijde store, soc 7.4.65 (noted '72-'79, to the main gate 4.80 for display).
F-84F Thunderstreak	FU-177	(ex 53-6888) ex Koksijde store, soc 27.8.70 (noted '72-'88 as "BA-04").
F-84F Thunderstreak	FU-181	(ex 52-6371) ex Koksijde store, soc 11.5.66 (noted '72-'79 as "BA-02", to Helchteren ranges by 1980).
F-84F Thunderstreak	FU-183	(ex 52-6403) ex Koksijde store, soc 26.8.68 (noted '72-'79 as "BA-06", to Helchteren ranges by 1980).
F-84F Thunderstreak	FU-185	(ex 52-6569) soc 13.1.65 (noted '72-'88 as "BA-07").
F-84F Thunderstreak	FU-188	(ex 52-6369) soc 3.10.64 (noted '72-'79, to 31 Esc for display by '82, still current in 1986).
F-84F Thunderstreak	FU-197	(ex 52-6584) soc 2.2.65 (noted '72-'83, to Keiheuvel by Chinook 5.83).

The long standing remains of a Hunter lingered on the fire dump until at least 1975 and could well have been F.4 ID-19 which was soc 11.2.60 and allocated to Kleine-Brogel.

By 1986 one of the decoy F-84Fs had been burnt to a crisp by the firemen. By a process of elimination, this should be FU-49.

There is also a report of the burnt remains of F-104G Starfighter FX-75 (c/n 9127, crashed at Peer 4.4.68) being noted here in 1984 but the compiler believes this to be in error. More likely, what was seen was one of the mock-up F-104 decoys which were in use here. Four were noted in 8.82 comprising "FX-01", "FX-42", "FX-49" and, significantly, "FX-75". These were still fooling the unwary enthusiast as late as 1986 being much more realistic than the two dimensional variety at Bierset.

F-104G Starfighter FX-04 (c/n 9019) was struck by a vehicle at Kleine-Brogel on 13.7.76 and withdrawn from use. The unfortunate aircraft then spent at least a further two years on the base sulking before eventually joining the Belgian AF road show of recruiting display airframes.

The less than substantial remains of burnt out F-16A wreck FA-35 were noted by the hangars in 1985 through to 1987 whilst parts of the unfortunate FA-14 (collided with FA-35 and crashed near Rochefort, Ardennes, on 19.1.82) were reported in use for bdr training in 1984.

KOKSIJDE

Displayed on the gate at a BelgAF barracks just across the road from the main base is Hunter F.4 ID-123 (c/n 8679), mounted in a flying attitude on a plinth made from the wing of another Hunter (noted '79-'89).

As well as the helicopters of 40 Esc, Koksijde houses the BelgAF's storage and disposal centre (Vliegtuigen Park). Having dealt with Hunters and Meteors in the sixties, the early seventies found the unit with some 95 F-84Fs and RF-84Fs. Several of the former escaped the axe to serve as decoys - probably into the nineties!
We will take up the story in the mid seventies and review those aircraft which have passed through Koksijde:-

A handful of Dakotas served with 21 Esc/15 Wg at Melsbroek into the seventies, the last being retired in 1976.

Douglas C-47B Dakota	K-1	(c/n 26501, ex 43-49240) ex 'OT-CWA', soc 11.12.73, N99346 ntu, dismantled 5.79 and to Gits.
Douglas C-47B Dakota	K-8	(c/n 25756, ex 43-48495) ex 'OT-CND', wfu early '76 and stored, soc 23.6.76, to SU-AZO, F-ODHB.
Douglas C-47B Dakota	K-10	(c/n 25851, ex 43-48590) 'OT-CWE', wfu early '76 and stored, soc 26.1.76, to SU-AZM.
Douglas C-47B Dakota	OO-SNC	(c/n 32664, ex 44-76332, K-28/OT-CNO) ex Transport Ministry, regn cancelled 15.1.75, stored, to SU-AZN.

The four DC-6As operated by 21 Esc were retired to Koksijde in 1976 and spent a relatively short time in storage before finding gainful employment with Secmafer of Nice.

Douglas DC-6A	KY-1	(c/n 45458) ex 'OT-CDA', to F-BYCG 2.77.
Douglas DC-6A	KY-2	(c/n 45518) ex 'OT-CDB', to F-BYCH 2.77.
Douglas DC-6A	KY-3	(c/n 44420) ex 'OT-CDC', to F-BYCI 2.77.
Douglas DC-6A	KY-4	(c/n 44421) ex 'OT-CDD', to F-BYCJ 2.77.

The field filled up with the old C-119G Packets in the early seventies, just as soon as the F-84s were disposed of. Most had met their fate at the hands of the scrap men by 1980 but a couple of derelict hulks seem determined to become a part of the scenery and remain to this day.

C-119G Packet	CP-9	(c/n 10689, ex 51-1700) ex 'OT-CAI', to 3C-ABA of Bata International Airways but ntu, flew out to Manston 9.4.81. Currently with Aces High at North Weald, UK, as G-BLSW/N2700.
C-119G Packet	CP-10	(c/n 10690, ex 51-2701) ex 'OT-CAJ', still current 1980, to 3C-ABB but not taken up. Reported to be one of the two surviving hulks.
C-119G Packet	CP-11	(c/n 10685, ex 51-2696) ex 'OT-CAK', still derelict in the scrapping area mid '89.
C-119G Packet	CP-12	(c/n 10692, ex 51-2703) ex 'OT-CAL', last noted '79.
C-119G Packet	CP-13	(c/n 10693, ex 51-2704) ex 'OT-CAM', last noted '79.
C-119G Packet	CP-15	(c/n 10695, ex 51-2706) ex 'OT-CAO', last noted '79.
C-119G Packet	CP-16	(c/n 10696, ex 51-2707) ex 'OT-CAP', last noted '79.

C-119G Packet CP-17 (c/n 10697, ex 51-2690) ex 'OT-CAQ', last noted '79.
C-119G Packet CP-18 (c/n 10680, ex 51-2691) ex 'OT-CAR', arr 7.73 - last BelgAF C-119 flight, last noted '79.
C-119G Packet CP-20 (c/n 11034, ex 52-6033) ex 'OT-CAT', last noted '77.
C-119G Packet CP-21 (c/n 10952, ex 52-6022) ex 'OT-CBA', last noted '73.
C-119G Packet CP-22 (c/n 10953, ex 52-6023) ex 'OT-CBB', last noted '75.
C-119G Packet CP-24 (c/n 11077, ex 52-6038) ex 'OT-CBD', last noted '75.
C-119G Packet CP-26 (c/n 11029, ex 52-6028) ex 'OT-CBF', last noted '75.
C-119G Packet CP-27 (c/n 10997, ex 52-6026) ex 'OT-CBG', last noted '75.
C-119G Packet CP-28 (c/n 11078, ex 52-6039) ex 'OT-CBH', last noted '75.
C-119G Packet CP-30 (c/n 10998, ex 52-6027) ex 'OT-CBJ', last noted '75.
C-119G Packet CP-31 (c/n 11036, ex 52-6035) ex 'OT-CBK', last noted '73.
C-119G Packet CP-32 (c/n 11084, ex 52-6045) ex 'OT-CBL', last noted '77.
C-119G Packet CP-33 (c/n 11033, ex 52-6032) ex 'OT-CBM', last noted '77.
C-119G Packet CP-34 (c/n 11118, ex 52-6050) ex 'OT-CBN', last noted '75.
C-119G Packet CP-35 (c/n 11120, ex 52-6052) ex 'OT-CBO', last noted '73.
C-119G Packet CP-38 (c/n 11119, ex 52-6051) ex 'OT-CBR', last noted '75.
C-119G Packet CP-39 (c/n 11085, ex 52-6046) ex 'OT-CBS', last noted '75.
C-119G Packet CP-40 (c/n 11146, ex 52-6058) ex 'OT-CBT', last noted '75.
C-119G Packet CP-41 (c/n 11246, ex 53-7829) ex 'OT-CEA', last noted '79.
C-119G Packet CP-42 (c/n 11260, ex 53-7843) ex 'OT-CEB', last noted '79.
C-119G Packet CP-43 (c/n 241, ex 53-8138) ex 'OT-CEC', last noted '79.
C-119G Packet CP-44 (c/n 244, ex 53-8141) ex 'OT-CED', last noted '77.
C-119G Packet CP-46 (c/n 254, ex 53-8151) ex 'OT-CEH', last noted '77, to Brussels museum.

A number of Magisters were made surplus with the procurement of the Alpha Jet. As can be seen below, of those in storage here the bulk were sold (through various middle men) to Israel for possible use in the AMIT programme, most being acquired by Aces High during 1988. Of those listed, all except MT-14 were in open storage by 7.80.

CM170 Magister MT-1 (c/n 258) arr 6.4.77, returned to service.
CM170 Magister MT-2 (c/n 259) arr 28.11.78, sold 1980.
CM170 Magister MT-4 (c/n 261) arr 6.4.77, returned to service.
CM170 Magister MT-5 (c/n 262) arr 20.9.79, sold 1980.
CM170 Magister MT-11 (c/n 268) arr 19.8.77, sold 1980.
CM170 Magister MT-12 (c/n 269) arr 27.6.78, sold 1980.
CM170 Magister MT-14 (c/n 271) arr 30.8.79, returned to service.
CM170 Magister MT-15 (c/n 272) arr 2.9.77, sold 1980.
CM170 Magister MT-16 (c/n 273) arr 2.3.79, sold 1980.
CM170 Magister MT-18 (c/n 275) arr 2.10.78, sold 1980.
CM170 Magister MT-21 (c/n 278) arr 2.7.79, sold 1980.
CM170 Magister MT-27 (c/n 284) arr 26.1.79, sold 1980.
CM170 Magister MT-32 (c/n 289) arr 20.8.79, sold 1980.

Replaced by the F-16, thirty eight F-104G Starfighters arrived at Koksijde for storage (a further eighteen aircraft were collected from Beauvechain by the Turkish AF). After several years of wheeling and dealing the airframes have gradually deteriorated and the chances of them flying again are remote to say the least. By the end of 1988 these machines had finally passed into the hands of Radcomm Inc who were offering them for sale at 250,000 Belgian Francs each. The first few disposals were taking place as this text was closed for press.

F-104G Starfighter FX-02 (c/n 9017) ex 31 Esc/10 Wg, arrived 14.6.83.
F-104G Starfighter FX-03 (c/n 9018) ex 23 Esc/10 Wg, arrived 3.11.81.
F-104G Starfighter FX-07 (c/n 9022) ex 31 Esc/10 Wg, arrived 7.7.83.
F-104G Starfighter FX-10 (c/n 9027) ex 350 Esc/1 Wg, arrived 5.2.81.
F-104G Starfighter FX-41 (c/n 9084) ex 31 Esc/10 Wg, arrived 10.5.83.
F-104G Starfighter FX-44 (c/n 9087) ex 350 Esc/1 Wg, arrived 7.5.81.
F-104G Starfighter FX-45 (c/n 9088) ex 31 Esc/10 Wg, arrived 13.5.82.
F-104G Starfighter FX-47 (c/n 9090) ex 31 Esc/10 Wg, arrived 4.8.83.
F-104G Starfighter FX-48 (c/n 9091) ex 350 Esc/1 Wg, arrived 14.4.81.

F-104G Starfighter	FX-51	(c/n 9094) ex 31 Esc/10 Wg, arrived 25.8.82.
F-104G Starfighter	FX-52	(c/n 9095) ex 31 Esc/10 Wg, arrived 29.6.83.
F-104G Starfighter	FX-57	(c/n 9100) ex 350 Esc/1 Wg, arrived 14.4.81.
F-104G Starfighter	FX-58	(c/n 9101) ex 350 Esc/1 Wg, arrived 15.9.80.
F-104G Starfighter	FX-59	(c/n 9102) ex 350 Esc/1 Wg, arrived 3.6.81.
F-104G Starfighter	FX-60	(c/n 9103) ex 23 Esc/10 Wg, arrived 19.2.82, to Hermeskeil, WG, 10.2.89.
F-104G Starfighter	FX-62	(c/n 9105) ex 349 Esc/1 Wg, arrived 29.5.80.
F-104G Starfighter	FX-64	(c/n 9107) ex 23 Esc/10 Wg, arrived 22.10.81.
F-104G Starfighter	FX-65	(c/n 9108) ex 23 Esc/10 Wg, arrived 19.11.81.
F-104G Starfighter	FX-67	(c/n 9113) ex 350 Esc/1 Wg, arrived 30.9.80.
F-104G Starfighter	FX-69	(c/n 9115) ex 349 Esc/1 Wg, arrived 18.7.80.
F-104G Starfighter	FX-70	(c/n 9119) ex 23 Esc/10 Wg, arrived 25.2.83.
F-104G Starfighter	FX-72	(c/n 9121) ex 350 Esc/1 Wg, arrived 14.4.81.
F-104G Starfighter	FX-74	(c/n 9126) ex 350 Esc/1 Wg, arrived 14.4.81.
F-104G Starfighter	FX-76	(c/n 9131) ex 23 Esc/10 Wg, arrived 14.8.81.
F-104G Starfighter	FX-78	(c/n 9133) ex 31 Esc/10 Wg, arrived 18.5.83.
F-104G Starfighter	FX-80	(c/n 9138) ex 350 Esc/1 Wg, arrived 14.4.81.
F-104G Starfighter	FX-81	(c/n 9139) ex 31 Esc/10 Wg, arrived 19.4.82.
F-104G Starfighter	FX-82	(c/n 9140) ex 31 Esc/10 Wg, arrived 21.10.82.
F-104G Starfighter	FX-83	(c/n 9141) ex 23 Esc/10 Wg, arrived 11.2.82.
F-104G Starfighter	FX-84	(c/n 9142) ex 23 Esc/10 Wg, arrived 10.12.81.
F-104G Starfighter	FX-85	(c/n 9146) ex 23 Esc/10 Wg, arrived 27.2.81.
F-104G Starfighter	FX-89	(c/n 9153) ex 350 Esc/1 Wg, arrived 14.4.81.
F-104G Starfighter	FX-90	(c/n 9154) ex 31 Esc/10 Wg, arrived 23.9.82, to Savigny-Les-Beaune, France, by 12.88.
F-104G Starfighter	FX-93	(c/n 9160) ex 31 Esc/10 Wg, arrived 6.4.82.
F-104G Starfighter	FX-94	(c/n 9164) ex 31 Esc/10 Wg, arrived 22.6.83.
F-104G Starfighter	FX-99	(c/n 9172) ex 31 Esc/10 Wg, arrived 26.9.83.
F-104G Starfighter	FX-100	(c/n 9176) ex 23 Esc/10 Wg, arrived 28.1.82.

All the surviving TF-104Gs were placed in store here and like their single seat colleagues waited for years to find a buyer.

TF-104G Starfighter	FC-01	(c/n 5786) ex 10 Wg, arrived 17.8.82.
TF-104G Starfighter	FC-02	(c/n 5787) ex 10 Wg, arrived 14.2.83.
TF-104G Starfighter	FC-03	(c/n 5788) ex 10 Wg, arrived 30.10.81.
TF-104G Starfighter	FC-04	(c/n 5101) ex 10 Wg, arrived 4.10.83, to Gosselies 21.12.84 but returned by road.
TF-104G Starfighter	FC-06	(c/n 5103) ex 10 Wg, arrived 16.2.83.
TF-104G Starfighter	FC-07	(c/n 5104) ex 10 Wg, arrived 4.5.83.
TF-104G Starfighter	FC-08	(c/n 5105) ex Evere/Melsbroek (C-130 loading trials) arr 26.3.81, to Savigny-Les-Beaune, France by 12.88.
TF-104G Starfighter	FC-10	(c/n 5107) ex 10 Wg, arrived 6.11.81.
TF-104G Starfighter	FC-11	(c/n 5108) ex 10 Wg, arrived 26.9.83, to Gosselies 21.12.84 but returned by road.
TF-104G Starfighter	FC-12	(c/n 5109) ex 10 Wg, arrived 25.3.83.

Most T-33A disposals were direct from Brustem but a couple of them deserve a mention here.

Lockheed T-33A	FT-03	(ex 51-4062) arrived 22.5.78, departed to the ranges at Vilseck, WG, 28.3.79 slung under CH-47C Chinook 20946.
Lockheed T-33A	FT-34	(ex 55-3043) arrived 24.7.78, to Brussels museum.

Having been gathered into storage at Koksijde, the Pembrokes were sold in the USA in 1978 and passed through the UK for fitment of long range tanks prior to crossing the Atlantic. Within a few years most of them had crashed whilst engaged on drug smuggling flights though RM-1 is now with the Yankee Air Museum and RM-2 is still flying from Denver.

Hunting Pembroke C.51	RM-1	(c/n 14) ex 'OT-ZAA' 21 Esc/15 Wg, arr 13.1.76, soc 6.4.76, to N51973 & dep 31.5.78.

Hunting Pembroke C.51	RM-2	(c/n 17) ex 'OT-ZAB' 21 Esc/15 Wg, arr 15.7.74, soc 26.2.75, to N51948 & dep 9.8.78.
Hunting Pembroke C.51	RM-3	(c/n 20) ex 'OT-ZAC' 21 Esc/15 Wg, arr 28.1.77, soc 31.3.77, to N51951 & dep 31.5.78.
Hunting Pembroke C.51	RM-5	(c/n 24) ex 'OT-ZAE' 21 Esc/15 Wg, arr 14.2.74, soc 12.11.74, to N51961 & dep 9.8.78.
Hunting Pembroke C.51	RM-6	(c/n 25) ex 'OT-ZAF' 21 Esc/15 Wg, arr 16.8.75, soc 29.9.75, to N51962 & dep 24.6.78.
Hunting Pembroke C.51	RM-8	(c/n 28) ex 'OT-ZAH' 21 Esc/15 Wg, arr 28.2.75, soc 22.4.75, to N51963 & dep 14.5.78.
Hunting Pembroke C.51	RM-9	(c/n 29) ex 'OT-ZAI' 21 Esc/15 Wg, arr 19.3.76, soc 28.4.76, to N51964 & dep 14.5.78.
Hunting Pembroke C.51	RM-10	(c/n 31) ex 'OT-ZAJ' 21 Esc/15 Wg, arr 13.5.76, soc 21.6.76, to N51966 & dep 31.5.78.
Hunting Pembroke C.51	RM-11	(c/n 32) ex 'OT-ZAK' 21 Esc/15 Wg, arr 22.6.76, soc 19.11.76, to N51970 & dep 14.5.78.
Hunting Pembroke C.51	M-12	(c/n 33) ex 'OT-ZAL' 21 Esc/15 Wg, arr 17.6.75, soc 3.9.75, to N51972 & dep 24.6.78.

The Sikorsky S-58/H-34/HSS-1 was based at Koksijde and operated by 40 Esc on behalf of the BelgAF and the Belgian Navy with the final aircraft being withdrawn from use in 7.86. Earlier disposals had found civilian employment in West Germany but of the recent retirements B-6 replaced the wrecked B-13 in the Brussels museum and three aircraft are still held in long term store.

Sikorsky UH-34G	B-4	(c/n SA145) ex 'OTZKD', wfu 5.12.84 and stored here.
Sikorsky UH-34G	B-5	(c/n SA146) ex 'OT-ZKE', to storage following an accident here on 29.8.85.
Sikorsky UH-34G	B-6	(c/n SA181) ex 'OT-ZKF', wfu 10.5.79, TT 3744 hrs, to Brussels museum 20.8.81.
Sikorsky UH-34G	B-8	(c/n SA185)ex 'OT-ZKH', wfu 19.7.86,TT 3489 hrs,stored.
Sikorsky S-58C	B-10	(c/n 58-333, ex OO-SHH) ex 'OT-ZKJ', wfu 25.5.76, dep 31.1.78 to D-HAUE.
Sikorsky S-58C	B-11	(c/n 58-356, ex OO-SHI) ex 'OT-ZKK', wfu 29.6.76, dep 22.3.78 to D-HAUF.
Sikorsky S-58C	B-12	(c/n 58-388, ex OO-SHL) ex 'OT-ZKL', wfu 20.7.76, dep 22.3.78 to D-HAUD.
Sikorsky S-58C	B-14	(c/n 58-850, ex OO-SHQ) ex 'OT-ZKN', wfu 10.6.76, dep 31.10.78 to D-HAUC.
Sikorsky S-58C	B-15	(c/n 58-826, ex OO-SHQ) ex 'OT-ZKP', wfu '76, dep 5.5.78 to D-HAUG.

The last few Stampe SV4Cs from long term storage were sold off in 1978/79 having replaced by the Siai-Marchetti SF260MB some eight years earlier.

Stampe SV4C	V-4	(c/n 1144) ex EVS, sold 6.12.78 to OO-EIR.
Stampe SV4C	V-43	(c/n 1185) ex EVS, sold 24.10.79, to OO-SVB.
Stampe SV4C	V-49	(c/n 1191) ex EVS, sold 24.10.79, to OO-SVA.
Stampe SV4C	V-52	(c/n 1194) ex Brustem, sold 6.12.78, to OO-BPL.

Former AdlA Mystere IVA 191/8-NK (ex ET.2/8) arrived here from Savigny-Les-Beaune on 16.11.88 for storage on behalf of the Brussels museum. It was involved in an exchange which took a couple of F-104s to Savigny. It joins ex CEV Meteor NF.11 NF.11-3 which arrived here for the museum in 7.87.

Spitfire LF.IX SG-29/MN-P (ex MK912) arrived here from Saffraanberg in '88 and moved on to Coltishall by C-130 on 22.6.89 in exchange for a Bristol Fighter.

LEOPOLDSBURG

Piper PA18-95 OO-DFS (c/n 18-1637, ex 51-15637 ALAT, CofA expired 8.3.78) was noted dismantled here in 8.86.

LONDERZEEL

Morane Saulnier MS885 Super Rallye OO-MUZ (c/n 5427) is stored next to a Mazda garage in the vicinity (on the N177 North of Brussels).

MARCINELLE

The fuselage of Bap-Air's MS317 Parasol OO-JUL (c/n 6530/276) is undergoing restoration here (on the Southern side of Charleroi). The wings are stored at Gosselies.

MOHIVILLE-HAMOIS

L-125 Sohaj 2 OO-ZPM (c/n 178) is in storage awaiting restoration at a private address here (off the N4 some 30kms South East of Namur).

MOLENHEIDE

Hunting Pembroke C.51 RM-7/OT-ZAG (c/n 27, ex 21 Esc/15 Wg) was flown to Kleine-Brogel upon retirement and soc 23.3.76. Originally intended for use as a range target, the aircraft was granted a reprieve and moved to the Molenheide leisure complex near Helchteren, a few miles South of Kleine Brogel and just off the N15. Although sitting atop several poles, the aircraft has suffered from vandals and the elements over the years.

MONS

PA28 Cherokee OO-LSP (c/n 28-3954) was described as 'withdrawn from use' here in 6.85 whilst Leonard 360M3 OO-BAZ is thought to be in store here following CofA expiry on 9.7.85.

MOORSELE

Noted at the airfield here in 5.83 was the wreckage of Beagle Pup OO-WRL (c/n B170, ex G-BBIB). More recently, Stampe SV4C OO-GWA (c/n 478) has been under restoration, assisted by the fuselage of F-BDCX (c/n 552).

OOSTENDE

Former Young Air Cargo Britannias OO-YCB (c/n 13456, ex XL659) and OO-YCE (c/n 13398, ex XL636) were derelict here for some time before being broken up for scrap mid 1980.

Derelict here in 5.81 was Convair VT-29A N39414 (ex 50-0183 and MASDC storage as park-code TB037 from 29.8.74-16.2.77). The aircraft spent a considerable time in the open at Stansted before staggering to Oostende where the aircraft was still derelict in 4.85 and was scrapped soon after.

Further derelicts noted here in 5.81 were Beagle B206 OO-EEL (c/n B026, ex G-ATKP, since to Snaaskerke) and Cessna UC-78 Bobcat OO-TIN (c/n 5253, ex 43-7703, HB-UEF). The Bobcat had been acquired by Aero Retro at St Rambert d'Albon, France, by 1984.

Cessna F150L OO-NZO (c/n F.0778) is dismantled here, having been stored since CofA expiry on 5.3.81.

Viscount 708 9Q-CAH (c/n 36, ex G-ARIR) of 3M Air Services was stored here by 6.86. She was still current up to 3.89 when the aircraft was blown up with dynamite and removed for scrap!

OUDENBURG

Stampe SV4C OO-CKZ (c/n 21) is undergoing restoration here at the owner's private premises (East of Oostende).

OUD-TURNHOUT

The wreckage of Scheibe SF27A Bergfalke OO-ZZB (c/n 6042) is stored in a hangar here.

OVERBOELARE

In use as a clubhouse and bar at the airfield here is Douglas DC-4 "N2893C" (built as C-54 42-72247) which was aquired after the war by American Airlines as N90443 "Flagship Texas". Following service with Eastern Airlines, the a/c went to Aerovias Panama Airways. On 14.6.63 the aircraft flew into Brussels with the fake registration "N2893C" on the fuselage (which it still wears - just!). The craft was impounded and sold at public auction, making her final flight from Brussels to

Overboelare on 5.7.67. She was still present in 10.84 and probably survives to this day.

PAAL

Stored here, probably at a private house are MS885 Super Rallye OO-AKA (c/n 145), the fuselage of MS893A Rallye OO-AMA (c/n 2601), the wreck of MS880B Rallye OO-VHF (c/n 2458), SV4B OO-LEL (c/n 1197 ex V-55), Jodel DR315 Petit Prince OO-NEW (c/n 364, dismantled), Cessna F172H OO-PPE (c/n F0557, wreck, crashed at Averbode 17.8.80), PA18 Super Cub OO-VVC (c/n 18-8286, crashed at Drongen 17.5.86), Cessna 150G N3162J (c/n 65862), Cessna FA150L Aerobat OO-WIR (c/n 0111), ex RLS Safirs PH-RLB (c/n 91368), PH-RLL (c/n 91377 - to fly again), PH-RLO (c/n 91380) and the fuselage of Cessna U206A OO-VDC (c/n 0575). This fellow sounds like the Belgian equivalent of Roger Windley!

RUMST

The fuselage of Piaggio P.149D OO-LWH (c/n 052, ex WGAF 9038) is thought to be in store here (South of Antwerp) with the dealers 'Gebroeders Van Der Auwera'.

SAFFRAANBERG

The BelgAF's technical school is located about a mile down the N3 from Brustem air base. On display near the main gate in 350 Sqn markings has been Spitfire LF.IX SM-29/"MN-P" (ex MK912, KLu H-59, H-119, fitted with wings from SM-22). The aircraft went via Koksijde to Coltishall (UK) on 22.6.89 in exchange or a Bristol Fighter.

Bolingbroke IVT	9895	(ex RCAF) arrived here from Brussels museum by 5.88 for restoration to static display condition.
Dornier Do 27J-1	DO-2	(c/n 2058) last flight 25.3.77, wfu at Butzweilerhof then arrived here 4.5.78, to Brasschaat '89.
CM170 Magister	MT-37	(c/n 312) arr 6.4.77 (current '89).
F-104G Starfighter	FX-01	(c/n 9016) nose section only, ex 1 Wg, crashed at Chapois-Leignon 26.1.71. Still current '82.
F-104G Starfighter	FX-12	(c/n 9029) arr Brustem 13.11.79 and roaded here 27.11.79, to Brussels Museum 4.5.83.
F-104G Starfighter	FX-15	(c/n 9034) ex 31 Esc/10 Wg, roaded here from Brustem on 4.5.83 (noted '87-'89).
F-104G Starfighter	FX-18	(c/n 9040) ex 1 Wg, Cat.4 accident at Beauvechain 23.5.78, rear fuse reported here 5.83, fuselage dumped here '87-'89.
F-104G Starfighter	FX-21	(c/n 9046) ex 349 Esc/1 Wg, arr Brustem 8.2.80 and roaded here 14.2.80 (noted '87-'89).
F-104G Starfighter	FX-39	(c/n 9079) ex 349 Esc/1 Wg, arr Brustem 9.1.80 and roaded here 14.2.80 (noted '87-'89).
F-104G Starfighter	FX-53	(c/n 9096) ex 349 Esc/1 Wg, arr Brustem 1.9.79 and roaded here 1.10.79 (noted '87-'89). By early '89 the aircraft was restored to the old silver colour scheme and replaced the Spitfire on display by the gate.
F-84F Thunderstreak	FU-174	(ex 53-6862) (noted '73-'79, then scrapped).
RF-84F Thunderstreak	FR-30	(ex 51-17015) ex 42 Esc (noted '78-'88).
RF-84F Thunderstreak	FR-31	(ex 53-7644) ex 42 Esc (noted '78-'87, to KLu by early '88).
RF-84F Thunderstreak	FR-32	(ex 53-7646) ex 42 Esc (noted '78-'82, to Bierset by '83).
RF-84F Thunderstreak	FR-33	(ex 53-7658) ex 42 Esc (noted '78-'88 - to the Musee de l'Air at Le Bourget '89).
Sud Alouette II	OL-A10	(c/n 1534) crashed at Butzweilerhof 14.6.66 (noted '77-'87).

ST GHISLAIN

Cherokee 180 OO-LSP (c/n 28-3954) is under restoration here (West of Mons).

ST HUBERT

Bellanca Decathlon OO-BNO (c/n 610-80) is under restoration at the owner's residence here following CofA expiry on 2.4.86.

ST KATELIJNE-WAVER

SNCAN/Caudron NC800 OO-ZVE (c/n 9912/252) is stored in a greenhouse here (South East of Antwerp).

ST NIKLAAS

In use as a garage here (South West of Antwerp) is the wingless fuselage of an ex Koksijde C-119G Packet.

SCHILDE

The fuselage of Wassmer WA51 Pacific OO-JCO (c/n 003) remains here (East of Antwerp) as a spares source since it was destroyed in an accident at Bissegem on 16.8.87. The fuselage of WA52 Europa LX-OUF (c/n 104) is also here (wings at Antwerp).

SENSENRUTH

Schneider Grunau Baby OO-ZPP is undergoing restoration at a private address here (off the N554 North of Bouillon).

SNAASKERKE

A scrapyard here held a large stock of dismantled Hunter F.4 hulks into the 1980s though it has now been almost totally cleared. Noted in 8.80 were the following.

Hawker Hunter F.4	ID-47	ex 9 Wg, soc 19.7.61 (rear fuselage '82).
Hawker Hunter F.4	ID-49	ex 1 Wg, soc 28.6.61.
Hawker Hunter F.4	ID-51	ex 'IS-Q' 9 Wg, soc 25.10.61 (front & centre fuselage
Hawker Hunter F.4	ID-52	ex 9 Wg, soc 25.7.61, parts to Feltham, UK.
Hawker Hunter F.4	ID-53	ex 1 Wg, soc 25.8.61, parts to Feltham, UK.
Hawker Hunter F.4	ID-54	ex 1 Wg, soc 30.10.61, parts to Staravia at Ascot, UK.
Hawker Hunter F.4	ID-55	ex 1 Wg, soc 7.8.61.
Hawker Hunter F.4	ID-57	ex 'G' 1 Wg, soc 9.11.61 (rear fuselage '82).
Hawker Hunter F.4	ID-62	ex 1 Wg, soc 28.9.61 (rear fuselage '82, parts to Feltham, UK).
Hawker Hunter F.4	ID-115	
Hawker Hunter F.4	ID-119	tail still here '88.
Hawker Hunter F.4	ID-121	
Hawker Hunter F.4	ID-127	(front & rear fuselage '80).
Hawker Hunter F.4	ID-128	(front & rear fuselage '80).
Hawker Hunter F.4	ID-129	
Hawker Hunter F.4	ID-...	ex '7-JC'

The hulk of Beagle B.206 OO-EEL (c/n B.026, ex G-ATKP) had arrived here from Oostende airport by 1988.

SPA

Fournier RF-3 OO-NSC (c/n 64) was written off in a crash at Jalhay on 6.10.85. The wreck is stored here.

STEVOORT

Jodel D120A OO-BDV (c/n 316) is stored dismantled in the owner's garden here (West of Hasselt).

TEMPLOUX

Stored in the Air-Technic hangar are PA28R Cherokee OO-BEN (c/n 28-7615052, dismantled), MS880B Rallye Club OO-FAF (c/n 1856, fuselage), MS880B Rallye Club OO-GYT (c/n 2260, CofA expired 2.5.85), Jodel D120A OO-FDM (c/n 264, dismantled) and MS880B Rallye OO-GOM (c/n 2479, fuselage only).

In open store outside the glider hangar is Scheibe L-Spatz 55 OO-ZIL (c/n 534) whilst Robin HR100/210 OO-BLD is stored somewhere on the field following CofA expiry on 24.11.86 as is Jodel D112F Club OO-JOB (c/n 1119) whose CofA expired 23.9.80.

MS880B Rallye OO-BTL (c/n 2424) is under restoration here following CofA expiry on 28.4.83 with MS885 Super Rallye OO-FTL (c/n 5395) in the same situation after its CofA expired 8.5.86. Piper J-3L Cub OO-UBU (c/n 4645) is stored, dismantled.

TESSENDERLO

Aeronca 11AC Chief OO-SGT (c/n 11AC-1604) is thought to be undergoing restoration here (North of Diest) at a private address.

TONGERLO

The Brussels museum has a storage/restoration facility in a military area here which looks after their 'heavy metal' items. Light aircraft such as the Cubs and Stampes are dealt with at Tielen and recent arrivals have gone to storage at Koksijde. The two ex Gosselies (qv) Meteor TT.20s which came here departed during 6.88 to Monsieur Pont's museum at Savigny-Les-Beaune, France as part of an exchange deal.

Former Beauvechain decoy F-84F Thunderstreaks FU-184 (ex 52-6430) and FU-186 (ex 52-6620) were both airlifted in by Chinook on 17.12.86 for use in future exchange deals.

TORHOUT

Former 21 Esc Douglas DC-4 KX-1/OT-CWU (c/n 10326) came here by road from Koksijde storage in 1973 for use as an attraction at a cafe. Regrettably, the aircraft was scrapped in 1978.

VERVIERS/THEUX

Stored in a hangar here are the unmarked fuselage of Jodel D11 OO-VIV (c/n CD.03), the wreckage of SZD-22B Mucha Standard OO-ZSR (c/n 521?) and the unmarked and dismantled Piper L-21B Super Cub OO-VIZ (ex 51-15507).

WEELDE

The 'bent' fuselage of Schleicher KA.4 Rhonlerche II OO-ZPW (c/n 235/56) is stored inside a hangar here.

WESTOUTER

Douglas C-47B Dakota K-31/OT-CNR (c/n 16064, ex 43-76991) was soc at Koksijde 19.10.71 and moved to a location near here (a few kilometres South of Poperinge, by the French border) where its fuselage still lay in 1989.

WEVELGEM

Noted here in 4.80 was Convair VT-29B N99653 (ex 51-5154, ex MASDC TB134). Was this W&R material and if so what happened to it?

By 6.83 Ryan Navion 4 OO-EXK (c/n NAV-4-1117) was derelict here whilst in 6.85 the wreck population comprised Jodel DR315 OO-BUK (c/n 443, stored dismantled, CofA expired 16.3.82) and Jodel OO-GRE.

Beech F33A Bonanza OO-EOD (c/n CE-291) was stored here by 1988 following a landing accident at Koln/Bonn, WG, in 1987. DH Chipmunk 22A OO-FFT (ex WG401) has been in store here since CofA expiry on 30.9.86.

The fuselage of Cherokee 235B OO-JVE (c/n 28-10894) has been stored in the Servisair hangar since it was badly damaged in a heavy landing here on 19.7.87.

WILRIJK

Wassmer WA52 Europa OO-GIN (c/n 71) is being restored here (on the Southern edge of Antwerp), its CofA having expired on 18.9.81.

ZELE

A private owner here (some 10 kms East of Kalken) has the fuselage of Lockheed T-33A FT-23 (ex 51-17539) which crashed near Oldenmark on 11.7.61 and subsequently appeared in the yard at Kalken. The aircraft is apparently available for hire as a travelling exhibit.

ZELLIK

There is a large BelgAF depot at Eckstein Kaserne (by the side of the Zellik - Relegem - Wemmel road) which has held a Hunter and a Stampe in recent years. Hunter F.4 ID-26 (ex 7 Wg, OVK, 9 Wg) was soc 19.2.60 and allocated to Wevelgem 8.11.60 for gate guard duties before arrival at Zellik. After a while in store here, the aircraft was placed on display on a pole within the base (noted 1983). Stampe SV4C V-57 (c/n 1199, Cat.4 17.5.56) was also reported here some years ago but was passed on to the Brussels Museum where she hangs in anonymous overall white colour scheme in memory of the famous escapee from occupuied Europe which became MX457.

ZEMST

Piaggio P.149D OO-LWI (c/n 154, ex WGAF 9132) made a wheels-up landing at Zwartberg on 31.5.82 and has since been positioned as an attraction at the owner's house here (between Brussels and Mechelen).

ZOERSEL

Eric Voormezeele's ex AdlA AD-4N Skyraider is kept here. Registered as OO-FOR, the a/c is ex Bu126965 (c/n 7765) and served with the USN, AdlA and Chad AF before returning to the AdlA for disposal via Chateaudun. The wings and fuselage of Stampe SV4C OO-SPM (c/n 349) are stored here, the CofA having expired on 15.12.77.

ZWARTBERG

Piper J-3C Cub OO-JAN (ex 43-30238) is under restoration here (North of Genk).

CYPRUS

Divided into Greek and Turkish sectors since the Turkish invasion during 1974, Cyprus also houses several Sovereign Base Areas retained as UK territory after independence. The SBAs are now included in our sister volume 'Wrecks and Relics' (the original) by Ken Ellis. Brief details only of the current situation are therefore included together with some rather old information for Nicosia airport. This airport is now situated in the buffer zone between the Greek and Turkish communities and access is limited. It is therefore most likely that the W&R situation is unchanged.

AKROTIRI

Wrecks and relics present over the last couple of years have comprised the following.

Avro Vulcan B.2	XL317	(8725M) (arrived '83, scrapped late '86, the bits lingering into '87).
Canberra B.6(Mod)	WJ768	ex 51 Sqn, mortal remains on fire dump.
Lightning F.6	XS929	ex 'BG' 11 Sqn, arrived 20.5.88 and preserved on the gate in 56 Sqn markings as 'L'.
Whirlwind HAR 10	XJ437	(8788M) ex "Clubs" 84 Sqn A Flt, bdr airframe by 11.87.

LARNACA

Whirlwind HAR.10 XD184 (8787M, ex "Spades" 84 Sqn) serves as a gate guard at the barracks here (noted '87).

NICOSIA

The following information dates from the early eighties but is thought still to remain valid. If anyone is able to supply an update it would be gratefull received.

For many years former Cyprus Airways HS Trident 2E 5B-DAB (c/n 2155) has occupied the large Cyprus Airways hangar here. The aircraft is complete but minus engines, instrumentation and is riddled with bullet holes gained during the Turkish invasion. On the far side of the field lie the burnt remains of Trident 2E 5B-DAE (c/n 2134) of which the wings and tail are the most substantial areas. Both these aircraft were damaged (or destroyed in the case of 'DAE) on 22.7.74.

In the same hangar was PA22 Colt 5B-CAQ (c/n 22-7470) looking very tatty and minus its wings.

Under the threshold of one of the runways are the remains of Canadair CL-44 HB-ITB (c/n 13232) which crashed here as long ago as 19.4.67. These remains are not too substantial but include the front fuselage and the engines.

DENMARK

A fascinating country for those with an interest in the classic fighters of the post war era as the Danish AF are most reluctant to scrap their aeroplanes at the end of their flying careers. Some relics still surviving on Danish air bases have been there for around three decades! Unfortunately the inevitable has happened in the last few years and many of these old warriors have recently gone for scrap or for use as range targets.

On the preservation scene, Denmark is fortunate to have several excellent museums possessing many rare aircraft. The most important development in recent times has been the establishment of a permanent museum for the Danmarks Flyvemuseum which has been located at Billund since 1987 and is at last able to publicly display airframes which have long been held in store.

It is rumoured that a Danish Starfighter is involved in an exchange deal to bring a Fairey Firefly from Sweden whilst a Norwegian museum is due to receive an F-86D from Karup.

The Danish section of this book takes the mid seventies as its starting point as there has not, to my knowledge, been any other publication dealing with the "W&R" situation in Denmark recently.

Finally, just a reminder that local spellings are used throughout, hence Alborg and Kobenhavn etc, rather than the anglicised Aalborg and Copenhagen.

ALBORG

Denmark's most Northerly air base, Alborg houses the RDanAF's Esk.723 and Esk.726 operating F-16s. The airfield can be found to the West of the city of Alborg to the South of the 11/55 highway.

The main gate is guarded by an F-86D Sabre marked as "F-326" (noted '75-'88) which is in fact F-947 (ex 51-5947) fitted with the tail of F-043 (ex 51-6043). The fake serial "F-326" was used because of the '3' for Esk.723 and the '6' for Esk.726. On a pole at the entrance to the Esk.726 area is F-84G Thunderjet 19966 (ex 51-9966) (noted '75-'88) painted in spurious Esk.726 codes as "KR-A". In fact this last saw service with Esk.728 as 'SI-Q' and is now allocated to the Flyvevabnets Historiske Samling (RDanAF Historical Collection).

Decoy aircraft at Alborg recently have comprised the following.

F-86D Sabre	F-470	(ex 51-8470) ex Esk.728, wfu 14.3.66 (noted '75-'88, then to fire dump).
F-86D Sabre	F-473	(ex 51-8473) ex Esk.728, wfu 14.3.66 (noted '75-'88, to Oksbol ranges 10.6.88).
F-86D Sabre	F-971	(ex 51-5971) ex Esk.728, wfu 14.3.66 (noted '75-'88, then to fire dump).
F-86D Sabre	F-994	(ex 51-5994) ex Esk.728, wfu 14.3.66 (noted '75-'88, to Oksbol ranges 10.6.88).
F-84G Thunderjet	110018	(ex 51-10018) ex 'SY-V' Esk.729, wfu 3.1.59 (noted pre '78).
F-84G Thunderjet	110209	(ex 51-10209) ex 'SE-X' Esk.730, wfu 13.12.58 (noted pre '78).
F-84G Thunderjet	110297	(ex 51-10297) ex 'KR-O' Esk.726, wfu 18.8.58 (noted pre '78).
F-84G Thunderjet	110614	(ex 51-10614) ex 'KP-C' Esk.725, wfu 8.7.58 (noted pre '78).

The four Thunderjets listed above had all left Alborg by 1978 having been sold as scrap a short time before.

CF-104 Starfighter	R-757	(ex RCAF 12757) ex Esk.726, wfu 1.7.83 (noted '85, to Tirstrup as decoy '86).
CF-104 Starfighter	R-758	(ex RCAF 12758) ex Esk.726, l/f 10.6.83 (noted '85, to Tirstrup as decoy '86).
CF-104 Starfighter	R-896	(ex RCAF 12896) ex Esk.723, l/f 28.6.83 (noted '85).
CF-104D Starfighter	RT-667	(ex RCAF 12667) ex Esk.723, l/f 28.12.82 (noted '85).

The following aircraft have been held in storage on the base in recent years.

Gloster Meteor F.4	43-461	(c/n G5/294) ex Aalborg Stn Flt, wfu 19.1.56 (noted '75-'85, to Billund 4.5.88).
Gloster Meteor TT.20	H-504	(c/n 5545, ex WM387) ex Karup Stn Flt, wfu 31.7.62 (noted '84, to Billund 8.10.86). Formerly displayed on the gate, this a/c was restored to NF.11 configuration as 51-504 and moved to the Danmarks Flyvemuseum at Billund on 8.10.86.
Hawker Hunter F.51	E-401	(c/n 41H/680260, ex 35-401) ex Esk.724, wfu 31.3.74 (noted '75-'81). Stored for Flyvevabnets Historiske Samling, has also been seen at Gronholt and was restored at Skrydstrup in '87 for the Danmarks Flyvemuseum at Billund where it should arrive during 88.
CF-104 Starfighter	R-814	(ex RCAF 12814) ex Esk.723, l/f 29.12.83, stored here until going to the Egeskov Veteran museum 6.4.87.
CF-104 Starfighter	R-825	(ex RCAF 12825) ex Esk.726, l/f 5.11.82, in use as decoy pending display in the Esk.726 area.
CF-104 Starfighter	R-832	(ex RCAF 12832) ex Esk.726, wfu 2.7.84, in use as a decoy prior to being placed on display in the Esk.723 area in 8.88.
CF-104 Starfighter	R-888	(ex RCAF 12888) ex Esk.723, l/f 22.12.83, stored here until moved to the Danmarks Tekniske Museum (at Alborg or at Helsingore?) on 11.11.86.

The ex Canadian Starfighters such as those above were bought outright by Denmark and were therefore disposed of locally at the end of their lives. The MDAP (Mutual Defense Aid Program) supplied Starfighters remained US controlled and were placed in store following their withdrawal on 30.4.86. The following aircraft were then disposed of to Taiwan and were shipped out from Arhus, the date shown being the official handover date.

F-104G Starfighter	R-340	(ex 62-12340) ex Esk.726, to CNAF 24.2.87.
F-104G Starfighter	R-342	(ex 62-12342) ex Esk.726, to CNAF 6.4.87.
F-104G Starfighter	R-345	(ex 62-12345) ex Esk.726, to CNAF 31.3.87.
F-104G Starfighter	R-347	(ex 62-12347) ex Esk.726, to CNAF 2.4.87.
F-104G Starfighter	R-348	(ex 62-12348) ex Esk.726, to CNAF 1.4.87.
F-104G Starfighter	R-349	(ex 62-12349) ex Esc.726, to CNAF 25.2.87.
F-104G Starfighter	R-645	(ex 63-13645) ex Esk.726, to CNAF 6.4.87.
F-104G Starfighter	R-646	(ex 63-13646) ex Esk.726, to CNAF 27.2.87.
F-104G Starfighter	R-647	(ex 63-13647) ex Esk.726, to CNAF 30.3.87.
F-104G Starfighter	R-699	(ex 63-12699) ex Esk.726, to CNAF 18.2.87.
F-104G Starfighter	R-702	(ex 63-12702) ex Esk.726, to CNAF 23.2.87.
F-104G Starfighter	R-703	(ex 63-12703) ex Esk.726, to CNAF 2.4.87.
F-104G Starfighter	R-707	(ex 63-12707) ex Esk.726, to CNAF 3.4.87.
F-104G Starfighter	R-754	(ex 64-17754) ex Esk.726, to CNAF 3.3.87.
F-104G Starfighter	R-755	(ex 64-17755) ex Esk.726, to CNAF 24.2.87.
TF-104G Starfighter	RT-682	(ex 63-12682) ex Esk.726, to CNAF 30.3.87.
TF-104G Starfighter	RT-683	(ex 63-12683) ex Esk.726, to CNAF 31.3.87.
TF-104G Starfighter	RT-684	(ex 63-12684) ex Esk.726, to CNAF 2.3.87.

R-707 was fitted with the tail from R-825 before delivery to Taiwan whilst R-825 (Alborg decoy) received the tail from R-896. To complete the exchange R-896 (Alborg decoy) received the tail of R-707.

One Lockheed built RDanAF Starfighter which did not go to Taiwan was F-104G R-756 (ex 64-17756) ex Esk.726, wfu 22.11.84 which was air-freighted from Alborg into Coventry on 30.4.87 by RDanAF C-130H for the Midland Air Museum.

On the fire dump in 1986 was CF-104 Starfighter R-851 (ex RCAF 12851, ex Esk.726, wfu 1.1.84) whilst CF-104D RT-664 (ex RCAF 12664, ex Esk.726, wfu 21.2.84) was in use for bdr training. As noted above, two of the decoy F-86Ds were relegated to the fire dump by 1988.

At the show in 1975 a crash compound near the tower held the wreckage of F-104G Starfighter R-759 (ex 64-17759, ex Esk.726, crashed 4 kms East of Thisted on 8.6.73). At the show in 1985, the mortal remains of three other Starfighters were in evidence, F-104G R-753 (ex 64-17753, ex Esk.723, crashed at Bjerget, near Gjol, on 14.10.80), CF-104s R-819 (ex RCAF 12819, ex Esk.723, crashed 2 kms North of Vildsund on 5.9.78) and R-887 (ex RCAF 12887, ex Esk.723, crashed at Fjerritslev on 18.8.82).

Near the base, in a large park to the West of Alborg and South of Skydebanevej (the road next to the park), lives F-84G Thunderjet 110622 (ex 51-10622). This machine last served with Esk.727 as 'KU-U' and was wfu on 9.6.59. She was still in reasonable condition in 1987.

At the civil field can be found the wreck of Beech 76 Duchess OY-BEU (c/n ME-399, ex N3834P, crashed at Maribo 17.10.83).

BALLERUP

Ballerup is a suburb of Copenhagen and can be found to the West of the city. DH Chipmunk T.20 P-126 (c/n C1/0105, ex FLSK, wfu 10.9.76) was sold to Sokilde Autos here on 30.9.76 possibly intended as a garage attraction but instead went Stateside as N22777 and now flies with Valiant Air Command in Florida.

BILLUND

The Danmarks Flyvemuseum (Danish Aviation Museum) finally opened here on 2.6.89. Several aircraft collected by this organisation have been stored at other locations (principally Kobenhavn/Osterbrogades Kaserne, Kongelunden, Egeskov and Kobenhavn/Kastrup) pending the establishment of a permanent museum. Aircraft already present, or expected to arrive here include the following.

Aero Commander 560E	OY-ADS	(c/n 612-40) (noted 6.87).
Boeing 720-025	OY-DSP	(c/n 18241) ex Conair.
PBY-6A Catalina	L-861	(Bu64035) ex Esk.721, wfu 13.11.70, to Engagergaard 6.10.77 for museum store, returning to Vaerlose 6.81, due here '88.
DH Chipmunk T.20	P-127	(c/n C1/0106) ex FLSK, Helsingore & Osterbrogades Kaserne, arrived 15.5.87.
DH Chipmunk T.20	P-143	(c/n C1/0881) ex Tirstrup Stn Flt, wfu 21.3.77, to FLKS as gia (due here from Vaerlose '88).
DH Dove 6	OY-DHZ	(c/n 04476, ex G-AOUF, D-IBYW) (noted 6.87).
Douglas C-47A Dakota	K-681	(c/n 9664, ex 42-23802, LN-IAP, 68-681) ex Esk.721, wfu 31.12.80, Vaerlose storage, flew to Billund museum 17.8.86 as 'OY-DDA' 'Svend Viking' for SAS jubilee.
Douglas C-47A Dakota	K-687	(c/n 19200, ex 42-100737, RNorAF, 68-687) ex Esk.721, wfu 8.1.81 (ex Vaerlose store, noted '88).
GAL Monospar	OY-DAZ	(c/n 95) completed her rebuild at Osterbrogades Kaserne on 15.12.87, due to come here.
Gloster Meteor F.4	43-461	(c/n G5/294) ex Alborg Stn Flt, wfu 19.1.56 (arr from Alborg 4.5.88).
Gloster Meteor F.4	43-469	(c/n G5/302) ex Alborg Stn Flt, wfu 7.1.56 (expected from Skrydstrup).
Gloster Meteor NF.11	51-504	(c/n 5545, ex WM387, 51-504, H-504) ex Karup Stn Flt, wfu 31.7.62 (arr from storage at Alborg 8.10.86, current '88).
Hawker Hunter F.51	E-401	(c/n 41H/680260, ex 35-401) ex Esk.724, wfu 31.3.74 (ex Skrydstrup restoration, arrived 31.5.88).
Hutter H17A	OY-AXH	(c/n 186, ex OY-61) arrived from Egeskov by '88.
CF-104 Starfighter	R-846	(ex RCAF 12846) ex Esk.726, wfu 11.7.84 (arrived from Vaerlose 7.6.88).
CF-104D Starfighter	RT-657	(ex RCAF 12657) ex Esk.726, wfu 15.11.84 (noted 6.87).

Lockheed T-33A	DT-491	(ex 51-4491) ex Vaerlose Stn Flt, wfu 7.10.74 and to FLKS for gia use (arrived from Vaerlose 11.10.88).
Lockheed T-33A	DT-497	(ex 51-6497) ex Karup Stn Flt, wfu 17.5.77 (due to come here from Vaerlose).
Lockheed T-33A	DT-923	(ex 51-8923) ex Vaerlose Stn Flt, wfu 19.2.75 (arrived from Vaerlose 18.10.88).
Harvard T.2B	31-309	(c/n 14A-966, ex 43-12667, FS826) ex Vaerlose Stn Flt, wfu 22.4.59 and to gia at Mathskolen, stored at Gronholt (eg 1980) but removed to Vaerlose by 6.84 and arrived here 14.10.86 (current '88).
F-86D Sabre	F-421	(ex 51-8421) ex Esk.728, wfu 14.3.66 (due from Vaerlose '88).
F-86D Sabre	F-028	(ex 51-6028) ex Esk.728, wfu 14.3.66 (arrived from Skrydstrup 7.3.89).
TF-100F Super Sabre	GT-927	(ex 56-3927) ex Esk.730, wfu 11.5.82 (arrived from Vaerlose '88).
F-84G Thunderjet	A-803	(ex 51-9803) ex Esk.725, wfu 5.7.61 (expected from Skrydstrup).
F-84G Thunderjet	A-777	(ex 51-10777) ex Esk.730, wfu 11.6.59 and used as a decoy at Skrydstrup, later allocated to Flyvevabnets Historiske Samling, to Billund by 8.88 and under restoration as 'SE-G'.
F-84G Thunderjet	A-047	(ex 52-3047)ex Esk.725,wfu 8.6.61,cockpit section only.
RF-84F Thunderflash	C-264	(ex 51-11264) ex Esk.729, wfu 7.9.71 (arrived here from Karup).
SAAB J 29F Tunnan	29487	ex '07' F 3, RSwedAF & Egeskov museum, arrived 6.87.
SAI KZ IIS	OY-DOU	(c/n 13) ex Egeskov, due from Sonderborg following restoration by Cimber Air.
SAI KZ III	61-611	(ex 61-611, OY-ACT) due from Sonderborg after restoration.
SAI KZ IV	OY-DZU	(c/n 70) ex Kobenhavn/Kastrup, arr '88.
SAI KZ VII	O-620	(c/n 182, 63-620) due here from Vaerlose '88.
SAI KZ VII	O-621	(c/n 183, 63-621) due here from Vaerlose '88.
SAI KZ VII	OY-ATK	(c/n 184, ex 63-622, O-622) ex Army (noted 6.87, due to go to Karup museum).
Sud Alouette III	M-388	(c/n 1388) ex Esk.722, wfu 21.9.80, arrived here 15.1.87 from Helsingore.

The entrance to Billund airfield is just across the road from the famous "Legoland" leisure park and perhaps appropriately the airfield gate was guarded by Cherokee 180C OY-BBH (c/n 28-4351) - a Lego aeroplane if ever there was! It was still current early in '88 but has since moved, probably into the Lego hangar at Billund airport.

Stored here with HO-Aero is former instructional airframe Chipmunk T.20 12-131 (c/n C1/0695, ex FLSK, wfu 7.1.54 for gi). It was sold to HO-Aero on 8.6.78 and remains in store here as a prospective sale in Sweden came to nothing (current 4.87).

Lying dumped on the field is Douglas DC-8-55F 5N-ATS (c/n 45817, crashed here 30.3.88).

At the 'Propellen' restaurant in Billund, the nose section of Douglas DC-7C OY-KNB (c/n 44929) serves as a bar in the discotheque. The remainder of the airframe is still dumped at Kastrup.

BJERRINGBRO

A number of ex Vaerlose T-33As were scrapped here during 1983. Refer to the T-bird listing under Vaerlose for details.

EGESKOV CASTLE

The <u>Egeskov Veteranmuseum</u> possesses a varied collection of aircraft, several of them on loan from other organisations. The museum can be found some 2km West of Kvaerndrup on the A8 (about 30 kms South of Odense).

Brodersen Homebuilt	-	
DH82A Tiger Moth	NL913	(c/n 86356, ex NL913, G-AOFR, SE-COX, OY-BAK, "S-11")
PT-26 Cornell	253	(ex 44-19258) ex LN-BIF.
Fa 330A-1 Bachstelze	60127	
Hawker Hunter F.51	E-426	(c/n 41H/680285, ex 35-426) ex Esk.724, wfu 31.3.74, cockpit section only, on loan from Flyvevabnets Historiske Samling.
Hollaender AH.1	OY-ADO	(c/n 1)
Hutter H17A	OY-AXH	(c/n 186) moved to Billund by '88.
CF-104 Starfighter	R-814	(ex RCAF 12814) ex Esk.723 (arrived from Aalborg store 6.4.87).
Mignet Pou-du-Ciel	-	replica
Moelhede-Petersen XMP-2	-	
Harvard T.2B	31-324	(c/n 14A-1420, ex 43-13121, FT380) ex Vaerlose Stn Flt, wfu 7.8.58 and to gia at Mathskolen, to Egeskov in '66 and went to Karup 6.5.82.
F-84G Thunderjet	A-792	(ex 51-9792) ex Esk.725, wfu 14.9.59 (fitted with tail from 110094), stored.
SAAB B 17A	17320	(c/n 17320, converted to L 17A, ex RSwedAF and SE-BWC) last flew 10.6.64, donated to Egeskov 5.5.70 and painted as B 17C code 'E' (for Egeskov) which was used by the Danish Brigade in Sweden during the Second World War.
SAAB J 29F	29487	ex '07' F 3, RSwedAF (to Billund museum 6.87).
SAI KZ IIS	OY-DOU	(c/n 13) to Sonderborg for restoration by Cimber Air prior to a move to Billund.
Spitfire HF.IX	41-401	(ex NH417)ex Esk.4,wfu13.4.51,on loan from Tojhusmuseet.

The Lockheed 12A L2-38 was displayed here until acquired by the Militair Luchtvaartmuseum at Kamp Zeist, Netherlands.

EGTVED

Mr NE Skaerlund has the following airframes here.

PA18-150 Super Cub	OY-BYM	(c/n 18-4650, ex D-ELED)
PA18-150 Super Cub	OY-EAM	(c/n 18-6796, ex N9694D)
Stinson L-5 Sentinel	-	(c/n VW2493,ex N...., D-ELKO)

FARUM

The NBC School here, a couple of kilometres North of Vaerlose, has for many years used F-84G Thunderjet 19978/SI-G for de-contamination exercises. The aircraft is ex Esk.728 and was wfu 19.9.58. She wears the name 'Ludvig' on the nose and was still present in 1987 though in poor condition. Her days are probably numbered in view of the delivery here of CF-104 Starfighter R-855 (ex RCAF 12855) in 1986. This aircraft was last used by Esk.723 and was wfu 1.1.84.

GRAM

Several years ago F-84G Thunderjet 19718/KP-A (ex 51-9718) ex Esk.725, wfu 11.10.58 was preserved in a playground here (some 20 kilometres West of Skrydstrup). As with so many others, this fine machine was eventually sold as scrap.

GRONHOLT

Gronholt airfield (about 30 kms North of Kobenhavn, between Fredensborg and Hillerod) is operated by the Bohnstedt-Petersen company which used to be the Piper agent in Denmark. The company have preserved L-4H Cub OY-AFG (c/n 10858, ex 43-29567, LN-MAP, SE-CEW) which is held in store here in a dismantled state. They also maintain ex Esk.721 C-47A Dakota K-682/OY-BPB (c/n 20019, ex 43-15553, LN-IAT, 68-682) which was wfu 30.7.82 and is owned by the FHS (Flyvabnets Historiske Samling or RDanAF Historic Collection).

Harvard T.2B 31-309 (c/n 14A-966, ex 43-12667, FS826, ex Vaerlose Stn Flt, wfu 22.4.59 and to gia at Mathskolen) was in hangar storage here for some time (eg 1980) for the FHS, was removed to Vaerlose by 6.84 but was back at Gronholt in 6.86. This nomadic aircraft has since moved to Billund, on 14.10.86.

Hunter F.51 E-401 (c/n 41H/680260, ex 35-401, ex Esk.724, wfu 31.3.74) has also been seen here in storage (eg 6.86) but now lives at Skrydstrup.

The fuselage of American Aviation AA-1A Trainer SE-FTN was noted here 6.86.

GUDSO

F-84G Thunderjet A-143 (ex 51-10143) ex Esk.728, wfu 31.8.60 was reported in use here for fire training during the seventies and in latter years was joined by F-86D Sabre F-307 (ex 51-8307, ex Esk.728, wfu 14.3.66). Both were still current in '88, the F-84G only just surviving.

HADERSLEV

F-84G Thunderjet A-598 (ex 51-10598, ex Karup Stn Flt, wfu 8.9.61) was preserved in a playground here (12 kms East of Skrydstrup) during the seventies but was eventually sold as scrap.

HELLEBEEK

During the seventies Harvard T.2B 31-306 (c/n 14-748, ex 42-12501, FH114, ex Vaerlose Stn Flt, wfu 25.5.59) was reported simply 'in a forest' here having been sold on 31.5.61 and sold to a Mr J Utzon (or rather, the Mr J Utzon, designer of the Sydney opera house). The aircraft eventually gravitated to the museum at Stauning for use as a source of spares for their ex Swedish AF Harvard 16126.

HELSINGORE

The Danmarks Tekniske Museum is located here and contains several experimental aircraft from the pioneering days of aviation. These comprise the Donnet-Leveque 'Magen 3' (with wings from the Magen 2, the remainder of which is in store), the Ellehammer II, Ellehammer Standard Monoplane and Ellehammer Helicopter, a Larsen glider, the Svendsen Glenten, a Grunau Baby and the Polyteknyk Polyt II OY-65.

Sud Alouette III M-388 (c/n 1388, ex Esk.722) came here from storage at Ostergrogades Kaserne but has since moved to Billund. Ex FLSK Chipmunk T.20 P-127 was here for a while in the late seventies/early eighties before moving to Osterbrogades Kaserne in Kobenhavn (and has also since gone to Billund).

HERNING

Preserved in a park here was F-84G Thunderjet 19844 (ex 51-9844, ex Esk.725, wfu 20.1.60) with the rear fuselage and tail from 110660. The airframe was eventually moved back to Karup for the fire dump (where "110660" was noted in '75) and the mortal remains have since been sold as scrap.

Dumped on the airfield are Beech Baron SE-FNR, Cessna F172P OY-SUD (c/n 2204, crashed en route Aero to Tasinge 11.5.85), Cherokee Six OY-BGL (c/n 32-7200048, crashed at Billund 23.7.86) and SAI KZ VII OY-AAP (c/n 152).

HOLSTEBRO

Yet another F-84G Thunderjet to end its days as a childrens' toy was 110016 (ex 51-10016) ex 'KR-D' Esk.726, wfu 2.12.58 which was scrapped some time ago.

The Civil Defence in the town were still using F-84G Thunderjet A-652 (ex 51-10652, ex Esk.728, wfu 31.8.60) during 1987, though it was in very poor condition by this time. Holstebro is located some 25 kilometres West of Karup.

JAGERSPRIS

Still extant here in 1987 were the mortal remains of three F-84G Thunderjets which had been expended as range targets.

F-84G Thunderjet	A-114	(ex 51-1114) ex Karup Stn Flt, wfu 4.9.61.
F-84G Thunderjet	19944	(ex 51-9944) ex 'SI-S' Esk.728, wfu 29.5.59.
F-84G Thunderjet	110753	(ex 51-10753) ex 'SE-K' Esk.730, wfu 20.6.58 (ex Vaerlose, tail from 110580).

KARUP

Located halfway between Viborg and Herning, Karup houses the RDanAF's two Draken squadrons, Esk.725 and Esk.729.

Several airframes have been preserved at a small museum on the base, comprising:-

Gloster Meteor F.8	44-491	ex Karup Stn Flt, wfu 13.4.61, soc 5.5.61 (arr '88, ex decoy here).
F-84G Thunderjet,	A-665	(ex 51-16665) ex Esk.728, wfu 31.8.60 but painted up as "110477/KP-A" in Esk.725 whose tail it acquired. The a/c was finally correctly repainted as A-665 in 1987 (current '88).
TF-100F Super Sabre	GT-949	(ex 56-3949) ex Esk.730, wfu 5.5.82, preserved by 1986 (current '88).
Lockheed T-33A	DT-905	(ex 51-8905) ex Karup Stn Flt, wfu 28.2.77, to Skrydstrup, returned to Karup 15.12.80 and allocated to the Flyvevabnets Historiske Samling 14.3.81 (current '88).
Harvard T.2B	31-324	(c/n 14A-1420, ex 43-13121, FT380) ex Vaerlose Stn Flt, wfu 7.8.58 and to gia at Mathskolen, to Egeskov Veteranmuseum '66, arr at Karup 6.5.82 on loan (current '88).
F-84G Thunderjet	A-477	(ex 51-10477) ex Esk.728, wfu 31.8.60, (tail from 116665) on the dump here until retrieved by the museum (current '88).
RF-84F Thunderflash	C-274	(ex 51-11274) ex Esk.729, wfu 1.4.71, ex decoy (see below) placed on display after restoration (noted '88).
RF-84F Thunderflash	C-054	(ex 51-17054) ex Esk.729, wfu 7.10.71, was on display but replaced by C-274.

Preserved in the Esk.729 area is RF-84F Thunderflash C-581 (ex 53-7581) ex Esk.729, wfu 31.12.71 (noted '75-'87).

Karup boasts an enviable decoy population, the following having been noted in recent years. There has been some movement of aircraft around the base and various conflicting descriptions have been applied to the decoy ares. These machines are therefore listed by type.

Gloster Meteor T.7	22-265	(c/n G5/354) ex Karup Stn Flt, wfu 13.4.61, soc 6.3.63, held in open store for Flyvevabnets Historiske Samling (noted '75-'86).
Gloster Meteor F.8	44-491	(c/n G5/365) ex Karup Stn Flt, wfu 13.4.61, soc 5.5.61, formerly displayed on the gate (pre 1977), open storage for RDanAF museum (noted '75-'87, undergoing restoration for the base museum, to museum '88).
Gloster Meteor F.8	B-499	(c/n G5/373) ex Karup Stn Flt, wfu 13.4.61, soc 6.3.63 (noted '75-'88) open storage for Flyvevabnets Historiske Samling.
F-86D Sabre	F-018	(ex 51-6018) ex Esk.728, wfu 14.3.66 (noted '75-'86).
F-86D Sabre	F-118	(ex 51-6118) ex Esk.728, wfu 14.3.66 (noted '75-'86).
F-86D Sabre	F-123	(ex 51-6123) ex Esk.728, wfu 14.3.66 (noted '75-'86).
F-86D Sabre	F-303	(ex 51-8303) ex Esk.728, wfu 14.3.66 (noted '75-'86).
F-86D Sabre	F-307	(ex 51-8307) ex Esk.728, wfu 14.3.66 (noted '75, to Gudso).
F-86D Sabre	F-427	(ex 51-8427) ex Esk.728, wfu 14.3.66 (noted '75-'86).
F-86D Sabre	F-474	(ex 51-8474) ex Esk.728, wfu 14.3.66 (noted '75-'86).
F-86D Sabre	F-500	(ex 51-8500) ex Esk.728, wfu 14.3.66 (noted '75-'86).
F-86D Sabre	F-504	(ex 51-8504) ex Esk.728, wfu 14.3.66 (noted '75-'86).
F-86D Sabre	F-952	(ex 51-5952) ex Esk.728, wfu 14.3.66 (noted '79-'86).
F-86D Sabre	F-953	(ex 51-5953) ex Esk.728, wfu 14.3.66 (noted '75-'86).
F-86D Sabre	F-977	(ex 51-5977) ex Esk.728, wfu 14.3.66 (noted '75-'86).
F-86D Sabre	F-984	(ex 51-5984) ex Esk.728, wfu 14.3.66 (noted '79-'86).

RF-84F Thunderflash C-054 (ex 51-17054) ex Esk.729, wfu 7.10.71 (noted '75-'79) then to base museum but since replaced there by C-274. Fate?
RF-84F Thunderflash C-248 (ex 52-7248) ex Esk.729, wfu 24.6.71 (noted '75-'86).
RF-84F Thunderflash C-253 (ex 52-7253) ex Esk.729, wfu 1.4.71 (noted '75-'86).
RF-84F Thunderflash C-264 (ex 51-11264) ex Esk.729, wfu 7.9.71 (noted '75-'82). This a/c was dismantled to permit restoration for the Karup museum but the fuselage was blown over in a storm. C-274 was selected as a replacement. C-264 is now expected to go to Billund imminently.
RF-84F Thunderflash C-274 (ex 51-11274) ex Esk.729, wfu 1.4.71 (noted '75-'86, to Karup museum).
RF-84F Thunderflash C-281 (ex 51-11281) ex Esk.729, wfu 6.9.71 (noted '75-'86).
RF-84F Thunderflash C-283 (ex 52-7283) ex Esk.729, wfu 24.6.71 (to MBB 1.73).
RF-84F Thunderflash C-324 (ex 52-7324) ex Esk.729, wfu 17.8.71 (noted '75-'86).
RF-84F Thunderflash C-473 (ex 52-7473) ex Esk.729, wfu 4.10.71 (noted '75-'86).
RF-84F Thunderflash C-649 (ex 53-7649) ex Esk.729, wfu 14.12.71 (noted '75-'86).
RF-84F Thunderflash C-651 (ex 53-7651) ex Esk.729, wfu 31.12.71 (noted '75-'86).
RF-84F Thunderflash C-670 (ex 53-7670) ex Esk.729, wfu 31.12.71 (noted '75-'86).
RF-84F Thunderflash C-865 (ex 51-1865) ex Esk.729, wfu 24.6.71 (noted '75-'86) preserved on the gate in '75, decoy by '85.
RF-84F Thunderflash C-937 (ex 51-1937) ex Esk.729, wfu 1.4.71 (to MBB, West Germany, 1.73).
F-84G Thunderjet A-330 (ex 51-10330) ex Esk.730, wfu 5.7.61 (noted pre '78, to Oksbol ranges).
F-84G Thunderjet A-504 (ex 51-10504) ex Esk.730, wfu 29.6.61 (noted pre '78).
F-84G Thunderjet A-520 (ex 51-10520) ex Esk.730, wfu 5.7.61 (noted pre '78).
F-84G Thunderjet 110629 (ex 51-10629) ex 'KU-J' Esk.727, wfu 30.10.58 (noted pre '78).
F-84G Thunderjet A-720 (ex 51-10720) ex Esk.725, wfu 26.6.61 (noted pre '78).
F-84G Thunderjet A-769 (ex 51-10769) ex Esk.730, wfu 12.5.61 (noted pre '78).

Apart from A-330 which ended up as a range target, the other five Thunderjets all went to the scrapman.

TF-100F Super Sabre GT-874 (ex 56-3874) ex Esk.730, wfu 2.3.82 (noted as decoy '85-'86).

By 1986 CF-104D Starfighter RT-655 (ex RCAF 12655, ex Esk.726, wfu 15.10.84) was in use here for bdr training.

In 1975 the crash compound held the wrecks of A-35XD Drakens A-013 (c/n 35.1013, ex Esk.725, crashed near Karup 21.11.74), A-015 (c/n 35.1015, ex Esk.725, crashed near Karup 27.7.71), F-100D G-778 (ex 55-2778, ex Esk.730, crashed at Limfjorden 11.8.70) and TF-100F GT-015 (ex 56-4015, ex Esk.727, crashed 2 kms East of Karup 20.3.70). A-015 was still to be seen during 1986.

By 1985, a scrap compound on the base held F-100D Super Sabres G-279 (ex 54-2279, ex Esk.730, wfu 18.7.77 and broken up for spares) and G-773 (ex 55-2773, ex Esk.730, wfu 18.7.77 and broken up for spares). Both were still current in '86.

Five S 35E Drakens were obtained from Sweden for spares recovery. These aircraft had previously served with F 21 at Lulea and were drawn from storage at Halmstad and Tullinge. Arrival dates were 35905 on 19.2.80, 35922 on 8.2.80, 35925 on 17.2.80, 35929 on 12.2.80 and 35931 on 6.2.80. The latter is now on the fire dump at Karup whilst 35905 has spent some time at Vaerlose for bdr purposes but has returned here.

The cockpit section of J 35F Draken 35552 was also delivered from Sweden for use in a Draken flight simulator. In addition, a Draken cockpit was temporarily displayed at Herning during 1988 with a radio-call indicating it to be the former '49' of F 16. This should make it J 35F 35420. Although their demise has often been prematurely reported, the continued existence of all seven Draken airframes mentioned above was confirmed during 1988.

In 1975 the fire dump held three F-84G Thunderjets for the entertainment of the base fire crews.

F-84G Thunderjet A-511 (ex 51-10511) ex Karup Stn Flt, wfu 8.9.61 (burnt out).

F-84G Thunderjet	19844	(ex 51-9844) ex 'KP-S' Esk.725 (fitted with tail of 110660) ex Herning.
F-84G Thunderjet	A-477	(ex 51-10477) ex Esk.728, wfu 31.8.60 (tail from 116665).

Only one aircraft was to be seen on the dump by 1979 and A-477 was still present in 1986. All the remains have now been sold for scrap.

Ex RSwedAF S 35E Draken 35931 was on the fire dump here during '87 (refer above).

A playground in Karup village received F-84G Thunderjet 19838 (ex 51-9838, ex 'SI-A' Esk.728, wfu 2.6.58) fitted with the tail of 110752. The aircraft was in poor condition by 1987.

KOBENHAVN

The Tojhusmuseet is located in the city centre near Christiansborg Castle. On display here are.

Avro 504N	110	(c/n 50) soc 1935.
Berg & Storm BS.III	-	soc 1914.
Hawker Dancock	158	soc 22.1.37.

The museum also owns Spitfire HF.IX 41-401 (ex NH417) which has been on loan to the Egeskov museum for some years.

In the Northern part of the city, several aircraft have been stored or renovated at Osterbrogades Kaserne for the Danmarks Flyvemuseum (see under Billund) and the Flyvevabnets Historiske Samling.

DH Chipmunk T.20	P-127	(c/n C1/0106) ex FLSK, to Danmarks Tekniske Museum at Helsingore, then to Osterbrogades Kaserne (stored for Flyvevabnets Historiske Samling). To Billund museum 15.5.87.
DH Dove 6	OY-DHZ	(c/n 04476) ex Sonderborg, Danmarks Flyvemuseum, to Billund by 6.87.
GAL Monospar	OY-DAZ	(c/n 95) Danmarks Flyvemuseum. Completed her rebuild 15.12.87, due to move to Billund.
Klemm Kl.35D	SE-AKN	(c/n 1873) Danmarks Flyvemuseum.
F-84G Thunderjet	A-777	(ex 51-10777) ex Esk.730, wfu 11.6.59 and used as a decoy at Skrydstrup, later allocated to Flyvevabnets Historiske Samling, to Billund by '88.
SAI KZ IIT	-	frame only, Danmarks Flyvemuseum. This anonymous a/c was at Vaerlose and a gia at Avno before that. It is probably c/n 121 which crashed following a collision with KZ VII 621 on 6.5.49 at Avno. The airframe has also been on display at Egeskov and (in '79) at Helsingor.
SAI KZ VII	OY-ATK	(c/n 184, ex 63-622, 0-622) ex RDanAF & Army loan, allocated to Flyvevabnets Historiske Samling but to Billund by 6.87.
Sud Alouette III	M-388	(c/n 1388) ex Esk.722, wfu 21.9.80, allocated to Flyvevabnets Historiske Samling but to Helsingore and then to Billund 15.1.87.

KOBENHAVN/KASTRUP

The Danmarks Flyvemuseum has access to restoration facilities here and owns three of the relics at Copenhagen's airport.

Hunting President	OY-AVA	(c/n 29, ex G-AOJG) ex RDanAF Pembroke 69-697 with Esk.722, to OY-AVA in 7.62, restored in the RAF colours it wore when used as a demonstrator by Hunting, but will be restored as OY-AVA for eventual display at Billund.
SAI KZ IV	OY-DZU	(c/n 70) in hangar storage, to Billund by '88.
SE210 Caravelle III	OY-KRD	(c/n 47) ex SAS (current 7.88).

Dumped and derelict airframes around the airfield in recent years have included the following.

Boeing 720-025	OY-DSP	(c/n 18241) ex Conair, stored '87 (current '88).
Convair 440	SE-BSS	(c/n 358) last flew 23.9.75,dumped 17.5.76 (scrapped'88).
Douglas DC-7C	OY-DMT	(c/n 44136, ex N315AA, N315A, CF-PWD) ex Conair, wfu '71 (current '88).
Douglas DC-6B	OY-BAV	(c/n 45199, ex N574) wfu '71 (current '88).
Douglas DC-7C	OY-KNB	(c/n 44929) dumped here minus nose (to Billund) and engines (current '88).
Douglas DC-8-32	LN-PIP	(c/n 45256) wfu by 10.84 (current '88).

KONGELUNDEN

The Danmarks Flyvemuseum have a store on a military site here but with the establishment of a permanent museum at Billund these airframes can be expected to gravitate to the new location. Known to have been stored here are the following.

DH89A Dragon Rapide	OY-AAO	(c/n 6775, ex NR676)
SG-38 Schulgleiter	OY-86	
DFS Weihe	OY-VOX	(c/n 216)
UC-61K Argus	OY-EAZ	(43-14998, HB724)
Hoglund-Olsen 2G	OY-ATX	(ex OY-100)
Lund HL-1	-	
Miles Gemini 1A	G-AKDK	(c/n 6469)
Percival Proctor III	62-605	(c/n H274, ex HM364, OY-ACP) to Egeskov.
Polyteknyk Polyt II	OY-98	(ex OY-98, OY-BEX)
Grunau Baby II	OY-DAX	(ex OY-29)
Grunau Baby II	OY-AHX	(ex OY-90)

OKSBOL

F-84G Thunderjet 19978/SI-G (ex Esk.726, but retained Esk.728 codes during its two months with 726, wfu 19.9.58) was preserved here for several years, but finally expired on the ranges at Tranum.

The last remains of the following Thunderjets were expiring on the ranges here in 1987 having arrived during '76. By the end of 1988 only 110362 and one other were still extant.

F-84G Thunderjet	A-181	(ex 51-10181) ex Skrydstrup Stn Flt, wfu 28.9.61 (tail from 19944), ex Skrydstrup decoy.
F-84G Thunderjet	A-330	(ex 51-10330) ex Esk 730, wfu 5.7.61, ex Karup decoy.
F-84G Thunderjet	110362	(ex 51-10362) ex 'SI-V' Esk.728, wfu 12.3.59, ex Skrydstrup decoy.
F-84G Thunderjet	10718	(ex 51-10718) ex 'SI-O' Esk.728, wfu 6.4.59, ex Skrydstrup decoy.

Since the end of their flying careers, 110362 and 110718 have been repainted with the new style serials (A-362 etc) which they did not carry in service.

New range targets arrived here during 1988 in the form of half a dozen Sabres from Alborg and Skrydstrup.

F-86D Sabre	F-473	(ex 51-8473) ex Esc.728, wfu 14.3.66 (arrived from Alborg 10.6.88).
F-86D Sabre	F-994	(ex 51-5994) ex Esc.728, wfu 14.3.66 (arrived from Alborg 10.6.88).
F-86D Sabre	F-016	(ex 51-6016) ex Esk.728, wfu 14.3.66 (ex Skrydstrup).
F-86D Sabre	F-034	(ex 51-6034) ex Esk.728, wfu 14.3.66 (ex Skrydstrup).
F-86D Sabre	F-346	(ex 51-8346) ex Esk.728, wfu 14.3.66 (ex Skrydstrup).
F-86D Sabre	F-431	(ex 51-8431) ex Esk.728, wfu 14.3.66 (ex Skrydstrup).

OVER JERSTAL

F-84G Thunderjet A-058 (ex 51-1058 ex Esk.730, wfu 12.5.61) ended its days as a childrens' toy in a playground here. It was scrapped during the seventies.

PADBORG

At the airfield here is the wreck of Cessna F150H OY-AHL (c/n 0341) which crashed near Thisted 14.10.82 after colliding with OY-AGV.

PLEJERUP

Consolidated PBY-5A Catalina L-857 (Bu08019, ex Esk.721, wfu 14.10.67 and stored in the open at Vaerlose) was sold to a Mr J Larsen in '82 and moved here. His plans to restore the Cat have so far come to nothing and the aircraft's fate remains in the balance.

RANDERS

The Civil Defence in the city have F-84G Thunderjet 110482 (ex 51-10482) which is fitted with the tail from 51-10209. 110482 last served as 'SE-A' with Esk.730 and was wfu 14.10.59. By 1987 the aircraft was in a very bad condition.

RASTED

Wrecks on the airfield during '87/'88 comprised the following.

MS880B Rallye Club	OY-DDT	(c/n 845)
PA32 Cherokee Six	OY-TOY	(c/n 32-7540130) crashed on Hesselo island 28..80.
SAI KZ VII	OY-AAS	(c/n 155, ex OY-AAS, D-EMES)

RIBE

A playground here was the last resting place of F-84G Thunderjet A-124 (ex 51-10124 ex Alborg TT Flt, wfu 9.1.62). The aircraft is no longer current having been sold as scrap during the seventies.

RYVANGEN

F-84G Thunderjet 22981 (ex 52-2981) (ex 'KP-K' Esk.725, wfu 2.9.58) was with the NBC school here during the seventies. It moved with the school to Farum but was replaced by 19978. 22981 was reported with a new museum at Slangerup as we closed for press.

SINDAL

The only wreck at the airfield is that of Beech King Air SE-GUU (c/n LJ-470, ex N490K).

SKRYDSTRUP

Skrydstrup is home to two squadrons of F-16s (Esk.727 and Esk.730) and is the most Southerly RDanAF base being situated some 15 kms West along highway 47 from the E3 motorway to the German border.

The main gate is guarded by F-84G Thunderjet 110603 (ex 51-10603) painted as "A-603/SK-P" (noted '75-'87). This machine last served with Esk.729 as 'SY-C' and was wfu 28.11.59 and is allocated to the Flyvevabnets Historiske Samling.

Displayed by the Esk.727 HQ is Meteor F.4 43-469 (c/n G5/302, ex Alborg Stn Flt, wfu 7.1.56, allocated to the Flyvevabnets Historiske Samling and due to go to Billund) whilst F-86D Sabre F-028 (ex 51-6028, ex Esk.728, wfu 14.3.66) also lives in their area (held for the Flyvevabnets Historiske Samling and allocated to Billund). TF-100F Super Sabre GT-908 (ex 56-3908, ex Esk.730, wfu 11.8.82) had been preserved in the Esk.727 area by '85 by which time GT-870 (ex 56-3870, ex Esk.730, wfu 11.8.82) was being similarly looked after by Esk.730. It has since been restored to the old Esk.730 colour scheme and has guarded the entrance to their area since 3.7.87. Another TF-100F, GT-961 (ex 56-3961, ex Esk.730, wfu 23.9.81) was stored on the base for a display at various air shows etc.

Hunter F.51 E-401 (c/n 41H/680260, ex 35-401, ex Esk.724, wfu 31.3.74) arrived here from Gronholt for storage by 1987 but departed to Billund on 31.5.88.

The decoy areas on the base have contained the following aircraft recently.

F-84G Thunderjet	A-181	(ex 51-10181) ex Skrydstrup Stn Flt, wfu 28.9.61 (noted '75, to Oksbol ranges '76).
F-84G Thunderjet	110362	(ex 51-10362) ex 'SI-V' Esk.728, wfu 12.3.59, painted in new style markings as "A-362" (noted '75, to Oksbol ranges '76).
F-84G Thunderjet	110718	(ex 51-10718) ex 'SI-O' Esk.728, wfu 6.4.59, painted in new style markings as "A-718" (noted '75, to Oksbol ranges '76).

F-84G Thunderjet	A-803	(ex 51-9803) ex Esk.730, wfu 5.7.61 (noted '75-'87, allocated to Flyvevabnets Historiske Samling and due to go to Billund for Danmarks Flyvemuseum but still here '88).
F-86D Sabre	F-016	(ex 51-6016) ex Esk.728, wfu 14.3.66 (noted '85 & '87, to Oksbol ranges '88).
F-86D Sabre	F-034	(ex 51-6034) ex Esk.728, wfu 14.3.66 (noted '85 & '87, to Oksbol ranges '88).
F-86D Sabre	F-346	(ex 51-8346) ex Esk.728, wfu 14.3.66 (noted '85 & '87, to Oksbol ranges '88).
F-86D Sabre	F-431	(ex 51-8431) ex Esk.728, wfu 14.3.66 (noted '85 & '87, to Oksbol ranges '88).
F-86D Sabre	F-946	(ex 51-5946) ex Esk.728, wfu 31.8.65 (noted '85).

In 1975 the fire dump held the badly burnt remains of F-84G Thunderjet A-138 (ex 51-10138, ex Skrydstrup Stn Flt, wfu 15.8.61) and the complete 110487 (ex 51-10487, ex 'SE-V' Esk.730, wfu 12.3.59). The latter was still extant in 1988 by which time 110138 was sold for scrap and F-86D Sabre F-946 was reported to have moved from the decoy area to meet a fiery fate.

By 1986, CF-104D Starfighter RT-662 (ex RCAF 12662, ex Esk.726, wfu 1.1.84) had arrived for battle damage repair training (current '87).

SONDERBORG

Dismantled Bf 108 Taifun OY-AIH (c/n 1561, ex F-BBRH) was here in 6.87 but has since returned to active use. SAI KZ IIS OY-DOU (c/n 13) was here in '88 for restoration by Cimber Air prior to display in the Billund museum. They have also been working on KZ III OY-ACT which will go to Billund when restored as 61-611.

STAUNING

This airfield is the home of the Dansk Veteranflysamlung whose museum displays the following aircraft.

Aeronca Champion	-	frame only noted 6.86, may become OY-ALA.
Aero Super 45	OY-EFC	(c/n 03-007) no longer here, sold as OH-EFC.
Auster J/1 Autocrat	-	(prototype, c/n 124, ex D-EKOM & G-AFWN) frame only (noted 6.86).
Beech D18S (C-45)	D-INOL	(c/n 4A1) wreck.
DH Chipmunk T.20	OY-ALZ	(c/n C1/0067, ex P-121)
DH Chipmunk 22	OY-DJH	(c/n C1/0470, G-AMMA) wreck, crashed at Marbaek, near Frederikssund, 26.4.87.
DH82A Tiger Moth	OY-ECH	(c/n 85234, ex OO-DLA)
DH82A Tiger Moth	OY-DVP	(c/n 85506)
DH87B Hornet Moth	OY-DEZ	(c/n 8040, ex G-AMZO)
Druine Turbulent	OY-AMG	(c/n 1)
Gumpert G-2	OY-BLX	(c/n 5) hung from the roof.
Hollaender HT.1	OY-FAI	(c/n 1)
Jurca Tempete	OY-CMB	
Lockheed T-33A	DT-884	(ex 51-8884) wfu 10.2.75 and to gia at Karup, arrived at Stauning 26.11.78 (current '88).
Mignet Pou-du-Ciel	-	marked 'Dansk Provelufttarttoj' (Danish Experimental Aircraft), to be made airworthy.
Miles Mercury 6	OY-ALW	(c/n 6268, ex G-AHAA, D-EHAB)
Harvard T.2B	31-306	(c/n 14A-748, ex 42-12501, FH114) ex Vaerlose Stn Flt, wfu 25.5.59, sold 31.5.61, to Hellebeek then to Stauning 6.78 for use as spares for 16126 (current '88).
AT-16 Texan	16126	ex RSwAF (current '88).
Piper J-3F Cub	OY-ABT	(c/n 2475)
Raab Doppelraab IV	OY-XIT	(c/n 03) hung from the roof.
Rearwin Sportster	OY-AVJ	(c/n 567D, ex SE-AGB) ex Malmo, under restoration in the workshops 6.86 (this machine served as a pattern for the Swedish licence-built version, the GV-38).

F-84G Thunderjet	A-057	(ex 52-3057) 'KP-X' ex Esk.730, wfu 1.5.61 (current '88).
F-84G Thunderjet	A-515	(ex 51-10515) ex Esk.730, wfu 29.6.61 (nose section only).
SAI KZ I	OY-KZI	replica/rebuild under construction in the workshops 6.86, on display 8.88. The registration OY-CMZ was allocated but ntu.
SAI KZ IIK	OY-AEA	(c/n 27)
SAI KZ IIT	OY-FAN	(c/n 110, ex 110, 102)
SAI KZ IIT	OY-FAM	(c/n 111) under rebuild 1986.
SAI KZ IIT	OY-ADM	(c/n 113, ex 113, 105, wfu 2.2.55) under rebuild.
SAI KZ IIT	OY-FAE	(c/n 119, ex 119, 111) under rebuild 1986.
SAI KZ III	OY-DZA	(c/n 66)
SAI KZ IV	OY-DIZ	(c/n 43) under rebuild in 1986.
SAI KZ VII	D-EBTO	(c/n 149, ex OO-AAB) wreckage of crash near Hov 18.7.83.
SAI KZ VII	OY-AVR	(c/n 176)
SAI KZ VII	O-624	(c/n 187) frame only in workshop area.
SAI KZ G1	OY-ASX	(c/n 44) hung from the roof.
Scheibe Spatz B	OY-AXU	(c/n 524) hung from the roof.
Scheibe Bergfalk II	OY-REX	(c/n 102) hung from the roof - also quoted as OY-AXS?.
Grunau Baby IIB	OY-AUX	(c/n PFG8) hung from the roof.
Stampe SV4B	OY-DBC	(c/n 1204, ex V-62 BelgAF)
Taylorcraft Plus D	OY-DSH	(c/n 228, ex D-ECOD, painted as "LB381")
Transavia Airtruk	OY-DRL	(c/n 1135) crashed, spares source for OY-DVZ.
Transavia Airtruk	OY-DVZ	(c/n 1238, ex VH-ETH) airworthy.

Noted on the field in 1985 were Stampe SV4B V-62 (ex BelgAF, arrived in Denmark on 4.6.77 having been exchanged for Chipmunk T.20 P-130 (ex gia at Avno, went to the Brussels museum on 8.6.77) and ex RDanAF Chipmunk T.20s P-121/OY-ALZ & P-147/OY-ALD still retaining their former military colour schemes. By 6.86 the Stampe had become OY-DBC and was part of the museum collection listed above as was Chipmunk OY-ALZ.

Around the hangars, the fuselages of Cessna F172M Skyhawk OY-AGW (c/n 1151) and Cessna 172C OY-DIW (c/n 48877) were noted here during 6.86. The latter was still current late '87/early '88 when the following were also recorded.

Cessna 337D	OY-AGU	(c/n 1049, ex N35989)
Fairchild Argus	OY-...	(c/n 464, ex 43-14500, FS583, HB-EAS, D-EDAV)
Piper J-3C Cub	OY-ANK	(c/n 9059)
Piper PA17 Vagabond	OY-AVW	(c/n 17-70)

Stauning Aero Service seem to be the repository for insurance write offs with the following wrecks noted recently.

Cessna 150F	LN-VYE	(c/n 62643, ex N8543G) (noted '86-'88).
Cessna F172	D-ECJW	due to become OY-BZC but scrapped instead(noted'86-'87).
Cessna F172H	OY-EGB	(c/n 0246) (noted '87).
Cessna F172G	OY-BYB	(c/n 0306, ex D-EJKI) (noted '87).
Cessna 310B	OY-PON	(noted '86-'88).
Mooney M.20	D-EMMO	(noted '87).
Piper PA22 Tri-Pacer	OY-DDN	(c/n 22-7506) (noted '87).
Piper PA22 Tri Pacer	PH-NGE	(noted '87).
Piper PA22 Tri Pacer	-	(noted '87, in addition to the other two).
Piper PA28 Cherokee	OY-BGA	(c/n 28-7225271) (noted '87).

Stored at the nearby private residence (just North of Stauning) of Mr Jens Toft, an avid collector, are the following (all reported late '87/early '88).

Auster J/5D Autocar	OY-DBL	(c/n 2912, ex HB-EOU, D-EMYD, D-EGHG)
Champion Tri-Traveler	OY-DBB	(c/n 454, ex N9922Y, D-....)
DH82A Tiger Moth	OY-ALT	(c/n 85621, ex DE680, G-ANBZ, (SL-AAF), D-ELYG)
Piper L-4 Cub	OY-EFM	
Piper J-3C Cub	-	new frame, c/n not known.
Piper J-3C-65 Cub	D-EHID	(c/n "11874"(really 12047) ex 44-79571, PH-NBP, (D-EKAB), (D-ECAX))

Piper J-3C-65 Cub	OY-EFM	(converted from TG-8 c/n G1/9144, ex 43-2009, NC46490, N46490, D-EMJG)
Piper PA22 Tri-Pacer	-	(c/n 22-6812)
Piper PA22 Tri-Pacer	-	possibly ex D-EASZ.

THISTED

The wreck of Cessna 182P OY-BFB (c/n 62477, ex N52241, crashed near Esbjerg 4.9.86) can be found here.

TIRSTRUP

As with the other Danish bases, Tirstrup has maintained an impressive decoy line up. Unfortunately the seven Thunderjets were all sold for scrap in 12.87. The tail from 19711 went to Oslo/Gardermoen to assist in the restoration of an F-84G for the RNorAF museum.

F-84G Thunderjet	19711	(ex 51-9711) ex 'AT-O' Alborg TT Flt, wfu 5.11.59.
F-84G Thunderjet	19949	(ex 51-9949) ex 'SI-Z' Esk.728, wfu 21.12.59.
F-84G Thunderjet	110076	(ex 51-10076) ex 'KP-E' Esk.725, wfu 20.11.59.
F-84G Thunderjet	110902	(ex 51-10902) ex 'SY-N' Esk.729, wfu 3.7.58 (tail from 19819).
F-84G Thunderjet	A-167	(ex 51-11167) ex Esk.730, wfu 12.5.61.
F-84G Thunderjet	23066	(ex 52-3066) ex 'SI-T' Esk.728, wfu 29.8.58.
F-84G Thunderjet	23079	(ex 52-3079) ex 'KP-Z' Esk.725, wfu 23.11.59.
F-86D Sabre	F-361	(ex 51-8361) ex Esk.728, wfu 14.3.66 (noted '85, to the fire dump).
F-86D Sabre	F-451	(ex 51-8451) ex Esk.728, wfu 14.3.66 (current '86).
CF-104 Starfighter	R-757	(ex RCAF 12757) ex Esk.726, wfu 1.7.83 (arrived '86).
CF-104 Starfighter	R-758	(ex RCAF 12758) ex Esk.726, wfu 1.7.83 (arrived '86).
CF-104D Starfighter	RT-660	(ex RCAF 12660) ex Esk.726, wfu 3.1.83 (current '86, used for bdr training).

As noted above, F-86D F-361 moved to the fire dump around '85/'86 and was still current during '88 though in a sorry state.

TONDER

DH Dove 5 OY-AJR (c/n 04474, ex XK897, G-AROI, N2410J, G-AROI) was here in 6.87 looking sorry for itself. By 4.88 the fuselage was at Vamdrup.

TRANUM

Preserved here prior to 1978 was F-84G Thunderjet 19819 (ex 51-9819, ex 'AT-L' Alborg TT Flt, wfu 16.7.58). The aircraft was sold for scrap during the late seventies (her tail was fitted to 110902 at Tirstrup at some stage).

VAERLOSE

The FLSP (Flyvevabnets Specialskole or RDanAF Technical Training School, formerly known as the FLKS - Flyvevabnets Konstabelskole) is located at Vaerlose and has utilised the following ground instructional airframes in recent years though only the CF-104D remains current.

DH Chipmunk T.20	P-130	(c/n C1/0109) ex FLSK, wfu 2.9.52 for gi here, to Brussels Museum on 8.6.77 in exchange for Stampe SV4B V-62).
DH Chipmunk T.20	12-131	(c/n C1/0695) ex FLSK, wfu 7.1.54 for gi, to Vaerlose depot 10.5.77, sold to HO-Aero at Billund 8.6.78 and due to go to Sweden. This fell through and the a/c remains at Billund.
CF-104D Starfighter	RT-654	(ex RCAF 12654) ex Esk.726, wfu 1.7.83, delivered to the school 22.7.83.
Lockheed T-33A	DT-491	(ex 51-4491) wfu 7.10.74, to Flyvevabnets Historiske Samling - see below.
F-86D Sabre	F-421	(ex 51-8421) to Flyvevabnets Historiske Samling - see below.

Almost the entire RDanAF T-bird fleet ended up here for storage and disposal, many surviving to this day as surface decoys.

Lockheed T-33A	DT-102	(ex 51-9102) ex Training Sqn, wfu 3.9.74 (noted '84-'88, to Slangerup by 6.89 - see 'Stop Press').
Lockheed T-33A	DT-289	(ex 51-9289) ex Karup Stn Flt, wfu 9.3.77 (noted '84-'88).
Lockheed T-33A	DT-404	(ex 51-4404) ex Vaerlose Stn Flt, wfu 2.12.76 (noted '85-'88).
Lockheed T-33A	DT-450	(ex 51-4450) ex Karup Stn Flt, wfu 30.8.74 (noted '85-'88).
Lockheed T-33A	DT-490	(ex 51-17490) ex Karup Stn Flt, wfu 19.1.77 (scrapped Bjerringbro '83).
Lockheed T-33A	DT-491	(ex 51-4491) wfu 7.10.74, to Flyvevabnets Historiske Samling and due to go to Billund but current as a decoy at Vaerlose '88.
Lockheed T-33A	DT-492	(ex 51-17492) ex Training Sqn, wfu 14.8.74 (noted '75 & '77, scrapped at Bjerringbro '83).
Lockheed T-33A	DT-497	(ex 51-6497) wfu 17.5.77, to Flyvevabnets Historiske Samling and also allocated to Billund. Current here as decoy during '88.
Lockheed T-33A	DT-516	(ex 51-17516) ex Karup Stn Flt, wfu 7.1.77 (noted '77, scrapped at Bjerringbro '83).
Lockheed T-33A	DT-566	(ex 51-8566) ex Karup Stn Flt, wfu 17.3.77 (airlifted to Northolt 31.7.79 & became G-TJET 8.1.82).
Lockheed T-33A	DT-571	(ex 51-6571) ex Karup Stn Flt, wfu 25.11.76 (to Sola, Norway 22.1.81, and displayed at Naval Base by 1985 in RNorAF marks as 'DP-A').
Lockheed T-33A	DT-728	(ex 51-8728) ex Karup Stn Flt, wfu 1.10.75 after a bird strike at Skrydstrup 14.8.75 (scrapped at Bjerringbro '83).
Lockheed T-33A	DT-835	(ex 51-8835) ex Training Sqn, wfu 3.9.74 (noted '75, scrapped at Bjerringbro '83).
Lockheed T-33A	DT-847	(ex 51-6847) ex Vaerlose Stn Flt, wfu 13.9.74 (noted '79-'88, to Slangerup by 6.89 - see 'Stop Press').
Lockheed T-33A	DT-923	(ex 51-8923) ex Vaerlose Stn Flt, wfu 19.2.75 (noted '75-'88, departed to Billund 18.10.88).
Lockheed T-33A	DT-974	(ex 51-9974) ex Karup Stn Flt, wfu 4.4.77 (noted '79, scrapped at Bjerringbro '83).

Just as a 'tail-piece', in 1973 DT-905 suffered a fire in the tail and received the tail from DT-102 as a replacement. Sometime between '73 and '76 the tail on DT-905 was changed for that from DT-492 and is current as such at Karup, with the serial '18905' on the fin. DT-102 remains here with the original tail from 18905 and DT-492 was scrapped during '83 when fitted with the tail of DT-102 wearing the serial '18905'. So there were three rear ends around all wearing the serial '18905'. Confused - you should be!

The following aircraft are held in store for the Flyvevabnets Historiske Samling (RDanAF Historical Collection).

CF-104 Starfighter	R-846	(ex RCAF 12846) ex Esk.726, wfu 11.7.84, to museum 10.7.84 (sheltered, departed to Billund 7.6.88).
PBY-5A Catalina	L-857	(Bu08019) ex Esk.721, wfu 14.10.67 and stored in the open at Vaerlose, to Plejerup c.1982.
PBY-6A Catalina	L-861	(Bu64035) ex Esk.721, wfu 13.11.70, to Engagergaard 6.10.77 for museum store, returning to Vaerlose 6.81 and currently under restoration inside prior to a move to Billund.
DH Chipmunk T.20	P-143	(c/n C1/0881) ex Tirstrup Stn Flt, wfu 21.3.77, to FLKS as gia, then to museum store (in Shelter 32) (current '88, due to go to Billund).

Douglas C-47A Dakota	K-681	(c/n 9664, ex 42-23802, LN-IAP, 68-681) ex Esk.721, wfu 31.12.80, open storage, flew to Billund museum 17.8.86.
Douglas C-47A Dakota	K-687	(c/n 19200, ex 42-100737, RNorAF, 68-687) ex Esk.721, wfu 8.1.81, open storage here. Flew to Billund 3.9.87 using parts borrowed from K-681/"OY-DDA".
Lockheed T-33A	DT-491	(ex 51-4491) ex Vaerlose Stn Flt, wfu 7.10.74 and to FLKS for gia use, (stored in Shelter 32, departed to Billund 11.10.88).
Lockheed T-33A	DT-497	(ex 51-6497) ex Karup Stn Flt, wfu 17.5.77, allocated to museum 18.8.77 (open storage, later in hangar 6). Due to go to Billund.
F-86D Sabre	F-421	(ex 51-8421) ex Esk.728, wfu 14.3.66 (in Shelter 33, current '88, due to go to Billund).
TF-100F Super Sabre	GT-927	(ex 56-3927) ex Esk.730, wfu 11.5.82 (in Shelter 31, current '88 but due to go to Billund).
Harvard T.2B	31-309	(c/n 14A-966, ex 43-12667, FS826) ex Vaerlose Stn Flt, wfu 22.4.59 and to gia at Mathskolen, stored at Gronholt (eg 1980) but removed to Vaerlose by 6.84 and to Billund museum 14.10.86.
SAI KZ VII	0-620	(c/n 182, ex 63-620) (in Shelter 33, poor condition, to go to Billund).
SAI KZ VII	0-621	(c/n 183, ex 63-621) in Shelter 32 (current '88) due to go to Billund).
Sikorsky S-55C	S-883	(c/n 55-1031, ex 88-883, wfu 31.1.66) ex Esk.722 (under restoration, air-freighted Northolt-Vaerlose 21.7.79 in a swop with Autair Helicopters for T-33A DT-566).
Sud Alouette III	M-388	(c/n 1388) ex Esk.722, wfu 1.9.80, allocated to Flyvevabnets Historiske Samling by 1.87, to Billund museum by 6.87.

Decoys at Vaerlose have included the following F-84G Thunderjets (as well as many of the T-33s noted above.

F-84G Thunderjet	19951	(ex 51-9951) ex Karup Stn Flt, wfu 31.8.61 (noted 1975, remains sold for scrap).
F-84G Thunderjet	110753	(ex 51-10753) ex 'SE-K' Esk.730, wfu 20.6.58 (tail from 110580), to Jagerspris ranges by 1987 - probably much earlier.

In 1975 the fire dump held F-84G Thunderjet 110731 (ex 51-10731, ex 'KP-R' Esk.725, wfu 7.6.60), PBY-5A Catalina L-852 (ex RCAF 11049, ex Esk.721, wfu 29.11.57, dumped 3.5.60) and Meteor F.8 44-481 (c/n G5/355, ex Alborg Stn Flt, wfu 30.7.57). The Catalina was sold for scrap in the late seventies whilst the Thunderjet and Meteor were still (just!) extant in 1988. The Meteor had been described as 'burnt out' as far back as 1979.

The fuselage of ex RSwedAF S 35E Draken 35905 was noted on the dump in '84 having been transported here for bdr exercises. It has since returned to Karup.

VAMDRUP

The fuselage of Dove 5 OY-AJR (c/n 04474, ex XK897, G-AROI, N2410J, G-AROI) had arrived here from Tonder by 4.88. It was scrapped later that year with some parts being donated to airworthy Dove 8 OY-BHZ.

VANDEL

Piper L-18C Super Cub Y-652 (c/n 18-3151, ex 53-4751) was wfu 9.2.77 and was described as 'preserved' on the base here in 1981. During 1987/88 it was under restoration to flying condition with the base flying club who already operate Y-654/OY-AZZ (c/n 18-3165, ex 53-4765, wfu 20.1.77).

The decoy areas at Vandel have recently contained the following.

F-84G Thunderjet	19681	(ex 51-9681) ex 'AT-D' Esk.725, wfu 6.7.60 (bad condition '87).
F-84G Thunderjet	A-043	(ex 51-10043) ex Esk.730, wfu 21.3.61 (bad condition '87).
F-84G Thunderjet	110503	(ex 51-10503) ex 'SY-S' Esk.729, wfu 25.5.60 (last reported 1985 though this report is doubted by our Danish correspondents as the aircraft had been sold for scrap).
F-84G Thunderjet	110651	(ex 51-10651) ex 'SI-C' Esk.728, wfu 22.8.60 (bad condition 1987).
F-84G Thunderjet	A-024	(ex 52-3024) ex Esk.728, wfu 31.8.60 (last reported 1985).
F-86D Sabre	F-026	(ex 51-6026) ex Esk.728, wfu 14.3.66 (not noted '85).
F-86D Sabre	F-060	(ex 51-6060) ex Esk.728, wfu 14.3.66 (noted '85).
F-86D Sabre	F-062	(ex 51-6062) ex Esk.728, wfu 14.3.66 (noted '85).
F-86D Sabre	F-096	(ex 51-6096) ex Esk.728, wfu 14.3.66 (noted '85).
F-86D Sabre	F-119	(ex 51-6119) ex Esk.728, wfu 17.7.65 (noted '85).
F-86D Sabre	F-469	(ex 51-8469) ex Esk.728, wfu 14.3.66 (noted '85).
F-86D Sabre	F-960	(ex 51-5960) ex Esk.728, wfu 14.3.66 (noted '85).
CF-104 Starfighter	R-704	(ex RCAF 12703) ex Esk.726, wfu 1.1.84 (arr 18.2.86).
CF-104 Starfighter	R-771	(ex RCAF 12771) ex Esk.726, wfu 1.1.84 (arr 18.12.86).
CF-104 Starfighter	R-812	(ex RCAF 12812) ex Esk.726, wfu 13.12.82 (arr 18.12.86).

The base fire section have been using F-86D Sabre F-429 (ex 51-8429, ex Esk.728, wfu 14.3.66) which was noted as such in 1985 and was still current during '88.

A museum close to Vandel air base has F-84G Thunderjet A-708 (ex 51-10708, ex Esk.728, wfu 31.8.60). The aircraft was still in reasonable condition in 1987.

VOJENS

Preserved in a playground in Ostergarde Street (East of the town centre) is F-84G Thunderjet A-525 (ex 51-10525, ex Esk.730, wfu 26.6.61). By 1987 the aircraft was in poor condition.

FINLAND

Maintaining a neutral position between East and West Finland has been able to draw on both sides for her military hardware, for example, MiG-21 pilots are currently trained on the BAe Hawk! As a result Finnish museums have a wide variety of types to offer including a Bristol Bulldog, Gloster Gauntlet and Blackburn Ripon of particular interest to British enthusiasts.

The flood of surplus Magisters is finding a ready market with the established 'warbird' fraternity in the States and has provided the first jet warbird on the civil registers of Eire and Finland.

AHTARI

Ex HavLv.31 Magister FM-71 is displayed in an amusement park here, about 100 kms North of Tampere (current '88).

HALLI

In the town square, Folland Gnat F.1 GN-103 (c/n FL16) is mounted in flying attitude (current '88).

The Air Force Technical School held the following ground instructional airframes during 8.88.

CM170 Magister	FM-43	ex 'G' IlmaSK.
MiG-21F	MG-78	on display outside.
SAAB J 35B Draken	35252	ex Swedish AF.

The school had used SAAB 91C Safir SF-7 as an instructional airframe but this was no longer current in '88 (last reported '83).

Fw 44J Stieglitz SZ-4 (ex SZ-4, OH-SZO) is preserved in one of the Air Force hangars in an airworthy state.

J 35BS Draken DK-206 (c/n 35266) was damaged in 1.74 due to an engine fire and was relegated to ground instructional use as "DK-942". Its permanent base is here but the aircraft moves around frequently as a travelling exhibit.

The storage and disposal of the Finnish AF Magister fleet has centred on Halli. Known disposal details are as follows.

CM170 Magister	FM-2	(c/n 182) ex 'T' IlmaSK, to N903DM Warplanes Inc.
CM170 Magister	FM-4	(c/n 186)
CM170 Magister	FM-5	(c/n 187)
CM170 Magister	FM-7	(c/n 189)
CM170 Magister	FM-14	(c/n 246)
CM170 Magister	FM-15	(c/n 248) ex HavLv.11.
CM170 Magister	FM-17	(c/n 253)
CM170 Magister	FM-18	(c/n 256) ex HavLv.21, to N805DM Warplanes Inc.
CM170 Magister	FM-26	to N16FM Exotic Aircraft Inc.
CM170 Magister	FM-27	to N604DM Warplanes Inc.
CM170 Magister	FM-28	ex 'O' IlmaSK, to N18FM Exotic Aircraft Inc then to EI-BXO at Shannon (Eire) 10.88.
CM170 Magister	FM-29	to N403DM Warplanes Inc.
CM170 Magister	FM-30	to N204DM Warplanes Inc.
CM170 Magister	FM-31	ex 'N' IlmaSK, to N19FM Exotic Aircraft Inc.
CM170 Magister	FM-32	ex 'C' IlmaSK, to N305DM Warplanes Inc(at Chino,CA,6.88
CM170 Magister	FM-35	ex 'H' IlmaSK, to N405DM Warplanes Inc.
CM170 Magister	FM-36	to N505DM Warplanes Inc.
CM170 Magister	FM-37	ex 'R' IlmaSK, to OH-FMA at Turku.
CM170 Magister	FM-38	to OH-FMB at Tampere-Pirkkala.
CM170 Magister	FM-39	to N19JV Exotic Aircraft Inc.

CM170 Magister	FM-42	for Finnish Aviation Museum.
CM170 Magister	FM-45	ex HavLv.31, last flying example, Halli based.
CM170 Magister	FM-46	ex HavLv.31.
CM170 Magister	FM-47	ex 'I' IlmaSK, to N605DM Warplanes Inc.
CM170 Magister	FM-49	to N804DM Warplanes Inc.
CM170 Magister	FM-51	to Oulu as OH-FMM.
CM170 Magister	FM-54	
CM170 Magister	FM-59	
CM170 Magister	FM-64	ex 'U' IlmaSK.
CM170 Magister	FM-66	
CM170 Magister	FM-67	
CM170 Magister	FM-71	ex HavLv.31, open store at Halli 6.86, to Ahtari.
CM170 Magister	FM-72	ex 'E' IlmaSK, to N404DM Warplanes Inc.
CM170 Magister	FM-73	ex 'A' IlmaSK, to N504DM Warplanes Inc.
CM170 Magister	FM-74	ex 'Y' IlmaSK.
CM170 Magister	FM-76	open store at Halli 6.86, to N705DM Warplanes Inc.
CM170 Magister	FM-78	ex 'L' IlmaSK, open store at Halli 5.87, sold to car dealer E Ikonen as a forecourt attraction.
CM170 Magister	FM-80	to N904DM Warplanes Inc.
CM170 Magister	FM-81	open store at Halli 6.86, to N303DM Warplanes Inc.

Adjacent to the VALMET works, is the Hallinportti Ilmailumuseo (Halli Aircraft Museum) with the following exhibits.

Bristol Bulldog IV	BU-59	(c/n 7810) (noted '87-'88).
Caudron G.III	1E-18	(noted '87-'88).
IVL D27 Haukka II	HA-41	(c/n 2) (noted '87-'88).
IVL C24	8F-4	(c/n 1) (noted '87-'88).
Karhu 48	OH-VKK	(c/n 5) (fuselage frame, noted '87-'88).
MiG-15UTI	MU-1	(c/n 922221) (noted outside '87-'88).
Rumpler 6B	5A-1	(ex Kauhava) (noted '87-'88).
VL Saaski II	LK-1	(c/n 2) (noted '87-'88).

Across the field in its own hangar lives Gloster Gauntlet II GT-400/OH-XGT (c/n G5/35957,ex K2571,noted'87-'88)which has been lovingly restored to flying condition.

Stored in a hangar on the airfield in 5.88 was damaged Pawnee 235 OH-PDZ (c/n 25-4163) which appeared to have suffered an accident. The aircraft has since been restored to health and now flies from Rayskala.

HAMEENLINA

Douglas DC-2 DO-1 (c/n 1354, ex PH-AKH, SE-AKE, DC-1) was here for many years serving as a coffee bar. In 11.81 the aircraft left for the museum at Tikkakoski.

HELSINKI/VANTAA

On the second floor of the main terminal Junkers A50ce Junior OH-ABB (c/n 3530, ex D-1915) of the Finnish Aviation Museum is displayed (noted '87).

Recently restored here by Finnair was VL Viima II OH-VII (ex VI-21) which is kept at the Finnair maintenance facility. Outside the complex is C-47A Dakota DO-8 (c/n 19309,ex 42-100846,OH-LCD) awaiting restoration in Finnair colours (noted '87-'88).

Just off the airport approach road is the Suomen Ilmailumuseo (Finnish Aviation Museum) which boasts the following.

Outside

Mil Mi-1 (SM-1SZ)	HK-1	(c/n A07060) (noted '87-'88).
Mil Mi-4	HR-3	(c/n 09114) (noted '88).
Mil Mi-8	HS-1	ex KuljLLv (arrived 5.88).

New Hangar

Convair 440	OH-LRB	(c/n 73) (noted '87-'88).
Douglas DC-2-200	DO-3	(c/n 1562, ex OK-AIC, D-AAIC, OH-DLB, OH-LDB) fuselage only, ex Loparo (noted '87-'88).
Folland Gnat F.1	GN-105	(noted '85-'88).
LET Z.37 Cmelak	OH-CMB	(c/n 04-09) (noted '87-'88).
Lockheed 18 Lodestar	OH-VKU	(c/n 2006, ex F-ARTF) ex Kar Air (noted '87-'88).
Schreder HP-16	OH-450X	(c/n 01) (noted 5.88).

SZD-10 bis Czapla OH-KCC (c/n W51) (noted 5.88).

Main Hall

Adaridi - (1924 vintage) (noted '87-'88).
Bell 47D-1 OH-HIA (c/n 646) (noted '87-'88).
DH Vampire T.55 VT-9 (c/n 15720) (noted '87-'88).
DFS108 Schulgleiter SG-1 (c/n 79) (noted '87-'88).
DFS108-49 Baby II OH-BAA (c/n 12/43) (noted '87-'88).
Eklund TE-1 OH-TEA (c/n 1) (noted '87-'88).
Fibera KK-le Utu OH-368 (c/n 21/68) (noted '87-'88).
Fieseler Fi 156K-1 OH-FSA (c/n 4230, ex ST-112, OH-VSF) (noted '87-'88).
Folland Gnat F.1 GN-106 (c/n FL28) (noted '87, to storage hangar).
Gloster Gamecock GA-58 fuselage only (noted '88).
Harakka II H-56 (c/n 24/52) (noted '87-'88).
Heinonen HK-1 Keltiainen OH-HKA (c/n 1) (noted '87-'88).
IVL A22 Hansa IL-2 (c/n 2 ex 4D-2) (noted '87-'88).
Kokkola Superupstart OH-XYY (c/n 01) (noted '87-'88).
Pik.3A OH-YKA (c/n 1/50) (noted '87-'88).
Pik.5B OH-PAR (c/n 16/50, ex OH-152) (noted '87-'88).
Pik.10 Moottoribaby OH-PXA (c/n 1) motorised version of Grunay Baby II OH-BAB '87-'88).
Pik.11 Tumppu OH-YMA (c/n 1) (noted '87-'88).
PA28R-180 Cherokee OH-PJN (c/n 28R-30885, SE-FDY ntu) (noted '88).
Polikarpov I-16UTI UT-1 (noted '87-'88).
SAAB 91C Safir SF-9 (c/n 91-355) (noted '87 & in storage hangar '88).
Schneider Grunau 9 G-36 (c/n 22/39) (noted '87-'88).
Grunau Baby II OH-BAA (c/n 12/43, ex OH-JAMI-5) (noted '88).
VL Viima II OH-VII (ex VI-21) (noted '88).
VL Tuisku TU-178 (noted '87-'88).
VL Pyry II PY-27 (c/n 26) (noted '87-'88).
WWS-1 Salamandra OH-SAA (c/n 1/47) (noted '87-'88).

Storage Hangar

Bristol Blenheim IV BL-180 rear fuselage only (noted '87-'88).
DFS108-70 Meise OH-OAA (c/n 1/45) (noted '87).
DFS Weihe OH-WAA (ex OH-JAMI-2) (noted '88).
DH Vampire FB.52 VA-2 (noted '85-'88).
Fibera KK-le Utu OH-KYC (noted '88).
Folland Gnat F.1 GN-106 (c/n FL28) (noted '88, ex Main Hall).
Kassel 12A "13" (c/n 1) ex Vesivehmaa storage (noted '88).
Klemm L-25 OH-KLA (c/n 137, ex K-SABA, OH-ABA).
Nyberg & Blomqvist Monoplane - (c/n 1)
Pik.12 Gabriel OH-318 (noted '87).
SAAB 91C Safir SF-9 (c/n 91-355) (noted '88, ex Main Hall).
SZD-9 Bocian OH-177 (noted '87-'88).
VL Pyry II PY-16 ex Vesivehmaa (noted 5.88).
VL Saaski II SA-131 (c/n 11/5) (under restoration when noted during '87).

Under restoration in one of the Finnair hangars at the airport during '88 was Karhumaki Karhu 48B OH-VKL (c/n 6, ex OH-KUA). With work completed this aircraft has now (by 11.88) returned to the museum but has not yet been confirmed on display or in store). Stored at the airport during 1988 were Douglas DC-3A OH-VKB (c/n 1975, ex SE-BAC) and DHC-2 Beaver OH-MVL (c/n 141). The latter at least had moved to the museum by 11.88. CM170 Magister FM-42 is due to come here from storage at Halli.

HYVINKAA

The major light aviation field in Southern Finland (about 25 kms North of Helsinki), a visit here in 5.88 found wrecks a plenty. Derelict outside in a damaged condition is MS880B Rallye Club OH-SCN (c/n 1330) whilst stored in the hangars, mostly in a dismantled state, were Cessna F150B OH-CCC (c/n 59462, wfu 2.1.86), Cessna A188 Agwagons OH-CCJ (c/n 0310, wfu 31.8.79), OH-CFD (c/n 00789, registration cancelled 30.1.81), and OH-CGR (c/n 019287) with Cessna F150H OH-CCR (c/n 0322, damaged beyond repair at Oulu 22.9.82). In the glider hangar during 5.88 was Schleicher ASK .21

OH-654 (c/n 21113) in a wrecked state.

ILMAJOKI

Klemm K125e OH-ILL (c/n 1045, ex SE-ANB) is undergoing restoration here.

JOENSUU

Pik.5B OH-PAT (c/n 18) was stored in a hangar here during 5.88.

KAUHAVA

CM170 Magisters FM-21 (ex HavLv.31) and FM-82 (ex 'M' IlmaSK) were allocated to the air base in 1987 for display purposes and by 1988 were mounted in flying attitude.

KUOPIO/RISSALA

MiG-21F MG-61 is preserved on a pole at the air base (noted 6.88). Fokker D.XXI FR-110 is undergoing restoration to static display standard at the base and will be unveiled at the Tikkakoski museum on 30.11.89 (the 50th aniversary of the start of the Winter War).

LOPARO

Douglas DC-2 DO-3 (c/n 1562, ex OK-AIC, D-AAIC, OH-DLB, OH-LDB) spent many years here as a children's playhouse. In the midst of dense vegetation and located on an island, this must have been one of the most inaccessible relics in Europe. The aircraft was eventually recovered ('87/'88) by Finnish AF Mi-8 and taken to the museum at Helsinki/Vantaa.

NUMMELLA

Pik.5B OH-PAC was in storage here in 5.88 with Grunau Baby IIB OH-BAF. In its own little hangar is MS885 Super Rallye OH-MRB (c/n 5161) which was cancelled from the register as withdrawn from use on 10.1.83 and has not flown since.

OULU

CM170 Magister FM-51 was noted here in 6.88, awaiting civil registration as OH-FMM.

PIEKSAMAKI

Pik.5B OH-PAV (c/n 20) was stored in a hangar here 5.88 (70 kms South of Kuopio).

RAYSKALA

SZD-9 Bocian OH-346 (c/n 876) was stored here in 5.88 with PIK-3C OH-233 (c/n 11) and Schneider Grunau Baby IIB OH-BAR.

ROVANIEMI

Gate-guard at the air base here is Folland Gnat F.1 GN-110 (c/n FL44) (noted '80-'88). In storage on the civil side in 5.88 was Schneider Grunau Baby IIB OH-BAY.

TAMPERE

In the town of Tampere, outside a VALMET factory, prototype VL Viima VI-1 (c/n 1) is preserved in a glass pagoda.

The Tampereen Teknillinen Museo (Tampere Technical Museum) has the following aircraft on display on the first floor (the ground floor is devoted to cars).

DH60X Moth	OH-ILA	(c/n 447, ex K-SALF ntu, K-SILA) (noted '87-'88).
Fokker D.10	FO-42	(ex 8E-3) frame only (noted '87-'88).
Mignet Pou-du-Ciel	OH-KAA	(c/n 1/35) (noted '88)
Mil Mi-1	HK-2	(WSK built, c/n A07030) (noted '87-'88).
Saaski	SA-95	(ex K-SASA) frame only (noted '87-'88).
VL Pyry II	PY-1	(c/n 1) (noted '87-'88).

A group of enthusiasts here are restoring Letov S.21B Smolik SM-141 (c/n 5/VL) to static display condition.

TIKKAKOSKI

North of Jyvasklya is the Luonetjarvi Air Force Base at Tikkakoski. On the military side of the field is the Keski-Suomen Ilmailumuseo (Central Finnish Aviation Museum). Inside the main hall are the following exhibits.

Avro 504K	AV-57	(ex E448, G-EBNU, IH-49) (noted '87-'88).
DH60X Moth	OH-EJA	(c/n 10/29, ex MO-100, OH-ILC, OH-MAH) (noted'87-'88).
DH Vampire T.55	VT-8	(c/n 15719) (noted '80-'88).
Folland Gnat F.1	GN-101	(c/n FL8, ex G-39-6) (noted '80-'88).
Gourdou-Lesseurre GL-21C1	8F-12	(c/n 60, ex GL-12) (noted '87-'88).
Hawker Hurricane I	HC-452	(ex N2394, HU-452) (noted '87-'88).
Ilyushin Il-28R	NH-4	(c/n 1106) (noted '80-'88).
Messerschmitt Bf 109G	MT-507	(c/n 167271) (noted '87-'88).
Mignet Pou-du-Ciel	-	(noted incomplete '87-'88).
Martinsyde F4 Buzzard	MA-24	(ex D4326) (noted '87-'88).
MiG-15UTI	MU-4	(c/n 722375) (noted '80-'88).
Mil Mi-1	OH-HRC	(c/n 1811) (noted '87-'88).
Mil Mi-4	HR-1	(c/n 07114) (noted '84-'88).
Morane MS-50C	MS-52	(ex 2G-7) (oted '87-'88).
Paatalo Tiira	-	(noted '87-'88).
Pik.5B	OH-PAX	(c/n 21/56) (noted 5.88, ex store).
Polikarpov Po-2	1	(Soviet c/s) (noted '87-'88).
SAAB 91D Safir	OH-SFB	(c/n 91-440, ex SF-31) (noted 5.88).
SAAB 91C Safir	SF-8	(c/n 91-354) cockpit only, ex store (noted '88).
Thulin D	F-1	(noted '88, ex store).
Valmet Vihuri II	VH-18	(noted '84-'88).
VL Humu	HM-671	(c/n 632567) (noted '87-'88).
VL Pyorremyrsky	PM-1	(c/n 1) (noted '87-'88).

The following machines have been stored in the open.

Douglas DC-2	DO-1	(c/n 1354, ex PH-AKH, SE-AKE, DC-1) (noted '84-'88).
Douglas C-47A Dakota	DO-4	(c/n 25515, ex 43-48254, ex OH-LCF) TT 28576 hrs (arr 27.5.82, current '88).
Folland Gnat F.1	GN-104	(c/n FL19) (noted '80-'88).
Hunting Pembroke C.53	PR-2	(c/n 70) (noted '84-'88).

MiG-21F MG-92 has joined the collection but has not as yet been noted on site.

Fokker D.XXI FR-110 will come here following restoration at Kuopio/Rissala.

A nearby shed, not open to the public, contains the museum store. A full list is not available due to the large number of aeroplanes and parts of aeroplanes packed into a small space making access difficult and well nigh impossible. Those items which were positively identified in 5.87 comprised:-

Bell P-39Q Airacobra	26	(ex 44-2664) Soviet colour scheme (noted '87-'88).
Bristol Blenheim IV	BL-200	(plus noses of 2 more, all noted '87-'88).
Cessna F172H	OH-CNH	(c/n 0519) (noted '87-'88).
DFS Weihe	OH-WAB	(ex OH-JAMI-3, OH-135) (noted '87-'88).
DH Vampire T.55	VT-6	(c/n 15756) (noted '87-'88).
Fokker C.X	FK-113	frame, plus two more (all three noted '87).
MiG-3	-	fuselage only (noted '88).
UC-64A Norseman	OH-NOA	(ex 44-70381, HB-UIK) fuselage only (noted '87-'88).
Pik.3B	OH-199	(c/n 5/59) (noted '87).
Pik.5B	OH-PAX	(c/n 21/56) (noted '87).
Pik.5B	OH-PBA	(noted '87).
SAAB 91C Safir	SF-2	(c/n 91-348) (noted '87-'88).
SAAB 91C Safir	SF-8	(c/n 91-354) cockpit section only (noted '84-'87, to main hall by 5.88).
SAAB 91D Safir	OH-SFD	(c/n 91-443, ex SF-34) (noted '87-'88).
SAAB 91D Safir	OH-SFE	(c/n 91-444, ex SF-35) (noted '87-'88).
Grunau Baby II	OH-BAD	(c/n 15/36) (noted '87-'88).
SZD 10 bis Czapla	OH-KCD	(c/n W39/59, ex OH-209) (noted '87-'88).
Thulin D	F-1	(noted '87, to Main Hall).
Tupolev SB-2	'12/117'	(Soviet c/s) sections only (noted '87-'88).
Valtion Tuisku	-	derelict (noted '88).
VL Pyry II	PY-35	(c/n 34) (noted '87-'88).

They should also have:-

DH Vampire FB.52	VA-6	(c/n V0696)
MiG-21F	MG-92	
MiG-21UTI	MK-103	stored on the military side during '88.
Valmet Myrsky II	MY-5	frame only
Valmet Myrsky II	MY-9	frame only
Valmet Myrsky II	MY-10	frame only
Valmet Vinka	370	prototype (noted '88)

It is expected that by the end of 1989 the museum will move to larger premises near Highway E4 (an old factory on the edge of Tikkakoski village).

TURKU

Preserved in flying condition here (by 5.88) is CM170 Magister OH-FMA (ex FM-37).

UTTI

Preserved here for many years is Messerschmitt Bf 109G-6 MT-452 (c/n 165227).

The fuselage of C-47A Dakota DO-5 (c/n 9799, ex 42-23937) is in use on the airfield for paratroop training (noted '85-'86).

The surviving Dakotas were gathered here for storage and disposal in 1984, details as follows.

C-47A Dakota	DO-6	(c/n 12050, ex 42-92268) sold 1.85, allocated G-BLXW 19.4.85 but to N57NA and flown to USA 18.5.85.
C-47A Dakota	DO-7	(c/n 19109, ex 42-100646, OH-LCB) wfu '83, to PH-DDA'84.
C-47A Dakota	DO-8	(c/n 19309, ex 42-100846, OH-LCD) last Finnish AF Dak flight 18.12.84, to Airveteran Oy at Helsinki/Vantaa.
C-53D Skytrooper	DO-9	(c/n 11750, ex 42-68823, OH-LCG) sold 1.85, allocated G-BLYA 19.4.85 but to N59NA and flown to USA 30.5.85.
C-53C Skytrooper	DO-11	(c/n 6346, ex 42-93096, OH-LCH) to Airveteran Oy and re-registered as OH-LCH 4.86.
C-47A Dakota	DO-12	(c/n 12970, ex 42-93096, OH-LCE) sold as SE-IOK 10.84 but allocated G-BLXV 19.4.85, became N58NA and flown to USA 18.5.85.

UUSIKAUPUNKI

SAAB 91C Safir SF-5 (c/n 91-351) was displayed at the local SAAB car factory here (50 kms North West of Turku) by 1983 (current '88).

VESIVEHMAA

The Finnish Aviation Museum Society have a storage hangar here (20 kms NE of Lahti) within which many of the country's more historic aircraft have survived over the years, gradually departing to good homes elsewhere in Finland. Apart from the Gnat and MiG-15 (relative newcomers) all are dismantled and unrestored.

Aero A11	AE-47	(noted '87).
Aero A32	AE-59	(noted '87).
Blackburn Ripon IIF	RI-140	(c/n 12) (noted '87).
Breguet 14A2	3C-30	(noted '87).
Caudron C59	CA-50	(ex 2E-5) (noted '87).
Caudron C60	CA-84	(c/n 24) (noted '87).
Caudron C.714	CA-556	(c/n 6)
Fokker C.VE	FO-75	fuselage only (noted '87).
Fw 44J Steiglitz	SZ-35	(noted '87).
Folland Gnat F.1	GN-112	(c/n FL47) (noted '87).
IVL Haukka 1	HA-39	(noted '87).
IVL K1 Kurki	-	(noted '87).
Kassel 12A (glider)	'13'	(c/n 1) to Helsinki/Vantaa by '88.
MiG-15UTI	MU-2	(c/n 822028) (noted '87).
Tupolev SB-2	'16/250'	fuselage, in Soviet markings (noted '87).
VL E30 Kotka II	KA-147	(c/n 4) (noted '87).
VL Pyry II	PY-16	(noted '87, to Helsinki/Vantaa by 5.88).
VL Pyry II	PY-26	fuselage frame (noted '87).

FRANCE

France is literally bursting at the seams with Wrecks and Relics and could easily justify a book of this size all to itself. We cannot devote the whole of this volume to France so I have had to be very selective in what is included and what I omit. Much has already been published about the French W&R scene both on the military side (eg my own French Military Wrecks and Relics published by BARG in 1986) and also the civil (witness the W&R section in the Air Britain French registers). Bearing this in mind I have in this section concentrated more on the current/recent scene rather than attempt to cover the last decade except where some historical perspective seems appropriate (eg Chateaudun). Mention of the large and ever growing number of aircraft 'collections' in France has also been kept to a minimum, my excuse being that some of their aircraft are already in flying condition and others are being actively restored to airworthiness, so many are not true 'W&R' material anyway. To have done otherwise would have increased the size of this section to unacceptable proportions and delayed the publication date significantly.

The bracketed numbers after each place name refer to the Departement (French administrative region) within which the location can be found. This gives the reader a good idea of whereabouts on the map to look to find a particular relic, so further directions are kept to an absolute minimum in this section. Once again may I recommend the Michelin series of maps to you.

Finally may I say a special thank-you to my good friend Patrick Vinot-Prefontaine (Wrecks and Relics editor for the excellent 'Le Trait d'Union' magazine) who despite serious illness has made an outstanding contribution without which the French section of this book would be much the poorer.

ABBEVILLE/DRUCAT (80)

A long standing landmark here is the Aero Club de la Somme's derelict MD450 Ouragan 215 (ex '2-EN' EC.2) which sits outside the Motel at the airfield (noted '67-'88).

AIRAINES (80)

N1101 Noralpha F-BLQZ (c/n 142) is preserved outside a BP petrol station on the RN901 (noted '84-'88).

AIRE-SUR-ADOUR (40)

By 1.88 CM170 Magister 167 had arrived at the CNES (who?) from the Fouga works.

AIX/LES-MILLES (13)

Preserved by the civil terminal was MD311 Flamant 281 (ex '316-KK' GE.316, soc 14.10.69). It was finally scrapped between '84 and 3.86. Guarding the gate on the military side (Base Aerienne 114) is Mystere IVA 289 (noted '83-'89) in EC.2 markings as "2-EY". It should not be confused with 105 which as at Le Bourget painted as "289".

On the dump, the firemen have trained on an H-34, a Flamant and a Noratlas in recent years. The dump is on the North West corner of the field and is easily missed.

MD312 Flamant	238	ex '91-CW' EB.91, soc 24.10.74 (noted '78-'86).
N2501 Noratlas	87	ex '64-KA' ET.64, fuselage pod (noted '84-'88).
Sikorsky H-34A	SA57	(noted '78-'86).

The preservationists Escadrille Pegase have their main base here and as their aircraft tend to move around a bit I have listed them all here for convenience. Where the aircraft is believed to be located elsewhere this is highlighted in the notes. Some aircraft are stored at Salon or are active at Vinon or Aspres-Sur-Buech (where the group has an active gliding section). Restoration work is often carried out at Le Castellet or La Mole.

Breguet 900	-	stored.
Brochet MB.83	F-PGLF	(c/n 6) at Le Castellet.
Brochet MB.70	F-BCZF	(c/n 01) under restoration at Cuers.
Castel C.25S	-	under restoration.
Caudron C.800	F-CADI	(c/n 352) at Aspres.
Caudron C.800	F-CBAF	(c/n 286) stored.
PBY Catalina	-	nose section reported here 4.89, probably the ex Protection Civile nose that used to be at Marseille years ago.
MD311 Flamant	250	(F-AZEN) often here but does not belong to Escadrille Pegase, refer to Le Castellet.
MD311 Flamant	274	(F-AZEH) ex '316-..' GE.316 (arr 27.6.86, noted here '89).
Super Mystere B.2	46	ex '12-ZY' EC.2/12, at Salon.
CM170 Magister	-	Patrouille de France c/s (noted here '89, compiler's educated guess at its identity is 545, but it could be 45 in spurious PdF colours. As we go to press it is reported that 545 is now displayed at Berlin/Tegel - the same a/c?).
Lockheed T-33S-C	21121	ex '314-UW' GE.314, & Apt (noted here '87-'89).
Morane MS500	-	stored at Salon.
MS505 Criquet	F-BJHV	(c/n 617/30) stored.
MS733 Alcyon	F-BDZY	(c/n 13) stored at Bergerac.
Nord NC858S	F-BBRP	(c/n 142) under restoration.
Nord NC858	F-BFSU	(c/n 74) under restoration at Salon.
N1101 Noralpha	197	ex 'CAN-15' DCAN, stored at La Mole.
N1101 Noralpha	F-BLEX	(c/n 189) stored at La Mole.
N1203 Norecrin	F-BEQE	(c/n 109) stored at Brignoles.
Nord 2000	F-CAUM	(c/n 36) at Aspres.
N2501 Noratlas	105	ex '63-VM' ET.63 (noted here '86-'89).
N2504 Noratlas	01	ex Aeronavale, arrived 26.6.88, allocated F-GFTS but instead became F-AZNA (current here '89).
Piel CP30 Emeraude	F-PFVY	(c/n 01) under restoration at Brignoles.
PA22 Tri-Pacer	F-BLOD	(c/n 22-7482) stored.
Schneider Grunau Baby	F-CRDT	(c/n 14) stored at Salon.
Stampe SV4C	F-BBQR	(c/n 195) under restoration at La Mole.
Stampe SV4C	F-BHGS	(c/n 1065) stored at La Mole.
Vautour IIN	338	ex '30-MN' ECTT.2/30 & Clermont-Ferrand.

Stored on the civil side in 6.89 was PA23-160 Apache F-BTDX (c/n 23-108),

ALENCON/VALFRAMBERT (61)

The Association de Voltige Alenconnaise acquired MD312 Flamant 160/F-AZDR (ex '319-DA' GE.319) from Chateaudun in 1984 and maintain it in airworthy condition along with Nord 3202 94/F-WZBB (ex Guyancourt) and MD311 Flamant 276/F-AZER. Their MH1521 Broussard 294/F-GDQV (ex Blois) had moved to storage at Herbault by '87.

ALES/DEAUX (30)

CM170 Magister 101 (ex '4-WB' SLVSV/EC.4) was preserved with the Aero Club here (noted '83) but it had turned up at Montelimar/Ancone by 7.89. During 4.86 damaged L-19E Bird Dog 24559/F-GDQZ was noted stored in a hangar.

AMBERIEU (01)

Preserved at Base Aerienne 278 is T-6G Texan 114688/RC (ex 51-14688) which came from the Escadrille de Souvenir at Etampes on 26.9.82 (current '87).

Breguet 941S 3/62-NC (ex ET.62 & Chateaudun store) arrived here for storage by 1974 and was still parked out during '87 though it was expected to be handed over to the firemen soon after.

The fuselage of an unidentified Sud Fennec (T-28) was noted on the base during 6.85. On the dump at this time was an equally anonymous N2501 Noratlas fuselage.

AMBOISE/DIERRE (37)

The Aero Club here, Les Ailes Tourangelles, used to display an Ouragan and Flamant but these were unfortunately sold for scrap (12,000F the pair) and dismantled c10.6.86 after their condition had deteriorated to the extent that they became dangerous to children. Although marked as "271" the Flamant is thought to have been 284 with the fins from 271. Both machines were soc at Chateaudun in '69 and some fin swopping is known to have taken place.

MD311 Flamant	284	ex 'N' GLA.45 (soc 14.10.69, scrapped 6.86).
MD450 Ouragan	308	ex 'UO' GE.314 (noted '73, scrapped 6.86).

The wreck of Robin ATL F-GFSI (c/n 89) lay here by 7.88.

ANCY-LE-FRANC (89)

The Musee Automobile in the chateau has a Pou-du-Ciel on display (built at Auxerre in 1936) (noted '87).

ANDERNOS (33)

Present during 7.87 were the wrecks of PA24-250 Comanches F-BJAG (c/n 24-359) and F-BLTZ (c/n 24-2753).

ANGERS (49)

Wrecks at the aerodrome during 1988 compised MS880 Rallyes F-GAYT (c/n 2909, crashed 8.84) and F-BPSD (c/n 1192) and the front fuselage of Cessna F150M F-GAGK (c/n 1334).

In a barracks (Caserne Berthezene) in the town, the Armee de Terre's 21 Regiment du Genie have a Vertol H-21C preserved. It has the legend 'Gaubourgs' on the fuselage sides and was still current during 11.88.

On the edge of the town, on the road to La Fleche, MS733 Alcyon F-BLXT (c/n 131) was noted in a yard in 3.87. It belongs to Monsieur Landreau who also has the three Alcyons at St Jean de Linieres.

On the South side of the N160 towards Cholet, a CM170 Magister is displayed atop a pole near the 'Cuir Centre' store (noted 5.88).

Ailes Anciennes - Anjou (previously Groupement pour la Preservation du Patrimonie Aeronautique) has been loaned some aircraft and gliders by the Musee de l'Air and has a large display hangar donated by the town council during 1989. Active aircraft have been omitted from the list below.

Breguet 901S	F-CCCP	(c/n 13) stored.
Breguet 901S	F-CCCS	(c/n 16) stored.
Castel C.25.S	-	stored.
Castel C.25.S	F-CRLP	(c/n 179) stored.
Castel 3010	F-CAIS	(c/n 1026) stored.
Castel 301.S	F-CBUG	(c/n 1089) stored.
Castel 310.P	F-CRJJ	(c/n 123) stored.
Castel 311.P	F-CALS	stored.
Caudron C.800	F-CAHD	(c/n 230) under restoration.
Caudron C.800	F-CAHE	(c/n 338) stored.
DFS SG38 Schulgleiter	-	(c/n 157) stored.
DFS Weihe	F-CBGT	(c/n 3) under restoration, loan from Musee de l'Air.
Fouga CM.8-13	F-CCHM	(c/n 01) stored, loan from Musee de l'Air.
Gardan GY201 Minicab	F-BGTH	(c/n 149) stored.
Gasnier	-	loan from Musee de l'Air.
SA104 Emouchet	F-CAIP	(c/n 250) stored.
SA104 Emouchet	F-CADP	(c/n 264) stored.
Jodel D120	F-BKJU	(c/n 214) under restoration.
Morane MS505 Criquet	F-BIPJ	(c/n 149) under restoration, loan from Musee de l'Air.
Nord 1300	F-CRNO	(c/n 71) stored.
Nord 1300	F-CRJI	(c/n 209) stored.
N2501 Noratlas	184	ex '328-EO' CIFAS.328, on the airfield '86-'89.
Nord 2000	F-CBGE	(c/n 48) stored.
Piper J-3C Cub	F-BHEB	(c/n 11343) under restoration.
Tipsy Nipper	F-OBYV	(c/n 61) stored.
Zlin 326	F-BMQU	(c/n 900) stored.

ANGOULEME/RUELLE (16)

The Aero Club de la Charente had MD312 Flamant 188/41-GD (ex ELA.41, soc 5.9.72) here. The aerodrome here closed with the opening of the new Brie/Charente airport nearby. As a result the Flamant was scrapped sometime after 7.81.

ANNECY/MEYTHET (74)

Sikorsky H-34A SA92 (ex CELAG/Grenoble) had arrived for the Musee des Deux Guerres by '87. The Aero Club d'Annecy received CM170 Magister 85/33-XC ex SALE/ER.33 on 9.7.86 (current '88).

ANNEMASSE (74)

A hangar held the wreck of Calvel-Piel CPM.01 Zef F-PTXL (c/n 01, ex F-WTXL) in 9.87 whilst stored here in 12.88 was the wreck of PA28 Cherokee Arrow G-AZSM (crashed 2.9.85).

APT/ST CHRISTOL (84)

At Base Aerienne 200, the gate is guarded by Sikorsky H-34A SA84/67-OB (ex EH.67). Sikorsky H-34A SA72 was stored here (noted '83) whilst expended on the dump was MD312 Flamant 233 (soc 9.4.70, disappeared post 1978). Lockheed T-33S-C 21121 (ex '314-VW' GE.314) was noted here during '82 and subsequently travelled to Aix/Les-Milles for Escadrille Pegase who re-assembled her on 24.2.87. This machine was allocated the US registration N12424 but obviously preferred to stay in France.

ATHIS-MONS (90)

The nose of ex Air France SE210 Caravelle III F-BHRU (c/n 58) was in use for instructional purposes here at an establishment called the CCR in '86.

AUBENAS (07)

On display at the Aero Club is CM170 Magister 124 (noted '86-'87). The fuselage of MS880B Rallye Club F-GBKA (c/n 3058) was here in '86 and still current in 7.87 by which time another MS880B, F-BKZZ (c/n 402) was also derelict.

AUBIGNY-SUR-NERE (18)

The Aero Club here were the recipients of MD312 Flamant 194 (ex '30-QL' ECTT.12/30, soc 23.5.72). It was recorded here in poor condition during 9.83 but had gone to a local scrap dealer by 5.84. An unidentified Pou-du-Ciel was stored here in 11.87.

AULNAY SOUS BOIS (93)

The Parc des Sports de la Rose des Vents had N2501 Noratlas 50 (ex '64-BH' ET.3/64) on display by 10.88, this machine having been discarded by the Musee de l'Air at Le Bourget.

AUTUN/BELLEVUE (71)

Adams RA.14 Loisirs F-PHLG (c/n 104) has been stored at the back of the hangar for years (current 8.89).

AVIGNON/CAUMONT (84)

Stored in the hangars on the far side of the field is SFERMA 60 Marquis F-BJSI (c/n 02, noted 6.87). Preserved by the tower is SE210 Caravelle III/48T "F-POHA" (c/n 242, ex F-BOHA) in Air France colours (noted '83-'89).

A new arrival in '84 was MD312 Flamant 156 (ex 'OG' CEV) for which the registration F-AZDY has been allocated (noted '85-'86). The machine belongs to the Musee de l'Air.

Ex 'Hanover Street' B-25J Mitchell N9455Z/"151863" (ex 44-30210) 'Big Bad Bonnie' blew a cylinder and was abandoned here by '82. After several years sunbathing it was restored to airworthiness and departed Stateside.

AVORD (18)

Preserved inside the gate at Base Ecole 702 is MD312 Flamant 229/319-DW (ex GE.319) (noted '85-'86). Another Flamant, MD312 146 (ex '319-CM' GE.319, soc 5.12.75) was displayed amongst the buildings on the East side of the base until at least 1983. It has since been repainted in camouflage colours with the code "319-GE" and has been re-positioned (still current '86). Mirage IVA 29/BB was preserved on the base by 7.88, restored to the old silver colour scheme (current 4.89).

The based pilot selection unit EFIPN.307 brought their CAP.10B instructional airframe with them from Clermont-Ferrand during 10.85. It comprises the fuselage of 2/VT (ex GI.312) with the wings from 19.

On the fire dump, MD312 Flamant 169 (ex '4-WA' EC.4/SLVSV, soc 24.11.66) had been consumed by 1983. It was superseded by MD312 201 (ex '319-DJ' GE.319) which first appeared in 1982 and by T-33SF 21105 (ex '314-YO' GE.314) which arrived in 1.83. They were not recorded during the open day in 1985 and nothing has been seen on the dump since.

A scrap compound here held a section of fuselage from the Nord 2200 (from the ETBS at Bourges) during the early eighties. Fortunately this was saved for preservation and moved to Savigny and then on to Vannes where Ailes Anciennes - Armorique will re-unite it with the rest of the airframe. It is then expected to go to the Aeronavale museum at Rochefort and may well be there by the time these words are read.

AVRANCHES (50)

The wreck of MS893A Commodore 180 F-BPHI (c/n 10798) was stored in the hangar here during 10.87 (current 10.88).

BARCELONNETTE/ST PONS (04)

The Aero Club here have MD312 Flamant 200 (ex '13-TA' EC.13/SLVSV, soc 14.12.71). Its continued existence was last confirmed during 10.84.

BEAUNE (21)

Ailes Anciennes - Beaune have acquired CAP.10B 19/313-SQ from Clermont-Ferrand (noted '86) though this hardly furthers their aim to set up a Jodel Museum here. The group have also obtained items from the disbanded Ailes Anciennes - Dijon, principally a Mignet HM.14 Pou-du-Ciel and the fuselage of a Morane-Saulnier MS230.

BEAUVAIS/TILLE (60)

Stored here by Dr Blondel is N1101 Noralpha 74 (ex 'LZ' CEV). He also has Caudron C-635 Simoun F-AZBO (c/n 342, ex F-DADY) under restoration.

BERCK (62)

The wreck of CEA DR315 Petit Prince F-BSBD (c/n 468) lay in the hangar here in 8.88.

BERGERAC/ROUMANIERE (24)

MD312 Flamant 236 (soc 13.8.73) is preserved just North of the aerodrome here having been donated to L'Association des Parents des Enfants Inadaptes de Bergerac (noted '86).

The collection Les Cages a Poules d'Aquitaine fly from here whilst an unidentified Stampe of theirs was derelict here about 1987.

BESANCON (25)

A military parachute training centre here uses a N2501 Noratlas fuselage (noted '83-'85).

BIARRITZ (64)

Mirage IIIA 06 is preserved at the AMD-BA (Dassault) factory here (noted '74-'86). Stored at a private location is a Payen Pa.61 Arbalete (noted '89).

BISCARROSSE (40)

Two ex Luftwaffe Dornier Do 24 flying boats were recovered from the Etang de Biscarrosse where they had lain since 1944 and were beached near the Musee des Hydravions (flying boat museum). 1007/W4+BH was still here in 7.85 whilst the fuselage of 1101/W4+DH had been scrapped (the wings and tail remained). All the remains of these two flying boats have now been scrapped due to heavy corrosion and vandalism.

The museum itself had Thurston Teal TU-TWA (c/n 16) on display by '88 (it was in store during '87).

BLANGY-LE-CHATEAU (14)

Sikorsky H-34 SA55/68-OA (ex EH.2/68) was reported at a private location here in '85 but had moved to St Philibert-Des-Champs by '87.

BLOIS/LE BREUIL (41)

Guarding the entrance to the civil aerodrome is MS733 Alcyon F-BMMV (c/n 117). This appeared by 8.87 replacing the quartet of ex military types which graced this field through the seventies. It was once part of an interesting quartet which was split up during the eighties when the A-26 was acquired by the Musee de l'Air, the Ouragan moved to Savigny-Les-Beaune and the C-45 and Flamant were unfortunately sold for scrap. The Ouragan has previously been reported as 208 but official records show that 230 was sold to the Aero Club here on 3.2.64 whilst 208 was scrapped.

Beech C-45	133	(ex 44-7133) soc 29.9.71, scrapped Spring '85.
MD312 Flamant	165	ex '44-GI' ELA.44, soc 3.8.71, scrapped Spring '85.
MD450 Ouragan	230	ex '4-US' EC.3/4 & 'TD' GE.314 (to Savigny 7.87).
A-26B Invader	39162	(c/n 6875, ex 41-39162) ex 'Z' CEAM, to Musee de l'Air '81.

Cessna F150M F-GAAY (c/n 1327) was in store here in 8.87 with Cessna 180A F-BCDQ (c/n 50037) and an anonymous Fournier RF-3. The Cessna 150 was still current in 8.88.

BORDEAUX/MERIGNAC (33)

Preserved around the base at BA106 have been the following airframes.

Mirage IIIR	346	ex '33-C.' ER.1/33 (noted '87-'89).
Mystere IVA	48	ex '314-ZF' GE.314 (preserved '77-'89, for Ailes Anciennes - Le Bourget).
Mystere IVA	306	ex '8-MW' ET.1/8 (noted '82-'89).
Super Mystere B.2	124	ex '21-LC' BA721 (stored '83, also noted '87).
A-26B Invader	35859	(c/n 29138, ex 44-35859) '328-EY' (noted '78-'89).
MH1521 Broussard	285	ex ETE.43 (noted '89).
Vautour IIB	636	ex '92-AW' EB.92 (noted '78-'89).
Vautour IIB	6..	stored, ex St Nazaire (noted '88, for the museum?).

On the dump in 7.85 was the burnt hulk of an anonymous N2501 Noratlas. In 9.86 a Mirage IVA fuselage was seen on the dump.

Parked out on the South West side of the base (near the EC.4/11 area) by 10.88 were desert camouflaged Mirage IIICs 35 and 70. Their subsequent fates are not known but undoubtedly their flying days are over.

A quartet of CM170 Magisters were in open store by the SOGERMA hangars by the end of 1985 having served for training foreign pilots. The four were 51/F-ZVLE, 69/F-ZVLF, 99/F-ZVLG, and 102/F-ZVLL. They were still current in 9.87 but have not been heard of since.

A museum is being set up on the former CIFAS.328 area adjacent to the airport terminal. The following aircraft have so far arrived here and I suspect that the Super Mystere and one of the Vautours listed above might also be for the museum.

MD312 Flamant	202	ex '319-CS' GE.319 (noted '88-'89).
Mirage IIIB	204	ex 'DG' CIFAS.328 (noted '88-'89).
CM170 Magister	117	(noted '88-'89).
MH1521 Broussard	228	(noted '88-'89).
N2501 Noratlas	111	ex '63-VF' ET.63, Chateaudun & Marmande (noted '88-'89).
N2501 Noratlas	200	nose section only.

Preserved by the airport terminal is SE210 Caravelle III/48T "F-CCIB" (c/n 152, ex F-BJTP) (noted '85, to SOGERMA for restoration '89, may then be used as a gia).

BORDEAUX/SOUGE (33)

The ALAT base within the Camp Militaire de Souge (West of Bordeaux/Merignac) had a preserved SNCASO S01221 Djinn by '84. It had gone by '87.

BOUILLY (10)

SO1221 Djinns FR103, FR117/CBA, FR128, FR130/CBC, FR137, and FR145 may still be in store at the former premises of the 'Phitagri' agricultural firm. FR117 was last reported during '86 whilst the other five were still current 12.87.

BOURGES (18)

The Etablissement Technique du Bourges (ETBS) (in the South East part of town between the D976 and RN76) was visited in 9.83 and found to contain seven dismantled Super Mystere B.2s. Three were in natural metal finish (one with dayglo areas) with the other four in camouflage with all identifying marks painted out except for the last letter of the code on the nose wheel door. Their identities are believed to be as listed below but confirmation would be welcome. They were accompanied by Sikorsky H-34A SKY525/68-0_ (ex EH.2/68) in 9.83 but this had disappeared by 5.84.

Super Mystere B.2	01	ex EPNER (current '88).
Super Mystere B.2	02	ex EPNER (current '88).
Super Mystere B.2	73	ex '12-ZI' EC.2/12.
Super Mystere B.2	83	ex '12-ZT' EC.2/12, to Savigny-Les-Beaune by '89.
Super Mystere B.2	91	ex '12-ZV' EC.2/12.
Super Mystere B.2	118	ex '12-YS' EC.1/12 (arr from Chateaudun post '85).
Super Mystere B.2	145	ex '12-ZR' EC.2/12, to Savigny-Les-Beaune by '89.

A visit in 7.88 found four camouflaged Super Mystere B.2s still present, two in poor condition but only 118 was identified.

The ALAT facility at Bourges had Nord 3202 'MDZ' (c/n ?) displayed outside the Ecole Superieure du Materiel during '87. L-19E Bird Dog 24523/BGS was on display by 8.89.

BRETIGNY-SUR-ORGE (91)

An unknown Sikorsky H-34A is preserved on the AdlA side (Base Aerienne 217) of this CEV operated airfield whilst a Lockheed T-33 is displayed in front of the Mess (probably on the same side of the field). Both were noted during '86 at which time the front fuselage of former Air France Boeing 707-328 F-BHSR (c/n 18245) was lying dumped on the South end of the field.

BRIARE (45)

The Musee Automobile de Briare (on the main road through the town) has L-19E Bird Dog 24710 (ex 'MDK' DCM, ALAT) in an overall pale blue colour scheme (noted '84-'89). The aircraft is kept in the open air.

BRIENNE-LE-CHATEAU (10)

Preserved adjacent to the Aero Club here is MD312 Flamant 235 (ex '319-DC' GE.319, arr 9.83; current 6.89).

The Musee Aeronautique de Champagne was set up here in the early eighties and has so far amassed the following exhibits (all were noted here 6.89 except the Vampire and NC856). An NC702 is expected, perhaps the example now abandoned at La Ferte Alais?

Beech C-45 (D.18S)	6250	(ex 43-35683, RCAF 1383) ex Kellerman Kaserne, Chateaudun, arrived 5.11.86.
Mystere IVA	28	ex '314-TY' GE.314, arrived 29.3.83.
DH Vampire	IB427	ex Indian AF (arr '88, stored off site).
CM170 Magister	7	ex '12-XJ' SLVSV/EC.12, arrived 5.5.82.
Gloster Meteor NF.11	NF11-1	ex CEV, arrived 28.7.85.
SP-2H Neptune	147563	ex 25F, arrived 29.7.83.
Lockheed T-33S-US	14115	(ex 51-4115) ex '314-TM' GE.314, arrived 12.4.83.
MH1521 Broussard	91	ex '8-OZ' SLVSV/ET.8.
N2501 Noratlas	31	ex 'B' (CEAM & ELA.44 badges), arrived 5.5.82.
NC856N Norvigie	57	also quoted as 93 (noted '87, c/n 57 appears on a plate on the fin).

The Reseau du Sport de l'Air (the French equivalent of the UK's Popular Flying Association) has a collection of homebuilts and gliders spread over a couple of hangars here and forming the Musee du Reseau du Sport de l'Air with the following.

Adam RA.14 Loisirs	F-PEVV	(c/n 35bis)

Breguet 904S	F-CCFT	(c/n 10) (noted '86).
Brochet Pipistrelle	-	(noted '86).
Carmam M.100S	F-CDDG	(noted '86).
Castel C25.S	-	
Castel C310.P	F-CRJF	(c/n 124) (noted '86).
Castel C310.P	F-CRHC	(c/n 152)
Caudron C282 Phalene	-	
Caudron C800	F-CBAM	(c/n 106)
Chanute glider	-	(replica)
Chapeau EC.19	-	(c/n 11) (noted '86).
Chatelain AC.10	F-PPPT	(c/n 01)
Croses EC.1	F-PIHL	(c/n 02)
Denize RD105	F-PKXD	(c/n 01)
DFS Schulgleiter	F-AZBJ	(c/n 19)
DFS 108-70 Meise	F-CACZ	(c/n 10)
Drezair Hang Glider	-	
Druine Turbulent	F-PMXN	(c/n 269)
Fauvel AV.36	F-CBZA	(noted '86)
Fleury Vedette	F-PEPR	(c/n 01)
Gardan Minicab	F-PJXT	(c/n A.225)
Gaucher Gaucho 620	F-PKXH	(c/n 01)
SA103 Emouchet	F-CRQD	(c/n 176)
SA104 Emouchet	F-CRGE	(c/n 251) (noted '86).
Grinvalds 801 Orion	F-PYKF	(c/n 01) (noted '86).
Lachassagne AL.7	F-WBBN	(c/n 01)
Leduc RL.19	F-PAGT	(c/n 01)
Lemaire RL.1	F-PPPN	(c/n 01) (noted '86).
Leopoldoff L.55	F-PHGT	
Max Williams Motorfly	F-WEAZ	(c/n 01) (noted '86)
Mignet Pou-du-Ciel	-	ex Lapierre (3 of these 5 Pous (Poux?) were noted '86)
Mignet Pou-du-Ciel	-	ex Metz
Mignet Pou-du-Ciel	-	ex Garsault
Mignet Pou-du-Ciel	-	Baude built, ex Dodier
Mignet Pou-du-Ciel	-	two seater, ex Garde
Mignet HM.360	F-PLUZ	(c/n 32) (noted '86).
Mirouze AM01 Pulsar	F-WTXF	(c/n 01) (noted '86).
Mirouze Aile Volante	-	(c/n 01)
Nord 2000	F-CABE	(c/n 90) (noted '86).
Nuville Gyrocopter	F-WSSP	(noted '86).
Piel CP.80	F-PVQF	(c/n 01)
Pottier P.170S	-	
Rigaud-Deproux RD.01	F-WSGU	(noted '86).
SFAN.2	F-PFOO	(c/n 01) (noted '86).
Schleicher ASK.16	F-CEGY	(c/n 16012)
Siren C.30	F-CCCZ	(c/n 03) (noted '86).
Siren C.34	F-CCAZ	(c/n 01) (noted '86).
SIPA 903	F-BGBS	(c/n 69)
Taylor Monoplane	-	
Tresy	-	(c/n 01) (noted '86).
Van Lith VI	F-PINX	

From time to time the aircraft on display may include active aircraft belonging to the Gyro Club de Champagne (GCC) or private owners.

BRIGNOLES (83)

Stored at the Securite Civile premises here is MD311 Flamant 266 (ex '316-KD' GE.316) (noted '84-'89).

In store at a private location with Monsieur Covield are Piel CP.30 F-PFVY (c/n 01) and N1203 Norecrin F-BEQE (c/n 109, here by '84) (both noted 12.87).

BRIOUDE (43)

On the edge of town, on the Clermont-Ferrand road, a scrapyard had the fuselage of Wassmer WA52 F-BTLG (c/n 53) during '87.

BRIVE (19)

Stored here in 8.87 were Gatard Statoplan AG.01 Alouette F-PFDA (c/n 01) and MS885 Super Rallye F-BKEO (c/n 55), both engineless. A further visit in 8.88 found the wrecked fuselage of Cessna F150L F-BURF (c/n 1009) and Wassmer WA40 F-BJPN (c/n 14).

BRUZ (35)

Mirage IIIC 8/2-FB (ex ECT.2/2) is displayed at CELAR (Centre d'Electronique de l'Armement) here having arrived from Rochefort/St Agnant by '83. A visit in 1986 failed to locate the Mirage but it is still thought to be here.

BUREAU CENTRAL DES RELATIONS EXTERIEURES

The AdlA's equivalent of the RAF Exhibition Flight travels la belle France equipped with CM170 Magisters 401/315-XV (ex GE.315), 55/312-HB (ex GE.312) and the nose of Mirage IIIA 08 (ex 'DZ' CEV). They are also thought to possess Mirage IIIC 11 and a Super Mystere B.2.

CAEN (14)

Within the Memorial de la Paix (War Memorial) here by 11.88 was a Hawker Typhoon 1B replica in 185 Sqn colours as JP656/BR-S. It was still current during 5.89 on which occasion its status as a replica was confirmed though it looks good enough to pass for an original.

CAEN/CARPIQUET (14)

The airport entrance has MD452 Mystere IIC 52/10-LF (ex EC.10) on display (noted '76-'86). This rare aircraft is now allocated to the Musee de l'Air. It was formerly accompanied by MD312 Flamant 161 (soc 1.1.72) which moved to a private collector in nearby Olendon by '83 then on to Falaise.

At the end of 1988 Transvalair obtained six N2501 Noratlas from Chateaudun. It is likely that most or all will be held in open store either as spares sources for their existing Noratlas fleet or awaiting their turn to be reactivated. The six aircraft, with the registrations worn for their delivery flight from Chateaudun are 96/F-WECE, 100/F-WFYF, 113/F-WFYI, 169/F-WFYJ, 179/F-WFYG and 180/F-WFYH. 179 was still at Chateaudun as late as 6.89.

CAHORS (46)

On display at the Gel Occitan works near the airport is MH1521C Broussard F-BLLD (c/n 30) whilst Boisavia 601L Mercurey F-BHVI (c/n 23) is stored engineless (both noted 3.89).

CAMBRAI/EPINOY (59)

Guarding the gate at Base Aerienne 103 since 1977 has been Super Mystere B.2 88 (ex '12-ZB' EC.2/12). Surprisingly, at the Open Day in 1988 its place had been taken by "148/12-YP" in EC.1/12 markings. Confirmation would be appreciated as to whether this is a change of aircraft or just a 'confuse-a-spotter' repaint (or as the French say, re-peinture-trompe-spotter!). The real 148 used to be preserved at Lyon/Mont Verdun and it is your compiler's opinion that this is the aircraft now on the gate. A silver Super Mystere B.2 marked "177/12-YA" appeared at the '89 Open Day and I believe this to be 88 with a new coat of paint. Mystere IVA 186/"12-UT" had arrived from Chateaudun by this time for display purposes.

During 1988 the Musee de l'Air despatched Spitfire IX BS464 and Dewoitine D.520DC 603 here for restoration by EC.12 (current 6.89).

On the dump, Vautour IIB 633/JC (ex EdR.05/106) arrived from Chateaudun during 1981. Only the wings and rear fuselage were still extant during 6.88. The wreck of Mirage F.1C-200 250/12-KQ (ex EC.3/12, crashed on the approach 21.3.84) was dumped here during 1985 but had gone by '88.

CANNES (06)

Mounted at the gate to the airport here is Beech E-18S "FBCCI" (without hyphen, c/n BA184, ex F-BUOP) (noted '85-'87). Other Wrecks and Relics here over the last few years have included.

AA1B Trainer	F-BVJN	(c/n 0369) dismantled (noted '87).
B65-88 Queen Air	F-BOHY	(c/n LP-42) (noted '85-'87).
B65 Queen Air	F-BJOK	(c/n LC-2) wfu (noted '85-'87).
MS894E Minerva	F-BVZA	(c/n 1202) derelict (noted '86-'87).
N1203 Norecrin	-	undergoing rebuild 6.89.
PA28-161 Warrior II	F-GBPH	(c/n 7916213) fuselage only (noted '89).
PA28-181 Archer II	F-GALX	(c/n 28-76903480 fuselage only (noted '89).
PA28-181 Archer II	F-GBGP	(c/n 7990108) fuselage only (noted '89).
PA30-160B	I-KLKL	(c/n 30-1293) crashed (noted '83).
PA38-112 Tomahawk	F-GBRG	(c/n 38-79A0535) (noted '87).

CAPTIEUX (40)

At least five Super Mystere B.2s were in use as range targets here during 1988. One was in 'Tiger' colour scheme and it has been suggested it may be 136. Personally, I would suggest it is more than likely 13 which was painted up as '136' in tiger scheme at Rochefort. This sighting does at least cast some light on the likely fate of several Super Mysteres which disappeared from Rochefort/St Agnant in the mid eighties.

Super Mystere B.2	50	ex '12-ZE' EC.2/12 (to Savigny-Les-Beaune 3.89).
Super Mystere B.2	60	ex '12-ZC' EC.2/12 (noted '89, for scrap).
Super Mystere B.2	69	ex '12-YG' EC.1/12 (to Savigny-Les-Beaune 10.88).
Super Mystere B.2	175	ex '10-SK' EC.1/10 (noted '89, for scrap).
Super Mystere B.2	179	ex '10-SJ' EC.1/10 (noted '89, for Ailes Anciennes Armorique).

CASTELNAUDARY (11)

N2501 Noratlas 201 landed here for the last time on 10.3.87 for onward road transport to the microlight field at Rieumajou for use as a club house. However, it was allocated the registration F-GFLJ during '88 and may yet fly again with the Association Miss Pacifique.

CASTELNAU/MAGNOAC (65)

The Aero Club de Castres received MD312 Flamant 220 (ex '319-CK' GE.319, soc 2.2.74). It was still extant in 7.88.

CAZAUX (33)

Base Aerienne 120 boasts three preserved aircraft. The H-34 is in the EH.1/67 area and the Mystere near main gate.

Mystere IVA	120	ex '8-ME' ET.1/8 (also marked "8-NE" ET.2/8) (arr 9.5.80, current '89).
Sikorsky H-34A	SA86	ex '67-OY' EH.1/67 (noted '78-'89).
Vautour IIB	615	ex '92-AK' EB.92 & Cazaux ranges (noted '87-'88).

By 7.89 the Vautour was described as 'by the fire station' so it may no longer be preserved. However, Mirage IIIC 32/10-RE (ex EC.2/10) and Mirage IIIR 309/33-CV (ex ER.1/33) were in the same area during the Open Day.

Cazaux has live weapons ranges to the North and South of the base with the vast Centre d'Essais des Landes military area only a few miles South. Many airframes have been expended as range targets and others as fire training aids. Those visible from the base over the years have included the following. The list is not exhaustive by any means.

MD Flamant	-	(noted '79-'87).
MD Flamant	-	(noted '87).
Mystere IVA	37	(to Savigny-Les-Beaune 3.87).
Mystere IVA	100	ex '8-NP' ET.2/8 (noted '79-'85).
Mystere IVA	111	ex '8-NY' ET.2/8 (noted '81-'85).
Mystere IVA	178	ex '8-NK' ET.2/8 (noted '81-'83, to Chateaudun).

Mystere IVA	279	ex '8-NZ' ET.2/8 (noted '79).
Mystere IVA	282	ex '8-NW' ET.2/8 (noted '83).
Mystere IVA	324	ex '8-NH' ET.2/8 (noted '81-'83).
EE Canberra B.6	318	ex 'AU' CEV (noted '80-'87).
Gloster Meteor T.7	F6	(to Savigny-Les-Beaune 1.88).
Gloster Meteor T.7	91	(noted '86).
Gloster Meteor T.7	92	(noted '86).
N2501 Noratlas	57	ex 'XC' GAM.56 (noted '79-'87).
N2501 Noratlas	-	(noted '87).
Vautour IIA	2	ex'92-AB'EB.92(noted'79-'87,to Savigny-Les-Beaune 8.88)
Vautour IIB	612	ex 'A' EdR.05/106 (noted '79-'83)
Vautour IIB	614	ex '92-AJ' EB.92 (noted '79-'83)
Vautour IIB	615	ex '92-AK' EB.92 (noted '79, preserved here by '87)
Vautour IIN	343?	ex 'L' (noted '79-'83)

At least two unidentified Vautours were still to be seen on the nearer ranges during '87. Of the more distant ranges little is known but photographs of the recovery of the Musee de l'Air's SE5000 Baroudeur from here in 1983 provided a tantalising glimpse of F-84F Thunderstreaks, F-84G Thunderjets, Mysteres and other types in the background, though only F-84G 51-11007 was identified. Ailes Anciennes - Toulouse were reported to have secured several items from here including a Canberra, F-84E and two Meteors but this now seems in doubt. The F-84E is particularly confusing since the airframe expected by Toulouse was quoted as a composite of which one section would be from 19572. The front half of this aircraft is definitely now at Savigny-Les-Beaune but is also quoted as the identity of the cockpit section at Perpignan! It is something of an understatement to say that further reports on this and any other Cazaux wrecks would be most welcome.

CHALONS/ECURY-SUR-COOLE (51)

Lying near the car park in 7.86 was the gutted fuselage of Robin DR400 F-GABI (c/n 93). MS505 Criquet F-BEJG (c/n 653) has been reported dismantled here (noted '85-'87, due to go to CELAG at Grenoble) whilst the fuselage of MH1521M Broussard 280/F-WKQV (ex 'AFR' & 'MHA' ALAT & Montauban store, noted '85-'87) has been stored in the rafters and sister-ship 150/F-BXCQ was gathering dust during '85 following sale from the ALAT at Montauban on 25.11.80.

Reported during 5.88 was the burnt out wreck of PA25-235B Pawnee F-WDPB (c/n 25-3109, ex N7202Z, F-GDPB).

CHAMBERY/AIX-LES-BAINS (73)

Base Aerienne 725 had closed by 1986 with the based helicopter unit CIEH.341 transferring to Toulouse/Francazal. Prior to closure, the gate was guarded by Mystere IIC 147/"5-OR" which was transferred to Istres by '84. Preserved on the base was Sikorsky H-34A SA154/68-DI (ex EH.68) which moved to Toulouse with CIEH.341.

Derelict on the airfield during '83 were MH1521 Broussards 95 and 207 with stored ex EH.3/67 Alouette II 336/67-SA (c/n 1728).

Hangared on the civil side during 6.89 were the wrecks of TB10 Tobago F-GBHY (c/n 41), Cessna F150M F-GAAL (c/n 1302) and PA28R-201T Turbo Arrow F-GBGN (c/n 7803312). Derelict on the field at this time was PA23-250 Aztec C F-BNTS (c/n 27-3348, ex N6136Y).

CHAMBON SUR VOUEYZE (23)

Preserved on a landing strip on a private estate here is the wingless and engineless Hurel-Dubois HD321 01 which made a night forced landing here 10.5.60. Its background is mysterious but the machine is believed to have been undertaking a secret mission for GAM.56. The engines were salvaged and the wings are still in a nearby barn.

CHARTRES (28)

Base Aerienne 122 has displayed the following aircraft in recent years.

Beech C-45	"MT10/122"	spurious serial based on Base Aerienne number (noted '83, to Etampes by '86).

MD312 Flamant	199	ex '41-GE' ELA.41 (soc 23.9.69, current '86, not seen '87).
Super Mystere B.2	90	ex '12-YQ' EC.1/12 (noted '83-'85).
CM170 Magister	62	(noted '87-'89).
Sikorsky H-34A	SA114	ex '68-OE' EH.2/68 (noted '81-'86, to Poitiers then Savigny-Les-Beaune 4.87).

On the civil side of the field, MH1521 Broussard 39 was to be seen in a derelict condition during 1984. In 7.89 Caudron C.601 Aiglon F-POIT (c/n P-2) was awaiting rebuild by Chartres Air Services for the Salis Collection.

In the past, the Musee de l'Air utilised some hangars at Chartres for storage purposes, however this facility was closed during 1986.

CHATEAUDUN (28)

Reported on display inside the military hospital in the town during 1986 was an anonymous MD312 Flamant.

In the town, the gate at Kellerman Kaserne was guarded by Beech C-45 6250 (ex 43-35683, RCAF 1383) from the early seventies 1984 when it was moved to the airfield for hangar storage prior to transfer (on 5.11.86) to Brienne-Le-Chateau for the museum there.

The aircraft listed below are all preserved around Base Aerienne 279. The Flamant is at the main gate, Mystere IVA 89 is by the control tower with 278 on the North side. The Thunderstreak sits by the East side hangars whilst the Super Mystere is on a pole outside the Officers' Mess on the other side of the Chateaudun-Orleans road to the air base.

MD315 Flamant	124	(soc 18.12.72, current '89).
Mystere IVA	89	(ex '8-NQ' ET.2/8) painted as "7-AM" (noted '84-'87).
Mystere IVA	186	appeared at open days in PdF colours '85-'87, to Cambrai by 6.89.
Mystere IVA	278	ex '8-MB' ET.1/8 (noted '84-'87).
Super Mystere B.2	79	ex '12-YU' EC.1/12 (noted '78-'89).
F-84F Thunderstreak	29061	(ex 52-9061) ex '1-ES' EC.1 (noted '78-'89).

During 1987 one of the hangars was seen to contain a number of Mirages for storage or bdr training. Those confirmed were Mirage F.1 02 (stored for Musee de l'Air), Mirage IIIC 91 plus one other (both for bdrt). The hangar also held some wreckage from crashed Mirage 2000s.

The resident Entrepot de l'Armee de l'Air 601 (EAA.601) is responsible for the overhaul, storage and disposal of many AdlA types. There are many storage hangars at Chateaudun where aircraft can be hidden away for years but the main attraction of this base to enthusiasts lies in the rows of aircraft which often lie outside awaiting disposal. From the mid seventies onwards the base has seen the demise of large numbers of C-45s, H-34s, Flamants, Noratlas's and other types, these superseding the Invaders, Dakotas and more Flamants during the sixties. To try and keep this listing to a manageable size, we will deal only with those aircraft stored in the open on the airfield and will concentrate on the post 1980 era.

MD312 Flamant	142	ex '319-DI' GE.319 (noted '79).
MD312 Flamant	153	ex '319-DV' GE.319 (noted '83, to Sezanne).
MD312 Flamant	155	ex '319-CH' GE.319 (scrap '79).
MD312 Flamant	158	ex '319-CF' GE.319 (noted '84-'87, to F-AZGE, to Savigny-Les-Beaune then to Nimes).
MD312 Flamant	160	ex '319-DA' GE.319 (noted '84, to F-AZDR at Alencon).
MD312 Flamant	164	ex '319-DB' GE.319 (noted '84, to gia at Montmirault).
MD312 Flamant	172	ex '319-DD' GE.319 (noted '84-'85, to F-AZAI at Montelimar).
MD312 Flamant	173	ex '319-CR' GE.319 (noted '84-'86, to F-AZFR).
MD312 Flamant	177	ex '319-DU' GE.319 (noted '84-'86, to F-WZEL at Pau).
MD312 Flamant	187	ex '319-CK' GE.319 (noted '79, scrap '80, to Dijon dump).
MD312 Flamant	202	ex '319-CS' GE.319 (noted '86, to Bordeaux).
MD312 Flamant	208	ex '319-CC' GE.319 (noted '79, scrap '79).

MD312 Flamant	210	ex '319-CE' GE.319 (noted '83, to Paray-Le-Monial).
MD312 Flamant	215	ex '319-DP' GE.319 (noted '83, to Reims).
MD312 Flamant	218	ex '319-CA' GE.319 (noted '84, to Eu-Sur-Mer).
MD312 Flamant	226	ex '319-CG' GE.319 (noted '84-'86, to Til-Chatel).
MD312 Flamant	227	ex '319-CX' GE.319 (noted '83, to Toulouse/Blagnac).
MD312 Flamant	228	ex '319-CP' GE.319 (noted '84-'86, to F-AZAI at Montelimar).
MD312 Flamant	232	ex '319-CB' GE.319 (noted '86, to Rodez).
MD312 Flamant	235	ex '319-DC' GE.319 (noted '83, to Brienne-Le-Chateau).
MD312 Flamant	237	ex '319-DC' GE.319 (noted '83, to Nevers, then Montceau-Les-Mines).
MD312 Flamant	240	ex '319-DY' GE.319 (noted '85, to gia at Toussus).
MD312 Flamant	248	ex '319-DH' GE.319 (noted '79, to Reims/Champagne).
MD312 Flamant	250	ex '319-CI' GE.319 (noted '86, to Le Castellet).
MD312 Flamant	251	ex '319-CZ' GE.319 (noted '84, to F-AZDE at Lons/Le-Saulnier).
MD312 Flamant	253	ex '319-CQ' GE.319 (noted '83, to Visan).
MD311 Flamant	257	ex '316-KG' GE.316 (scrap '78).
MD311 Flamant	258	ex '316-KA' GE.316 (scrap '78).
MD311 Flamant	260	ex '316-KB' GE.316 (noted '85, to Nancy/Essey).
MD311 Flamant	262	ex '316-KK' GE.316 (noted '77, scrap '78).
MD311 Flamant	263	ex '316-KN' GE.316 (scrap '78).
MD311 Flamant	266	ex '316-KD' GE.316 (noted '81, to Brignoles).
MD311 Flamant	270	ex '316-KC' GE.316 (noted '77, scrap '78).
MD311 Flamant	274	ex '316-KH' GE.316 (noted '85-'86, to F-AZAH at Aix/Les-Milles).
MD311 Flamant	276	ex '316-KC' GE.316 (noted '85, to F-AZER at Alencon).
MD311 Flamant	278	ex '316-KC' GE.316 (noted '80, scrap '81).
MD311 Flamant	280	ex '316-KM' GE.316 (noted '85-'86, to Musee de l'Air).
MD311 Flamant	286	ex '316-KO' GE.316 (noted '85-'86, to Montceau-Les-Mines).
MD311 Flamant	287	ex '316-KF' GE.316 (noted '77, scrap '78).
MD311 Flamant	288	ex '316-KP' GE.316 (noted '77-'80, to Rocamadour).
MD311 Flamant	290	ex '316-KL' GE.316 (noted '80-'83, to Romans-Sur-Isere).
MD311 Flamant	291	ex '316-KS' GE.316 (noted '81, to F-AZCB at La Ferte Alais).
Mirage IIIC	41	(noted '87).
Mirage IIIE	449	ex '13-QL' EC.13 (noted '87-'88).
Mirage IIIE	560	(noted '88).
Mirage IIIR	303	ex '33-TM' ER.3/33 (noted '88-3.89).
Mirage IIIR	304	ex '33-TN' ER.3/33 (noted '88-3.89).
Mirage IIIR	309	ex '33-CV' ER.1/33 (noted '88, to Cazaux by 7.89).
Mirage IIIR	324	ex '2-ZN' ECT.2/2 (noted '87-3.89).
Mirage IIIR	327	ex '33-CO' ER.1/33 (noted '87).
Mirage IIIR	329	ex '33-CM' ER.1/33 (noted '87-'88).
Mirage IIIR	330	ex '33-CC' ER.1/33 (noted '87-'88).
Mirage IIIR	333	ex '33-CB' ER.1/33 (noted '87).
Mirage IIIR	334	ex '33-CG' ER.1/33 (noted '87, to Musee de l'Air, for loan to Nancy/Essey).
Mirage IIIR	335	ex '33-TK' ER.3/33 (noted '87).
Mirage IIIR	340	ex '2-ZH' ECT.2/2 (noted '88).
Mirage IIIR	348	ex '33-CM' ER.1/33 (noted '87-3.89).
Mirage IIIR	349	(noted '88).
Mirage IIIR	350	ex '2-ZG' ECT.2/2 (noted '87).
Mirage IIIRD	356	(noted 3.89).
Mirage IIIRD	359	ex '33-TH' ER.3/33 (noted 88).
Mirage IIIRD	360	(noted '88-3.89).
Mirage IIIRD	367	(noted 6.89).
Mystere IVA	24	(noted '86-'87).

Mystere IVA	39	(noted '87).
Mystere IVA	45	(noted '87).
Mystere IVA	116	(noted '86-'87).
Mystere IVA	142	(noted '86, to scrap compound here).
Mystere IVA	178	ex Cazaux (noted '85-'87).
Mystere IVA	191	(noted '87, to Savigny-Les-Beaune).
Mystere IVA	287	(noted '86-'89).
Mystere IVA	293	(noted '86-'87, to Savigny-Les-Beaune).
Super Mystere B.2	53	ex '12-YO' EC.1/12 (noted '81-'84).
Super Mystere B.2	118	ex '12-YS' EC.1/12 (noted '81-'85, to ETBS Bourges).
CM170 Magister	38	ex '2-HB' (noted '87, to Montelimar).
CM170 Magister	52	ex '2-HC' (noted '87, to Montelimar).
CM170 Magister	78	(noted '87).
CM170 Magister	126	(noted '87, to Montpellier '88).
CM170 Magister	143	(noted '88, to Scaer/Guiscriff).
CM170 Magister	160	ex '3-KE' (noted '87, to St Malo 19.5.87).
CM170 Magister	209	ex '30-QH' SALE/EC.30 (noted '89).
CM170 Magister	224	(noted '89).
CM170 Magister	237	ex '315-PY' GE.315 (noted '88-'89).
CM170 Magister	310	ex '315-QO' GE.315 (scrapped '85, to fire dump here by 5.86).
CM170 Magister	326	(noted '88-'89).
CM170 Magister	334	ex '91-GB' EB.91 (noted '89).
CM170 Magister	336	ex '11-OC' SALE/EC.11 (noted '88-'89).
CM170 Magister	352	ex '315-QR' GE.315 (noted '87).
CM170 Magister	356	ex 'GH' (noted '87-'89).
CM170 Magister	363	ex '7-JH' SALE/EC.7 (noted '89).
CM170 Magister	379	ex '315-XR' GE.315 (noted '87, to Le Castellet).
CM170 Magister	383	ex '315-PV' GE.315 (noted '88-'89).
CM170 Magister	387	(noted '89).
CM170 Magister	388	ex '315-II' GE.315 (noted '88-'89).
CM170 Magister	398	ex '315-QV' GE.315 (noted '89).
CM170 Magister	413	ex '128-VM' BA.128 (noted '89).
CM170 Magister	438	ex '312-TW' GI.312 (noted '89).
CM170R Magister	443	(noted '87).
CM170R Magister	454	(noted '88).
CM170R Magister	458	ex '312-AR' GI.312 (noted '88-'89).
CM170R Magister	459	(noted '88, to F-WGGE 27.4.89 for Nancy/Essey).
CM170R Magister	460	ex '312-TB' GI.312 (noted '88-'89).
CM170R Magister	463	(noted '88-'89).
CM170R Magister	471	(noted '88, to F-WFPK).
CM170R Magister	478	(noted '88-'89).
CM170R Magister	483	(noted '89).
CM170R Magister	520	ex '312-UA' GI.312 (noted '88-'89).
CM170R Magister	522	(noted '87-'88, to F-WFTX & to Visan).
CM170R Magister	524	(noted '88).
CM170R Magister	525	(noted '89).
CM170R Magister	526	ex '312-TS' GI.312 (noted '89).
CM170R Magister	532	(noted '88-'89).
CM170R Magister	533	(noted '89).
CM170R Magister	538	(noted '88).
CM170R Magister	561	(noted '89).
CM170R Magister	569	(noted '88-'89).
MH1521 Broussard	50	(scrap '81-'82 - but reported as '41-AB' 8.85, confirm?).
MH1521 Broussard	113	(scrap '81-'82).
MH1521 Broussard	186	ex '5-MP' SLVSV/EC.5 (scrap '81-'82).
MH1521 Broussard	306	ex '721-EP' BA.721 (scrap '81-'82).
N2501 Noratlas	1	ex '340-HG' CIET.340 (noted '75-'77, scrap '78).

N2501 Noratlas 6 ex '312-BJ' GI.312 (noted '76-'77, scrap '78).
N2501 Noratlas 7 ex '118-ID' CEA, (noted '72-'77, scrap '78, to Evreux).
N2501 Noratlas 8 ex '340-VA' CIET.340 (noted '75-'77, scrap '78-'79).
N2501 Noratlas 10 ex '340-VD' CIET.340 (noted '75, to Rochefort).
N2501 Noratlas 11 ex '312-BE' GI.312 (noted '76-'77, scrap '78-'79).
N2501 Noratlas 12 ex '64-BL' ET.64 (noted '76-'77, scrap '78, to St Peravy).
N2501 Noratlas 13 ex '340-VF' CIET.340 (noted '73, to Rochefort).
N2501 Noratlas 14 ex '340-VE' CIET.340 (noted '75, to Rochefort).
N2501 Noratlas 15 ex '070-MC' EdC.70 (noted '76-79).
N2501 Noratlas 16 ex '340-VY' CIET.340 (noted '75-'79).
N2501 Noratlas 17 ex '312-BF' GI.312 (noted '76-'77, scrap '78, to Evreux).
N2501 Noratlas 19 ex '340-HJ' CIET.340 (noted '75-'77, scrap '78-'79).
N2501 Noratlas 20 ex '312-BH, GI.312 (noted '74-'79).
N2501 Noratlas 21 ex 'XG' GAM.56 (noted '75-'77, scrap '78).
N2501 Noratlas 23 ex '312-BE' GI.312 (noted '81-'82, to Poitiers).
N2501 Noratlas 24 ex '312-BJ' GI.312 (noted '81-'82, to Rouen).
N2501GABRIEL Noratlas 25 ex EE.54 (noted '80).
N2501 Noratlas 27 ex '62-QA' ET.62 (noted '77-'79).
N2501 Noratlas 29 ex 'BJ' CEV (noted '77, to Orleans).
N2501 Noratlas 32 ex '64-BY' ET.64 (noted '82-'83, scrap '83).
N2501 Noratlas 33 ex '63-VC' ET.63 (noted '84, scrap '85-'86).
N2501 Noratlas 36 ex '63-VC' ET.63 (noted '80, scrap '81).
N2501 Noratlas 37 ex 'AC' Djibouti AF (scrap '83).
N2501 Noratlas 38 ex '64-IA' ET.64 (noted '76-'77, scrap '78).
N2501GABRIEL Noratlas 39 ex EE.54 (noted '77, scrap '78).
N2501 Noratlas 43 ex '340-VI' CIET.340 (noted '77-'79).
N2501 Noratlas 44 ex '64-BI' ET.64 (noted '77, to F-BZCK 18.5.78).
N2501 Noratlas 46 ex '59-CB' GMT.59 (noted '76-'79).
N2501 Noratlas 47 ex '64-IG' ET.64 (noted '76-'79).
N2501 Noratlas 51 ex '340-VD' CIET.340 (noted '76-'77, scrap '78).
N2501 Noratlas 52 ex '44-GD' ELA.44 (noted '77, to F-BZCL 18.5.78).
N2501 Noratlas 53 ex '312-BI' GI.312 (noted '77-'79).
N2501 Noratlas 55 ex '118-IC' CEAM (noted '77, to F-BZCM 18.5.78).
N2501 Noratlas 56 ex '312-BK' GI.312 (noted '77, to F-BZCN 18.5.78).
N2501 Noratlas 58 ex '64-IJ' ET.64 (noted '77, to F-BZCO 18.5.78).
N2501 Noratlas 60 ex '64-BX' ET.64 (noted '77, to F-BZCP 18.5.78).
N2501 Noratlas 61 ex '340-VJ' CIET.340 (noted '76-'77, scrap '78).
N2501 Noratlas 64 ex '62-KI' ET.62 (noted '77, to F-BZCQ 18.5.78).
N2501 Noratlas 65 ex '340-VO' CIET.340 (noted '77, to F-BZCR 18.5.78).
N2501 Noratlas 72 ex '62-WO' ET.62 (noted '77, to F-BZCS 18.5.78).
N2501 Noratlas 75 ex '63-VB' ET.63 (noted '81-'82, scrap '83-'84).
N2501 Noratlas 76 ex '62-WD' ET.62 (noted '77, to F-BZCT 18.5.78).
N2501 Noratlas 77 ex '312-BG' GI.312 (noted '77, scrap '78).
N2501 Noratlas 78 ex '312-BE' GI.312 (noted '77-'78, to Nimes/Courbessac).
N2501 Noratlas 80 ex '64-IY' ET.64 (noted '81, scrap '81-'82).
N2501 Noratlas 81 ex '055-KA' ETOM.55 (noted '83, scrap '84).
N2501 Noratlas 83 ex '63-KF' ET.63 (noted '83, scrap '83).
N2501 Noratlas 84 ex '63-VR' ET.63 (noted '79-'80).
N2501 Noratlas 85 ex '63-WG' ET.63 (noted '83, to the fire dump here).
N2501 Noratlas 86 ex '63-WS' ET.63 (noted '83, scrap '83-'84).
N2501 Noratlas 87 ex '64-KA' ET.64 (noted '83, fuselage to Aix/Les-Milles by '84).
N2501 Noratlas 88 ex '64-IX' ET.64 (noted '80).
N2501 Noratlas 89 ex '63-WE' ET.63 (noted '80, scrap '81).
N2501 Noratlas 90 ex '55-KB' ETOM.55 (noted '83, scrap '83).
N2501 Noratlas 92 ex '64-IT' ET.64 (noted '83) .
N2501 Noratlas 94 ex 'YF' EE.54 (noted '87).

N2501 Noratlas	95	ex '64-KU' ET.64 (noted '80, scrap '81-'82).
N2501 Noratlas	96	ex '63-VH' ET.63 (noted '87-'88, to F-WECE at Caen).
N2501 Noratlas	97	ex '63-WB' ET.63 (noted '82, to Nancy/Essey).
N2501 Noratlas	99	ex '64-KJ' ET.64 (noted '80, scrap '81).
N2501 Noratlas	100	ex '63-VC' ET.63 (noted '86-'88, to F-WFYF at Caen).
N2501 Noratlas	103	ex '64-IB' ET.64 (noted '77, to Gyrafrance 18.5.78).
N2501 Noratlas	106	ex '118-IC' CEAM (noted '82, scrap '83-'84).
N2501 Noratlas	107	ex '328-EP' CIFAS.328 (scrap '83-'84).
N2501 Noratlas	108	ex '328-EF' CIFAS.328 (noted '80, scrap '81).
N2501 Noratlas	109	ex '312-BN' GI.312 (noted '83).
N2501 Noratlas	110	ex '64-BV' ET.64 (scrap'83-'84).
N2501 Noratlas	111	to Bordeaux/Merignac museum.
N2501 Noratlas	112	ex '328-EB' CIFAS.328 (noted '86-'88).
N2501 Noratlas	113	ex '63-VN' ET.63 (noted '86-'87, to F-WFYI at Caen).
N2501 Noratlas	116	ex '64-IB' ET.64 (scrap '83).
N2501 Noratlas	117	ex '64-BU' ET.64 (scrap '83).
N2501 Noratlas	119	ex '64-BS' ET.64 (noted '81-'82, scrap '83-'84).
N2501 Noratlas	120	ex '63-VA' ET.63 (noted '86).
N2501 Noratlas	121	ex '64-IL' ET.64 (noted '80-'81, scrap '81).
N2501 Noratlas	123	ex '312-BH' GI.312 (noted '83, scrap '84-'86).
N2501 Noratlas	125	ex '64-BH' ET.64 (noted '83, scrap '84, fuselage still current '89).
N2501SNB Noratlas	127	ex '328-EA' CIFAS.328 (noted '80-'81, scrap '81).
N2501SNB Noratlas	128	ex '328-EC' CIFAS.328 (noted '84-'87).
N2501 Noratlas	129	ex '316-FA' GE.316 (noted '86-'87, to Merville).
N2501 Noratlas	131	ex '63-KF' ET.63 (noted '84-'85, to F-GEXP).
N2501SNB Noratlas	132	ex '328-ED' CIFAS.328 (noted '85, scrap '86).
N2501 Noratlas	134	ex '316-FT' GE.316 (noted '77, scrap '78-'79).
N2501SNB Noratlas	135	ex '63-VS' ET.63 (noted '84-'85, to F-GEXR).
N2501 Noratlas	136	ex '328-EA' CIFAS.328 (noted '84-'86).
N2501 Noratlas	137	ex '316-FM' GE.316 (noted '77, scrap '78-'79).
N2501 Noratlas	138	ex '63-WN' ET.63 (scrap '81).
N2501 Noratlas	139	ex '64-IE' ET.64 (scrap '84-'86).
N2501 Noratlas	141	ex '64-IJ' ET.64 (store '83, scrap '84-'86, fuselage current '89).
N2501 Noratlas	142	ex '63-VP' ET.63 (noted '85, to F-GEXS).
N2501 Noratlas	144	ex 'XA' GAM.56 (sold to Gyrafrance 23.2.78).
N2501 Noratlas	145	ex '63-WR' ET.63 (noted '83, scrap '84-'85, to Istres).
N2501 Noratlas	146	ex '63-WV' ET.63 & 'MC' EdC.70 (noted '86-'89).
N2501 Noratlas	148	ex '328-EI' CIFAS.328 (noted '85-'87).
N2501 Noratlas	149	ex 'XB' GAM.56 (noted '83).
N2501 Noratlas	151	ex '63-WF' ET.63 (noted '83, scrap '84-'85, fuselage in revetments '85).
N2501 Noratlas	154	ex '64-KJ' ET,64 (noted '83, to Saintes).
N2501SNB Noratlas	155	ex '328-EH' CIFAS.328 (noted '86, fuselage to Orleans).
N2501 Noratlas	157	ex '63-WK' ET.63 (noted '86-'87, to Musee de l'Air and preserved at Finkenwerder, WG, as "62-KS").
N2501 Noratlas	158	ex '312-BN' GI.312 (scrap '83-'84).
N2501 Noratlas	159	ex '63-WB' ET.63 (noted '83, scrap '84-'85).
N2501 Noratlas	160	ex '64-IN' ET.64 (noted '84, to Vannes/Meucon).
N2501 Noratlas	161	ex '64-IM' ET.64 (noted '80, to Pau/Uzein).
N2501 Noratlas	162	ex '63-VP' ET.63 (noted '86-'87, to Musee de l'Air).
N2501SNB Noratlas	163	ex '328-EM' CIFAS.328 (noted '83, scrap '84-'86).
N2501 Noratlas	164	ex '63-VN' ET.63 (noted '82, scrap '83-'84).
N2501 Noratlas	165	ex '63-VK' ET.63 (noted '87).
N2501 Noratlas	166	ex '63-VB' ET.63 (noted '83, booms only scrap '84-'85, fuselage on a lorry 19.5.84).
N2501 Noratlas	167	ex '64-BX' ET.64 (scrap '83-'84).
N2501 Noratlas	168	ex '64-KB' ET.64 (scrap '83).

N2501 Noratlas	169	'-' (noted '86-'87, to F-WFYJ at Caen).
N5201 Noratlas	171	ex '316-FR' GE.316 (noted '86-'89).
N2501 Noratlas	173	ex '64-KW' ET.64 (noted '80, booms only scrap '81-'83).
N2501 Noratlas	175	ex '63-WU' ET.63 (noted '80, scrap '83-'84).
N2501 Noratlas	176	ex '312-BG' GI.312 (scrap '84-'85).
N2501 Noratlas	179	ex '63-WH' ET.63 (noted '84-'88, due to go to Caen as F-WFYG but still here 6.89, the last example on the storage line where so many came to die).
N2501SNB Noratlas	180	ex '63-VB' ET.63 (noted '86-'87, to F-WFYH at Caen).
N2501 Noratlas	184	ex '328-EO' CIFAS.328 (noted '84-'85, to Angers).
N2501SNB Noratlas	186	ex '328-EJ' CIFAS.328 (noted '84, to Mont-De-Marsan).
N2501 Noratlas	188	ex '316-FS' GE.316 (noted '86).
N2501 Noratlas	189	ex '316-FN' GE.316 (noted '86-'87, to Nancy/Essey).
N2501 Noratlas	193	ex '328-..' CIFAS.328 (noted '87, to Pau/Uzein).
N2501 Noratlas	194	ex '316-FP' GE.316 (noted '86-'88).
N2501 Noratlas	197	ex '316-FU' GE.316 (noted '77, scrap '78).
N2501 Noratlas	199	ex '63-WM' ET.63 (noted '86, returned to service briefly as 'MF-070' EdC.70 6.87, to Landsberg, WG, 9.87).
N2501SNB Noratlas	203	ex '328-EL' CIFAS.328 (scrap '83-'84).
N2501 Noratlas	205	ex '328-EA' CIFAS.328 (noted '85-'86).
N2501 Noratlas	207	ex 'XD' GAM.56 (noted '83, scrap '84-'86).
Vautour IIB	632	ex 'JB' EdR.05/106 (noted '80, to St Nazaire).
Vautour IIB	633	ex 'JC' EdR.05/106 (noted '80, to Cambrai dump).

In recent years the firemen here have utilised the following airframes to practice their trade.

Mirage IIIE	589	ex '4-AJ' EC.1/4 & scrap compound (noted '86-'87).
CM170 Magister	310	ex '315-QO' GE.315 (noted '85-'86).
Lockheed T-33SF	21477	ex '314-UC' GE.314 (noted '81-'85).
N2501 Noratlas	85	ex '63-WG' ET.63 (noted '83-'86).
Vautour IIN	318	ex '30-MF' ECTT.2/30 (noted '78-'80).

Near the main gate there is a scrap compound which has held the wrecks of various accident victims, former bdr airframes and scrapped fighters. The Magister is of particular interest since although it was seen here a year after its last sighting at Rochefort/St Agnant, a close examination of photographic evidence leads to the conclusion that the two '36's are not the same aeroplane (the real 36 was soc 10.6.66 for instructional use at Rochefort). Any explanations would be gratefully received.

Mirage IIIC	..	discarded bdrt fuselage (noted '87).
Mirage IIIE	552	crashed 26.2.69 (noted '85).
Mirage IIIE	589	ex '4-AF' EC.1/4, crashed 28.1.82 (noted '83-'85, to the fire dump).
Mystere IVA	45	(noted '83).
Mystere IVA	142	(noted '83-'87, to Savigny-Les-Beaune).
CM170 Magister	36	fuselage only (noted '87).
Jaguar	...	(noted '83).

CHATEAUROUX (35)

Ex Corse Air SE210 Caravelle VI-N F-BYCD (c/n 67) arrived here in 2.87 for display at the airport but had gone by early '89.

CHATELLERAULT (86)

CM170 Magister 133/- (ex '128-VN' BA128, Metz/Frescaty) arrived during 10.85 for display with the Aero Club (current '89).

Preserved at SOCATA/SNECMA factory on the N10 just North of the town is CM170 Magister 338/315-IB (ex GE.315) (noted '87-'88).

About 9kms out of Chatellerault on the Monthoiron road a collector of military equipment has an H-34 and a Flamant (noted 10.87).

CHATILLON-EN-DIOIS (26)

Preserved at a campsite at the edge of town is ex EC.4/11 F-100D Super Sabre

52734/11-YP (ex 55-2734, noted '87) which was obtained in exchange for parts of a DFS230 glider now with Ailes-Anciennes - Dugny for the Musee de l'Air.

CHAVENAY/VILLEPREUX (78)

The Collection Jean Bertin has a hangar here with the following aircraft under restoration or in store (the list is not exhaustive).

T-6G Texan	114674	(ex 51-14674) (noted '84, flying by '89 as F-AZEZ).
AT-6D Texan	F-BJBD	(c/n 88-15564) ex Paris/Vilgenis (noted '84).

The Group Aerien Victor Tatin are also based here.

Other items noted in recent years have comprised the following.

Aero 45	-	(c/n 4904) stored 5.88.
Fournier RF-3	F-BMTH	(c/n 63) stored 5.88.
Grinvalds Orion	-	stored 5.88.
Jodel D112 Club	F-BHPU	(c/n 540) stored engineless 5.88.
MS880B Rallye 100T	F-BXYA	(c/n 2671) wfu by 8.89.
Nord 1001 Pinguin	75	(noted 2.87).
N1203 Norecrin	F-BEBM	(c/n 43) stored 5.88.
Pottier P.70S	F-WYJB	(c/n 014) fuselage only, stored 5.88.

CHENEVIERES (94)

The Bourdon scrapyard (on the RN4) held N1203 Norecrin F-BEMQ and MS572 F-BEJI when examined in 9.88.

CHERBOURG/MAUPERTUS (50)

MD312 Flamant 170/319-CR (ex GE.319, soc 24.1.74) was preserved at the Aero Club de Cherbourg et de la Manche. During 1985 it was handed over to the airport firemen and but the hulk still lingered on during 10.88.

CLERES (76)

The Musee Automobile de Cleres (at the Chateau de Cleres) should still have T-6G Texan 115102 (ex 51-15102) in a 'home-grown' colour scheme provided it hasn't rusted away yet. It was looking somewhat the worse for wear in '85 but was still to be seen in 6.87. The musee also has Potez 53 F-AMJP (c/n 3322) and Stampe SV4 F-BMME (c/n 109) (all were seen during '87).

CLERMONT-FERRAND/AULNAT (63)

Mystere II 013 served as a gia here until '82 when it was noted in the nearby scrapyard of M Reccia. It was subsequently sold to Monsieur Pont and is now on display at Savigny-Les-Beaune.

On the base, Mystere IVN 01/F-ZXRM acted as gate guard at AIA (Atelier Industriel de l'Aeronautique) (noted '78-'87, to Musee de l'Air). It was succeeded by Mirage F.1 prototype 03 (noted '88-'89).

AIA have also been storing Vautour IIN 338/30-MN (ex ECTT.2/30) pending its collection by the group Escadrille Pegase (she has perhaps moved on by now). It used to be accompanied by Transall prototype V2/YD (ex CEV) which was unfortunately scrapped during '82.

CLOYES (28)

The remains of ex Chateaudun Breguet 941S 1/62-NA and 2/62-NB were still to be found in a scrapyard here during '87.

COETQUIDAN (56)

The St Cyr military academy has had two Vertol H-21Cs for years. They have not been confirmed since 1980 and remain anonymous.

COGNAC/CHATEAUBERNARD (16)

With the replacement of GE.315's extensive 'Maggie' fleet with the new Epsilon, CM170 Magister 198/315-GC was preserved behind the GERMaS (Maintenance) hangar at BA709 by 6.88 with 324/315-QD preserved on a pole near the Epsilon ramp by 9.88.

Sikorsky H-34A SA116 was painted up as "58-002/GR" to represent the original 58-002 which was lost during the Algerian War and for many years was displayed behind the hangars here (noted '82-'86). By 10.87 it had gone to Toulouse/Blagnac for Ailes Anciennes - Toulouse.

For ground instructional purposes GE.315 utilise Epsilon 02/VJ.

On the fire dump, an unidentified Flamant, Broussard and Magister were present during 1983.

COLMAR/MEYENHEIM (68)

Guarding the entrance to BA132 is Mirage IIIC 13/"13-EC" (current '89) which was first noted during '87. Despite the seemingly contrived c/n it is thought to be the genuine article with EC.13 just being lucky to find an appropriate aircraft.

In use as a spares source here is Mirage IIIE 427/13-QB ex EC.1/13 which was wfu following a heavy landing on 16.9.86 (current '89).

Still present on the dump here is ex EB.92 Vautour IIB 602/92-AB which was first noted in the late seventies and was still current during '89 hidden away in the North East shelter area.

COMPIEGNE (60)

Stored here during 5.88 were Cessna 310K F-BNLS (c/n 0210, ex N3810X) fuselage minus tail & u/c), Navion F-BAVX (c/n 2147B), Navion F F-BAVY (c/n 1947), Navion 4 F-BFVI (c/n 4-1455) and Zlin 326 Trener F-BMQV (c/n 901). The Navions were all wfu by '84.

COULOMMIERS/VOISINS (77)

The fuselages of Jodel DR250-160 Capitaine F-BMZG (c/n 6) and MS893A Commodore 180 F-BNSP (c/n 10613) were noted here in 5.88. By 10.88 PA23-250 Aztec C F-BNDK (c/n 27-2598) was lying derelict. Several other airframes were hangared and stored in a dismantled state. These comprised PA38-112 Tomahawk F-GBLI (c/n 38-82A0117, ex N9227A, 6V-AFK), PA34-200 Seneca F-BTMH (c/n 34-7250135) and two Fourniers.

COULONGES-SUR-L'AUTIZE (79)

A night club here has ex Air France SE210 Caravelle III F-BHRI (c/n 17) as an attraction (noted '86).

COUTURES (49)

Stored at a private location in 3.89 were Gasne RG.3 F-WBGN (c/n 01, built 1942) and a 1928 vintage Masson Avionnette (a Mignet HM.8 derivative).

CREIL/SENLIS (60)

Now reduced to care and maintenance status (since 1.6.85), the gate at Base Aerienne 110 is no longer guarded by Super Mystere B2 139. Formerly '12-YB' with EC.1/12 it was painted up as "10-RE/10-SE" in EC.1/10 and EC.2/10 marks during its sojourn here. It was noted between '78 and 2.88 but had gone later in the year and is thought now to be stored here.

The following airframes have been noted dumped at various locations in the last few years. Several relics were removed with the closure of the airfield.

Lockheed T-33SF	21009	ex '314-YP' GE.314 (noted '82-'83, to Ailes Anciennes, Armorique, at Vannes/Meucon).
N2501 Noratlas	..	fuselage only (noted '80-'89).
F-84F Thunderstreak	29078	ex '1-EH' EC.1 (noted '82, was gate guard here '63-'72).

Over on the North side, former IGN Hurel-Dubois HD.34 F-BICV (c/n 8) is displayed by the Aero Club (noted '88-'89).

CREPY-EN-LAONNAIS (02)

Sikorsky H-34A SA162 is preserved at this military camp North West of Laon (noted 12.87). It was not found when searched for in mid '89 so any further details on its location would be appreciated.

CRESSANGES (03)

MH1521 Broussard 15 is kept at a private location here (noted '89).

CUERS/PIERREFEU (83)

Preserved at this Aeronavale maintenance facility is ex DCAN N1101 Noralpha 181/CAN-12 (noted '83-'87). Of the other DCAN Noralphas, 192/CAN-14 was sold off to a group of preservationists (which one?), 197/CAN-15 went to La Mole for Escadrille Pegase and 125/CAN-10 was still here during '87.

Discarded from the Aeronavale facility have been the wrecks of F-8E(FN) Crusaders 14 (noted '87, w/o 8.5.85), 30 (noted '89, w/o 9.5.85?) and the fuselages of Alizes 27 and 34 (both noted '85) of which 27 was roaded to Hyeres during 11.85.

Brochet MB.72 F-BCZF (c/n 01) came here from Mauguio for restoration by Lionel Dupays.

DAX (40)

The ALAT Museum is housed in Hangar H7 here. It is hoped that by the 1990 season it will have moved to another part of the base which will permit public access.

Agusta-Bell 47G	056	'CAN-7' ex DCAN (noted '86-'87, on floats).
Agusta-Bell 47G-2	160	'ZP' ex Ecole de Specialisation et d'Application, Bourges, (noted '86-'87).
Bell 47G-1	1314	'BDM' ex ESALAT (noted '86-'87).
L-19E Bird Dog	24521	recovered from Central Africa by '87, stored.
L-19E Bird Dog	24530	"CEA" ex 'CCA' ESALAT and storage at ERGM Montauban, (noted '86-'87).
L-19E Bird Dog	24725	"BUA" ex 'AQK' ESALAT (noted '86-'87).
Hiller UH-12A	133	ex F-OAHB, on loan from M Poiree (noted '86-'87).
MH1521 Broussard	266	ex AdlA, Metz, due '89.
MH1521 Broussard	269	ex 'MIA' ESALAT (noted '86-'87).
MS505 Criquet	656	"UA" ex F-BDQQ, on loan (noted '83-'87).
Nord NC856	-	sections only, recovered 3.88 from M Piracchi of Bordeaux.
Nord 3202	66	"JR" ex 'AJR' ESALAT (noted '86-'87).
Nord 3202	99	ex Patrouille ALAT and Montauban gate (arr 3.88).
Nord 3400	75	'MFA' ex ESALAT and storage at Montauban (noted '78-'87).
Piper L-18	-	incomplete, donated by Belgian Army (noted '87).
Sikorsky H-19D	55-1085	"AVW" painted in colours of GH.2 (noted '86-'87).
Sikorsky HSS.1	143	(c/n SA143) ex 33F, Aeronavale, flew in from St Mandrier 11.9.79 (noted '86-'87).
Stampe SV4C	496	"1" ex F-BDIZ at CEV, Bretigny (noted '86-'87).
Sud Alouette II	-	"BBC" recovered from Gendarmerie store at Le Blanc, possibly ex 1234/JAR though c/n 1076 has also been quoted (noted '86-'87).
Sud Alouette III	1001	ex Cazaux.
SO1221 Djinn	-	"BVV" (noted '86-'87).
SO1221 Djinn	FR116	ex 'CBB', recovered from a farm at Nailloux (wreck stored '86).
SO1221 Djinn	FR149	ex 'BNG', recovered from 1 GSALAT Phalsbourg (noted '86).
Vertol H-21C	FR94	ex ESALAT, painted as "BEJ" in GH.2 marks (noted '86-'87).
Vertol H-21C	FR106	ex 5 GALAT Lyon/Corbas, arrived '86, due to go to Toulouse/Blagnac on loan.

One of the L-19E Bird Dogs is due to be exchanged for a Piper Tri-Pacer.

The preservation group Amicale des Anciens d'ALAT operates Bell 47Gs 722/F-BVKQ, 1302/F-BVPX and L-19E Bird Dogs 24582/F-BIFB, 24588/F-GEJQ, 24728/F-GDPC in military markings.

DIEPPE (76)

The fuselage of Beech B.24R Sierra F-GCMT (c/n MC-158, ex G-BAXM) was noted here during 8.89.

DIJON (21)

Stored in the locality with the Escadrille du Souvenir is a Sud Fennec (T-28) which is believed to have been obtained from Saintes. Its identity is unconfirmed but is probably 51-7749 (SFERMA 135).

Ailes Anciennes - Dijon are believed to have disbanded, their few airframes going to Ailes Anciennes - Beaune except for a Caudron Fregate under restoration at Dijon/Longvic.

DIJON/DAROIS (21)

Wrecks here during 7.87 comprised Robin DR400/160 F-BTKN (c/n 715) and Robin R3140 F-WZJY (c/n 001).

Stored in the Robin factory at this time were the Dyke Delta JD2 Manta F-WYBZ (c/n 02, to be F-PYBZ) and prototype Robin DR200P F-BLKP (c/n 01).

During 6.89 the following Robin ATLs were in store at the factory, engineless and with the wings stacked in front of the fuselages. They comprised F-GFND (c/n 04), F-GFNI (c/n 09), F-GFOD (c/n 28), F-GFOF (c/n 30), F-GFOM (c/n 37), F-GFOQ (c/n 41) and F-GFRD (c/n 53).

DIJON/LONGVIC (21)

Displayed in 'Patrouille de France' colours on the gate at Base Aerienne 102 is Mystere IVA 290 (arrived '84, current '89).

On the dump in 1984 was the front fuselage of a Mirage III, probably the remains of an accident victim. Other occupants at this time comprised a long standing F-84F and Flamant together with a more recently arrived Flamant from Chateaudun.

MD312 Flamant	187	ex '319-CK' GE.319 (noted '80-'84).
MD312 Flamant	221	ex '319-CM' GE.319 (noted '84-'89).
F-84F Thunderstreak	29113	(ex 52-9113) ex '4-VP' EC.4 (noted '74-'84).

By 6.89 a burnt Flamant and Mirage IIIB had appeared in a scrap compound near the civil hangars, presumably Flamant 187 and the Mirage III referred to above.

On the civil side, Sud Fennec (T-28) 51-7692 (SFERMA No 142) from Pont d'Ain has been rebuilt as F-AZFV. The owner, Monsieur JC Calvet also has Fennec 51-6301 (SFERMA No.67) to restore now that 142 is finished.

The local branch of the Escadrille de Souvenir keep their Fennec 51-7749 in the area, probably on the base.

DINAN (22)

CM170 Magister 80 (ex '2-HB' EC.2/SALE) arrived here on 14.10.86 for preservation with the Aero Club de Dinan (current 3.89). Stored here in 6.88 was Cessna F150J F-BRBG (c/n 0499) whilst MS733 Alcyon F-BNEJ (c/n 156) was under restoration.

DINARD/PLEURTUIT (35)

The wreck of Aeronavale Nord 262A 85 (ex 2S) was dumped here in the early eighties but was cut up for scrap by 1986.

MS880B Rallye Club F-BKKL (c/n 117) was lying wrecked on the TAT apron here during 12.87 and was still there in 9.88. Cessna 172C Skyhawk HB-CRT (c/n 49163) was in storage here during 9.88 but is to be restored.

During 9.88, the unmarked fuselage of a wrecked Fokker F.28 was on the TAT apron, the subject of a very slow, optimistic, rebuild.

CIPRA overhauled eighteen T-33ANs for the Bolivian AF here during 1985/86. The last six were never delivered due to financial problems and to the best of my knowledge they remain in store here. They are 21088, 21132, 21152, 21182, 21195 and 21307.

DIORS (36)

Displayed at the Musee des Trois Guerres is an MS505 which was obtained from the Musee de l'Air.

ECROUVES/BLATZEN (54)

On the N4 just West of Toul, an Armee de Terre barracks has Vautour IIN 308/30-MC (ex ECTT.2/30) displayed just inside the gate (noted '78-'89).

ECUEILLE (36)

The wreck of MS472 Vanneau 251 was still extant (just!) in a scrapyard here in 1.87.

EPERNAY (51)

Heintz Zenith F-PYOY was derelict here during 5.88.

EPINAL (88)

Stored here in 11.85 was SE210 Caravelle VI-N F-BYCY (c/n 233, ex YU-AHG). It was due to be converted as a bar and may well have been transformed by now.

ESCATALENS (82)

The preservation group 'Epsilon' are based here, basically forming a flying branch of Ailes Anciennes - Toulouse. They have restored Auster 5/J2 Arrow F-AZDZ (c/n 2354) and are working on a Nord 3400. In the vicinity, Philippe Cassaigne is tackling the restoration of Potez 36 F-PHZN.

ETAIN/ROUVRES (55)

An H-19 (or Westland Whirlwind) appeared at the 6.89 Open Day on a trailer. It may not necessarily reside on the base. Traces of the previous code 'CYX' were discovered together with the digits 7615 which may or may not be connected with the helicopter's identity.

ETAMPES (91)

This popular field houses four active preservation groups, Escadrille du Souvenir, Les Coucous Beaucerons, Mecaniciens et Pilotes d'Aeronefs Anciens and the Aero Club Les 733. As mentioned in the Introduction to this section, many of their aircraft are active and are not strictly W&R territory, however the following relics have been recorded here in recent years.

Agusta-Bell 47G	094	(F-BNFB) ex 'BTR' ALAT.
Beech C-45	-	formerly "MT122" at BA122, Chartres (noted '88-'89).
Beech C-45	-	anonymous, GAEL badge, first noted here 6.89.
Bell 47G	019	stored 5.88.
Bell 47G-2	F-BSIA	(c/n 1629)
CEA DR220A 2+2	F-BOZE	(c/n 62) wreck in main Club hangar 8.89.
Cessna 180E	F-BFVX	(c/n 51093) derelict '89.
DH82A Tiger Moth	"K2570"	(c/n 83097, ex R5238, G-ANRZ, OO-SOG)
Dewoitine D.520DC	650	stored '78, to Toussus by '86.
Hiller 360 (UH-12)	158	ex 'H' in Viet Nam, F-BEEF and Chambery, under restoration.
Hurel-Dubois HD34	F-BHOO	(c/n 01, ex F-WHOO)
Jodel D92 Bebe	F-PIIE	(c/n 292) on rebuild 8.89.
Jodel D120	F-BHYZ	(c/n 69) derelict '89.
Jodel D140B	F-BJQU	(c/n 69) stored 5.88.
DR315 Petit Prince	F-BSBG	(c/n 472) fuselage only, stored 5.88.
MH1521 Broussard	64	stored 6.89.
Morane MS504 Criquet	F-BCME	(c/n 600)
Morane MS505 Criquet	F-BCMD	(c/n 599)
MS733 Alcyon	165	(F-AZAE) ex Aeronavale.
MS733 Alcyon	190	(F-AZAF) ex Aeronavale.
MS733 Alcyon	F-BDZV	(c/n 10) derelict '88-'89.
MS733 Alcyon	F-BKOM	(c/n 36) stored 8.89.
MS733 Alcyon	F-BMMG	(c/n 67) stored 8.89.
MS880B Rallye Club	HB-EDF	(c/n 77) in use as a spares source '89.
MS733 Alcyon	F-BNEH	(c/n 147) stored 8.89.
NC702 Martinet	315	ex CEV.
N1002 Pingouin	F-BFUY	(c/n 69) dismantled 8.89.
N1101 Noralpha	15	(F-BYAX) ex 'NM' CEV.
N1101 Noralpha	87	ex 'BR' CEV (stored '78-'89).
N1101 Noralpha	106	(noted '89).

N1203 Norecrin	F-BERY	(c/n 353) stored 5.88.
N1203 Norecrin	F-BBKB	(c/n 3) stored 8.89.
N2501 Noratlas	98	ex '64-BC' ET.64 arr 7.1.80 (current '89).
Nord 3202	71	(F-WZBD)
Nord 3202	101	(F-WZBE)
Nord 3400	99	ex 'JBW' Gendarmerie (on Musee de l'Air charge).
Nord 3400	108	ex 'JBY' Gendarmerie (on Musee de l'Air charge).
Nord 3400	131	ex 'CUC' ALAT
T-6G Texan	21475	(F-AZBG) (ex 52-1475) (noted '89).
T-6G Texan	114387	(F-AZEF) (ex 51-14387) ex Paris/Vilgenis.
T-6G Texan	34579	(ex 53-4579) ex La Ferte Alais.
PA-18A Super Cub	F-BFES	(c/n 18-3293) derelict '89.
SIPA S903	F-BGAA	(c/n 26) stored '88-'89.
SNCASO SE535 Mistral	50	"7-BM" ex Ecole des Transissions, Auxerre (noted '78-'89).
Stampe SV4A	38	ex FZJCF CEV.
Stampe SV4A	F-BISY	(c/n 82)
SO1221 Djinn	FR46	w/o 3.6.67 as CS-MAA) ex Brienne-Le-Chateau.
SO1221 Djinn	FR92	(c/n 1042, allocated F-BSEY) ex Brienne-Le-Chateau.
SO1221 Djinn	FR146	(owned not by the group but by one of its members) ex Brienne-Le-Chateau.
Zlin 326	F-BNMU	(c/n 910)

By 8.89 the MPAA had flown in three AD-4N Skyraiders from storage in Chad (125716/F-AZFN, 126935/F-AZFO, 126959/F-AZFP). These were previously languishing at N'Djamena with 126998/F-AZKY and 126880/F-AZGA, also destined for repatriation to France.

Adjacent to the aerodrome, a petrol station on the Southbound carriageway of the RN20 displays Wassmer WA52 F-BSNS (c/n 41) as an eye-catcher (noted '85-'89).

EU-SUR-MER/LE TREPORT (76)

On display with the Aero Club by 9.84 was MD312 Flamant 218 (ex '319-CA' GE.319) (noted '84-'88).

EVREUX/FAUVILLE (27)

Preserved at Base Aerienne 105 are N2501 Noratlas 172 (ex 'XR' GAM.56, within the GAM.56 area) and Sikorsky H-34A SA167/68-OC (ex EH.2/68, at the GAM.56 gate).

Preserved at the Aero Club is Breguet 765 Sahara 501/64-PE (ex ET.64, soc 18.8/69) (noted '74-'88). A second Sahara, 504/64-PH (ex ET.64, soc 26.8.69) was stored on the field until 8.85 when a lengthy period of dismantling commenced prior to transport to Ailes Anciennes - Toulouse.

On the Northern side of the field two Noratlas fuselages lay derelict from '78 until '86. They are 7 (ex '118-ID' CEAM, soc 12.8.76) and 17 (ex '312-BF' GI.312, soc 16.8.76). They were moved to a position in the middle of the field during '86.

The dump held Noratlas 79/64-IO (ex ET.64) by late '84. Three aircraft were standing wfu by 5.84 of which one was presumably 79. It is not certain whether the other two were disposed of locally or via Chateaudun.

EYMOUTIERS (87)

A vintage car enthusiast here also had Zlin XII F-AQII (c/n 194), dismantled but in good condition, during '87. It has gone to Diest/Schaffen (Belgium) for restoration.

FALAISE (14)

Monsieur du Valleroy received MD312 Flamant 161 (ex Caen/Carpiquet and Olendon) by 1984. It is thought to be at his house.

FEURS/CHAMBEON (42)

Wrecks here in 8.88 comprised MS880B Rallye Club F-BPDC (c/n 1139) and MS893E Rallye 180GT F-GBCM (c/n 13107) whilst Jodel D112 F-PJXE (c/n 1041) was incomplete and in pieces. By 7.89 only the rear fuselage of Rallye F-GBCM remained.

FLERS (61)

MD315R Flamant 51/30-QS (ex ECTT.12/30) was soc 5.10.72 and presented to the Aero Club de Basse Normandie. By early '87 it had moved to St Gatien Des Bois.

FONTENAY/TRESIGNY (77)

Used as a bar by the local Aero Club is Br 763 Provence 306/82-PP (ex ETOM.82, wfu 24.8.67). A visit in 6.85 found her in a sorry state but by 6.87 she had benefitted from a new coat of paint with the spurious registration "F-BACC" and was still current as such in 5.88. The aerodrome is 3 kms East of the town to the North of the N4.

An anonymous Holste MH52 was in store here during 5.88.

FREJUS/ST RAPHAEL (83)

Preserved on the civil side is MD315 Flamant 113 (ex '30-QY' ECTT.12/30, soc 7.8.72) which was still current 6.89. Nearby, at the entrance to the Aeronavale area is Sikorsky HSS-1 149 (c/n SA149) (noted '83-'87).

Instructional airframes with the Aeronavale here have included WG13 Lynx 03/XX904 (ex FZKCU, to Rochefort/Soubise by '87) and 04/XX911 which was damaged at Nimes/Garons on 29.3.79.

Stored on the civil side in '85 were Beech 23 F-BNFO (c/n M-763) and Robin HR100/210 Safari F-BUPG (c/n 162).

Dumped in the bushes by the civil hangar (6.87) was Beech 35-33 G-DEBY (c/n CD-214) which was only registered for five weeks before plunging to a watery fate in the Med nearby.

FUMEL/MONTAYRAL (47)

CEA DR315 Petit Prince F-BSJZ (c/n 522) was in store here during 6.86.

GAP/TALLARD (05)

MD312 Flamant 185 (ex '319-CO' GE.319, soc 19.11.73) was displayed at the Aero Club until at least 10.84 but has unfortunately since been scrapped.

Cessna 180 F-BISE (c/n 32239) lay wrecked here during 1986.

GAVRES (56)

An anonymous Sikorsky HSS-1 (in blue/yellow colours) and a Bell 47G (overall dayglo) have been standing on the ranges here (over the river from Lorient) since at least 1982 and probably for a lot longer. They were still present in late '88.

GRAMAT (46)

Southeast of Rocamadour on the N140, the Centre de Recherche de l'Armee de l'Air uses Mirage IIIA 07 (ex CEV) for EMC (Electro-Magnetic Compatibility) trials (noted '87). They have also used CEV Mirage IIIR 02 during '83 but it returned to active use at Bretigny by '84.

GRAULHET (81)

The fuselage of MS880B Rallye Club F-BUZI (c/n 2403) was stored here during 8.88.

GRAY (70)

DR340 Major F-BRVN (c/n 434) was stored here in '86 in a damaged condition.

GRENOBLE/LE VERSOUD (38)

The Centre d'Etude et de Loisirs Aerospatiaux de Grenoble (CELAG) have the following helicopters in store on the airfield.

Cessna L-19E Bird Dog	24720	ex ALAT (stored '86).
Sikorsky H-19D	"3RHC"	ex 3 RHC, ALAT at Verdun/Etain (noted '87).
Sikorsky H-34A	SA92	ex '68-OE' EH.68, wreck only, to Annecy by '87.
Sikorsky H-34A	SA177	ex '67-VR' EH.67 (noted '87).
Sud Alouette II	1440	ex '236-DY'
Vertol H-21C	FR41	ex 'ARB' ALAT & Carcassonne/Salvaza dump (noted '87).

GUISCRIFF/SCAER (56)

The Aero Club here, Les Ailes Armoricaines, received MD315R Flamant 50/30-QU (ex ECTT.12/30, soc 15.9.72, fitted with fins from 43). Regrettably this grand old lady was scrapped between 6.84 and 6.85.

On 10.10.88 CM170 Magister 143 flew in for display purposes (the Aero Club had been hoping for a Noratlas).

GUYANCOURT (78)

Another of the prolific Paris general aviation fields, wrecks and relics here in recent years have comprised the following.

Aermacchi AL.60B-2	F-BLGE	(c/n 31/6211) (noted 5.88).
B.35-33 Debonair	F-BJOG	(c/n CD-208) fuselage only (noted 8.89).
Jodel DR1050	F-BJYK	(c/n 281) engineless (noted 5.88).
MS885 Rallye	F-BKUM	(c/n 239) fuselage (noted 5.88, current 8.89).
CP301 C1 Emeraude	F-BTEO	(c/n 559) no propeller (noted 5.88).
PA34-200 Seneca	F-BVES	(c/n 34-7450062) (noted '88).
Stampe SV4A	F-BDNF	(c/n 661) engineless (noted 5.88).
Stampe SV4C	F-BFZU	(c/n 377) dismantled (noted 5.88).
Wassmer WA81 Piranha	F-GAIM	(c/n 810) fuselage only, stored (noted 5.88).

HENIN-BEAUMONT (62)

Displayed in the Parc Municipal by the main road through the town is MD452 Mystere IIC 104/10-SQ (ex EC.1/10) (noted '78-'89).

HERBAULT (41)

The fuselage of MH1521 Broussard F-GDQV (c/n 294, ex 'MYU' ALAT) was stored in a hangar here alongside the A10 autoroute by 11.87 in a blue and yellow colour scheme. The aircraft suffered an accident in 8.85.

HOURTIN (33)

Preserved at the Naval Base is an unidentified Sikorsky HSS-1 (noted 4.86).

HYERES/LE PALYVESTRE (83)

Preserved at the Aeronavale base are ex 59S Alize 16 (noted '83-'88) and CM175 Zephyr 18 (noted '85-'88).

The fuselage of Alize 27 arrived from Cuers/Pierrefeu during 11.85 for spares recovery and fire practice.

INGRE (45)

An unidentified Mirage IIIC has been reported stored in a hangar in the industrial estate (noted '86).

ISSOIRE (63)

A visit in 8.87 found the wrecks of CE43 Guepard F-BXCZ (c/n 471), Wassmer WA80 F-WVKR (c/n 01) and dismantled WA40 Super IV F-BHJN (c/n 12). Noted a month earlier were the wrecks of WA81 Piranha F-GAIS (c/n 821) and WA51A Pacific F-BSNZ (c/n 18) together with four stored WA81 fuselages which had never been completed.

Cessna F172H F-BOGO (c/n 0384) was in storage here during 8.88 awaiting an uncertain future following a minor accident.

ISSOUDON (36)

MD312 Flamant 224 (ex '319-DM' GE.319, soc 13.3.69) was in a scrapyard here until 1982 when it was finally chopped up. Sister aircraft 222 (ex '319-DY' GE.319, soc 14.12.72) suffered a similar fate around the same time having previously been displayed at the Aero Club at Issoudon/Le Fay aerodrome.

ISTRES/LE TUBE (13)

The gate at Base Aerienne 125 is guarded by MD452 Mystere IIC 147/CM (ex Chambery, noted '84-'88).

Ex EPNER Lockheed T-33S-US 35061 was parked out on the GERMaS.15/093 apron during 1986 pending transport to the musem at Nancy/Essey.

The fire dump here has dealt with the following in recent years.

MD315 Flamant	6	ex 'BR' CEV (noted '77-'79).
N2501 Noratlas	145	fuselage only (noted '84-'88).
Vautour IIN	621	ex '92-AN' EB.92 (noted '79-'88).

The wreck of P-38J Lightning 43-28537 was raised from the Mediterranean and stored with the CEV. It has not been heard of recently and may have ended up as a pile of scrap.

In the industrial estate, the yard of Etablissements Fondi holds stored ex CEV H-34A SA95 (noted '87).

JACOU (34)

Preservationists Aero 34 had obtained the hulk of Alouette III F-BRAQ (c/n 1447) from Heli-Union by 2.88. Their SO1221 Djinn FR132 is stored awaiting restoration and the group have parts of FR111/CAA and another anonymous airframe to assist in this (all from Phitagri at Bouilly and noted '87). All these were still current during 12.88. The group also have facilities at Le Cies.

LA BAULE/ESCOUBLAC (44)

Preservation group Ailes Anciennes - La Baule have the following airframes.

Caudron C275 Luciole "F-APLM" (F-AZCT, c/n 7474,ex F-BBCF) airworthy.

Super Mystere B.2	179	ex '10-SJ', expected from Captieux ranges.
Lockheed T-33S-US	53091	(ex 55-3091, returned to USAF charge 4.10.82) ex '338-HD' CEVSV.338, on display (current '89).
MH1521 Broussard	133	ex 'ABX' ALAT, Montauban store & Toulouse, spares source for F-BMJO.
MH1521 Broussard	F-BMJO	(c/n 19, ex F-BNEN) ex Soulac, airworthy.
Mauboussin 123C	F-PJDH	(c/n 159) active.
Mauboussin 129	F-PJKQ	(c/n 189) stored, parts possibly donated to F-PJDH.
N1101 Noralpha	177	ex 'BQ', from Musee de l'Air.

LA CHICOTIERE (69)

On pole outside a scrapyard is MS880B Rallye Club F-BPHP (c/n 1188) with the spurious registration "G-GINET" (noted '85-'87).

LA COURNEUVE (93)

The Aerospatiale works held preserved AS355 Ecureil 2 F-WZLA (c/n 001) during 1.87.

LA FERTE ALAIS (91)

This aerodrome (which now appears to prefer to be called Cernay) houses L'Amicale Jean-Baptiste Salis better known as the Salis Collection, an enormous collection of airworthy and derelict aircraft, some very old. Several other groups house their aircraft on the base but for our purposes here they are all regarded as Salis aircraft. This list does not attempt to record all the active antique aircraft here but concentrates on those which are non-airworthy, derelict or recognisably part of the Salis museum collection.

Aero Z.131 (Bu 131)	I-BRAK	crash wreck (noted '88).
Agusta-Bell 47G	024	ex 'BCG' ALAT (noted '80).
Albatros C.II	F-AZAV	(c/n 005, ex F-WZBH) replica (noted '85-'89).
Albatros C.II	F-AZAX	(c/n 004, ex F-WZBG) replica (noted '85-'89).
Antonov An-2TD	F-AZDJ	(c/n 11801, ex Polish AF & F-BTOM) (noted '85-'88).
Beech C-45 (E.18S)	F-AZEJ	(c/n BA-359, ex F-BTCS) one-time painted in Luftwaffe colours as "BT+CS", more recently in RAF c/s as "43-6904" (noted '85-'89).
Bell 47G	F-WIPA	(c/n 01) (noted '85-'89).
Boeing Stearman	41-8094	(F-AZCK) "205" (noted '84-'88).
Boeing Stearman	F-AZGM	(noted '89).

Boeing N2S-5 Stearman	F-AZDI	(c/n 75-5238, ex 42-17075, N5817N, F-AZDI) "6116/238" (noted '88-'89).
Breguet XIVP	F-AZBH	(replica built '78) to Thai AF Museum '86 in exchange for Bearcat 122095, itself passed on to Duxford, UK.
CASA 1-131E (Bu 131)	E.3B-532	ex '781-13' SpanAF & Granada/Armilla (noted '89).
CASA 1-131E (Bu 131)	E.3B-538	ex '781-83' SpanAF & Granada/Armilla (noted '89).
L-19E Bird Dog	24519	allocated F-WNRQ (noted '85-'86).
L-19E Bird Dog	24550	(noted '85-'86).
FG-1D Corsair	88297	(N88297) (noted '86, to Duxford by '89).
F4U Corsair	124724	(NX4901E, ex FAH-605 Honduran AF) "P/22" VC-3 colours (noted '86-'89).
MD311 Flamant	291	(F-AZCB) ex '316-KS' GE.316 (noted '81-'89).
DH Chipmunk T.22	"WB557"	(c/n C1/0702, ex RDanAF P-132) (F-AZCH) (noted '80-'89).
DH89A Dragon Rapide	F-AZCA	(c/n 6541, ex G-ALZF, F-BGON) RAF c/s (noted '87-'89).
Deperdussin 1913	F-AZAR	(c/n 1) replica (noted '87-'89).
AD-4N Skyraider	124143	(F-AZDP) ex Gabon AF, painted as "RM/205" of VA-176/USN (noted '84-'89).
AD-4N Skyraider	126922	(F-AZED) ex Gabon AF, painted as "JS/937" VA-152/USN (noted '86-'89).
Douglas C-47B Dakota	13142	(ex 42-93251, F-BAXG, F-BLOX) ex CNET (noted '80-'89).
UC-61A Argus	"43-14499"	(F-AZCF) "OKI-E" (noted '83-'86).
UC-61K Argus	F-AZCI	(c/n 998, ex 44-83087, KK380, F-BEXC) (noted '85-'89).
Fokker DR.1	F-AZAQ	(c/n 1) replica (noted '89).
Hatry-Opel RAK-1	"D-125"	replica (noted '85-'89).
Jodel D120 Paris-Nice	F-BMIA	wreck (noted '88).
MH1521 Broussard	021	(F-BVSS) ex ALAT & Montauban (noted '81, to Lorient).
MH1521 Broussard	022	(F-BVSU) ex 'MAB' ALAT & Montauban (noted '81-'89).
MH1521 Broussard	293	(F-BXCS/F-AXCS) ex 'BPD' ALAT & Montauban (noted '81-'89).
Morane MS138	F-AZAJ	(c/n 3220/138?) (noted '89).
Morane MS185	F-AZAZ	(c/n 3672/01, ex F-AJRQ) (noted '89).
Morane MS230	F-AZAK	(noted '89).
Morane MS317	F-BCNL	(c/n 273/6527) (noted '85-'89).
Morane MS317	F-BCNU	(c/n 351) (noted '85-'89).
Morane MS505 (Fi 156)	F-BBUJ	(c/n 263/23) (noted '85-'89).
Morane MS505 (Fi 156)	F-BJQD	(c/n 120/40) (noted '85-'89).
UC-64A Norseman	F-AZBN	(c/n 774, ex 44-70509, I-AIAK, YE-AAD, I-AIAK, EC-ANO, CN-TEE) painted as "D-ANBZ" '88 (noted '87-'89).
NC702 Martinet	331	ex 'PN' CEV (arr from Avernes '85, dumped outside '89).
N1101 Noralpha	19	ex 'DG' CEV (noted derelict '78-'80).
N1101 Noralpha	67	ex 'CY' CEV (arr from Merville '86, stored '89).
N1101 Noralpha	120	ex 'NR' CEV (noted '80-'86).
N1101 Noralpha	134	ex 'DZ' CEV (noted '78-'86).
N1203 Norecrin	F-BMHZ	(c/n 194) derelict '88.
Nord 3202	8	ex 'AJH' ALAT (derelict '76-'86).
Nord 3202	9	ex 'MDB' ALAT (derelict '76-'81).
Nord 3202	11	ex ALAT (derelict '76-'86).
Nord 3202	14	ex 'AJB' ALAT (derelict '76-'86).
Nord 3202	15	(F-WZBA) ex 'AJV' ALAT (noted '78-'89).
Nord 3202	18	ex 'ALB' ALAT (derelict '76-'86).
Nord 3202	19	ex 'AJC' ALAT (noted '76-'81, to Luneville).
Nord 3202	20	(F-WZBY) ex 'AIE' ALAT (noted '76-'86).
Nord 3202	23	ex 'AIG' ALAT (derelict '76-'86).
Nord 3202	26	ex 'AJA' ALAT (derelict '76-'86).
Nord 3202	G-BEFH	(c/n 80) (noted '89).
Nord 3400	37	ex 'MIB' ALAT (noted '85, to Coventry, UK).
Nord 3400	87	ex 'MAB' ALAT (noted '85-'86).
Nord 3400	121	ex 'MJB' ALAT (noted '85, to Coventry, UK).
AT-6C Texan	F-AZBE	(c/n 88-12127, ex 41-33606, EX633, BelgAF H-29, F-BJBI, F-WJBI) mocked up as a Hellcat (noted '86-'88).

T-6G Texan	92901	(ex 49-2901) ex 'DQ' (derelict '76-'86).
T-6G Texan	01289	(ex 50-1289) ex 'WV' & Etampes (noted '83).
T-6G Texan	114367	(F-AZBK ex 51-14367, F-BUQD) (noted '79-'89).
T-6G Texan	114374	(ex 51-14374) ex 'DD' (derelict '77-'86).
T-6G Texan	114454	(ex 51-14454) (derelict '77).
T-6G Texan	114700	(ex 51-14700) (derelict '76-'86).
T-6G Texan	114707	(ex 51-14707) ex 'KN' (derelict '76-'86).
T-6G Texan	114718	(ex 51-14718) ex 'DC' (derelict '76-'77).
T-6G Texan	114740	(ex 51-14740) (derelict '76-'86).
T-6G Texan	114811	(ex 51-14811) ex '13' (derelict '76-'77).
T-6G Texan	114839	(ex 51-14839) ex 'YJ/KQ' (derelict '76-'86).
T-6G Texan	114848	(F-AZBQ ex 51-14848, F-BOEO) ex Merville (noted '87-'89).
T-6G Texan	114979	(ex 51-14979) ex 'Q' (derelict '76-'86).
T-6G Texan	115017	(ex 51-15017) ex 'RD' (derelict '76-'86).
T-6G Texan	115049	(F-AZAS, ex 51-15049, F-BMYP) painted in USN style as "3-F-1" (noted '80-'88).
T-6G Texan	115113	(F-AZAU, ex 51-15113, F-BNAU) "MH-038" USAAF marks (noted '79-'89).
T-6G Texan	34572	(ex 53-4572) ex 'KA' (derelict '76-'86).
T-6G Texan	34579	(ex 53-4579) ex 'DJ' (derelict '76-'86).
T-6G Texan	34592	(ex 53-4592) ex 'RA' (derelict '76-'86).
T-6G Texan	34593	(ex 53-4593) ex 'KH' (derelict '76-'86).
T-6G Texan	34594	(ex 53-4594) (derelict '76-'79).
T-28 Fennec	-	(noted dismantled '80-'81).
Percival Proctor I	R7524	(c/n H.20) (G-AIWA) crashed here 9.6.84 (wreck in woods '86).
Piel CP301 Emeraude	F-PKXE	crashed 17.5.86 (wreck noted '86).
Piel CP1310	TU-TFE	fuselage only, stored '88.
Pilatus P2-05	U-116	(F-AZCD) Luftwaffe c/s (noted '81-'89).
Pilatus P2-06	U-152	(F-AZCE) Japanese c/s (noted '81-'89, now in Luftwaffe c/s as "4").
Piper J-3C-65 Cub	F-BEGG	(c/n 12866, ex 44-80590) (noted '84-'89).
Polikarpov Po.2	045	(F-AZDB) ex Yugoslav AF (noted '84-'89).
Poullain PJ.5B	F-BAQC	(c/n 6) (noted '87-'89).
RAF SE.5A	F-AZCY	(c/n 3) "1", replica (noted '85-'89).
P-47D Thunderbolt	44-90368	ex Venezuela (noted '83-'85, to Charles Osborn, Louisville, KY).
Salmson D.6	F-AZAB	(c/n 9, ex F-BFNG) (noted '89).
SFCA Govin Taupin G	F-AZBG	(c/n 10) (noted '85-'89).
Soko 522	210	ex Yugoslav AF (noted '85-'89).
SPAD XIII	"159"	(c/n 4377) ex Belgian military (noted '89).
Stampe SV4A	F-BDCQ	(c/n 54) (noted '89).
Stampe SV4C	F-BCQT	(c/n 411) (noted '89).
Stinson 108 Voyager	F-BFPM	(c/n 5080) (noted '87-'89).
Yakovlev Yak C11	511	(noted '84-'86)
Yakovlev Yak C11	529	
Yakovlev Yak C11	532	
Yakovlev Yak C11	533	to St Rambert d'Albon.
Yakovlev Yak C11	536	
Yakovlev Yak C11	539	to F-YAKA at St Rambert d'Albon.
Yakovlev Yak C11	540	
Yakovlev Yak C11	542	
Yakovlev Yak C11	543	
Yakovlev Yak C11	563	
Yakovlev Yak C11	564	
Yakovlev Yak C11	565	
Yakovlev Yak C11	570	
Yakovlev Yak C11	579	

Yakovlev Yak C11	580	
Yakovlev Yak C11	581	
Yakovlev Yak C11	582	
Yakovlev Yak C11	588	
Yakovlev Yak C11	589	
Yakovlev Yak C11	593	
Yakovlev Yak C11	607	
Yakovlev Yak C11	667	
Yakovlev Yak C11	704	stored '89
Yakovlev Yak C11	706	stored '89
Yakovlev Yak C11	707	
Yakovlev Yak C11	708	stored '89
Yakovlev Yak C11	709	
Yakovlev Yak C11	790	to OO-YAK with BAP Air (Gosselies, Belgium).
Yakovlev Yak C18M	607	(noted '86)
Yakovlev Yak C18M	627	to Coys of Kensington as G-BMJY 21.1.86.
Yakovlev Yak C18M	640	(noted '86)

Individual details on Yak disposals are few, but one has gone to AMPA at Lausanne (Switzerland) and approximately 10 went to the USA (one is N11SN). A total of approximately 39 Yak 11s and 4 Yak 18 were recovered from Egypt early in '84. Anyone with further details please write!

L'AIGLE (61)
The Aero Club de l'Aigle have MD311 Flamant 275/316-KC (ex GE.316, soc 6.10.69) preserved at the aerodrome. It was still current during 9.88 in poor condition.

LALINDE (24)
The preservation group 'Les Cages a Poules d'Aquitaine' have an unknown Nord 3400.

LA MOLE (83)
In 6.87 Lockheed 12 F-BUIE (c/n 1226, ex EI-ALV) was dumped amongst the trees. The airfield is also used by the preservation group Escadrille Pegase (refer to Aix/Les Milles for more details of their collection).

LANDIVISIAU (29)
In use for ground instructional purposes in a small outbuilding between the two flight lines is Super Etendard prototype 01 (rebuilt from Etendard IVM 68, soc for gia use 5.11.80, noted '82-'88).

LANVEOC/POULMIC (29)
Ex 32F Sikorsky HSS-1 7 (c/n 58-1007/SA50) is displayed at the entrance to the Aeronavale base (noted '83-'88).

LAON (02)
A Mignet type aircraft wearing the registration F-WTET was in store at the Aero Club here by 2.89.

LAPALISSE (03)
The Aero Club have the wreck of Cessna 207A F-GAMY (c/n 00381, crashed 2.1.84, noted '85-'88). Also noted on 7.88 was an anonymous, dismantled, all silver PC6 Porter. A visit in 7.89 found Cessna 207 F-BXLX (c/n 00290) acting as a spares source.

LA PETITE CALADE (13)
A couple of kilometres south of Lignane on the RN7, the only AISA I-115 in France sits on the roof of a building in wrecked condition (noted '87).

LA REOLE (33)
Noted here in 1.83 was the fuselage only of Piper PA25 N7202Z.

LA ROCHELLE (17)
Noted here in 9.86 were the wrecks of MS885 F-BKEN (c/n 52) and Cessna F172P F-GCYK (c/n 2094).

LA ROCHE SUR YON (85)
The cannibalised hulk of Merlin F-GEJY (c/n T-222) was to be seen here during 11.87.

LA TRESNE (33)
The Ecole Technique here are due to receive the Mirage F.1E prototype from Avions Marcel Dassault.

LAVAUR (81)
A N1101 Noralpha was displayed at an Elf petrol station on the CD112 during 1.87.

LE BLANC (36)
SIAI S205/20R F-BTOG (c/n 4-282) was derelict here during '87 with Cessna FTA337E F-BSHC (c/n 0001). Previously recorded relics in the form of Cessna 180C F-BMSG (c/n 50898) and Cessna 310Q CS-AOR (c/n 0803) had by this time disappeared.

LE CASTELLET (83)
Stored out on the field by 6.89 were CM170 Magisters 350 and 379. On the roof of an office inside a hangar at this time was MS881 Rallye 105 F-BMNB. Also stored was MS880B Rallye F-BVZX (c/n 2555). Aircraft from the preservation group Escadrille Pegase can also be found here, refer to Aix/Les-Milles for details.

Based here with the Association Co-operative des Pilotes de Provence (but often at Aix) is MD311 Flamant 250 (F-AZEN).

LE HAVRE (76)
AD-4N Skyraider 126924/"RM-20" is undergoing a slow restoration outside the hangars here (noted '87).

LE LUC (83)
Preserved at the entrance to this ALAT base is Vertol H-21C FR107/"LRZ" (noted '73-'89). Sikorsky H-19 55-864 (c/n, not US serial) was hangared here at the Open Day in 6.89 with the H-21, the latter presumably only removed from the gate for the occasion.

LEMPDES (63)
Preserved at the 'Concorde' supermarket on the N89 (near Clermont Ferrand) is Viscount 708 F-BOEA (c/n 12) which crashed at Clermont-Ferrand/Aulnat on 28.12.71 (noted '85-'89).

LENS (62)
The fuselage of Cessna F172F F-BMRM (c/n 0104) was stored here in 5.88.

LE PETIT BORDEAU (17)
Jean-Claude Leger has the Leger JCL.01 F-PVQX (c/n 1, last flew 3.7.83) in store at a private location here (noted 5.86).

LE PLESSIS/BELLEVILLE (60)
PA28-180E Cherokee TR-LWU (c/n 28-5776) has been stored here since at least 1985 (still current '88). Beech 65 Queen Air F-BNAT (c/n LC-74) was abandoned in the long grass by 5.88.

LESCAR (64)
SFERMA 60A Marquis F-BLLQ (c/n 11) is displayed on a pole at the Carosserie du Moulin, a scrap dealer on the RN117 West of Pau (noted '87-'88).

LES MONTILS (41)
Monsieur Lerin had a Mignet HM.8 in store here during 11.86.

LES MUREAUX (78)

N2501 Noratlas 202 (ex '63-VE' ET.63) was preserved at the Aerospatiale works here by 7.86.

LESSAY (50)

Beech C-45 753/AL (ex CEV) was standing on three concrete pillars here from 1976 and by 1983 was in a sorry state. Despite reports of its acquisition by Ailes Anciennes - Toulouse to assist in the restoration of their own 085 this was not to be and the aircraft was scrapped c.1986.

LES VERNES (89)

A N1203 Norecrin was on display here during 6.88 modified as a 'tail-dragger'. It could possibly be F-BEBH (c/n 38).

LILLE/LESQUIN (59)

The wreck of Beech A100 F-GEFR (c/n B-220) was lying here in 3.87 having been written off on 28.8.86.

LILLE/MARCQ (59)

A visit here in 5.88 found two Pou-du-Ciel fuselages (but only one wing), the long-lost fuselage of Max Holste MH52R F-BDXO (c/n 10, here since 1979), engineless PA18-95 Super Cub F-BMCU (c/n 18-1429), engineless SIAI S205 c/n 110, WA40 Super IV F-BKAF (c/n 18), Jodel DR1050 F-BKHZ (c/n 298), the fuselage of Jodel DR300/108 F-BSOH (c/n 569) and DR400/2+2 F-BUPC (c/n 821).

LIMOGES (87)

Guarding the gate at Base Aerienne 274 Limoges/Romanet is CM170R Magister 477/AJ (ex GI.312, crashed 22.12.65) (noted '83-'86).

The Musee de la Resistance du Centre has ex Luftwaffe Reggiane Re2002 OV+BI which was restored by Ailes Anciennes - Clermont Ferrand and then stored for a while at BA274.

LOGNES (77)

The fuselage of Wassmer WA41 F-BOBR (c/n 142) was in store here during 6.85 and was still current 4.89.

LONS/LE SAULNER (39)

The preservation groups Air Memorial, Retro Air Franche Comte and Alcyons all have a presence here with various airframes, some in flying condition. During '87 Air Memorial received MD312 Flamant 210/F-AZEO which had been preserved at Paray-Le-Monial. Thus was followed in 7.88 by another MD312, 217, which flew in from Redon where it had been maintained in excellent condition by the Aero Club. Aircraft of particular interest here recently have included.

MD312 Flamant	210	(F-AZEO) 'Night Mission' SVNAF c/s (noted '88).
MD312 Flamant	217	ex Redon (noted '88).
MD312 Flamant	251	(F-AZDE) ex '319-CZ' GE.319 (noted '84).
HA1112 Buchon	-	(licence built Me 109).
MH1521 Broussard	224	(F-GBEN)

The group Alcyons were wound up following disagreements among the membership. Their two Texans (49-3037/F-AZCQ & 51-14456/F-AZCV) were stored by the Aero Club hangar here by 10.88.

LORIENT (56)

Preserved within the Ecole des Fusilliers-Marins (within the naval arsenal alongside the River Blavet) is Sikorsky HSS-1 144 (noted '86-'89).

LORIENT/LANN-BIHOUE (56)

This vast Aeronavale base has a generous number of preserved aircraft. The Alize and Neptune are inside the main gate, the JRB-4 (C-45) is in the 2S area and the Texan (displayed near the civil terminal during the seventies) is next to the 52S hangar.

Beech JRB-4 (C-45)	85104	'4' ex Rochefort/Soubise (noted '86-'89).
Breguet Alize	86	ex 4F (noted '80-'89).
SP-2H Neptune	147567	ex 25 F (noted '83-'89).
SNJ-5 Texan	43981	restored in '81 and preserved in 2S marks (current '89).

The SP-2H Neptunes of 25F were gradually wfu between 1981 and '84. By '85 the dump here held 147562, 147568, 147570 (burnt out) and 148332. All were still there in '86 but by late '88 only 147562 and 147568 remained.

The Aeronavale's last airworthy Neptune, ECM aircraft 147569, was wfu here during 1984 and remained parked in the same dispersal area in late '88, still in good condition. It is to be hoped that this grand old lady finds a good home.

An anonymous Sud Fennec (T-28) appeared in the civil hangars here during '83 and continues on long term rebuild (still current '85). An anonymous C-45 was noted in a dispersal on the base during the open day in '83 but has not been reported before or since.

In the civil area here the wreck of Alouette II F-BIES (c/n 1116) and stored MS881 Rallye 105 F-BMNF (c/n 431) were reported during 8.88.

LORIOL-SUR-DROME (26)

Nord 3400 ../MFA was displayed in Dubost's scrapyard here by '87. It was available for sale.

LUCHEUX (80)

Super Mystere B.2 154/12-YA (ex EC.1/12) is preserved at the radar station CDC.05/925 here, parented by BA925 at Doullens (noted '77-'89).

LUNEVILLE/CROISMARE (54)

A visit in 6.88 found the fuselage of Jodel D112 F-BIPK (c/n 896), two Stampes undergoing restoration one of which was SV4A F-BDMI (c/n 639), and the hulks of Boisavia Mercureys F-BIRF (c/n 110) plus one other.

LUXEUIL/ST SAUVEUR (70)

By 11.88 a Mirage IIIE coded '4-BI' (ex EC.2/4) had been placed on display within the base following EC.4's re-equipment with the Mirage 2000N. The last known '4-BI' was 568 but confirmation is required that this is the aircraft concerned.

The firemen here received MD312 Flamant 166 (ex '319-DF' GE.319) by 6.83 and it was still current on the dump in '87.

Former CEV Vautour IIN 358 arrived by air on 18.6.87 and is now on display at the City Museum in the town.

LYON/BRON (69)

MS880B Rallye F-BPSI (c/n 1193) was under rebuild here during 7.89.

LYON/CORBAS (69)

MD312 Flamant 189 (ex '319-CU' GE.319) arrived mid 1983 for preservation with the Aero Club here (current '89). Also in their hangar by 6.85 was CM170 Magister 57/13-TD (ex EC.13/SLVSV) of the preservation group ASPAA (and previously displayed in a public park in Lyon). By 6.87 it was parked outside in the long grass and had progressed to Montelimar/Ancone by 6.89.

Vertol H-21C FR26 was preserved within the ALAT base on the other side of the field but by 1986 it had been acquired by the Section Retro de l'Aero Club de Villeurbanne and was removed between 9.85 and 9.87.

Another Vertol H-21C, FR106, was also preserved at the ALAT base, but was transferred to the ALAT museum at Dax in '86 who should be loaning it to Ailes Anciennes - Toulouse.

LYON/MONT VERDUN (69)

Perched on top of the highest hill for miles around is the AdlA Air Traffic Control radar at Base Aerienne 942. Displayed here for several years was Super Mystere B.2 148 (ex '12-YH' EC.1/12) (noted '83-'86). By 6.88 a Super Mystere B.2 marked "148/12-YP" had appeared on the gate at Cambrai replacing 88 there. It is almost certainly the genuine 148 from here.

LYON/SATOLAS (69)

Preserved here is SE210 Caravelle III F-BHRM (c/n 37, with 'Aeroport de Satolas' titles, noted '80-'89). Lying wrecked here during 10.88 was the fuselage and centre section of ex Air Service Nantes Fairchild F-27J F-GDXY (c/n 85, ex N172C).

MARENNES (17)

Mignet HM296 F-PFRH (c/n 04) was in store here during 9.86.

MARMANDE (47)

On display at the aerodrome here with Sahel Amities by 3.89 was N2501 Noratlas 111 (ex Chateaudun and Bordeaux/Merignac).

MARQUISE (62)

L1049G Super Constellation F-BGNF (c/n 4515) was preserved at the "Disco Bar Tango Charlie" but was unfortunately scrapped in 1986.

MARSEILLE/MARIGNANE (13)

On display at the airport is former Air Inter SE210 Caravelle III F-BNKE (c/n 224, noted '80-'85).

Aerospatiale have a group of helicopters in open store on the South side for a possible museum.

Sikorsky HSS-1	944	(noted '80-'89).
SA321F Super Frelon	F-BTRP	(c/n 01) (noted '83-'87).
SA360	F-WSQL	(c/n 001) (noted '86-'87).
SA361H	F-WZAK	(c/n 1012) (noted '86-'87).
SA321 Super Frelon	-	(noted '87).
SO1221	-	(c/n 001) (noted '89).
SO1221-PS	FC-22	(c/n 013) (noted '87).

A nearby hangar appears to have a number of helicopters in store including some apparently unfinished SA321s, SA341 Gazelle 1515/F-WXFI and an Alouette II coded 'AR'.

Behind some pallets and containers beside the Securite Civile hangar, ex Italian AF S-2A Trackers MM148297/41-40 (ex Naples) and one other are used as a source of spares for the Securite Civile Conair Firecat (Tracker) fleet. The unidentified airframe is marked '42' in the cockpit (noted '85-'87). It is unlikely to be (as sometimes reported) 133103 which has been reported dumped at Brindisi both before and after the appearance of '42' here.

Mystere IVA 315/"1-DF" (F-AZDF, ex '8-MQ' ET.1/8) arrived on 26.9.83 for the late Roland Fraissinet's Les Ailes Francaises de la Chasse.

A scrap compound on the far side has held the wreck of Firecat F-ZBEI/T-6 (ex 136448) following its crash on 20.8.85.

The wreck of PA38 Tomahawk F-GJHT was here in 6.89.

MAUBEUGE/LA SALMAGNE (59)

The wreck of Dornier Do 27A-4 F-BSGH (c/n 434, ex 5708) was recorded with the Aero Club here during 7.88.

MEAUX/ESBLY (77)

CM170 Magister 31 (ex '30-QG' EC.30/SALE) is on display with the Aero Club (noted '88). Noted here in 5.88 was tail-less Cessna F150K F-BRXU (c/n 0630) and stored PA34-200 Seneca F-BTOJ (c/n 7250340).

MELUN/VILLAROCHE (77)

Vautour IIN 337 (ex CEV) arrived at the SNECMA factory here during 2.88 and has since been placed on display.

MENGAM (29)

The Thompson-CSF facility here (near Brest) have a Mirage 2000 perched up a pole for use in ECM trials (noted 6.88). It is not known whether this is a genuine airframe or a test rig.

MERVILLE (59)

The Institut Amaury de la Grange aircraft engineering school has utilised the following ground instructional airframes.

Agusta-Bell 47G	028	ex Guyancourt (stored '87).
Beech 65 Queen Air	F-BKBU	(c/n LC-78) (noted '85).
Beech 65 Queen Air	F-BRPL	(c/n LC-143) (noted '85).
Boeing 707-328	F-BHSF	(c/n 17618) (arr 13.5.77, current '88).
Cessna 310	F-BKBS	(c/n 35260) converted to Link Trainer (noted '85).
Super Mystere B.2	167	ex '12-YD' EC.1/12 (noted '79-'88).
Super Mystere B.2	173	ex '12-YP' EC.1/12 (noted '79-'86).
N1101 Noralpha	67	ex 'CY' CEV (noted '79, to La Ferte Alais '86).
N1101 Noralpha	77	ex 'NP' CEV (noted '79, to St Rambert d'Albon by '86).
N2501 Noratlas	129	ex Chateaudun, flew in 21.8.87 (current '89).
T-6G Texan	114314	(ex 51-14314) (noted '79, to Metz by '85).
T-6G Texan	114391	(ex 51-14391) ex 'DL' (noted '79, to ....).
T-6G Texan	114401	(ex 51-14401) ex 'DI' (noted '79, to Paris/Vilgenis by '86).
T-6G Texan	114848	(ex 51-14848, F-BOEO) (noted '79, to F-AZBQ at La Ferte Alais).
T-6G Texan	114898	(ex 51-14898) ex 'KW' (noted '79).
T-6G Texan	34618	(ex 53-4618, F-BRGA) (noted '79).
SE210 Caravelle III	F-BHRT	(c/n 55) (noted '85-'88).
Vickers Viscount 708	F-BMCF	(c/n 54) (noted '79-'88).

METZ/FRESCATY (57)

Preserved at Base Aerienne 128 are four airframes of which the Thunderstreak is within the main base area, the Noratlas in the EE.54 area and the H-34A next to the EH.67 hangar. The T-6G is to be further restored by Ailes de France.

N2501 Noratlas	42	ex EE.54 (placed on display 29.3.89).
T-6G Texan	114314	(ex 51-14314, F-BOEN) "VM" ex Merville, restored by BA128 to the markings of ELA.12/72 (noted '85-'87).
F-84F Thunderstreak	28879	(IRAN No551) ex Ecrouves, painted in EC.1/9 marks as "9-AU", installed 11.9.78 (current '88).
Sikorsky H-34A	SA170	ex '67-EH' EH.67 (noted '81-'88).

On the fire dump the hulk of F-84F Thunderstreak 29003/4-SA (ex 52-9003) ex EC.4 was present between '77 and '88 but it has moved on to join the expanding collection at Savigny-Les-Beaune.

A scrap compound on the base contained the wreck of MH1521 Broussard 244/41-AC (ex ETE.41) in 6.85.

A nearby Armee de Terre caserne (housing the 1er Regiment de Livraison par Air) had the fuselage of a N2501 Noratlas during the early eighties but it has since moved on.

MEYZIEU (69)

Cessna 182 D-ECIX was stripped for spares by Monsieur Raffin to assist in the construction of his homebuilt CP.1320. The hulk was scrapped circa 1984/84 when it was of no further use.

MONTAIGU (85)

Stored here in 5.87 was Vintras Joker F-PTXE (c/n 01).

MONTAUBAN (82)

Nord 3202 66/AJO was preserved here but moved on to the ALAT museum at Dax by '86. Similarly Nord 3202 99/MAZ was preserved at the at ERGM entrance here (noted '86) but had also made the move to to Dax by 3.88. It was replaced here by a so far unidentified Nord 3202 obtained from the ERGM at Bourges. Vertol H-21C 'Flying Banana' FR15 should still be in store here (last reported 6.86).

The ERGM here is the main unit responsible for the overhaul, storage and disposal of ALAT aircraft. During the eighties this has involved Broussards, the last few Nord 3400s and almost the entire L-19E Bird Dog fleet.
On the civil side in 8.88 was the wreck of Jodel D119 F-BIBH (c/n 626) and the stored fuselage of Jodel DR1050 F-BMPY (c/n 621).

MONTCEAU-LES-MINES (71)

The preservation group SV.4 Aero (to be precise 'l'Association de Restauration d'Aeronefs et de Collectionneurs de Materiel Aeronautique du Musee SV.4 Aero') were dealt a savage blow with the death of two members in the crash of MD311 Flamant 286/F-AZEP. The group have since obtained MD312 Flamant 237 (ex '319-DM' GE.319) from Nevers and continue to work on their SV.4 c/n 31, an unidentified Norecrin, a Mignet Pou-du-Ciel and GY201 Minicab F-PINM (c/n A.144).

MONT-DE-MARSAN (40)

Preserved around Base Aerienne 118 recently have been the following.

Mirage IVA	43	ex 'BP' (noted '88 - on Musee de l'Air charge).
Mystere IVA	234	ex '8-NW ET.2/8 (noted '84-'88).
Super Mystere B.2	153	ex 12-YY' EC.1/12 (noted '79-'87 - not to be confused with the aircraft in the Musee de l'Air which also wears this c/n).
A-26B Invader	39223	(c/n 6936, ex 41-39223) ex Saintes, painted as '0' of GB.1/19 (noted '82-'87).
Vautour IIB	364	ex '92-AY' EB.92 (noted '86-'87).

The Invader is now undergoing restoration to flying condition (excellent!) by the organisation Memorial Flight.

CM170 Magister 410 (ex Rochefort) was parked out on the field in '83 but has not been recorded since. Noratlas 118 (ex '118-IE' CEAM) was expended on the fire dump between 1983 and '85.

N2501 Noratlas 186 (ex '328-EJ' CIFAS.328) arrived in '85 and has subsequently been placed on display at 6 RCP's barracks in the town (noted '88).

MONTELIMAR/ANCONE (26)

MD312 Flamant 172 arrived here from Chateaudun late '85 for the Aero Club de Montelimar with the ferry registration F-AZAI (since re-used on 228). It has since been taken over by the Musee Europeen de l'Aviation de Chasse which has gathered the following aircraft here (though the Broussard belongs to four members of the museum and Flamant 172 and Magister 52 both belong to the Aero Club). A hangar is currently being built to house the collection.

Beech C-45G	F-BHMM	(c/n AF-465) (noted '89)
MD312 Flamant	172	ex '319-DD' GE.319 (noted '85-'89).
MD312 Flamant	228	(noted '87-'89, airworthy as F-AZAI).
Mirage IIIR	-	expected.
MD450 Ouragan	214	ex 'UG' GE.314 and Tours/Sorigny (noted '87-'89).
DH Vampire T.11	XD613	(ex 8122M & CATCS) ex Cosford, UK (arr 12.6.89).
Fiat G-91	-	ex Italian AF. Expected.
CM170 Magister	38	ex '2-HB' SALE/EC.2 (noted '87-'89).
CM170 Magister	52	ex SALE/EC.2 (noted '87-'89).
CM170 Magister	57	ex '13-TD' EC.13/SLVSV & Lyon/Corbas (noted '89).
CM170 Magister	101	ex '4-WB' EC.4/SALE & Ales (noted '89).
F-104G Starfighter	-	expected.
Mauboussin 123.C	48	under restoration at Chomerac '87.
Mauboussin 129	F-PCIP	(c/n 183) under restoration at Chomerac '87.
MH1521 Broussard	211	(noted '89).
Nord 1002	F-BEAZ	(c/n 90) under restoration, belongs to Dr Strubi (noted '87).
N2501 Noratlas	-	expected.

MONTLUCON (03)
The Zeland-Gazuit factory had an Ouragan on display by 1.87.

MONTMIRAULT (91)
Ground instructional airframes at the Lycee d'Enseignement Alexandre Denis (a couple of kms from La Ferte Alais airfield by the side of the road to Etampes) comprise the following. All were confirmed during 6.89.

MD312 Flamant	164	ex '319-DB' GE.319, arr from Chateaudun 16.10.84.
CM170 Magister	83	ex '10-KG' EC.10/SLVSV, arr 16.10.84.
MH1521 Broussard	179	arr 15.2.83.
MH1521 Broussard	191	arr 22.2.83.
MS892A Commodore 150	F-BPQH	(c/n 10803) rear fuselage.
T-6G Texan	F-BJBG	(c/n 88-16151) ex Paris/Vilgenis, arr 10.1.83.
Robin HR200/100	F-WSQP	(c/n 01) arr 9.2.83.
Sikorsky HSS-1N	1376	(c/n 58-1376) ex 'AN' CEV, from Bretigny.

MONTPELLIER (34)
Used for instructional purposes at the Lycee J Mermoz is Super Mystere B.2 72 (ex Rochefort, noted '87-'88). CM170 Magister 126/F-WZLQ was noted at the airport here in 9.88 having flown in from Chateaudun store and is thought to be either for display at the airport or instructional use with the Lycee.

Monsieur Taillefer is restoring the sole SIPA S.251 Antilope, F-BJSS (c/n 01) at a private location here (noted 4.89).

MONTPELLIER/L'OR (34)
Also known as Caudillargue or Mauguio! Nord NC858S F-BEZG (c/n 100) was under restoration here during '87 following recovery from a scrapyard at Puricoud. Another NC858S, F-BEZF, was stored in the AARCAM hangar with Castel C.301S c/n 1057 hanging from the ceiling. The fuselages of Cherokee Warrior OO-ELF and PA28-181 Cherokee Archer II F-GCTQ (c/n 28-8090297, ex N82002, OO-HLZ) were also here at this time.

The fuselage of Cessna 310P F-BRIH (c/n 0152) had left here for a scrapyard by '87.

MOURMELON LE GRAND (51)
The hulk of prototype SA330 Puma F-ZWWR (c/n 05) lies derelict in a military camp here (noted 9.88).

MULHOUSE (68)
At the Musee National de l'Automobile was former BEA Vickers Viking 1B G-AIVG (c/n 220, painted as "G-AJBR") which was damaged beyond repair on 12.8.53 after bursting a tyre at Le Bourget. By the time these words are read it should have gone to the Brooklands museum in the UK.

MURET (31)
Piper PA22 Tri-Pacer F-BMXY (c/n 2013) was stored at the Aero Club by 4.89.

NANCY/ESSEY (54)
Many aircraft are stored on the West side of the field (in the hangars near the civil terminal) and elsewhere pending the establishment of a permanent building for the Musee Aeronautique de Nancy due for 1992. Some of the museum's aircraft are currently exhibited at the Parc de Haye, Merville (about 10 kms West of Nancy). These are marked with an asterisk (*) whilst those in open store at Nancy/Essey are marked +. Locations are as noted 6.89.

Agusta-Bell 47G	046	ex 'BDS' ALAT & Montauban. *
Antonov An-2	-	expected from USSR.
Beech D.18S (C-45)	-	expected.
Boeing 727	-	expected from Air France.
Breguet 904S	F-CCFS	(c/n 9) ex St Auban. *
Bu 181 Bestmann	F-PCRL	(c/n 112/121) ex Luneville. *
Castel C.25S	F-CRMI	(c/n 169, ex F-CBAY) ex Thionville. *

Castel C.311P	F-CBEL	(c/n 300) ex St Dizier.
L-19E Bird Dog	24504	ex ALAT Etain, flown in as F-WZXB (noted '84-'86).
L-19E Bird Dog	24508	(F-GCSB) ex ALAT, stored in Aero Club hangar following a heavy landing.
L-19E Bird Dog	24...	under restoration (noted '83-'89). *
MD311 Flamant	260	ex '316-KB' GE.316 (noted '85-'89). +
MD312 Flamant	148	ex '319-DE' GE.319, flew in as F-WZXA (noted '83-'89). +
Mirage IIIR	334	expected.
Mystere IVA	23	ex '314-ZK, GE.314, painted as "7-CP" (noted '83).
Super Mystere B.2	113	ex '21-GR' BA721, arrived 22.6.85 (noted '88).
DFS SG38 Schulgleiter	-	ex Nancy.
Fairchild F.24R Argus	F-BEXU	(c/n 1063, ex 44-83102, KK445) ex Dieuze. *
Fiat G-91R/3	3093	(c/n 357) ex Lekg.43/LVR.6, WGAF, on loan from Musee de l'Air (noted '84).
CM170 Magister	24	(noted '86).
CM170 Magister	30	arr '82 as F-WDHG.
Fouga CM173/Potez 94A	01	ex Chartres, on loan from Musee de l'Air (noted '84).
Gasnier 2	-	replica.
Gloster Meteor NF.11	NF11-9	ex 'BF' CEV (noted '84).
SA103/4 Emouchet	"F-CRDI"	(c/n "26", composite of Guerchais-Roche SA103 F-CAXX c/n 23 and SA104 F-CRDI c/n 247). *
MH1521 Broussard	198	ex AdlA. *
MH1521 Broussard	...	a second example is stored at Essey.
Leduc 0.22	02	expected (front fuselage only).
F-104G Starfighter	2196	(c/n 7065) expected from WGAF.
SP-2H Neptune	148334	ex 25F, arr 26.7.83 (noted '83-'89). +
Lockheed T-33S-US	35061	(ex 53-5061) ex EPNER (stored at Essey '87).
Lockheed T-33S-F	21255	ex '314-VH' GE.314. *
Lockheed T-33S-C	21127	ex Strasbourg/Entzheim (noted '87-'89). +
Lockheed RT-33A	41553	ex '33-XU' ER.33/SLVSV (stored Essey '83).
F-4E Phantom	-	expected (wished for?) from USAF.
HM.14 Pou-du-Ciel	-	ex Nancy. *
HM.14 Pou-du-Ciel	-	stored.
MS505 Criquet	F-BDQT	(c/n 700/36) ex Montagne Noir. *
MS733 Alcyon	173	(wings from 186) ex Aeronavale. *
NC856 Norvigie	51	ex 'AYM' ALAT, ex Besancon.
NC856 Norvigie	108	ex FSDYS, on rebuild. *
N2501 Noratlas	54	ex '63-WX' ET.63 (noted '84-'89). +
N2501 Noratlas	97	ex '63-WB' ET.63 (noted '82-'89). +
N2501 Noratlas	189	ex '316-FN' GE.316 (noted '88). +
Nord 3202	59	ex ALAT.
Nord 3202	64	ex EPNER. *
Nord 3202	100	ex 'AJE' ALAT & Montauban, on rebuild. *
Nord 3400	100	ex 'FIA/MIA' (on either side) ALAT. *
F-84F Thunderstreak	"28946"	painted as "3-IV" EC.1/3, this is almost certainly former Florennes decoy FU-76 (ex 53-6536).
SAAB 91 Safir	-	expected from Toussus.
H-19A Chickasaw	-	*
Sikorsky H-34A	SA59	ex '59-DK' GMT.59. *
SNCASO SO1221 Djinn	FR144	ex ALAT. *
Sud Alouette II	65	ex'67-JL' EH.67, *
SE210 Caravelle III	F-BHRY	(c/n 61) ex Air France, arr 14.11.81 (noted '89). +
SO4050 Vautour IIN	307	ex CEV (noted '88). +
Vertol H-21C	-	expected from ALAT.

NANCY/OCHEY (54)

The base acquired a gate guard by 6.88 in the form of an unidentified Mystere IVA (possibly 123 or 183?).

The F-84F Thunderstreak "28946" (see Nancy/Essey) appeared here at the Open Day in 6.85.

In 6.85 the scrap compound here held the wreck of Mirage IIIBE 264/2-ZD (ex ECT.2/2) which was written off on 16.4.85 in collision with ER.3/33 Mirage IIIRD 365/33-TM over Luneville.

NANGIS (77)

Noted here during 5.88 were wrecked MS883 Rallye 115 F-BRMY and MS880B Rallye Club F-BUGT (c/n 2243).

NANTES/CHATEAU BOUGON (44)

Former Air Fret L1049 Super Constellation F-BRAD (c/n 4519, ex F-BGNJ, EC-BEN) was roaded in from Nimes during the '70's and preserved at the airport (current 4.89, restored in Air France colours). Stored here in 6.88 was the fuselage of Piel CP211 Pinocchio F-PJCM.

In the city itself, a N2501 Noratlas was in use as a gia at Richemond Caserne during 10.85.

NARBONNE (11)

Super Mystere B.2 54/"5-NO" (ex Rochefort) was reported on display at Base Aerienne 944 (a non-flying AdlA facility) during 4.89.

NEUVILLE-SUR-OISE (95)

The Chabrillan-Bouffort Elytroplan was stored here in 5.89 with Monsieur D'Harambure.

NEVERS/FOURCHAMBAULT (58)

The Aero Club here, L'Aeronautique de Nivernais, received MD312 Flamant 237/319-DC (ex GE.319) from Chateaudun in 1984. By 3.88 it had been acquired by the group SV.4 Aero from Montceau-Les-Mines.

NICE (06)

Preserved just outside the airport is SE210 Caravelle III F-WJTH (c/n 124, ex F-BJTH, arr 7.7.81) at one time wearing both Air France and Air Inter colours (though she arrived in her original Air Charter International scheme). She has now been repainted yet again in an aluminium/yellow/black scheme (by 9.88).

NIMES/COURBESSAC (30)

Preserved on the airfield are N2501 Noratlas 78/312-BE (ex GI.312, soc 18.10.77) and MD450 Ouragan 232/TP (both current '88).

Across the road at Base Aerienne 726 F-84E Thunderjet 9600 (ex 51-9600, painted as "9654/3-NW" and allocated to the Musee de l'Air) and Mystere IIC 143 (ex '5-OP' EC.5) are on the gate (both current '88).

Thought still to be in use as ground instructional airframes here are Sikorsky H-34As SKY479, SA163 and CM170 Magister 17, certainly SKY479 and the Maggie were still current at the open day in 6.88 and SA163 was noted during 9.87.

Stored on the civil side during 12.88 was Cessna F172H F-BOGT (c/n 0340).

NIMES/GARONS (30)

Preserved on the West side of the field are Alize 5 (noted '82-'88) and ex 56S C-47 Dakota 87 (c/n 4579, ex 41-18487, noted '85-'88).

An unidentified Alize was lying on the dump during 1980 and ex 59S Alize 1 was noted derelict here in 9.87 (reported as preserved by the tower in 2.87).

In the civil area during '87 were derelict SE210 Caravelle VI-R F-GAPA (c/n 99, ex Minerve) and cannibalised DC-8-33 TU-TCA (c/n 45670, here since '85 at least). Both are believed still to have been in existence during mid '88.

Stored DH Rapide F-BCDB (c/n 6897) departed to Amsterdam, Neths, during 1988 whilst Cessna F172H F-BOGT (c/n 0340) sat covered in dust in the Aero Club hangar by mid '88.

NOYANT-SUR-ALLIER (03)

MH1521 Broussard 156 was displayed in a municipal park here by 1.87.

NYONS (26)

S01221 Djinn FC18 (c/n 10) was in store here during 12.87 (perhaps with aspirations of becoming F-AZAC).

ORANGE/CARITAT (84)

Super Mystere B.2 121/"5-OL" in EC.2/5 markings guards the gate at BA115 (noted '78-'89).

ORLEANS/BRICY (45)

Two aircraft have been reported as preserved at BA123. Of the Noratlas there is no doubt but the Super Mystere has not been seen during any open days and seems an unlikely choice for this transport base. Confirmation would be appreciated.

Super Mystere B.2	9	ex CEV (reported 2.85 & 6.86?).
N2501 Noratlas	29	ex CEV, soc 9.6.77, painted as "61-QP" (noted '78-'89).

An arrival here by early '89 was C-160V Transall F-WESE (c/n V3, ex WGAF 5002 and TR-LWE) from storage at Le Bourget. It is presumed to be required for spares recovery and/or bdr training.

The fuselage of N2501 Noratlas 155 lies in front of the hangars here (noted '88-'89).

ORLEANS/ST DENIS DE L'HOTEL (45)

The remains of MS880B Rallye F-BTIN (c/n 1955) lay in the glider hangar during 7.89 while Jodel D119 F-PTXA (c/n 1276) was dismantled.

OYONNAUX (01)

Stored at the Aero Club here in '85 was Cessna F150M F-GASY (c/n 1386).

PARAY-LE-MONIAL (71)

During '84 the Aero Club de Charollais received MD312 Flamant 210/319-CE (ex GE.319) from Chateaudun. In '87 it was registered to Air Memorial as F-AZAO, and has been ferried across to Lons/Le Saulnier.

PARAY-VIEILLE-POSTE (91)

An Air France training centre here has the fuselage of Boeing 707-328 F-BHSD (c/n 17616) (presumably for cabin crew training). It was last reported in '85.

PARIS (75)

The Musee National des Techniques at 292 Rue St Martin displays the following.

Ader Avion III	-	on long term restoration with the Musee de l'Air.
Bleriot XI	01	original channel crossing aircraft (current 4.89).
Breguet RU.1	40	(current 4.89).
REP 1907 monoplane	-	(current 4.89).

The Breguet RU.1 is the sole surviving French military aircraft from the period prior to the First World War which still survives.

At the Cafe Touring Club de France in the Bois de Boulogne, MD312 Flamant 168 (soc 3.3.71) was preserved. Unfortunately it was sold for scrap in the early eighties.

In 'The Wiz' night club (formerly 'Bobinos' music hall) at 14 Rue de la Gaite (14th Arrondissement), an MD312 Flamant had been suspended from the ceiling by 9.88. No doubt this will attract a more discerning clientele. The aircraft no doubt originated from Chateaudun.

On display at 'Le Zenith' music hall by the Boulevarde Peripherique on the East side of Paris is N1203 Norecrin F-BEQP (c/n 150, noted 4.89) which came from the preservation group Orion at Marmande.

PARIS/CHARLES DE GAULLE (95)

Brand new Boeing 747-3B3 F-GDUA (c/n 22870) caught fire on the ground here shortly after delivery. The aircraft could have been repaired but was declared an insurance loss. She was derelict here during 11.85 and the hulk was still being broken up here during 1.87.

PARIS/ISSY-LES-MOULINEAUX (92)

Monsieur Dechaux is restoring SO1221 Djinn FR114 here. His two Dechaux Helicopjets were both stored in a hangar here during '83.

PARIS/LE BOURGET (93)

From 5.78, Gyrafrance stored a number of ex Chateaudun Noratlas here. They were 44/F-BZCK, 52/F-BZCL, 55/F-BZCM, 56/F-BZCN, 58/F-BZCO, 60/F-BZCP, 64/F-BZCQ, 65/F-BZCR, 72/F-BZCS, 76/F-BZCT, 103/64-IB (ex ET.1/64) and 144/XA (ex GAM.56). Without a buyer, all were scrapped in '81/'82 except for 72 and 144 which lingered until 1984 and 44 which is now with Ailes Anciennes.

Ex Aeronavale Douglas DC-6AC 44063 was stored outside the SLD hangars for some time until being broken up for scrap in 5.84.

Parked out on the field in open storage by 5.87 were ex Senegalese AF C-47 Dakotas F-GEFU (c/n 19074), F-GEFY (c/n 14152/25597) and C-160V Transall F-WESE (c/n V3, ex WGAF 5002, TR-LWE). The Daks were still present in 3.89 whilst the Transall had gone to Orleans/Bricy, possibly for bdr training. With the Daks by this time was stored Fairchild FH-227 F-OGJB (c/n 103).

The front fuselage of Douglas DC-8 N805E (previously stored at Roissy) was lying by the rotor test rigs at the North East end of the field by '87 (current '89).

A scrap compound next to Aero Stock had Cessna F172M F-BVBG (c/n 1117), Lear Jet 24B F-BRNL (c/n 24B-183, fuselage only, w/o Toulouse 12.85) and the cabin of AB206A Jet Ranger F-BRSI (c/n 8213) during '87. The Lear Jet was still present during 2.89 accompanied by ex Lead Air Piper Cheyanne F-GFLE (c/n 31T-752002).

The superb Musee de l'Air et de l'Espace collection is listed below. Not all are on display at any one time and the museum has extensive storage and restoration facilities at Dugny (on the far side of Le Bourget) with a store at Villacoublay. Locations given at the end of some of the entries (eg 'Hall A', 'Gallery', 'O/S' - for Outside) are as noted during '88. The outside exhibits made their usual migration to the storage area for the duration of the 1989 Paris Salon, but very few have since returned to the museum proper. With the erection of a chain link fence across the museum apron it appears that there will be fewer exhibits outside in this area in future.

Aircraft with Ailes-Anciennes - Le Bourget are included in this list (and identified as such) as almost all are Musee de l'Air airframes anyway. The Ailes Anciennes organisations (see Introduction) spend a lot of their time on restoration projects for the Musee de l'Air.

AAC.1 (Ju 52/3m)	216	ex Aeronavale, painted as "334/DG" of GT.1/64, stored Dugny '85, to Rochefort for Aeronavale museum.
Ader Avion III	-	under restoration, ex Musee National des Techniques.
Ader Avion III	-	replica, ex Salis, Gallery.
Aero 3	40156	(F-AZEB, ex YU-DAJ) Ailes Anciennes.
Aerospatiale SA360	001	Dauphin prototype, expected.
Agusta-Bell 47G	40	ex F-YEEA DCAN, arr 27.10.87.
Agusta-Bell 47G	076	'TE' Hall E.
Air 102	"F-ZABY"	(possibly c/n 403) Hall E.
Air 102	F-CBHG	(c/n 27) stored.
Amiot homebuilt	-	arrived from Vaux de Cernay 8.85
Amiot 351	117	arrived from Vaux de Cernay 8.85
Arado 96B	-	'PD+EJ' ex Luftwaffe, recovered from Etang d'Aureilhan but subsequently corroded away.
Avia 15A	-	stored.
Avia 40P	-	Hall A.
Avro Lancaster B.7	WU-21	(ex NX664) recovered from Hihifo, Wallis Island, under restoration by Ailes Anciennes, Ile de France.
BAC/Sud Concorde	F-WTSS	(c/n 001) arr 19.10.73, O/S.
Beech JRB-4	44676	(ex N61909) '56S.18' stored Dugny '85.
Beech C-45	-	(FSDSF) stored at Dugny '85.
Beech C-45	-	stored at Villacoublay '85.
Beech JRB-4 (C-45)	44676	(ex N61909) "56S.18"

Bell 47G	710	ex Chambery
Bernard 191GR	F-AJGP	(c/n 02) Hall A.
Biot Massia	-	1879 vintage glider, Gallery.
Bleriot XI	-	ex Madame Bleriot, Gallery.
Bleriot XI	-	composite.
Bleriot XI-2	878	stored at Villacoublay '85.
Bleriot XI-2	686	'Pegoud', Gallery.
Bleriot XII	-	under restoration by Ailes Anciennes.
Bleriot XXXVI	-	fuselage only, stored.
Bleriot SPAD 54	F-AHBE	(c/n 8) Hall E.
Bloch MB.152	-	hulk recovered near Chateauroux.
Boeing B-17G Fortress	F-BGSO	(ex 44-8889) arr 8.9.76, ex IGN, O/S.
KC-97L Stratocruiser	53-0280	(ex N49549) ex Missouri ANG, arr '85, O/S.
Boeing PT-17	41-8860	ex USAF/Air Force Museum, arr 18.4.83, Hall E.
Boeing 707-328B	F-BLCD	(c/n 18941) ex Air France, arr 18.4.83, O/S.
Boeing 707	-	nose section, ex Air France.
Boisavia Mercurey	F-BIRE	(c/n 102) ex Cherence, stored at Villacoublay '85.
Breguet G.III	F-WFKC	"0" Hall C.
Breguet 19 Grand Raid	1685	Hall A.
Breguet 19 Super Bidon	-	Hall A.
Breguet 1001 Taon	02	ex Salon, 'E', O/S
Breguet Alize	10	ex 4F, O/S.
Breguet XIV.A2	2016	(ex F-WAHR) Gallery.
Breguet XIV.A2	-	
Breguet 900	-	static test airframe, stored.
Breguet 901	F-CAJA	Hall E.
Breguet 904.S	F-CAGU	(c/n 11) active at Bourges with Les Planeurs du Souvenir
Breguet 905 Fauvette	-	stored, arr 25.2.86.
Breguet 906 Choucas	F-CCGP	(c/n 01) stored.
Breguet 941S	4	ex '62-ND' ET.62, O/S.
Bristol Bolingbroke	9947	ex Belgium.
Brochet MB30/50	F-PHFI	(c/n 1) ex Etampes.
Brochet MB.83	F-BGLG	(c/n 7) stored at Villacoublay '85.
Bruhel-Duhamel-Molinari	F-WEPH	(c/n 01) stored.
Bu 181 Bestmann	"SV+NJ"	(c/n 330844, ex F-BBNA) Hall E.
Bu 181 Bestmann	F-WBYU	(c/n 53/144) stored.
CAP.20	1	ex 'VU' GI.312 (arr '89).
CASA 2.111	BR.21-129	ex Spanish AF, stored Dugny '85.
Castel C.24R	-	(c/n 4)
Castel C.25S	F-CRQR	(c/n 111) stored.
Castel C.25S	F-CREM	(c/n 164) under restoration.
Castel C.25S	F-CRMM	(c/n 194) stored.
Castel C.25S	F-CRFX	(c/n 203) stored.
Castel C.301S	F-CBYM	(c/n 1054) Hall E.
Castel C.301S	F-CBUO	(c/n 1078) stored.
Castel C.301S	F-CRBH	(c/n 1137) stored.
Castel C.310P	F-CRBS	(c/n 131) stored.
Castel C.311P	F-CAYN	(c/n 19) stored.
Caudron C.60	F-AINX	(c/n 6184) Hall E.
Caudron C.109	F-PFLN	(c/n 6192, ex F-AIQI) Hall A.
Caudron C.277 Luciole	F-AOFX	(c/n 7156/14) Hall E.
Caudron C.282 Phalene	F-AMKT	(c/n 6770)
Caudron C.366	-	Hall A.
Caudron C.510 Pelican	-	stored.
Caudron C.600 Aiglon	F-AZCO	(c/n P.3, ex F-BCEV) wreck.
Caudron C.600 Aiglon	F-PNZE	(c/n 64) ex Morlaix.
Caudron C.635 Simoun	"F-ANRO"	(c/n 428?, ex CS-ADG) Hall A.
Caudron C.713	7357/01	Ailes Anciennes.
Caudron C.714	8537/5	"CA-553" arr from Finland 18.1.83, Ailes Anciennes.

Caudron C.714R	01	Hall A.
Caudron C.800	F-CCCA	(c/n 261) stored.
Caudron C.800	334	ex Salon, Hall E.
Caudron C.801	-	stored.
Caudron G.III	324	Gallery.
Caudron G.IV	C-1720	Gallery.
Chanute 1896	-	replica, Gallery.
Cierva C.8L Mk.II	G-EBYY	Hall E.
Colomban MC10 Cri-Cri	F-PTXJ	(c/n 01) stored.
Croses Mini Criquet	F-PVQI	(c/n 01) Hall E.
Curtiss CW1 Junior	F-AZBR	(c/n 1089, ex N10907).
Dassault Falcon 20	F-WLKB	(c/n 01) O/S.
MD311 Flamant	-	(nose only) stored Villacoublay '85.
MD311 Flamant	280	ex GE.316, O/S.
MD315 Flamant	130	ex 'OF' CEV.
MD312 Flamant	156	(F-AZDY) ex CEV, located at Avignon '86.
MD312 Flamant	241	ex '319-CV' GE.319.
Dassault Hirondelle	F-WPXB	stored Dugny '85.
MD450 Ouragan	02	"2" ex Chambery.
MD450 Ouragan	154	painted as '4-LT' EC.4, ex 'UU' GE.314, Hall D.
Mystere IIC	52	ex '10-LF', reservation - located at Caen/Carpiquet.
Mystere IVA	01	Hall C.
Mystere IVA	48	ex Bordeaux/Merignac, Ailes Anciennes.
Mystere IVA	105	(ex '8-MZ' ET.1/8) painted as "289/2-EY" Hall D (see Aix/Les Milles).
Mystere IVA	210	(nose only) ex F-ZAGO CEV and BCRE.
Mystere IVA	245	ex '8-NN' ET.2/8, arr 25.4.80.
Mystere IVA	299	ex ET.1/8, arr 26.6.79, stored Dugny '85.
Mystere IVN	01	(F-ZXRM) ex Clermont-Ferrand/Aulnat.
Super Mystere B.2	11	ex '12-ZW' EC.2/12, thought to be the example displayed in Hall D as "153/12-YY", the real 153 being at Mont-De-Marsan.
Super Mystere B.2	59	ex '12-ZS' EC.2/12.
Mirage IIIA	01	ex CEV, arr 9.12.78, Hall C.
Mirage IIIC	7	ex '2-FD' ECT.2/2 (painted as "10-SC" EC.2/10) Dugny.
Mirage IIIC	70	ex Djibouti, expected here but see under Bordeaux.
Mirage IIIC	74	O/S
Mirage IIIC	87	stored.
Mirage IIIC	-	reservation
Mirage IIIR	334	ex '33-CC' ER.1/33, for Nancy/Essey.
Mirage IIIR	-	reservation
Mirage IIIV	01	Hall C.
Mirage IVA	02	O/S
Mirage IVA	9	'AH' reserved.
Mirage IVA	-	reserved, for Koblenz, WG.
Mirage IVA	-	reserved, for Elvington, UK.
Mirage F.1	02	expected (stored at Chateaudun 9.87).
Mirage G.8	01	Hall C.
Mirage 2000C	01	O/S
De Havilland DH.9	F1258	Gallery.
DH80A Puss Moth	F-ANRZ	(c/n 2151, ex CH-271)
DH82A Tiger Moth	"K2570"	(c/n 83097, ex R5238, G-ANRZ, OO-SOG) stored at Etampes.
DH89A Dragon Rapide	F-BHCD	(c/n 6706, ex HG721, G-ALGB) Hall E.
DH Vampire T.55	185	ex Irish Air Corps (arr 3.2.78, to Savigny-Les-Beaune).
DH Venom Mk.4	J-1636	ex Swiss AF.
Deperdussin B	-	built 1910, Gallery.
Deperdussin Monocoque	"334"	(c/n 934) Gallery.
Dewoitine D.7	16	ex Monsieur Dewoitine.
Dewoitine D.520	408	(F-ZWVB) painted as "90/2", crashed at Vannes 13.7.86.

Dewoitine D.520	603	painted as "277/6" of GC.III/6, ex Hall B, to Cambrai for restoration '88, current there 5.89.
Dewoitine D.520	862	painted as Aeronavale "AC.1", stored Dugny '85, to Rochefort for Aeronavale museum '89.
Dewoitine D.530	F-AJTE	(c/n 06) Hall A.
DFS Weihe 50	01	"F-CBGR" Hall E.
DFS 108-14 SG-38	"45"	(c/n 31) Hall E.
DFS 108-14 SG-38	173	Hall E.
DFS 108-30 Kranich	1399	stored at Etampes '88.
DFS 108-49 Grunau Baby	-	stored.
DFS 108-53 Habitsh II	"F-CAEX"	(c/n 1) Hall E.
DFS 108-70 Meise	F-CRBT	(c/n 12/259) Hall E.
DFS Weihe	F-CBGT	(c/n 3) under restoration at Angers with GPPA.
DFS Weihe	-	(c/n 42) stored.
DFS Weihe 50	-	(c/n 01)
DFS GP Zogling	-	(c/n SG.24) stored.
DFS 230 C1	36-16	ex 'H4+..' ex Chatillon en Diois, under restoration by Ailes Anciennes.
DFS 230 C1	-	ex 'H4+..' ex Vassieux en Vercors, wreck, Ailes Anciennes.
DFS 230 B2	-	ex 'H4+..' ex Chatillon en Diois (cockpit only), Ailes Anciennes.
Donnet Leveque A	-	Gallery.
Dornier Do 28B-1	3032	F-ZBBF ex Douanes Francaises.
Douglas C-47A Dakota	92449	(c/n 12551, ex 42-92449) ex 'FA', O/S.
Douglas C-47A Dakota	71	(c/n 12471, ex 42-92647) ex 56S, Aeronavale.
Douglas C-47B Dakota	49194	(c/n 15010/26455, nose only, ex 43-49194) ex GTLA.2/60, soc 16.7.70, Hall B.
Douglas DC-6B	45473	(nose only) ex '64-PL' ET.64, allocated N72534 but Ntu.
Douglas DC-7C-AMOR	45061	ex 'CA' CEV, O/S.
AD-4N Skyraider	126979	(SFERMA 53) ex 'MK' EdC.70, painted as "22-DD", arr 6.76.
Douglas A-26B Invader	39162	(c/n 6875, ex 41-39162) ex CEAM & Blois, stored Dugny '81-'85.
Douglas A-26B Invader	34773	(c/n 28052, ex 44-34773) ex 'N', stored Dugny '85.
EE Canberra B.6	763	ex 'AM' CEV, O/S.
Fabre Hydravion	01	Gallery.
Farman F.60 Goliath	F-HMFU	(c/n 2) fuselage only, Hall A.
Farman F.192	"F-AJJB"	(c/n 7248/4, F-BAOP) arr 4.4.60, Hall A.
Henri Farman HF-20	-	ex Belgian military, Gallery.
Farman F455 Moustique	F-AOYL	(c/n 01) Hall E.
Fauvel AV.22S	F-CCGK	(c/n 1) active at Angers with GPPA.
Fauvel AV-36	F-CRRB	(c/n 102) Hall E.
Fauvel AV-36	F-CBRX	(c/n 123) active.
Fauvel AV-36	-	stored.
Fauvel AV.45	F-CCHR	(c/n 02) stored.
Ferber 6 bis	-	replica, Gallery.
Fiat G-91R/3	9939	(c/n 515) ex FDG, WGAF, O/S.
Focke-Achgelis Fa 330	-	Hall B.
Focke-Achgelis Fa 330	-	stored.
Fokker D.VII	6796/18	Gallery.
CM170 Magister	23	on a pole at museum entrance (PdF colours).
CM170 Magister	26	ex '33-XE' ER.33/SALE, on a pole at museum entrance (PDF colours).
CM170 Magister	28	now front fuselage only (noted '89).
CM170 Magister	29	on a pole at museum entrance (PdF colours).
CM170 Magister	40	ex '12-XL' SALE/EC.12.
CM170 Magister	401	used by the BCRE (see Bureau Centrale etc entry).
CM170 Magister	-	for exchange.

CM170 Magister	-	for exchange.
CM170 Magister	-	exchanged in USA for NAA,64/BT-9.
CM173/Potez 94A	F-ZWWL	(c/n 01) loaned to Nancy museum.
Fouga CM8/13	F-CCHM	(c/n 01) stored.
Fournier RF-2	F-BJSY	(c/n 02) Hall E.
Gary Gyrocopter	F-WYDD	(c/n 01) Hall E.
Gasnier	"3"	Gallery (also reported on loan to GPPA, Angers, this is probably more recent information).
Gloster Meteor NF.11	NF11-5	ex CEV, arr 12.2.85, O/S.
Gloster Meteor NF.11	NF11-14	ex CEV, to Manching, WG, 6.5.87.
Gloster Meteor NF.11	NF11-24	(ex WM301) ex F-ZAGM of CEV
Gloster Meteor NF.13	NF13-365	ex CEV.
Gloster Meteor NF.14	NF14-747	ex CEV.
Gordou-Leseurre B-7	F-APOZ	(c/n 3) Hall A.
SA103 Emouchet	F-CRHB	(c/n 69) stored.
SA103 Emouchet	F-CROF	(c/n 94) stored.
SA104 Emouchet	F-CRPP	(c/n 106) stored.
SA104 Emouchet	F-CRLL	(c/n 253) Hall E.
Grassi	-	stored.
HFB320 Hansa Jet	1607	(c/n 1024) ex FBS, WGAF, arr 28.11.87 as 'F-WZIH', O/S.
Hanriot HD.14	F-AMBP	stored Villacoublay.
Hawker Hunter F.4	ID-44	ex BelgAF & Brussels Museum, to Savigny-Les-Beaune.
Heinkel He 46D	-	stored, ex Diors.
Heinkel He 162A	120223	'3' Hall B.
Henry Farman HF.20	-	Gallery.
Hiller UH.12B	158	ex ALAT, F-BEEF & Chambery.
Hirsch 100	F-WGVC	(c/n 01) arr 16.7.71, Hall C.
HA1112M-1L Buchon	C.4K-156	(c/n 156) ex '471-28' Spanish AF, Hall B.
Hurel Aviette	F-WTXS	man-powered aircraf.
Hurel-Dubois HD.10	F-BFAN	(c/n 01) Hall C.
Hurel-Dubois HD.34	F-BICR	(c/n 4) ex IGN, arr 22.6.78, O/S.
Jodel D9 Bebe	F-PEPF	(c/n 01) arr 12.62, Hall E.
Jodel D112	F-BFCG	(c/n 320) arr 6.86.
Jodel D119	F-PINS	(c/n 613) Hall E.
Junkers F.13	-	Hall A.
Junkers J.9D1	5998/18	Gallery.
Kellner-Bechereau E60	01	Hall A.
Lacroix 2LB7 Autoplan	01	(F-WFOQ) previously known as the Dumolard Autoplan.
Leduc 0.16	01	painted as Leduc 0.10 "03", arr 19.1.54, Hall C.
Leduc 0.22	"01"	(c/n 01 or 02) Hall C.
LeO C-302 Autogyro	F-BDAD	(c/n 15) Hall E.
Levavasseur Antoinette	-	Gallery.
Lilienthal glider	-	replica, built 1928.
L749 Constellation	2503	ex F-ZVMV CEV/ENSA, arr 17.7.75, O/S.
L1049 Constellation	N6931C	(c/n 4813) nose only, ex Guadeloupe.
F-104G Starfighter	2240	(c/n 7118) ex Jbg.34/LVR.1, WGAF, TT 3600 hrs (arr 14.10.86), O/S.
SP-2H Neptune	148335	ex 25F, arr 21.7.83, O/S.
F-5G Lightning	44-53247	(recce version of P-38) arr by C-5 26.5.89 in exchange for the Packard Lepere C2, ex Pima County, Tucson, AZ.
Lockheed T-33S-US	35055	(ex 53-5055) ex 'GC' CEV/EPNER, O/S.
Lockheed T-33S-US	35211	(ex 53-5211) ex CEV.
Lockheed T-33S-F	21029	(ex RCAF 21029) ex '314-YG' GE.314 (to Savigny-Les-Beaune).
Lockheed T-33S-C	21064	(ex RCAF 21064) supercritical wing test a/c, stored Dugny '85).
LVG C.VI	9041/18	Gallery.
B-26 Marauder	-	ex Air France Tech School, stored at Villacoublay
MATRA Cantiniau MC101	-	stored.

Mauboussin 121	F-AMHR	(c/n 3358) stored.
Maurice Farman MF.7	446	ex Belgian AF, under restoration.
MH1521 Broussard	07M	ex '11-OB' EC.11/SLVSV, arr 27.3.72 (stored at Villacoublay).
MH1521 Broussard	-	four examples due 1989, three for exchange.
MiG-15	-	ex Finnish AF.
Mignet HM-8	-	Hall E.
Mignet HM-8	-	stored.
HM14 Pou-du-Ciel	-	Hall A.
HM280 Pou-Maquis	-	
Morane A1	-	stored Villacoublay '85.
Morane type H	-	Gallery.
Morane MS.29-R1	1598	fuselage only, stored Villacoublay.
Morane MS.30	F-ABAO	(c/n 2283) Hall A.
Morane MS.30 (A-1)	F-AZAO	(c/n 03) replica, active at Etampes.
Morane MS149	F-AJFJ	(c/n 29) stored.
Morane MS230	F-BGMQ	(c/n 1048) Hall E.
Morane MS315	F-BCBR	(c/n 312) stored Villacoublay '85.
Morane MS317	F-BCNM	(c/n 6582/328) Hall E.
Morane MS406	J-277	(Swiss built as the D-3801) ex Swiss AF, Hall B.
MS472 Vanneau	122	(front fuselage only) ex Perigueux, Hall D.
MS472 Vanneau	254	ex Avord, stored Villacoublay '85
MS472 Vanneau	283	ex CET Jean-Mermoz, Bourges, stored at Villacoublay
Morane MS500 Criquet	"D-EMAW"	(c/n 1034) Hall B.
MS505 Criquet	F-BAOU	active at Angers.
MS505 Criquet	F-BBAT	(c/n 2039) under restoration by Ailes Anciennes.
MS505 Criquet	F-BCMD	(c/n 599) stored at Etampes.
MS733 Alcyon	F-BLXS	(c/n 114) ex St Yan.
MS760 Paris	-	expected.
MS880 Rallye	F-BJSF	(c/n 03) arr 26.5.77, Hall C/D.
MS1500 Epervier	01	ex Turbomeca, Pau.
Muynet M360 Jupiter	F-BLKE	(c/n 01) ex Toussus.
Nieuport 2N	-	Gallery.
Nieuport XI Bebe	976	Gallery.
Nieuport Delage 29.C1	N-1284S	(010) "R251" Hall A.
Nord 260	01	(nose only) ex 'GG' CEV, stored Dugny '85.
NC701 Martinet	-	(nose only) stored at Villacoublay '85.
NC702 Martinet	282	ex 'BN' CEV, stored at Villacoublay.
NC856A Norvigie	101	(ex F-BNAT) identity uncertain, ex St Cyr, Ailes Anciennes.
NC900 (Fw 190)	62/7298	(c/n 7298) Hall B.
N1002 Pingouin	F-BGZH	(c/n 135) stored.
N1101 Noralpha	135	ex 'LX' CEV, Hall D.
N1101 Noralpha	177	ex 'BQ' CEV, loaned Ailes-Anciennes - La Baule.
N1203 Norecrin	F-BICY	(c/n 373) arr 27.2.78, Hall C, to fly again.
Nord 1300	F-CRBZ	(c/n 26) stored.
Nord 1300	F-CREO	(c/n 40) stored.
Nord 1300	F-CRKX	(c/n 90) stored.
Nord 1300	F-CRQU	(c/n 159) stored.
Nord 1500 Griffon II	02	"I" Hall C.
Nord 2000	F-CBGB	(c/n 79/10409) Ailes Anciennes.
N2501 Noratlas	44	ex F-BZCK & Gyrafrance, Ailes Anciennes.
N2501 Noratlas	50	ex '64-BH' ET.3/64, to Aulnay Sous Bois '88.
N2501 Noratlas	157	expected.
N2501 Noratlas	162	replaced 50, O/S.
N2501 Noratlas	194	
Nord 3202	42	ex 'AIA', stored at Etampes.
Nord 3202	57	ex 'AYG' Hall E.
Nord 3202	67	ex 'AJC', stored at Etampes.

Nord 3202	92	now active as F-AZFL with Epsilon group at Escatalens.
Nord 3400	01	stored.
Nord 3400	99	ex 'JBW' Gendarmerie, stored at Etampes.
Nord 3400	108	ex 'JBY' Gendarmerie, stored at Etampes.
North American BT-9	N3415C	(c/n 2224) '415' arr '87 in exchange for a Magister.
TB-25N Mitchell	44-86701	(ex N7681C) painted as "151790", ex Dinard, stored Dugny '85.
P-51D Mustang	44-14291	ex 'CL-P', w/o 26.8.44, wreck only, recovered from Cap Ferret, with Ailes Anciennes.
P-51D Mustang	44-63871	(ex N9772F) painted as "466318/MO-C", Hall B.
T-6G Texan	-	Ailes Anciennes.
T-6G Texan	114522	(ex 51-14522) painted as "14915/RM", ex Cognac, Hall D.
T-6G Texan	114351	(ex 51-14351) ex '56', from Saintes.
F-86K Sabre	54841	(ex 55-4841) ex '13-PI' EC.13 & Colmar gate, Hall D.
F-100D Super Sabre	52736	(ex 55-2736) ex '11-MR', painted as "11-EF", Hall D.
Oemichen Helicostat	1	stored.
Oemichen Helicostat	2	stored.
Oemichen Helicostat	3	stored.
Oemichen Helicostat	6	
Oemichen Helicostat	7	stored.
Omnipol Aero 45	F-AZCL	(c/n 4927) active at Etampes.
Packard Lepere C2	SC42133	(c/n 6) to USA '89 in exchange for the F-5G (P-38).
Paul Schmidt 1915	-	fuselage only, stored Villacoublay '85.
Paumier 1912	-	Gallery.
Payen Pa.49 Katy	F-WGVA	(c/n 01) arr 3.6.67, Hall C.
Perrin Helicion III	-	stored Villacoublay.
Perrin Helicoptere III	-	stored Villacoublay.
Pescara F.3	3	stored.
Pfalz D.XII	3.173/140	Gallery.
Piel CP1310 Emeraude	F-BMJJ	(c/n 938) Hall E.
Piper J-3C Cub	-	Ailes Anciennes.
L-18 Super Cub	18-1430	(ex 51-15430) ex ALAT, painted as "N1957C", Hall E.
Polikarpov I-153	"9"	ex Soviet AF, Hall B.
Potez 36/13	F-ALQT	(c/n 2620) Hall A.
Potez 43/7	F-APXO	(c/n 3588) Hall E.
Potez 53	"10"	(c/n 3402) Hall A.
Potez 58/2	F-ANYA	(c/n 3875) stored.
Potez 60	F-PVQB	(c/n 1) active at Angers with GPPA.
Potez 842	F-BNAN	(c/n 3) O/S.
RAF BE.2C	9969	Gallery.
Renard	-	replica, stored.
REP type D	-	built 1910, displayed without fabric, Gallery.
REP type K	-	Gallery.
F-84E Thunderjet	9600	(ex 49-0600) "9654/3N-W" due from Nimes/Courbessac '90.
F-84F Thunderstreak	28875	(ex 52-88750, IRAN No 727) ex '4-VA', Hall D.
RF-84F Thunderflash	FR-33	(ex 53-7658) expected from Saffraanberg, Belgium.
F-105G Thunderchief	63-8300	under restoration by Ailes Anciennes, Ile de France.
P-47D Thunderbolt	44-20371	Hall B.
SAAB J 29B Tunnan	29665	ex Swedish AF, stored at Villacoublay.
SAAB J 35B Draken	35069	ex '36' F 16, Swedish AF, O/S.
SAAB 91 Safir	F-BHAK	(c/n 91-299) identity uncertain, stored at Toussus.
Santos-Dumont 14bis	-	replica
S-D Demoiselle	-	Gallery.
S-D Demoiselle	-	replica, stored.
S-D Demoiselle	-	replica, stored.
Ka2 Rhonschwalbe	-	(c/n 33) ex AdlA, stored.
Ka6 Rhonsegler	-	(c/n 333) stored.
Schreck FBA	F-AJOR	(c/n 195) Hall A.
SEPECAT Jaguar A	A04	ex 'E' CEAM, O/S.

Short Sandringham 7	F-OBIP	(c/n SH-57C) arr 3.11.78, stored Dugny '85.
Sikorsky H-19D	55-864	(c/n 55-864) stored, appeared at Le Luc show 6.89.
Sikorsky H-34	SA53	ex CEV/EPNER, stored Villacoublay.
Sikorsky H-34A	SA101	ex '68-ON' EH.68, stored Dugny.
Sikorsky HSS-1	121	(c/n SA121) ex 'Y' 31F, stored Dugny.
Siren C-34	F-CCAY	(c/n 02) Hall E.
SNECMA Atar Volant	-	"Z" Hall C.
Sopwith 1A2	556	"1263" (built by Liore et Olivier) Gallery.
SPAD VII	254	mount of the French ace Guynemer, Gallery.
SPAD VII	-	fuselage only.
SPAD XIII.C1	S-15295	Gallery.
SPAD-Herbemont 52	3125	Hall A.
Stampe SV4C	1084	'84' ex Chartres store.
Stampe SV4C	F-BBQL	(c/n 149) Hall E.
Stampe SV4A	F-BMMJ	(c/n 691) Ailes Anciennes, may have gone to the Aeronavale museum at Rochefort as "51S.15".
SUC.10 Courlis	F-BEKH	(c/n 31) under restoration with Ailes Anciennes.
Sud Fennec (T-28)	17491	(ex 51-7491, SFERMA 121) ex Saintes, to be restored by M Calvet of the group Orion.
Sud Ludion	-	Hall C.
SA3210 Super Frelon	01	'F-ZWWE' Hall C.
SA321J Super Frelon	01	expected.
SE Alouette II	329	(c/n 1703) ex '341-RO' CIEH.341, arr 27.1.87.
SE Aquilon 203	53	ex '16F.16' 16F and preservation at Lorient. Under restoration with Ailes Anciennes.
SE210 Caravelle	F-BHHI	(c/n 02) nose only, Hall C.
SE210 Caravelle III	F-BJTR	(c/n 22) ex Air France, arr 29.12.80, O/S.
SE210 Caravelle III	141	(FRAFG) ex GLAM, arr 28.3.80, O/S.
SE212 Durandal	01	stored at Villacoublay.
SE535 Mistral	4	ex '7-CE' EC.7, arr 19.2.63, Hall D.
SE3101	F-WFDQ	(c/n 01) Hall E.
SE5000 Baroudeur	3	ex 'V', recovered from Cazaux ranges, under restoration with Ailes Anciennes.
SO30P Bretagne	18	ex 'BI' CEV & La Roche Sur Yon, stored Dugny '79-'85.
SO1110 Ariel II	F-WFRQ	(c/n 01) Hall C.
SO1220 Djinn	F-WGVD	(c/n 02) Hall C.
SO1221S Djinn	FR101	ex 51 ALAT, stored.
SO4050 Vautour IIN	330	ex '30-ML' ECTT.2/30, O/S.
SO4050 Vautour IIB	634	ex EdR.05/106, stored Dugny.
SO6000 Triton	03	(with parts of 05/F-WFKX) "F-WFKY" Hall C.
SO9000 Trident	01	ex 'Y' Hall C.
Spitfire IX	BS464	"GW-S" 340 Sqn marks, to Cambrai '88.
Spitfire XVI	RR263	"GW-B" 340 Sqn marks, painted as "TB597", Hall B.
SZD-24 Foka	F-CCHX	(c/n W-150) Hall E.
Vertol H-21C	FR69	ex Montauban, stored Villacoublay.
"Villa"	-	stored.
VMA.200 Milan (Weihe)	F-CBGR	(c/n 30)
Voisin 1907	-	replica built 1919, Gallery.
Voisin LA5.B2	-	Gallery.
Vuia 1906	-	Gallery.
Wassmer WA21 Javelot	58	ex 'XO', stored.
WA22A Super Javelot	114	ex 'XB', stored.
Wassmer WA51 Pacific	F-BPTT	(c/n 01) Hall E.
Westland Lysander	-	ex Belgium, stored Dugny.
Wright Baby	-	Gallery.
Wright Flyer	-	replica, Gallery.

Yakovlev Yak-3	"4"	ex Soviet AF, Hall B.
Zeppelin C.IV	01	stored Villacoublay.
Zlin 326	F-BNMU	(c/n 910) active at Etampes.
Zlin 326	F-BORT	(c/n 923) Hall E.

PARIS/ORLY (94)

Preserved by the terminal here were SE210-3 Caravelle prototype F-BHHH (c/n 01, arrived 6.66) and Concorde prototype F-WTSA (c/n 02, arrived 22.5.76, Air France colours). The Caravelle was scrapped during late 10.86 much to the consternation of French preservationists. By 2.89 the Concorde was parked by the side of the RN7 on the South side of the airport with ex Corse Air SE210 Caravelle VI-N F-BVPZ (c/n 218). Both are now part of the Athis Aviation museum founded by Roland Payen. He hopes to set up a museum of delta winged aircraft and is building a Payen Pa.100 replica.

PARIS/VILGENIS (91)

The Centre d'Instruction de Vilgenis (Air France Technical School) is located West of Orly airport on the D120 between Massy and Vilgenis. The following airframes have been used for instructional purposes over the last few years. The aircraft are kept inside and the premises are not accessible to the casual visitor.

Boeing 707-328	F-BHSL	(c/n 17919) ex Air France (noted '77-'85).
Lockheed T-33S-US	16520	(ex 51-6520) ex '338-HC' CEVSV.338 (noted '82-'85).
Lockheed T-33S-US	16524	(ex 51-6524) ex '3-KB' EC.3/SLVSV (noted '82-'85, to St Dizier).
Lockheed T-33S-US	16525	(ex 51-6525) ex 'WN' CIFAS.328 (noted '82-'85).
Lockheed T-33S-US	18693	(ex 51-8693) ex '13-TF' EC.13/SLVSV (noted '81-'85).
Lockheed T-33S-US	29867	(ex 52-9867) ex '314-WL' GE.314 or '338-HO' CEVSV.338 (noted '81-'85).
Lockheed T-33S-US	35339	(ex 53-5339) ex '12-XC' EC.12/SLVSV (noted '82-'85).
AT-6C Texan	F-BJBJ	(c/n 88-12046) (noted '68-'85).
AT-6D Texan	F-BJBH	(c/n 88-15778) (noted '68-'85).
T-6G Texan	114387	(ex 51-14387) to Etampes.
T-6G Texan	114401	(ex 51-14401) ex 'DI' & Merville (noted '78-'86)
T-6G Texan	114674	(ex 51-14674) to Chavenay by '82
SAAB Safir	F-BHAH	(c/n 91-296) (noted '83-'85 under restoration).
SAAB Safir	F-BHAJ	(c/n 91-298) (noted '83-'85, spares source).
SE210 Caravelle III	F-BHRA	(c/n 1) wfu 19.12.75 (noted '76-'85).
SE210 Caravelle III	F-BJTO	(c/n 148) nose & tail only (noted '82-'85).

PAU/UZEIN (64)

The preservation group Squadron 64 have the following on display here.

MD312 Flamant	177	(F-AZEL) ex '319-DU' GE.319 (noted '87-'89).
Mirage IIIR	310	ex '33-TF' ER.3/33 (noted '86-'89).
Super Mystere B.2	173	ex '12-YP' EC.1/12 & Merville (noted '89).
CM170 Magister	14	(noted '87-'89).
N2501 Noratlas	193	ex '328-..' CIFAS.328 & Chateaudun (noted '88-'89).
Sud Alouette II	258	(c/n 1505) ex '341-RL' CIEH.341 (noted '87-'89).

On the dump on the military side, MH1521 Broussard 159/118-IV (ex CEAM) appeared during '85 and was still current in '86.

N2501 Noratlas 161 (ex '64-IM' ET.1/64, noted '81-'89) is displayed at the ETAP.

PERPIGNAN (66)

Former AdLA pilot Charles Noetinger keeps an interesting collection of aircraft (the Musee d'Avions du Mas Palegry) at his vineyard here in the hamlet of Mas-Palegry (5kms South of Perpignan just East of the RN114).

Boyer BF.01	F-PMXM	(c/n 01) 'Le Pezoul'
Caudron C.800	F-CBXF	(c/n 192)
Caudron C.275 Luciole	F-PPHO	(c/n 7496/20)
DH Vampire FB.5	VX950	ex Rochefort and Kerneis' scrapyard, Laz, arr 5.76
CM170 Magister	05	ex Cognac.

MS505 Criquet	-	derelict.
Morane MS603	F-PHJC	(c/n 1) fuselage only, the rest at Pont s/Yonne.
MS733 Alcyon	F-BMQG	(c/n 101)
F-84E Thunderjet	-	cockpit section.
RF-84F Thunderflash	11928	(ex 51-1928, tail from 52-7457) "3-43", ex ItAF.

The serial 51-9572 has been suggested for the F-84E though this is the identity of the front fuselage section at Savigny-Les-Beaune. Perhaps it has moved - confirmation? See also under Cazaux.

PERPIGNAN/LLABANERE (66)

Perpignan has housed many derelicts over the years, mostly around the EAS maintenance base from whence a few have escaped back to active use.

Dornier Do 27Q-5	F-BKVT	(c/n 2062) (noted '85-'87).
Dornier Do 28A-1	F-BGYT	(c/n 3042, ex D-IBEV, F-OBYT) (under restoration'85-'87).
Dornier Do 28A-1	F-BHZZ	(c/n 3038, ex D-IBOD, F-OBZZ) (stored '77-'87).
HP Herald 210	F-BLOY	(c/n 173, ex G-ASPJ, HB-AAK, F-OCLY) (stored '78-'88, to G-SCTT).
HP Herald 210	F-BOIZ	(c/n 188, ex HB-AAL, F-OCLZ) (stored '78-'88, to G-STVN).
HP Herald	F-BVFP	(c/n 191, ex PP-SDL, G-BDZV) (noted '84-'87).
SE210 Caravelle VI-N	F-BXOO	(c/n 76, ex OO-SRF) (noted '84-'87).
SE210 Caravelle VI-N	F-GBMJ	(c/n 149, ex LV-PVU, LV-HGZ, ArgAF TC-92, N46SB) (noted '84-'87).
SE210 Caravelle VI-N	F-BYCA	(c/n 66) (fuselage noted '87).
SE210 CAravelle 10B3	F-GFBA	(c/n 243, ex F-WJAM, D-ABAV) (noted '87).
Vanguard 953F	TR-LZA	(c/n 715, ex G-APEL, F-BYCF ntu) (noted '86, to F-GEJF Intercargo Service by '87).
Vanguard 953F	F-BYCE	(c/n 716, ex G-APEM) (noted '79-'86, returned to service by '87 with Air Bridge Carriers as G-APEM).
Vanguard 952	F-BXAJ	(c/n 725, ex CF-TKB, TF-JES, G41-1-72, G-AYFN) (noted '79-'87).
Vanguard 952F	G-AZRE	(c/n 729, ex CF-TKF) allocated F-BXOF (noted '75-'87).
Vanguard 952F	TR-LBA	(c/n 730, ex CF-TKG, G-AYLD, SE-FTH, G-AYLD, F-BUFT) (noted'82-'86, to F-GEJE with Intercargo Service by'87).
Vanguard 952	G-AXNT	(c/n 737, ex CF-TKN) (noted '79-'87).
Vanguard 952	F-BXOG	(c/n 739, ex CF-TKP, G-BAFK, PK-MVR, G-BAFK) (noted '80-'87).
Vanguard 952	F-BVRZ	(c/n 741, ex CF-TKR, F-OCUB) (noted '80-'87).
Vanguard 952	PK-MVH	(c/n 746, ex F-BTOV) ex Merpati Nusantara, arr '87.

PEZENAS/NIZAS (34)

The Aero Club de Pezenas-Nizas received MD315R Flamant 66/30-QW (ex ECTT.12/30, soc 14.9.72) for display. It was still current during 1.87. Morane-Saulnier MS317 F-BCBC (c/n 323) was wfu here by 7.88 but has since gone to Ailes Anciennes - Toulouse. The aerodrome is 5kms North of the town amid a maze of minor roads.

PHALSBOURG (67)

Preserved here at the time of the Open Day in 6.89 was a Sikorsky H-19 (or Westland Whirlwind with no visible c/n but wearing the spurious code "MST" with the previous code 'APY' showing through the paint. It used to be displayed by the main gate here many years ago.

Withdrawn from use here by 6.89, with long grass growing round it, was MH1521 Broussard 38/MJC.

PLASSAC (17)

Monsieur Francis Bouyer's car dismantlers yard (on the RN137 South of Saintes) was visited in 6.87 and held the hulk of a Djinn together with Sikorsky H-34A SA91/"P-96" (last reported at Saintes 10.86) though with the fuselage marked "P-99" and "P-96" appearing on the rear fuselage. If anyone has the opportunity to inspect this airframe closely, confirmation of its identity would be appreciated.

PLOENIS (29)
Serving as an attraction at the "Le Moulin" discotheque here (near Quimper) is ex Air France L1049 Super Constellation F-BHBG (c/n 4626, current 8.87). The aircraft is in poor condition and has been painted in inaccurate Air France colours.

POITIERS (86)
The Chez Manuel museum is on the RN10 1km North of the Poitiers Nord exit on the A10 autoroute. Sikorsky HSS-1 142 (ex 31F & Rochefort/Soubise) is here (noted '86) with an anonymous SNCASO SO1221 Djinn .

The Armee de Terre caserne in the town has the fuselage of N2501 Noratlas 23 (ex '312-BE' GI.312) which came from Chateaudun (noted '83-'85).

PONS/AVY (17)
Abandoned outside a hangar here during 8.87 were Cessna F150M F-BVXY (c/n 1155, current 8.88), MS893E Rallye 180GT F-GACG (c/n 12702, current 8.88), Gardan GY80-160 Horizon F-BLPZ (c/n 65, current 8.88) and an anonymous Jodel D112. The latter might be F-PHQS (c/n 468) which was stored here during '86.

The wrecked fuselage of Cessna F172H F-BOQC (c/n 0446) was here in 8.88.

PONT D'AIN (01)
The fuselage of Sud Fennec (T-28) 51-7692 (SFERMA No 142) lay atop a roof at a camp site here (noted '85). By 1.87 the same location had MS733 Alcyon F-BLYC (c/n 96) following an exchange with the preservation group Alcyons '86 who carried off the Fennec to Villeneuve sur Lot. Later on, the Fennec went to the Orion group.

PONTOISE/CORMEILLES (95)
The fuselages of Beech 35-33 Debonair F-BJOG (c/n CD-208) and MS880B Rallye Club F-BONV (c/n 861) were stored in the Aero Club hangar during '87.

POURVILLE-SUR-MER (76)
The Musee du Aout 19, just along the coast South of Dieppe, has NC856 Norvigie 94/AGM (ex ALAT) preserved inside the windowless building (noted '86).

PRECIGNE (72)
Stored at a farm here (Ferme de la Grande Hiltiere) is a Pou-du-Ciel (built at Montelimar in 1937) with a Monsieur Neveu (noted '87-'89).

REAUX (17)
Monsieur Michaud has GY80 Horizon F-BGMF (c/n 107, ex Jonzac) in store (noted '87).

REDON (35)
The Aero Club Redonnais received MD312 Flamant 217 (ex '319-CJ' GE.319) on 12.6.82 and maintained it in airworthy (but unflown) condition. In 7.88 the aircraft left for Lons for the preservation group Air Memorial.

REIMS (51)
Displayed at the Centre de Controle Aerienne (ATC Centre) is MD312 Flamant 215 (ex '319-DP' GE.319) (noted '84-'87).

The Musee St Remy in the city received an MH1521M Broussard on 16.1.89 (they were built at Reims/Prunay).

REIMS/CHAMPAGNE (51)
The gate at Base Aerienne 112 is guarded by Vautour IIN 347/30-FB ex ECTT.3/30. It was officially dedicated on 8.6.74 and was still current in '88.

On the dump, the fuselage of an MD312 Flamant coded '319-DH' (probably 248) was ceremonially burnt at the '81 Open Day. The firemen have also had the benefit of F-84F Thunderstreak 28769/1-NQ (ex 52-8769, minus rear fuselage, noted '77-'87). The compiler has need of a photo of this airframe if anyone can oblige.

The wreck of ex EC.3/30 Mirage F.1C 46/30-FO (crashed 3.4.85) was lying by some buildings on the base in 6.86.

REIMS/PRUNAY (51)

TB10 Tobago F-GBHY (c/n 41) was lying dismantled here during 10.88 pending a decision on its future (it crash landed in a field on 15.6.88 having run out of fuel). At the same time, Campbell Cricket F-WSYR/"1451" was partially dismantled and seemingly forgotten.

RENNES/ST JACQUES (35)

The fuselage of N2501 Noratlas 187 (ex '64-IS' ET.1/64) had arrived in the ALAT area of the airport by 1983. It appears to be in use for paratroop training and was still current during 4.89.

Two of the ex Swiss AF EKW C-3605s from the sale at Lodrino in 12.87 have gravitated here. They are C-493/F-AZGC and C-550/F-AZGD both being noted during 3.89.

RIEUMAJOU (31)

Noratlas 201 landed at Castelnaudary on 10.3.87 for road transport to this micro-light airfield as a club house. It may never appear here having since been registered as F-GFLJ with Association Miss Pacifique who may succeed in returning her to airworthiness.

RION-DES-LANDES (40)

Nord 1002 282 (F-AZBX reserved) was noted during 7.87 undergoing a lengthy restoration with Monsieur Faugere.

ROANNE (42)

Air France SE210 Caravelle III F-BHRF (c/n 12) arrived here on 6.6.81 for preservation (current '87).

ROCAMADOUR (46)

On the gate at BA607 in 1981 were MD311 Flamant 288 (ex '316-KP' GE.316, soc 25.5.78), Mystere IVA 182 (ex Rochefort) and CM170 Magister 21 (also ex Rochefort). By 1985 the Army had taken over the base and the Flamant had disappeared, probably for scrap, the Mystere had moved to Toulouse/Lhers and only the Magister remained.

ROCHEFORT (17)

Near the railway station, between the railway line and a disused dock, is a large scrapyard which has dealt with a few aircraft from the bases at Soubise and St Agnant. Recorded here on a couple of visits in '85 and '86 were the following.

MD312 Flamant	65	fuselage, identity unconfirmed.
MD312 Flamant	302	fuselage, ex Soubise.
Mirage IIIC	..	remains of a blue/grey example.
CM170M Esquif	01	fuselage, ex Soubise.
N2501 Noratlas	14	wreck, ex Soubise.

ROCHEFORT/SOUBISE (17)

Rochefort was the joint AdlA/Aeronavale technical training school until 1978 when the AdlA opted out and set up its own organisation at the newly constructed BA721 Rochefort/St Agnant just down the road. AdlA airframes then in use were either scrapped or transferred to the new base. Since the split, the following ground instructional airframes have been noted here with the CEAN (<u>Centre Ecole de l'Aeronautique Navale</u>).

Beech JRB-4 (C-45)	66425	'425' (noted '78-'88, to museum).
Beech JRB-4 (C-45)	85104	'4' (noted '78-'80, to Lorient).
Beech JRB-4 (C-45)	134709	'709' (noted '78-'86, to museum).
Breguet Alize	04	(noted '72-'83).
Breguet Alize	3	ex 6F (noted '76-'88).
Breguet Alize	4	(noted '80-'88).

Breguet Alize	5	to Nimes/Garons by '82.
Breguet Alize	8	ex 3S (noted '78-'87, preserved by HQ block '88).
Breguet Alize	15	ex 6F (noted '80-'88, to museum).
Breguet Alize	21	ex 4F (noted '80-'88).
Breguet Alize	40	(noted '80-'88).
Etendard IVM	01	(noted '78-'88).
Etendard IVM	03	(noted '72-'87 - but also reported scrapped).
Etendard IVM	05	(noted '78-'88, to museum).
Etendard IVM	06	(noted '78-'88).
Super Etendard	02	(arr 4.81, current '88).
MD312 Flamant	294	ex 11S (noted '78-'88, to museum).
C-47 Dakota	716	(c/n 33448, ex 44-77116) ex 56S (noted '85-'88, to museum).
CM170M Esquif	01	to the scrapyard in the town by 1980.
CM170M Esquif	02	(noted '78-'87).
CM175 Zephyr	1	(noted '86-'88, to museum).
CM175 Zephyr	10	(noted '78-'88).
CM175 Zephyr	20	(noted '88).
CM175 Zephyr	24	(noted '86-'88).
SP-2H Neptune	144688	(noted '80-'88, to museum).
MS760 Paris	31	ex SLD (noted '78-'88).
N2501 Noratlas	14	ex '340-VE' CIET.340 (noted dumped '80, to the scrapyard in Rochefort town).
SNJ-5 Texan	3820	'820' (noted '78-'88, to museum).
Sikorsky H-34A	7	(c/n 58-1007/SA50) (noted '80, to Lanveoc/Poulmic).
Sikorsky HSS-1	135	(c/n SA135) ex 31F (noted '80-'87).
Sikorsky HSS-1	140	(c/n SA140) (noted '80).
Sikorsky HSS-1	148	(c/n SA148) ex 33F (noted '80-'87).
Sikorsky HSS-1	150	(c/n SA150) ex 31F (noted '80-87, to museum).
Sikorsky HSS-1	512	(c/n 58-512) ex 20S (noted '78-'87).
Sikorsky HSS-1	640	(c/n 58-640) ex 20S (noted '80-'87).
Sikorsky HSS-1	641	(c/n 58-641) ex 33F (noted '80, to St Rambert d'Albon).
Sikorsky HSS-1	688	(c/n 58-688) ex 33F (noted '80-'87).
Vought F-8A Crusader	143719	"01" (noted '78-'85, relegated to dump by 6.86).
F-8E(FN) Crusader	16	(arr 6.86, current '87).
F-8E(FN) Crusader	-	(arr '86, current '87).
Westland WG13 Lynx	XX904	"03", ex Frejus/St Raphael (noted '87-'88).

The wreck of CAP.10B 107 was lying by the 51S area during '88 following its crash at St Junien.

After a long gestation period, the Musee de Tradition de l'Aeronautique Navale was officially opened on 30.9.88 (though not to the public as yet) with the following aircraft on display most of which have been drawn from the local stock of ground instructional airframes.

AAC.1 (Ju 52)	216	expected from Musee de l'Air.
Beech JRB-4 (C-45)	25	(ex 66425)
Beech C-45	709	(ex 134709)
Breguet Alize	15	stored.
Caudron C.800	F-CAFB	(c/n 215)
Etendard IVM	05	
MD312 Flamant	294	ex 11S
Dewoitine D.520	862	loan from Musee de l'Air.
C-47 Dakota	716	(c/n 33448, ex 44-77116) ex 56S .
CM175 Zephyr	1	
SP-2H Neptune	144688	ex 24F.
MH1521 Broussard	258	ex 'CAN-16' DCAN.
Nord 2200	01	ex Vannes/Meucon.
T-6 Harvard II	820	(c/n 3820)
SEPECAT Jaguar M	M-05	'J' ex Rochefort/St Agnant.
Sikorsky HSS-1	150	
SE Aquilon 203	53	ex Le Bourget (restored by Ailes Anciennes).

ROCHEFORT/ST AGNANT (17)

This new base was completed in 1978 following the AdlA decision to withdraw from the joint AdlA/Aeronavale technical training facility at Soubise and to go its own way. Some airframes retain their former unit markings whilst others have gained local codes based on the Base Aerienne number (BA721). Training airframes noted here since the base's inception are as follows.

MD312 Flamant	163	ex '319-CN' GE.319 (noted '80-'83).
MD312 Flamant	196	ex '319-DZ' GE.319 (noted '84-'86).
MD312 Flamant	203	ex '319-CY' GE.319 (noted '84-'86).
MD312 Flamant	239	ex '319-DN' GE.319 (noted '80-'83, to Toulouse/Francazal dump by '84).
MD312 Flamant	246	ex '319-DT' GE.319 (noted '80-'84).
Mystere IVA	118	preserved on base (noted '78-'87).
Super Mystere B.2	13	"136" '21-HG' painted in Tiger c/s as per the original 136. Ex '12-YH' EC.1/12 (noted '80-'82, to Captieux?).
Super Mystere B.2	22	'21-BU' ex '12-YE' EC.1/12 (noted '80-'84).
Super Mystere B.2	48	'21-BT' ex '12-YM' EC.1/12 (noted '80, to Toulouse).
Super Mystere B.2	54	'21-FD' ex '12-YD' EC.1/12 (noted '80-'83, to Narbonne).
Super Mystere B.2	55	'21-LI' ex '12-YU' EC.1/12 (noted '78-'87, preserved on base).
Super Mystere B.2	72	'21-LM' ex '12-YO' EC.1/12 (noted '80-'83, to Montpellier).
Super Mystere B.2	74	'21-CP' ex '12-YS' EC.1/12 (noted '80-'84).
Super Mystere B.2	77	'21-LJ' ex '12-YW' EC.1/12 (noted '80-'84).
Super Mystere B.2	85	'21-HL' ex '12-YF' EC.1/12 (noted '80-'84).
Super Mystere B.2	99	'21-LH' ex '12-YJ' EC.1/12 (noted '80-'83,to Savigny-En-Septaine).
Super Mystere B.2	109	'21-CN' ex '12-YL' EC.1/12 (noted '80-'81).
Super Mystere B.2	111	'21-HO' ex '12-YR' EC.1/12 (noted '80-'84).
Super Mystere B.2	112	'21-GR' ex '12-YC' EC.1/12 (noted '80-'83).
Super Mystere B.2	113	'21-RB' ex '12-YO' EC.1/12 (noted '80-'84, to Nancy/Essey).
Super Mystere B.2	124	'21-LC' ex '12-YX' EC.1/12 (noted '80-'82, to Bordeaux).
Mirage IIIC	1	ex '10-SA' EC.1/10 (noted '78-'86).
Mirage IIIC	5	ex '10-RC' EC.2/10 (noted '78-'84).
Mirage IIIC	8	ex '2-FB' ECT.2/2 (noted '80-'82, to Bruz).
Mirage IIIC	32	ex '10-RE' EC.2/10 (noted '82-'86).
Mirage IIIC	46	(noted '78-'84).
Mirage IIIC	55	ex '10-RN' EC.2/10 (noted '86).
Mirage IIIE	429	ex '2-LO' EC.3/2 (noted '86).
Mirage IIIE	454	ex '13-QD' (noted '86).
Mirage IIIE	563	ex '4-BK' EC.2/4, w/o 4.6.71 (noted '80-'86).
Mirage IIIR	319	ex '33-NR' ER.2/33 (noted '84).
Mirage IIIR	321	ex '33-CJ' ER.1/33 (noted '84).
Mirage IIIR	337	(nose only) ex '33-CF' ER.1/33, w/o 6.2.70 (noted '78-'84).
Mirage IIIR	343	ex '33-CP' ER.1/33 (noted '84-'86).
Mirage IIIR	345	ex '33-CN' ER.1/33 (noted '84-'86).
Mirage IIIT	01	Preserved at main gate (noted '78-'89).
CM170 Magister	36	ex 'AV' (noted '80-'86 - but see Chateaudun).
CM170 Magister	162	(noted '84-'86).
CM170 Magister	165	(noted '84-'86).
CM170 Magister	166	ex '10-KK' EC.10/SALE (noted '84-'86).
CM170 Magister	222	ex '315-IM' GE.315 (noted '84-'86).
CM170 Magister	332	(noted '84-'86).
CM170 Magister	349	(noted '84-'86).
N2501 Noratlas	10	ex '340-VD' CIET.340 (noted '78, since scrapped).
N2501 Noratlas	122	ex '63-WD' ET.63 (noted '82-'87).
SEPECAT Jaguar E	E02	ex FZWRC/BAe Warton (arr 7.6.80, current '86).

SEPECAT Jaguar M	M05	ex FZWRJ, (noted '80-'86, to Musee de l'Aeronautique Navale).
Alouette II	62	(c/n 1067) ex Aeronavale, frame only (noted '80).
Alouette II	89	(c/n 1111) (noted '80).
Transall C-160	V1	ex 'DK' CEV (noted '80-'89).

RODEZ (12)

MD312 Flamant 232 had arrived from Chateaudun by 8.87 for preservation at the aerodrome (current 8.88). Stored here in 8.88 was crash damaged AA1B Trainer F-BUUT (c/n 0332).

ROMANS-SUR-ISERE (26)

Preservation group Aero Phoenix are based at the aerodrome (4 kms North east of the town on the N92).

With their collection are the following.

MD311 Flamant	290	ex '316-KL' GE.316 (noted '80-'86).
NC702 Martinet	350	ex 'PR' CEV, ex St Martin d'Hostun.
Pilatus P2-05	U-106	(F-AZCG, c/n 26) ex Swiss AF.

The fuselage of prototype MS890B Commodore F-BJSG (c/n 01) lay dismantled in a hangar here during 9.87.

The preservation group Amicale Romanaise d'Aviation Ancienne is based here but all their aircraft are now airworthy and thus well beyond the scope of this volume.

ROMILLY-SUR-SEINE (10)

Under restoration here in 1.87 were Brochet MB.83 F-BGLA and Larrieu JL2 F-PHQH whilst the fuselage of Robin HR200 F-BUQM (c/n 09, ex Meaux) was in store.

ROMORANTIN/PRUNIERS (41)

This airfield houses the AdlA depot EAA.602 which has MD450 Ouragan 297/UG (ex GE.314) preserved outside the Head Quarters block (noted '78-'89). Mirage IIIR 331/33-TK (ex ER.3/33) was out on the airfield by 6.85 and has since been preserved near the main gate (current 4.89).

A couple of Broussards were dumped here in '82/'83 but had gone by 6.85. One was 128 whilst the other was never identified but was coded 'X-' (possibly 'XB' or 'XG') and may well be ex EC.12.

On the civil side, Zlin Z326 Trener-Master F-BMQU (c/n 900) was gathering dust in 8.87. Stored on their noses were Jodel D112s F-BHYX (c/n 555), F-BNCT (c/n 1317) (both since to Tours/Sorigny) and the wreck of Jodel DR250/160 F-BMZJ (c/n 11).

ROUEN (76)

Outside some military offices in the Rue Louis Blanc sits N2501 Noratlas 24 (ex '312-BJ' GI.312) (arr 9.82, current '87).

ROUEN/BOOS (76)

Stored here in 1.87 was GY80 Horizon 180 F-BNYQ (c/n 191)

ROUEN/GRAND QUEVILLY (76)

The Parc des Loisirs in this Rouen suburb contained MD315 Flamant 58/118-IS (ex CEAM, soc 25.9.72) for many years. Following considerable vandalism and the ravages of time it was declared unsafe and scrapped between 9.84 and 6.85.

SAINTE-ADRESSE (76)

In 1983 a Vertol H-21C was reported in a fort here (a western suburb of Le Havre).

ST BRIEUC (22)

C-47A Dakota F-GESB (c/n 13835, ex 43-30684, NC88732, N48V, Aeronavale 35) was stored at the new airfield here (noted 9.86) whilst DC-3 F-BHKX was languishing on the old airfield, now disused, at the same time.

ST CHAMOND (42)

Noted here during 8.88 were the wrecked fuselage of crashed Piper PA18-95 Super Cub F-BKRU (c/n 18-1456, ex 51-15456) and the hulk of MS880B Rallye Club F-BOVN (c/n 1111) being stripped for spares. Both were still current in 7.89 when Jodel D112 F-PJXR (c/n 1107) was on rebuild with MS880B Rallye F-BSCN (c/n 1577) awaiting its turn. Stored in the roof is a Chanute glider built by the airfield owner when he was a teenager.

ST CYRAN DU JAMBOT (36)

A Mignet HM.14 and HM.290 were reported in store here with Monsieur Turmeau during 11.86.

ST CYR L'ECOLE (78)

Preserved out on the field is Sikorsky H-34A SA85 (ex '68-RA' EH.68) which arrived as long ago as 25.10.75 (current 6.89).

Stored in one of the hangars here are/were Agusta-Bell 47Gs 052/BCS and 067/BDD (both ex ALAT) (noted '78-'80). The former may be the "05" reported here in 9.88.

Stored in a shed behind the 'flight line' here were a number of ex ALAT Hiller UH-12Bs. They were reported here in 1981 and a visit in '82 identified the following.

Hiller UH-12B	133	ex F-OAHB, to Dax by '86 on permanent loan.
Hiller UH-12B	157	ex 'ABB' & F-BFPZ.
Hiller UH-12B	158	to Chambery.
Hiller UH-12B	667	current 6.86, F-BNGL reserved '82.
Hiller UH-12B	669	current 6.86, F-BNGM reserved '82.

Three were noted in early '89 of which only 157 was positively identified but 667 and 669 are almost certainly the other two.

Other relics seen here have included the following.

AB206B Jet Ranger	F-BTDU	(c/n 8324) noted 12.87 partially dismantled and crash-damaged (current '88).
MS733 Alcyon	F-BKOH	(c/n 63) stored 5.88.
MS880B Rallye Club	F-BOVX	(c/n 898) dismantled 5.88.
MS880B Rallye Club	F-BVHD	(c/n 2503) stored 5.88 minus engine & undercarriage.
MS893E Commodore 180	F-BUZM	(c/n 12319) (noted '88).
MS885 Super Rallye	F-BLSB	(c/n 388) (noted '88).
PA38-112 Tomahawk	F-GCLZ	(c/n 38-80A0069) crash wreck (noted 5.88).
Poullin PJ.5	F-PDVD	(c/n 1) crash wreck (noted 5.88).
DR221 Dauphin Srs3	F-BPRT	(c/n 128) fuselage only (stored 5.88).
SIAI S205-20/R	F-BOEU	(c/n 227) dumped '88.
SO1221 Djinn	FR112	stored at Heli-Club Maurice Ripoche (noted 12.87).

ST DALMAS DE TENDE (06)

Near the Italian border, on the RN204, the town was presented with CM170 Magister 125 by '84. The aircraft was displayed amongst some buildings when last noted in 9.86 and is very hard to find. The Gendarmerie station is the best landmark to look out for but the last report said the aircraft was in poor condition and likely to be scrapped.

ST DIE (88)

SO6025 Espadon 01/C was under restoration here but moved to Ailes-Anciennes, Toulouse, at Toulouse/Blagnac by 1988 after the preservation group here disbanded. It was stored for some time in a technical college in the town after the group folded.

ST DIZIER/ROBINSON (52)

The home of EC.7's Jaguars, BA113, is guarded by an ex Chateaudun Thunderstreak. Elsewhere on the base is a T-33A from the Air France technical school at Vilgenis and a Magister.

Mystere IVA	14	ex '314-TX' GE.314, marked as "7-AI" (noted '87).
CM170 Magister	46	(noted '87).
Lockheed T-33S-US	16524	(51-6524) ex '338-H.' & Vilgenis (noted '87).
F-84F Thunderstreak	28897	(ex 52-8897) (IRAN No. 725) ex '1-ET' EC.2/1 (noted '74-'87).

The fire dump still has two long standing residents.

MD312 Flamant	252	ex '319-DQ' ex GE.319 (noted '76-'87).
Vautour IIN	345	ex '30-MP' ECTT.2/30 (noted '76-'87).

ST ETIENNE/BOUTHEON (42)

Fuselage of Orion c/n 160 dumped at the back of the hangars 6.87. Having failed to gain certification it was due to be scrapped. The wreck of MS880B Rallye Club F-BUVQ (c/n 2333) was here in 6.89.

ST FLOUR (15)

In store at the Aero Club during 8.88 were the fuselages of Jodel D112 F-BIQC (c/n 576), Jodel D120 F-BNCR (c/n 302) and CEA DR253 Regent F-BPRG (c/n 134).

ST GATIEN DES BOIS (14)

MD315R Flamant 51/30-QS (ex ECTT.12/30) had arrived here from dereliction at Flers by early '87. The aircraft is in a terrible state and can be found in the car park at the 'Top Gun' disco.

ST GEOIRS (38)

A new arrival at this Grenoble airfield in 6.87 was CM170 Magister 119 for preservation (current 6.89).

ST JACQUES DE GRASSE (06)

Monsieur Huitric acquired CM170 Magister 135 in '83 (possibly on 1.6.83 when it was seen by the compiler leaving Aix-Les-Milles by road). It was noted in his garden during 3.86.

ST JEAN DE CARDONNAY (76)

Aero Commander 680E F-BJAR (c/n 687-16) arrived from Rouen/Boos on 5.10.80 and was still lying here during '87 at a scrapyard on the RN15.

ST JEAN DE LINIERES (49)

In a scrapyard on the RN23 (about 5kms from Angers) are MS733 Alcyons F-BKOY (c/n 44, ex F-BHCU), F-BMQA (c/n 144), F-BMQI (c/n 116). All were current in 4.89 though the rudders have been swopped around so not all the c/ns and registrations tie up correctly.

ST MALO (35)

CM170 Magister 160 arrived by road from Chateaudun on 19.5.87 and is displayed with the Aero Club (current '89). Monsieur Guineheux was restoring a Brochet (80 or 100) here during 3.89.

ST MARTIN D'HOSTUN (26)

Stored here (15kms East of Romans-Sur-Isere) with Aero Phoenix is NC702 Martinet 350 (ex 'PR' CEV) which was retrieved from Valreas-Plage (near Beziers) in 1979. It will move to Romans after restoration.

ST NAZAIRE/MONTOIR (44)

Adjacent to the airport here is a SNIAS factory which has maintained a private museum holding Vautour IIB 632 (ex 'JB' EdR.5/106), former CEV SO30P Bretagne 37 (recovered from Istres, painted as "F-BANZ") and Fouga 90 prototype 01/FWZJB.

All were outside during 3.89.

The museum is being dispersed with the Bretagne promised to Ailes-Anciennes - Toulouse whilst a second (unidentified) Vautour IIB departed here on 1.10.87 for Bordeaux/Merignac.

ST OMER (62)

The hulk of Piper J3C-65 Cub F-BHMQ (c/n 10885, ex 43-29594) was here in 9.87.

ST PERAVY-LA-COLOMBE (45)

Halfway betwen Chateaudun and Orleans, behind the Total petrol station in this tiny village sits the fuselage of N2501 Noratlas 12 (ex '64-BL' ET.3/64, soc 12.8.76) which arrived here from the dump at Chateaudun (noted '81-'89).

ST PHILIBERT-DES-CHAMPS (14)

Monsieur Joseph has Sikorsky H-34A SA55/68-OA (ex Blangy-Le-Chateau) at a private location here (noted '87).

ST PIERRE D'OLERON (17)

MD315R Flamant 79/30-QX (ex ECTT.12/30) arrived here on 29.9.72 for the Aero Club, Les Ailes Oleronnaises. It survived until Spring '85 when it was broken up for scrap.

ST RAMBERT D'ALBON (26)

Aero Retro were founded on 24.5.77 and have the following collection based here, some airworthy, some static and others under restoration.

Boeing Stearman	-	unknown a/c under rebuild 7.89.
Bu 131 Jungmann	F-AZDL	(c/n 78) (noted '87-'89).
Caudron Luciole	F-AZAL	(c/n D16, ex F-PJKE) (noted '87-'89).
L-19E Bird Dog	F-GECB	(c/n 24658) ex ALAT (noted '87-'89).
Cessna T-50 Bobcat	OO-TIN	(c/n 5253, ex 43-7703, HB-UEF) ex Ostend, fuselage frame for rebuild (noted '86-'89).
DH Chipmunk T.20	1321	ex PortAF (noted '89).
AD-4N Skyraider	126956	(F-AZDQ) ex Gabon AF, painted in USMC colours as "RM-3" of VMC-1 (noted '86-'89).
CM170 Magister	206	ex '315-QX' GE.315, flew in as F-WDUD, to F-WMOM (noted '87-'89).
Morane MS315	F-AZAH	(c/n 254, ex F-BBZO) (noted '86-'89).
Morane MS502	F-AZCP	(c/n 320, ex F-BBUS) Aeronavale c/s (noted '87-'89).
Morane MS505	F-AZDA	(c/n 226/2, ex F-BBUG) (noted '81-'89).
MS733 Alcyon	F-BLEV	(c/n 68) painted in Aeronavale c/s as "68/51S" (noted '86-'87).
Nord NC854S	F-BFSY	(c/n 77) (noted '89).
N1101 Noralpha	77	(F-WZCZ) ex 'NP' CEV & Merville (noted '86-'89).
P-51D Mustang	44-72035	(F-AZMU) (noted '89).
T-6 Texan	F-WZBM	mocked up to resemble a Zero, painted as "3-189" (noted '89).
AT-6C Texan	F-BJBC	(c/n 88-12326) (noted '86-'89).
SNJ-5 Texan	F-AZBL	(ex 42-85886, Bu 90669) came from a French scrapyard, painted as "09905/56S.42" (noted '86).
T-6C Harvard	F-AZDK	(c/n 80-10570, ex 41-33449, EX476, H-8, F-BJBE) "12" in USN colours (noted '86-'89).
Pilatus P2-05	U-117	(F-AZCC, c/n 37) ex Swiss AF, painted in spurious Luftwaffe colours as "W/Nr 4381" (noted '86-'89).
Piper J-2 Cub	F-AZBM	(ex L-4H c/n 12332, ex 44-80036, F-BDTH) (noted '89).
Piper J-3C	-	(c/n 12856) (noted '89).
Sikorsky H-34A	641	(c/n 58-641) ex Rochefort/Soubise (noted '86-'89).
SIPA CP.901	F-BEYZ	(c/n 22) (noted '87-'89).
SIPA S.903	F-AZEK	(c/n 99, ex F-BGHY) (noted '89).
Stampe SV4C	F-BDCV	(c/n 551) (noted '87-'89).
Yak C.11	533	ex Egyptian AF & La Ferte Alais, spares for F-YAKA (noted '86-'88, to Duxford, UK).
Yak C.11	539	(F-YAKA) ex Egyptian AF & La Ferte Alais (noted '85-'87).
Yak C.18	640	ex Egyptian AF (noted '86-'87).

Two Yaks registered F-AZFG and F-AZJB were recorded in 6.89, probably two of the above. In store in the locality during 6.87 were MH1521 Broussard F-BIEN (c/n 43), Nord 1002 F-BAUF (c/n 173) and one other.

ST VALERY EN CAUX (76)

CM170 Magister 13 (ex '30-QI' EC.30/SALE) is hangared at the Aero Club here (noted '83-'87).

SAINTE-MERE-EGLISE (50)

The Airborne Troops Museum here (in the town centre) received C-47 Dakota "315159" (c/n 19288, ex 42-100825 & Aeronavale 25) from 56S on 13.1.83. They also display WACO CG-4A 45-17241.

SAINTES/THENAC (17)

Base Aerienne 722 houses the Ecole d'Enseignement Technique de l'Armee de l'Air (EETAA). Preserved around the base have been the following.

A-26B Invader	39223	(c/n 6936, ex 41-39223) ex 'S', to Mont-De-Marsan 1.82.
MD312 Flamant	175	ex '41-GB' ELA.41, (to the dump '83 and burnt).
Super Mystere B.2	156	ex '12-YK' EC.1/12 (noted '85-'86).
Lockheed T-33S-C	21113	(ex RCAF 21113) ex '314-UV' GE.314 (noted '82-'88).
N2501 Noratlas	124	ex '64-BP' ET.64 (soc 7.10.69) (noted '79-'88).
N2501 Noratlas	170	ex '63-WT' ET.63 (noted '85-'88).

Instructional airframes utilised by the EETAA since 1980 have comprised the following.

MD312 Flamant	207	ex '319-CV' GE.319, soc 6.7.73, (dumped '83 & burnt).
Mirage IIIC	64	(blue fuselage, desert camo wings) (noted '87).
Mystere IVA	11	ex '314-TQ' GE.314 (noted '76-'88).
CM170 Magister	376	ex 'AQ' CEV (noted '85-'86).
CM170 Magister	384	ex 'AR' EPNER/CEV (noted '85-'86).
N2501 Noratlas	154	ex '64-KJ' ET.2/64 (noted '83-'88).
Sikorsky H-34A	SKY615	ex '68-OK' EH.68, to "P92" (noted '75, dumped '85-'86).
Sikorsky H-34A	SA91	ex '68-DK' EH.68, to "P96" (noted '75, dumped '85, to Plassac).

SALON-DE-PROVENCE (13)

At the Ecole de l'Air (Base Aerienne 701) are preserved Mirage IIIC 3/2-FA (ex ECT.2/2) (noted '83-'86) and CM170 Magister 150 (noted '86-'88).

The preservation group Escadrille Pegase have a storage/restoration facility on the air base, refer to Aix/Les Milles for a listing of their aircraft.

On the dump here is CM170 Magister .../31.-ID (noted '87-'88). It has been reported as '312-ID' but that does not fit GI.312's code ranges so '315-ID' seems more likely.

SALON/EYGUIERES (13)

A visit here in 6.89 found the wrecks of Robin DR400/120 Dauphin F-GDEF (c/n 1555) and Fournier RF-3 F-BMDS (c/n 41). Preserved with the Aero Club was CM170 Magister 44 (ex '7-JD' SALE/EC.7).

SARLAT/DOMME (24)

MD315R Flamant 39/30-QR (ex ECTT.12/30, fitted with fins from 41) is preserved at the airfield entrance with the Aero Club du Sarladais (noted '78-'87). The airfield lies South East of Domme, East of the D46E.

The wreck of crashed CEA DR380 Prince F-BROT (c/n 395) was to be found here in 8.87.

SARREBOURG (57)

The wreck of Zlin 326 F-BMQR (c/n 893) was stored in the roof of a hangar here during 6.88.

SARRE-UNION (67)

Preserved at the small aerodrome here with the Aero Club de Sarre-Union is MD311 Flamant 255/316-KN (ex GE.316) which was soc 31.10.69 and still present in '89. The airfield lies on the East side of the N61 to the north of the town.

SAUMUR (49)

SO1221 Djinn FR116/CBB arrived from the Musee de l'ALAT at Dax in '86 for restoration at the ALAT base here.

SAVIGNY-EN-SEPTAINE (18)

Preserved with Entrepot de l'Armee de l'Air 605 (current 4.89) is Super Mystere B.2 99/21-LH (ex BA721 Rochefort/St Agnant). By 12.87 it had been restored to its former EC.1/12 colours as "12-YJ".

SAVIGNY-LES-BEAUNE (21)

Monsieur Pont with the Association des Amis du Musee du Chateau has set up an excellent museum at the Chateau here over the last two years. Arrivals so far are listed below. This place is obviously worth keeping an eye on with Polish MiGs and an ex Leuchars Lightning reportedly next on the list of aquisitions. It is also worth noting that the Chateau (built c.1340) also has a large collection of racing cars and over 400 motor cycles. They also produce high quality Burgundy wines here.......

MD312 Flamant	158	ex '319-CF' GE.319 & Chateaudun, became F-AZGE. Departed Savigny to Monsieur Villa of Nimes '88.
Mirage IIIB	216	ex Rochefort, restored with parts of 218 and a third, camouflaged, a/c (arr 6.88).
Mirage IIIC	50	ex '3-10-LD' EC.3/10 (arr 1.89 from Djibouti).
Mirage IIIR	323	ex '33-TB' ER.3/33 (arr 7.86).
Mirage IVA	18	ex 'AQ' (arr from Bordeaux 3.87).
Mystere IIC	013	ex Monsieur Reccia's scrapyard at Clermont Ferrand (arr 3.87).
Mystere IVA	"47"	wears dayglo colours and thus could be the real 47 ex GE.314 & Chateaudun store but is also quoted as 37 (from fuselage c/n plate) ex '8-QE', with the fin from 47. Take your pick. This machine arrived 3.87.
Mystere IVA	142	ex '8-NU' ET.2/8 (arr 4.88, in the 'wreck' area).
Mystere IVA	191	ex '8-MS' ET.1/8 (arr 4.88, reported to have gone to Koksijde for the Brussels Museum 16.11.88 but code quoted as '8-NK' for this example).
Mystere IVA	293	ex '8-NG' ET.2/8, arr from Chateaudun 5.89, on a trailer here 6.89 and available for exchange.
Super Mystere B.2	50	ex '12-ZE' EC.2/12 & Captieux ranges (arr 3.89).
Super Mystere B.2	69	ex '12-YG' EC.1/12 & Captieux ranges (arr 10.88).
Super Mystere B.2	83	ex '12-ZT' EC.2/12 & ETBS Bourges (arr 6.88, with fin from 118, for exchange).
Super Mystere B.2	145	ex '12-ZR' EC.2/12 & ETBS Bourges (arr 8.87, to Koksijde, Belgium, for Brussels Museum store by 6.89).
MD450 Ouragan	230	ex '4-US' EC.3/4, 'TD' GE.314 & Blois (arr 7.87).
DH Vampire T.55	185	ex Irish Air Corps & Musee de l'Air (arr 3.87).
Gloster Meteor T.7	F.6	ex Cazaux ranges (arr 1.88).
Gloster Meteor NF.11	SE-DCF	(AWA built) ex Gosselies & Brussels museum (arr 3.88).
Gloster Meteor NF.11	SE-DCH	(AWA built) ex Gosselies & Brussels museum (arr 6.88).
Hawker Hunter F.4	ID-44	ex Belgian AF & Musee de l'Air (arr 3.89).
F-104G Starfighter	FX-90	ex BelgAF & Koksijde store (arr 11.88).
TF-104G Starfighter	FC-08	ex BelgAF & Koksijde store (arr 11.88).
Lockheed T-33S-C	21...	ex '314-UZ' GE.314 (arr from Strasbourg 12.87 but not the oft reported 21127 which is current at Nancy/Essey).
Lockheed T-33SF	21029	ex '314-YG' GE.314 & Musee de l'Air.
Mignet HM.14	-	built 1934 (arr from Toucy 7.87).
F-100D Super Sabre	42130	(ex 54-2130) ex '11-YF' EC.4/11, arr Le Havre 29.1.89 on the 'Ville de Rouen' from Djibouti (fin from 52739).
F-100D Super Sabre	52739	(ex 55-2739) ex '11-YL' EC.4/11, arr Le Havre 29.1.89 on the 'Ville de Rouen' from Djibouti (fin from 42130, for exchange).
F-100D Super Sabre	.....	ex '11-EA' EC.1/11, wreck, possibly 63187 which is believed to have crashed as '11-EA' (arr from Orleans 3.88).
F-100F Super Sabre	63937	(ex 56-3937) ex '11-YH' EC.4/11, fin from 42235 (arr from Djibouti via Marseille 3.89).

F-100F Super Sabre 64017 (ex 56-4017) ex '11-YB' EC.4/11 (arr from Djibouti via Marseille 3.89, for exchange).
F-84F Thunderstreak FU-21 (ex 52-7170) ex decoy at Brustem, Belgium.
F-84F Thunderstreak FU-45 (ex 52-7210) ex decoy at Florennes, Belgium.
F-84F Thunderstreak FU-116 (ex 53-6738) ex decoy at Bierset, Belgium (arr 22.5.89 in exchange for a Mystere IVA for Brussels museum).
F-84F Thunderstreak 29003 (ex 52-9003) ex '4-SA' EC.4 & Metz fire dump (tail from FU-21, for exchange).
F-84F Thunderstreak ..... ex '4-VF', arr from Beaune 12.87, no longer current.
RF-84F Thunderstreak FR-26 (ex 51-1886) ex Kalken, Belgium (arr 9.88).
F-84E Thunderjet 19572 (ex 51-9572) with rear fuselage from another a/c. Arr from Cazaux ranges 12.88 (but see also under Perpignan).
Sikorsky H-34A SA114 ex '68-OE' EH.68, ex Chartres & Poitiers (arr 4.87).
Vautour IIA 2 ex '92-AB' EB.92 & Cazaux ranges (arr 8.88).
Vautour IIN 304 ex CEV (flown to Dijon & arr 9.88, on loan from Musee de l'Air).
Westland Whirlwind WAD130 ex 'CUV' ALAT, Sainteny & Poitiers (arr 3.87).

As so many enthusiasts seem to have visited here at the time of the Dijon Open Day in 6.89 it is worth pointing out that the aircraft present at that time comprised all the above except as follows. The Flamant had departed together with F-84F '4-VF' and Super Mysteres 50 and 145, the latter now being at Koksijde in store for the Musee de l'Air. The Mystere IVAs continue to pose problems as mentioned in the notes against each aircraft. Several other c/ns have been quoted but the listing here is believed to be correct following extensive correspondence. However, I am not yet happy about 47/37 and would welcome concrete evidence either way.

SEDAN/DOUZY (08)
The fuselage of a Grinvalds Orion was in store here by 2.89.

SEMUR EN AUXOIS (21)
AM69/70 F-PTXB (c/n 01) was in store here by '87.

SEZANNE/ST REMY (51)
The Aero Club Sezannais received MD312 Flamant 153 (ex '319-DV' GE.319) by 1.84 (Still current '87). The aerodrome is off the D53 South of the town.

SISSONNE (02)
A Sikorsky H-19 was reported derelict at a military base here during 1981.

SISTERON (04)
The wreck of MS893A Commodore 180 F-BRRK (c/n 11439) was noted here in '86. By 6.89 it had been repaired with a new set of wings, the old ones remaining here. Lying between the hangars in 6.89 was the wreck of MS893A Commodore 80 F-BOTO (c/n 10684).

SOLENZARA (20A)
Preserved on BA126 is Vautour IIN 370 "30-QY" which was officially dedicated on 11.7.85 (still current '88).
Vautour IIN 354/92-AA (ex EB.92) was derelict here in 12.79 but has since been scrapped.

SOULAC-SUR-MER (33)
An MH1521 Broussard lies derelict by the parachute club, thought to be F-BNEN (c/n 19) or F-BMSB (c/n 87).

STRASBOURG (67)
Under restoration with Monsieur Le Reverend at a private location is SO1221 Djinn FR146 (noted 9.88).

STRASBOURG/ENTZHEIM (67)
Preserved outside the Operations block at BA124 are Mirage IIIRD 361/33-TJ (ex

ER.3/33) (noted '75-'88) and ex ER.1/33 RF-84F Thunderflash 37577/33-CK (ex 53-7577) (noted '78-'88).

Three T-birds were derelict on the field by 8.82 two of which entered preservation with the museum at Nancy/Essey. 35790 was offered to the group Ailes Anciennes - Alsace but was broken up in indecent haste before anything could be done.

Lockheed RT-33A	35790	(ex 53-5790) ex '33-XV' ER.33 (noted '82, scrapped '85).
Lockheed RT-33A	41553	(ex 54-1553) ex '33-XU' ER.33 (noted '82, to Nancy).
Lockheed T-33S-C	21127	(ex RCAF 21127) (noted '82-'84, to Nancy/Essey).

Parked out in the centre of the field during 6.88 was an unidentified Flamant in an overall green colour scheme. There was no sign of this in 5.89 but Mirage IIIC 11 had appeared outside apparently in use as a bdr airframe.

STRASBOURG/NEUHOF (67)

The group Ailes Anciennes - Alsace are based here. They hope to set up a Musee de la Reconnaissance Aerienne in view of the proximity of the AdlA's sole fighter-recce unit (ER.33) at nearby Strasbourg/Entzheim.

Mystere IVA	33	ex '312-UR' GI.312, painted as "57/10-RE" (noted '86-'88).
Mirage IIIR	3..	expected.
P-38 Lightning	-	replica (noted '87).
F-84F Thunderstreak	-	expected.

SUIPPES (51)

The ALAT's 15 RA have a Sikorsky H-19 (or Westland WS-55) preserved at the entrance to the base in Algerian War colours (noted '81-'87).

TARBES/LALOUBERE (65)

Dismantled here in 8.87 were Robin DR400/140B Major F-BXVL (c/n 1100), Fournier RF4D F-BPLI (c/n 4.121, here since '84), the wreck of MS880B Rallye Club F-BTPV (c/n 2057) and the gutted fuselage of TB10 Tobago N105A (c/n 590). Also noted was an unknown home-built type marked "F-PEKD".

TARNOS (40)

A CM170 Magister arrived at the Turbomeca factory here during '83. It has since been painted in Patrouille de france colours and mounted on a pole within the factory (current '87).

TAVERNY (95)

Super Mystere B.2 158/12-YP (ex EC.1/12) is displayed outside the Centre de Commandement des Forces Strategiques at Base Aerienne 921 in the suburbs of Paris (current '89). It is now painted in 'air superiority blue'!

TIL-CHATEL (21)

Preserved at the aerodrome by 1987 was MD312 Flamant 226 (ex '319-CG' GE.319) which was previously stored at Chateaudun. By 6.89 the aircraft was under active restoration to fly as F-AZES.

TOUL (54)

A scrapyard here held the hulks of two T-33As from Nancy/Ochey in 9.83. One of them was identified as 35060.

TOULON/ST MANDRIER (83)

The gate at this Aeronavale helicopter base is embellished by Sikorsky HSS-1 182 (ex 'W' 31F) (noted '83-'86).

TOUL/ROSIERES (54)

Preserved on a pole near the main entrance to Base Aerienne 136 is ex EC.2/11 F-100D Super Sabre 42131/11-MJ (ex 54-2131) which took up this task on 27.6.77 (current '88).

In use for bdr training with GERMaS 15/011 by 6.88 was Mirage IIIR 316/- (ex ER.2/33 & Chateaudun) painted in 'tiger' colours.

TOULOUSE (31)

The Ecole Nationale Superieure de l'Aeronautique (ENSAE, or SupAero) should still use Mirage IIIA 02/C and CM170 Magister 178 (arr 1.71) for instructional purposes. Both were last confirmed in 2.85.

The Centre d'Etudes des Materiels Aeronautiques (CEMA) use an unidentified Mirage IIIC as an instructional airframe (noted 7.86) whilst the CEAT (Centre d'Essais Aeronautique de Toulouse) have Mirage F.2 01 which came from ENSAE (noted 2.85).

TOULOUSE/BLAGNAC (31)

Near the Dassault-Breguet hangars, Ailes Anciennes - Toulouse have the following collection which is to form the basis of the forthcoming Musee des Transports de Toulouse.

BAC/Sud Concorde	F-WTSB	(c/n 01)
Beech C-45	085	ex F-ZJAD CEV.
Br 765 Sahara	504	ex '64-PE' ET.64 & Evreux (noted '88).
Castel C.310	-	composite a/c, ex Nogaro.
MD312 Flamant	227	ex '319-CX' GE.319, arr 2.11.83 (current '88).
Mystere IVA	1	ex Ecole Technique Bordeaux, arr 29.10.83 (noted '88).
Mystere IVA	44	ex '314-UU' GE.314, arr 27.4.83 (current '88).
Super Mystere B.2	48	ex '21-BT' BA721 (noted '86-'88).
DH Vampire T.11	XE950	ex Croydon ATC, arr by Transall 14.11.86 (noted '88).
EE Canberra B.6	318	may be recovered from Cazaux ranges.
CM170 Magister	103	ex '3-KA' EC.3/SLVSV, arr 2.11.83 (current '88)
Fournier RF-3	-	stored.
Gloster Meteor T.7	91	may be recovered from Cazaux ranges.
Gloster Meteor T.7	92	may be recovered from Cazaux ranges.
Gloster Meteor NF.11	NF11-8	(AWA built) ex 'BG' CEV, arr 2.1.84 (current '88)
Hispano HA200 Saeta	-	expected.
Jodel D112	-	stored.
F-104G Starfighter	2...	due from Manching.
Lockheed T-33SF	14230	ex '314-VV' GE.314, arr 9.1.84 (current '88).
MH1521 Broussard	133	ex 'ABX' ALAT & Montauban (noted '83, to La Baule by '85).
MH1521 Broussard	139	ex 'ABZ' & Montauban, arr 23.10.82 (noted '88).
Merville SM.30	F-CCHN	(c/n 01) arr 12.8.84.
Mignet HM.8	-	
Mignet HM.14	-	stored.
Morane MS317	F-BCBC	(c/n 323) may still be at Pezenas/Nizas.
MS733 Alcyon	F-BMMT	(c/n 106) arr 9.5.81 (noted '88).
MS893A Rallye	F-BPMF	(c/n 10761) stored.
N1101 Noralpha	81	ex 'DR' (or 'BR' ??) CEV, arr from Cazaux 26.6.80 (noted '88, but to Manching for transport to Koblenz museum).
N1101 Noralpha	88	ex 'DD' CEV & ENSICA.
Nord 1300	F-CROE	
Nord 1300	F-CRQH	
N2501 Noratlas	191	ex '88-JD' ETOM.88, arr 25.4.84 (current '88)
Nord 3400	130	ex 'MCA', arr from Montauban 18.9.82.
Nord 3400	140	under restoration.
T-6G Texan	"102"	arr 11.11.80, ex Jean Salis, restored at Labege, (noted here '88).
ONERA Deltaviex	F-WBHA	(c/n 01) arr 30.9.84.
Piper J-3C Cub	F-BETX	(c/n 12763, ex 44-80467, D-EBOR) arr 3.86, on loan.
F-84E Thunderjet	19572	(ex 51-9572) arr 6.82, recovered from the ranges at Cazaux (noted '88). Includes parts of another F-84 from Avord.
F-84F Thunderstreak	FU-125	(ex 53-6760)ex Beauvechain,Belgium,arr by C-160 9.3.88.

Sikorsky H-34A	SA116	"58-002/GR" ex Cognac (noted '88).
Vautour IIB	640	ex CEV, arr 4.2.81 (current '88).
SO30P Bretagne	37	expected to come here from St Nazaire.
SO6025 Espadon	01	'C', due from St Die.
Vertol H-21C	FR106	ex Lyon/Corbas.

In 1988 the museum launched an appeal fund to obtain an F-105 (once based in France) from Davis Monthan.

TOULOUSE/FRANCAZAL (31)

Preserved at the main gate of BA101 is N2501 Noratlas 208 (ex '63-VX' ET.63) painted up as "340-HB" in CIET.340 markings. Preserved on the base are MD311 Flamant 282 (ex '316-KY' GE.316) and Sikorsky H-34A SA154 (ex '68-DI' EH.68 and Chambery). All were current during 9.88.

On the fire dump in recent years have been the following.

MD312 Flamant	180	ex '319-CI' GE.319 (noted '82-'83).
MD311 Flamant	293	(soc 25.10.73) (noted '74-'83).
MD312 Flamant	239	ex '319-DN' GE.319 (ELAS.1/44 badge) (noted '84).
N2501 Noratlas	91	ex '63-WT' ET.63 (noted '82-'83).
N2501 Noratlas	174	ex 'XZ' GAM.56 (noted '83).

Engineless Noratlas 114/316-FQ (ex GE.316) was lying engineless out on the field by '87 whilst 115/63-VA (ex ET.63) has been parked out on the East side from at least '83 to '87. It is allocated to the BOMAP paratroop barracks in the city but presumably it is easier to get the troops to the aeroplane rather than vice versa. Both these 'Norries' were current in 10.88.

TOULOUSE/LASBORDES (31)

MD312 Flamant 216/319-DK (ex GE.319) came here for the Association pour la Sauvegarde des Avions Anciens Tarnais with the registration F-AZDD.

TOULOUSE/LHERS (31)

On the gate at Base Aerienne 292 is Mystere IVA 182 (ex '8-MZ' ET.1/8, current 1.87) which arrived from Rocamadour circa 1982/83.

TOURS/ST SYMPHORIEN (37)

The home of GE.314 with the Alpha Jet, Base Ecole 705 preserves several examples of the unit's former equipment.

MD450 Ouragan	187	ex 'UI' GE.314 (noted '74-'89).
MD450 Ouragan	227	ex 'UN' GE.314 (noted '74-'89).
Mystere IVA	22	ex '314-TG' GE.314 (noted '73-'89).
Lockheed T-33SF	21330	(ex RCAF 21330) ex '314-UM' GE.314 (noted '83-'89).

On the dump, T-33S-C 21032/314-VG (ex GE.314) was consumed between '79 and '81. By 7.81 it was joined by T-33SF 21002/314-UK. By 9.82 only one burnt out wreck remained and this had gone by 6.83. A visit in 8.84 found the hulk of a T-33 coded '314-UO' (probably T-33SF 14420 which crashed on 10.2.81).

TOURS/SORIGNY (37)

Preserved with the Aero Club de Touraine is MD450 Ouragan 214/UG (ex GE.314) (noted '78-'86). It moved to Montelimar/Ancone during 2.87.

Robin HR100-285 F-WSQV (c/n 001) had appeared on display on a pole here by 7.88. At the same time Jodel D112s F-BMAK (c/n 1220), F-BNCT (c/n 1317) and F-BHYX (c/n 555) were all stored here. The fuselage of Robin ATL F-GFSO (c/n 95) was stored here by 5.89.

TOUSSUS-LE-NOBLE (78)

Toussus is the major Parisian general aviation airfield (and there are several!) and predictably has a substantial W&R population. Recent inmates are listed in tabular form for ease of reference.

AS355F Ecureil	F-OBUV	(c/n 5066) (wreck, outside Heli-Union 7.88).
Aerostar 601P	F-GBBZ	(c/n 61P-0489-199) (wreck noted 7.88).

Agusta-Bell 47G-2	F-BXXV	(c/n 161) stored rotorless (noted 5.88).
Cessna F150M	F-BXNG	(c/n 1248) spares source (noted '88-8.89).
Cessna FP172D	F-BLKC	(c/n FP172-0001) stored (noted 5.88).
Cessna F172N	F-GBQC	(c/n 1829) gia (noted 7.88).
Cessna F177RG	F-BXQG	(c/n 0141) fuselage only, stored (noted 5.88).
MD312 Flamant	240	ex '319-DY' GE.319 (noted '86-'89, for preservation).
DH 104 Riley Dove 2	F-BGOA	(c/n 04344) gia (noted 7.88).
CM170 Magister	100	gia (noted '87-'88).
Hughes 269C	F-GBLT	(c/n 19-0757) cabin only, stored noted 5.88).
N1101 Noralpha	139	'CAN-11' ex DCAN (noted '84, fuselage only '85).
PA23-250 Aztec C	F-BXSB	(c/n 27-3655) (noted '87).
PA27-250 Aztec C	HB-LCF	(c/n 27-3141) with NEAS for spares 7.88.
PA28 Cherokee 140E	F-BTQD	(c/n 28-7225314) spares source (noted '88-8.89).
PA34-200 Seneca	F-BTYT	(c/n 34-7350089) (wreck noted '85-'88).
SAAB 91 Safir	F-BHAG	(c/n 91-295) stored 5.88.
SAAB 91 Safir	F-BHAI	(c/n 91-297) stored 5.88.
SAAB 91 Safir	F-BHAK	(c/n 91-299) stored 5.88.
Sikorsky H-34A	SKY705	ex '68-OH' EH.2/68, gia (noted '81-'88).
Sud Alouette II	D-HOBU	gia (noted 7.88).
Sud Alouette II	1654	ex 'JAG' Gendarmerie, gia (noted 7.88).
Sud Alouette II	-	gia noted 7.88, possibly a mock-up).
Sud Alouette III	HC-BLK	(c/n 1914) Heli Union (noted '89).
Sud Alouette III	HC-BLQ	(noted '89).
SO1221 Djinn	FR134	stored '88, at rear of Helidan hangar 8.89, due to be restored.

It is expected that the two Alouette IIIs may be rebuilt to form one airframe from the best parts of the two.

TROYES (10)
Stored here in 6.88 was PA12 Super Cruiser F-BFQO (c/n 3492). The fuselage of ST10 Diplomate F-BSXJ (c/n 127) was derelict in 3.89.

VALENCE (26)
MH1521 Broussard 24 (ex 'GG') is preserved by the entrance to this joint civil/ALAT airfield (noted '83-'89).

VALENCIENNES/PROUVY (59)
An unidentified Super Cub was reportedly derelict here by 7.88.

VANNES/MEUCON (56)
N2501 Noratlas 160/64-IN (ex ET.1/64) arrived during 1984 for the preservation group Ailes-Anciennes - Armorique. It is preserved adjacent to the civil terminal. The group have also received Lockheed T-33SF 21009 (ex '314-YP' GE.314) from Creil/Senlis (by 12.87). This was the sole camouflaged T-bird in the AdlA, being painted up for the TV series 'Les Chevaliers du Ciel'. Nord 2200 01 came here from the ETBS at Bourges, or at least the front and rear portions of it did in 1980. The centre section arrived from Savigny on 27.6.88. It is expected to move to the newly formed Aeronavale museum at Rochefort/Soubise on completion but was still here 3.89 as were the Noratlas and T-bird. The group also have a stored Nord 1300, Nord 2000 F-CBGB (c/n 79) and a DFS SG38 Schulgleiter F-CAJB (c/n 35).

Monsieur J Frelaut recovered Seafire III PP972 from the firing ranges at Gavres in 1965. It has moved through various locations over the years on a protracted restoration and moved here from Malestroit in the mid eighties. The aircraft was fully restored as "1F.9" in Aeronavale markings and went to Doug Arnold's collection at Biggin Hill during late '88.

Cessna F172H F-BPEY (c/n 0495) was in a sorry state here during 12.87 with the wreck of Swearingen SA226T Merlin F-GFMS (c/n T-296, crashed here 8.11.87).

VASSIEUX-EN-VERCOURS (26)

Leftover from the Second World War are the frames of some DFS230 gliders. In '87 there were two by the Mairie, one by the church and one at the museum. A Gotha Go 242 frame was also displayed by the museum.

VERDUN/ETAIN (55)

At the open day in 10.81 a derelict L-19E Bird Dog was to be seen on the West side of the field with the forward fuselage of an Alouette II. The only relic found at the 1989 open day was an S-55/Whirlwind which was totally anonymous and mounted on a trailer so it may not necessarily reside here.

VIAPRES-LE-PETIT (10)

An anonymous ex ALAT NC856 Norvigie may still be stored in a barn here (noted '78-'83).

VIC-SUR-AISNE (02)

An anonymous HM.14 Pou-du-Ciel is stored with Monsieur Cochet at a private location here (current '85).

VIERZON (18)

The Aero Club here, Les Ailes Vierzonnaises received MD312 Flamant 191 (ex 'XA' GAM.56, soc 25.11.71) which was still current in 6.89.

VILLACOUBLAY (78)

Preserved outside the Head Quarters building of ET.60 on Base Aerienne 107 is N1101 Noralpha 11/F-BLTE (current '87). Outside the EH.3/67 area on the other side of the field is Sikorsky H-34A SKY507/67-SV (ex EH.3/67, current '88). N2501 Noratlas 198/"62-SV" (ex '64-IN' ET.1/64) was preserved here during the early eighties but was moved to the fire dump in 1984 and perished shortly after.

Next to the motorway on the North side an NC702 Martinet and a C-45 were preserved. The C-45 was last noted in mid '80 whilst the Martinet passed into the hands of the Musee de l'Air during 1983 and is held in store at Villacoublay for them. The store contains a substantial number of airframes which for ease of reference are dealt with under the Le Bourget entry with the museum proper.

Apart from the Noratlas noted above, the fire dump has also consumed a second, anonymous, Noratlas fuselage (noted '81-'84) and ex ET.2/65 Broussard 181/65-CD (noted '81-'83).

VILLEBON-SUR-YVETTE (91)

The Ecole Technique Aeronautique here has at least two ground instructional airframes.

Super Mystere B.2	21	(noted '87).
CM170 Magister	-	(noted '87).

VILLEPERDUE (37)

Located some 30 kms South of Tours on the D21 (off the RN10), a scrapyard in the town was visited in '85 and found to hold an H-21C 'Flying Banana' and a scrapped T-bird. By 1986 they had been joined by the wreckage of a Broussard.

Lockheed T-33S-F	21028	ex '314-UR' GE.314 (noted '85-'86)
MH1521 Broussard	182	crashed at Tours 7.6.85 (noted '86)
Vertol H-21C	FR60	ex 'MDL' ALAT and Dax gate (fin from FR94).

VILLEURBANNE (69)

In this Lyon suburb, MH1521 Broussard 11 was displayed in a public park until disposal as scrap (last noted '83). Its place was taken by CM170 Magister 57/13-TD (ex EC.13/SLVSV) which was retrieved by the preservation group ASPAA and moved to the airfield at Lyon/Corbas for restoration.

VINON-SUR-VERDON (83)

Stored here in 6.89 was the wreck of Navion Rangemaster G F-BJSD (c/n 2354).

VISAN (84)

MD312 Flamant 253 has been displayed at the aerodrome since 2.85 at least. By 6.89 CM170R Magister 522/F-WFTX had arrived from Chateaudun

VITROLLES (13)

The Lycee P Mendes-France have been using the following ground instructional airframes.

CM170 Magister	372	arr 27.11.85.
MH1521M Broussard	114	
N2501 Noratlas	205	ex 'A', arr 21.5.86.
SA365 Dauphin	F-WVKD	

The Lycee also has some light aircraft and airliner fuselages (not necessarily complete!) which have not been reported. The registration F-GFJY was reserved by the Lycee for MH1521M Broussard 296 on 18.10.88.

The photographs on pages 129 to 160 and 289 to 320 are arranged by country in alphabetical sequence as with the main text. Within each country there is no special order except that where possible they are arranged in what might loosely be called "interest groups".

AUSTRIAN GLASNOST

The first of the many, ex Polish AF MiG-15 1326 at Graz started their mass migration to the West *(Colin Walford)*

Antonov An-2 CCCP-44998 at Wiener Neustadt Ost, a present from Gorbachov *(Dr. Gottfried Holzschuh)*

Ex Polish AF An-2 2919 at Graz *(Colin Walford)*

AUSTRIA

The Air Classik Viking 1A G-AGRW, formerly a restaurant in Holland, is now on display at Vienna Airport *(Dr. Gottfried Holzschuh)*

SAAB J 29 Tunnan 29560 is in an amusement park at Hubhof *(Dr. Gottfried Holzschuh)*

Dove 5 OE-BVM resides in the Technical Museum in Vienna *(Dr. Gottfried Holzschuh)*

BELGIUM

Three residents of the excellent Brussels Museum -

Mosquito NF.30 MB-24 seen during restoration work *(Mike Bursell)*

Hanriot HD.1 HD-78, beautifully restored *(Chris Michell)*

Hurricane IIc LF658 displayed as 'LF345/ZA-P' *(Phil Stevens)*

BELGIAN JETS

Starfighter FX-79 can be found in a haulage contractor's yard at Beervelde *(Otger v/d Kooij)*

F-84G Thunderjet FZ-107 seen 6.83 during one of its outings from Brussels to Bierset, painted as 'FZ-153/JE-C' *(Mike Bursell)*

RF-84F Thunderflash FR-34 by the entrance to the Administration site at Bierset air base *(Mike Bursell)*

BELGIAN DECOYS

A brace of F-84Fs doing their well known impression of a Mirage 5 at Bierset *(Mike Bursell)*

Thunderstreak FU-156, also at Bierset *(Mike Bursell)*

A 'droop-snoot' Thunderstreak. The modifications to resemble a Mirage have not stood the test of time on FU-67/'BA-03' at Kleine Brogel *(Mike Bursell)*

BELGIAN CIVILIANS

Britannia OO-YCE awaiting the scrapman at Oostende in 1980 *(Mike Everton)*

C-47B Dakota K-1/OT-CWA was rescued from Koksijde and is preserved at Gits *(Otger v/d Kooij)*

Beagle 206 OO-EEL seen here derelict at Oostende has now gravitated to the scrapyard at Snaaskerke *(Mike Everton)*

CYPRUS/DENMARK

Sadly no more is this Vulcan which wore the markings of all the fighter squadrons to visit Akrotiri on APC *(Jim Simpson via Ken Ellis)*

The remains of DC-7C OY-KNB at Kastrup; the nose serves as a bar in Billund *(John Wegg)*

The fuselage of Dove OY-AJR at Vamdrup, April 1988 *(Per Thorup Pedersen)*

DANISH EX-MILITARY

Catalina L-861 at Vaerlose under restoration for the Billund museum *(Dave Weinrich)*

Texan 31-306 seen here at Stauning serves as a spares source *(Dave Lee)*

TF-100F Super Sabre GT-874 still survives at Karup *(Dave Weinrich)*

DANISH EX-MILITARY

Dakota K-681, neglected here at Vaerlose, later flew to Billund *(Dave Weinrich)*

Veteran F-84G A-525 - a children's plaything in a park at Vojens *(Dave Weinrich)*

Meteor F.4 43-469 stored at Skrydstrup in 1985 by the FHS *(Dave Weinrich)*

DENMARK

F-86D Sabre F-947 guards the gate at Alborg, masquerading as 'F-326' *(Dave Lee)*

The trees around F-84G Thunderjet 23079/KR-Z show just how long she was parked out at Tirstrup; sadly the aircraft is no more *(Dave Weinrich)*

RF-84F Thunderflash C-253 heads an impressive decoy line of the type at Karup in 1985 *(Dave Weinrich)*

FINLAND

Mil Mi-1 HK-1 and Mi-4 HR-3 are preserved together outside at the Finnish Aviation Museum, Helsinki *(Joe Evans)*

An impressive gate guard at Kuopio/Rissala is MiG-21MF MG-61 *(Joe Evans)*

LET Z.37 Cmelak OH-CMB is seen here outside the museum at Helsinki. It has since been reassembled in the new building *(John Davis)*

FINNISH MUSEUMS

Gloster Gauntlet GT-400/OH-XGT, impeccably restored to fly at Halli *(John Davis)*

Douglas DC-2 DO-1 at Tikkakoski awaiting restoration *(John Wegg)*

'Twin-stick' MiG-15UTI MU-1 is preserved at Halli *(John Davis)*

FINNISH MUSEUMS

Sole surviving Blackburn Ripon RI-140 in store at Vesivehmaa *(John Davis)*

Folland Gnat F.1 GN-105 in the Finnish Aviation Museum *(John Davis)*

Ilmailuvoimien A22 Hansa IL-2, also in the museum at Vantaa *(John Davis)*

FRANCE - CIVILIANS

Ex Air Inter Viscount 707 F-BMCF serves as a ground instructional aid at Merville *(Joe Evans)*

The wreck of Percival Proctor I G-AIWA/R7524 at La Ferte Alais following an accident there on 9 June 1984 *(Mike Everton)*

Alcyon F-BKOY, with the fin fron F-BMQI, is one of three examples in a yard at St.Jean de Linieres *(Phil Stevens)*

FRANCE - CIVILIANS

Ex Air France Caravelle F-BHRY is stored at Nancy/Essey for the prospective museum *(Mike Bursell)*

The stripped out hull of Robin DR400 F-GABI lay at Chalons in 1986 *(Mike Everton)*

Ryan Navion F-BAVY has lain at Compiegne for the last three years and shows no sign of moving again *(Mike Everton)*

FRANCE - MILITARY TWINS

Radar-nosed N2501SNB Noratlas 189, one of three at Nancy *(Mike Bursell)*

MD312 Flamant 229/319-DW on the gate at Avord *(Mike Bursell)*

Ex-GLAM Caravelle 141/FG now with the Musee de l'Air *(Mike Bursell)*

FRANCE - MILITARY TWINS

SP-2H Neptune 147568 out to grass at Lorient, mid-'86 *(Mike Bursell)*
C-45 85104, a former Rochefort gia, preserved at Lorient *(Mike Bursell)*
Breguet 941 04/62-ND preserved with the Musee de l'Air *(Mike Bursell)*

FRENCH JETS

SE535 Mistral 50/'7-BM' after lengthy restoration at Etampes *(Mike Bursell)*

Meteor NF.11 SE-DCH now in the museum at Savigny-les-Beaune *Mike Bursell)*

A chateau is a strange home for an Irish Vampire - 185 at Savigny *(Mike Bursell)*

FRENCH JETS

F-100D 52734/11-YF ex EC.4/11 in Djibouti, now at Chatillon *(P Couderchon)*

New replaced by 148/12-YP, Super Mystere B.2 88 on Cambrai's gate *(Andy Thompson)*

Mystere IVA 315/1-DF, sole French jet warbird so far, at Dijon 1984 *(Mike Bursell)*

FRENCH JETS

Ex GE.314 Ouragan 308/UO at Amboise/Dierre was sold for scrap in mid '86 *(Mike Bursell)*

The unique Mirage IIIT 01 is preserved by the main gate at Rochefort/St.Agnant *(Mike Bursell)*

Vautour IIB 636/92-AW preserved at its old base of Bordeaux *(J-C Oge)*

FRENCH JETS

Mystere IIC 104/10—SQ survives in the municipal park at Henin-Beaumont *(Mike Bursell)*

BA 120 chose Mystere IVA 120/'8-ME'/'8-NE' for retention when the Alpha Jet replaced the type with EC.8 *(Mike Bursell)*

Recent addition to storage at Nancy/Essey is ex CEV Vautour IIN 307, a former radar test bed *(Mike Bursell)*

FRENCH MILITARY

Frustrated Bolivian T-33AN 21182 at Dinard after CIPRA rework *(Alain Rabiller)*

Magister 101, ex '4-WB', has gone to the Aero Club at Ales *(Mike Bursell)*

Alize 86 inside the main entrance to Lorient/Lann Bihoue *(Mike Bursell)*

FRENCH MILITARY HELICOPTERS

Sikorsky HSS-1 144 inside a Naval Arsenal at Lorient *(Patrick V Prefontaine)*

Sikorsky H-19D c/n 55-1085 'AVW' with the ALAT Museum, Dax *(Claude Petit)*

Vertol H-21C FR-60 survives in a scrapyard at Villeperdue *(Mike Bursell)*

FRENCH MUSEUMS

This original Gasnier is preserved by Ailes Anciennes - Angers *(C Ravel)*

Rare Polikarpov I-153 Chaika '9' is preserved inside the Musee de l'Air at Le Bourget *(Mike Bursell)*

Also in the Musee de l'Air is this Breguet G.III gyroplane F-WFKC *(Patrick Vinot Prefontaine)*

FRENCH MUSEUMS

Yak C11 F-AZFJ/29 at La Ferte Alais was one of the batch recovered from Egypt in 1984 *(Mike Bursell)*

Preserved at the ALAT Museum, Dax is Stampe SV.4C 496 *(Claude Petit)*

Vautour IIA 2 was recovered from the Cazaux ranges for M Pont's museum at Savigny-Les-Beaune *(Mike Bursell)*

FRENCH VINTAGE

Ex Gabonese AD-4 Skyraider 126924 under restoration to fly at Le Havre *(Mike Bursell)*

Under restoration at Dugny is Caudron C714 No.5 c/n 8537 *(P Couderchon via Patrick V Prefontaine)*

Texans returning to nature at La Ferte Alais *(Phil Stevens)*

GREECE

Curtiss Helldiver 83321 at the Hellenic War Museum, Athens *(Chris Michell)*

Dakota 92641, not very thoroughly restored at Katahas *(Paul Jackson)*

F-86D Sabre 51-6171 also at the Hellenic War Museum *(Chris Michell)*

ICELAND

Ex 57th FIS F-102A 56-1378 on the Keflavik dump after several years on display at the base *(Ken Ellis)*

Nose section of ex Iscargo DC-6B TF-OAA at Reykjavik *(Ken Ellis)*

Ogn biplane TF-OGN hangs in Keflavik's civil terminal *(Ken Ellis)*

ITALIAN MILITARY

Texan MM54106 painted as 'MM53802/53-22' (airworthy in France) is preserved at Cameri *(Dave Lee)*

SH-34J MM149082/4-04, one of a trio stored at Luni NAS *(Frank McMeiken)*

Agusta-Bell 47J MM80257/53-95, formerly with 653 SC, at Cameri *(Dave Lee)*

ITALIAN JETS

F-84F MM36845 at Rivolto in 'Diavoli Rossi' aerobatic team colours *(John Grech)*

Canadair Sabre 4 MM19668 at Cameri in 'Lanceri Negri' colours *(John Grech)*

Fiat G-80-3B MM53882 at the Museo Storico never wore 'RS-22' in service; this part of the fuselage is from a G-82 *(Mike Bursell)*

ITALIAN JETS

RF-84F Thunderflash MM52-7390/ 3-19 is preserved at Milano/ Bresso with the Gruppo Amatori Volo *(Mike Bursell)*

This Tiger striped Starfighter at Cameri is believed to be MM6504 *(Dave Lee)*

F-86K Sabre MM38301/5-52 at Rimini/Miramare *(via Fred Martin)*

ITALIAN MILITARY

Macchi MB323 MM554/RS-10 at the Museo Storico at Vigna di Valle *(Mike Bursell)*
Fiat G-46-1B MM52790 ex I-AEHL now preserved at Forli as 'SV-3' *(Frank McMeiken)*
Lockheed T-33A MM51-17534/534 preserved at Cameri *(Dave Lee)*

GREECE

Firstly, it cannot be overstressed that Greece is not a country which understands our interest in military aircraft. Photography or note taking at Greek military bases without permission will be interpreted as espionage and is likely to result in an extended stay in prison. You have been warned.

On the brighter side, 1988 saw the first (to my knowledge) official visits to Greek military bases by British enthusiasts. Perhaps the climate is beginning to change. A further welcome development has been the arrival of former Greek 'decoy' aircraft in the UK and West Germany as museum pieces and battle damage repair training airframes. Hopefully this will continue - how about an Albatross or F-102 for the UK?

ARAXOS

Serving as decoys on the air base in 1983 were two F-86D Sabres serialled ..182 and ..392.

ATHENS

In the city, between the Chandris Hotel and the Greek Planetarium, F-84F Thunderstreak 26729 (ex 52-6729) was on display in 6.83 but had gone by 4.85.

The Hellenic War Museum (Polemico Moussio) is located in the city centre on the corner of Vassilissis Sofias and Rizari streets. It has the following aircraft on display in the open air:-

SB2C-5 Helldiver	83321	(noted '82-'88).
DH82A Tiger Moth	G776	(noted '82-'88).
F-104G Starfighter	6695	'FG-695' (noted 5.88-10.88 - full identity needs to be confirmed as ex KLu 6695 was at Athens Airport at the same time).
Lockheed T-33A	16771	(ex 51-6771) (noted '82-'87, to Athens Airport by '88).
F-86D Sabre	16171	(ex 51-6171) (noted '85-'88).
T-6G Texan	"32803"	(ex 49-3500) (noted '82-'88).
Spitfire IX	MJ755	(noted '82-'88).

ATHENS AIRPORT

On the road into Athens from the East Terminal (about a mile from the airport buildings) in 6.83 were B-23 Dragon N86E (c/n 2745) and C-82 Packet N127E (c/n 10150). They were originally operated by the John W Mecom oil company until abandoned at Athens in the late sixties. These two relics had gone by 6.88 by which time a new road had been built over the ground they used to occupy.

Olympic's Skyvan 3s SX-BBN (c/n SH1869, ex G-14-41, G-AXLB) and SX-BBO (c/n SH1870, ex G-14-42, G-AXLS) were wfu on the Olympic ramp by 6.88.

Stored for several years in a compound opposite the Olympic terminal here were six ex Olympic Boeing 720s, details as follows:-

Boeing 720-051B	SX-DBG	(c/n 18352) (noted '82-'87).
Boeing 720-051B.	SX-DBH	(c/n 18353) (noted '82-'87).
Boeing 720-051B	SX-DBI	(c/n 18355) (noted '81, dep to Shannon, Eire, 13.12.84 for scrapping).
Boeing 720-051B	SX-DBK	(c/n 18356) (noted '82-'87).
Boeing 720-051B	SX-DBL	(c/n 18420) (noted '82-'87).
Boeing 720-051B	SX-DBM	(c/n 18687) (noted '81-'87).

Noted in 2.84 were ex Greek CAA C-47B Dakota SX-ECD (c/n 14787/26232, ex 43-48971) and C-47C SX-ECF (c/n 33206, ex 44-76874, Bu99836, N7071C, N29, N17, N73) (both still current 8.87). SX-ECD was still present in 6.88 by which time SX-ECF had been immaculately restored and preserved in the grounds of the Hellenic CAA on the side of the road from the airport to Glyfada.

HU-16D Albatross 137909 was engineless and derelict on the field by 1980 but had gone for scrap by 11.83.

In 9.83, the light aircraft park held the fuselage of Cessna 188 Agwagon N8102V (a long term relic - still here 2.84) and derelict PA38-112 Tomahawk SX-AJN (not noted 2.84). By 6.88 the General Aviation ramp had been tidied up and these two relics had been relegated to a position near the Boeing 720s which they shared with Cessna 337 SX-BDH.

The military side of the field (Hellenikon) houses a maintenance facility which has handled a variety of Hellenic AF types. In the mid eighties large numbers of F-84F Thunderstreaks gathered here possibly in storage pending a slot on the overhaul line but in many cases ending up on the scrap heap. Invariably, visitors to Athens see more aircraft at this facility than they are able to positively identify and one can seldom be sure whether an aircraft is fair "Wrecks and Relics" game or whether it is still active. Bearing this in mind, the following notes may be of use:-

F-84F Thunderstreak 11812 (ex 51-1812) (noted 10.84).
F-84F Thunderstreak 26362 (ex 52-6362) (noted 8.83, unconfirmed).
F-84F Thunderstreak 26425 (ex 52-6425) (noted 2.84, 9.88).
F-84F Thunderstreak 26439 (ex 52-6439) (noted 6.88-9.88, 26438 noted 2.84).
F-84F Thunderstreak 26467 (ex 52-6467) (noted 10.84, 5.85 & 9.88).
F-84F Thunderstreak 26541 (ex 52-6541) (noted '82, to Usworth, UK).
F-84F Thunderstreak 26611 (ex 52-6611) (noted '82, 8.83, 2.84 & 10.84).
F-84F Thunderstreak 26621 (ex 52-6621) (noted '82, 8.83, 2.84 & 10.84).
F-84F Thunderstreak 26622 (ex 52-6622) (noted '82, 8.83, 2.84 & 5.85).
F-84F Thunderstreak 26681 (ex 52-6681) (noted 8.83, 2.84 & 9.88).
F-84F Thunderstreak 26686 (ex 52-6686) (noted 3.83 as 36686 & 2.84).
F-84F Thunderstreak 26688 (ex 52-6688) (noted 10.84 - confused with 26686?).
F-84F Thunderstreak 26703 (ex 52-6703) (noted 10.87 & 9.88).
F-84F Thunderstreak 26727 (ex 52-6727) (noted 6.88-9.88).
F-84F Thunderstreak 26761 (ex 52-6761) (noted 3.83, 2.84, 10.84 & 9.88).
F-84F Thunderstreak 26773 (ex 52-6773) (noted 2.84, 5.85 & 9.88).
F-84F Thunderstreak 26797 (ex 52-6797) (noted 10.87 & 7.88).
F-84F Thunderstreak 26811 (ex 52-6811) (noted 10.84 & 7.88).
F-84F Thunderstreak 26812 (ex 52-6812) (noted 4.88).
F-84F Thunderstreak 27086 (ex 52-7086) (noted 6.88-9.88),
F-84F Thunderstreak 27091 (ex 52-7091) (noted 10.87 & 9.88).
F-84F Thunderstreak 27763 (ex 52-7763) (noted 2.84).
F-84F Thunderstreak 37182 (ex 53-7182) (noted 8.83, 2.84, 10.84, 5.85 & 7.88).
F-84F Thunderstreak 37203 (ex 53-7203) (noted 5.85).
F-84F Thunderstreak 37206 (ex 53-7206) (noted 10.87).
F-84F Thunderstreak 37209 (ex 53-7209) (noted 3.83, 10.84 & 9.88).
F-84F Thunderstreak 37216 (ex 53-7216) (noted 10.84).
F-84F Thunderstreak 37589 (ex 53-7589) (noted 9.85).
F-84F Thunderstreak 38209 (ex 53-8209) (noted 2.84 & 10.87).
RF-84F Thunderflash 117011 (ex 51-17011) (noted 5.85).
RF-84F Thunderflash 28730 (ex 52-8730) (noted 6.88-9.88).
RF-84F Thunderflash 28740 (ex 52-8740) (noted 5.85, 10.87 & 9.88).
RF-84F Thunderflash 37683 (ex 53-7683) (noted 9.88).

In 1.83 there were over thirty Thunderstreaks parked in the open, and as can be seen from the known details listed above several of them at least appear to have been in long term store. Similar quantities of 'streaks and 'flashes continued to be seen around the facility until a visit in 2.86 when the area resembled a scrapyard with the remains of one F-84F and several T-33As visible together with the fuselage of F-104G Starfighter FG-6700 (ex KLu D-6700). The fuselages of three ex WGAF F-104Gs had been seen here in 1983 and it may be that as well as the plant handling the acceptance/modification of second hand Starfighters for the Hellenic AF, some airframes may have been acquired purely as a source of spares. Finally, in 10.87 ex WGN F-104G 2188 was seen here on its belly and in a sorry state - a possible accident victim, or just scrapped? It was still present in 11.88 with the fuselage of 2210.

By 6.88 six Dakotas were present of which three were engineless. All may well end up with the scrap man. They comprised KN575 (c/n 33199, ex 44-76867), KP255 (c/n 33557, ex 44-77225), 92621, 92622, 92625 (c/n 4409) and 92637 (c/n 19983, ex 43-15517, NC62386). By 9.88 these had been joined by KJ690, KK156 (c/n 26740, ex 43-49479) plus one other whilst 92621 and 92637 were described as tail-less.

By 4.88 Lockheed T-33A 16771/TR-771 had arrived here from the Hellenic War Museum and by 8.88 was reportedly preserved here along with F-84F Thunderstreak 26659 (ex 52-6659).

ATHENS/MARATHON AIR PARK

Cessna A185F 5B-CCA (c/n 02666) was noted here in 6.88 dumped in the long grass.

CORFU

Cessna A188B Agwagon SX-AIO (c/n 01442) was noted here in 6.83 in a decidedly derelict condition.

ELEFSIS

Preserved outside the Officers' Mess by 4.88 was C-47 Dakota 92628 (ex 49-2628) (But reported as 92626 11.88!).

This, the main Hellenic AF transport base, has seen the wholesale destruction of the Noratlas fleet in the early eighties. By 1985 approximately 18 aircraft, all with serials removed, were dumped on the airfield awaiting the bulldozer. By 7.86, only seven remained. Details are inevitably incomplete, but the following sightings have been reported.

N2501D Noratlas	52-121	(c/n 023, ex WGAF 5221) stored/dumped 9.82.
N2501D Noratlas	52-122	(c/n 024, ex WGAF 5222) stored/dumped 9.82.
N2501D Noratlas	52-127	(c/n 029, ex WGAF 5227) stored/derelict 9.85.
N2501D Noratlas	52-128	(c/n 030, ex WGAF 5228) wfu by 11.85, still present 11.88 (calibration a/c).
N2501D Noratlas	52-131	(c/n 033, ex WGAF 5231) being broken up 5.85, dump 7.85, gone 9.85.
N2501D Noratlas	52-135	(c/n 037, ex WGAF 5235) being broken up 5.85, dump 7.85, gone 9.85.
N2501D Noratlas	52-138	(c/n 040, ex WGAF 5238) stored/dumped 5.81 & 9.82.
N2501D Noratlas	52-140	(c/n 042, ex WGAF 5240) being broken up 5.85, dump 7.85, gone 9.85.
N2501D Noratlas	52-151	(c/n 057, ex WGAF 5251) stored/derelict 9.82.
N2501D Noratlas	52-153	(c/n 061, ex WGAF 5253) stored/derelict 5.81 & 9.82.
N2501D Noratlas	52-163	(c/n 072, ex WGAF 5263) being broken up 5.85, dump 7.85, gone 9.85.
N2501D Noratlas	52-172	(c/n 081, ex WGAF 5272) stored/derelict 9.82, dumped '85.
N2501D Noratlas	52-189	(c/n 107, ex WGAF 5289) stored/derelict 9.85.
N2501D Noratlas	52-222	(c/n 141, ex WGAF 5322) being broken up 5.85 (calibration a/c), dump 7.85, gone 9.85.
N2501D Noratlas	52-234	(c/n 157, ex WGAF 5334) being broken up 5.85, dump 7.85-7.88.
N2501D Noratlas	52-239	(c/n 162, ex WGAF 5339) being broken up 5.85, dump 7.85-7.88.

C-47A Dakota 13012 (c/n 13012, ex 42-93134, KG529, G-AJBD, SX-BBD) was withdrawn from use here by 1981 and was noted being broken up in 3.83 (but still there 7.88) adjacent to a large pile of aeronautical scrap which could have been the mortal remains of further Daks or perhaps Noratlas.

Surface decoys here have comprised the following.

F-102A Delta Dagger 60981 (ex 56-0981) (noted '78-'86).

F-102A Delta Dagger 61007 (ex 56-1007) (noted '78-'88).

F-102A Delta Dagger 61025 (ex 56-1025) (noted '78-'86).

F-102A Delta Dagger 61031 (ex 56-1031) (noted '78 - may still be current - sightings?).

F-102A Delta Dagger 61052 (ex 56-1052) (noted '78-'86).

F-102A Delta Dagger 61059 (ex 56-1059) (noted '78-'85).

F-102A Delta Dagger 61125 (ex 56-1125) (noted '78-'86, to Ramstein by 10.87).

F-102A Delta Dagger 61232 (ex 56-1232) (noted '78-'86).

F-102A Delta Dagger 61233 (ex 56-1233) (noted '78 - may still be current - sightings?).

TF-102A Delta Dagger 54035 (ex 55-4035) (noted '78-'88).

TF-102A Delta Dagger 62326 (ex 56-2326) (noted '78-'85).

TF-102A Delta Dagger 62327 (ex 56-2327) (noted '78-'88).

TF-102A Delta Dagger 62355 (ex 56-2335) (noted '78-'88).

In 1985 Canadair CL215 1015 lay derelict on the Eastern boundary of the field. Dornier Do 28D/2 4092 was recorded with the CL215 on one occasion but its condition is not confirmed and it may well have been an airworthy aircraft just parked nearby.

By 11.88, Do 28D/2s 4082, 4100, 4102, 4131, and 4166 were to be found here, also apparently wfu. Perhaps these are aircraft awaiting a slot on the rework cycle?

HERAKLION

On the island of Crete, the airport here has a small military presence. In use for decoy purposes (noted '85) are an F-86 Sabre and two F-84F Thunderstreaks. No serials are known and the aircraft are only visible from the sea!

KALAMATA

Preserved on the gate at this Hellenic AF training base (equipped with Cessna T-37s and Rockwell T-2Es) is Lockheed T-33A 35786/TR-786 (ex 53-5786) (noted '85-'88).

KATAHAS

By the roadside here, some 45 miles South of Thessaloniki is preserved (though wingless) C-47 Dakota 92641 (49-2641) (Noted '83).

LARISSA

Dumped in the middle of the base in '82, presumably in use as decoys, were nine F-84F Thunderstreaks (including 26679, 26710, 26808, 26908, 26915, 27107, 36686, 36687), five Lockheed T-33As (including 16867, 21397 (T-33AN), 35845 and 41574) and three F-86 Sabres.

Preserved at a nearby barracks in 7.85 (& 8.88) was F-104G Starfighter 6668/FG-6668 (c/n 6668, ex KLu).

MEGARA

Preserved by the gate in 3.83 was L-21B Super Cub Eξ-268 whilst the upturned cockpit section of an AB205/UH-1 lay near the perimeter fence.

PREVEZA

Over recent years this joint civil airport/military reserve airfield has acquired an enviable collection of fifties vintage fighters which deserve a better fate than that which seems to await them. The difficulties in identifying those aircraft which have appeared here are considerable and the following list has been collated from several sources. As of mid 1987 the airfield housed some forty F-84F Thunderstreaks, one F-84G Thunderjet and six F-86 Sabres (four of which were burnt out).

F-84G Thunderjet "17014" (store '87).

F-84F Thunderstreak ..225 (store '87).

F-84F Thunderstreak ..351 (noted '83).

F-84F Thunderstreak ..4.7 (noted '83).

F-84F Thunderstreak ..503? (store '87).

F-84F Thunderstreak ..623 (noted '83).

F-84F Thunderstreak ..663 (store '87).

F-84F Thunderstreak	..709?	(store '87).
F-84F Thunderstreak	..800?	(store '87).
F-84F Thunderstreak	..892	(store '87).
F-84F Thunderstreak	..904	(store '87).
F-84F Thunderstreak	..923	(store '87).
F-84F Thunderstreak	..962?	(store '87).
F-84F Thunderstreak	26540	(ex 52-6540) (store '87).
F-84F Thunderstreak	26556	(ex 52-6556) (store '86-'87).
F-84F Thunderstreak	26585	(ex 52-6585) (store '87-'87).
F-84F Thunderstreak	26611	(ex 52-6611) (store '86-'87).
F-84F Thunderstreak	26689	(ex 52-6689) (store '86-'87).
F-84F Thunderstreak	26809	(ex 52-6809) (store '86-'87).
F-84F Thunderstreak	26828	(ex 52-6828) (store '86-'87) marked '820' on port side.
F-84F Thunderstreak	26831	(ex 52-6831) (store '86-'87).
F-84F Thunderstreak	26832	(ex 52-6832) (store '86-'87).
F-84F Thunderstreak	26848	(ex 52-6848) (store '87).
F-84F Thunderstreak	26857	(ex 52-6857) (store '86-'87).
F-84F Thunderstreak	26872	(ex 52-6872) (store '86-'87).
F-84F Thunderstreak	26883	(ex 52-6883) (store '86-'87).
F-84F Thunderstreak	26890	(ex 52-6890) (store '86-'87).
F-84F Thunderstreak	26891	(ex 52-6891) (store '87).
F-84F Thunderstreak	26926	(ex 52-6926) (gate '86 until 7.87, to store by 8.87).
F-84F Thunderstreak	26939	(ex 52-6939) (store '87).
F-84F Thunderstreak	26941	(ex 52-6941) (store '86-'87).
F-84F Thunderstreak	26951	(ex 52-6951) (store '86-'87).
F-84F Thunderstreak	26960	(ex 52-6960) (store '86-'87).
F-84F Thunderstreak	27114	(ex 52-7114) (store '86-'87).
F-84F Thunderstreak	28776	(ex 52-8776) (store '86-'87).
F-84F Thunderstreak	28778	(ex 52-8778) (store '86-'87).
F-84F Thunderstreak	28827	(ex 52-8827) (store '86-'87).
F-84F Thunderstreak	36641	(ex 53-6641) (store '86-'87).
F-84F Thunderstreak	36753	(ex 53-6753) (store '87).
F-84F Thunderstreak	36871	(ex 53-6871) (store '87).
F-84F Thunderstreak	37173	(ex 53-7173) (store '86-'87).
F-84F Thunderstreak	37175	(ex 53-7175) (store '86-'87).
F-84F Thunderstreak	37201	(ex 53-7201) (store '86-'87).
F-84F Thunderstreak	37222	(ex 53-7222) (store '86'87).
F-84F Thunderstreak	37225	(ex 53-7225) (store '87).
F-84F Thunderstreak	37230	(ex 53-7230) (store '86-'87).
F-86D Sabre	16149	(ex 51-6149) (noted '83, dumped '87).
F-86D Sabre	18297	(ex 51-8297) (noted '83, dumped '87).
F-86D Sabre	.....	(noted '83, burnt on dump '87).
F-86D Sabre	.....	(noted '83, burnt on dump '87).
F-86D Sabre	.....	(noted '83, burnt on dump '87).
F-86D Sabre	.....	(noted '83, burnt on dump '87).

SOUDHA BAY

The wreck of Lockheed T-33A 17521/TR-521 (ex 51-17521) was noted at this A-7 base on the island of Crete in 1981 and was still to be seen in 1988.

TANAGRA

Prior to 1977, F-102A Delta Dagger 61106 (ex 56-1106) was preserved here with an F-86 Sabre marked "52235". Their fate is not known.

Hellenic Aerospace Industries operate a training school on the air base which utilises a number of instructional airframes.

Bell 47G-5	Eξ-738	(noted '83).
F-102A Delta Dagger	61056	(ex 56-1056) (noted '82-'88).
T-33AN Silver Star	21269	(ex RCAF 21269) 'TR-269' (noted '82-'86).

Piper L-21B Super Cub 219 (noted '83).
Piper L-21B Super Cub 244 (noted '83).
F-84F Thunderstreak 26722 (ex 52-6722) (noted '82-'88).
A number of Delta Daggers serve as decoys.
F-102A Delta Dagger 61001 (ex 56-1001) (noted '78-'88).
F-102A Delta Dagger 61024 (ex 56-1024) (noted '78-'86, to the fire-dump by '88).
F-102A Delta Dagger 61034 (ex 56-1034) (noted '78-'88).
F-102A Delta Dagger 61039 (ex 56-1039) (noted '78-'86).
F-102A Delta Dagger 61040 (ex 56-1040) (noted '78-'86).
F-102A Delta Dagger 61079 (ex 56-1079) (noted '78-'88).

TATOI/DEKELIA

T-6G Texan 92424 is preserved on the parade ground by the Academy HQ here (noted '83-'88) whilst F-84F Thunderstreak 26837 (ex 52-6837) was seen to be preserved by the base entrance here in 6.88.

Several airframes are held here by 123 Pterigha Technikis Ekpaidefsis (123 Technical Training Wing) for ground instructional purposes.
Bell OH-13H 5385 (c/n 2398, ex 58-5385) (noted '84-'88).
Bell OH-13H 4964 (noted '88).
Douglas C-47B Dakota KK169 (c/n 26860, ex 43-49599) (noted '84-'88).
Douglas C-47B Dakota 349111 (c/n 14927/26372, ex 43-49111) (noted '84-'88).
F-104G Starfighter 6699 (ex KLu D-6699) 'FG-699' (noted '84-'88).
Lockheed T-33A 16714 (ex 51-6714) 'TR-714' (noted '84-'88).
N2508 Noratlas 53-258 (c/n 001A, ex WGAF 5358) (noted '84-'88).
F-84F Thunderstreak 26361 (ex 52-6361) 'FU-361' (noted '84-'88).
F-84F Thunderstreak 26743 (ex 52-6743) 'FU-743' (noted '84-'88).
F-84F Thunderstreak 32716 (ex 53-2716) 'FU-716' (noted '84-'88).
A visit in 4.88 noted two Texans on the fire dump of which T-6G 93514 (ex 49-3514) was identified. A couple of months later, a further visitor described "several unidentified Texans" as being dumped on the field.

THESSALONIKI/MIKRA

By 4.88 C-47 Dakota 92613 (ex 49-2613) was preserved at the local Aero Club as was CL-13 Sabre 2 19494 (Probably the same example was was noted parked on the light aircraft apron in '83).

At least seven Sabre 2s served as decoys here until 1977 or later, serials including 19168, 19198, 19237, 19347 and presumably also 19494 mentioned above.

ICELAND

The character of Iceland's Wrecks and Relics population is a direct result of the lack of a local air arm coupled with the inhospitable terrain which has fostered the growth of private flying in this country. The Iceland Aviation Historical Society have plans for the establishment of a museum at the Loftleidir Hotel, but most relics are non-airworthy light aircraft, some of which are the subject of rebuilding plans many years after their apparent demise. Several machines are at locations unknown to the compiler, in most cases at the owner's home.

AKUREYRI

Auster 5 TF-LBP (c/n 1577, ex RAF TJ592) was in a dismantled condition here late in 1987, awaiting restoration. At the same time, Beech C-45H TF-JMP (c/n AF-602, ex 52-10672, TF-JME) was undergoing restoration.

KEFLAVIK

The gate at the military side of Keflavik is guarded by ex USN Keflavik Base Flt C-117D Skytrooper (or "Super Dak") 17191. This veteran (and former Mildenhall resident) was first placed on display in late '78 and was still current in '87. She was built as C-47A 42-93105 c/n 12980 then rebuilt for the Navy, emerging in 1952 as R4D-8 (later C-117) 17191 with the new c/n 43379.

17191's predecessor on the gate was ex 57 FIS F-102A Delta Dagger 61378 (56-1378) which was retained for display purposes when the 57th transitioned from the F-102A to the F-4C Phantom in 1973. The Dagger remained as gate guardian until 1983 when she fell from her perch due to severe corrosion. The airframe was then dumped near the base fire station where she was still complete and unburnt in 4.87.

C-118A Liftmaster 533257/JT (USAF aircraft transferred to the USN, ex VR-52) arrived at Keflavik to replace C-118B 131592 with the Base Flight. The unfortunate 533257 caught fire in a hangar here on 1.10.83 whilst being prepared for service. Whilst the aircraft still appeared intact, the fuselage was gutted by fire inside. Consequently both C-118s were relegated to the dump where they were last noted in 3.85, still standing on their undercarriages and unburnt.

On the civil side of the field, Ogn homebuilt TF-OGN is preserved in the terminal building. The aircraft was suspended from the roof in 3.87 when the new terminal was completed.

Another former NAF Keflavik C-117D, 39096, was relegated to the dump here by 1978 and was last noted there in 4.81. EC-121T Constellation 50121 (55-0121) of 79 AEW&CS caught fire on the ground here on 15.3.78 (unintentionally!) and her remains were subsequently placed on the fire dump. By 1979 the wreckage was scattered and she also was last recorded in 4.81

In the early sixties the 57th FIS operated the F-89J Scorpion, eventually graduating to the F-102A. Ten of the F-89s were dumped on the field at the end of their flying careers and duly disappeared over the next few years. Amazingly, all ten were rediscovered in 1979 when some bulldozing work was being carried out in the soft ground around the dump. Serials of these machines were 40210, 40217, 40226, 40228, 40240, 40242, 40244, 40248, 40254 and 40256 (all FY54). They remained visible on the dump until 4.81 and are believed to have gone to a local scrapyard soon after, certainly by 1983 when the dump was cleared to make way for a new passenger terminal.

REYKJAVIK

The Iceland Aviation Historical Society has a store here, the largest items in which are the battered centre section and remains of Miles Martinet TT.1 TF-SHC (ex RAF

MS902 - suffered an accident in 1952 and subsequently lay derelict at Reykjavik) together with Brantly 305 TF-DIV (c/n 1037) which was wfu following damage in 1975.

The society has plans to open a museum near to the Hotel Loftleidir at Keflavik. Aircraft on display will include the recently restored WACO YKS-6 NC15613 (c/n 4505, ex NC15613) which is painted up as "TF-ORN" representing a YKS-7 floatplane which was Flugjelag Akureyrar's (now Icelandair) first aircraft. Stinson SR-7D NC16123 has also been restored to represent "TF-AZX", Loftleidir's first aircraft.

REYKJAVIK AIRPORT

Noted here in 1979 was the wreck of Sikorsky HH-52A TF-GNA (c/n 62-096, ex USCG 1411) which retained its high visibility USCG colour scheme. It was still present in 8.80 but was not noted on a visit in 4.81 and had probably expired.

Dismantled in a corner of a hangar here in 1983 (still current '87) was ex Icelandair DC-3 TF-ISB (c/n 9860, ex 42-23998, FD939, G-AIBA, FD939, G-AKSM) which was wfu in 1979 and is now in long term storage for future restoration. This machine used to act as a source of spares for Landgraedslan's airworthy C-47A TF-NPK which earns its keep as a crop-duster in the Summer season.

Two ex Iscargo Douglas DC-6 cockpit sections are to be found here, DC-6B TF-OAA (c/n 45060, ex N93117, JA6207, TF-FRA) sits on a trailer in very battered condition whilst DC-6A TF-IUB (c/n 44907, ex N37592, LN-FOL) is with the Iceland Aviation Historical Society (in a hut near TF-OAA).

The wreck of a single engined Beech light aircraft, N6937Q, was noted on the field in 4.87 - details?

Reykjavik is home to a goodly proportion of the Icelandic civil register, and as such houses a large number of light aircraft wrecks and relics. These are listed in tabular form for ease of reference.

Beech C-45H	TF-JMD	(c/n AF-598, ex 52-10668, TF-JMO) stored here with engines and outer wings removed.
D50B Twin Bonanza	TF-ESD	(c/n DH-204, ex TF-FSD) in store, not flown for some ten years.
Stearman A75N-1	TF-KAU	(c/n 75-1556, ex 41-7997) undergoing restoration here following an accident in 1953!
Cessna 140	TF-AIB	(c/n 13825) undergoing lengthy repairs following an accident in 1984 but will fly again.
Cessna 140	TF-AIG	(c/n 9421) in store, only partly repaired after an accident in 1974.
DH82C Tiger Moth	TF-KBD	(c/n 1447, RCAF 1204) last flew as long ago as 1955 but remains dismantled here.
Ercoupe 415C	TF-RCK	(c/n 478, ex TF-ROK) hulk only, noted here 8.80.
Ercoupe 415C	TF-KBA	(c/n 598) stored on the airfield in poor condition.
Fleet 168 Finch II	TF-KAN	(c/n 651, RCAF 4772) under restoration.
Temco Twin Navion	TF-AIP	(c/n 4.1832, ex G-ARIT) fuselage only, lies among the 'lock-ups'.
Piaggio P.149D	TF-LWE	(c/n 135, ex WGAF 9114, D-ENAW, D-EHOM, OO-LWK) burnt out at Reykjavik 29.9.85, burnt hulk only.
J-3C-65 Cub	TF-TPR	stored since 1977.
PA22 Colt	TF-EVA	stored, damaged in 1966 and partially repaired.
Republic RC-3 Seabee	TF-RKH	(c/n 171) derelict.

SELFOSS

J-3C-65 Cub TF-DYR is under restoration here following an accident circa 1964/65.

VESTMANNAEYAR

Preserved in the terminal here is the first aircraft ever to land on the Westmann Islands, Klemm L.25E TF-SUX. She was wfu in 1940 but restored and flew again in 1978.

UNKNOWN LOCATIONS

Aeronca 7BC	TF-IVR	(ex N4492E) under restoration following an accident in 1975.
Auster J/1	TF-ACC	(c/n 2207, ex G-AIGV) damaged 1974 and stored since then.
Fleet Finch II	TF-KAL	(c/n 293, RCAF 4491) damaged in 1950, currently under restoration.
PA18A-150 Super Cub	TF-AFI	(c/n 18-6968, ex TF-KAZ) undergoing extended repairs following an accident in 1984.
PA18 Super Cub	-	(unregistered, ex ALAT, D-ELAT) under restoration.
PA20 Pacer	TF-IBM	(c/n 20-148, ex N7040K) under restoration after an accident 4.87.
SAI KZ.VIIU-2	TF-JON	(c/n 156, ex OY-AIR) in storage, last flown 1978.
Stinson 108-1 Voyager	TF-AIM	(c/n 1070, ex NC97070, TF-KAR) under restoration.

ITALY

Italy is one of those wonderful countries from a W&R point of view where it is still possible to discover the unexpected. The country is vast and in the South relatively unpopulated providing many hiding places for dead and dying aeroplanes. It is also noticable that in Italy the traditional method of aircraft disposal is to park the machine in a deserted corner of the aerodrome and wait 20 years or so for it to rot away. This is particularly true of US supplied military aircraft where the original terms of supply give the US a say in the disposal of the aircraft.

Aircraft preservation in Italy is attracting increasing support, the country has after all a rich aeronautical past, and the group GAVS (Gruppo Amici Velivoli Storici) deserve a special mention. Their quarterly Italian language journal 'Ali Antiche' has been of particular help in compiling this section and this debt is gratefully acknowledged. Frank McMeiken also merits a special 'thank you' and readers seeking further information are referred to 'Ali Antiche' (contact address Largo Lucio Apuleio 11, 00136 Roma) and to Frank's superb 'Italian Military Aviation' published by MCP.

ALBENGA

Preserved at the aerodrome here (about 80 kms West of Genova, on the coast) is Fiat G-46-4B I-AEHJ/MM53404 (c/n 164) (noted '87).

ALESSANDRIA

Located some 80 kms North of Genoa, derelict outside a garage here in 1982 was Fairchild 24R-46A Argus 3 I-AIAT (c/n 1041, ex 44-83080, KK423, I-FULN). In 1987 it was to be found at Via Marengo 169, perhaps the same location?

The Instituto Tecnico A Volta Di Alessandria have F-86K Sabre MM53-8274/5-57 as a gia together with Macchi M416 I-AEPW (c/n 5932, ex MM53167).

ALESSANDRIA/ACQUI TERME

Preserved at the airfield (about 25 kms South West of Alessandria) and cared for by the preservation group Associazione Arma Aeronautica is T-6G Texan MM53766/RM-10 ex 1 RVR (noted '86-'87).

AMENDOLA

By the middle of '88 ex SVBAA Fiat G-91T/1 MM6348/SA-48 had been installed as a gate guard here (current 6.89).

Fiat G-91T/1 MM6321/SA-21 (crashed 21.7.77) was dumped here by 4.78. By 11.82 there were three ex SVBAA Fiat G-91Ts dumped here of which only MM6338/SA-38 was unidentified and things had not changed by 7.84. The situation appeared unchanged in 4.86 when MM6321/SA-21, MM6338/SA-38 and MM6.../SA-96 were noted, however in 4.89 MM6321/SA-21, MM6338/SA-38 and MM54413/SA-113 were recorded.

By 6.89 Fiat G-91T/1 MM6332/SA-32 had been stripped of spares and dumped behind a hangar with the scapped remains of another example.

ANZOLA EMILIA

Preserved at a private house here (near Bologna) is Piaggio P.136F I-TEMA (c/n 109, ex MM80004) (noted 10.84).

ATINA

Between Atina and Cassino in 1987 at the Valentino Corsi furniture shop on the SS509 was T-6H-4M Texan MM53835/SC-74 (ex 51-17218) which came from the Castrette scrapyard.

AVIANO

Preserved in the town is F-86D Sabre 53-8189 painted in USAF markings with "MY" code (applied by 347 TFW crews during a deployment here) and the incorrect serial "63-8189" (noted '83).

For bdr training the base has received the following airframes.

F-4C Phantom	63-7512	ex 163 TFS/Indiana ANG on 10.7.86 (still current 2.88).
Lockheed T-33A	17483	(ex 51-17483) ex AdlA (noted '83-'89).
F-105G Thunderchief	62-4442	ex 128 TFS/Georgia ANG & MASDC FK090, painted as "67-040/AV" (noted '85-'88).

The 'Thud' arrived by road from Venice on 24.6.85 whence it had been delivered as deck cargo.

On the dump in '83 and still current in '89 was ex AdlA Lockheed T-33A 53104 (ex 55-3104).

BAREGGIO

By 1986 RF-84F Thunderflash MM52-7471/3-14, formerly in a sports complex near the Castrette yard, had arrived for display at the Silvani di San Martino di Bareggio company.

BARI

Three Texans were offered for sale (number 50-6139) as scrap on 25.9.86 having lingered in open storage since withdrawal by 3 RVR. They were offered for tender a second time on 27.1.87 but may still be here.

T-6H-4M Texan	MM53806	ex 'RB-3' 3 RVR (wfu here by 7.79, TT 5540 hrs).
T-6H-2M Texan	MM54135	ex 'RB-1' 3 RVR (wfu here by 7.79, TT 7356 hrs).
T-6H-2M Texan	MM54136	ex 'RB-2' 3 RVR (wfu here '79, TT 8045 hrs).

A total of seven Texans were seen around the field in 8.88 and 4.89 though not all were identified on each occasion. It remains to be confirmed whether the missing aircraft is MM53694 or one of the three above. Comments?

T-6H-2M Texan	MM54101	ex 'RB-11' 3 RVR (noted '76-'88).
T-6H-2M Texan	MM54110	ex 'RB-8' 3 RVR (noted '78-'88).
T-6G Texan	MM54111	ex 'RB-7' 3 RVR (noted '76-'89).
T-6D Texan	MM53143	ex 'RB-6' 3 RVR (noted '76-'89).
T-6G Texan	MM53694	ex 'RB-3' 3 RVR (noted '76-'84).

On the dump in 5.80 was Siai S208M MM61972/RB-77 (crashed here 15.10.75) whilst the remains of Beech C-45s MM61679/RB-15 and MM61692/RB-14 lingered at least as late as 1984.

At the University, T-6C Texan MM53866/RB-5 was with the Facolta di Ingegneria dell Universita di Bari in '84 as an instructional airframe.

Lohner L-1 L-127 was with the Museo Storico di Bari for many years but departed to Lecce for rebuild.

BERGAMO

The Museo del Risorgimento di Bergamo (in the old town) has Ansaldo A-1 Balilla 16553 on display.

BERGAMO/ORIO AL SERIO

The gate here used to be guarded by F-86K Sabre MM53-8299/"51-6" (ex '51-61' 51 Stormo) which had progressed to Gallarate by 1983.

Offered for sale by the US Defense Logistics Agency at Camp Darby (Livorno) on 16.7.81 (though physically located here) was T-6H-4M Texan MM53802/RM-2 ex 1 RVR (TT 5625 hrs, to G-BJMS 5.10.81) together with a further five examples described on the sale brochure as 6000kg of scrap. Others were sold off from here around the same time, including the following.

T-6C/D Texan	MM53432	ex 'RM-11' 1 RVR, to Staverton (UK) for D Baker.
T-6G Texan	MM53652	ex 'RM-1' 1 RVR, to UK 11.81.
T-6G Texan	MM53664	ex 'RM-9' 1 RVR, to G-BKRA at Sandown (UK).
T-6H-4M Texan	MM53795	ex 'SC-66' Scuola Centrale, to G-BJST at Kemble(UK).

T-6H-4M Texan	MM53796	ex 'SC-52' Scuola Centrale, to Kemble as spares for G-BJST.
T-6H-2M Texan	MM54137	ex 'RM-12' 1 RVR, to G-CTKL at Dorchester.

In storage here with 3 RRALE by 6.84 was Agusta-Bell AB47G-3B-1 MM80421/EI-50 (ex 44 GSERI).

Noted on the dump here in 5.85 was Beech C-45 MM61682. Only a few charred bits remained in '87 and the aircraft was not seen on a visit in 7.88.

BIELLA

Grumman HU-16A Albatross MM50-174/15-2 (ex 84 Gruppo/15 Stormo) was preserved on this civil airfield (noted '79-'88). During 7.88 the aircraft was dismantled for shipment to the collection of preserved aircraft at Cameri.

BOLOGNA/BORGO PANIGALE

Four Siai SM1019Es were wfu here with 2 RRALE by mid '87, one of which is MM57226/EI-433. Three were on the dump in 3.89 when MM57201/EI-408, MM57250/EI-457 and the hulk of MM57264/EI-471 were recorded.

By 6.88 seven Agusta-Bell AB204Bs appeared in open storage of which only MM80324/- and MM80333/SA-3 were identified. More AB204s have subsequently been despatched here for storage following their replacement with the A109 and a visit in 3.89 found the following derelict here. AB204Bs MM80288/EI-205, MM80303/1-03, MM80316/EI-216, MM80333/SA-3, MM80381/EI-227, MM80388/EI-234, MM80472/1-72, MM80.../72-51 and MM80.../72-65.

Dumped here in '86 was the skeletal fuselage of Macchi M416 (Fokker S.11) I-AENS (c/n 1022, ex MM53224). It was still to be seen by the control tower during 1987.

Wrecks noted here in early '87 were Macchi AL.60 I-TZAN, Partenavia P.64 Oscar I-PASS and the sole P.66B Oscar 100 I-PAOC.

BONATE SOTTO

Outside the Barbisu restaurant, Partenavia P66B Oscar I-MARP (c/n 31) was noted on display during '85.

BRACCIANO

The ALE's 1 RRALE stores some of the Esercito's surplus aircraft here, sometimes in the open air as was the case with the Super Cubs which were disposed of in the early eighties.

Agusta-Bell AB204B	MM80399	ex '245/UN' UNFIL (noted '83, dumped '86-'87).
Agusta-Bell AB204B	MM80400	ex '246/UN' UNFIL (noted '83, dumped '86-'87).
Bell OH-13H	MM80810	ex 'EI-72' SVE (dumped '86-'87).
L-18C Super Cub	MM51-15304	ex 'EI-53' 1 RRALE (noted '77, sold 16.7.81 to N3267W).
L-18C Super Cub	MM52-2403	ex 'EI-76' SVBAE (noted '80, sold 16.7.81 to N1384R).
L-18C Super Cub	MM52-2405	ex 'EI-78' SVBAE (noted '80, sold 16.7.81 to N3134F).
L-18C Super Cub	MM52-2407	ex 'EI-80' SVBAE (noted '80, sold 16.7.81 to N3267Y).
L-18C Super Cub	MM52-2408	ex 'EI-81' SVBAE (noted '80, sold 16.7.81 to N27363).
L-18C Super Cub	MM52-2409	ex 'EI-82' SVBAE (noted '80, sold 16.7.81).
L-18C Super Cub	MM52-2413	ex 'EI-83' SVBAE (noted '80, sold 16.7.81).
L-18C Super Cub	MM52-2414	ex 'EI-84' SVBAE (noted '80, sold 16.7.81 to N3268N).
L-18C Super Cub	MM52-2420	ex 'EI-89' SVBAE (noted '80, sold 16.7.81 to N917CS).
L-18C Super Cub	MM52-2421	ex 'EI-90' SVBAE (noted '80, sold 16.7.81 to N917AS).
L-18C Super Cub	MM52-2423	ex 'EI-92' SVBAE (noted '80, sold 11.81 to I-NACA).
L-18C Super Cub	MM52-2425	ex 'EI-94' SVBAE (noted '80).
L-18C Super Cub	MM52-2426	ex 'EI-95' SVBAE (noted '80, sold 16.7.81 to N917ES).

BRENO
In the Camonica Valley, North of Bergamo, SE210 Caravelle VI-N I-DAXU (c/n 79, wfu 14.9.76, TT 30,002 hrs) is in use as the 'Ristorante Caravelle'. The cockpit is more or less intact whilst the passenger cabin serves as the restaurant itself (noted '88).

BRESCIA/REZZATO
Preserved at a monument to aviators here by 1983 was Lockheed T-33A MM51-17484/6-30 (ex 606 SC/6 Stormo & Ghedi store).

BRINDISI
Near the gate by 3.85 was Fiat G-91R MM6242 (ex '2-77' 2 Stormo) painted as "32-13" with the fin painted in 'Frecce Tricolori' colours and coded "26" on one side and "31" on the other. It was not recorded on a visit in 6.89 but may not be visible from outside.

HU-16A Albatross	MM51-7157	ex '15-10' 84 Gruppo/15 Stormo (dumped '80-'86).
HU-16A Albatross	MM51-7175	ex '15-11' 84 Gruppo/15 Stormo (dumped '80-'89).
HU-16A Albatross	MM51-7252	ex '15-12' 84 Gruppo/15 Stormo (dumped '80-'86).
Grumman S-2A Tracker	MM133078	ex '41-40' 41 Stormo (dumped '82-'86).
Grumman S-2A Tracker	MM133103	ex '41-42' 41 Stormo (dumped '82-'86).
Grumman S-2A Tracker*	MM136735	ex '41-56' 41 Stormo (dumped '83, to San Antonio (Texas) by 3.87).
Grumman S-2A Tracker*	-	overall brown c/s (dumped '82-83).
Lockheed T-33A	MM51-6660	ex '36-64' 636 SC/36 Stormo (derelict in the bushes by 32 Stormo hangar '81-'88, on the dump by 6.89).

One of the two Trackers marked with an asterisk was still current during 1986.

BUSSOLENGO
Preserved outside a restaurant here during 1982 was RF-84F Thunderflash MM52-7471/3-46 (ex 132 Gruppo/3 Stormo). By 1986 it had moved on to San Martino di Bareggio.

CAGLIARI
Macchi MB308 I-ACSA (c/n 5838/65, ex MM52920) is preserved with a private owner here, on the island of Sardegna (current '88).

CAGLIARI/ELMAS
Gate guardian here is Grumman S-2A Tracker MM144716/AS-12 (ex 86 Gruppo/41 Stormo, noted '81-'82).

CAMERI
The base boasts a generous collection of preserved aircraft. In 6.89 all except the Tornado were displayed on an area near the control tower.

Agusta-Bell AB47J	MM80257	ex '53-95' 653 SC/53 Stormo (noted '84-'89).
HU-16A Albatross	MM50-174	ex '15-2' 84 Gruppo/15 Stormo & Biella, began arriving in bits 7.88 (current '89).
F-104G Starfighter	MM6504	"53-21" ex '3-05' 18 Gruppo/3 Stormo, arr by 6.87, painted in 'tiger' colours and displayed on a pole. May not be the real MM6504 (current '89).
Lockheed T-33A	MM51-17534	ex '534' 653 SC/53 Stormo (noted '84-'89).
F-86E(M) Sabre Mk.4	MM19668	(ex XB814) 'Lanceri Neri' c/s (noted '77-'89, incorporates parts from MM19509).
F-86K Sabre	MM53-8316	"51-21" (ex '51-53', by 21 Gruppo hangar '80-'89).
T-6G Texan	MM54106	painted as "CN53802/53-22", ex '53-27' 653 SC/53 Stormo (noted '80-'89).
Panavia Tornado	MMX587	(c/n P09) by 1 RMV facility '87 but hangared and coded "6-10" by 7.88. Used for temporary exhibitions and may change codes (current 6.89).
Piaggio P.166M	MM61886	ex '53-76' 653 SC/53 Stormo (noted '85-'89).

Displayed here at the 1987 Open Day was Macchi MC205 MM91818 (restored to airworthiness as "MM92214"/I-MCVE but w/o 23.7.86) which was painted as "MM92215" for the Open Day but later re-painted as "MM9327/81-5" in the colours of 81 Squadriglia/1 Stormo. It has since been donated to the Museo Nazionale della Scienza e della Tecnica in Milan.

The wreck of F-104S Starfighter MM6805/53-10 ex 53 Stormo was here during 1985 as was the burnt out hulk of another F-104S likely to be MM6793 of 21 Gruppo/53 Stormo which caught fire here during pre-flight checks on 30.10.84. The nose section only of the former was recorded here again during '89.

T-6H-2M Texan MM54142/RM-1 (ex 653 SC/53 Stormo) was in store here by 1977 until its acquisition by the Caproni Museum at Vizzola Ticino. The aircraft had moved to the museum by 1987 (probably much earlier).

Piaggio P.166M MM61928/53-34 ex 653 SC/53 Stormo was reported as wfu here in 3.87.

CAMPOFORMIDO

Preserved at a restaurant here (5 kms South West of Udine) is Fairchild C-119G MM52-6029/46-93 (ex 98 Gruppo/46 Aero) (noted '86).

CAMPO MORONE

The wreck of Piper J-3C Cub I-TESO (c/n 12296, ex 44-80000) was with a private owner here during '86.

CAPPANELLE

The hulk of P-51D Mustang MM4292/64 (ex Roma/Ciampino) was abandoned on a Vigili del Fuoco (Fire Service) training area here (near Roma) by 1962. In 1982 the hulk was shipped to the UK for the Robs Lamplough.

CAPUA

Located at the Scuola Specialisti (part of the AMI's Scuola Sottufficiali AM or AMI NCO School) are the following ground instructional airframes.

Douglas DC-6	MM61922	(c/n 43216) ex '31-26' 31 Stormo, arr 3.7.81 (current '89).
Fiat G-91R	MM6282	ex '2-34' 2 Stormo.
Grumman S-2A Tracker	MM133069	ex 'AS-2' 41 Stormo (noted '81-'89).
Lockheed T-33A	MM51-9033	'SS-1' Scuola Specialisti (noted '89).
Lockheed T-33A	MM51-6576	'SS-2' Scuola Specialisti (noted '89).
Macchi MB326	MM572	ex 'RS-16' RSV (noted '81-'86).
Macchi MB326	MM54188	(noted '89).
Macchi MB326	MM54220	ex '32-53' 632 SC/32 Stormo (noted '89).
F-86E Sabre	MM19523	(ex XB620) ex '4-50' 4 Stormo (noted '81, to Grazzanize by '87, fitted with tail of 19664).
F-86E Sabre	MM19664	(ex XB810) ex '13-3' 13 Gruppo/2 Aero (noted '81, to Rivolto by '87 marked as "19685").
F-86E Sabre	MM19841	(ex XB954) ex '4-44' 4 Stormo (noted '81, to Grosseto by '87).
F-86K Sabre	MM53-8297	ex '51-60' 51 Stormo (noted '89).
T-6G Texan	MM53679	ex 'SL-36' Scuola Lecce (noted '79-'89).
Piaggio P.148	MM53733	ex '27' & Latina store (noted '81).
Piaggio P.148	MM53741	ex '21' (noted '81).
Piaggio P.166M	MM61875	(noted '89).
Piaggio P.166M	MM61884	ex 653 SC/53 Stormo (noted '86).
F-84F Thunderstreak	MM53-7633	ex '50-28' 50 Stormo (noted '89).
RF-84F Thunderflash	MM52-7395	ex '3-12' ex 18 Gruppo/3 Stormo (noted '81-'89).

It is interesting to note that F-86E Sabre "MM19664/4-50" (refer MM19523 and MM19664 above) was reportedly current here in '89. Further comment welcomed!

CARPANETO PIACENTINO

Partenavia P.66B I-MEGA (c/n 26) was erected as a monument here (15 kms South of Piacenza) by 4.86.

CARPI
Fiat G-91PAN MM6264 (ex '6' 'Frecce Tricolori') was acquired by the Aero Club at Budrione aerodrome and was placed on display by 1984. It was still current during 9.87. Carpi is of the E6 motorway North of Modena.

CASALE
An F-84F Thunderstreak can be found here (off the A26 motorway between Vercelli and Alessandria) comprising the fuselage of MM53-6970/36-40 (ex 156 Gruppo/36 Stormo with the rear fuse/tail of MM53-6579).

CASCINO
Displayed on the SS.509 road between Cascino and Atina (near Frosinone) by 1987 was T-6H-4M Texan MM53835/SC-74 (ex Scuola Centrale) which came from the Castrette scrapyard.

CASERTA
Located at the main gate of the Scuola Sottufficiali AM (AMI NCO School) is F-86E(M) Sabre Mk.4 MM19596/4-46 (ex XB710) (current '89). Other ground instructional airframes recorded here in mid 1987 were the following.

Agusta-Bell AB47G	MM80049	(current '89).
Agusta-Bell AB47J	MM80213	ex 'SE-40' SVE (current '89).
Agusta-Bell AB204B	MM80335	ex 'SE-31' SVE (current '89).
Agusta-Bell AB204B	MM80339	(wreck - used for winch training, current '89).
Bell OH-13H	MM80791	(ex 58-5392) ex 'SE-7' SVE (current '89).
Macchi MB326	MM.....	

Note that although an AB204B coded 'SE-31' was here in '87 and MM80335 in overall olive drab without codes or serials was recorded in '89, the tie up between code and serial is an assumption and requires confirmation. They are however believed only to have the two on charge.

CASTEL DEL RIO
A war museum here (25 kms South West of Imola) had acquired T-6H4M Texan MM54149 from Roma/Guidonia by 1987. The aircraft still carries USAAF markings and code "TA-143" acquired during the filming of 'La Pelle' at Guidonia.

CASTELLO DI ANNONE
T-6G Texan MM53670/RM-16 (ex 1 RVR & Bergamo store) is preserved here (20 kms West of Alessandria) with 3 Magazzino Sussidiario, AMI (noted '84-'86). Also noted in 4.86 were derelict Piaggio P.166Ms MM61888/RM-80 (ex 653 SC/53 Stormo) and MM61907/53-75 (ex 653 SC/53 Stormo).

CASTRETTE
The celebrated Petrimetal scrapyard (at Villorba, 5 kms North of Treviso) specialises in buying up surplus aircraft and re-selling them for use as attractions at garages etc. As far back as 1977 the yard held 11 F-84Fs and 13 RF-84Fs. Late in '88 it was announced that the yard owner, Gianni Petrin, intends to establish a museum here in which the C-119 and G-91 will be amongst the first exhibits.

It should be noted that although the yard is widely known as Castrette, its correct address is Via Roma 149/A, 31050 Villorba. Occupants have included the following.

Agusta-Bell AB204B	MM80331	ex '15-26' 15 Stormo (hulk, arr 5.7.88).
C-119J Packet	MM51-8121	ex '46-50' 46 Aero (arr from preservation at Turin/Caselle 7.88).
Fiat G-91R	MM6276	ex '2-75' 2 Stormo and Treviso/Sant Angelo dump (noted 11.88).
F-86K Sabre	"MM41256"	"51-50" (front fuselage of 55-4815/51-50, rear fuse of 53-8298/51-79, fin from 54-1256) (noted '81-'85, to Megliadino di San Fidenzo 4.87).
T-6G Texan	MM53657	ex 'SC-61' & Grottaglie (noted '81-'87).

T-6H-4M Texan	MM53785	(ex 51-17106) ex 'SC-62' & Grottaglie (noted '81-'84, to I-TSIX).
T-6H-4M Texan	MM53792	(ex 51-17103) ex 'SC-65' & Grottaglie (noted '81-'84).
T-6H-4M Texan	MM53797	ex 'SC-67' & Grottaglie (noted '81).
T-6H-4M Texan	MM53820	ex Grottaglie (noted '81-'85).
T-6H-4M Texan	MM53823	ex 'SC-20' & Grottaglie (noted '81, to San Pelagio).
T-6H-4M Texan	MM53828	ex 'SL-69' Scuola Lecce (noted '84).
T-6H-4M Texan	MM53832	ex 'SC-72' & Grottaglie (noted '81-'84).
T-6H-4M Texan	MM53835	(ex 51-17218) ex 'SC-74' & Grottaglie (noted '81-'85, displayed on the SS509 near Atina by '87).
T-6H-4M Texan	MM53841	ex 'SL-9' & Grottaglie (noted '81-'85).
T-6H-4M Texan	MM53844	(ex 51-17225) ex 'SL-30' Grottaglie (noted '81-'84).
T-6H-4M Texan	MM53847	(ex 51-17228) ex 'SC-77' & Grottaglie (noted '81-'88).
T-6H-4M Texan	MM53849	ex 'SC-78' & Grottaglie (noted '81, to Lancenigo by late '83).
T-6H-2M Texan	MM54144	ex 'SL-51' & Grottaglie (noted '81-'84 - restored).
F-84F Thunderstreak	MM53-6619	ex '50-19' 155 Gruppo/50 Stormo, tail from "2052" (noted '81-'87).
RF-84F Thunderflash	MM..-....	ex '3-17' 18 Gruppo/3 Stormo (noted '87)
RF-84F Thunderflash	MM52-7399	ex '3-16' 18 Gruppo/3 Stormo (marked '27456' on port fin and '27469' on stbd) (noted '81).
RF-84F Thunderflash	MM52-7585	ex '3-07' 18 Gruppo/3 Stormo, tail from 36972 (noted '81-'87).
RF-84F Thunderflash	MM..-....	ex '3-09' 18 Gruppo/3 Stormo (noted '81).

Three F-86K Sabres arrived here in 5.87 for restoration and sale. They were recorded at Istrana in 8.72 (with five others) and subsequently noted in a scrapyard at Godega/S. Urbano in 5.75 but disappeared soon after. They comprise the following.

F-86K Sabre	MM55-4869	ex '51-56' 51 Stormo (tail from 54858).
F-86K Sabre	MM55-4858	ex '51-51' 51 Stormo (tail from 54869).
F-86K Sabre	MM54-1288	ex '51-72' 51 Stormo.

Former Air Gabon SE210 Caravelle VI-R TR-LWD (c/n 114, ex N1020U, OY-SBZ) was wfu at Venice during 1983 and was reported in the yard here by '87. Former Alitalia examples I-DABT and I-DAXU also passed through, being seen during 3.84 with the fuselage of I-DABT still present in '85.

On display at a nearby sportsground in 1981 was RF-84F Thunderflash MM52-7457/3-14 (fin serial '27471' on starboard side and '27479' on port). By 1986 it had resurfaced at Bareggio.

CATANIA/FONTANAROSSA

Preserved here are Agusta A106 MM5001N/5-01 near the gate with MM5002N/5-02 under restoration inside (noted '85-'88). They also have AB204AS MM80518/3-30 (noted '88).

Substantial quantities of Trackers have been stored here since their withdrawal from 41 Stormo on 31.8.78.

Grumman S-2A Tracker	MM133106	ex '41-23' (derelict '78-'88).
Grumman S-2A Tracker	MM133113	ex '41-25' (derelict '78, dump '83-'86).
Grumman S-2A Tracker	MM136558	ex '41-28' (derelict '78-'86, no engines).
Grumman S-2A Tracker	MM136728	ex '41-29' (derelict '79-'86, no engines).
Grumman S-2A Tracker	MM136727	ex '41-30' (derelict '79-'86, no engines).
Grumman S-2A Tracker	MM144702	ex '41-31' (derelict '77-'86).
Grumman S-2A Tracker	MM144696	ex '41-32' (derelict '78-'83, no engines).
Grumman S-2A Tracker	MM148301	ex '41-36' (derelict '78-'86, no engines).
Grumman S-2A Tracker	MM148303	ex '41-38' (derelict '79-'86, no engines).
Grumman S-2A Tracker	MM133085	ex '41-41' (derelict '78, dump '83-'86).
Grumman S-2A Tracker	MM148294	ex '41-43' (derelict '78-'86, no engines).

Grumman S-2A Tracker MM133097 ex '41-44' (derelict '78-'86).
Grumman S-2A Tracker MM136561 ex '41-45' (derelict '83).
Grumman S-2A Tracker MM148299 ex '41-46' (derelict '80-'88).
Grumman S-2A Tracker MM144717 ex '41-57' (derelict '78-'86, no engines).
Grumman S-2A Tracker MM136734 ex 'AS-10' (derelict '78-'86).
Several AB204ASWs were withdrawn from use and placed in open storage here by 4.86 when MM80301/3-01, MM80363/3-03, MM80366/3-05, MM80371/3-10, MM80372/3-11, MM80375/3-14, MM80376/3-15 and MM80518/3-30.

The dump has contained the rear half of F-104S Starfighter MM6927/5-34 ex 23 Gruppo/5 Stormo which crashed nearby 4.3.79 (noted 12.80-4.86). Noted in 1988 was the hulk of Dornier Do 27B I-BZPA (c/n 308, ex WGAF 5633, D-ELUY).

CERVIA/SAN GIORGIO

Preserved here is F-84F Thunderstreak MM53-6619/"8-34" (ex '50-19', noted '77-'86). Fiat G-91Y "8-06" (MM6441??) was damaged in an incident here during 11.87 and by 9.88 was hangared here for bdr training.

CINGOLI

Douglas DC-6B MM61965 (c/n 44251, ex I-DIMA) which last served as '31-5' with 306 Gruppo/31 Stormo arrived here (also described as Mummumiola, near Macerata - Cingoli is about 12 kms from Macerata) by early '88 following years of storage at Roma/Ciampino. The aircraft is modified for use as a dance bar and wears the spurious registration "I-LOVE". The same owner also took Agusta-Bell 47G MM80166 and AB47J MM80304 from Roma/Quarto Miglio (qv).

CONEGLIANO D'OTRANTO

Preserved in some gardens in this village (near Lecce) in 1987 was SNJ-5 Texan MM54292/SC-79 (ex Scuola Centrale and Grottaglie store). This, the sole Italian SNJ-5 was by this time in very poor condition.

CUNEO/LEVALDIGI

Preserved on the airfield is HU-16A Albatross MM50-180/15-6 (ex 84 Gruppo/15 Stormo, noted '80-'88).

DECIMOMANNU

Preserved at the gate of this well known NATO base is T-33A MM51-17455/SST-1 (ex Sezione Standardizzazione Tiro) (noted '81-'85). By 1983 RT-33A MM53-5668 was preserved on the base (current '85).

Agusta-Bell AB47J MM80256/SE-47 (ex SVE) was apparently wfu in a hangar here by 1.84. By 12.88 it was displayed on the gate in white c/s with AWTI titles but no code.

F-104G Starfighter 2514 (ex Memmingen decoy) arrived here aboard a Transall during 9.88 and has been placed on display in front of the control tower.

Derelict by the SAR hangar in 1979 were T-6Gs Texans MM53692/-, and MM54099/RR-56 (ex 2 RVR, arr Lyneham 1.7.87). Both were rescued from an uncertain future and airlifted to the UK in late '87 for restoration.

A scrap compound on the base in 1983 held the front fuselage of the unfortunate WGAF F-104G Starfighter 2553 (ex Jbg.32) which suffered a 'nasty' whilst on weapons camp here on 7.10.78. By 4.85 it had been joined by the wreck of an Italian G-91T thought to be MM6353/SA-53 (ex SVBAA) which crashed here 8.2.84. The "Deci" volume in the "Superbase" series makes reference to the dump being piled high with G-91s but unfortunately neglects to illustrate this - comments?

The wreck of TF-104G Starfighter 2710 (c/n 5711, ex 61-3040) was dumped behind the WGAF hangars here following a crash on approach to Deci whilst on an APC.

FAGIOLI DI SAN ILARIO D'ENZA

Five ex West German Choctaws were to be found here (in Reggio Emilia province) during '86, in a haulage contracter's yard. They arrived in Italy during 1975 in a frustrated Middle Eastern deal. Details as follows.

H-34G-III Choctaw 8072 (c/n 58-1553) TT 2260 hrs, last flew 10.6.78.
H-34G-III Choctaw 8093 (c/n 58-1605) TT 2355 hrs, last flew 10.6.78.
H-34G-III Choctaw 8203 (c/n 58-1619) TT 1469 hrs, last flew 17.6.78.
H-34G-III Choctaw 8204 (c/n 58-1733) TT 1470 hrs, last flew 18.6.78.
H-34G-III Choctaw 8205 (c/n 58-1737) TT 1517 hrs, last flew 10.6.78.
With my limited knowledge of Italian it is just possible that the company is called Fagioli and it may be located at San Ilario d'Enza. Be warned!

FALCONARA
Former Altair SE210 Caravelle I-GISE (c/n 208) was in use as a pizzeria at the airport here (on the coast, just North of Ancona) by 1988. The owners are also looking for an AB47G and AB47J.

FOLIGNO
In 1987 the OMA company had two complete ex ALE O-1E Bird Dogs and several engineless Siai SM1019Es at the airfield here (20 kms South East of Perugia).

FORLI
Preserved in the AAAV (Italian state ATC service) compound at this civil airport is Fiat G-46A MM52790/"SV-3" (c/n 23, ex I-AEHL, noted '83-'88) while a second example in the form of MM53312 (c/n 188, ex I-LEOR, noted '77-'88) is derelict on the field with some wrecked Macchi M416s (Fokker S.11s).

FROSINONE
Two Bell 47Gs and two AB204s were reported wrecked on the base during '87.

FURBARA
Douglas DC-6B MM61900/31-6 (c/n 43152, ex I-LIKE, I-DIMC) was abandoned on this Roma airfield by 1982 (noted '82-'86). The prototype General Avia SF600, I-CANG, was dumped here by '87 having crashed on 8.2.85.

GALLARATE
Displayed here (30 kms North West of Milano) by 2 Deposito Centrale AM are the following.

Agusta-Bell AB47G	MM80...	Medevac a/c (noted '85).
Agusta-Bell AB47J	MM80224	ex'RM-93' 1 RVR (noted '85).
Agusta-Bell AB204B	MM80...	ex 'SE-56' SVE (noted '85).
Fiat G-91PAN	MM6...	ex '2' 'Frecce Tricolori' (noted '85, probably MM6239 or MM6244).
Macchi MB326	MM.....	(noted '87).
F-86K Sabre	MM53-8299	"51-6" ex '51-61' 51 Stormo and Bergamo gate (noted '85).
T-6H-2M Texan	MM54143	ex 'RB-3' 3 RVR and Guidonia store (noted '85).
Piaggio P.166M	(MM61882)	marked "MM61822", ex 653 SC/53 Stormo (noted '85).

The unit also has premises at nearby Malpensa but no aircraft were visible from the outside at either location when visited in 7.88.

GAMBETTA
A scrapyard here was investigated in 7.82 and produced the wrecks of the following.

Agusta-Bell AB47J	MM80188	ex 'SC-2' Scuola Centrale.
Fiat G-91R	MM6399	ex '2-21' 2 Stormo.
F-104S Starfighter	MM6707	ex '51-05' 22 Gruppo/51 Stormo, crashed at Istrana 13.5.74).

Two Macchi M416s (license-built Fokker S.11s) and three Fiat G-46s remained unidentified, though a further visit in mid '84 confirmed the continued existence of the G-91 and unearthed the following.

Fiat G-46-3B	I-AEHD	(c/n 175, ex MM53299)
Fiat G-46-1B	MM52798	(c/n 31) ex 'ZP-15'

Fiat G-46-1B	MM52777	(c/n 10) ex 'ZP-24'
Macchi M416	I-AEMB	(ex MM53172)
Macchi M416	I-AEMN	(ex MM53230)
Macchi M416	I-AEPO	(ex MM53164)

GARDOLO
A garage here, near Trento, displayed Nardi FN305 I-DASM (ex MM52757) for many years. It was recovered by the preservation group GAVS in 2.86 and taken to Roma/Urbe for restoration.

GARDONE
The Museo Vittoriale di Gardone at Gardone Riviera (some 30 kms North East of Brescia) displays an anonymous Ansaldo SVA.5.

GHEDI
By 6.83 F-104G Starfighter MM6601/6-26 (ex 154 Gruppo/6 Stormo) was being prepared for gate guard duties having been replaced by the Tornado. She was in position on the gate by 1984 and still there in '89.

Preserved inside the base is F-84F Thunderstreak MM53-6740/"6-83" (noted '84-'86) which was previously at Livorno.

Withdrawn from use here by 1986 was Macchi MB326 MM54165/6-62 (ex 606 SC/6 Stormo). This may be the broken up example seen on the dump in 6.89.

GIGLIO DI VEROLI
Between Sora and Frosinone on the SS214, the '4R Rufa' furniture store has SE210 Caravelle VI-N I-DABU (c/n 77, wfu 26.9.76, TT 30,859 hrs) as an attraction (noted 12.87). The aircraft was formerly stored at Roma/Fiumicino.

GIOIA DEL COLLE
Preserved at the base here is F-84F Thunderstreak MM53-6858/36-39 (ex 36 Stormo) (noted '78-'86). On the gate by 6.89 was an F-86K Sabre marked "MM53-8303/36-06", presumably in spurious markings as the real 53-8303 was w/o on 20.4.56.

With the withdrawal of the AMI T-33s, several aircraft have languished out on the field with one being rescued for preservation.

Lockheed T-33A	MM51-9253	ex '36-65' 636 SC/36 Stormo (noted '83, preserved with 636 SC '84-'89 - but parked near the scrap compound).
Lockheed T-33A	MM54-1603	ex '36-69' 636 SC/36 Stormo (scrap '84).
Lockheed RT-33A	MM53-5396	ex '36-69' 636 SC/36 Stormo (stored '83, dump '84-'89).
Lockheed RT-33A	MM53-5430	ex '36-68' 636 SC/36 Stormo (stored '83, dump '84-'89).
Lockheed RT-33A	MM53-5525	ex '36-63' 636 SC/36 Stormo (scrap '84).

Three Piaggio P.166Ms were stored here in '84 whilst the type suffered some propeller problems. Perhaps co-incidentally, near the dump in early '86 were P.166Ms MM6190/36-73, MM61871/36-74, and MM61888/36-76 accompanied by a T-33A and an F-104S coded '36-07' which is thought to be MM6718. The P.166Ms and F-104 were still on the dump in 6.89 together with the two RT-33s noted above.

GORIZIA
Grumman HU-16A Albatross MM51-037/15-9 ex 84 Gruppo/15 Stormo was retired here (on the Yugoslav border) and flew in on 31.8.79 (current '80).

GRAZZANISE
The gate is guarded by Lockheed T-33A MM55-2980/9-33 (ex 609 SC/9 Stormo, formerly derelict here) which was here by 9.87. This replaced F-86E Sabre MM19841/4-44 (ex XB954, ex 4 Stormo) whuch arrived from Capua by 1983 but was later sent to Grosseto.

F-86E Sabre MM19523 (ex XB620, ex '4-50' of 4 Stormo but wears '13-30' of 13 Gruppo/2 Aero) had arrived here from Capua by '87, fitted with the rear fuselage and tail of 19664.

T-6H-4M Texan MM54098/SL-37 (ex Scuola Lecce and gia here) lay derelict here in early '83 but was rescued from an uncertain future and displayed outside the 609 SC hangar as "9-04" (or "9-09"?) later in the year (still current '88).

Lockheed RT-33A	* MM53-5587	ex '9-32' 609 SC/9 Stormo (derelict '83-'86).
Lockheed T-33A	* MM55-3077	ex '9-30' 609 SC/9 Stormo (derelict '83-'86).
Lockheed T-33A	* MM51-17470	ex '9-31' 609 SC/9 Stormo (derelict '83-'86).
Lockheed T-33A	MM55-2980	ex '9-33' 609 SC/9 Stormo (derelict '83-'86, displayed on the gate by '87).
Lockheed T-33A	MM55-3033	ex '4-033' 604 SC/4 Stormo (derelict '83-'88).

Those aircraft marked with an asterisk were offered for tender as scrap on 25.9.86 in DLA sale 50-6139. An enterprising scheme by the Italian preservationists GAVS to exchange the RT-33A in the USA for a P-39 foundered due to Italian red tape.

On the dump in '83 were the wrecks of two unidentified F-104 Starfighters.

GROSSETTO

The base acquired a gate guard in mid 1985 in the form of an anonymous TF-104G Starfighter wearing the code "20". MM54231 (last reported as '20-7' 3.82) would seem to be the most likely candidate but confirmation is required. The aircraft was still current during 6.89. F-86E Sabre MM19841/4-44 (ex XB954, ex 4 Stormo) had arrived here from Grazzanise by 1987, for preservation (current '89).

4 CMP undertake Starfighter overhauls here and by 1980 were using F-104S MM6931/51-12 (ex 51 Stormo) as a source of spares (current '85).

Offered for sale as scrap on 25.9.86 was Lockheed T-33A MM51-8829 which had been wfu here by 4.78.

Three F-104S Starfighters were in cocoon storage here by 5.87. A visit in 6.89 found a charred mess on the dump which may once have been a '104 whilst the visitors were informed that two dumped '104s had been cleared from the dump some months previously.

GROTTAGLIE

Offered for sale by the US Defense Logistics Agency office at Camp Darby (Livorno) in 3.81 and 7.81 were the following T-6 Texans which were in storage here at that time.

T-6C Texan	MM53418	(noted 3.81).
T-6G Texan	MM53655	'SC-69' (noted '77-3.81).
T-6G Texan	MM53657	'SC-61' (sold 16.7.81, TT 4275 hrs, to Castrette 10.81).
T-6H-4M Texan	MM53785	'SC-62' (sold 16.7.81, TT 5162 hrs, to Castrette 10.81).
T-6H-4M Texan	MM53792	'SC-65' (sold 16.7.81, TT 4959 hrs, to Castrette 10.81).
T-6H-4M Texan	MM53795	'SC-66' (noted '77-3.81, to Kemble, UK, becoming G-BJST).
T-6H-4M Texan	MM53796	'SC-52' (noted 3.81, to Kemble, UK).
T-6H-4M Texan	MM53797	'SC-67' (sold 16.7.81, TT5213 hrs, to Castrette 10.81).
T-6H-4M Texan	MM53816	'SC-63' (wrecked, noted '76-3.81).
T-6H-4M Texan	MM53820	(sold 16.7.81, TT 5381 hrs, to Castrette 10.81).
T-6H-4M Texan	MM53823	ex 'SC-70' (sold 16.7.81, TT 4771 hrs, to Castrette 10.81).
T-6H-4M Texan	MM53829	ex 'SC-73' (wreck noted '76, sold 3.81, to C-FCLJ at Vancouver Technical School).
T-6H-4M Texan	MM53832	ex 'SC-72' (sold 16.7.81, TT 5321 hrs, to Castrette 10.81).
T-6H-4M Texan	MM53833	ex 'SL-18' (noted 3.81).
T-6H-4M Texan	MM53835	ex 'SC-74' (sold 16.7.81, TT 5556 hrs, to Castrette 10.81).
T-6H-4M Texan	MM53841	ex 'SL-9' (sold 16.7.81, TT 5412 hrs, to Castrette 10.81).

T-6H-4M Texan MM53844 ex 'SL-30' (sold 16.7.81, TT 4940 hrs, to Castrette 10.81).
T-6H-4M Texan MM53847 ex 'SC-77' (sold 16.7.81, TT 6001 hrs, to Castrette 10.81).
T-6H-4M Texan MM53849 ex 'SC-78' (sold 16.7.81, TT 529 hrs, to Castrette 10.81).
T-6H-2M Texan MM54144 ex 'SL-51' (sold 16.7.81, to Castrette 10.81).
Also stored here at some time was the sole Italian AF SNJ-5 Texan.
SNJ-5 Texan MM54292 ex 'SC-79' to Conegliano d'Otranto by 1987.

IMOLA

T-6H-2 Texan MM54146 is preserved in a war museum at the Palazzo Alidosi painted as "284491/TA-491' (noted '87).

ISOLA SACRE

Convair 440 MM61833/31-1 (ex 306 Gruppo/31 Stormo) was expected to come here (near Roma/Fiumicino airport) after spending several years derelict at Roma/Ciampino.

ISTRANA

Preserved by the gate are the following.
Lockheed RT-33A MM53-5322 ex '51-76' 651 SC/51 Stormo (last flew 11.12.80, noted '81-'89).
F-86K Sabre MM55-4863 ex '51-60' 51 Stormo (painted as "MM53-8276/51-01") (noted '81-'85).
F-84F Thunderstreak MM53-7604 ex '50-04' 50 Stormo, painted as "51-26" (noted '75-'85).
Derelict on the field in recent years have been the following.
Agusta-Bell AB47J MM80162 ex '53-94' 651 SC/51 Stormo (wfu 3.82, scrap c.1986).
Agusta-Bell AB47J MM80246 ex '51-84' 651 SC/51 Stormo (wfu '83, scrap c.1986).
Lockheed T-33A MM51-9037 ex '51-86' 651 SC/51 Stormo, (wfu 23.2.79, fire dump '88-'89).
Lockheed T-33A MM51-9030 ex '51-85' 651 SC/51 Stormo (wfu by 10.79, dumped '87-'89).
Lockheed T-33A MM51-8936 ex '51-86' 651 SC/51 Stormo (last flt 1.7.80, burnt on fire dump '87).
Lockheed T-33A MM52-9898 ex '5-898' 651 SC/51 Stormo (wfu 11.79, allocated to air cadets 1987 for display as "51-86").
Lockheed RT-33A MM53-5238 ex '51-78' 651 SC/51 Stormo (wfu by '81, in use for bdr '88).
Macchi MB326 MM54216 ex '51-78' 651 SC/51 Stormo, wfu by 5.88.
The AB47Js and the unlucky T-birds were sold to a local scrap dealer, the helicopters subsequently appearing in a nearby scrapyard. T-birds 51-9037 and 53-5238 were offered under the Defense Logistic Agency's sale 50-6139 on 25.9.86 but obviously failed to attract a buyer. They were offered again in sale 50-8023 on 7.1.88.

T-6G Texan MM54096/RR-58 (ex 2 RVR) arrived for the fire dump in 9.82.

LAMPEDUSA

Preserved on the island of Lampedusa (in the Southern Mediterranean) is HU-16A Albatross MM50-177/15-4 (ex 84 Gruppo/15 Stormo) which flew in on 2.11.79 after several months storage at Roma/Ciampino (and was in poor condition by mid '85). This machine made the last AMI HU-16 flight.

LANCENIGO

One of the Texans from Castrette (qv) was displayed outside a shop here by '84.

LA RIVIERA

Preserved in '86 with a religious order (monastery or seminary perhaps?) at Zubie-na-Fraz is the fuselage of Stinson L-5 Sentinel I-AEFO (ex 42-98994, MM56694)

LATINA

Preserved on the North side by 6.83 was C-47 Dakota MM61778/SP-11 (ex SVBAE). The aircraft was still current in '85 but was processed by scrap dealers Nicola Del Prete from Cisterna early in 1988. Piaggio P.166M MM61873/SP-30 ex SVBAE (see below) was preserved on the gate by 8.85.

By the early eighties, the middle of the field boasted a long line of stored P.166s and P.148s, the latter looking very much the worse for wear. In early '88, six were sold to the same dealer who took the C-47 (the rest are probably still here). Known details are included in the list below. MM53544 has since been re-sold to another dealer.

Piaggio P.148	MM53544	ex '2' SVBAE (noted '78-'86, sold early '88 to a scrap dealer in Albano).
Piaggio P.148	MM53545	ex '3' SVBAE (noted '78-'86, to Sabaudia early '88).
Piaggio P.148	MM53546	ex '16' SVBAE (noted '78-'86, to Sabaudia early in '88).
Piaggio P.148	MM53547	ex '19' SVBAE (noted '78-'86, for Vigna di Valle).
Piaggio P.148	MM53549	ex '72' SVBAE (noted '78-'86, for San Pelagio).
Piaggio P.148	MM53550	ex '9' SVBAE (noted '78-'86).
Piaggio P.148	MM53551	ex '4' SVBAE (noted '78-'86).
Piaggio P.148	MM53558	ex 'RR-71' CMVV (noted '78-'86).
Piaggio P.148	MM53560	ex '75' SVBAE (noted '78-'86).
Piaggio P.148	MM53561	ex '18' SVBAE (noted '78-'86).
Piaggio P.148	MM53562	ex '26' SVBAE (noted '78-'86).
Piaggio P.148	MM53566	ex '74' SVBAE (noted '78-'86).
Piaggio P.148	MM53568	ex '8' SVBAE (noted '78-'86).
Piaggio P.148	MM53570	(noted '78-'80).
Piaggio P.148	MM53572	ex '25' SVBAE, (noted '78-'86 for ONFA at Cadimare).
Piaggio P.148	MM53580	ex '14' SVBAE (noted '78-'83).
Piaggio P.148	MM53573	ex '6' SVBAE (noted '78-'86).
Piaggio P.148	MM53582	ex '7' SVBAE (noted '78-'86).
Piaggio P.148	MM53583	ex 'RR-74' CMVV (noted '78-'86).
Piaggio P.148	MM53584	ex '29' SVBAE (noted '78-'86).
Piaggio P.148	MM53587	ex '11' SVBAE (noted '78-'86).
Piaggio P.148	MM53589	ex 'RR-73' CMVV (noted '78-'83).
Piaggio P.148	MM53590	ex '12' SVBAE (noted '78-'86).
Piaggio P.148	MM53593	ex 'RR-72' CMVV (noted '78-'86).
Piaggio P.148	MM53724	ex '15' SVBAE (noted '78-'86).
Piaggio P.148	MM53725	ex 'RR-78' CMVV (noted '78-'86).
Piaggio P.148	MM53726	ex '79' SVBAE (noted '78-'86, sold early '88 & preserved at Mario Caponera's nearby car showroom).
Piaggio P.148	MM53727	ex '22' SVBAE (noted '78-'86).
Piaggio P.148	MM53729	ex '20' SVBAE (noted '78-'86).
Piaggio P.148	MM53733	ex '22' SVBAE, to Capua by '81.
Piaggio P.148	MM53734	ex '71' SVBAE (noted 78-'86).
Piaggio P.148	MM53736	ex '3' SVBAE (noted '78-'86).
Piaggio P.148	MM53737	ex '28' SVBAE (noted '78-'80).
Piaggio P.148	MM53739	ex '23' SVBAE (noted '78-'86).
Piaggio P.148	MM53740	ex '77' SVBAE (noted '78-'86).
Piaggio P.148	MM53743	ex '10' SVBAE (noted '78-'86).
Piaggio P.166M	MM61878	ex 'SP-35' SVBAE (noted '83-'86).
Piaggio P.166M	MM61877	ex 'SP-37' SVBAE (noted '83-'86).
Piaggio P.166M	MM61872	ex 'SP-81' SVBAE (noted '83-'85).
Piaggio P.166M	MM61873	ex 'SP-39' SVBAE (noted '83, preserved on gate by '86).
Piaggio P.166M	MM61904	ex '303-31' 303 Gruppo (noted '85).
Piaggio P.166M	MM6.....	ex '303-16' 303 Gruppo (noted '86).
Piaggio P.166M	MM6.....	ex '303-36' 303 Gruppo (noted '86).

LECCE/GALATINA

On the gate by 7.84 were T-6H Texan MM53831/"SL-25" (Scuola Lecce marks) and former SVBIA Macchi MB326 MM54154/85. Both were still current in '89. By mid '85 a further MB326 coded '90' had arrived (probably from Naples) was parked outside the 3 RTA hangar with the forward fuselage of another example coded '23'.

10 CMP (formerly 3 RTA) have utilised their expertise and facilities to complete a number of restorations, several for the Museo Storico at Vigna di Valle. These include the following.

Fiat G-59	MM53265	(c/n 74) (being restored to G-55 standard) ex 'RB-49' (noted '85-'87).
Lohner L	L.127	captured 1919, ex Bari (noted '84-'87).
Messerschmitt Bf 109	-	wings and fuselage section in poor condition, stored '85 pending availability of a complete fuselage.
P-47D Thunderbolt	MM4653	(ex 44-89746) ex '51-19' 51 Stormo and Pisa University as gia, last flew 19.5.53 (noted '78-'85).
Spitfire LF.IX	MM4084	(ex MK805) ex Nettuno and Poligono di Foce Verde (noted '83-'88).

Four Macchi MB326s were noted on the dump during 11.82.

LECCE/SAN CATALDO

Preserved at the Aero Club by 1987 was Macchi MB308 I-ATAB (c/n 5853/80, ex MM52932).

LIDO-DI-JESOLO

On display in the resort is RF-84F Thunderflash MM52-7399/3-4 (rear fuselage from MM52-7546) (ex 18 Gruppo/3 Stormo).

LIVORNO/CAMP DARBY

Also known as Pisa/Tombolo, the US Defense Logistics Agency office here has in the past handled AMI Sikorsky H-19D disposals & some scrap F-84s. In the more recent past, the ALE's Super Cub fleet has largely passed through here onto the civil market.

Sale 11.2.81:

L-18C Super Cub MM51-15302 ex 'EI-51' to Walkeridge Farm (UK) becoming G-BJTP.
L-18C Super Cub MM51-15303 ex 'EI-52' to Walkeridge Farm (UK) becoming G-BIYJ.
L-18C Super Cub MM52-2379 ex 'EI-58' to Walkeridge Farm (UK) becoming G-BIYY.
L-18C Super Cub MM52-2380 ex 'EI-59' to Walkeridge Farm (UK) becoming G-BPJH.
L-18C Super Cub MM52-2385 ex 'EI-64' to Walkeridge Farm (UK) becoming G-BJWX.
L-18C Super Cub MM52-2388 ex 'EI-66' to Walkeridge Farm (UK) becoming G-BJEI.
L-18C Super Cub MM52-2390 ex 'EI-67' to Walkeridge Farm (UK) becoming G-BKET.
L-18C Super Cub MM52-2392 ex 'EI-69' to Walkeridge Farm (UK) becoming G-BKDG.
L-18C Super Cub MM52-2398 ex 'EI-71' to Walkeridge Farm (UK) becoming G-AMEN.
L-18C Super Cub MM52-2401 ex 'EI-74' to Walkeridge Farm (UK) becoming G-BIZV.
L-18C Super Cub MM52-2422 ex 'EI-91' to Walkeridge Farm (UK) becoming G-BJFE.

Offered for sale in 3.81 were O-1E Bird Dogs MM61-2988 and MM61-2991 with T-6H-4M Texan MM53846/RM-22 (ex 1 RVR, wfu 13.2.79). The Texan was allocated G-BIWX on 29.4.81 for Robs Lamplough.

Sale 50-1096 16.7.81:

O-1E Bird Dog MM61-2961 ex 'EI-22' (TT 2605).
O-1E Bird Dog MM61-2969 ex 'EI-16' (TT 2084).
L-18C Super Cub MM51-15304 ex 'EI-53' (TT 1611, ex Bracciano) to N3267W.
L-18C Super Cub MM51-15306 ex 'EI-55' (TT 1968, ex Bracciano) to N2703W.
L-18C Super Cub MM51-15307 ex 'EI-56' (TT 1653, ex Bracciano) to N1384N.
L-18C Super Cub MM52-2386 ex 'EI-65' (TT 2221, ex Bracciano) to N3268A.
L-18C Super Cub MM52-2403 ex 'EI-76' (TT 1885, ex Bracciano) to N1384R.
L-18C Super Cub MM52-2405 ex 'EI-78' (TT 2522, ex Bracciano) to N3134F.
L-18C Super Cub MM52-2407 ex 'EI-80' (TT 1830, ex Bracciano) to N3267Y.

L-18C Super Cub MM52-2408 ex 'EI-81' (TT 2000, ex Bracciano) to N27363.
L-18C Super Cub MM52-2409 ex 'EI-82' (TT 2070, ex Bracciano).
L-18C Super Cub MM52-2413 ex 'EI-83' (TT 2362, ex Bracciano).
L-18C Super Cub MM52-2414 ex 'EI-84' (TT 1792, ex Bracciano) to N3268N.
L-18C Super Cub MM52-2419 ex 'EI-88' (TT 2015, ex SVBAE) to N3134G.
L-18C Super Cub MM52-2420 ex 'EI-89' (TT 1783, ex Bracciano) to N917CS.
L-18C Super Cub MM52-2421 ex 'EI-90' (TT 2275, ex Bracciano) to N917AS.
L-18C Super Cub MM52-2426 ex 'EI-95' (TT 1856, ex Bracciano) to N917ES.
L-21B Super Cub MM52-2383 ex 'EI-62' (TT 2424) to N1394R.
L-21B Super Cub MM53-7718 ex 'EI-101' (TT 1999) to I-LOBO.
L-21B Super Cub MM53-7724 ex 'EI-106' (TT 2210) to N811CG.
L-21B Super Cub MM53-7735 ex 'EI-116' (TT 2520, ex Bracciano) to N....
L-21B Super Cub MM53-7739 ex 'EI-120' (TT 3100) to I-BTRE.
L-21B Super Cub MM53-7740 ex 'EI-121' (TT 2666) to N1383N.
L-21B Super Cub MM53-7757 ex 'EI-135' (TT 1948, ex Bracciano) to N1394Y.
L-21B Super Cub MM53-7759 ex 'EI-137' (TT 2422, ex Bracciano) to N3907E.
L-21B Super Cub MM54-2316 ex 'EI-154' (TT 2342, ex Bracciano) to N27036.
L-21B Super Cub MM54-2321 ex 'EI-158' (TT 3630, ex Bracciano) to N1394V.
L-21B Super Cub MM54-2369 ex 'EI-181' (TT 2505) to SX-ASM.
L-21B Super Cub MM54-2382 ex 'EI-193' (TT 3343, ex Bracciano).
L-21B Super Cub MM54-2396 ex 'EI-205' (TT 2046).
L-21B Super Cub MM54-2400 ex 'EI-209' (TT 2897, ex Bracciano).
L-21B Super Cub MM54-2506 ex 'EI-211' (TT 1857) to N1421B.
L-21B Super Cub MM54-2528 ex 'EI-232' (TT 2586) to N27039.
L-21B Super Cub MM54-2530 ex 'EI-233' (TT 2582) to N13824.
L-21B Super Cub MM54-2546 ex 'EI-247' (TT 2275).
L-21B Super Cub MM54-2551 ex 'EI-251' (TT 1423) to N1383W.
L-21B Super Cub MM54-2555 ex 'EI-253' (TT 3356) to N13835.
L-21B Super Cub MM54-2581 ex 'EI-259' (TT 2008, ex Bracciano).
L-21B Super Cub MM54-2582 ex 'EI-260' (TT 2062) to I-BUNO.
L-21B Super Cub MM54-2611 ex 'EI-269' (TT 1719, ex Bracciano).
L-21B Super Cub MM54-2618 ex 'EI-275' (TT 2429) to N2227C.
L-21B Super Cub MM54-2629 ex 'EI-285' (TT 2633, ex Bracciano) to N2621K.

Sale 11.81
L-18C Super Cub MM52-2423 ex 'EI-92' to I-NACA.
TL-21B Super Cub MM53-7731 ex 'EI-113' to N2719B.
L-21B Super Cub MM54-2318 ex 'EI-155' to C-GFRI.
L-21B Super Cub MM54-2320 ex 'EI-157'
L-21B Super Cub MM54-2354 ex 'EI-168' to N3021L.
L-21B Super Cub MM54-2388 ex 'EI-197' to N3267N.
L-21B Super Cub MM54-2392 ex 'EI-201' to N2474Z.
L-21B Super Cub MM54-2509 ex 'EI-214' to N85DC.
L-21B Super Cub MM54-2510 ex 'EI-215' to N3267P.
L-21B Super Cub MM54-2568 ex 'EI-258' to N3020F.

Sale early '86
O-1E Bird Dog MM61-3001 ex 'EI-10'

Sale 30.9.87
O-1E Bird Dog MM61-2977 ex 'EI-28' (TT 1911, ex CALE).

LORETO
F-104G Starfighter MM6632/3-24 (ex 3 Stormo) was at Villafranca early in '89 reportedly allocated to the AMI Scuola Perfezionamento Sottufficiali here (near Ancona) as a gate guard. It was joined by Fiat G-91R MM6301/2-25 (ex 2 Stormo) from Treviso/San Angelo in early 5.89.

MACERATA
Preserved at the SARAM (Scuola Addestramento Reclute AM) here in '85 were Macchi MB326 MM54153/84 and an anonymous T-6G Texan coded '303-56' (ex 303 Gruppo).

MARINA DI CAMPO

Westland-Bell 47G-3B1 I-ELDE (c/n WA519, ex XT182) was displayed outside a newsagents here on the island of Elba by 1987.

MEGLIADINO DI SAN FIDENZO

F-86K Sabre MM54-1256/51-50 (ex 51 Stormo) arrived here (near Padova) on 15.4.87 from the yard at Castrette having been purchased by the Barolo company in Via Longo Pasquali.

MILANO

At the Museo Alfa Romeo di Arese some 12kms North West of Milan, Alfa Romeo display a considerable number of cars and a lone aircraft in the form of SAI Ambrosino S.111 Grifo "I-ASSI". This is a partial replica using parts of I-RANN (c/n 11).

The Museo Nazionale della Scienza e della Tecnica (National Museum of Science & Technology) holds the following airframes.

Bleriot XI	-	replica (noted '77-'88).
Breda Ba.15	-	(noted '77-'88).
Caproni TM2	MM511	(c/n 2) (noted '77).
Caproni-Campini CC.2	-	fuselage only (noted '77).
Cierva C.30A	I-CIER	(c/n 753, ex G-ACXA, I-CIER, MM30030) (noted '77-'88).
DH80A Puss Moth	I-FOGL	(c/n 2114) (noted '77-'88).
DH Vampire FB.52A	MM6112	'76' (noted '88).
DH Venom FB.50	MM6153	composite with parts from MM6154 (noted '77).
Farman C.IVA	I-FARM	replica (noted '77-'88).
Junkers J4	-	fuselage only (noted '77-'88).
MC205V Veltro	MM92166	(ex EgyptAF 1243) painted as "MM9327/81-5" (noted '77-'88).
Macchi-Nieuport Ni10	I-BORA	(c/n 15179) (noted '77-'88).
Magni PM 3/4 Vale	MM253	(noted '77-'88).
Muegyetemi M.24	I-TITI	(noted '77-'88).
Nardi FN.333 Riviera	-	(noted '77-'88).
T-6G Texan	MM54114	ex 'RM-18' 1 RVR and Bergamo store (noted '77-'88).
F-86K Sabre	MM55-4812	(c/n NC52) "51-3", ex '5-57' 5 Stormo, wfu 10.4.73 (noted '88).
Pasotti F9 Sparviero	I-HAWK	(c/n D2) (noted '77-'88).
F-84F Thunderstreak	MM53-6805	ex '50-30' 50 Stormo (noted '77-'88).
Ricci 6	-	replica (noted '77-'88).
SAI Ambrosini S.7	I-PAIN	(c/n 1/01) (noted '77-'88).
Saiman 202M	I-CUPI	(ex MM52162) (noted '77-'88).
SM.102	I-GION	(c/n 17, ex MM61810) (noted '77-'88).

MILANO/BRESSO

Preserved on the airfield by 1979 (and still current 7.88) was RF-84F Thunderstreak MM52-7390/3-19 (ex 18 Gruppo/3 Stormo, last flew 17.7.73) with the Gruppo Amatori Volo. The group have Piaggio P.136L I-FRLV (c/n 212, ex MM80082, I-SASO) and a Caproni Ca.100. Plans are in hand for a hangar to house several preserved aircraft here, including the Piaggio P.148 prototype I-DIDA.

By 1987 an unidentified Fiat G-46 was preserved at the entrance to the ALE's 3 Raggruppamento area.

MILANO/LINATE

Undergoing restoration to fly here in 1987 was Piper L-18C Super Cub MM52-2402/EI-75 to become I-ARMY.

MILANO/MALPENSA

C-130H Hercules MM62000/46-14 (ex 50 Gruppo/46 Stormo) jumped chocks here on 23.1.79 during post overhaul engine runs. The badly damaged airframe was written off for spares use and was still present during '89, the nose now being fitted to MM61995.

Dumped here is an ex Altair SE210 Caravelle which crashed during the mid '80s (current 7.88).

MONDAINO

Signor Carlo Bulli has Macchi MB308 I-PINI (c/n 5819) preserved here (near Forli) at the Hotel Montebello (noted '87).

MONTE SAN SAVINO

Preserved at a factory near the station is O-1E Bird Dog MM61-2988/EI-23 (noted '84-'85). Monte San Savino is off the E6 motorway some 80 kms North of Ovieto.

NAPLES/CAPODICHINO

Gate guardian here is Lockheed T-33A MM51-17536/4-16 (ex 604 SC/4 Stormo) (noted '85).

The AMI's 5 RTA are believed to have handled the disposal of some life-expired MB326s in the mid eighties. Further details would be welcome.

Several Trackers have been long-term inhabitants of the dump, comprising the following.

Grumman S-2A Tracker	MM136558	ex '41-28' (noted '83).
Grumman S-2A Tracker	MM144696	ex '41-32' (noted '83).
Grumman S-2A Tracker	MM144710	ex '41-33' (noted '80-'88).
Grumman S-2A Tracker	MM148295	ex '41-35' (noted '80-'88).
Grumman S-2A Tracker	MM148297	ex '41-40' (noted '80, to Marseille (Fr) by '85).
Grumman S-2A Tracker	MM148299	ex '41-46' (noted '83).

Dumped here in '84 were T-33As MM51-17455/36-66 and MM..-..../36-67 (both ex 636 SC/36 Stormo). Both were still current in '86.

NOVARA

Nardi FN305 I-TOMI (c/n 007) is privately preserved in a barn near here.

ORZINUOVI

At this small town near Ghedi, RF-84F Thunderflash MM27397/3-13 (ex 18 Gruppo/3 Stormo) is preserved at the war memorial in the town centre (noted '77-'83).

OSPEDALICCHIO

On the SS75 road, the Falaschi furniture shop here had engineless Piaggio P66B I-PALE on display by 1985.

PADOVA/SAN PELAGIO

The Nido delle Aquile Air Museum at Castello di San Pelagio (about 12 kms South West of Padova) holds the following airframes.

Agusta-Bell AB47J	MM80227	(c/n 1122) ex 'SE-40' SVE (noted '85-'86).
Agusta-Bell AB204B	MM80281	(c/n 3049) ex '15-25' 15 Stormo (arrived 8.86).
Alaparma AM.10	I-CARD	(c/n 001) (noted '86).
Avia FL.3	I-AIAD	(c/n A-10) (noted '86).
Aviamilano P.19	-	(stored, dismantled '86).
CVV8 Canguro	I-TRIW	(c/n 0003, ex MM100005) (noted '86).
EC38-56C Urendo	I-AVMM	(c/n 008) (noted '86).
UC-61K Argus	I-FRIF	(c/n 1036, ex 44-83075, KK418) (noted '86).
Fauvel AV.36	I-DAWN	(c/n 42) (noted '86).
HU16A Albatross	MM51-7253	ex '15-14' 84 Gruppo/15 Stormo, flew to Padova/Brusegana 19.6.79 (TT 7053 hrs) and airlifted here by CH-47 6.5.81 (noted '86).
Macchi MB308	I-ATAA	(c/n 5851/78, ex MM52931) (noted '86).
T-6H Texan	MM53823	ex 'SC-70' (ex Castrette) (noted '82-'86).
RF-84F Thunderflash	MM52-7339	ex '3-03' 18 Gruppo/3 Stormo and Carita (noted '86).

PALERMO

The engineering faculty at the University had Fiat G-59-4A MM53530/RR-73 (c/n 115) in 1985 though another source gives it as G-59-4B MM53535/RM-73 (c/n 135).

PERDASDEFOGU

In 1981 Lockheed T-33A MM51-8832/51-87 (ex 651 SC/51 Stormo) was airlifted by ALE CH-47 from Decimomannu to the ranges here for gate-guard use. It was current during 1988.

PESCARA

By 1985 Fiat G-91R MM6253/2-71 (ex 2 Stormo) was preserved at the aerodrome here (current '86).

PERUGIA

Piaggio P.136L-1 MM80077/84-12 has been reported to be preserved here (eg '83).

PISA

The local technical college (ITI Da Vinci) have F-86E Sabre MM19782/4-83 (ex XB894, ex 4 Stormo) for instructional purposes (noted '64-'88).

PISA/SAN-GIUSTO

A reminder of 46 BA's earlier days is preserved on the gate in the form of Fairchild C-119G MM53-3200/46-38 (ex 2 Gruppo/46 Aero) (noted '83-'89).

Beech C-45	MM61707	ex 'RR-04' 2 RVR (noted '80-'89).
Fairchild C-119G	MM52-6002	ex '46-31' 2 Gruppo/46 Aero (noted '79-'86, sold for scrap '86).
Fairchild C-119J	MM51-8125	ex '46-51' 50 Gruppo/46 Aero (noted '80).
Fairchild C-119J	MM51-8128	ex '46-52' 50 Gruppo/46 Aero (noted '80).
Fairchild C-119J	MM51-8130	ex '46-53' 50 Gruppo/46 Aero (noted '80).
Fairchild C-119J	MM51-8140	ex '46-54' 50 Gruppo/46 Aero (noted '80).
Fairchild C-119J	MM51-8152	ex '46-56' 50 Gruppo/46 Aero (noted '80).
Fairchild C-119J	MM51-8156	ex '46-58' 50 Gruppo/46 Aero (noted '72-'80).
Fairchild C-119J	MM52-5866	ex '46-61' 50 Gruppo/46 Aero (noted '80).
Fairchild C-119J	MM52-5897	ex '46-65' 50 Gruppo/46 Aero (noted '80).
Fairchild C-119J	MM52-5947	ex '46-66' 50 Gruppo/46 Aero (noted '80).
Fairchild C-119J	MM53-8098	ex '46-67' 50 Gruppo/46 Aero (noted '80).
Fairchild C-119J	MM53-8103	ex '46-68' 50 Gruppo/46 Aero (noted '80).
Fairchild C-119J	MM51-8113	ex '46-69' 50 Gruppo/46 Aero (noted '80).
Fairchild C-119G	MM52-6024	ex '46-91' 98 Gruppo/46 Aero (noted '79-'85).
Fairchild C-119G	MM53-7845	ex '46-94' 98 Gruppo/46 Aero (noted '77-'89).
Fairchild C-119G	MM52-6030	ex '46-95' 98 Gruppo/46 Aero (noted '79-'88 but offered for sale as scrap '86).
Fairchild C-119G	MM53-3219	ex '46-96' 98 Gruppo/46 Aero (noted '77-'89).
Fairchild C-119G	MM53-7828	ex '46-97' 98 Gruppo/46 Aero (noted '77-'88).
Fairchild C-119J	51-8046	acquired for spares only (noted '77-'85).
Fairchild C-119J	5.-...	acquired for spares only, probably marked '66' (noted '77-'85).

Withdrawn from use here by 9.85 (and still current 6.89) were Piaggio P.166Ms MM61876/303-32 and MM61902/303-36 (both ex 303 Gruppo). The airfield has been littered with withdrawn C-119s since the late seventies and the last handful still linger, along with a solitary C-45). The two 'spares-ship' C-119Js which remained in '83 were both ex USAF aircraft, though unfortunately, no-one seems ever to have identified the second one. 51-8046 was found to be non-airworthy on arrival and spent several years in use as a cockpit procedure trainer before being relegated to the dump. The hulk of one of this pair was still extant (just!) in 6.89.

Agusta-Bell AB205 MM80776/CC-35 was damaged on 10.9.88 and its wreck was with 4 Elinucleo Carabinieri here during 12.88.

PORTOGRUARO

The Instituto Professionale Statale Industriale ed Artigiano di Portogruaro (off the A4 motorway about 50 kms North East of Venezia) has Fiat G-46-4B I-AEHY (c/n 178, ex MM53302) (noted '78-'85).

PORTOMAGGIORE

A wrecked Stinson L-5 was to be seen in a scrapyard here (near Ferrara) during 1987. No identity could be found on the complete but battered airframe.

PRATICA DI MARE

In recent years an increasing number of aircraft have been preserved here, as shown by the list below.

Agusta-Bell AB47J	MM80212	ex 'RB-47' 512 Sq (noted '87-'88).
Douglas C-47	MM61775	ex '14-40' 8 Gruppo/14 Stormo (preserved at 8 Gruppo '82-'86).
Fiat G-91PAN	MM6248	noted '84, reported in '87 to be going on display by the RSV HQ.
Fiat G-91T proto	MM6288	ex 'RS-01' RSV (preserved with 311 Gruppo/RSV '84-'86).
Fiat G-91Y proto	MM579	ex 'RS-11' RSV (noted '86, at the entrance to the CTA/TLC-AV or Centro Tecnico di Addestramento alle Telecomunicazioni e Assistenza di Volo).
F-104G Starfighter	MM6660	ex 'RS-02' RSV (preserved with 311 Gruppo/RSV '84-'86).

Reported preserved inside a building by the Servizio Aereo del Carabinieri in 1987 were the following.

Agusta-Bell AB47G-3B1	MM80482	ex 'CC-13' (c/n 1615).
Agusta-Bell AB47J	MM80294	ex 'CC-1' (c/n 2039).

The Guardia di Finanza have a substantial presence on the base and by 1988 had preserved one of their early helicopters here.

Agusta-Bell AB47G	MM80084	ex 'GdiF-1' (w/o 19.4.72, noted '88).

The preserved aircraft are outnumbered by a large quantity of derelicts, mostly hidden away in various nooks and crannies around the field. One wonders where they find room for any active aircraft! Reportedly derelict in recent years are the following.

Agusta-Bell AB47G-3B1	MM80489	(c/n 1635) ex 'CC-22' Carabinieri (noted '86)*.
Agusta-Bell AB47J	MM80139	ex 'RS-29' RSV (noted '86).
Agusta-Bell AB47J	MM80140	ex 'RS-29' RSV (noted '86).
Agusta-Bell AB47J	MM80...	ex 'RS-29' RSV (noted '86).
Agusta-Bell AB47J	MM80185	ex '31-34' 31 Stormo (noted '86).
Agusta-Bell AB47J	MM80199	ex '31-32' 31 Stormo (noted '86).
Agusta-Bell AB47J	MM80198	ex 'SE-51' SVE (noted '86)*.
Agusta-Bell AB47J	MM80218	ex '512-44' 512 SC (noted '86)*.
Agusta-Bell AB47J	MM80...	ex '15-34' 15 Stormo (noted '86)*.
Agusta-Bell AB47J	MM80...	ex '15-35' 15 Stormo (noted '86)*.
Agusta-Bell AB47J-3	MM80404	ex 'CC-..' Carabinieri (noted '86)*.
Agusta-Bell AB205A-1	MM80777	(c/n 4173) ex 'CC-33' Carabinieri (noted '84, sold for scrap '88)*.
Agusta-Bell AB205A-1	MM80783	(c/n 4259) ex 'CC-39' Carabinieri, crashed at Catanzaro 31.10.77 (noted '84).
Agusta-Bell AB206	MM80925	rear only, ex 'CC-47 Carabinieri (noted '86)*.
Beech C-45	MM61643	ex 'CR-30' Centro Radiomisure (noted '86, but MM61758/CR-30 reported '84!).
Bell OH-13H	59-4956	ex USAREUR (noted '86)*.
Bell 47D-1	MM80042	ex 'EL-4' Centro Elicotteri (noted '88).
C-47 Dakota	MM61800	(c/n 4260, ex 41-7773) ex 'CR-51' Centro Radiomisure (scrap compound '83-'86).
C-47 Dakota	MM61825	(c/n 4221, ex 41-7742) ex '14-50' 8 Gruppo/14 Stormo (noted '83-86)*.
Fairchild EC-119G	MM53-8146	ex '46-35' 71 Gruppo/14 Stormo (noted '83-'86).
Fiat G-222 proto	MM582	ex 'RS-06' RSV (noted '83-'86).
Lockheed T-33A	MM51-4418	ex '418' 14 Stormo (noted '82-'86).
Lockheed T-33A	MM51-4514	ex '14-22' 14 Stormo (noted '82-'86).
Lockheed T-33A	MM51-9140	ex '6-31' 606 SC/6 Stormo (noted '82-'86).

Lockheed T-33A	MM54-1602	ex '602' (noted '84-'86).
Macchi AL.60C-4	MM581	ex 'RS-23' RSV, also marked I-MACP (noted'81-'86)*.
Macchi MB326	MM54166	derelict '84.
Sikorsky HH-3F	MM80982	rear only (noted '86 but MM80987/15-16 reported in damaged state here 8.85-4.86 following accident c.19.8.84)*.

The aircraft marked with an asterisk were in 9.86 described as wrecks belonging to the Magazzino Speciale Aeronautico (a storage facility).

The burnt remains of F-84F Thunderstreak MM53-6801/50-24 were sold for scrap late in 1988 (along with AB205A-1 MM80777 noted above). Both are believed to have gone to a scrapyard in Naples. Just to confuse the issue, F-84F MM51-7029/50-24 was reported wrecked here in '84 (perhaps another composite airframe?).

PRATO

At Casale, a hamlet a few kilometres from Prato (itself about 10 kms North West of Firenze) the dismantled hulk of F-84F Thunderstreak MM53-6579/36-40 was discovered in 1987. It is alongside, but not visible from, the A11 autostrada.

RAVENNA

The wrecks of Macchi 416s (Fokker S.11s) I-AELC (c/n 1052, ex MM53755) and I-AEFX were dumped here during '87.

RIETI

Preserved on the military side of the aerodrome here (some 70 kms North East of Roma) by 1985 was Fiat G-91R MM6277/2-70 (ex 2 Stormo).

RIMINI

In front of a hotel in the town centre is F-84F Thunderstreak "MM64974/69-4" which is made up from the front fuselage of MM53-6637/50-10 and the rear of MM53-6695/36-35 (noted '82-'88).

RIMINI/MIRAMARE

Preserved on the base in 6.84 were F-84F Thunderstreak MM53-6856/50-13 (ex 102 Gruppo/50 Stormo) and F-86K Sabre MM53-8301/5-52 (ex 23 Gruppo/5 Stormo). The latter was still current 7.88 (marked as "5-18") whilst the former had been relegated to the dump. It replaced F-86K Sabre "MM55-4820/5-53" which was a composite of MM55-4906/5-53 (front) and MM55-4820/51-52 (rear). It was reported on the fire dump in '82.

Lockheed T-33A MM51-17477/477 ex 605 SC/5 Stormo was dumped here by 1980 following an accident here on 10.6.78 (current '87).

RIVOLTO

The home of the Frecce Tricolori has an extensive base museum here displaying mostly aerobatic aircraft.

Fairchild C-119G	MM52-6020	ex '46-84' 98 Gruppo/46 Aero (noted '78-'88).
Fiat G-91PAN	MM6241	ex '3' 'Frecce Tricolori' (noted '81-'88).
Lockheed T-33A	MM55-3080	ex '51-85' 651 SC/51 Stormo. (arr 2.4.82, current '88).
Lockheed RT-33A	MM53-5795	ex '36-68' 636 SC/36 Stormo (noted '82-'88).
T-6H-4M Texan	MM53822	painted as "303-23" 303 Gruppo marks (ex 'SC-53' SCIV) (noted '80-'88).
F-86E Sabre	MM19664	(ex XB810) ex '13-3' but painted as "MM19685/4-20" in the colours of the 'Cavallino Rampante' team (noted '82-'88).
F-86E Sabre	MM19724	(ex XD723) ex '4-25', painted in 'Frecce Tricolori' colours (noted '77-'86).
F-86E Sabre	MM19680	(ex XB826) ex '2-37' and Malignani technical institute at Udine (noted '88 in 'Lanceri Neri' colours, might only be here temporarily).

F-86K Sabre	MM54-1292	ex '5-65' 5 Stormo, fitted with rear fuselage from MM55-4818 and marked as "MM55-4818/51-36" (noted '77-'88).
F-84F Thunderstreak	MM53-6845	one side in 'Diavoli Rossi' c/s, the other in 'Getti Tonanti' scheme) (noted '77-'88).
RF-84F Thunderflash	MM52-7474	ex '3-18' (parts from 52-7463, noted '82-'88).

ROMA

On the Via del Mare between Roma and Ostia is a building supplies depot which had received the five airframes listed below by 1983.

Macchi MB308	I-GIPI	front fuselage only.
Macchi MB308	I-AERO	(c/n 5820/47, ex MM52905) ex Lugo di Romagna Aero Club.
Partenavia P.66	I-MAZZ	(c/n 54) ex Modena.
Partenavia P.66	I-NOLI	ex Modena.
PA23-150 Aztec	I-HUNT	(c/n 23-151, ex N1311P) ex Biella.

In 1987, Salvatore Profeta's scrapyard at Grande Raccordo Anulare (between the SS Flaminia and SS Salaria roads) had Siai S205-20R I-SPQS (c/n 4-136) from Rome/Urbe, PA22 Tri Pacer G-ARCU (c/n 22-7471, crashed at Naples 6.9.71) and Partenavia P.66B I-HERO (last noted derelict at Roma/Urbe in 1980). The S205 at least was still current in 6.89 and is visible from the Roma ring road near Cassia.

The Instituto Tecnico Galileo Galilei (Tech College) were using a Fiat G-46-1B coded 'AA-77' (probably MM52795 c/n 28) and Sabre Mk.4 MM19666/4-11 during '83 (with the Sabre still current 5.86). Also in 1983, another Tech College, the IAS F de Pinedo had Viscount 798 I-LIRG (c/n 284, ex N6594C) and Fiat G-46-1B MM52778 (c/n 11, ex I-AEHP, I-DEPI).

The Museo Storico della Motorizzazione Militare at the 'Cecchignola' barracks has Agusta-Bell AB47J-3B-1 MM80263/EI-24. They have also had L-21B Super Cub MM54-297/EI-206 and an unidentified L-18C coded "EI-00" (both noted '83) but these may have moved on. An AB204B is expected.

Preserved at the Museo del Genio di Roma is Bleriot XI "1" c/n 412 (noted '83).

ROMA/CIAMPINO

Home of the AMI's VIP transport units, the base has housed many long term relics over the years.

Convair CV 440	MM61833	(c/n 442) ex '31-1' 306 Gruppo/31 Stormo (noted '78-'87, to Isola Sacre).
Convair CV 440	MM61898	(c/n 392) ex '31-4' 306 Gruppo/31 Stormo (noted '78-'87, sold for scrap 28.11.86).
Convair CV 440	MM61899	(c/n 407) ex '31-21' 306 Gruppo/31 Stormo (noted '78-'87, sold for scrap 28.11.86).
Convair CV 440	MM61901	(c/n 450) ex '31-22' 306 Gruppo/31 Stormo (noted '78-'87, sold for scrap 28.11.86).
Douglas DC-6B	MM61964	(c/n 44253) ex 'SM-23' 306 Gruppo/31 Stormo (on fire dump '75-'87)
Douglas DC-6B	MM61965	(c/n 44251) ex '31-5' 306 Gruppo/31 Stormo (noted '78-'87, to Cingoli as "I-LOVE").
HU-16A Albatross	MM51-035	ex '15-8' 84 Gruppo/15 Stormo (noted '79-'88, preserved by SAR HQ on South side by '86).
Lockheed T-33A	MM51-9249	ex '51-88' 651 SC/51 Stormo, flew in 3.4.82 and stored pending transport to Museo Storico (noted '83-'84).
Lockheed RT-33A	MM53-5594	ex '9-35' 609 SC/9 Stormo (noted '84, to Vigna di Valle).

ROMA/FIUMICINO

An AMI depot near the airport has T-6H-4M Texan MM53801/"4-01" (spurious 4 Stormo marks, really ex 'RB-6' 3 RVR) which came from the store at Guidonia by 1987.

SE210 Caravelle III I-DABU (c/n 77) was preserved in the Alitalia area at the airport by '83. In '85 it was sold for use as a bar.

ROMA/GUIDONIA

Preserved on the gate by 1983 was T-6H-4M Texan MM53825/303-50 (still there '86). The aircraft last served as 'RR-55' with 2 RVR and retired to 2 RTA at Guidonia by 4.78.

Under restoration in 1986 was a composite Vampire single seater being prepared for the Museo Storico at Vigna di Valle by the Servizio Tecnico of 303 Gruppo (ex 2 RTA). The fuselage nacelle came from the Galileo Galilei technical college in Rome, with other sections being retrived from the old airfield at Roma/Furbara.

In recent years the airfield has been littered with large quantities of redundant aircraft, principally C-45s, C-47/C-53s, T-6s and P.166s. In 1983 there were some 14 C-45s, 7 Daks, 16 Texans and 7 P.166s. In mid '87 the field could still muster 11 C-45s and 7 Texans with an unspecified number of Daks and Piaggios. It must be pointed out that some of the Daks recorded in '83 were sectioned fuselages and could easily be overlooked. Near them were the barely recognisable remains of some Macchi M416s (licence-built Fokker S.11) which appeared to have been left to rot many years before.

Some years earlier, in 1978, a large number of C-45s were to be seen piled up in a scrapyard adjoining the airfield but these had all expired by 1983. As well as those C-45s listed below, an aircraft noted as "R.-33" was recorded during 6.89, perhaps MM61677 plus a little heat haze? A total of 9 Texans remained by this time.

Noted around the field in recent years have been the following.

Beech C-45	MM61644	ex 'RR-15' 2 RVR (noted '77-'83 in USAF marks for filming purposes). Probably still current '89 when an "RR-15" was recorded.
Beech C-45	MM61646	ex 'RR-23' 2 RVR (noted '77-'89).
Beech C-45	MM61672	ex 'CR-36' 14 Stormo (noted '77-'88, scrapped)
Beech C-45	MM61675	ex 'RR-50' 2 RVR (noted '77-'83 - last flew 28.7.77). This a/c was previously 'RM-50' and could be the example noted 6.89 as 'RM-50' allowing for a bit of faded paintwork.
Beech C-45	MM61677	ex 'RR-22' 2 RVR (noted '77-'88, scrapped)
Beech C-45	MM61693	ex 'RR-16' 2 RVR (noted '78-'89).
Beech C-45	MM61708	ex 'RR-16' 2 RVR (noted '83 in USAAF marks for filming purposes).
Beech C-45	MM61710	ex 'CR-35' 14 Stormo (sold for scrap '88)
Beech C-45	MM61714	ex 'RR-18' 2 RVR (noted '78-'89).
Beech C-45	MM61716	(noted '87 - confirmation?).
Beech C-45	MM61717	ex 'RR-26' 2 RVR (noted '78-'89).
Beech C-45	MM61722	ex 'RR-27' 2 RVR (noted '77-'89).
Beech C-45	MM61727	ex 'RM-51' 1 RVR (noted '77-'88, scrapped)
Beech C-45	MM61743	ex '..-53' (noted '80-'87, to the airline Alisarda in '88 for restoration as "I-SARE").
Beech C-45	MM61754	ex 'RR-28' ex 2 RVR (noted '77-'89).
Beech C-45	MM61755	ex 'RR-12' ex 2 RVR (noted '78, painted in USAAF c/s for film, to Udine 28.5.82).
Beech C-45	MM61762	ex 'RR-11' 2 RVR (noted '74-'88, under restoration by 303 Gruppo). Painted in USAAF colours for film c.1982.
Douglas C-53D	MM61764	ex '14-48' 8 Gruppo/14 Stormo (noted '83, sold for scrap '88).
Douglas C-53D	MM61765	(c/n 11681, ex 42-68754) ex '14-49' 8 Gruppo/14 Stormo (noted '82-'88, scrapped)
Douglas C-53D	MM61766	ex 'RR-04' 2 RVR (noted '77-'88, scrapped)
Douglas C-47 Dakota	MM61776	ex '14-45' 8 Gruppo/14 Stormo (noted '86-'89).
Douglas C-47A Dakota	MM61777	(c/n 9910, ex 42-24048) ex '14-43' 8 Gruppo/14 Stormo (noted '86-'89).
Douglas C-47B Dakota	MM61799	(c/n 15293, ex 43-49477) ex '14-41' 8 Gruppo/14 Stormo (noted '83-'89).

Douglas C-47B Dakota	MM61815	(c/n 15355, ex 43-49539) ex '14-47' 8 Gruppo/14 Stormo (noted '86-'89).
Douglas C-53	MM61818	(c/n 7397, ex 42-15880) ex 'RR-02' 2 RVR (noted '77-'88, scrapped)
Douglas C-47 Dakota	MM61826	(c/n 4380, ex 41-18342) ex '14-44' 8 Gruppo/14 Stormo (noted '86-'89).
Douglas C-47 Dakota	MM61894	(c/n 4261, ex 41-7774) ex 'CR-50' Centro Radiomisure (noted '77-'88, scrapped)
Douglas C-47 Dakota	MM61895	(c/n 6011, ex 41-18650) ex '14-42' 8 Gruppo/14 Stormo (noted '83-'89)
Douglas C-47 Dakota	MM61897	(c/n 4291, ex 41-7799) ex 'CR-53' Centro Radiomisure (noted '77-'88, scrapped)
Douglas DC-6B	MM61923	ex '31-8' 306 Gruppo/31 Stormo (stored '83-'89).
HU-16A Albatross	MM50-182	ex '15-7' 84 Gruppo/15 Stormo (stored '80-'89).
Macchi MB326	MM54155	ex '40' (noted '86, stored for static displays).
Macchi MB326	MM54...	ex '15' (noted '89, apparently dumped).
T-6D Texan	MM53043	ex 'RR-57' 2 RVR (noted '77-'83, to Vignola by '85).
T-6G Texan	MM53659	ex 'RB-9' 3 RVR (noted '77-'89).
T-6H-4M Texan	MM53665	ex 'RR-66' 2 RVR (noted '77-'86).
T-6G Texan	MM53669	ex 'RR-70' 2 RVR (dismantled in hangar '86, outside 6.89).
T-6H-4M Texan	MM53786	ex 'RB-13' 3 RVR (sold 8.3.83, TT 4682 hrs) (noted 8.83).
T-6H-4M Texan	MM53794	ex 'RM-2' 1 RVR (noted '77-6.83, sold 8.3.83, TT 3879 hrs).
T-6H-4M Texan	MM53801	ex 'RB-6' 3 RVR (noted '78-80, to Roma/Fiumicino).
T-6H-4M Texan	MM53811	ex 'RR-63' 2 RVR (noted '78-6.83, sold 8.3.83, TT 6587 hrs).
T-6H-4M Texan	MM53815	(noted '80, to Roma/Urbe by '84).
T-6H-4M Texan	MM53821	ex 'RR-51' 2 RVR (noted '83).
T-6H-4M Texan	MM53839	ex 'RB-1' 3 RVR (noted '77-'83, "RR-1" noted 6.89).
T-6H-4M Texan	MM53850	ex 'RM-3' 1 RVR (noted '77-'86).
T-6H Texan	MM53863	ex 'RR-64' 2 RVR (noted '77-'86).
T-6G Texan	MM54102	ex 'RR-51' 2 RVR (noted '77-'83).
T-6G Texan	MM54105	ex 'RR-54' 2 RVR (noted '77-'86).
T-6G Texan	MM54108	ex 'RR-68' 2 RVR (noted '77-'86).
T-6G Texan	MM54109	ex 'RR-56' 2 RVR (noted '80-'83).
T-6H-2M Texan	MM54141	ex 'RR-58' 2 RVR (noted '77-'89).
T-6H-2M Texan	MM54143	ex 'RB-3' 3 RVR & Bari store (noted '80, to Gallarate).
T-6H-2M Texan	MM54145	ex 'RM-5' 1 RVR (noted '79-'83, sold 8.3.83, TT 6681 hrs, still present 8.83).
T-6H-2M Texan	MM54148	ex 'RR-54' 2 RVR (noted '83).
T-6H-2M Texan	MM54149	ex 'RR-64' 2 RVR (noted '78-'83, sold 8.3.83, TT 5998 hrs, still present 6.83 as "TA-143" USAAF marks for film 'La Pelle', to Castel del Rio).
Piaggio P.166M	MM61874	to Vigna di Valle 6.83.
Piaggio P.166M	MM61879	ex '36-75' 636 SC/36 Stormo (noted '83-'89).
Piaggio P.166M	MM61881	ex 'SP-34' SVBAE (noted '83-'88).
Piaggio P.166M	MM61885	ex '303-33' 303 Gruppo, scrapped by '87.
Piaggio P.166M	MM61887	scrapped by '87.
Piaggio P.166M	MM61889	ex 'SP-31' SVBAE (noted '83-'89).
Piaggio P.166M	MM61890	ex 303 Gruppo, to Vigna di Valle 10.83.
Piaggio P.166M	MM61904	ex '303-31' 303 Gruppo (noted '89).
Piaggio P.166M	MM61905	ex 'SP-33' SVBAE (noted '83-'89).
Piaggio P.166M	MM61906	ex '53-72' 653 SC/36 Stormo (noted '83-'86).
Piaggio P.166M	MM61908	ex '53-73' 653 SC/36 Stormo (noted '83-'88,scrapped).

Piaggio P.166M MM61909 ex '303-28' 303 Gruppo (noted '83-'84).
Piaggio P.166M MM61... ex '303-38' 303 Gruppo (noted '86-'88, scrapped)
Piaggio P.166M MM61910 ex 'SP-41' SVBAE (noted '83-'86).
Piaggio P.166M MM61911 ex 'SP-36' SVBAE (noted '83-'89).
Piaggio P.166M MM61927 ex '15-43' 15 Stormo (noted '86).
Those aircraft scrapped late in 1988 (C-45s, Dakotas and P.166s) were bought by a scrap dealer from Napoli.

ROMA/QUARTO MIGLIO

Along the SS Appia in this Rome suburb in 7.87 were the following ex Guardia di Finanza helicopters, all up for sale at 2 million Lire each!

Agusta-Bell AB47J MM8018..
Agusta-Bell AB47G-2 MM80128 ex 'GdiF-10' *
Agusta-Bell AB47G-2 MM80166 ex 'GdiF-16' incomplete, to Cingoli.
Agusta-Bell AB47G-2A MM80417 ex 'GdiF-43'
Agusta-Bell AB47J-3 MM80296 ex 'GdiF-33' to Cingoli.
Agusta-Bell AB47J-3 MM80304 ex 'GdiF-36'
Agusta-Bell AB47J-3 MM80414 ex 'GdiF-40' *
Nardi-Hughes NH500MC MM81016 ex 'GdiF-87'

The two machines asterisked were sold a few days later - fates for these or any of the above would be of interest. Only MM80296 and an unidentified 'G' still remained in 2.88.

ROMA/URBE

T-6H-4M Texan MM53815/"51-15" (ex Guidonia) was preserved at the entrance to the military area here by 10.83 (still current '88).

Nardi FN305 I-DASM/MM52757 arrived here from Gardolo (Trento) on 26.2.86 for restoration by the preservation group GAVS (Gruppo Amici Velivoli Storici) this being completed on 10.6.88. GAVS have also obtained ex SVBIA Piaggio P.148 MM53545/3 from a scrapyard at Cisterna early in 1988 and restored it in its original codes '9-75'. Later in '88 the P.148 was exchanged for a Saiman 202M, the former now being preserved near Verona.

Just outside the airfield perimeter and overgrown with vegetation are the wrecks of a Beech C-45 which crashed on the approach during the '60s and Auster 5 I-FOTO (c/n 1814, ex TW472, F-OAJP, TS-BJP). The former was stripped for spares and abandoned in situ whilst the latter is considered to be màterial evidence in a police investigation and cannot be interfered with! Both were re-discovered by the preservation group GAVS during 1984.

RONCADELLO

Macchi MB308 I-ACSL (c/n 5867/94, ex MM52945) was displayed in a public park here (noted '88) but has since gone.

ROVERETO

The Museo Storico Italiano della Guerra Rovereto (located in the Castello di Rovereto, itself about 50 kms up the A22 from Verona) displays Macchi-Nieuport Ni10-18mg 13469.

SABAUDIA

About 15 kms South of Latina, F-84F Thunderstreak MM53-6988/50-19 (ex 50 Stormo) is preserved with the Scuola di Artiglieria Contra-Aerea (noted '83-'86). A couple of Piaggio P.148s from Latina (qv) are reported to have come to this area.

SALERNO

A large quantity of AB47G/AB47Js were reported in store here by 1984 (and again in '88).

SALTO DI QUIRRA

On the island of Sardinia, 672 Squadriligia were reported to possess two AB47Js marked as 'PI-02' and 'PI-04' in 7.85. These were formerly in service with the Poligono Interforce.

SAN MARTINO DI BAREGGIO

Preserved here by 1986 was RF-84F Thunderflash MM52-7471/3-46 (ex 132 Gruppo/3 Stormo) which was previously displayed at Bussolengo.

SAN VITTORIA

Aviamilano P19 I-GONO (c/n 307) was noted by the roadside here (near Alba) during '85 but disappeared later in the year.

SARSINA

Macchi MB308G I-LATT (c/n 5914) is preserved at the premises of the Fotoaerea Valvasssori company near Forli (noted '86).

SARZANA/LUNI

Agusta-Bell AB47G MM80087/1-01 (ex Grupelicot 1) was wfu 19.12.72 and preserved on the gate of the Naval Air Base here (though it has been suggested this may not be the real MM80087!). Agusta A106 MM5001N/5-01 (ex 2 Grupelicot and storage at Catania/Fontanarossa) was preserved here by 9.86 but has since returned to Catania.

In open storage on the field here are three ex 5 Grupo H-34s, all of which were wfu during 6.79. During '86 MM153622 was undergoing restoration prior to display at the entrance.

Sikorsky SH-34J	MM149082	ex '4-04' (noted '79-'86).
Sikorsky SH-34J	MM153618	ex '4-10' (noted '79-'86).
Sikorsky SH-34J	MM153622	ex '4-14' (last flew 28.6.79, noted '79-'86).

The wreck of Agusta-Bell AB212ASW MM81084/7-39 was reported on the dump here in 5.83.

SAVONA

Signor Flavio Cabib at Via Nostra Signora del Monte 60 has a composite F-84F Thunderstreak acquired from Castrette in 1977 (current '86). The front fuselage is from MM53-6695/36-35 with parts from 53-6972 and 53-6623.

SIENA

Former ALE O-1E Bird Dog MM61-2991/EI-4 was in a car scrapyard on the SS326 road from Siena to Betolle (about 1 km out from Siena) by 1984. She had gone by '85, probably sold elsewhere rather than scrapped.

SIGONELLA (SICILY)

Stored/derelict here in '78 was S-2A Tracker MM148300/41-37 ex 41 Stormo which by '79 had been joined by MM133212/41-27. Both were still current in '86.

Former Danish AF F-100D Super Sabre G-290 (ex 54-2290) went u/s here on 6.11.81 during its delivery flight to the Turkish AF and was still here in 7.84. The aircraft was recovered later in the year by the Museo Storico at Vigna di Valle.

SPAGNOLIA

Preserved in the Citta della Domenica park here (near Perugia) in 1982 were Macchi M416 I-IGAB (c/n 1042, ex MM53244) and Fiat G-59-4A MM53526/RR-80 (c/n 131). The G-59 was recovered by the Museo Storico by '83.

STAGNO

In Livorno province, Siai S205-20R I-SIAQ (c/n 4-116) stands on a concrete plinth outside a factory (noted '84).

TARANTO

The old seaplane base here acquired a Macchi MB326 for display on the gate by the end of 1988. At the same time AB204AS MM80363/3-02 was preserved at the Centro Addestramento Aeronavale.

By 6.89 a Macchi MB326 coded '89' was displayed in the town centre.

TAVAZZANO
Angelo Valente (a local enthusiast) obtained an ex Alitalia SE210 Caravelle late in '82 for use as a children's plaything here (near Milan). By '84 it had moved to Torricella di Magione.

TERAMO
Macchi MB308 I-ATAI (c/n 5847/74, ex MM52927) is preserved at a BMW dealer's here (current '88).

TERME DI MIRADOLO
Preserved in Signor Felici's garden is Macchi 416 (Fokker S.11) MM54129/I-AEPE (c/n 6080/118) in good condition (noted '84).

TERNI
Cessna 172 I-ALJD was preserved outside an EBRO store here during '86.

TORINO
F-86E Sabre Mk.4 MM19534/4-74 (ex 4 Stormo) has been displayed at the Presidio Militare di Torino in Via Beinette for some 20 years. It was restored by the preservation group Associazione Arma Aeronautica di Torino in late '83 and was still here in '87. By late '88 the aircraft had gone to Torino/Caselle.

TORINO/CASELLE
Fairchild C-119J MM51-8121/46-50 (ex 98 Gruppo/46 Aero) flew in on 28.2.73 for preservation at the AMI enclave near the civil terminal. The aircraft was dismantled in mid '88 with large sections, if not all of the airframe, going to the yard at Castrette. By late '88 it had been replaced by F-86E Sabre Mk.4 MM19534/4-74 (see under Torino).

Near the Aeritalia facility on the South side of the field in 1983 (still current '85) was the dumped fuselage of a Fiat G-91Y marked only "Y-12". It has been suggested that this airframe was damaged on the production line and that a replacement aircraft was built for the AMI.

Civil wrecks here in '87 were Partenavia P.66Cs I-IADB, I-IACH, Siai S.205-20R I-GHEE, Cessna 310F I-ALJB and Zlin Z526F Akrobat I-JOKE.

TORRICELLA DI MAGIONE
The Caravelle mentioned under Tavazzano was preserved here in fictitious "Alidelta" colours as "I-ALBA" in 1984.

TRAPANI/BIRGI
Withdrawn from use here by 7.85 was ex SVE Agusta-Bell AB47J MM80259/SE-59.

TRENTO
The frame of PA18-150 Super Cub I-PATN (c/n 18-8999) was hanging on a hangar wall here in 7.88. Other wrecks here at this time were MS880B Rallyes I-MASL (c/n 1305), I-RALH (c/n 2355), I-ACUC (c/n 903) and an unidentified Stinson L-5.

TREVISO/LANCENIGO
T-6H-4M Texan MM53849/SC-78 was noted in Signor Bettiol's market garden here (near the Treviso Nord autostrada exit) during 1988 and has probably been here since its departure from the Castrette scrapyard in 1983.

TREVISO/SAN ANGELO
Preserved in front of the Officers' Mess by 7.83 was Fiat G-91R-1 MM6285 (ex '2-30', marked '2-30' on the starboard side and "2-60" on the port) (current '89).

With the imminent demise of the 'Gina' and its replacement with the AMX, several tired looking G-91s have been appearing on the field over the last few years.

Fiat G-91R	MM6265	ex '2-34' wfu by 2.89.
Fiat G-91R	MM6267	ex '2-34' dumped by Met Building 2.84, to Modena.

Fiat G-91R	MM6269	ex '2-67' wfu by 12.88 (current 6.89).
Fiat G-91R	MM6274	ex '2-35' dumped by Met Building 2.84-2.87, to Trino Vercellese (Vercelli) 14.5.87 for preservation.
Fiat G-91R	MM6275	ex '2-30' wfu by 11.88 (current 6.89).
Fiat G-91R	MM6276	ex '2-75' wfu by '84 and still parked by the 103 Gruppo flight line in 3.85. Being cannibalised 5.85 and on the dump 3.88.
Fiat G-91R	MM6280	ex '2-33' wfu by 3.85 (still here 6.89, hangared with one side sectioned to show the interior at open days etc).
Fiat G-91R	MM6283	ex '2-70' wfu by 10.88 (current 6.89).
Fiat G-91R	MM6287	ex '2-31' wfu by 11.88 (current 6.89).
Fiat G-91R	MM6290	ex '2-26' wfu by 4.89.
Fiat G-91R	MM6291	ex '2-24' wfu by 9.88 (current 6.89).
Fiat G-91R	MM6292	ex '2-22' wfu by 11.88, to Vicenza 8.2.89.
Fiat G-91R	MM6298	ex '2-26' wfu by 9.88 (current 6.89, for Milano).
Fiat G-91R	MM6301	ex '2-25' wfu on 14 Gruppo flight line by 10.87, to Loreto 5.89.
Fiat G-91R	MM6303	ex '2-63' wfu by 11.88 (current 4.89).
Fiat G-91R	MM6306	ex '2-23' wfu by 12.87 (current 6.89, for FIAT).
Fiat G-91R	MM6311	ex '2-62' wfu on 103 Gruppo flight line by 12.87 (current 6.89).
Fiat G-91R	MM6312	ex '2-61' wfu by 12.87, current for rescue training 12.88.
Fiat G-91R	MM6314	ex '2-57' wfu 12.87-12.88, to Grontardo (Cremona).
Fiat G-91R	MM6375	ex '2-41' wfu by 7.88 (current 6.89).
Fiat G-91R	MM6376	ex '2-01' wfu by 9.88.
Fiat G-91R	MM6377	ex '2-12' wfu by 12.88 (current 6.89).
Fiat G-91R	MM6388	ex '2-42' wfu by 12.88.
Fiat G-91R	MM6391	ex '2-54' wfu by 11.88, to Orte c.2.89.
Fiat G-91R	MM6417	ex '2-10' wfu by 9.88.
Fiat G-91R	MM6418	ex '2-11' wfu by 11.88 (current 6.89).
Fiat G-91R	MM6420	ex '2-43' wfu by 11.88 (current 6.89).
Macchi MB326	MM54202	ex '2-83' 602 SC/2 Stormo, wfu by 7.88 (current 6.89).

Hangared here at the 1985 open day was F-86E Sabre MM19680 (borrowed from the ITI Malignani in Udine) in the black overall colours of the 'Lanceri Neri' aerobatic team.

On the civil side, ex Spanish AF T-6G Texan E16-71/793-8 (ex Esc.793 and Cuatro Vientos store) underwent restoration to fly as I-TSEI (begun by 1985, completed by 1988). Near Treviso, former Castrette inmate T-6H-4M Texan MM53785/SC-62 (ex Scuola Centrale) is under long term rebuild to fly.

In the town in 5.85 Fiat G-91R MM6272/2-31 (ex 14 Gruppo/2 Stormo) was on temporary display and is believed to be a non-airworthy airframe.

TRINO VERCELLESE

Fiat G-91R MM6274/2-35 (ex 14 Gruppo/2 Stormo) arrived here from Treviso/San Angelo on 14.5.87 for preservation.

UDINE

Macchi MC205V Veltro MM91818 was in use here as one of several gias here with the Instituto Tecnico A Malignani (the A Malignani Technical Institute) until going to Aermacchi for restoration (as "MM92214"). In return, the institute received the OH-13H, AM-3C and MB326 listed below.

Aermacchi AM-3C	I-AEAM	(c/n 6530) arr 28.7.79.
Beech C-45	MM61755	arr 28.5.82.
Bell OH-13H	MM80798	(ex 56-2180).
Fiat G-46B	MM52792	(c/n 25) arr 4.8.59.

Fiat G-91R	MM6272	ex '2-31' 2 Stormo, arr 19.9.85 from Treviso/San Angelo.
Macchi MB326	MM54266	ex '12' SVBIA, arr 17.3.80.
F-86E Sabre Mk.4	MM19680	(ex XB826) ex '2-37' 2 Stormo, arrived 22.1.64, to Rivolto by '88 in 'Lanceri Neri' colours. This may be only a temporary move as the aircraft was also displayed at Rivolto in '75 and Treviso in '85.

VEDELAGO

Near a shop in this small town just to the West of Istrana, F-84F Thunderstreak MM53-6646 painted as "36634/51-30" is preserved (noted '77-'89). The spurious tail serial arises from some swopping of tails in the Castrette scrapyard. By 8.87 the aircraft had been re-painted with the code "51-37" applied.

VENEGONO

By the end of 1988 the Aermacchi factory here had acquired an ex SVBIA MB326 for display purposes.

VENEZIA

A Bleriot XI and a SPAD are suspended from the ceiling in the Palais Grassi.

VENEZIA/LIDO

Fiat G-59-4B MM53774/RB-76 is under restoration to flying condition here.

VENEZIA/TESSERA

Engineless UAEAF Fiat G-222 301 was still languishing outside in 6.89 having been here for some time.

VERGIATE

Near the Siai Marchetti works on the West side of the field, several Fairchild C-119s sat derelict for many years since withdrawal in the early seventies. They were still complete in 6.84 but by 6.85 had been dismantled and piled up in a scrap compound on the field. They comprised C-119Js MM52-8144/46-55, MM52-5849/46-59, MM52-5851/46-50, MM52-8158/46-62 all ex 50 Gruppo/46 Aero; EC-119J MM52-5896/46-64 ex 2 Gruppo/46 Aero and EC-119J MM52-5884/46-63 which last served with 71 Gruppo/14 Stormo at Pratica di Mare. All were still present during 7.88.

Dumped on the far side of the field (noted '83-'86) is Beech C-45 MM61702/RB-20 (ex 3 RVR).

Stored and derelict Siai SF260s have been a feature of Vergiate for years. In 6.89 a batch of 13 SF260TPs were stored in crates with the wings lying alongside. They were c/ns 695, 696, 697, 699, 700, 701, 702, 705, 733, 758, 759, 761 plus one other. A second batch of 16 SF260s included c/ns 791, 793, 800, 804, 805 also stored in crates. About six SF260s were on the dump at this time.

Derelict here during '87 was Siai S.210 I-SJAV.

VERONA

Preserved near here is ex GAVS Piaggio P.149 MM53545/9-75 (ex '3' SVBAE and Latina store)

VERONA/BOSCOMANTICO

The remains of L-21B Super Cubs MM54-2378/EI-189 and MM54-2512/EI-217 (both ex Boscomantico store) were with the Aero Club in 10.82 and were still there in '86. At least one remained in 7.88. They are thought to serve as 'Christmas trees' for the airworthy I-LOBO (ex MM53-7718/EI-101).

VICENZA

Fiat G-91R MM6292/2-22 (ex 14 Gruppo/2 Stormo) arrived here from Treviso/Sant Angelo on 8.2.89 for gate guard duties.

For several years 10 SRA (now redesignated 10 GME) have used an unidentified AB204B coded '15-10' as in instructional airframe here (still current '87).

VIGNA DI VALLE

The Museo Storico is situated on the Southern shore of Lake Bracciano, at the old seaplane base. Not all the airframes are on display at any one time as the site includes restoration and storage facilities not normally open to the public. This listing includes aircraft on display, stored on site or under restoration on or off site.

Aerfer Ariete	MM569	(c/n 2) ex RSV & Torino (noted '77-'87).
Aerfer Sagittario II	MM561	(c/n 2) ex RSV (noted '77-'87).
Aerlualdi L.59	MM576	(c/n 1) ex CALE & Viterbo store (noted '83-'89).
Agusta A102	I-ECIN	(c/n 004, ex MM80201) (arr 20.8.74, current '87).
Agusta-Bell AB47G-2	MM80113	(c/n 196) ex '12' SVE (noted '77-'87).
Agusta-Bell AB47J	MM80187	ex 'SE-38' SVE (arr 7.83, current '87).
Agusta D'Ascanio ADA	-	ex Frosinone, restored by Elicotteri Meridionali (arr '84, current '87).
Ansaldo AC.2	MM1208	ex Centocelle, painted as "94-6" (noted '77-'87).
Ansaldo SVA.5	11721	ex Milano (noted '77-'87).
Avia FL.3	I-ADOD	(c/n A34-28) (noted '87).
Beech C-45	MM61734	ex 'RR-25' 2 RVR (noted '77-'87).
Bleriot-SIT XI-2	"BL246"	"semi-original" (noted '77-'87).
Caproni Ca.3	23174	ex Torino, painted as "4166" (noted '77-'87).
Caproni CC.1	1	(noted '77-'83).
Caproni CC.2	MM487	(c/n 4849) (noted '84).
Caproni Trento F.5	MM553	(c/n 1, ex I-FACT) ex Torino (noted '77-'87).
CRDA Cant Z.506S	MM45425	ex '84-4', painted as "MM45442" ex 84 Gruppo (noted '77-'87).
CVV6 Canguro	MM100028	ex 'VV-10' (noted '77-'87).
CVV8 Bonaventura	MM100042	(noted '87).
Curtiss A.1 Triad	-	replica (noted '77-'87).
DH Vampire NF.54	MM6152	ex Torino (noted '77-'87).
UC-61K Argus	MM56698	(ex I-FAMA) (noted '84).
Fiat C-29	MM130	(c/n 2) (noted '77-'87).
Fiat G-5bis	MM290	(c/n 5, ex I-BFFI) (noted '84).
Fiat G-46-3B	MM53090	(c/n 140) ex 'SM-80' (noted '84).
Fiat G-46-4A	MM53283	(c/n 189) ex Torino (noted '77-'87).
Fiat G-46-4A	MM53286	(c/n 192, ex I-AELM) (noted '77-'84).
Fiat G-46-4A	MM53292	(c/n 198) ex 'ZR-2' (noted '84).
Fiat G-49-2	MM556	(c/n 2, ex I-FIAT) (noted '87).
Fiat G-59-2A	MM53265	(c/n 74) ex 'RB-49' & Novara, to be rebuilt as G-55
Fiat G-59-4B	MM53276	ex Torino (noted '77-'87).
Fiat G-59-4A	MM53526	(c/n 131) ex 'RR-80 & Spagnolia (noted '83-'84).
Fiat G-59-4B	MM53772	(c/n 179) ex 'RS-25' RSV (noted '77, sold '84, to Frank Sanders, Chino, California).
Fiat G-59-4B	MM53774	(c/n 181) ex 'RR-76' (noted '84, away with Aeronavali, Venezia by '86 for restoration).
Fiat G-80-3B	MM53882	(c/n 2) ex 'RS-22' RSV (noted '77-'89).
Fiat G-82	MM53885	(c/n 2) ex 'RS-18' RSV (noted '77-'87).
Fiat G-82	MM53886	(c/n 3) ex 'RS-19' RSV (noted '77-'89).
Fiat G-82	MM53888	(c/n 5) ex 'RS-21' RSV (noted '77-'89).
Fiat G-91PAN	MM6250	(c/n 16) ex Frecce Tricolori (arr 9.82, current '87).
Fiat G-91Y	MM580	(c/n 2002) ex 'RS-11' RSV (noted '83-'89).
Fiat G-212CA	MM61804	(c/n 19) ex '142-5' 142 Sq, soc 26.1.59 (noted '77-'87).
Fiat G-222	MM583	(c/n 4002) ex 'RS-07' RSV (arrived '83, current '89).
HU-16A Albatross	MM50-179	ex '15-5' 84 Gruppo/15 Stormo, wfu 14.5.78 (noted '80-'89).
Grumman S-2F Tracker	MM136556	ex '41-6' 41 Stormo (noted '80-'87).
GVV Siai 3V-1 Eolo	I-BIGI	(noted '87).

Hanriot HD.1	19309	(c/n 76, Macchi built) '515' (noted '77-'83).
Helio Courier	MM91001	ex Roma/Furbara (arr '84).
Hispano HA 132L	328	'VIII-92' (license-built Fiat CR.32) (noted '77-'87).
IMAM Ro.43	MM27050	ex 'ORB-23' Scuola Idro di Orbetello (noted '77-'87).
F-104G Starfighter	MM6501	(c/n 9998) ex '3-11' 3 Stormo (noted '85-'87).
Lockheed T-33A	MM53-5594	ex '9-35' 609 SC/9 Stormo (noted '86-'87).
Lockheed RT-33A	MM51-9249	ex '51-88' 651 SC/51 Stormo (flew to Ciampino 4.4.82) (arr 4.85, current '89).
Macchi C200	MM8307	painted as "MM7707/359-8" (noted '77-'87).
Macchi C202T-AS	MM9667	painted as "MM7844/91-3", ex Pisa University (noted '77-'87).
Macchi MB323	MM554	(c/n 1) ex 'RS-10' RSV (noted '77-'87).
Macchi MC205V	MM9546	painted as "MM9345/155-6" (noted '77-'87).
Macchi M39-II	MM76	(c/n 5) (noted '77-'87).
Macchi M67	MM105	(c/n 3) fuselage only (noted '77-'87).
Macchi MC72	MM181	(c/n 5) ex Milano (noted '77-'87).
Macchi M416	MM53444	(c/n 6005/61, ex I-AEPF) (noted '84).
Macchi M416	MM53457	(c/n 6013/69, ex I-AELS) (noted '84).
Macchi M416	MM53761	(c/n 1058, ex I-AELI) (noted '84).
Macchi M416	MM53762	(c/n 1059, ex I-AELY) license-built Fokker S.11 (noted '77-'87).
Milti MB3 Leonardo	I-MIBO	(c/n 1) (noted '84-'87).
Nardi FN305	-	stripped fuselage frame & wings donated by Nardi many years ago, stored (noted '77).
F-86E(M) Sabre Mk.4	MM19792	(ex XB915) ex '13-1' 13 Gruppo (noted '77-'87).
F-86K Sabre	MM54868	(c/n 128) ex '51-62' 23 Gruppo/51 Stormo (noted '77-'87).
F-100D Super Sabre	42290	(ex 54-2290, RDanAF G-290) ex THK (briefly - went u/s on dely!) & Sigonella dump (noted '86-'89).
P-51D Mustang	MM4323	ex 'RR-11' 2 RVR, last flew 30.9.64 (noted '77-'87).
T-6G Texan	MM54097	ex 'RR-67' 303 Gruppo (noted '77-'87).
P.53 Aeroscooter	I-REDI	(c/n 1) (noted '77-'87).
Piaggio P.136F	MM80005	(c/n 110) ex '140-6' 140 Sq (noted '77-'83).
Piaggio P.136L1	MM80078	(c/n 204) ex '140-15' 140 Sq (noted '77-'83).
Piaggio P.136L1	MM80083	(c/n 213) ex '84-16' (noted '84).
Piaggio P.150	MM555	(c/n 1, ex I-PIAR) (noted '77-'87).
Piaggio P.166M	MM61874	(c/n 382) ex '53-79' 653 SC/53 Stormo & Guidonia (noted '83-'89).
Piaggio P.166M	MM61890	(c/n 398) ex 303 Gruppo & Guidonia (arr 10.83, current '89).
F-84F Thunderstreak	MM36892	ex '36-38' 156 Gruppo/36 Stormo (noted '77-'87).
RF-84F Thunderflash	MM27458	(ex 52-7458) ex '3-05' 18 Gruppo/3 Stormo (noted '77-'87).
F-84G Thunderjet	MM111049	(ex 51-11049) "51-18" 51 Stormo markings (noted '77-'87).
P-47D Thunderbolt	MM4653	(ex 44-89746) ex '51-19' 51 Stormo and Pisa University as gia, last flew 19.5.53, restored at Lecce by 3 RTA (arr 6.85, current '87).
SAAB J 29F Tunnan	29543	ex '19' F 20, Swedish AF, damaged at Napoli in '68 and donated to ItAF (noted '77-'89).
SAI-Ambrosini Grifo	-	fuselage only (noted '77-'87).
SAI-Ambrosini Super S.7	MM558	ex Torino (noted '77-'87).
Saiman 202M	MM51497	(c/n 508, ex I-SARD) (noted '84).
S-M S.56	I-AEDA	(c/n 5611) ex Caproni Museum loan (arr 5.85, current '87).
S-M SM.79	L-112	ex Lebanese AF & Rayak Road, Beirut, painted as "MM24327" (noted '77-'87).

S-M SM.82/PW MM61187 painted as "MM61850/14" (noted '77-'87).
Spad S.VII S.1420 (noted '77-'87).
Stinson L-5 MM52848 (ex I-AEEU) (noted '84-'87).
Spitfire IX MM4084 (ex MK805) ex Nettuno & restoration at Lecce, painted as "MM4079/MJ996" "A-32" (noted '85-'88).

VIGNALE

A priest here (in the Asti area) has T-6D Texan MM53043/RR-57 (ex 41-33334, EX361, ex 2 RVR and Guidonia store) in his garden.

VILLAFRANCA

Two RF-84F Thunderflashes are preserved on the field as a reminder of 3 Stormo's earlier days. MM27403/"3-28" (ex '3-15' 18 Gruppo/3 Stormo) is displayed in the 28 Gruppo area whilst MM27466/3-06 (ex 132 Gruppo/3 Stormo) can be found elsewhere on the field. Both were seen in '82 and were still current 6.89.

The T-birds of 603 SC/3 Stormo were left derelict on the field following their withdrawal.

Lockheed T-33A MM51-9141 ex '3-141' (noted '81-'89).
Lockheed T-33A MM51-9145 ex '3-145' (noted '81-'89).
Lockheed T-33A MM55-3030 ex '3-030' (noted '79-'89).

With the transition of 6 Stormo at nearby Ghedi to the Tornado in 1982, redundant Starfighters congregated at Villafranca to await disposal or absorption into the overhaul cycle. In the mid eighties a line up of a dozen or so stored or derelict '104s was a common sight here. The following machines have been of long duration but others have been only temporary and the full story on the many Starfighters to have passed through here is not available.

F-104G Starfighter MM6502 ex '6-25' (stored '83, derelict '84-'88, dumped '89).
F-104G Starfighter MM6504 ex '3-05' (stored '86, to Cameri gate guard by 6.87, assuming it wears the correct serial!).
F-104G Starfighter MM6524 ex '3-45' (wfu on 10.6.87).
F-104G Starfighter MM6525 ex '3-01' (stored '83-'88, marked "3-01"/"3-30" - as a travelling exhibit. By the dump 6.89.
F-104G Starfighter MM6544 ex '3-07' (dumped '89).
F-104G Starfighter MM6547 ex '3-34' (stored '89).
F-104G Starfighter MM6559 ex '3-41' (dumped '89).
F-104G Starfighter MM6561 (stored '89).
F-104G Starfighter MM6565 ex '6-05' (stored '82-'84, derelict '86, dumped'89).
F-104G Starfighter MM6568 ex '6-07' (stored '82-'83, derelict '84-'86, dumped '89).
F-104G Starfighter MM6577 ex '6-16' (stored '82-'86, wingless '87-'88).
F-104G Starfighter MM6578 ex '3-06' (stored, tail-less '89).
F-104G Starfighter MM6588 ex '3-07' (taxying accident 14.12.88, wfo 1.2.89 as a spares source).
F-104G Starfighter MM6590 ex '3-11' (wfu 18.2.89, stored).
F-104G Starfighter MM6632 ex '3-24', wfu by 9.88, to go to Loreto.
F-104G Starfighter MM6633 ex '3-26' (stored '87-'88, dumped '89).
F-104G Starfighter MM6634 ex '3-33' (stored '89).
F-104G Starfighter MM6651 ex '3-47' (wfu 7.3.89, stored).

Recent occupants of the dump have comprised the following. These are now being joined by Starfighters already listed above.

Macchi MB326 MM54200 ex '55' SVBIA (noted '83-'84, rear fuselage still extant '88).
F-104G Starfighter MM6582 ex '3-35' (crashed 3.7.82, noted '83, parts '84).
F-104G Starfighter MM6644 ex '3-22' (crashed 9.9.75, parts noted '84).

VITERBO

Preserved on the gate of the Centro ALE here is T-6H-4M Texan MM53818/"303-31" (ex 'SC-51' Scuola Centrale and Bergamo store) (noted '82-'83). In 1988 Agusta Bell

AB47G-3B-1 MM80492 and L-18C Super Cub MM52-2378/I-EIMU were seen to be preserved here at the main gate.

T-6H-2M Texan MM54139/"TA-141" (ex 'RB-2') was also reported to be preserved here during '83 in USAF markings following use in the film 'La Pelle', however its location was given as the Scuola VAM which may well be in the town rather than at the base. By '85 she was repainted in fictitious marks as "RR-02".

Noted here in 6.83 were derelict ex CALE L-18C Super Cubs MM52-2415/EI-85 and MM52-2425/EI-95.

By 6.85 O-1E Bird Dog MM61-2956/EI-21 (ex CALE) was held here in a state of preservation and is a likely candidate to appear on the gate. The front half of another Bird Dog was in use for fire fighting instruction at this time along with L-18C Cub "MM54-0000/EI-00" and the rear half of SM1019E MM57239. Agusta-Bell AB206A MM80586/"EI-000" (ex 'EI-525') has also been reported in use as a gia on the base.

VIZZOLA TICINO

The Caproni Museum here is situated on the Western side of Milano/Malpensa airport in a hangar within the Caproni factory. At the moment entry is by prior permission only but moves are afoot to provide a permanent public museum site. The Dove and F-86 are outside with the remainder indoors.

Aerolombarda Asiago	I-ZUME	(ex MM30096) (noted '85-'88).
Aerolombarda Asiago	I-VERG	(c/n 02/GS/04) (noted '85-'88).
Aerolombarda Asiago	I-DASI	(ex MM30098) (noted '85-'88).
Ansaldo A-1 Balilla	16552	(noted '88).
Avia FL3	I-AIAE	(c/n A-16) (noted '85-'88).
Bu 131B Jungmann	I-CERM	(c/n 57, ex Swiss AF A-45, HB-UTN) (noted '85-'88).
Caproni Ca.6	-	(noted '85-'88).
Caproni Ca.9	-	(noted '85, loaned to NASM, Washington DC, from '87).
Caproni Ca.53	-	(noted '85-'88).
Caproni Ca.100	I-GTAB	(c/n 1) (noted '85-'88).
Caproni Ca.100	I-DISC	(c/n 3752, ex MM56273) (noted '85-'88).
Caproni Ca.113	I-MARY	(c/n 3473) (noted '85-'88).
Caproni Ca.163	I-WEST	(noted '85-'88).
Caproni Ca.193	I-POLO	(c/n 5736, ex MM56701) (noted '85-'88).
Re2000 Falco 1	MM8287	(noted '85-'88).
DH Dove 6	I-ANIC	(c/n 04495) (noted '85-'89).
Fairchild F.24 C8C	I-GENI	(c/n 2662) (noted '85-'88).
Macchi M20	I-AABO	(ex I-BERG) (noted '85-'88).
Macchi MB308	I-ACSN	(c/n 5885/112, ex MM53065) (noted '88).
Manzolini Libellula 1	I-MANN	(noted '88).
F-86K Sabre	MM53-8300	ex '5-55' 23 Gruppo/5 Stormo, soc 18.4.73 (noted '82-'88).
T-6H-2M Texan	MM54142	ex 'RM-1' 653 SC/53 Stormo & Cameri (arr '86, current '88).
P.53 Aeroscooter	I-SELI	(c/n 002) (noted '85-'88).
Republic RC-3 Seabee	I-SIBI	(c/n 331, ex HB-SEA) (noted '85-'88).
SAI Ambrosini S.2S	I-LANC	(noted '85-'88).
Saiman 202M	I-BIOL	(c/n 5, ex MM52163) (noted '85-'88).
Savoia-Marchetti SM80	I-ELIO	(c/n 30003, ex I-TATI) (noted '85-'88).
S-M SM102	I-AEVO	(ex MM61829) (noted '85-'88).
Viberti Musca 1	I-DIAN	(c/n 12) (noted '85-'88).
Vizzola II	I-RENI	(c/n 003) (noted '85-'88).

LUXEMBOURG

Only a couple of brief comments are necessary, firstly to note that no relics have been brought to my attention at the 'other' Luxembourg airfield at Wiltz. Secondly, it is worth pointing out that Findel is a popular venue for the storage of 'geriatric jets'. So far these all seem to have been only short term residents and have not gained inclusion in this volume but perhaps there may be more to report in the future.

LUXEMBOURG/FINDEL

Five T-6G Texans from surplus Spanish AF stocks had arrived here by 12.83 and were stored on the field with all markings overpainted except their serials. Only two remained by 1987, both having been acquired by the preservation group Patrimonie Aeronautique Nationale (which also expects an L-19 Bird Dog and L-18C Super Cub). One of the Texans joined the civil register on 2.9.87 as LX-PAE and another is believed to be acting as a source of spare parts. The fate of the other three is not known, perhaps someone would care to enlighten me?

T-6G Texan	E.16-63	ex '793-6' Esc.793 (noted 12.83).
T-6G Texan	E.16-86	(ex 49-3337) ex '793-19' Esc.793 (noted '83-'87, spares source for LX-PAE?).
T-6G Texan	E.16-106	(ex 49-3453) ex '793-12' Esc.793, rebuilt for civil use as LX-PAE (noted '83-'87).
T-6G Texan	E.16-110	ex '793-6' Esc.793 (noted 12.83).
T-6G Texan	E.16-114	(ex 49-3382) ex '793-7' Esc.793 (noted 12.83).

Finally, the wreck of crashed Cessna 172 N1189U was noted on the field during 9.85.

MALTA

This popular holiday destination has a Wrecks and Relics population out of all proportion to its size. Only a Sea Gladiator and the mortal remains of a Spitfire remain from the Second World War but the activities of the International Fire and Safety Training School and Newcal Aviation involve a good many tired propliners. Some of Newcal's Cariboux are relatively short stayers, pausing only long enough for a complete rebuild prior to re-sale elsewhere. All their Cariboux are included here for the sake of completeness for as well as the transients several of them have been a feature of the landscape for years and will most certainly never fly again.

BIRZEBBUGA

To the North West of the village is a scrapyard which in 12.82 was found to hold the mortal remains of ex Luqa Station Flight Canberra T.4 WT482 which had previously been held in crated storage at Hal Far for the National War Museum from at least '76 to '78. These remains were accompanied by the fuselages of Dakotas N3101Q (C-53 Skytrooper c/n 4911, ex 42-6459, NC16565, WGAF XA-117, wfu Hal Far by 1970), N3102Q (C-53D Skytrooper c/n 11654, ex 42-68727, NC14959, N66Y, N7654, N485F, derelict at Hal Far 1977) and an anonymous Beech 18. A further visit in 10.87 found a new addition in the form of an Aero Commander (N491F from Luqa would seem to be the obvious candidate) whilst the Canberra and Beech 18 were still present. Reported on this occasion were two "DC-4s" which one assumes to be the Dakotas previously seen here.

HAL FAR

The International Fire and Safety Training School is based in the old Fleet Air Arm control tower here using the following airframes. The Dakotas were all brought in by road from Safi/Luqa - no mean feat considering the roads!

Douglas DC-6A	N90703	(c/n 42856) ex MIACO, wfu 2.77. This was the 6th DC-6 built and is now in a terrible state (not noted on a quick look 8.88 but may still be here).
C-47A Dakota	C-FITH	(c/n 20228, ex 43-15762, NC9033H, ZS-DLX, N9033H, ZS-DLX, CF-ITH, VP-KLU) ex Terra Surveys, to be refurbished for static display in the colours of the school (current, unmarked, 8.88).
C-47A Dakota	N535M	(c/n 20558, ex 43-16092, NC1050M, CU-T-265, YV-C-AVR) ex Conoco, for rescue training (current 8.88).
C-47B Dakota	N565	(c/n 14955/26400, ex 43-49139, NC66655) ex Conoco, for fire training (current 8.88).

LUQA

The current Luqa airport utilises the former airfields of RAF Luqa and RAF Safi which were joined together by the extension of Luqa's runway 14/32 during the seventies. Valetta C.2 VX574 occupied the dump at RAF Luqa throughout the seventies but was finally reduced to only a few charred components by the end of 1982.

The fire damaged remains of Egyptair Boeing 737-266 SU-AYH (c/n 21191) remained here following the conclusion of the hi-jack on 24.11.85 when several grenades were detonated in the cockpit and passenger cabin. The aircraft was sold to Air Ground Equipment Sales who commenced dismantling on 11.5.87 and shipped all useable components (including the fuselage and wings!) to New York. By 7.87 only a few fuselage sections remained on site and these were removed soon after.

The fuselage of G44 Widgeon N750M (c/n 1341) and the complete N3103Q (c/n 1218) were both dumped here in 1.87 on the Safi side of the field but were awaiting shipment to Ipswich, UK, where they arrived on 29.4.87. N3103Q is currently being restored to flying condition (as G-DUCK) using the second fuselage as a spares source.

Ex Air Malta Boeing 720-040B, 9H-AAM (c/n 18378), was wfu by late '82 and stored on the field minus engines and with titles and registration removed. The aircraft was subsequently painted in spurious markings for use in a film and was still parked out on the field in 8.88.

Other aircraft dumped at Luqa in 1.87 comprised ex Pyramid Airlines Aero Commander 690 N491F (possibly since to the scrapyard at Birzebbuga), Cessna 172s(?) N494F, N3548D and Aero Service Cessna 404 N80DS of which only the latter had a sporting chance of flying again.

Near Luqa airport, on the former RAF Safi site sits L1049 Super Constellation "5T-TAF" (c/n 4618, ex TAP CS-TLC) in use as a bar/restaurant. She arrived in Malta on 16.2.68 during the Biafran civil war and was impounded. The crew were arrested as the aircraft was found to be flying under a false registration, but they were eventually smuggled out of the country whilst the aircraft was disposed of by auction on 10.1.73. The aircraft was still serving as a restaurant in 8.88.

Newcal Aviation (formerly MIACO) occupy one of the old RAF Safi hangars and specialise in the refurbishment of surplus DHC-4 Caribou aircraft. Most of these linger for years rather than months and some indeed appear to have taken root.

DHC-4 Caribou	5H-AAC	(c/n 11) ex JW9014 Tanzanian AF, allocated N3262X 8.82 for John Woods Inc but not taken up (noted '84, derelict fuselage only by 1.87, current 8.88).
DHC-4 Caribou	9J-NAA	(c/n 216) ex 303 Zambian AF (noted '84).
DHC-4 Caribou	9J-NAC	(c/n 219) ex 304 Zambian AF (arr 28.7.86, allocated N999NC, in work 8.88) "Jayne".
DHC-4 Caribou	N600NC	(c/n 237) ex 201 Kenyan AF & 5Y-BEM (noted '86, departed 25.7.87 to USA via Denham, UK) "Araminta".
DHC-4 Caribou	5Y-BEV	(c/n 238) ex 202 Kenyan AF (arr 28.6.87, current 8.88).
DHC-4 Caribou	5Y-BER	(c/n 240) ex 204 Kenyan AF (noted '86) "Suzanne". Noted at Ipswich, UK, 4.89 as N400NC "Lisa-Suzanne".
DHC-4 Caribou	5H-AAB	(c/n 244) ex JW9003 Tanzanian AF, allocated N3262W 8.82 for John Woods Inc but not taken up, derelict fuselage (noted '84-'88).
DHC-4 Caribou	N84893	(c/n 282) ex 303 Abu Dhabi AF (noted '84, to USA 16.9.86).
DHC-4 Caribou	N84897	(c/n 283) ex 304 Abu Dhabi AF (noted '84-'87, fuselage only 8.88).
DHC-4 Caribou	N84899	(c/n 300) ex 305 Abu Dhabi AF (noted '84, complete but engineless 8.88).
DHC-4 Caribou	5Y-BEU	(c/n 302) ex 205 Kenyan AF (arr 14.7.86, allocated N50NC, in work 8.88) "Donna Lee".
DHC-4 Caribou	5Y-BET	(c/n 303) ex Kenyan AF 206 (arr 4.7.86, allocated N300NC, current 8.88).

Three ex Spanish AF aircraft were acquired early in 1987 and have proved to be relatively short term inmates.

C-7A Caribou	N90NC	(c/n 24, ex 60-5433, T.9-24) ex '371-04' Esc.371 (arr 6.3.87, dep 29.8.87).
C-7A Caribou	N88NC	(c/n 38, ex 60-5444, T.9-17) ex '353-17' Esc.353 (arr 17.3.87, dep 12.3.88 to Lydd, UK).
C-7A Caribou	N95NC	(c/n 135, ex 62-4191, T.9-30) ex '371-10' Esc.371 (arr 3.8.87, departed 8.88 to Moorsele, Belgium.

These were joined in 4.88 by a further three ex Spanish AF examples as follows:-

C-7A Caribou	N555NC	(c/n 15, ex 60-3764, T.9-13) ex '353-13' Esc.353 (arr 11.4.88).
C-7A Caribou	N666NC	(c/n 27, ex 60-5436, T.9-26) ex '371-06' Esc.371 (arr 18.4.88).
C-7A Caribou	N888NC	(c/n 58, ex 61-2398, T.9-28) ex 371-08' Esc.371 (arr 6.4.88).

Dumped outside the old MIACO hangar (also on the Safi side of the airfield) by 1.87 were the following Dakotas.

C-47A Dakota	N9050T	(c/n 12472, ex 42-92656, KG437, G-AGYX, PH-MAG, 5N-ATA) ex Nigeria Trade Wings.
C-47A Dakota	SU-BFY	(c/n 19754, ex 43-15288) ex Pyramid Airlines.
C-47A Dakota	C-FITH	(c/n 20228, ex 43-15762, NC9033H, ZS-DLX, N9033H, ZS-DLX, CF-ITH, VP-KLU) ex Terra Surveys.
C-47A Dakota	N535M	(c/n 20558, ex 43-16092, NC1050M, CU-T-265, YV-C-AVR) ex Conoco.
C-47B Dakota	N565	(c/n 14955/26400, ex 43-49139, NC66655) ex Conoco.

The first three were moved to the International Fire and Safety Training School at Hal Far by 2.87 whilst N9050T remains here (as of 8.88) in the forlorn hope of attracting a buyer. SU-BFY flew out for the Dutch Dakota Association as PH-DDZ 'Sleeping Beauty' arriving at Schiphol 10.5.87 and is to be put into very long term storage to preserve a flying example of the type for future generations. The 'Sleeping Beauty' is to be woken in time for the 75th anniversary of the Dak's first flight in 2010.

Stored in the military area by 1984 were three Libyan Alouette IIIs, LC2288 (c/n 2288), LC2295 (c/n 2295) and LC2315 (c/n 2315).

VALLETTA

The National War Museum at Fort St Elmo displays the fuselage of Sea Gladiator N5520 (claimed to be 'Faith' of Faith, Hope & Charity fame, retrieved from a quarry at Kalafrana) and the corroded forward fuselage of Spitfire Vc BR108 (ex 603 Sqn, shot down by a Bf 109 8.7.42 and recovered from Marsalforn Bay, Gozo, in 1973) amongst other smaller exhibits.

NETHERLANDS

Holland is just about the most air-minded nation in Europe, if not the world. This is reflected in the aviation heritage preserved in the country (though inevitably many treasures failed to survive the Second World War) and in the tenacity with which recent preservation projects have been pursued, witness the efforts of the Dutch Dakota Association.

Once again there is a strong F-84 presence on the W&R scene reflecting the importance of this breed in the post-war NATO air forces. Each Dutch base received four Thunderstreaks for surface decoy duties and a few of these can still be found. As this text was being finalised, the next generation of KLu fighters was being farmed out into W&R territory in the form of eighteen Starfighters stored at Ypenburg since their final withdrawal during 1984 with quantities of NF-5s entering storage at Woensdrecht and Gilze-Rijen.

Mention must be made of the excellent 'Dutch Wrecks and Relics' of which three editions have so far been published by Airnieuws Nederland. These have proved a valuable reference during the compilation of this section and this debt is gratefully acknowledged. The reader is also referred to these publications for more dated information together with a wealth of detail on the individual aircraft concerned. The contribution made by the Aviation Society of the Netherlands also deserves a special acknowledgement. For this many thanks.

AMSTERDAM/SCHIPHOL

The Aviodome museum at Schiphol airport was opened on 10.7.71 and displays a comprehensive collection of aircraft encompassing the development of aviation in Holland (prior to 1971 a few aircraft were displayed at Schiphol-Oost). As well as the Aviodome itself, the museum makes use of storage and restoration facilities at Schiphol-Oost (ie the East side of the airport) and at Badhoevedorp. On display here have been the following.

Auster J/5	PH-NFH	(c/n 1845, ex PH-NAA, PH-LPS) (arr 6.1.77, current '89).
Beagle Pup 121	PH-VRV	(c/n B120) ex Haarlem, used as childrens' plaything (current '89).
Bleriot XI	BAPC105	replica, ex Salisbury Hall, UK, & Rosmalen (noted '81-'89, on loan from Mosquito Museum).
Cierva C.30A	SE-AFI	(c/n 735, ex G-ACVC, LN-BAD, RNorAF 99) crashed 13.12.51 at Eskilstuna (arr '62, current '89).
DHC-2 Beaver	"JZ-PAD"	(c/n 1288, ex N7904C) ex TH Delft, marked "NNGLM" and "Kruinduif", fuselage only used as childrens' plaything (current '89).
DH Sea Devon C.20	"PH-MAD"	(c/n 04453, ex XJ350) painted as a Martins Air Charter DH Dove, arr 9.11.82, last flight 29.12.82 (current '89).
DH104 Dove 6	OO-SCD	(c/n 04117, ex VP-KDE, G-AMFU) cockpit section only, remainder scrapped (arr late '75, current '89).
DH82A Tiger Moth	A-38	(c/n 83101, ex R5242) soc 24.3.61 (noted '71-'89).
Douglas DC-3C	"PH-TCB"	(c/n 19434, ex 42-100971, PH-PBA) ex Royal Flight (arr 4.2.76, current '89 in KLM colours).
Eich JE2	PH-GYR	(c/n 18/01) (arr 18.1.89, current).
Evans VP-1	"PH-VPI"	(noted '88-'89).
Fokker C.VD	634	(ex 312, "618") (arr '60, current '89).
Fokker DR.1	-	replica, built '77 (current '88).
Fokker F.VIIA	"H-NACT"	(c/n 5054, ex CH-159, OY-DED, SE-ASE, OY-ASE) KLM

		colours, may be restored to airworthiness (noted '78-'89).
Fokker F-27-100	PH-FCX	(c/n 10183, ex TC-TEC) F-27 Friendship Association, ex Ypenburg store & KLM gia (arr 6.5.88, current '89).
Fokker S.11	"E-42"	(c/n 6198, ex PH-UET, OO-TIM, PH-UET, (PH-BEB ntu)) ex St Jacobiparochie (arr early '83, current '89).
Fokker S.11	E-24	(c/n 6215) soc 3.9.73 (noted '74-'84, to Assen).
Fokker S.14	"K-1"	(c/n 6289, ex PH-XIV) ex NLR (arr mid '71, current '89 in KLM c/s).
Fokker Spin 3	-	replica, built 1936 (arr '60, current '89). The original Spin came home from Poland on 1.8.86 and will eventually be displayed here following restoration at the Fokker Bedrijfsschool.
Gloster Meteor F.8	I-189	(c/n 6468) "7E-5" soc 9.4.58 (noted '71-'88, to Gilze-Rijen).
Grumman US-2N Tracker	159/V	(c/n 720, ex 148281) ex 320 Sqn, soc 7.1.76 (arr 18.12.75, current '89).
Hawker Sea Fury Mk.51	6-43	(c/n 6310) soc 18.4.57, ex TH Delft (arr 3.71 in a swop for the incomplete 6-14, current '89).
Sea Hawk FGA.6	"118/D"	(c/n 7474, ex WV828) ex AES Lee-On-Solent, painted in MLD colours as an FGA.50 of 860 Sqn (arr 4.7.78, current '89).
Hawker Hunter F.51	"WV395"	(c/n 680269) '69' in 4 FTS marks. Composite airframe, mostly ex RDanAF E-410 with rear fuselage of WV395 and wings of XE584, arr from BAe as G-9-438 (arr '79, current '88).
Lilienthal glider	-	replica of 1893 model, built '57 (noted '59-'89).
Mignet Pou-du-Ciel	"G-AEOF"	(c/n WM.1, BAPC.22) ex Newark, UK (arr 19.3.78, current '89).
NHI Kolibri	PH-NHI	(c/n 3001) (arr '64, current '88).
Harvard T.2B	B-73	(c/n 14A-1268, ex 43-12969, FT228) ex TH Delft (noted '84, to Veghel late '88).
Harvard T.2B	B-182	(c/n 14A-808, ex 43-12509, FS668) masquerading as a P-47 for "A Bridge Too Far") (arr 3.6.75, dep 9.75, back 12.76, to Gilze-Rijen '85).
Piasecki HUP-2	130082	(c/n 259) painted in USN marks "UR/42", ex Aeronavale & Antony Fokker School (arr 12.77, current '89).
Piper L-4J Cub	PH-NLA	(c/n 12772, ex 44-80476, OO-GEI, OO-AVL) (noted '80-'84, to Veghel).
RC680 Commander	OO-SID	(c/n 357-46, ex NC6846S) (arr 30.10.85, current '89).
Rienks R-1B	-	(arr '82, current '89).
RRG Zogling	"PH-1"	replica (arr '60, current '89).
SAAB 91D Safir	PH-RLN	(c/n 91-379) ex RLS (noted '88-'89).
Sikorsky HO4S-3	076/V	(ex 133777, 8-2) 'Salome', soc 11.12.63, ex KLM Bedrijfsschool (arr mid '75, current '89).
Slingsby Grasshopper	WZ872	(arr 12.2.88, current '89).
SE210 Caravelle III	PH-TRO	(c/n 33, ex F-WJAM, HB-ICW) cockpit section only remainder scrapped at Schiphol 3.76 (noted '76-'89).
Spitfire LF.IXc	H-8	(c/n CBAF IX 970, ex MJ271) soc 4.6.56, ex AFS Den Haag, sometime painted as "H-53/MH424" (arr 23.3.78, current '89).
Tipsy T.66 Nipper	"OO-NIC"	(c/n 11, ex OO-NIC, D-EMEC) (noted '88-'89).
VO3 De Reiger	PH-1A6	(c/n 1/NVAV29) (noted '89).
Wright Flyer	-	replica, built '57 (noted '59-'89).

The KLM Bedrijfsschool (KLM apprentice school) in Hangar 9 maintains several instructional airframes - painted in KLM colours!

US-2N Tracker	"190"	(c/n 712, ex 147641, 151) ex 320 Sqn, soc 7.1.76 (arr from De Kooij 14.3.78, current '89).

SP-2H Neptune	210	(c/n 7263) ex 320 Sqn, soc 1.6.82, arr 16.12.83 (current '89).
Harvard T.2B	B-103	(c/n 14A-1459, ex 43-13160, FT419) (noted '72 dep 23.10.86 to Valkenburg for restoration, then to MLM Kamp Zeist as "099/K" in MLD colours).

The Fokker Bedrijfsschool (Fokker apprentice school) has one and a half Thunderstreaks kept on the second floor of the apprentice school. There are also many parts of Fokker S.11s here (including major components) which provide a stock of spares for the Fokker Four display team.

F-84F Thunderstreak	P-172	(ex 53-6678) soc 7.9.70, ex 315 Sqn, LETS & DVM (arr 18.5.84, current '89).
F-84F Thunderstreak	P-230	(ex 53-6726) soc 2.10.70, rear half only (remainder at DVM, Gilze-Rijen) (noted '87-'89).

The school are also restoring the original Fokker Spin (1911 vintage) which returned home from Poland on 1.8.86.

The Dutch Dakota Association (operators of 'flyer' PH-DDA) received C-47A Dakota PH-DDZ (c/n 19754) on 10.5.87 and have placed it in very long term store. Former RAAF Douglas DC-2 A30-14 was offloaded from the 'Zuiderkruis' in Den Helder docks and roaded here for restoration by the DDA on 19.12.88 following the long voyage from Australia. It is currently stored at Schiphol-Oost.

Morane-Saulnier MS505 N156EB (c/n 752, ex F-BAYE) had arrived here by 4.87 from Gilze-Rijen and will probably end up in the Aviodome. It is currently stored in Hangar 8 under plastic sheets with DH89A Dragon Rapide F-BCDB (c/n 6897, ex NR833, YI-ABD, G-AKDW) from Nimes, France (noted '88). The cockpit section of Fokker F.XVIII PJ-AIS (ex PH-AIS) arrived from Willemstad (on the island of Curacao) in late '88 for a three year restoration job by KLM.

APELDOORN

Fairchild F24R-1 HB-EIM (c/n 418) is under restoration here.

ASSEN

The Auto Museum here(some 25 kms South of Groningen) has acquired the following aircraft for display here. The Super Cub arrived from DVM storage at Gilze-Rijen in 1980 and was still here in '89 on permanent loan from the Militaire Luchtvaart Museum. The rest arrived from the MLM's storage facility at the DVM, Gilze-Rijen, early in 1989.

DH L-20B Beaver	S-9	(c/n 965, ex 55-4585) soc 3.9.74, ex 300 Sqn.
Fokker S.11	E-24	(c/n 6251) soc 3.9.73, ex Aviodome & Gilze store.
Hawker Hunter F.4	N-122	(c/n 8622) soc 10.5.60.
Hawker Hunter T.7	N-305	(c/n 41H-693457) to AFS 28.2.67, soc 8.9.67, to museum store at Woensdrecht, then Gilze-Rijen, to MLM '81-'83, then Gilze-Rijen store.
Piper L-18C Super Cub	R-87	(c/n 18-3185, ex 53-4785, BLa OL-L111) wfu 12.67, arr from DVM early '80, hanging from ceiling.
F-84G Thunderjet	K-6	(c/n 1358, ex 51-9583) soc 16.11.56, ex TH Delft & Gilze-Rijen store, marked as "TP-25".
F-84F Thunderstreak	P-248	(ex 53-6584) soc 25.9.70, ex LETS & DVM store.

BADHOEVEDORP

The Aviodome has a storage facility here (near Schiphol airport) where many small items are kept together with some aircraft components and occasionally complete airframes. The following have been recorded recently.

Bensen B6 Gyroglider	-	acquired 1975.
Fi 156 Storch	D-EDEC	(c/n 5802, ex MM12822, I-FAGG) to Guy Black 29.9.83.
Fokker S.IV	108	(ex LVA) under restoration to flying condition with the registration PH-SIV reserved.
Fokker S.11	E-9	(c/n 6200, PH-HOS ntu) soc 17.8.72, ex Seppe (noted'87).
Fokker S.12	PH-NDC	(c/n 6287) arr from Westzaan '82 for restoration, to Lelystad by '88.

Mignet Pou-du-Ciel	"PH-POU"	built 1935, arrived '84.
B-25D Mitchell	B-9	(c/n 100-20754, ex 42-87261, FR199, A-22, M-9, B-9) '2-9', soc 8.7.54, nose section only, to Veghel '88.
Harvard T.2B	B-82	(c/n 14A-1188, ex 43-12889, FT148) soc 13.3.62, ex Leeuwarden dump, arrived 11.83, reduced to spares and scrapped.
Harvard T.2B	B-163	(c/n 14-664, ex 42-12417, FE930) soc 15.11.65, ex Nyverdal (noted '84, to UK '87).
Harvard T.2B	B-168	(c/n 14-718, ex 42-12471, ex FH150) soc 18.7.66, arr from Myverdal mid '80s, to UK '87.
Harvard T.2B	B-182	(c/n 14A-808, ex 43-12509, FS668) soc 21.11.66, masquerading as a P-47, ex Westzaan, to the Antony Fokker School mid '83).
Rhonlerche II	PH-251	(c/n 226) stored '84.
Grunau Baby IIB	PH-170	(c/n 6052) stored '84.
Grasshopper TX.1	XP462	arrived 12.2.88 with one other.
Spitfire LF.IX	H-25	(ex MK732, 3W-17) soc 4.6.56, hulk ex St Athan, arrived 13.4.84, to Gilze-Rijen store '86 and returned to UK during '88.

BEEK (MAASTRICHT AIRPORT)

Three ex Bursa Hava Yollari DC-8s arrived here for storage during 1981, destined never to fly again.

Douglas DC-8-21	TC-JBV	(c/n 45429, ex N8608, EC-CDB, A6-SHA) arr 8.4.81, scrapped here by Omega Air 12.84.
Douglas DC-8-52	TC-JBY	(c/n 45694, ex N8061U) arr 25.3.81, scrapped here by Omega Air 12.84.
Douglas DC-8-52	TC-JBZ	(c/n 45693, ex N8060U) arr 25.3.81, sold to Maastricht Airport 12.84 and broken up 24-26.5.85.

BREDA

Lockheed T-33A M-54 (ex 51-17411, soc 26.5.72) was preserved here for many years at the KMA (Koninklijke Militaire Academie/Royal Military Academy) barracks in Kasteelplein (the square in which the barracks is situated) (noted '72-'84). It has now moved to Woensdrecht, being replaced by F-104G Starfighter D-8245 (c/n 8245, ex 312 Sqn, soc 10.7.84) (noted '84-'89).

BUDEL

On display near the entrance to this West German AF base on the road from Eindhoven to Weert, the home of Ausbildungsregiment 2, is ex Jg.73 CL-13B Sabre Mk.6 JC-240 (c/n S6-1704) (noted '67-'89). After 20 years on its undercarriage, the Sabre was lifted onto a pole during 1988 with the aid of a CH-53G.

CRAILO

The barracks at Kamp Crailo (some 6 kms North of Hilversum) received Hunter F.4 N-129 (c/n 8629, soc 7.6.60) from Soesterberg during 1984 where it had served as gate guardian. The airframe is used for NBC decontamination training and was still current during '89.

DEELEN

MBB-105CB B-65 (c/n S.265) of 299 Sqn crashed on 2.10.85. The cockpit was salvaged for use as a simulator and is thought to be located here.

L-21B Super Cub R-115 (c/n 18-3605, ex 54-2405) was allocated the registration PH-KNA in 1978 and moved here for service as a glider tug. It remained in store, unconverted, for almost a decade but was re-activated by mid '88.

Standing out on the airfield is finless F-84F Thunderstreak P-243 (ex 53-6748, soc 30.9.70, gia with LETS '71-'83) (noted '83-'88) in use for bdr training and decoy duties.

On an annexe (Groot Heidekamp) to the South of the base is the LETS (Luchtmacht Elektronische en Technische School/KLu Technical & Electronic School) which has used the following complement of ground instructional airframes recently.

F-104G Starfighter	"LETS-1"	(c/n 8224, ex WGAF 2475) wfu after crash landing 7.2.66, arr here late '60s, to Leeuwarden 19.11.80.
F-104G Starfighter	D-8061	(c/n 8061) ex 312 Sqn, soc & arr 21.11.83.
F-104G Starfighter	D-8098	(c/n 8098) ex 322/323 Sqn, w/o at Wildenrath 21.11.78, to Leeuwarden 8.3.79, arr here 20.11.80, used as paint-spraying trainer.
F-104G Starfighter	D-8244	(c/n 8244) ex 312 Sqn, soc & arr 21.11.83.
F-104G Starfighter	D-8256	(c/n 8256) ex 312 Sqn, soc & arr 4.4.84.
F-104G Starfighter	D-8318	(c/n 8318) ex 312 Sqn, arrived 21.11.83.
Northrop NF-5A	K-3003	(c/n 3003) ex VUD, arr from Gilze-Rijen 22.1.87.
F-84F Thunderstreak	P-172	(ex 53-6678) soc 7.9.70, to DVM 28.12.83 then to KLM Bedrijfsschool 18.5.84.
F-84F Thunderstreak	P-192	(ex 53-6921) ex Eindhoven decoy, arrived 13.8.84, not seen 11.87, perhaps to the fire school?
F-84F Thunderstreak	P-226	(ex 53-6612) soc 20.10.70 (noted '83, to Kamp Zeist).
F-84F Thunderstreak	P-243	(ex 53-6748) soc 30.9.70, to Deelen airfield (see below).
F-84F Thunderstreak	P-263	(ex 53-6780) soc 29.9.70, to DVM Gilze-Rjen '85.
Sud Alouette III	A-274	(c/n 1274) ex 298 Sqn, crashed at Seedorf, WG, 2.3.67. Arr from DVM 1980 with boom (in 'Grasshoppers' c/s) of A-350.

The BWS (<u>Brandweerschool</u>/Fire School) here trains KLu firemen in the skills of tackling aircraft fires. Not all training airframes are actually set on fire and some may survive in this role for years. Airframes in use here over the last few years have comrised the following.

Grumman CS-2A Tracker	185/H	(c/n DH-5-6, ex RCN 1507) soc 1.8.71, used as rescue trainer (noted '72-'78, scrapped).
Hawker Hunter F.4	N-150	(c/n 8652) soc 9.6.59 after Cat.5 accident, ex Leeuwarden Stn Flt & LETS (noted '72-'88).
RF-104G Starfighter	D-8133	(c/n 8133) ex 306 Sqn, w/o after a bird strike at Jever 1.12.81 (noted '86-'87, upside down on dump).
Lockheed T-33A	14114	(c/n 5408, ex 51-4114) ex 32 TFS bdr airframe (fuselage section & wings arr '85, to Oirschot '88).
Lockheed T-33A	18756	(c/n 6540, ex 51-8756) obtained for spares use by KLu and never flown, used as gia at Woensdrecht (arr '81, current '88).
F-84F Thunderstreak	(P-116)	(ex 52-7164) ex Soesterburg decoy, arrived '79 and burnt soon after.
F-84F Thunderstreak	(P-140)	(ex 52-7191) ex Soesterburg decoy, arrived '79 and burnt soon after.
F-84F Thunderstreak	"P-149"	(really P-152, ex 52-10510) ex Soesterburg decoy, wears 334 Sqn badge (noted '79-'88).
F-84F Thunderstreak	(P-155)	(ex 52-10536) ex Soesterburg decoy, arrived '79 and burnt soon after.
F-84F Thunderstreak	P-165	(ex 53-6557) ex Leeuwarden decoy, arrived 26.6.78 and burnt soon after.
F-84F Thunderstreak	P-169	(ex 53-6671) ex Leeuwarden decoy, arrived 26.6.78 and burnt soon after.
F-84F Thunderstreak	P-194	(ex 53-6925) ex Leeuwarden decoy, arrived 6.78 and burnt soon after.
F-84F Thunderstreak	P-213	(ex 53-6533) ex Leeuwarden decoy, arrived 26.6.78 and burnt soon after.
F-84F Thunderstreak	P-244	(ex 53-6752) soc 7.9.70, ex Gilze-Rijen decoy (arr '85, burnt out nose remained '88).

DE KOOIJ

It is hoped to recover Sikorsky SH-34J 143/D (ex 147634) from the scrapyard at Seifertshofen, WG, and display it on the gate. An ex Royal Navy Wasp HAS.1 is also sought.

DELFT

The TU Delft (Technische University Delft, formerly the TH Delft, Technische Hoogschool) has an Aeronautical Engineering department (in Kluyverweg, within the university campus) which has used the following complete or substantial airframes together with many smaller components. Some of those listed below may well be dismantled and spread around the department, only the two F-104s are complete.

Beagle 121 Pup	PH-VRS	(c/n B119) fuselage only (noted '74-'88).
Dornier Do 27A	"OC-054"	(c/n 231 ex CC-054) fuselage only, in two pieces (noted '66-'80).
Dornier Do 28A-1	5N-ACQ	(c/n 3006, ex D-IHYL, PH-ACU) fuselage only (noted '78-'88).
Grumman G164A Ag Cat	PH-LIZ	(c/n 680, ex ET-ADY, 5Y-API, N67072) crashed 14.2.81 (noted '81).
Grumman CS-2A Tracker	193/H	(c/n DH-4-21, ex RCN 1522) soc 9.6.70 (noted '79-'88).
SP-2H Neptune	207/V	(c/n 7257) ex 320 Sqn, soc 9.3.81, front fuselage section (noted '81-'87).
SP-2H Neptune	218/V	(c/n 7157, ex 146438) ex 320 Sqn, soc 28.8.81. Sections only - remainder of airframe displayed at Kamp Zeist (noted '81-'87).
F-104G Starfighter	D-8048	(c/n 8048) soc 12.10.84, ex Ypenburg (arr early '89).
F-104G Starfighter	D-8114	(c/n 8114) soc 18.6.84, (noted '84-'89).
Harvard T.2B	B-73	(c/n 14A-1268, ex 43-12969, FT228) (noted '78, to Aviodome 10.83, then Veghel).
F-84E Thunderjet	K-6	(ex 51-9583) ex 'TP-25' 306 Sqn, soc 16.11.56 (noted '70-'85, to DVM Gilze-Rijen, then Assen).
F-84F Thunderstreak	P-227	(ex 53-6550) ex 306 Sqn, soc 7.2.57. Sections (noted '79-'88).
SAAB 91A Safir	PH-UEA	(c/n 91-125, ex SE-BFU) crashed 15.8.62, front fuse only (noted '84).
SE210 Caravelle III	PH-TRP	(c/n 43, ex HB-ICY) large section of rear fuse & wing (noted '76-'88).

In 1987 Spitfire LF.IX PL344 (or to be precise, a rather small centre fuselage section and part of a wing!) which had been in storage with the TU Delft for many years were obtained by Charles Church to form the basis for his third Spitfire restoration project (G-IXCC) at Micheldever, UK.

A scrapyard in Broekmoleweg processed CS-2A Tracker 183 (c/n DH-5-4, ex RCN 1505) when it was discarded by the TNO at Rijswijk in '79.

DEN HAAG

On the Eastern side of the city, on the border between Voorburg and Rijswijk, the Antony Fokker School is located at Brinckhorstlaan 251. The school has employed a varied selection of airframes to teach the skills of aeronautical engineering.

Cessna 150E	"PH-SKS"	(c/n 60797, ex N6097T, OO-SIM, PH-ALB, "PH-AFS") (arr 13.5.77, current '89).
DH L-20B Beaver	S-6	(c/n 959, ex 55-4582) ex 300 Sqn, soc 9.9.74 (arr 18.9.75, current '89).
Fokker S.11	E-14	(c/n 6205, PH-HOO ntu) soc 9.73 (arr from Veen 10.11.75, to Ypenburg 15.10.82 and restored to airworthiness with the 'Fokker Four' as PH-AFS.
Grumman CS-2A Tracker	184/H	(c/n DH-5-05, ex RCN 1506) soc 28.6.72 (arr from De Kooij 26.5.73, current '89).
F-104G Starfighter	D-8259	(c/n 8259) ex UFO, soc 11.10.84 (arr 8.9.85, current'89).
TF-104G Starfighter	D-5810	(c/n 5810) ex UFO & Ypenburg store, soc 23.11.84 (arr 11.6.88, current '89).
Lockheed T-33A	M-50	(c/n 5679, ex 51-4384) ex TVO, soc 8.6.72 (arr 29.7.72, current '89).
Harvard T.2B	"50"	(really c/n 14-764, ex 42-12517, FH130, B-165, "PH-AFS") ex VVO & Woensdrecht store, soc 18.7.66 (arr 26.9.72, current '89 in USN style c/s).

Harvard T.2B	B-181	(c/n 14-543, ex 42-12296, FE809) ex VVO, soc 23.12.66 (arr 3.2.77, to Gilze-Rijen early '80s).
Harvard T.2B	B-182	(c/n 14A-808, ex 43-12509, FS668) soc 21.11.66, DVM store, to LETS '72, to Aviodome 3.6.75, rebuilt as a "P-47" for "A Bridege Too Far", returned to Aviodome by 12.76 as P-47 "MX-W", arr here 12.83 for rebuild to Harvard configuration. To Gilze-Rijen by '86.
PA27-250 Aztec	5N-AEZ	(c/n 27-2053, ex PH-EDG, D-IGOG) ex Schreiner-Nigeria (arr 26.11.77, current '89).
F-84F Thunderstreak	P-134	(ex 52-7185) ex 314 Sqn, soc 21.12.66 (arr 23.4.79 from Fokker in exchange for S.14 L-11, current '89).
F-84F Thunderstreak	P-254	(ex 53-6600) ex 315 Sqn, soc 2.10.70 (arr 20.4.71, current '89).
SAAB 91D Safir	PH-RLE	(c/n 91-372) (noted '82-'89, painted as "PH-AFS").
Sikorsky UH-34J	134/V	(c/n 58-1597, ex 150729, N266) ex 8 Sqn, soc 28.6.72 (arr 25.5.73, current '89).

DEN HAM

The hulk of Beech D-18S PH-UBY (c/n A.101, ex NL-501) arrived here (near Groningen) in the early seventies after storage at Eelde. The aircraft still survives, painted in a 'psychedelic' colour scheme.

DE PEEL

Two Super Cubs have spent several years in store at this KLu reserve air base.

Piper L-21B Super Cub	LX-PAA	(c/n 18-3815, ex 54-2415, R-125, allocated PH-KNC) ex Malden store (noted '86).
Piper L-21B Super Cub	R-160	(c/n 18-3850, ex 54-2450, allocated PH-KNM) ex Malden store (noted '80-'83).

EINDHOVEN

Preserved at the main gate are F-84F Thunderstreak P-231 (ex 53-6742, soc 2.11.70) repainted in "Double Dutch" colours during '88 (noted '79-'88) and F-84G Thunderjet K-85/"TB-1" (ex 51-10178, soc 3.7.55, ex 'TC-1') (noted '78-'88, also now in "Double Dutch" c/s). Displayed in flying attitude outside the Officers' Mess is Spitfire LF.IXc H-15 (c/n CBAF IX 1970, ex MK959, soc 4.6.54, installed 16.6.64 as "MJ289/VL-V", repainted '71, current '89). They were due to be joined by Northrop NF-5A K-3068 (c/n 3068) as this text was being prepared.

The KLu's Thunderstreaks gathered here at the end of 1970 following their final withdrawal. Four were allocated as surface decoys to each KLu base, Eindhoven retaining these four.

F-84F Thunderstreak	P-164	(ex 53-6547) (noted '70-'78).
F-84F Thunderstreak	P-192	(ex 53-6921) (noted '70, to LETS 13.8.84).
F-84F Thunderstreak	P-200	(ex 53-6932) (noted '70-'78).
F-84F Thunderstreak	P-231	(ex 53-6742) soc 2.11.70 (noted '70-'84, to main gate for display).

More recently, F-84F Thunderstreak P-277 (ex 53-6924) has arrived here (by 1985) from Gilze-Rijen. It was parked out on the field by 1986.

In use as a ground instructional airframe here is ex 314 Sqn NF-5A K-3068 which suffered a bird-strike at Hopsten on 16.1.87, was roaded to the DVM at Gilze, then on to Eindhoven 18.3.87. In use earlier was NF-5A K-3071/'NAC-7' (ex 316 Sqn) which suffered a bird-strike here on 3.10.73 and was rebuilt (under crew chief 'Nico') as 'NAC-7' (for "Nico's Aircraft Corporation"). It moved to Gilze in early '85 for use as weapon-loading trainer.

On the civil side, the Dynamic Air hangar held the wreck of AA5A Traveler PH-CDW (c/n 0648) in 6.88.

GILZE-RIJEN

Recent years have seen the gate guarded by a Hunter and later a Thunderstreak. No doubt the NF-5 will be a strong contender the next time a change is due.

Hawker Hunter F.6	N-258	(c/n 8934) ex 316 Sqn (noted '75-'79, to Soesterberg).
F-84F Thunderstreak	P-191	(ex 53-6916) soc 2.10.70, served as a decoy here from '71 (noted on the gate '79-'89).

The DVM (Depot Vliegtuig Materieel, equivalent to an RAF Maintenance Unit) is housed at Gilze and is the main KLu storage/overhaul centre and crash investigation unit. The NF-5 fleet is gathering here and at Woensdrecht for storage and disposal following replacement with the F-16. NF-5 arrivals here so far comprise the following.

Northrop NF-5A	K-3007	(c/n 3007) VUD badge.
Northrop NF-5A	K-3008	(c/n 3008) 314 Sqn badge.
Northrop NF-5A	K-3020	(c/n 3020) VUD badge.
Northrop NF-5A	K-3056	(c/n 3056) 313 Sqn badge.
Northrop NF-5A	K-3063	(c/n 3063) 314 Sqn badge.
Northrop NF-5A	K-3065	(c/n 3065) 316 Sqn badge.
Northrop NF-5B	K-4003	(c/n 4003) VUD badge.
Northrop NF-5A	K-4010	(c/n 4010) VUD badge.
Northrop NF-5A	K-4011	(c/n 4011) 316 Sqn badge, to MLM Soesterburg 7.89.
Northrop NF-5A	K-4018	(c/n 4018) VUD badge.
Northrop NF-5A	K-4021	(c/n 4021) no badge.

In use for battle damage repair training have been the following.

F-104G Starfighter	D-8133	(c/n 8133) ex 306 Sqn, crash landed at Jever 1.12.81 following a bird strike (noted '84-'86, to Deelen).
F-104G Starfighter	D-8282	(c/n 8282) ex UFO (noted '84-'86, to the Dutch base at Blomberg, WG, 12.88).
Northrop NF-5A	K-3034	(c/n 3043) ex 314 Sqn, w/o in landing accident at Eindhoven 4.2.85.

NF-5A K-3071/"NAC-7" (ex 316 Sqn, suffered bird-strike at Eindhoven 3.10.73) arrived in early '85 for use as a weapons loading trainer following several years as a gia at Eindhoven.

The DVM stores aircraft for the MLM at Kamp Zeist, for loan to museums and for use at air displays etc. The following have been noted recently.

Auster III	"R-5"	(c/n 350, ex MZ236, R-11, "R-55") to Veghel '88.
Auster 5	PH-NET	(c/n 965) (noted '83-'84).
Avro Anson C.19	"D-26"	(ex VM352) ex RAE Llanbedr, arrived Soesterberg 28.5.71 (noted '83-'86, to Rosmalen).
DH L-20B Beaver	S-9	(c/n 965, ex 55-4585) ex 300 Sqn, wfu 9.9.74 (noted '76-'89, to Assen).
Fokker S.11	E-24	(c/n 6215) to Assen early '89.
Fokker S.14	L-17	(c/n 7362) ex Woensdrecht store (noted '86).
Gloster Meteor T.7	I-19	(ex WH233) soc 15.5.59 (noted '84-'88, to Twenthe).
Gloster Meteor F.8	I-189	(c/n 6468) "7E-5", arrived from the Aviodome '88.
Hawker Hunter F.4	N-122	(c/n 8622) soc 10.5.60, arr from Soesterberg '83 (noted '83-'86).
Hawker Hunter F.4	N-144	(c/n 8644) soc 29.5.59 (noted '83, to Kamp Zeist '84).
Hawker Hunter T.7	N-305	(c/n 693457) soc 8.9.67 (stored since early '70s, at MLM '81-'84, current here '86).
TF-104G Starfighter	D-5803	(c/n 5803) soc 26.11.84 (arr from Ypenburg mid '89).
TF-104G Starfighter	D-5804	(c/n 5804) soc 23.11.84 (arr from Ypenburg 4.89).
TF-104G Starfighter	D-5805	(c/n 5805) soc 2.5.84 (noted '84-'88, displayed at Twenthe/Zuidkamp '88, swopped for D-5803 and back into store here early '89).
Morane MS505	N156EB	(c/n 752, ex F-BAYE) noted '85, to Schiphol by '87)
Harvard T.2B	B-71	(c/n 14A-1444, ex 43-13145, FT404) soc 18.7.66, to LETS, arr here 11.79 for storage, rebuilt to flying condition, flew again 19.3.83 as "Fokker D.XXI" "218". Returned to Harvard configuration and flown again as PH-MLM '87. Owned by MLM.

Harvard T.2B	B-103	(c/n 14A-1459, ex 43-13160, FT419) soc 20.3.63, KLM marks, ex KLM Bedrijfsschool, Schiphol (noted '86, to MLM Kamp Zeist as "099/K").
Harvard T.2B	B-177	(c/n 14-733, ex 42-12486, FE999) soc 21.11.66, arrived from Leeuwarden 21.12.78, displayed outside the DVM hangars from 5.83, removed early '88 and stored inside.
Harvard T.2B	B-179	(c/n 14A-807, ex 43-12508, FS667) soc 7.12.82, ex Antony Fokker School, Den Haag (arr early '80s, very little now left).
Harvard T.2B	B-182	(c/n 14A-808, ex 43-12509, FS668) soc 21.11.66, DVM store, to LETS '72, to Aviodome 3.6.75, modified 9.75 to resemble a P-47 as "43-12509/W-MX", Aviodome 12.76, to Antony Fokker School 12.83 for rebuild to Harvard standards, DVM store '85, modified to resemble a Fokker D.XXI and displayed at Kamp Zeist as "141" in '87, returned to store here late '88).
Harvard T.2B	B-184	(c/n 14A-1100, ex 43-12801, FS960) soc 18.7.66, stored here, to Soesterburg museum, later at Kamp Zeist, returned to storage '85.
Piper L-21B Super Cub	R-120	(c/n 18-3810, ex 54-2410) (noted '86).
Piper L-21B Super Cub	R-138	(c/n 18-3828, ex 54-2428, PH-KNG ntu) wfu 18.5.76, spares source for R-126 (noted '79-'87, sold as G-BLIH '88).
Piper L-21A Super Cub	R-213	(c/n 18-568, ex N7197K, 51-15682) soc 25.9.68, displayed at Soesterburg museum '71-'78, to Rosmalen '78, to DVM store, exchanged for RF-84F Thunderflash FR-31 and dep to Grimbergen 10.3.89 becoming OO-OAA (OO-OOA ntu).
Piper L-21A Super Cub	R-218	(c/n 18-555, ex N7184K, 51-15669) stored.
F-84E Thunderjet	K-6	(ex 51-9583) soc 16.11.56, ex TU Delft (noted '85-'88, to Assen early '89).
F-84F Thunderstreak	P-172	(ex 53-6678) ex LETS (arr 28.12.83, to KLM Bedrijfsschool 18.5.84)
F-84F Thunderstreak	P-226	(ex 53-6612) 314 Sqn marks (noted '84, to Kamp Zeist '85).
F-84F Thunderstreak	P-230	(ex 53-6726) soc 2.10.70, ex MLM Kamp Zeist, (noted '85-'88, rear half to KLM Bedrifsschool, Schiphol, in '87, nose remains here).
F-84F Thunderstreak	P-248	(ex 53-6584) soc 25.9.70, ex LETS (noted '71-'88, to Assen early '89).
F-84F Thunderstreak	P-263	(ex 53-6780) (noted '83-'87, loaned to Autotron, Rosmalen '87).
RF-84F Thunderflash	FR-31	(ex 53-7644, WGAF EA-311) ex BelgAF, received from Saffraanberg 11.87 in exchange for L-21A Super Cub R-213. For eventual display at aun unknown location.
Spitfire IX	H-25	(ex MK732, 3W-17) soc 4.6.56, arr from Badhoevendorp '86, to UK '88.

The group Stichting Vliegsport Gilze-Rijen base their collection of restored ex KLu aircraft here along with a number of machines used for spares or awaiting their turn for restoration. In most cases the allocated civil registrations are very small or worn on one side only.

Auster III	R-18	(c/n 344, ex MZ231,) also PH-NGK (noted '88).
Fokker S.11	E-20	(c/n 6211) airworthy, also PH-GRB.
Harvard T.2B	B-118	(c/n 14A-1467, ex 43-13168, FT247) soc 17.5.66, LETS '65-'76, stored here '76-'79, airworthy as PH-IIB.
Harvard T.2B	B-176	(c/n 14-719, ex 42-12472, FE985) soc 21.11.66, arr from Nijmegen '84 (noted '84-'86, incomplete, used as a spares source by Stichting Vliegsport).

Harvard T.2B	B-181	(c/n 14-543, ex 42-12296, FE809) soc 23.12.66, ex Antony Fokker School, Den haag (arr early '80s, incomplete airframe in storage, noted '86).
Piper L-21B Super Cub	R-109	(c/n 18-3537, ex 54-2337) airworthy, also PH-GAZ.
Piper L-21B Super Cub	R-116	(c/n 18-3606, ex 54-2406) fuselage only, in store (noted '74-'84).
Piper L-21B Super Cub	R-122	(c/n 18-3812, ex 54-2412) in store (noted '74-'84).
Piper L-21B Super Cub	R-181	(c/n 18-3871, ex 54-2471) airworthy, also PH-GAU.
Piper L-21A Super Cub	R-206	(c/n 18-575, ex N1004A, 51-15658) stored (noted '74-'84).

The base received the usual ration of four F-84F Thunderstreaks in 1971 for use as surface decoys.

F-84F Thunderstreak	P-170	(ex 53-6673) soc 2.10.70 (noted '78, to Woensdrecht'80).
F-84F Thunderstreak	P-191	(ex 53-6916) soc 2.10.70 (noted '71-'79, to the gate for display '79).
F-84F Thunderstreak	P-244	(ex 53-6752) soc 7.9.70 (noted '71-'85, to Deelen).
F-84F Thunderstreak	P-277	(ex 53-6924) soc 7.9.70 (noted '71-'85, to Eindhoven by '86).

GOES

In the De Poel industrial estate, on the island of Walcheren, the Jacob Boer company display Piaggio P.149D OO-LWG (c/n 050, ex WGAF 9036).

GRONINGEN/EELDE

SAAB 91D Safir PH-RLS (c/n 91-371) is displayed up a pole at the entrance to the RLS (Rijks Luchtvaartschool) (noted '86-'88).

The fuselage of another Safir, PH-RLH (c/n 91-375), was in a workshop here in 7.86.

The cockpit of Beech F33C Bonanza PH-BNR (c/n CJ-149, crashed 23.4.87) is in a workshop here as a training aid.

HAARLEM

In mid 1980 a scrapyard in the industrial estate here received five Harvards and a Fokker S.11 from storage with a private owner at Weesp.

Fokker S.11	E-4	(c/n 6193)
Harvard T.2B	B-163	(c/n 14-664, ex 42-12417, FE930) to Nyverdal, then to Badhoevedorp 12.11.83, then on to Windsor, UK.
Harvard T.2B	B-168	(c/n 14-718, ex 42-12471, FE984) to Nyverdal, then to North Weald, UK.
AT-6F Harvard	OO-JBS	(ex 44-81775, F-BJBS) ex GOGEA.
AT-6F Harvard	OO-JBT	(ex 44-81690, F-BJBT) ex COGEA.
AT-6F Harvard	OO-JBU	(ex 44-81730, F-BJBU) ex COGEA.

The Hogere Technische School (Technical High School) has been using the following instructional airframes.

Auster J/5B	PH-NEH	(c/n 2932) arr 1973, no longer current.
Beagle Pup 100	PH-VRV	(c/n B120) crashed 29.10.70, to the Aviodome by '89.
NHI Kolibri H-3	PH-NFT	(c/n 2001) ex TH Delft (current '89).
SAAB 91 Safir	PH-RLR	arr late '88, ex Eelde store.

HEINO

At the De Schaarshoek holiday camp SAAB 91A Safir PH-UED (c/n 91-137) is displayed on a pole with the spurious registration "PH-NEP" (noted '80-'86). Heino is about 10 kms South East of Zwolle.

HILVERSUM

In the roof of the glider hangar (on the South side of the field) L-21B Super Cub R-131 (c/n 18-3821, ex 54-2421, soc 30.9.76, allocated PH-KND) is stored (noted '78-'88). Breguet AV36 Fauvel OO-ZJM (c/n 159) was stored here from 1980 and may still be around.

On the opposite side of the field, the frame of Auster III PH-UFM (c/n 577, ex NJ957, R-4, A-31, U-31) is under restoration in the smaller of the two hangars (noted 6.88) whilst Slingsby Cadet TX.3 WT871 has been in store since its arrival during '88.

HOEVEN

The Bosbad Hoeven (a leisure centre just down the road from Seppe airfield) has always had an affinity with aircraft, the following having been displayed in the grounds in recent years.

PB2B-1 Catalina	16-212	(ex USN 46521, MLD 321 Sqn & 8 Sqn, soc 8.7.57) ex 321 Sqn (arr 2.8.57, noted '82, to MLM and displayed at Kamp Zeist from '83 following restoration work at Valkenburg).
CS-2A Tracker	"151"	(Really a re-paint of 190 c/n DH-5-14, ex RCN 1515) soc 17.10.68, ex Schiphol (arr 15.5.79, current '89).
Hawker Hunter F.6	N-226	(c/n 8858) soc 11.2.63, ex Nieuw Milligen & DVM (arr 5.83 in exchange for the Catalina, current '89).

HOOGEVEEN

Two Piper Cub frames were undergoing restoration here during 5.86.

LEEUWARDEN

Guarding the gate here has been Gloster Meteor T.7 I-320 (ex VW417, soc 1.12.58, arr 11.11.78, current '89) formerly derelict at Maastricht/Beek for many years. It was relocated near the control tower during the mid eighties and now wears its correct serial again following a spell as "I-323" courtesy of the locally based 323 Sqn. Displayed in front of the 322 Sqn HQ building is F-104G Starfighter D-8257 (c/n 8257, soc 22.5.84 after use as gia, noted '83-'89).

Serving as an aircraft towing training aid is F-104G Starfighter "LETS-1" (c/n 8224, ex WGAF 2475, noted '80-'89). This machine was wfu following a crash landing on 7.2.66 and served as a gia with the LETS during the late sixties and seventies. She moved to Leeuwarden on 19.11.80 in exchange for F-104G D-8098 which was more suitable for the LETS. During 1983 she was marked "PH-TED" for a while.

The base received its quota of F-84F Thunderstreaks in 1971. The burnt out remains of the last one were still here in '88.

F-84F Thunderstreak	P-165	(ex 53-6557) soc 11.9.70 (noted '71, to Deelen 26.6.78).
F-84F Thunderstreak	P-169	(ex 53-6671) soc 10.9.70 (noted '71, to Deelen 26.6.78).
F-84F Thunderstreak	P-194	(ex 53-6925) soc 1.7.70 (noted '71, to fire dump here 6.78-'88).
F-84F Thunderstreak	P-213	(ex 53-6533) soc 1.7.70 (noted '71, to Deelen 26.6.78).

The fire service here received three KLu Harvard T.2Bs in the early seventies of which B-82 (c/n 14A-1188, ex 43-12889, FT148) proved the toughest. She survived until 11.83 when the battered remains were moved to the Aviodome's store at Badhoevedorp for use as spares. The firemen continued to practice with ex decoy F-84F Thunderstreak P-194 (see above). This was in very poor condition by 6.88.

LELYSTAD

Dismantled in the Martinair Flying Club hangar in 5.86 were PA18-150 Super Cubs PH-MBC (c/n 18-5373), PH-MBD (c/n 18-5381), PH-MBE (c/n 18-5383). In 6.88, Fuji FA200-160 PH-GLA (c/n 137) was parked out on the field looking very much the worse for wear and with the grass growing round it.

The Keep 'm Flying museum collection (also known as Stichting Vroege Vogels/Early Birds Society) have had the following on display in their hangars recently. Those that are not yet airworthy are for the most part under active restoration.

Museum Hangar

Beech D18S	N5369X	RCAF colours (arr Schiphol 31.5.88).

A75N Stearman	N59257	(c/n 75-2764, ex 41-25275, N49948, C-FUCB) (noted '88).
DHC-1 Chipmunk 22	G-BBMO	(c/n C1/0550, ex WK514) (noted '85-'88).
DH Devon C.2/2	N531WB	(c/n 04266, ex WB531, G-BLRN) (noted '88).
Fokker S.11	PH-AFS	(c/n 6205, E-14, alloc PH-HOO) Fokker Four (noted '88).
Fokker S.11	PH-HOG	(c/n 6275, ex (PH-NFA), E-39, 199, alloc PH-HOI) Fokker Four (noted '88).
Fokker S.11	PH-HOK	(c/n 6272, ex E-29) (noted '88).
Fokker S.11	PH-HOL	(c/n 6270, ex E-27) Fokker Four (noted '88).
Fokker S.12	PH-NDC	(c/n 6287, ex E-41) under restoration to fly (noted '85-'88).
Klemm Kl.35D	D-ECCI	(c/n 1904, ex SE-BHX, RSwedAF 5069) (noted '88).
Pou-du-Ciel	"PH-POU"	built 1935, ex Badhoevendorp.
Harvard T.2B	PH-KLU	(c/n 14A-1184, ex 43-12885, FT144, B-59) (noted '85-'88).
PA18-95 Cub	PH-VCY	(c/n 18-3601, ex R-111) (noted '88).
Piper L-21B Super Cub	N83GR	(c/n 18-3851, ex R-161) (noted '88).
PA30 Twin Comanche	PH-COM	(ex 30-279, ex G-ASOB, G-MAAG) (noted '88).
Pottier P.80S	PH-JML	(c/n NVAV-34) (noted '88).
Skyin Sherpa II	PH-IMI	(c/n 8311/1049) (noted '88).
Starduster Too SA300	G-KEEN	(c/n 800) (noted '88).
Earlybirds Hangar		
CASA 1131E	N131EB	(CASA built Bu 131, c/n 2012, ex Spanish AF E.3B-478) (noted '85-'88).
DH60G Gipsy Moth	N168G	(ex A7-44, VH-AFN)
DH82A Tiger Moth	N82AM	(c/n 86568, ex PG671, F-BDOS)
DH82A Tiger Moth	ZS-DLK	(c/n 83912, ex T5902, SAAF 562, ZS-DLK, (PH-DLK))
Fleet 2 Finch	NC724C	(Brewster built, c/n 290) (noted '82).
Fokker DR.1	N5505V	(c/n 102) replica (noted '85-'88).
Mooney 20A	N8382E	(c/n 1560, ex N8382E, PH-HRC)
PA28R-201 Cherokee	PH-WCU	(c/n 28R-7703094) wreck.
Pietenpol Aircamper	N1858	(c/n A7-1968) ex Wings & Wheels, Orlando, FL (noted '82-'88).

A Sea Vixen FAW.2 is due here from storage in the Coventry area.

MAASBRACHT

On display in flying attitude atop a pole at the entrance to a shipyard here (off the E39 motorway North of Maastricht) is Harvard T.2B B-178 (c/n 14-739, ex 42-12492, FH105) (noted '78-'89). She arrived from storage at Soesterburg during the early seventies.

MIDDEN-ZEELAND

The fuselage of Cherokee 140F OO-JPA (c/n 28-7325491) was noted dumped here in 6.86. Two years later, in 6.88, PA34-220T Seneca III PH-KDW (c/n 34-8233148) was standing derelict minus engines and wing tips and with fading paintwork.

MOLENSCHOT

Next door to a scrapyard, the yard owner has Cessna F150H PH-VRL (c/n 0292) located on the roof of his garage (noted '81-'88). The town of Molenschot is on the edge of Gilze-Rijen air base.

MOORDRECHT

Mr PH Hofman (once the owner of many ex AAC Skeeters) stores his homebuilt autogyro "PH-MUG" here. The machine crashed during its test flight on 16.5.74 and remains stored in a shed here (about 15 kms North East of Rotterdam).

NIEUW LOOSDRECHT

The wreckage of former Skylight Harvard T.2B PH-KMA (c/n 14A-1216, ex 43-12917,

FT176, B-56, MLD 043) has been stored here (adjacent to Hilversum airfield) with Mr J Daams following its collision with Spitfire V AB910 at Bex (Switz) on 20.8.78. It will eventually be restored to flying condition with the aid of a spare fuselage obtained in France. Mr Daams also stores SAAB 91A Safir PH-UEG(c/n 91-143,ex SE-BNS) whilst Auster III PH-UFM has left here for rebuild at Hilversum (qv).

NIEUW MILLIGEN

Hawker Hunter F.6 N-226 (c/n 8858, soc 11.2.63) used to be preserved outside the "DutchMil" Air Traffic Control Centre here (noted '75-'81) but was involved in an exchange with the Catalina at Hoeven and was installed in its new home during 1983 following a period in storage with the DVM at Gilze-Rijen.

NIEUW VENNEP

A scrapyard here (about 10 kms South West of Schiphol airport) received the hulk of Cessna 150C PH-NAC (c/n 59976, ex N7876Z, OO-DEF) in 1983. It was thought to be for use as an eyecatcher rather than for scrap and may therefore still survive.

NIJMEGEN

Preserved at the gate of the LIMOS barracks (Luchtmacht Instructie en Opleidingsschool/KLu Basic Training School) in Gelderselaan since 14.4.78 was F-84F Thunderstreak P-205 (ex 53-6567, soc 22.10.70, ex Deelen decoy, current '89). By 9.88 this 'streak had been removed from its usual position and was re-located some 50 meters to the right to make room for ex Ypenburg storage F-104G Starfighter D-8053 (c/n 8053, soc 8.11.84, noted 1.89 in "F-16" style colours).

Just around the corner in Postweg Harvard T.2B B-176 (c/n 14-719, ex 42-12472, FE985, soc 21.11.66) was displayed in the grounds of a military compound (noted '69-'84). It moved to the DVM at Gilze-Rijen during '84 and has not been replaced.

In use as an attraction at the Kleyngeld car dismantlers yard in Kastanjelaan is Beech D-18S PH-UBX (c/n A-105, ex NL-505) which arrived in 1972 and was still in good condition here in the mid eighties.

Perhaps inspired by Mr Kleyngeld, at Xhofleer's scrapyard in Hogelandsweg is Aermacchi AL-60B.2 D-EKPL (c/n 71/6251) which arrived in 1980 and stands wingless near the entrance.

NIJVERDAL

Under restoration here by Early Birds is Nord 1101 Noralpha F-BLLO (c/n 179) which arrived from Lille in 4.88 (noted '84-'88). Two Harvard T.2Bs recovered from a scrapyard in Haarlem came here for storage late in 1980 (see under Haarlem for details). B-163 went to Windsor (via North Weald) for restoration whilst B-168 went to Badhoevedorp then on to North Weald during '88 for spares use with the Harvard Team.

OIRSCHOT

On 26.11.88 the hulk of former AdlA Lockheed T-33A 14114 (ex 51-4114) arrived at the Dutch Army base here (just to the North West of Eindhoven) from the BWS at Deelen. The airframe had previously served at Soesterburg as a bdr airframe for 32 TFS.

OOSTWOLD

The fuselage of L-21A Super Cub R-216/PH-GAT (c/n 18-856, ex 51-15691) was stored here (near Winschoten) by '81 and was still current during '87.

OSS

Preserved with a model aircraft club (Delta Mini Airport) in Frankenbeemdweg is F-84F Thunderstreak P-276 (ex 53-7000) which was soc 1.7.70 and served as a decoy at De Peel.

It was moved here during 1980, wearing a 315 Sqn badge, and is thought to be still current. Frankenbeemdweg is just outside the town on the North West side whilst Oss is halfway between Nijmegen and s'Hertogenbosch.

OUDERKERK

Stored here for the preservation group Vereeniging voor Historische Vliegtuigen (VHV) are the following.

DFS Meise Olympia	OO-ZJB	(c/n 6058) Fokker built.
NHI Kolibrie H-3	PH-NGV	(c/n 3007) ex TH Delft.

OUD VALKEVEEN

Convair 240 LN-KLT (ex 51-7898, N40CE, N406E) was for several years an eye catcher at a scrapyard near Bergen-Op-Zoom until moving to a park here during April 1981. It was finally scrapped at the end of 1988.

OVERLOON

The Oorlogsmuseum (National War and Resistance Museum) here (some 25 kms South East of Volkel) has had the following airframes on display. The Spitfire PR.XI has gone to the UK for restoration to flying condition whilst its replacement was restored to static display condition at Ludham, UK.

B-25D Mitchell II	FR193	(c/n N987-8957, ex 42-30792, FR193, A-17, M-6, B-6) soc 8.7.54, arrived here still coded '2-6' but painted in RAF 320 (Neths) Sqn marks post '78 as 'NO-L' (noted '59-'88).
Harvard T.2B	"12964"	(c/n 14-610, ex 42-12363, FE876, B-199) soc 28.11.62, ex AFS Den Haag, painted in USAAF markings. Restored with parts from B-69 & B-179 (noted '79-'88).
Spitfire PR.XI	PL965	(noted '60-'87, to Nick Grace).
Spitfire XIV	NH649	"3W-F" ex Indian AF, restored to static condition at Ludham, UK, and exchanged for PL965 (Noted '87-'88).

PRINSENBOSCH

The KLu NBC school here (a few kms South West of Gilze-Rijen) used to have Hunter F.4 N-135 (c/n 8635, soc 1962) for instructional use. It had disappeared by 1983. F-104G Starfighter D-8084 (ex Ypenburg) was on display at the gate by 19.5.89.

PURMEREND

The fuselage of ex Air Afrique DC-8-53 TU-TCB (c/n 45671, ex F-BJCB) arrived here (about 30 kms North of Amsterdam) 2.11.85 from Luxembourg where it had been stored since 1983. It has been converted as a restaurant by Dolf de Kuizer and Henk Grol.

RAAMSDONKSVEER

Displayed at the Dutch National Motor Car Museum here (about 25 kms North of Breda) is Koolhoven FK.43 PH-NAK (c/n 6168). The aircraft has been with the museum since 1950 and used to be displayed (eg 1979) at the museum's former premises in Leidschendam. They also have a Bleriot XI replica bought at the Christie's auction on 31.10.86.

REEK

The Mineurs en Sapeurs School (a Dutch Army school for military engineers, about 15 kms North of Volkel) has two 'streaks which are used for teaching soldiers how to camouflage aircraft in the field. P-224 is painted overall dark green whilst P-229 is dark green on the starboard side and retains its former colours on the port side but with the serial changed to "P-312" by 312 sqn. The base is in a heavily wooded area and the aircraft are not visible from outside.

F-84F Thunderstreak	P-224	(ex 53-6604) soc 2.10.70, ex De Peel decoy (noted '79-'87).
F-84F Thunderstreak	P-229	(ex 53-6582) soc 1.7.70, ex Volkel decoy (noted '79-'87).

ROSMALEN

The Lips Autotron car museum here (just North of s'Hertogenbosch) has displayed a number of aircraft, mostly on a temporary basis, with many being loaned from the museum store at Gilze-rijen. The more permanent exhibits have included the following.

Auster III	PH-POL	(c/n 458, ex NX534, R-17) (stored '87-'88).
Avro Anson C.19	"D-26"	(c/n 292655, ex VM352) ex RAE Llanbedr, arrived Soesterburg 28.5.71 for museum, to DVM store then Rosmalen during mid '80s.
Fokker S.11	"PH-HOE"	(c/n 6195, ex E-6, PH-HOT ntu) (noted '78-'84).
Nieuport 11	"N220"	replica, ex "N1540" with the Salis Collection (noted '81).
F-84F Thunderstreak	P-263	(ex 53-6780) soc 29.9.70, to LETS, to DVM store '83, arrived here 8.87.

Fokker S.14 L-17 (c/n 7362) was displayed here in '87 on loan from the DVM as was F-84F Thunderstreak P-263 (ex 53-6780).

ROTTERDAM

On display at a car breaker's yard in Charloisse-Legendijk, Rotterdam-Zuid is/was ex Aeronavale Piasecki HUP-2 Retriever 130076 (c/n 253, ex 76 Aeronavale). It arrived here from Veen in '73 and was still current in '89 painted in a red/white/blue scheme.

ROTTERDAM/ZESTIENHOVEN

PA31-350 Navajo F-BTQA (c/n 31-813) arrived at Rotterdam airport by road for storage on 21.3.83 following an accident at Valenciennes in 3.81. It was still present in the KLM hangar in 7.88 with the wings stacked against the fuselage.

Stored with the Vliegclub Rotterdam is the Dykman Dulkes FB-25 which made a single unofficial flight on 13.9.69 wearing the equally unofficial registration "PH-COR". It was previously stored in the loft of a Mr Van Ham in Assendelft.

SCHAARSBERGEN

The Koninklijke Kader School Luchtmacht (KKSL, or KLu basic training school) has Hunter F.4 N-138 (c/n 8638, soc 17.6.60, arr '64 ex Deelen gate) preserved on the gate (noted '63-'88).

The Kaderschool borders on to Deelen air base.

SCHIEDAM

Stored here (on the West side of Rotterdam) with Mr Kraan is/was Jodel D.112 Club PH-GHE (c/n 751, ex F-BGIP) (noted '83).

SEPPE

Wrecks noted here in 7.88 were Cessna F150M PH-LEG (c/n 1403) and PA28 Cherokee 161 PH-SRZ whilst Robin R.2112 Alpha PH-RGA (c/n 167, ex F-GBUB) was still in store, having been here for several years.

Bolkow Bo 208C Junior PH-KAS (c/n 628, ex D-EKAD) lies in the garden of a private house adjacent to the aerodrome (noted '80-'84).

SOESTERBERG

There has been a Hunter preserved at Soesterberg for as long as most of us can remember, though not always the same machine as can be seen from the list below. There is also a Meteor preserved next to a war memorial near the 334 Sqn (F-27) hangars.

Gloster Meteor F.8	I-187	(c/n 6466) soc 28.5.58, incorrectly marked as "I-147" for a while in the early '80s.
Hawker Hunter F.4	N-122	(c/n 8622) soc 10.5.60, arrived from store at Gilze early '80s and placed by the gate, returned to Gilze'83.
Hawker Hunter F.4	N-129	(c/n 8629) soc 10.5.60, mounted on a pole near the gate until replaced by N-122 early '80s and removed to Crailo '84 after a while in store here.
Hawker Hunter F.6	N-258	(c/n 8934) soc 8.9.67, ex Gilze-Rijen gate, preserved on pole at the main gate.

F-104G Starfighter D-8331 arrived here 27.6.88 (ex Ypenburg store) for onward transport to the USA for the Oklahoma Air Space Museum. In the event this was not proceeded with and the aircraft was roaded to Volkel during 3.89.
The USAFE's 32 TFS operates the F-15 Eagle from here under KLu control and in common with other USAFE units has been the recipient of several airframes for battle damage repair training.

F-4C Phantom	63-7453	ex 171 FIS/Michigan ANG (arr 13.6.86, current 10.87).
F-105F Thunderchief	62-4417	ex 128 TFS/Georgia ANG & MASDC FK080 (arr by 2.85, current 7.88).
Lockheed T-33A	51-4114	(c/n 5408) ex AdlA, (noted '80-'84, to Deelen by '85).

For the record, Soesterberg received the obligatory quartet of decoy Thunderstreaks during 1971 in the form of P-116, P-140, P-152 and P-155. For some inexplicable reason, they were repainted with the incorrect serials "P-147", "P-149", "P-234" and "P-251". All were relegated to the Brandweerschool (fire school) at Deelen during '79 (see under Deelen for more details).

The Militaire Luchtvaart Museum (Military Aviation Museum) is located in a barracks at Kamp Zeist, a mile or so South of Soesterberg air base and only accessible through Soesterberg village. The museum was previously housed at the air base and known as the KLu Museum, moving to Kamp Zeist during '80/'81. The change from KLuM to MLM also permitted the display of MLD aircraft as well as those of the KLu. The exhibits here change from time to time, often as airframes go to and from the museum store at Gilze-Rijen.

Where arrival dates quoted are prior to 1980, these refer to arrival at the KLu Museum at Soesterberg air base. During early 1989 the museum floor was being renewed causing some exhibits to be temporarily moved outside. The locations within the museum are as noted during '88.

Outside

PB2B-1 Catalina	16-212	(c/n 1824, ex Bu46521) (arr 28.10.83, current '88).
Douglas C-47A Dakota	"X-5"	(really ex RDanAF K-688, c/n 20118, ex 43-15652, RNorAF, RDanAF 68-688) flown to Soesterberg 16.12.82, painted in KLu c/s coded "ZU-5" (noted '83-'88).
SP-2H Neptune	201/V	(c/n 7241) ex 320 Sqn, MLD, flown to Soesterberg 11.11.81, soc 13.11.81 (noted '83-'88).
Lockheed 12A-26	L2-38	(c/n 1306, ex "BX238", L2-38, T-2, SE-BXR, OH-ETA, LN-BFS, OY-AOV) ex Egeskov, to Gilze 11.81 (arr '84, current '88).
F-84F Thunderstreak	P-226	(ex 53-6612) 314 Sqn marks, ex LETS & Gilze store (noted '85-'88).
F-84F Thunderstreak	P-230	(ex 53-6726) ex 314 Sqn and Gilze-Rijen (noted '84, to Gilze-Rijen by 5.85, front half stored there and rear half to Schiphol).

General C.J. Snijden Hall (Hall A)

Auster III	"R-55"	(c/n 350, ex MZ236, PH-NGH) ex Gilze-Rijen. Initially painted as "R-55" ('81) but re-painted as "R-5" ('83) (noted '81-'83, now at Veghel).
DH82A Tiger Moth	A-10	(c/n 86587, ex PG690, PH-UFC, soc 16.1.61) ex Autotron, Rosmalen (noted '81-'88).
Farman MF.20	-	fuselage only, on loan from Brussels museum (noted '88).
Farman HF.22	"LA-2"	replica, marked "LA-16" in '83-'87 (noted '81-'88).
Fokker D.VII	"F-266"	(ex 2528/18, N4729V) (noted '82-'88).
"Fokker D.XXI"	"219"	re-worked from Harvard T.2B B-64 (c/n 14-641, ex 42-12394, FE907, B-64, PH-FAR) (noted '81-'87, removed for rework to T-6 configuration as B-64/(PH-LSK)).
"Fokker D.XXI"	"141"	re-worked from Harvard B-182 (c/n 14A-808, ex 43-12509, FS668) (noted '87). See Gilze-Rijen.
Fokker D.XXI	"221"	replica (noted '88).
Fokker G.1A	"330"	replica, built c.'85 (noted '87-'88).

B-25J Mitchell	M-464	(c/n NA108-37234, ex 44-31258, N5-264) ex AURI, arr in Netherlands 12.5.71 (noted '81-'88).
Northrop NF-5B	K-4011	ex 316 Sqn & DVM store at Gilze-Rijen (new arrival by 7.89).

H.A. Vreeburg Hall (Hall B)

Beech D-18S	"G-10"	(really PH-UDT, c/n A-472) masquerading as a T-7 Navigator (noted '81-'88).
DH89B Dominie	V-3	(c/n 6740, ex NF869, PH-RAE, V-3, PH-VNC, V-3, PH-TGC, PH-OTA) 'Gelderland' (noted '69-'88).
Fokker S.11	E-22	(c/n 6213) ex EVO, soc 3.9.73 (noted '78-'88).
Fokker S.14	L-11	(c/n 7355) soc 7.7.64, ex Antony Fokker School (noted '81-'88).
Gloster Meteor T.7	I-19	(ex WH233) soc 15.5.59 (noted '81-'84, to Gilze-Rijen, later Twenthe).
Gloster Meteor F.4	I-69	(ex VZ409) ex 323 Sqn, soc 1.3.53, to KLuM 12.5.68 (noted '81-'88).
Grumman US-2N Tracker	160/V	(c/n 721, ex 148282) ex 320 Sqn, soc 30.9.75 (noted '81-'88).
Hawker Hunter F.4	N-144	(c/n 8644) soc 29.5.59, ex Gilze (arr '84, current '88).
Hawker Hunter T.7	N-305	(c/n 693457) soc 8.9.67 (noted '81-'84, to Gilze-Rijen).
Hiller OH-23C	O-36	(c/n 937, ex 57-6521) ex 299 Sqn, soc 14.4.65 (noted '68-'87).
F-104G Starfighter	D-8022	(c/n 8022) ex 312 Sqn, last flew/soc 15.3.84 (noted '84-'88).
SP-2H Neptune	218/V	(c/n 7157, ex 146438) ex 320 Sqn, fuselage section - other components with the Technical University at Delft (noted '81-'88).
Lockheed T-33A	M-5	(c/n 6812, ex 51-9028) ex TVO, soc 2.6.72 (noted '81-'87, to Rosmalen).
Harvard T.2B	B-175	(c/n 14-765, ex 42-12518, FH131) soc 21.11.66, bare fuselage frame (noted '81-'88).
Harvard T.2B	B-184	(c/n 14A-1100, ex 43-12801, FS960) (noted '81-'88).
Harvard T.2B	"099/K"	(really B-103, c/n 14A-1459, ex 43-13160, FT419) soc 20.3.63, ex KLM Bedrijfsschool at Schiphol & Gilze (noted '87-'88).
F-86F Sabre	"25385"	(ex PortAF 5307) arr Soesterburg 11.79 for 25th anniversary of 32 TFS, to MLM '81 in 32 TFS marks (noted '81-'88).
F-86K Sabre	"Q-305"	(c/n 33, ex 53-8305, MM6217) obtained from Italian AF in '73 and painted to represent the KLu's "Q-305" which was 54-1305 (noted '73-'88).
F-86K Sabre	Q-244	cockpit section marked "6726" (noted '83-'87).
P-51K Mustang	H-307	composite airframe from parts of 4 ex AURI P-51s, mostly 44-12125, assembled by the TH delft (arr 12.5.68, current '88).
F-84E Thunderjet	K-8	(ex 51-9591) ex 'TP-2', soc 2.6.56, ex TH Delft, incomplete (noted '83-'88).
F-84F Thunderstreak	P-109	(ex 52-7140) w/o 1.10.57, cockpit only (noted '78-'88).
RF-84F Thunderflash	"P-5"	(ex 51-1253) ex 348 Moira, Greek AF. Due here 6.89 following respray at Valkenburg in her original KLu c/s.
F-84G Thunderjet	"K-40"	(ex 51-10806, K-171) soc 14.4.58, ex Gilze store, painted as "K-40/DU-24" '81 (noted '78-'88).
Spitfire LF.IX	H-1	(c/n CBAF IX 907, MJ243) soc 4.6.54 (noted '70-'88).

TEUGE

The wrecks of the crashed PA31-350 Navajo PH-ASU (c/n 31-7752058) and Cessna 421B

D-IMMI (c/n 0915) were lying here in 6.86. Stored here late '88 were unmarked Cessna F172L PH-MRH (c/n 0831, ex D-ECRK) and Schneider Grunau Baby IIB PH-212 (c/n 91).

TWENTHE

Preserved on the civil side is F-86K Sabre Q-283 (ex 54-1283, soc 2.10.64) in 700 Sqn marks (noted '65-'88). From 14.2.89 it was assisted by former instructional airframe NF-5A K-3029 (c/n 3029, crashed on t/o from Ramstein 11.7.75, to gia as "TPG-29") which now guards the main gate on the other side of the field.

Preserved in the 315 Sqn area (with 315 Sqn badge) since the mid eighties is former decoy F-84F Thunderstreak P-171 (ex 53-6687, soc 10.6.70).

Two bdr/instructional airframes are presently derelict on the base, a former decoy Thunderstreak and a more recently acquired '104.

F-104G Starfighter	D-8338	(c/n 8338) soc 5.6.84 (current '89).
F-84F Thunderstreak	P-209	(ex 53-6568) soc 23.9.70, ex decoy here, no serial worn (current '89).

The other surviving F-84F Thunderstreak here is P-166 (ex 53-6606, soc 30.9.70) which arrived from Eindhoven in 5.71 and was still current as a decoy during '88.

At Zuidkamp (about 1 km from the civil side of the base) is a small museum which has displayed various aviation archaeology and historical items for several years, the largest of which was a section of fuselage from Typhoon RB396/XP-W. This is set to expand with the acquisition of Meteor T.7 I-19 (soc 15.5.59, ex DVM, arr mid '88) and F-104G Starfighter D-8268 (ex Ypenburg store).

Twenthe received TF-104G Starfighter D-5805 (c/n 5805, soc 2.5.84) from storage at Gilze-Rijen on 8.9.88 for display at Zuidkamp in the old 'Dutch Masters' colour scheme from the sixties.

VALKENBURG

The demise of the Neptune in MLD service at least provided the MLD base here with a 'quality' gate-guard in the form of SP-2H 216/V (c/n 7143, ex 144692, ex 320 Sqn, soc 11.7.80, placed on the gate 11.2.81, current '89).

The Neptune was gradually withdrawn from use with 320 sqn between 1979 and '82, most of the remaining aircraft being broken up at Valkenburg with some going to preservation or instructional duties. 202 was still current on the fire dump here during 1989.

SP-2H Neptune	202/V	(c/n 7245) soc 21.9.80, to fire dump 12.83 (current'89).
SP-2H Neptune	205/V	(c/n 7252) soc 25.1.82, parts to AFS Den Haag '84, remainder scrapped.
SP-2H Neptune	207/V	(c/n 7257) soc 9.3.81, scrapped 12.81.
SP-2H Neptune	209/V	(c/n 7261) soc 9.4.80, scrapped '81.
SP-2H Neptune	210/V	(c/n 7263) soc 6.82, to KLM Bedrijfsschool 16.11.83.
SP-2H Neptune	211/V	(c/n 7265) soc 23.1.79, scrapped '80.
SP-2H Neptune	213/V	(c/n 7268) soc 18.12.79, scrapped '81.
SP-2H Neptune	214/V	(c/n 7269) soc 21.5.81, scrapped 12.81.
SP-2H Neptune	215/V	(c/n 7142, ex 144691) soc 13.5.76, scrapped '80.
SP-2H Neptune	217/V	(c/n 7153, ex 146434) soc 12.2.80, scrapped 12.81.
SP-2H Neptune	218/V	(c/n 7157, ex 146438) soc 28.8.81, sections to Kamp Zeist and TU Delft.

Previous occupants of the dump were CS-2A Trackers 182/H (c/n DH-5-3, ex RCN 1504 soc 1.8.71, dumped 6.75, scrapped by 12.81), and before that 180/H (c/n DH-5-1, ex RCN 1502, soc 1.3.71, dumped 4.74, scrapped by 10.75).

For completeness, we should also record 321 Sqn's Atlantics which for the most part spent at least a year in open storage following withdrawal prior to their sale to France.

SP-13A Atlantic	250/V	(c/n 55) soc 12.84 & stored, to France 7.5.86.
SP-13A Atlantic	251/V	(c/n 56) soc 12.84 & stored, to France 7.3.86.
SP-13A Atlantic	252/V	(c/n 57) soc 6.12.84 & stored, to France 11.4.86.
SP-13A Atlantic	254/V	(c/n 61) soc 12.84 & stored, to France 6.2.86.
SP-13A Atlantic	256/V	(c/n 63) soc 12.84 & stored, to France 20.12.85.
SP-13A Atlantic	258/V	(c/n 65) soc 12.84 & stored, to France 6.12.85.

VEGHEL

The Bevrijdende Vleugels (Wings of Liberation) museum here (near Volkel) displays the following, all seen mid '88. There is also a Spitfire replica which was one of several used in the film 'A Piece of Cake'.

Auster III	"R-5"	(c/n 350, ex MZ236, 8A-13, R-11, PH-NGH, MZ236, "R-55") ex MLM, arrived here '88.
Harvard T.2B	FT228	(c/n 14A-1268, ex 43-12969, FT228, B-73) arrived from the Aviodome late '88.
B-25D Mitchell II	B-9	(c/n 100-20754, ex 42-87261, FR199, A22, M-9) soc 8.7.54, cockpit to TH Delft as a simulator, to Aviodome '81 & stored at Badhoevedorp (nose section only, arrived '88).
Piper L-4J Cub	PH-NLA	arr late '88 (returned by the Aviodome to its owner who loaned it here).

VOLKEL

Preserved in flying attitude inside the main gate of this F-16 base is F-104G Starfighter D-8279 (c/n 8279, noted '82-'88) which was written off after striking some trees on the approach to Gutersloh on 1.3.79. The aircraft was roaded back to Volkel for instructional use and following restoration work was officially installed as gate guard on 1.4.82.

On 29.7.88 RF-84F Thunderflash 11253 (ex 51-1253) of 348 Moira, Greek AF, made its last flight and returned here to its former operators the KLu. 11253 entered KLu service in 1956 as P-5 and was handed over to the Greek AF on 23.4.63. This classic machine will now be restored to Dutch markings and will go on display at the MLM, Kamp Zeist, from 6.89.

A landmark here throughout the seventies was a converted Hunter known as the "Starhunter" and wearing the serial "D-4711" after the well known perfume. The craft featured shortened wings and a pointed "F-104 type" nose and was used for teaching drivers how to tow Starfighters. After many years in this role the machine was finally relegated to the fire dump and was burnt in the early eighties, its identity never having come to light. It was always believed to be ex KLu but another theory to emerge describes the aircraft as a former 4 Sqn example which suffered an accident here whilst on an exchange. Comments welcome!

Replacing the "Starhunter" is F-104G Starfighter D-8341 (c/n 8341, arr from Gilze-Rijen '79, current '88) which was written off following a collision with D-8098 on the runway at Wildenrath on 21.11.78.

In use for battle damage repair training since '84 is F-104G Starfighter D-8063 (c/n 8063, soc 23.11.84). Another '104 here is D-8331 (c/n 8331, soc 8.11.84). This machine was moved to Soesterburg from storage at Ypenburg on 27.6.88, then on to Volkel where she was collected by C-141B 60130 on 9.6.89 for transport to the Oklahoma Air Space Museum.

WESTERBORK

Ex RLS SAAB 91D Safir PH-RLH can be found here at Roodhasterweg 2.

WESTERSCHOUWEN

Preserved on a pole at the entrance to the Duinrand camping site in Hogeweg (street name) is Harvard T.2B B-193 (c/n 14-770, ex 42-12523, FH136) soc 18.7.56 (noted '70-'89). She arrived from storage at Gilze-Rijen during the late sixties. Westerschouwen is the West end of the island of Schouwen in the Schelde estuary.

WOENSDRECHT

Gate guard here from 1985 is Lockheed T-33A M-54 (c/n 7150, ex 51-17411, soc 8.6.72) which is painted in 'Whiskey Four' colours as "M-52/51-6953" and appeared as such at the KLu 75th Anniversary at Deelen in 7.88. It was formerly on display at the KMA barracks in Breda.

In 1981 Fokker S.14 L-17 arrived from the DVM at Gilze-Rijen for use as a ground instructional airframe. In the process it was completely refurbished and returned to

Gilze-Rijen by '88. By 1986 the Fokker Bedrijfsschool (Apprentice school) had acquired SAAB 91D Safir PH-RLD (c/n 91-370) from Eelde for use as a gia.

Parked in the centre of the airfield as a surface decoy was F-84F Thunderstreak P-170 (ex 53-6673, soc 2.10.70) ex Gilze-Rijen decoy and KLM gia (noted '80-'88). It is now used by the Fokker fire brigade here but they are treating her gently (see photos).

In store awaiting a further lease of life with a new air force are the following NF-5s. Greece, Turkey and Venezuela have all been mentioned as prospective recipients but as with the Belgian '104s things seem to be happening very slowly, if at all.

Northrop NF-5A K-3011 (c/n 3011) ex 313 Sqn.
Northrop NF-5A K-3013 (c/n 3013) ex 313 Sqn.
Northrop NF-5A K-3015 (c/n 3015) ex 313 Sqn.
Northrop NF-5A K-3018 (c/n 3018) ex 313 Sqn.
Northrop NF-5A K-3022 (c/n 3022) ex VUD.
Northrop NF-5A K-3023 (c/n 3023) ex 314 Sqn, to THK 27.6.89.
Northrop NF-5A K-3027 (c/n 3027) ex 316 Sqn.
Northrop NF-5A K-3030 (c/n 3030) ex 316 Sqn.
Northrop NF-5A K-3032 (c/n 3032) ex 313 Sqn.
Northrop NF-5A K-3035 (c/n 3035) ex VUD.
Northrop NF-5A K-3040 (c/n 3040) ex VUD.
Northrop NF-5A K-3041 (c/n 3041) ex 314 Sqn, to THK 27.6.89.
Northrop NF-5A K-3043 (c/n 3043) ex VUD.
Northrop NF-5A K-3044 (c/n 3044) ex 314 Sqn.
Northrop NF-5A K-3045 (c/n 3045) ex 313 Sqn.
Northrop NF-5A K-3048 (c/n 3048) ex 313 Sqn.
Northrop NF-5A K-3057 (c/n 3057) ex VUD.
Northrop NF-5A K-3060 (c/n 3060) ex 313 Sqn.
Northrop NF-5A K-3067 (c/n 3067) ex 314 Sqn, to THK 27.6.89.
Northrop NF-5A K-3070 (c/n 3070) ex 313 Sqn.
Northrop NF-5B K-4002 (c/n 4002) ex VUD.
Northrop NF-5A K-4005 (c/n 4005) ex 316 Sqn, to THK 27.6.89.
Northrop NF-5B K-4008 (c/n 4008) ex VUD.
Northrop NF-5A K-4012 (c/n 4012) ex 316 Sqn.
Northrop NF-5B K-4020 (c/n 4020) ex 314 Sqn.
Northrop NF-5B K-4025 (c/n 4025) ex 316 Sqn, to THK 27.6.89.
Northrop NF-5B K-4028 (c/n 4028) ex 316 Sqn.
Northrop NF-5B K-4030 (c/n 4030) ex VUD.

WOUDENBURG

A dealer here has dealt in aircraft parts and scrap. Outside his premises in 1983 was Cessna 172A PH-MVB (c/n 47425, ex N7825T, SX-ADB) which is displayed without any registration. There is also a DC-8 cockpit section on the premises which are to the South of Woudenburg on the road to Masasbergen (current '88).

YERSEKE

In the industrial estate here (some 30 kms West of Bergen-Op-Zoom), SAAB 91D Safir PH-RJB (c/n 91-309) is to be found next to the main office of Skadoc Submersible Systems (noted '80-'88).

YPENBURG

On display within the base is Fokker S.14 L-18 (c/n 7363, soc 21.7.66) which arrived from Soesterburg on 25.4.67 and was placed on a pole soon after (current '88).

Stored here as a potential glider tug is L-21B Super Cub R-158 (c/n 18-3848, ex 54-2448, allocated PH-KNK). It has wfu 22.9.76 and has gathered dust here since 1978.

The KLu's last airworthy Starfighters were flown here for storage at the end of 1984 in the hope of attracting a buyer. As with the Belgian machines, many rumoured deals all came to nothing and disposals began during 1988. Disposal plans were changing by the minute as this text was closed for press.

F-104G	Starfighter	D-8048	(c/n 8048) arr/soc 12.10.84, to TU Delft early '89.
F-104G	Starfighter	D-8051	(c/n 8051) arr/soc 08.11.84, for storage at Gilze-Rijen.
F-104G	Starfighter	D-8053	(c/n 8053) arr 11.10.84, soc 8.11.84, to LIMOS barracks, Nijmegen by 1.89.
F-104G	Starfighter	D-8062	(c/n 8062) arr 25.10.84, handed over to Van Weerden Poelman Air Scouts 26.11.88, kept at Ypenburg.
F-104G	Starfighter	D-8084	(c/n 8084) arr/soc 18.10.84, to Gilze-Rijen 12.5.89 and on the gate at Prinsenbosch by 19.5.89.
F-104G	Starfighter	D-8091	(c/n 8091) arr/soc 25.10.84, to become a mobile display a/c, parented by Eindhoven.
F-104G	Starfighter	D-8258	(c/n 8258) arr/soc 26.11.84, for Hoger Nautisch Onderwijs in Amsterdam.
F-104G	Starfighter	D-8266	(c/n 8266) arr/soc 09.11.84, to go to a museum in Texel during 1990 but had left here by 5.89.
F-104G	Starfighter	D-8268	(c/n 8268) arr/soc 25.10.84, for display at Twenthe.
F-104G	Starfighter	D-8281	(c/n 8281) arr/soc 01.11.84, for LETS.
F-104G	Starfighter	D-8300	(c/n 8300) arr/soc 01.11.84, for display at KLu base Stolzenau, WG, from 9.89.
F-104G	Starfighter	D-8312	(c/n 8312) arr/soc 18.10.84, for Prins Maurits Laboratories, Rijswijk.
F-104G	Starfighter	D-8326	(c/n 8326) arr/soc 02.11.84, for preservation at Volkel.
F-104G	Starfighter	D-8331	(c/n 8331) arr 08.11.84, to Soesterberg 27.6.88, then Volkel for shipment to Oklahoma Air Space Museum.
TF-104G	Starfighter	D-5803	(c/n 5803) arr/soc 26.11.84, to DVM store mid '89.
TF-104G	Starfighter	D-5804	(c/n 5804) arr/soc 23.11.84, to Gilze-Rijen 4.89.
TF-104G	Starfighter	D-5806	(c/n 5806) arr/soc 18.10.84, due to go to Hoger Nautisch Onderwijs, in Amsterdam.
TF-104G	Starfighter	D-5810	(c/n 5810) arr/soc 23.11.84, to Antony Fokker School in Den Haag 11.6.88.

NORWAY

Considering the size of the country, the W&R population of Norway is relatively small. No doubt this is largely due to the fact that most of Norway's post-war military aircraft have been supplied under US aid schemes and have been passed on to other NATO members or returned to the US at the end of their service. The pattern set by the C-119, RF-84F, T-33 and HU-16 is now being followed by the F-5 and F-104. Only in the case of the CF-104s bought outright by the Norwegians are these airframes passing into the W&R realm as museum pieces, decoys etc.

The preservation movement in the country has received a major boost with the opening in 1984 of the Norwegian Air Force Museum at Gardermoen (and soon to move into new premises elsewhere). There has also been an upsurge of interest in the recovery of Second World War relics - witness the collection of Ju 52s at Gardermoen.

ANDOYA

CF-104 Starfighter 755 (ex RCAF 12755) arrived here on 22.7.85 (by sea) from storage at Sola. By 5.89 the wingless aircraft was in use with the Andoya Videregaende School as a gia, though it remains housed in Hangar F on the base. The Videregaende Schools are secondary schools which also provide a technical education and sometimes have instructional airframes allocated for this purpose. Some are housed on active bases due to lack of space in the schools.

BANAK/LAKSELV

On the fire dump here (140 kms South East of Hammerfest, near the Finnish border) in 1977 was RF-84F Thunderflash 27332/AZ-S (ex 52-7332, ex 717 Skv). The aircraft arrived at Banak on 16.3.69 when it struck a tree during a low pass over the field and was forced to make an emergency landing, being officially soc on 29.5.70. By 1985 the aircraft was listed as part of the RNorAF museum collection and is therefore probably now preserved on the base here.

BARDUFOSS

Preserved on the base (some 80 kms North of Narvik) in recent years have been, ex 339 Skv F-86K Sabre 41313/SI-O (ex 54-1313, noted '83-'88) and composite UH-1B Iroquois 995 (tail) 584 (fuselage) which was noted in 3.87 wearing both serials. 995 (ex 62-1995) was 'SI-C' with 339 Skv when it crashed on 4.12.68, the wreck moving on to Kjevik for ground instructional use. 584 (ex 60-3584) was last noted as 'SI-J' with 339 Skv. Note that UH-1B 995 was seen here in '85 and reported to be for Gardermoen. I assume this aircraft is the same one as the composite above, and that whilst probably on the RNorAF Museum's books it is staying at Bardufoss at least for the time being. Further comments would be welcomed.

CF-104 Starfighter 836 (ex RCAF 12836) arrived by boat from storage at Sola on 25.6.85 for instructional use with the Bardufoss Videregaende School here.

BERGEN

Preserved at Flesland Air Station is ex 332 Skv F-86F Sabre 31082/AH-A (ex 53-1082, current 5.89). The wreck of Focke-Wulf Fw 190F-8 931862 (shot down by a 144 Sqn Beaufighter on 9.2.45) was recovered from its resting place on Litlehesten mountain with the aid of a Sikorsky S-61 in 9.83. It was brought here and is now being brought up to display condition for the RNorAF museum.

CF-104D Starfighter 4632 (ex RCAF 12632) arrived by sea from Sola storage on 26.6.85 for unspecified purposes. It departed to the USA by C-130 during 11.88 and is to fly again.

BODO

Guarding the gate at the RNorAF's former '104 base (now re-equipped with the F-16) is F-104G Starfighter "104" (c/n 9010, ex WGAF 2564, current 5.89) which was acquired from the DFVLR at Braunschweig, West Germany, and airlifted in by RNorAF Hercules on 15.11.77 (current '88).

Preserved here in '83 were Spitfire LF.IXe MH350/"FN-T" (in spurious 331 Skv markings, MH350 was 'AH-V', 'A-BM' then 'FN-M'), Haerens Flyvemaskinfabrik FF9 Kaie 33 (c/n 121) and F-86K Sabre 41245/RI-Z (ex 54-1245, ex 334 Skv, soc 18.8.67). The Kaie 33 and F-86K were still current in 5.89, the latter spending a lot of its time hangared when not in use for training aircraft tug drivers. The Spitfire had by this time moved to Oslo/Akershus, the Sabre following by 1988.

Several Starfighters congregated here after the re-equipment of the resident Starfighter squadrons (331 Skv & 334 Skv) with the F-16. All those remaining are Canadian built machines which previously equipped 334 Skv. 870 and 4637 were retained here following their withdrawal.

CF-104 Starfighter	800	(ex RCAF 12800) last flew 1.4.84, TT 3450 hrs, arrived here by sea from Sola store 25.6.85.
CF-104 Starfighter	870	(ex RCAF 12870) last flew 1.12.82, TT 3379 hrs, allocated to the RNorAF museum (current here 7.88).
CF-104 Starfighter	890	(ex RCAF 12890) TT 3134 hrs, arrived here by sea from Sola store 25.6.85.
CF-104D Starfighter	4637	(ex RCAF 12637) last flew 1.4.83, TT 2975 hrs.

The latter three were still current in 5.89 whilst 800 has gone to the Asphaugen Videregaende School located between the base and the town where she was also current in 5.89.

EVJE

Also known as Kristiansand South, preserved here are Schneider Grunau Baby LN-GGH (c/n 4) from Baerum and Taylorcraft A LN-FAG (c/n 416) which came here from Krogstadelven.

GEITERYGGEN

DH Heron 1Bs LN-BFX (c/n 14020, CofA expired 30.6.72) and LN-BFY (c/n 14015, registered 10.2.72 but never obtained Norwegian CofA) were both derelict here in the late seventies. LN-BFX was rescued by the Norsk Flyhistorisk Forening and its forward fuselage is now on display at the Norsk Teknisk Museum in Oslo painted in Braathens colours as "LN-PSG" (but see also Sola - were both Herons rescued and are they both painted as LN-PSG?).

HOKKSUND

Cessna A185F LN-DBJ (c/n 03369) was stored here (some 30kms SW of Oslo) in 6.88 whilst three Cessnas were noted in hangar storage but were not identified.

In a supermarket adjacent to the airfield, a glider was suspended from the ceiling in the main food hall (different!) in the form of Antonov A-15 OH-GBM (c/n 0304).

HOLTER

Preserved near Ullensaker (some 30 kms NE of Oslo) are/were DH82A Tiger Moth T7794 (now restored to airworthiness as LN-MAX) and NorskFlyindustri C-5 Polar LN-DBW (c/n 01) which is being restored by Wideroe (at Bodo?).

HVALSMOEN

Preserved here (North East of Honefoss, about 40 kms NW of Oslo) is ex 334 Skv F-86K Sabre 41241/RI-Z (ex 54-1241).

JARLSBERG/TONSBERG

Preserved here (110 kms S of Oslo) are/were Interstate S.1A Cadet 505 (c/n 203/1041, to Gardermoen museum by '88), UH-19D Chickasaw 64279/HA-B (ex 56-4279) ex 330 Skv and LTBS Kjevik (to Gardermoen by 8.85), Scheibe SF28A Tandem Falke LN-GAT (c/n 5765, ex OY-XMV) and Rolladen-Schneider LS-6 LN-GBH (c/n 6022).

KJELLER

Located some 20 kms North West of Oslo, this LFK (Luftforsvarets Forsynings Kommando or Air Force Logistics Command) base is to become the new home for the RNorAF Museum, currently located at Gardermoen.

Northrop RF-5A 113 (ex 68-9113) is reportedly stored on the base here.

The firemen here had F-86K Sabre 41272/RI-F (ex 54-1272, ex 334 Sqn, soc 17.1.68) to play with but it was expended several years ago.

On the civil side, the fuselages of Cessna F172H LN-NAK (c/n 0604) and F172E LN-AEJ (c/n 0036) were present in 6.88.

KJEVIK

Kjevik (near Kristiansand) houses the RNorAF's LTBS (Luftforsvarets Tekniske Bifols Skole), the equivalent of the RAF's No.1 School of Technical Training at Halton, but on a much smaller scale. Guarding the gate is RF-84F Thunderflash 117055/AZ-H (ex 51-17055, ex 717 Skv, soc 29.5.70, current 6.89).

Ground instructional airframes with the LTBS in recent years have included the following.

Bell UH-1B Iroquois	995	(ex 62-1995, ex 'SI-C' 339 Skv, w/o 4.12.68 (current '83 but tail of this a/c displayed at Bardufoss by 3.87 joined to the cabin of 584). The Kjevik a/c is reportedly (eg 1.83) a composite with the tail from 957 (ex 62-1957).
Bell UH-1B Iroquois	588	(ex 63-8588) (noted 6.89).
Cessna O-1A Bird Dog	641	(ex 51-12641) wingless (noted 6.89).
F-104G Starfighter	12238	(ex 62-12238) ex 331 Skv, damaged 17.1.78, arrived 10.10.78, (current '83, but has since been broken up).
CF-104 Starfighter	818	(ex RCAF 12818) ex Sola store, arrived by road 17.6.85, current on the dump for bdrt 6.89.
Northrop F-5A	563	(ex 65-10563) (current 6.89).
Northrop F-5A	572	(ex 65-10572) ex 338 Skv (arrived '74, current 6.89).
Northrop F-5A	900	(ex 67-14900) (arrived '78, current as bdr airframe 6.89, on the dump).
Northrop RF-5A	102	(ex 68-9102) (current 6.89).
Northrop RF-5A	105	(ex 68-9105) ex Rygge (current 6.89).
Piper L-18C Super Cub	845	(ex 53-4845, c/n 18-3245) (arrived 7.78, to Gardermoen '83).
RF-84F Thunderflash	117050	(ex 51-17050) ex 'AZ-D' 717 Skv, soc 29.5.70 (current '78, scrapped).
RF-84F Thunderflash	117051	(ex 51-17051) ex 'T3-E' 717 Skv, w/o in wheels-up landing at Sola 8.12.56 (put into the fire training area in '76 but still current '83, to Gardermoen by 9.87).
SAAB 91B Safir	6326	(c/n 91-326) ex 'U-AG' Primary Flying School, w/o 26.1.62 (current '82, to Stavanger '83).
SAAB 91B Safir	57-333	(c/n 91-333) for RNorAF Museum (current 6.89).
Sea King Mk.43	068	(c/n WA749) ex 330 Skv, w/o 10.11.86 (noted 6.89).

BE.2e 133 (ex A1325) came here from Gardermoen by 1979, moving on to the Mosquito Air Museum at Salisbury Hall, UK, in 1.83. It probably yielded a few parts for the rebuild of 131 (ex A1380) which was restored here for the Gardermoen museum, being completed in early 1980. The craftsmen have since turned their attention to Avro 504K 103 which arrived from Gardermoen in 1983.

PT-19 Cornell 261/LD-M (ex 43-36487) was stored here prior to moving to the Gardermoen museum.

KROER/AS

Starck Turbulent D LN-AET (c/n 130, wfu on CofA expiry 31.3.65) is preserved here.

LILLESTROM

CF-104 Starfighter 766 (ex RCAF 12766) had arrived here (20 kms East of Oslo) by

8.88 (presumably for preservation) following storage at Sola. This machine had left Sola for Kjeller by C-130 on 26.3.85.

LISTA

In 1978 there were two preserved aircraft at this RNorAF reserve base. F-86F Sabre 31220/AH-L (ex 53-1220, ex 332 Skv, soc 15.7.67) and F-86K Sabre 41266/ZK-L (ex 54-1266, w/o 27.10.58 and to Kjevik for instructional use, then here). A report dated 1983 lists only the latter aircraft, though it has since turned up with the Flyhistorisk Museum at Sola.

MO-I-RANA

PA18-95 Super Cub LN-KCX (c/n 18-2062, ex 52-2462, R-76) has been stored here (just South of the Arctic Circle) since its crash on 1.8.83.

NOTODDEN

Three wrecks were discovered lurking behind a hangar here in 6.88, Rockwell Commander 112A LN-BFH (c/n 422) with fuselage sections of a Cessna 150 ..-AG. (presumably LN-AG.) and a Cessna 206.

ORLAND

Preserved at this base are F-84G Thunderjet 22912/MU-J (ex 52-2912, ex 338 Skv) and F-86K Sabre 25202/MU-F (ex 52-5202) also ex 338 Skv.

OSLO

The Sogn Videregaende school has used two airframes for ground instructional purposes. These are PT-26B Cornell LN-OAU (ex 43-36254, FZ204, RCAF 10757, RNorAF 205, L-CL) which was cancelled from the register 6.6.63 as wfu and ex 334 Skv F-86K Sabre 41274/RI-T (ex 54-1274). The latter was reported with the RNorAF museum at Gardermoen in 8.85 having been 'replaced' with the school by Safir 336 (ex Primary Flying School) though the Safir remains in store at Oslo/Fornebu where all the school's remaining aircraft should now be housed.

OSLO/AKERSHUS

The Forsvarsmuseet (Military Museum) is located in Akershus Castle (in the city centre by the harbour). The following have been exhibited recently though some are on loan from the Norsk Flyhistorisk Forening and the RNorAF collection and are therefore liable to change.

DH82A Tiger Moth	151	(c/n doubtful, could be 131 or 161, ex SE-ANL) (noted '85-'89, on loan from Norsk Flyhistorisk Forening).
DH Vampire FB.52	V0184	(c/n V0184, soc 14.2.57) ex 'ZK-U' & Vaernes (noted '85-'89, on loan from RNorAF).
Fieseler Fi 103	-	(V1 flying bomb) (noted '88).
Henschel Hs 293	21816	
F-86K Sabre	41245	(ex 54-1245, ex 'RI-Z' 334 Skv, soc 18.8.67) ex Bodo, arrived by '88.
SAAB 91B Safir	LN-FMU	(c/n 91-267, ex RSwedAF 50058, RNorAF 53-058) stored, since to Gardermoen.
Spitfire LF.IXe	MH350	(c/n CBAF 5400, 331 Skv marks as 'FN-T') ex Bodo (noted '85-'89, on loan from RNorAF).

OSLO/FRYSJA

In the Northern part of Oslo (next to Kjelsas railway station) is the Norsk Teknisk Museum (Norwegian Technical Museum) which holds the following aircraft.

Aero C.104 (Bu 131)	LN-BWT	(c/n 189) loan from Bjart Lyssand (noted '88).
Bell AB.47J	LN-ORD	(c/n 1562) (noted '88).
Bleriot XI	-	(c/n 794) 'Nordsjoen'.
DH Heron 1B	LN-BFY	(c/n 14015) ex Geiteryggen, fuselage only on display in '88 painted in Braathens-Safe colours as "LN-PSG" but see also under Sola.

DH Vampire F.3	P42459	(c/n EEP42459, ex VV214) ex LTBS, 336 Skv marks as 'PX-H' (nose section only on display in '88-'89).
Deperdussin A	-	(noted '88).
DFS108-70 Meise	LN-GAR	(c/n 527/1944)
Farman MF1 Longhorn	F.16	(noted '88).
FF.7 Hauk	-	(license built Hannover CL V by Haerens Flyvemaskinfabrik) front fuselage only on display in '88.
Grumman G.44A Widgeon	LN-HAL	(c/n 1332, ex SE-ARZ) ex Gardermoen loan (noted '88) .
CF-104 Starfighter	759	(ex RCAF 12759) ex Sola storage (arr 16.6.85, current 6.89).
Loening C2 Air Yacht	LN-BAH	(c/n 308, ex NR10239) ex Gardermoen loan (noted '88).
Miles Gemini 1A	LN-TAH	(c/n 6528, ex G-AKKA)
Rumpler Taube	-	(noted '88).
Scheibe SF26	LN-GLR	(c/n 5045, ex D-5010, D-5853) (noted '88).
SE210 Caravelle III	LN-KLH	(c/n 3) wfu 29.8.74, ex Gardermoen loan (noted '88).

OSLO/FORNEBU

SAAB 91B-2 Safir 336 (c/n 91-336, ex Primary Flying School) was retired in 1982 and allocated to the Sogn Videregaende Skole (see Oslo above) though it has remained stored at Fornebu and should now be accompanied by the rest of the School's airframes.

Across the road from the airport, in 7.85 the seaplane harbour held the wrecks of Luscombe 8F LN-VYF (c/n 4891) and Piper J-3C-65 Cub LN-SAI (c/n 12579, ex 44-80283, crashed 24.2.72, registration cancelled 4.5.77) (both float equipped) nestling amongst the bushes. At the same time PA18 Super Cub c/n 18-2062 and one other were undergoing rebuild in a nearby boathouse. Either of these may turn out to be related to J-3C Cub LN-IKJ (CofA expired 30.9.74, registration cancelled 30.6.78) which was here in a wrecked condition in 6.88 with Cherokee 180 LN-NPN (c/n 28-3247, ex SE-EYT, crashed 13.11.78).

DH Heron 1B LN-BFX (c/n 14020) was found in a wrecked condition inside a derelict hangar during 6.88 having moved here from Geiteryggen. This machine is also quoted as being on display at the Norsk Teknisk Museum in Oslo as "LN-PSG" but in view of the sighting of LN-BFX here the compiler takes the view that it is more likely to be 'BFY on display in Oslo. Confirmation would be welcomed.

In use with the airport firemen for rescue training is Convair 440 LN-KLG (c/n 506) which was cancelled from the register on 16.4.75 and was still extant in 8.88.

The fuselage of Convair 440 SE-BSX (c/n 396) is reported to have moved from here to Gardermoen by mid '87, probably for the benefit of the firemen there.

OSLO/GARDERMOEN

The home base of 335 Skv equipped with the C-130H Hercules and Falcon 20, Gardermoen is located some 55 kms North West of Oslo. Outside 335 Skv's Head Quarters building is displayed F-86K Sabre 41290/ZK-A (ex 54-1290, soc 17.1.66, current '88).

F-86K Sabre 41313/RI-A (ex 54-1313) was allocated to the base during the mid sixties for training in NBC de-contamination procedures. It has the rear end from 41334/RI-T. The aircraft was still complete in 1978 and is now officially part of the RNorAF museum collection though it is believed still to continue in its former occupation.

The Kongelige Norsk Luftforssvaret Collection (RNorAF museum) can be found just opposite the terminal here and was officially opened on 16.6.84 (most of the exhibits having gravitated here over the preceding couple of years). The collection is scheduled to move to a new location nearer to Oslo at an unspecified date in the future. On display recently have been the following.

Arado Ar 66C	-	frame only in '83.
Avro 504K	105	possibly ex B5405 (noted '83-'89).
Bell 47D-1	-/BE-D	(c/n 642, ex KK-R, BE-D, LN-ORM) composite a/c, ex Rygge (current '89).
DH82A Tiger Moth	N6972	(c/n 82210, ex 6317M) (current '89).

DH Vampire F.3	P42408	(c/n EEP42408, ex VT833) 336 Skv markings as "PX-E". (w/o 23.3.55 as 'SI-D') (current '89).
DH Vampire T.55	28456	ex '93' F 5, RSwedAF (current '89).
DHC-3 Otter	C-FIKT	(c/n 81) obtained in exchange for an F-5, to be displayed in RNorAF markings (current '88).
Douglas C-47A Dakota	93797	(c/n 13749, ex 42-93797) ex 'BW-L' 335 Skv (current'89).
M-62/PT-19 Cornell	103	(c/n T-40-208, ex 42-76477, 103, 208, 'L-AB', 103) 'L-AB' modified from PT-26A, ex Vaernes (current '89).
M-62A/PT-26B Cornell	36487	(c/n T-43-64872, ex 43-36487, FZ708, 261, 119, 'L-AI', LN-BIS, 'L-DM') 'L-DM') incorporates parts from PT-19 c/n T-40-269 (current '89).
Farman F46-80R	25	(c/n 25) (current '89).
Farman MF1 Longhorn	F.16	'Olaf Tryggveson', on loan from Norsk Teknisk Museum, returned to Oslo by '88.
Fokker C.VD	349	(c/n 133, ex SE-ALS) ex Fornebu store (current '89).
Gloster Gladiator II	N5641	ex 'HE-G' 263 Sqn (current '89).
Glider	-	uncompleted pre-war homebuilt found at Hitra, stored.
Gotha 45	-	remains of several aircraft recovered Summer '88 and crated here pending restoration into at least one airframe.
Heinkel He 111P-2	5J+CN	(c/n 1526) ex Luftwaffe (current '89).
Interstate S1A Cadet	505	(c/n 203/1041) ex Jarlsberg/Tonsberg.
Junkers Ju 52/3mg4e	CA+JY	(c/n 6657) ex Luftwaffe, recovered from Lake Hartvikvann near Narvik 10.6.83 (current, under restoration, '89).
Junkers Ju 52/3mg4e	CO+EI	(c/n 6134) ex Luftwaffe, recovered from Lake Hartvikvann '86 (current '89, open store).
Junkers Ju 52/3mg4e	1Z+BY	(c/n 55657) ex Luftwaffe, recovered from Lake Hartvikvann '86 (current, under restoration, '88).
Junkers Ju 52/3mg4e	VB+UB	(c/n 6791) ex Luftwaffe, recovered from Lake Hartvikvann '86 (open store '89).
Junkers Ju 88	-	recovered from mountains, for restoration (noted '89).
Kjolseth P.K. X-1	-	(c/n 1) (Norwegian helicopter).
Larsen Special	-	uncompleted homebuilt 4 seat jet! (current'88).
Lockheed 18 Learstar	N283M	(built as C-60A 42-55983, c/n 2444, ex N69898, N105G, N283M, OH-MAP, OH-SIR, G-BMEW) to be restored in Lodestar configuration (arrived 15.9.86, noted '88).
CF-104 Starfighter	801	(ex RCAF 12801) ex 334 Skv, arrived 13.7.82, TT 3358 hrs (current '88).
CF-104 Starfighter	882	(ex RCAF 12882) ex 334 Skv and Sola storage, TT 2995 hrs, arrived 2.7.85 (current '89).
TF-104G Starfighter	469	(c/n 5779, ex 63-4869, ex WGAF 2771) ex 334 Skv, arrived 13.7.82, TT 2744 hours (current '89).
Lockheed T-33A	117546	(ex 51-17546) ex '314-UB' GE.314, AdLA, painted in RNorAF marks as "DP-K", arrived 16.11.81, current '89. Served with RNorAF from 30.4.54 to 17.12.68.
UC-64A Norseman IVM	2491	(c/n 64, ex RCAF 2491, LN-BDP, SE-FUP) 'RA-V', under restoration in '82, current '89.
F-86F Sabre	25069	(ex 52-5069) ex 'AH-D' 332 Skv (first noted '88, current '89).
F-86F Sabre	31206	(ex 53-1206) ex 'FN-D' 331 Skv (current '89).
F-86K Sabre	41274	(ex 54-1274) ex 'RI-T' 334 Skv & Sogn Videregaende Skole, Oslo, arrived by 8.85. Note: This a/c was w/o 30.8.57 when struck by a tractor but was not soc until 17.1.68 when it went to the Yrkesskole, Oslo (current '89).
T-6J Texan	"8570"	(c/n CCF4-491, ex 52-8570, ex WGAF AA-622) ex WGAF Museum Uetersen, painted in RNorAF markings coded "M-BS", arrived '83 (current '89).

Northrop F-5A	207	(ex 66-9207) ex 336 Skv (arrived by 6.89).
Northrop N-3PB	320	(c/n 320) ex '(GS-)U' 330 Skv, crashed in the River Thorsa, Iceland, on 1.4.43, recovered 1979 and rebuilt by the manufacturer at Hawthorne, CA (current '89).
Piper L-18C Super Cub	845	(c/n 18-3245, ex 53-4845) 'F-AI' (current '89).
Piper L-18C Super Cub	895	(ex 53-4895) stored '83 (fuselage frame current '88).
RF-84F Thunderflash	117051	(ex 51-17051) ex 'T3-E' 717 Skv, w/o in wheels-up landing at Sola 8.12.56 and to Kjevik for ground instruction. Dumped there in by '76 but to Gardermoen (minus rear fuselage) and in open store by museum 9.87 (current 6.89).
RF-84F Thunderflash	117053	(ex 51-17053) ex 'AZ-G' 717 Skv, soc 29.5.70. (ex Vaernes) (current '89).
F-84G Thunderjet	111209	(ex 51-11209) ex 'MU-S' 338 Skv & Vaernes (current '89).
F-84G Thunderjet	28465	(ex 52-8465) ex 'MU-P' 338 Skv, incomplete (noted '83-'89).
RAF BE.2e	131	(ex A1380, 59) soc 11.11.24, TT 110.59 hrs (current '89).
SAAB 91B Safir	57-329	(c/n 91-329) ex 'UA-B' Primary Flying School (current '89).
SAAB 91B Safir	LN-FMU	(c/n 91-267) (ex RSwedAF 50058, RNorAF 53-058) ex Oslo/Akershus (current '88).
Scheibe Bergfalke II	LN-GBH	(c/n 202) (current '88).
UH-19D Chickasaw	64279	(ex 56-4279) ex 'HA-B' 330 Skv, LTBS Kjevik and Jarlsberg/Tonsberg (arrived by 8.85, current '89).
Spitfire PR.XI	PL979	(c/n 6S/583719, wfu 18.5.54) ex 'A-ZB' 717 Skv (current '89).

The fuselage of Convair 440 SE-BSX (c/n 396) reportedly arrived from Oslo/Fornebu by mid '87, probably for the airport fire service.

RAUFOSS

An ammunition factory here received Northrop RF-5As 101 (ex 68-9102), 110 (ex 68-9110) and 112 (ex 68-9112) from storage at Sola for testing purposes. Further details are unknown.

RYGGE

Spitfire PR.XI PL979/A-ZB (ex 717 Skv, wfu 18.5.58, TT 460 hrs) was preserved here by 1964 until approximately 1981 spending the Summers outside the Officers' Mess and Wintering in the hangars. By 1982 the aircraft was displayed in the RNorAF museum at Gardermoen.

Stored here for the RNorAF museum were the following aircraft.

Bell 47D-1	-/BE-D	(c/n 642, ex KK-R, BE-D, LN-ORM) composite a/c, to Gardermoen by 1983.
DH Vampire FB.52	P42408	(c/n EEP42408) ex 'SI-D', arr from Vaernes in '77 and displayed outside the Officers' Mess, to Gardermoen by '83.
F-86F Sabre	25069	(ex 52-5069) ex 'AH-D' 332 Skv, reported here in '83 (with tail from 25377), it had moved to Gardermoen by '88.
RF-84F Thunderflash	117045	(ex 51-17045) ex 'AZ-N' 717 Skv, soc 29.5.70 (noted . '78-'83, to Flyhistorisk Museum Sola).

The RNorAF's surplus RF-5As were gathered together here in the early eighties for storage and disposal, many eventually finding a new home with the Turkish AF (THK).

Northrop RF-5A	100	(ex 68-9100) TT 3198 hrs, to THK via Ramstein 1.12.87.
Northrop RF-5A	101	(ex 68-9101) to Raufoss.
Northrop RF-5A	103	(ex 68-9103) TT 2842 hrs, to THK 16.12.87.
Northrop RF-5A	104	(ex 68-9104) fate not known.

Northrop RF-5A	105	(ex 68-9105) to Kjevik.
Northrop RF-5A	106	(ex 68-9106) TT 2700 hrs, to THK 16.12.87.
Northrop RF-5A	107	(ex 68-9107) TT 2744 hrs, to THK 16.12.87.
Northrop RF-5A	108	(ex 68-9108) to N75FT.
Northrop RF-5A	109	(ex 68-9109) fate not known.
Northrop RF-5A	110	(ex 68-9110) to Raufoss.
Northrop RF-5A	112	(ex 68-9112) to Raufoss.
Northrop RF-5A	489	(ex 68-10489) TT 2895 hrs, to THK via Ramstein 1.12.87.
Northrop RF-5A	490	(ex 68-10490) TT 2653 hrs, to THK 16.12.87.

The base received CF-104 Starfighter 886 (ex RCAF 12886) from Sola storage on 9.12.82. By 5.89 it was in use for bdr training.

SKIEN

PA18-95 LN-KCT (c/n 18-2069, ex 52-2469, KLu R-58) has been stored here (about 100 kms SW of Oslo) since its accident on 10.1.78.

SOLA

The gate at Sola Air Base (near Stavanger) was guarded by F-84G Thunderjet 110161 between at least '78-'85. By 1989 it had joined the Flyhistorisk Museum Sola which has been set up here with the following complete or substantial airframes as well as smaller sections of other aircraft (eg Ju 52, Wellington III BK309, Bf 110, Seabee).

BN-2A-21 Islander	LN-MAF	(c/n 441, ex G-BCZS) fuselage only.
DH Heron 1B	"LN-PSG"	(really LN-BFY, c/n 14015) ex Geiteryggen, here by '84 (current 5.89 but see Oslo/Frysja).
CF-104 Starfighter	730	(ex RCAF 12730) ex 334 Skv & Sola store (current 6.89).
Lockheed T-33A	(16571)	(ex 51-6571, RDanAF DT-571) painted in RNorAF marks as "DP-X", ex Stavanger naval base (current 6.89).
Messerschmitt Bf 109	-	undergoing restoration following recovery from the sea (noted 5.89).
Morane MS500/502	-	parts of MS502 F-BDHZ c/n 540 and an anonymous MS500 to be combined to produce one Storch (noted '89).
Harvard T.2B	FE621	(c/n 14-355, ex 42-818) 'BE-M' ex RCAF, minus forward fuselage.
F-86K Sabre	41266	(ex 54-1266) ex 'ZK-L', w/o 27.10.58, to gia at Kjevik, to Lista, then here (current 6.89).
F-84G Thunderjet	110161	(ex 51-10161) ex 'MU-Z' 338 Skv & Sola gate (current 6.89).
RF-84F Thunderflash	117045	(ex 51-17045) ex 'AZ-N' 717 Skv soc 29.5.70, ex Rygge (current 6.89).

The MDAP (Mutual Defense Aid Program) supplied Starfighters were passed on to the Turkish AF (THK) in 1981 but the ex Canadian Armed Forces CF-104s were bought outright by Norway and brought to Sola for storage and disposal at the end of their career with 334 Skv at Bodo. At least three are reported to be destined for the USA to provide high speed target facilities and/or test pilot training on a commercial basis whilst others have gone for preservation.

CF-104D Starfighter	4632	(ex RCAF 12632) arrived 19.11.82, TT 2623 hrs, to Flesland by ferry 26.6.85, to USA by C-130 11.88.
CF-104D Starfighter	4633	(ex RCAF 12633) arrived 9.12.82, TT 2487 hrs, to Chino (California) by container freight 8.86.
CF-104 Starfighter	717	(ex RCAF 12717) arrived 17.1.83, TT 3150 hrs. To Godalen School, Sola, as gia a but stored in a shelter on the base (current 5.89).
CF-104 Starfighter	730	(ex RCAF 12730) arrived 14.3.83, TT 3219 hrs, to display at Sola.
CF-104 Starfighter	755	(ex RCAF 12755) arrived 7.1.83, TT 3543 hrs, to Andoya by sea 22.7.85.

CF-104 Starfighter	759	(ex RCAF 12759) arrived 22.11.83, TT 3413 hrs, to Norsk Teknisk Museum in Oslo 16.6.85.
CF-104 Starfighter	766	(ex RCAF 12766) arrived 29.11.82, TT 2807 hrs, to Kjeller 26.3.85, then Lillestrom.
CF-104 Starfighter	818	(ex RCAF 12818) arrived 3.12.82, TT 3147 hrs, to gia at Kjevik 17.6.85.
CF-104 Starfighter	836	(ex RCAF 12836) arrived 17.11.82, TT 3156 hrs, to Bardufoss 25.6.85.
CF-104 Starfighter	850	(ex RCAF 12850) arrived 6.12.82, TT 3483 hrs, current in shelter storage 5.89.
CF-104 Starfighter	882	(ex RCAF 12882) arrived 22.12.82, TT 2995 hrs, to RNorAF museum at Gardermoen by 2.7.85.
CF-104 Starfighter	886	(ex RCAF 12886) arrived 9.12.82, TT 2923 hrs, to Rygge 2.7.85.
CF-104 Starfighter	890	(ex RCAF 12890) TT 3134 hrs, to Bodo by sea 25.6.85.
CF-104 Starfighter	900	(ex RCAF 12900) arrived 3.1.83, TT 3135 hrs. Fate?

With the partial withdrawal of the RNorAF F-5s in favour of the F-16, since 1983 F-5s have been withdrawn here for storage and disposal. Most of these birds have since migrated South for further service with the Greek (HAF) and Turkish (THK) Air Forces.

Northrop F-5A	125	(ex 69-7125) TT 2558 hrs, to THK 1.12.87.
Northrop F-5A	129	(ex 69-7129) fate?
Northrop F-5A	156	(ex 67-21156) TT 3186 hrs, to THK 18.8.83.
Northrop F-5A	164	(ex 67-21164) TT 3662 hrs, to HAF 12.6.86, d/d via Aviano 27-29.8.86.
Northrop F-5A	165	(ex 67-21165) TT 3174 hrs, to THK 6.7.83, d/d 12.8.83.
Northrop F-5A	209	(ex 66-9209) TT 3514 hrs, to HAF 12.6.86, d/d via Aviano 27-29.8.86.
Northrop F-5A	211	(ex 66-9211) TT 3118 hrs, to THK 6.7.83, d/d 12.8.83.
Northrop F-5A	212	(ex 66-9212) TT 3592 hrs, to THK 26.2.85, d/d via Aviano 27.2-10.3.85.
Northrop F-5A	214	(ex 66-9214) TT 3758 hrs, to THK via Aviano 16.4-24.4.85.
Northrop F-5A	224	(ex 66-9224) TT 2892 hrs, to THK 30.6.83, d/d 12.8.83.
Northrop F-5A	227	(ex 66-9227) TT 3573 hrs, to THK 26.3.85.
Northrop F-5A	228	(ex 66-9228) TT 3372 hrs, to HAF 28.4.86, d/d via Aviano 29.4-1.5.86.
Northrop F-5A	229	(ex 66-9229) TT 3105 hrs, to THK 18.8.83, d/d 15.9.83.
Northrop F-5A	368	(ex 64-13368) TT 3744 hrs, to THK 6.7.83, d/d 12.8.83.
Northrop F-5A	369	(ex 64-13369) TT 3976 hrs, to THK 26.3.85, d/d via Aviano 16.4-24.4.85.
Northrop F-5A	370	(ex 64-13370) TT 4185 hrs, to THK 26.3.85.
Northrop F-5A	371	(ex 64-13371) TT 3755 hrs, to HAF 12.6.86, d/d via Aviano 27-29.8.86.
Northrop F-5A	372	(ex 64-13372) fate?
Northrop F-5A	373	(ex 64-13373) TT 3738 hrs, to THK 15.4.85, d/d via Aviano 16.4-24.4.85.
Northrop F-5A	374	(ex 64-13374) TT 3582 hrs, to THK 15.4.85, d/d via Aviano 16.4-24.4.85.
Northrop F-5A	375	(ex 64-13375) TT 3777 hrs, to THK 26.2.85, d/d via Aviano 27.2-10.3.85.
Northrop F-5A	376	(ex 64-13376) TT 3676 hrs, to HAF 28.4.86, d/d via Aviano 29.4-1.5.86.
Northrop F-5A	562	(ex 65-10562) TT 3162 hrs, to THK 30.6.83, d/d 13.7.83.
Northrop F-5A	565	(ex 65-10565) TT 3736 hrs, to THK 26.3.85.

Northrop F-5A	566	(ex 65-10566) TT 3380 hrs, to HAF 28.4.86, d/d via Aviano 29.4-1.5.86.
Northrop F-5A	567	(ex 65-10567) TT 3096 hrs, to THK 26.2.85, d/d via Aviano 27.2-10.3.85.
Northrop F-5A	568	(ex 65-10568) fate?
Northrop F-5A	569	(ex 65-10569) TT 3715 hrs, to HAF 12.6.86, d/d via Aviano 27-29.8.86.
Northrop F-5A	570	(ex 65-10570) TT 3044 hrs, to THK 26.2.85, d/d via Aviano 27.2-10.3.85.
Northrop F-5A	571	(ex 65-10571) fate?
Northrop F-5A	574	(ex 65-10574) TT 3737 hrs, to HAF 7.4.86, d/d via Aviano 27-29.8.86.
Northrop F-5A	575	(ex 65-10575) TT 3723 hrs, to THK 15.4.85, d/d via Aviano 16.4-24.4.85.
Northrop F-5A	576	(ex 65-10576) TT 3278 hrs, to THK 30.6.83, d/d 13.7.83.
Northrop F-5A	577	(ex 65-10577) TT 3195 hrs, to HAF 28.4.86, d/d via Aviano 29.4-1.5.86.
Northrop F-5A	578	(ex 65-10578) TT 3381 hrs, to THK 30.6.83, d/d 13.7.83.
Northrop F-5A	579	(ex 65-10579) TT 3228 hrs, to THK 21.7.83, d/d 15.9.83.
Northrop F-5A	580	(ex 65-10580) TT 3451 hrs, to THK 30.6.83, d/d 13.7.83.
Northrop F-5A	897	(ex 67-14897) TT 2972 hrs, to THK via Ramstein 1.12.87.
Northrop F-5A	901	(ex 67-14901) TT 2702 hrs, to THK 16.12.87.
Northrop F-5A	904	(ex 67-14904) TT 3010 hrs, to THK via Ramstein 1.12.87.
Northrop F-5A	905	(ex 67-14905) to Combat Jet & Aerospace Museum, Chino, CA, as N91011 passing through Prestwick 11-12.7.87.

In store here for a local school by 5.89 was Bell UH-1B Iroquois 580 (ex 60-3580).

STAVANGER

By 1983, SAAB 91B-2 Safir 6326/U-AG (c/n 91-326, w/o 26.1.62) had been discarded by the LTBS at Kjevik and arrived here for the Godalen Videregaende Skole. On display at the Naval Base in the town was ex RDanAF Lockheed T-33A DT-571 (ex 51-6571) painted in Norwegian markings as "DP-X" of 718 Skv (arrived 22.1.81, current '85). It has since gone to Sola for the Flyhistorisk Museum Sola.

TORP

In use for rescue training with the firemen at this RNorAF reserve base is RF-84F Thunderflash 28723 (ex 52-8723, ex 'AZ-X' 717 Skv, soc 29.5.70). By 1978 the aircraft was painted white overall and though looking sorry for itself was still supported by its main undercarriage with some makeshift support under the nose. This machine was still current in '83 and was listed as part of the RNorAF museum collection by 1985.

TRONDHEIM

SAAB 91B-2 Safir 323 (c/n 91-323) ex Primary Flying School was retired to the Tambartun Blindeskole here in 1982.

VAERNES

Located some 25 kms North East of Trondheim, Vaernes housed some of the RNorAF museum collection pending the establishment of a permanent museum at Gardermoen.

DH Vampire FB.52	V0184	(soc 14.2.57) ex 'ZK-U', to Oslo/Akershus by '82.
Fairchild Cornell	103	(ex 42-76477) 'L-AB' to Gardermoen by '83.
F-86F Sabre	31082	(ex 53-1082) unconfirmed report - comments?
RF-84F Thunderflash	117053	(ex 51-17053) ex 'AZ-G' 717 Skv, soc 29.5.70, to Gardermoen by '83.
F-84G Thunderjet	111209	(ex 51-11209) ex 'MU-S' 338 Skv, to Gardermoen by '83.
SAAB 91B Safir	53-058	(c/n 91-267) ex Primary Flying School, to Gardermoen by '88.

Derelict amongst the trees on the North side of the base in '85 and '87 was RF-84F Thunderflash 117047 (ex 51-17047, ex 'AZ-A' 717 Skv). It is used for NBC training.

PORTUGAL

Most airfields in this delightful country, whether civil or military, have a strong W&R presence. The military bases are liberally sprinkled with ex WGAF Fiat G-91s serving as decoys or as spares sources for the active 'Gina' fleet. Most civil fields possess their fair share of wrecks either long abandoned or awaiting a new owner to start a major rebuild. Air transport relics are almost unknown with only a Convair 880 and former gun-running Constellation to record.

Mention must be made of the excellent Museu do Ar which has a wide ranging selection of former Portugese AF equipment and holds numerous airframes for use in exchanges to fill gaps in the collection.

Recent reports suggest that the Portugese will receive substantial quantities of new military aircraft in the near future, F-16s, Epsilons and helicopters. Hopefully the aircraft they replace will give us plenty of W&R items to record in the future.

ALVERCA

Alverca, is the home of OGMA (Oficinas Gerais de Material Aeronauticao), the Portugese AF's repair and overhaul organisation. As well as OGMA's extensive hangars and manufacturing facilities, the complex also houses a military depot, the Museu do Ar and finally the famous compound which holds a wealth of interesting aircraft which await restoration for the Museu do Ar or which are retained as 'currency' to trade for future acquisitions.

On display in the Museu do Ar recently have been the following aircraft.

Auster D5/160	3553	(c/n OGMA 50) (noted '83, to store).
Auster D5/160	3564	(c/n OGMA 66) (noted '81-'87).
Caudron G.III	-	replica (noted '84-'87).
DFS108 Schulgleiter	PE-1	(noted '87).
DH82A Tiger Moth	111	(c/n OGMA P1) (noted '83-'87).
DH Vampire FB.9	"5801"	ex South African AF, (noted '81 & '87, see below).
Fairey IIID	"17"	replica (noted '81-'87).
Grumman G.44 Widgeon	129	(c/n 1251) (noted '81-'87).
Jodel D.9 Bebe	CS-AXA	(c/n 436) (noted '86-'87).
Maurice Farman MF-4	-	replica (noted '84-'87).
Oliveira Nikkus Monoplane	-	(noted '84).
Piper L-21B Super Cub	3212	(c/n 18-2562, ex 52-6255) (noted '83-'87).
Santos Dumont XX Demoiselle	-	replica (noted '84-'87).
Schneider Grunau Baby	CS-PAE	(c/n 3567) (noted '84-'87).

Also displayed in the museum building are the tail boom and rotors from UH-19A 9101 together with various instrument panels and other artifacts.

The contents of the museum storage compound have changed very little in recent years.

AAC.1 (Ju 52)	6311	(c/n 005) (noted '83-'87).
AAC.1 (Ju 52)	6315	(c/n 205) ex Sintra (noted '83-'87).
Auster D5/160	3548	(noted '82, to Sintra by '84).
Beech C-45H	2513	(c/n CA76, ex RCAF 2278) (noted '83-'87).
Beech C-45H	2517	(c/n CA94, ex RCAF 2296) (noted '80-'87).
DH Chipmunk T.10	1323	(c/n OGMA 13) (noted '79-'82, returned to service by '84).
DH Vampire FB.9	"5801"	ex SAAF, (noted '83-'84, to museum proper by '87).
Dornier Do 27A-4	3487	(c/n 141) (noted '83-'87).
Dornier Do 27A-4	3489	(c/n 251) (noted '83-'87).
Douglas C-54A	6606	(ex 41-37279) ex AB.1 (noted '80-'87).
Douglas DC-6B	6706	(c/n 44116) ex AB.1 (noted '80-'87).

Douglas A-26B Invader	7104	(ex 44-34726) (noted '83-'87).
Fiat G-91R/4	5412	(c/n 0149, ex WGAF BD-372) (noted '79-'82).
Junkers Ju 52/3mg3e	6300	ex BA.3. (noted '83-'87).
Junkers Ju 52/3mg3e	6301	(noted '83-'87).
Junkers Ju 52/3mg3e	6304	(ex Coimbra, first noted '87).
Junkers Ju 52/3mg3e	6305	(noted '83-'84 to........).
Junkers Ju 52/3mg3e	6306	(c/n 5664) ex BA.6 (noted '83-'87).
Junkers Ju 52/3mg3e	6309	(c/n 501196) (noted '83-'84, to Sabena Old Timers 29.3.85, arriving at Brussels 24.4.85).
Junkers Ju 52/3mg7e	6310	(c/n 501219) (noted '83-'87 - since to Sabena Old Timers).
Lockheed RT-33A	1916	(c/n 8813, ex 53-5474) (noted '84-87).
T-33AN Silver Star	1951	(ex RCAF 21045) (noted '81-'87, to Beja by 7.88).
PV-2C Harpoon	4620	(noted '83-'87).
Nord 2502A Noratlas	6403	(c/n 7, ex F-BGZG) (noted '82-'87).
Nord 2502 Noratlas	6412	(c/n 006) (noted '83-'87).
Nord 2501 Noratlas	6417	(c/n 059) (noted '83-'87).
Nord 2501 Noratlas	6420	(c/n 032) soc 25.2.77 (noted '82-'87).
AT-6D Texan	1527	(noted '79-'87).
AT-6C Texan	1662	(c/n 88-16336, ex 42-84634, EZ341) (noted '83-'87).
T-6J Texan	1737	(noted '82-'87).
T-6J Texan	1769	(c/n CCF4-517, ex 52-8696) (noted '82, to Montijo).
F-86F Sabre	5333	(ex 52-5184) (noted '79-'87).
F-86F Sabre	5337	(ex 52-5199) (noted '79-'87).
F-86F Sabre	5338	(ex 52-5204) (noted '79-'87).
F-86F Sabre	5347	(ex 53-1083) (noted '79-'87).
F-86F Sabre	5360	(ex 53-1190) (noted '79-'87).
F-86F Sabre	5361	(ex 53-1204) (noted '79-'87).
F-84G Thunderjet	5176	(ex 51-9928) (noted '83-'87).
L-21B Super Cub	"CS-207"	(c/n 18-1290, ex 51-15290, ex 3201/CS-ALQ) (frame & tattered fabric, noted '84-'87).
F-84G Thunderjet	5216	(ex 51-10838) (noted '82-'87).

Adjacent to the museum storage compound is a Portugese AF crash compound which held the wrecks of the following accident victims in 6.87. All were still current during 2.89.

Cessna T-37C	2418	(ex 62-5943) ex Esq.102, crashed 15kms North of Beja 5.11.86.
DH Chipmunk T.10	1322	(c/n OGMA 12) ex Esq.101.
Fiat G-91R/4	5433	(c/n 0119, ex WGAF BD-245) ex Esq.303.

The wreck of Esq.301 Fiat G-91R/3 5456 was reported here by 7.88 following an accident on 16.6.88.

There is another dump on the far side of the airfield, on the banks of the Rio Tejo. The following aircraft have been noted as 'dumped' in recent years, though some of them may well have been in the crash compound noted above. Noted from 1980 to 1983 was Douglas DC-6B 6707 (c/n 43533, ex AB.1) whilst dumped in '84 were four ex WGAF Fiat G-91R/3s and ex USN Rota Convair C-131F 141002. Reported in 1985 were ex USN RA-5C Vigilante 156620/606, two ex WGAF G-91R/3s, G-91R/4 5410 (c/n 0131, ex BD-363) and G-91T/3 3456 (c/n 616) which was parked near the hangars apparently withdrawn from use .

Standing on top of a building on the far side of the field (and not easy to see) in 6.87 was the wreck of an unidentified Harvard.

Dumped outside the helicopter overhaul hangar at the OGMA facility in 6.87 (and 7.88) was the wreck of SA330C Puma 9501 (c/n 1001, ex Esq.751, w/o 6.86).

Long term storage inmates in the helicopter hangar comprise Alouette IIIs 9314 (c/n 1621), 9337 (c/n 1661), 9358 (c/n 1750), 9395 (c/n 1896) and ex Heer Alouette IIs 7596 (c/n 1532), 7625 (c/n 1612), 7632 (c/n 1632), 7700 (c/n 1847). These former German Army Alouettes are the last of a batch received by 1984 and progressively overhauled for the GNR (National Guard) and Brigada Transita, all the others having now entered service with those units.

The wreck of Fournier RF10 1204 (c/n 13, ex Esq.802, crashed at Tancos 29.3.85) lay in one of the overhaul hangars here in 4.85.

OGMA have a gutted Alouette III in use as a ground instructional airframe. This also doubles as a centrepiece for the OGMA stand at various exhibitions, air displays etc. The airframe is mostly from 9258 (c/n 1116) with additional parts from 9265 (c/n 1138, crashed in '66).

DH82A Tiger Moth 102 (c/n 3650) had arrived with OGMA by 2.89 from the museum store at Sintra. It was undergoing restoration here and may well be returned to flying condition.

The Portugese AF depot here has a compound opposite the main entrance to OGMA. On a pallet here in 6.87 (amidst many other containers, pallets and assorted equipment) was the fuselage of Fiat G-91R/3 5450 (c/n 428, ex WGAF 3160). It was still in situ in 7.88.

A scrapyard in Alverca town at the rear of the Sta Iria Ceramica ceramics works was visited 10.80, located a few kilometres towards Lisbon from the airfield. Dealing with scrap from OGMA, the yard held at that time a DC-6 (in three sections), a complete Ju 52 fuselage (with a Tancos badge) together with large piles of T-6s, PV-2 Harpoons and Do 27s. Those identified were Texans 1501, 1536, 1546 and one coded '109' (though 1546 seems rather unlikely as it is now preserved at Sintra), Dornier Do 27A 3488 and camouflaged PV-2 Harpoon 4618.

BEJA

The WGAF were reported to have F-104G Starfighter 2004 (c/n 2004, ex LVR.1) here for battle damage repair training (noted '87). It has not (to my knowledge) been seen here since so confirmation would be welcome.

By 7.88, T-33AN 1951 (ex RCAF 21045) had arrived for display on the main gate. It was confirmed during 4.89 by which time F-104G Starfighter 2381 (c/n 8080) (or at least an F-104G marked as 2381) was also preserved here.

BENEDITA

Approximately halfway between Ota and Monte Real, at the side of the N1 highway, are the premises of scrap and surplus dealers Amarino A Mendes Lda. The yard is actually out in the middle of nowhere but the next turn off as you head South is to the village of Benedita. Anyway, noted here during 1987 was the hulk of Chipmunk T.10 1370 (c/n OGMA 60, ex Esq.101) which suffered an accident at Ota and was stripped of spares there early in 1985.

BRAGA

In 11.80 the wreck of Auster D5/160 CS-AMY (c/n 95) was noted at the airfield (some 50 kms North East of Porto).

CARVOEIRA

Some miles North West of Sintra on the N247 road to Ericeira, Fiat G-91R/3 3088 (c/n 352, ex WGAF and Tancos decoy) can be found by the side of the main road through the village. The aircraft is on concrete blocks, preserved at a school.

The identity of this aircraft is not yet confirmed and 3088 was reported still at Tancos in 4.89. The aircraft here could conceivably be a mis-identification of 3082 or 3083 both of which are also Tancos decoys. All have been reported at Tancos since the G-91 arrived here but significantly have not all been seen at once. Comments?

CASCAIS

F-86F Sabre 5344 (ex 52-5267) was presented to the children of Cascais by the USAF in 1968. After almost twenty years in this role, displayed by the entrance of this small civil airfield (10 kms West of Lisbon), the aircraft was in very poor condition when viewed in 1987. Final disposal to a scrapyard may not be long in coming.

Eight ex AdlA T-6G Texans attempted to transit here in the late sixties whilst en-route from France to join the Biafran AF. The aircraft were embargoed here and spent some 14 years derelict on the airfield. They were last noted in '83 and had gone by '84 but a substantial rear fuselage/tail section from 51-14794 was noted in a scrapyard at Sintra in 6.87, so perhaps all eight were dealt with at that yard. Serials were 51-14770, 51-14794, 51-14800/21, 51-14959/KK, 51-14991, 51-15046, 51-15083 plus one other.

Jurca MJ-2B Tempete CS-AXB (c/n 9) was noted here withdrawn from use in 10.80, never in fact having flown.

CHAVES

T-33AN Silver Star 1952 (ex RCAF 21228) was noted displayed on a pole in a park here (100 kms North East of Porto) in '78 and was still here in '85.

COIMBRA

Junkers Ju 52/3mg3e 6304 (c/n 5661) was on display in the Portugal dos Pequeninos playground by 1977 and was still current in 1985. The aircraft has quite a history, being one of ten Ju 52s bought direct from the manufacturer in 1937 as night bombers. In 6.87 this aircraft was noted in the Museu do Ar storage compound at Alverca.

The civil aerodrome here held L.13 Blaniks EC-BIW, EC-CIS (c/n 025601, damaged) and EC-CSR (c/n 026153) in 11.80. By 1983 the field was littered with wrecks, the following being noted.

Auster D5/160	CS-AMW	CofA expired 31.7.71.
Auster D5/180	CS-ANE	CofA expired 16.11.72.
Auster J/1 Autocrat	CS-ACI	(c/n 2349, ex G-AJRA)
Cessna A188T Agtruck	CS-AOG	(c/n 01086T) crash wreck.
Cessna A188T Agtruck	CS-ARF	crash wreck.
Culver V	CS-ACY	(c/n 348) CofA expired 26.5.56!
Ercoupe 415CD	CS-ACO	(c/n 4757) CofA expired 15.12.63.
Dornier Do 27A-3	CS-AQT	(ex PortAF 3460 & WGAF 5524) damaged beyond repair - wreck dumped.
Paulistinha 56-C1	CS-ALB	(c/n 1162) under rebuild.
Paulistinha 56-C1	CS-ALC	(c/n 1214) wreck, CofA expired 2.1.69.
Piper PA25-260C	CS-AHD	(c/n 25-5381) wfu.
PA11 Cub Special	CS-AAJ	(c/n 11-233) CofA expired 13.10.75.

ESPINHO

An unidentified Auster D4 fuselage was in store here (20 kms South of Porto) in 1980 with a couple of J-3C Cub frames. Recorded as withdrawn from use were the following.

DH82 Tiger Moth	CS-AFF	(c/n DHTM.18A) CofA expired 9.1.77, also noted 3.83, to Sintra museum by '84.
PA12 Super Cruiser	CS-ABA	(c/n 12-65) CofA expired 20.12.72, also noted 3.83.
Piper J-3C-65 Cub	CS-ABK	(c/n 17674)
Piper J-3C Cub	CS-ABW	(c/n 17242)
Paulistinha 56-C1	CS-ALH	(c/n 1144) fuselage only, also noted 3.83.

EVORA

Another Junkers Ju 52/3mg3e, 6303, was preserved by a swimming pool here (100 kms East of Lisbon) in the late seventies and was still current in 4.85.

FARO

L1049 Super Constellation "5N-83H" (c/n 4616, ex CS-TLA) was in use as a bar at the airport here for many years after a shady existence running guns to Biafra, however it has since moved as it was seen from a train window in 6.87 by a roadside approximately halfway between Faro and Albufeira. Whether or not this is to be its final resting place remains to be seen as the aircraft was still on the back of a lorry and the train would not stop!

FUNCHAL

On high ground near the airport at Funchal on the island of Madeira lies the fuselage of an unidentified Noratlas. The centre section lies nearby but there is no sign of the wings or tail. Quite why it should be sitting beside the road in the middle of no-where has yet to be explained. Its identity is also open to speculation but it is almost certain to be ex Portugese AF. This mystery ship was first reported in 1985.

FURADOURO

Beech C-45H 2511 was noted preserved here in the late seventies (the type was withdrawn in 1976). The aircraft was not found on a search in 4.85.

LISBOA (LISBON)

Preserved in Monsanto Park in 1980 was ex Portugese Navy Grumman G.44 Widgeon 2401. The aircraft was still current in '87.

The Museo de Marinha is located on the N6 (the main coastal highway along the North bank of the Tejo) a short distance West of the bridge. Amongst the vast collection of Naval exhibits are three aircraft.

Fairey IIID	17	(c/n F402)
Grumman G.44 Widgeon	128	(c/n 1242)
Schreck FBA	2	(c/n 203)

Adjacent to Lisbon Airport is the fuselage of ex Onyx Aviation Convair CV880 N8806E (c/n 21) which flew into Lisbon on 9.3.80 and was wfu due to technical problems on 4.5.80 (still in basic Delta colours). She was later sold for use as a bar (noted 6.87). At the airport itself, Aero Commander AC560F G-ARDK (c/n 992-6) has not moved for many years and was still parked there in 6.87. The registration CS-AJL was allocated but not taken up.

MONTE REAL

The main gate at BA.5 (Base Aerea 5) is guarded by F-86F Sabre 5301 (ex 52-5168, noted '82-'89). A second Sabre, F-86F 5320 (ex 52-5268), serves as a training aid for aircraft tug drivers (noted '82-'89).

At least two Fiat G-91s are to be found on the base, G-91R/3 3055 (c/n 313, ex WGAF, noted '84-'88) sits around the flight line in reasonable condition whilst a second, unidentified, a/c was noted in the woods in '87 and had been used for fire practice.

In 1983 the fire dump contained Lockheed T-33A 1912 (ex 55-3090) ex Esq.103 whilst in 1984 the unit were seen to have withdrawn from use 1910. Both were noted on a fire dump here in 8.87 and again in '88 but cannot be very easy to find as a good many visitors to the base in 6.87 failed to find them.

A scrap compound held the remains of LTV A-7P Corsair II 5535 (w/o 26.5.86) in 6.87, with parts of another (probably 5543 which crashed 26.5.85).

MONTIJO

Preserved on the main gate of BA.6 (Base Aerea 6) in 7.84 was Fiat G-91R/4 5423 (c/n 0146, ex WGAF BD-378). By 6.87 this aircraft had been replaced by Fiat G-91R/3 5463 (c/n 384, ex WGAF 3118). Preserved by the control tower in the Esq.301 area is a second Gina, Fiat G-91R/4 5404 (c/n 0117, ex WGAF BD-243) which sports a sharks mouth. Both were still current 4.89.

Maintained in airworthy condition here for the Museu do Ar are T-6J Texans 1769 (c/n CCF4-517, ex 52-8696) and 1774 (c/n CCF4-486, ex 52-8565).

Dumped amongst the dispersals on the South side of the base in '84 were four Fiat G-91s comprising two G-91R/3s and two G-91T/3s but unfortunately no serials were obtained. By 1985 there were five a/c present comprising G-91R/3s 3253 (c/n 522, ex WGAF), 3266 (c/n 536, ex WGAF) plus one other and two anonymous G-91T/3s. A close look in 6.87 found G-91R/3s 3065 (c/n 326, ex WGAF and Sintra store), 3241 (c/n 510, ex WGAF) and G-91T/3s 3414 (c/n 0016, ex WGAF), 3460 (c/n 620, ex WGAF). A check in 4.89 confirmed that 3241, 3414 and 3460 were still current. All of these had been extensively cannibalised for spare parts. The above just goes to show that unless these decoy airframes are positively identified, its very easy to jump to the wrong conclusion.

OTA

The main gate at BA.2 (Base Aerea 2) is guarded by F-84G Thunderjet 5201 (noted '79-'87).

A technical training school here (the Formacao de Especialistas Tecnicos) uses the following ground instructional airframes.

Beech C-45H	2516	(noted '84-'87).
DH Chipmunk T.10	1319	(c/n OGMA 9) (noted '82-'84).
Fiat G-91R/3	3004	(c/n 0057) ex WGAF (noted '84-'87).
Fiat G-91R/3	3285	(c/n 555) ex WGAF (noted '84-'87).
T-6J Texan	1766	(noted '79-'87).
T-6J Texan	1770	(noted '79-'82).
F-86F Sabre	5319	(ex 52-5262) (noted '82-'87).
Sud Alouette III	9379	(c/n 1835) (noted '82-'84 - wears spurious c/n 1612).

Noted here in a damaged condition in 4.85 was DH Chipmunk T.10 1370 (c/n OGMA 60). The aircraft subsequently appeared in a scrapyard near Benedita (qv).

Decoy aircraft at Ota comprise the following Fiat G-91s of which 3445 inhabits its own dispersal with the rest parked in a row along a taxiway through the dispersal area.

Fiat G-91R/3	3038	(c/n 0102) ex WGAF (noted '84-'88).
Fiat G-91R/3	3078	(c/n 340) ex WGAF (noted '84-'88).
Fiat G-91R/3	3207	(c/n 475) ex WGAF (noted '84-'88).
Fiat G-91R/3	3220	(c/n 488) ex WGAF (noted '84, to fire dump by '87).
Fiat G-91R/3	3227	(c/n 496) ex WGAF (noted '84-'88).
Fiat G-91R/3	3274	(c/n 544) ex WGAF (noted '84, to 5474 - see note).
Fiat G-91T/3	3443	(c/n 603) ex WGAF (noted '84-'88).
Fiat G-91T/3	3445	(c/n 605) ex WGAF (noted '84-'88).
Fiat G-91T/3	3448	(c/n 608) ex WGAF (noted '84-'88).
Fiat G-91T/3	3450	(c/n 610) ex WGAF (noted '84-'88).
Fiat G-91T/3	3457	(c/n 617) ex WGAF (noted '84-'88).
Fiat G-91T/3	3458	(c/n 618) ex WGAF (noted '84-'88).

Note that although 3274 was, according to one source, allocated the serial 5474 and has certainly disappeared from Ota, it has never been noted either in service or at Alverca. Perhaps the airframe was rejected as unsuitable for rebuild and may have been scrapped or reduced to spares. Comments please!

On a hill behind the control tower can be found a further five G-91s in use for fire training. 3030 is positioned separately, a short distance from the other group of four.

Fiat G-91R/3	3030	(c/n 0088) ex WGAF (noted '84-'87).
Fiat G-91R/3	3220	(c/n 488) ex WGAF (noted '87 - ex decoy area).
Fiat G-91R/3	3239	(c/n 508) ex WGAF (noted '84-'87).
Fiat G-91R/3	3287	(c/n 558) ex WGAF (noted '84-'87).
Fiat G-91T/3	3442	(c/n 602) ex WGAF (noted '84-'88).

PEDROUCOS

This suburb of Lisbon (close to the river, to the West of the city) houses the Institute of Higher Military Studies. Mounted at the gate in 8.81 was T-33AN 1953.

PORTO/PEDRAS RUBRAS

In 10.80 J-3C-65 Cub CS-AAQ (c/n 22021, ex G-AKBU), Auster D4/108 CS-AMJ (c/n 36), EoN Baby 1 CS-PAM (c/n EON/B/035) and Stampe SV4C G-AXME (c/n 545, ex F-BDCP) were all here in a non-airworthy condition.

SEIXAS

In 1984 T-6G Texan 1765 was noted here, preserved on a pole in the town centre.

SINTRA

Part of the Museu do Ar collection is located at Sintra where they have the use of one hangar with the overflow sunning themselves outside. The Fiat G-91s are available to trade for other types which the museum is seeking.

Inside

Auster D5/160	3548	ex Alverca (noted '84-'87).
Avro Cadet	501	(noted '84-'87).
DFS Kranich	CS-PAD	(c/n 983) (noted '84).
DFS Weihe A-3	CS-PAF	(c/n 244) (noted '84).
DH82A Tiger Moth	102	(c/n 3650) (noted '84-'87, to Alverca by 2.89).
DH82 Tiger Moth	CS-AFF	(c/n DHTM.18A) ex Espinho (noted '84-'87).
DH87B Hornet Moth	CR-AAC	(c/n 8104) (noted '84).
DH89A Dragon Rapide	2307	(c/n 6899) (noted '84-'87).
Dornier Do 27A-1	3358	(c/n 235, ex WGAF 5585) (noted '84-'87).
MH1521 Broussard	3303	(c/n 53C) wrecked (noted '84).
MH1521 Broussard	3304	(c/n 54C) (noted '83-'87).
Piper L-18C Cub	3218	(noted '84-'87).
Piper J-3C Cub	CS-ABY	(c/n 17243) (noted '84-'87).
Sikorsky H-19D	MM57-5979	ex 'CS-10' ItAF & Brussels Museum (noted '84-'87).

Also noted in '84 were two Tiger Moth frames (probably CS-AEF c/n 3650 and CS-AEL c/n OGMA P65). The H-19D came from Brussels in exchange for an ex Portugese AF F-86F Sabre.

Outside

Beech AT-11	2504	(c/n CLM-1431) (noted '79-'87).
Beech C-45H	2515	(noted derelict in '83 & '85 behind museum hangar).
Douglas C-47A Dakota	6157	(c/n 19755, ex 43-15289) (noted '79-'87).
Fiat G-91R/3	3049	(c/n 306) ex WGAF (noted '84-'87).
Fiat G-91R/3	3065	(c/n 306) ex WGAF (noted '84-'85, to Montijo by '87).
Fiat G-91R/3	3265	(c/n 535) ex WGAF (noted '84-'87).
Fiat G-91R/3	3277	(c/n 547) ex WGAF (noted '84-'87).
Fiat G-91R/3	3279	(c/n 549) ex WGAF (noted '84-'87).
Fiat G-91T/3	3454	(c/n 614) ex WGAF (noted '84-'87).
Fiat G-91T/3	3459	(c/n 619) ex WGAF (noted '84-'87).
SP-2E Neptune	4711	(c/n 5283, ex 134722, MLD 19-31, 096) ex BA.5 (noted '79-'87).
MH1521 Broussard	3301	(c/n 51C) (noted '79-'87).
Harvard T.2B	1512	fuselage only (noted '84 & '85 derelict behind museum hangar).
F-84G Thunderjet	5187	(ex 51-9928) (noted '79-'87).

Preserved aircraft on the base comprise Fiat G-91R/3s 5457 (c/n 464, ex WGAF 3196) on a pole outside the Air Force Academy whilst 5472 (c/n 559, ex WGAF 3288) and 5473 (c/n 590, ex WGAF 3319) are displayed on the AFA parade ground. All were noted in '84 and were still current in '87. Near the Esq.102 flight line, Harvard T.2B 1546 is preserved (current '89).

A scrapyard outside the Western perimeter of the base (not far from the stored museum aircraft) was investigated in 6.87 and produced the following list. All were dismembered into small pieces and were almost unrecognisable, although the rear fuselages of the Sabres had suffered less than the rest. It is thought that at least one Sabre remained unidentified though with front fuselages, rear fuselages and wings dotted around amongst piles of cars and industrial scrap it is difficult to be certain. The Texan remains were from one of eight aircraft abandoned at Cascais whilst en-route to the Biafran AF. It seems reasonable to suppose that the other aircraft may well have been processed through this yard.

BN-2A Islander	CS-???	
Douglas DC-6B	CS-TAK	(c/n 43535, ex PortAF 6709)
SP-2E Neptune	4701	(c/n 5273, ex 134671, MLD 19-21, 086) ex BA.5.
F-86F Sabre	5305	(ex 52-5178) ex Alverca.
F-86F Sabre	5309	(ex 52-5189)
F-86F Sabre	5326	
F-86F Sabre	5330	
F-86F Sabre	5331	
F-86F Sabre	5346	(ex 53-1073)
F-86F Sabre	5353	(ex 53-1209)

F-86F Sabre	5358	ex Alverca.
F-86F Sabre	5359	
F-86F Sabre	5365	ex Alverca.
T-6G Texan	114794	(ex 51-14794) rear fuselage only.

TANCOS

First noted here in 7.84 were the following Fiat G-91R/3 decoys which were parked by the Alouette hangar.

Fiat G-91R/3	3082	(c/n 345) (noted '84-'88).
Fiat G-91R/3	3083	(c/n 346) (noted '84-'88).
Fiat G-91R/3	3088	(c/n 352) (noted '84, to Carvoeira but also reported at Tancos 4.89!).
Fiat G-91R/3	3179	(c/n 447) (noted '84-'88).
Fiat g-91R/3	3250	(c/n 519) (noted '84-'89).
Fiat G-91R/3	3254	(c/n 524) (noted '84-'89).
Fiat G-91R/3	3276	(c/n 546) (noted '84-'89).
Fiat G-91R/3	3283	(c/n 553) (noted '84-'88).
Fiat G-91R/3	3298	(c/n 569) (noted '84-'89).

Decoy G-91s in Portugal continue to be the subject of conflicting sightings. Apart from the problem with 3088 above, 3278 was reported here for the first time in 4.89.

VILA REAL

Located some 110 kms East of Porto, Fiat G-91R/3 5462 (c/n 301, ex WGAF 3044) was on display in the town square in 7.84 but was in fact borrowed from the front line for the annual Air Force Week and gains a mention only to avoid confusion!

Preserved at the entrance to the civil airfield at Vila Real is ex PortAF Fiat G-91R/3 5470 (c/n 339, ex WGAF 3077) (noted '84-'85).

VISEU

About 100 kms South of Vila Real, preserved on a pole at the aerodrome entrance is Fiat G-91R/4 5408 (c/n 0153, ex WGAF BD-385) ex PortAF (noted '84-'85).

SPAIN

Spain has seen an upsurge of interest by European aviation enthusiasts in recent years, largely due to the restoration of democracy in this country which has made the observation of aircraft here a less hazardous occupation. The superb Museo del Aire collection, long hidden from view, has now been opened to the public (though one still has to obtain permission for photography in advance from the Ministry of Defence). Apart from this museum and a number of aircraft preserved within Spanish AF bases, aircraft preservation in Spain is virtually unknown.

One legacy of the Franco era is that aircraft photography is still sometimes regarded with a degree of suspicion. Permission should always be obtained in advance to avoid embarrassment.

ALBACETE/LOS LLANOS

The Spanish AF's first tanker aircraft were three ex USAF Boeing KC-97L Stratocruisers which served with Esc.123 of Ala.12 here. The first of these, KC-97L TK.1-1/123-01 (ex 53-0172, noted '84-'85) was preserved in a playground about half way between the base and the city of Albacete (on route C3211) but moved to a location by the A7 motorway North of Barcelona by late '88. TK.1-3/123-03 (ex 53-0189), was preserved on the base here with Ala Logistica 53 (noted '79-'84) but was moved to Cuatro Vientos for the Museo del Aire by 4.87.

There were also a couple of surplus C-97Gs delivered here as spares sources only (the USAF had cut through the wings to ensure they were never made airworthy). 53-0241 went from here to Sotillo De La Adrada whilst 53-0275 is believed to have been scrapped on site.

Offered for sale by auction here on 16.9.88 were CASA 1131E Jungmanns E.3B-153 (ex '781-75' Esc.781 and Granada/Armilla storage), E.3B-321, E.3B-408, and E.3B-429.

ALCANTARILLA

Preserved inside the base here is CASA 352L (Ju 52) T.2B-181/721-10 (ex Esc.721, noted '83-'88).

In the Esc.721 area lies the fuselage of an unidentified CASA 212, thought to be in use for paratroop training. This may well be a mock up.

ALICANTE

Stored here in '83 were Dakotas EC-AQB (DC-3C, c/n 12844, ex 42-92983, NC54705, EC-WQB) ex Aeroflete and EC-BUG (TC-47B, c/n 32734, ex 44-76402, KN366, N86441, SpanAF T.3-47) ex Aertransporte de Espana. Both were still current during '87.

A lean-to next to the Guardia Civil station held dismantled AISA I-115s E.9-74/903-74 (ex Esc.903) and E.9-93/221-31 (ex Esc.221) in 1985 (still there '87).

BADAJOZ

A couple of kilometres down the road to Sevilla (N432/E102) a Stinson 108-3 is displayed on the gate of the SADI SA chemical works.

BARCELONA/SABADELL

The fuselage of Piper J-3C-65 Cub EC-ALG (c/n 12240, ex 44-79944, HB-OIZ) was here in 4.83 with stored DH89A Dragon Rapide EC-AKO (c/n 6345, ex G-AERN - stored here since 1971!), the wrecks of Bellanca 17-30 Cruisair EC-BPL (c/n 30-140), Macchi MB308 EC-AGM (c/n 5807/34, ex I-MACC) and an unmarked Fairchild Argus (probably EC-AEN). The Dragon Rapide at least was still current at the end of 1986 when Sikorsky S-51 Dragonfly N9986Z was noted in store here, minus various parts. It is apparently intended to restore this machine to flying condition, a considerable task.

Alongside the A7 motorway to the North of the city by late '88 were Boeing KC-97Ls TK.1-1/123-01 (ex 53-0172) from Albacete and TK.1-2/123-02 (ex 53-0225) from Tarancon. They are both preserved at the 'Saint Cugat Airport', a huge discotheque equipped with runway lights, hangars, restaurant, swimming pool etc!

BENIDORM
The "Star Garden" discotheque contains WS55 Whirlwind Srs.2 ZD.1B-21 (c/n WA396) ex '803-03' Esc.803 which has been here since at least 1974. It is thought to have arrived from a scrapyard at San Martin de la Vega.

BETERA
Bell OH-13S HE.7B-27/ET-059-103 (c/n 3903, ex 65-13007) had arrived from storage at Colmenar by 1987 for restoration and eventual display on the gate with Unidad de Helicopteros II. During 11.88 it was not yet on display.

BILBAO
Former Trans Europa Douglas DC-7C EC-BCI (c/n 44880) was converted to a bar/restaurant during 1970 and was positioned near Sondica Airport. Its subsequent fate is not known - any offers?

CANDAS
Former Aviaco Douglas DC-8-52 EC-AUM (c/n 45657) arrived here (between Gijon and Aviles) by road from Madrid on 13.7.87 to be converted into a bar for the 'Pub San Francisco'.

COLMENAR/VIEJO
Preserved on the base here is Bell OH-13S HE.7B-26/ET-102 (c/n 3902, ex 65-13006, noted '85-'88).

The wreck of MBB105 HR.15-26/ET-145 was still to be seen here in 5.84 following an accident on 11.11.82. It was not noted on a visit in 3.85 and is thought to have been reduced to spares and produce.

Held in store here were five Bell 47s at least four of which have now moved on.

Bell OH-13S	HE.7B-27	'ET-059-103' (c/n 3903, ex 65-13007) (noted '84-'85, to Betera).
Bell OH-13S	HE.7B-28	'ET-059-104' (c/n 3904, ex 65-13008) (noted '84-'85, to El Copero).
Bell OH-13S	HE.7B-29	'ET-059-105' (c/n 3905, ex 65-13009) (noted '84).
Agusta-Bell 47G-3B	HE.7B-31	'ET-059-107' (c/n 1613) (noted '84, to EC-DZL).
Agusta-Bell 47G-3B	HE.7B-32	'ET-059-108' (c/n 1614) (noted '84, to EC-DZK).

In mid 1982 the hulk of ex US Army Europe UH-1B Iroquois 03558/ET-E01 (ex 60-3558) was discovered here, serving as a ground instructional airframe. By 7.86 the airframe had moved to the museum store at Cuatro Vientos.

CORDOBA
Lying at the airfield here during 1981 were the wrecks of Grumman G164A Ag Cat EC-BGY (c/n 430, ex N909X) and PA25-260 Pawnee EC-CVD (c/n 25-7405725, ex N9598P).

CUATRO VIENTOS
Located some 10 kms South West of Madrid, the base at Cuatro Vientos houses the Museo del Aire (Spanish AF museum) which was opened to the public on 14.3.82. The following aircraft have been recorded with the museum recently.

Aerotecnica AC-12	Z.2-6	'75-6' (noted '87-'89).
Aerotecnica AC-12	Z.2-7	'75-7' (noted '78-'89).
Aerotecnica AC-12	Z.2-11	'75-11'(noted '78-'87,to Villanueva y la Geltru early '87).
Aerotecnica AC-14	Z.4-06	(noted '83-'89).
Agusta-Bell 47G-2	HE.7-13	'751-4' ex Esc.751 (King Juan Carlos did his first solo in this machine) (noted '88-'89).
Agusta-Bell 47G-3B	HE.7B-21	'782-11' ex Esc.782 (storage compound '88, gone by 2.89, probably to Villanueva y la Geltru).

Agusta-Bell 47J-3B	HD.11-1	(c/n 2094, ex EC-AYN, EC-SSA, Z.11-1) (arrived '83, current '89).
Avro 504K	"M-MABE"	replica (noted '88-'89).
AISA I-11B Peque	EC-AKL	(c/n 006) (noted '82-'89).
AISA I-11B Peque	EC-BLD	(c/n 159) (noted '82-'83, stored in AF area).
AISA I-115	E.9-119	(noted '78-'89).
Bell UH-1B Iroquois	60-3558	(c/n 204) 'ET-E01' (ex Colmenar gia, storage compound 7.86-'89).
Boeing KC-97L	TK.1-3	(ex 53-0189) ex '123-03' Ala.12 (noted in car park 4.87-'89).
Breguet Grand Raid	12-72	(CASA built, c/n 42) (noted '78-'89).
Bu 133C Jungmeister	E.1-14	'513-20' (noted '78-'89).
CASA 101 Aviojet	XE.25-01	(ex EC-ZDY) (noted '88-'89).
CASA 352L (Ju 52)	T.2B-211	(c/n 102) '911-16' (noted '78-'88, to the active side of the base and restored to flying condition, f/f 19.4.88).
CASA 352L (Ju 52)	T.2B-254	'721-14' (noted '83, in storage compound 12.87-2.89).
CASA 1131H (Bu 131)	E.3B-...	(c/n 203) (noted '82-'89).
CASA 2.111H (He 111)	T.8B-97	(c/n 108) '462-04' (noted '78-'89).
CASA 207A Azor	T.7-6	'405-15' ex Esc.405 & Tablada (noted 3.85-'89).
CASA 207C Azor	T.7-17	(c/n 17) ex '405-17' Esc.405 (arrived 9.81, noted '89).
Cessna L-19A Bird Dog	L.12-2	(c/n 22426, ex 51-12112) ex '407-2' Esc.407, wfu 15.11.80 (noted '82-'89).
Cierva 19 Mk.IVP	EC-AIM	(license built Avro 620, c/n 5158, ex G-ABXH, EC-W13, EC-ATT, 30-62, EC-CAB) (noted '78-'83, away for painting 2.89).
DH60G Moth Major	EC-AFQ	(ex EE.1-89) (noted '78-'89).
DH82A Tiger Moth	-	(noted '87-'89).
DH89 Dragon Rapide	G-ACYR	(c/n 6261) (noted '78-'89).
DHC C-7A Caribou	T.9-25	(ex 61-2394) ex '371-05' Esc.371, wfu '86 (noted '87-'88, storage compound 2.89).
DFS.108 Schulgleiter	-	
DFS Kranich III	EC-ODK	(noted '82-'89).
DFS Weihe	EC-RAB	(noted '82-'89).
DFS Weihe	EC-RAJ	probably in store, not seen at Cuatro Vientos.
DFS Weihe	EC-RAM	probably in store, not seen at Cuatro Vientos.
DFS Weihe	EC-RAQ	probably in store, not seen at Cuatro Vientos.
Dornier Do 24T	HD.5-2	(c/n 5341, ex 65-2, HR.5-2) '58-02' (noted '78 and in pond by '83, current '89).
Dornier Do 28A-1	U.14-1	(c/n 3014) ex '407-7' Esc.407 (noted '82-'89).
Douglas C-47B Dakota	T.3-36	(c/n 20600, ex 43-16134, N86444) ex '721-9' Esc.721 (noted '78-'89).
C-54D Skymaster	T.4-5	(c/n 10824, ex 42-72719) nose section (noted '82-'89).
C-54A Skymaster	T.4-10	(c/n 10366, ex 42-72261, Bu50844, NC88934, N88934) ex '911-10' Esc.911 (noted '78-'89).
Fiat CR.32	262	(composite of a CR.32 and Hispano HA132L, marked "3-52" on one side & 262 on the other) (noted '78-'89).
Williams Fokker DR.1	D-EAWI	"425/17" (noted '88-'89).
HU-16B Albatross	AD.1B-8	(ex 51-5304) ex Esc.801 (noted '78-'89).
Gurripato II	-	(noted '83-'89).
Gurripato II	-	probably in store, not seen at Cuatro Vientos.
Heinkel He 111E-1	B.2-82	(c/n 2940) "25-82" ex '14-16' (noted '78-'89).
Hispano HA1112K-1L	C.4J-10	'94-28' (noted '78-'89).
Hispano HA1112M-1L	C.4K-158	(c/n 226) ex '471-23' (noted '78-'89).
HA200R-1 Saeta	XE.14-2	(ex EC-ANN) (noted '78-'89).

HA220D Super Saeta	A.10C-104	(c/n 22-100) (noted '82-'89).
Hispano-Suiza HS.34	EC-AFJ	(c/n 1) (noted '78-'89).
Huarte-Mendicoa HM1B	"HM-1"	(E.4-161, c/n 161) (noted '78-'89).
Huarte-Mendicoa H-2B	-	probably in store, not seen at Cuatro Vientos.
Lockheed T-33A	E.15-38	(ex 57-0652) ex '41-26' Grupo 41 (ex Zaragoza, in storage compound '88-'89).
Lockheed T-33A	E.15-48	(ex 57-0662) ex '41-16' Grupo 41 (ex Zaragoza, front fuselage in storage compound 2.89 with tail of E.15-19, since to Villanueva y la Geltru).
Lockheed T-33A	E.15-51	(ex 53-4921) ex '41-8' Grupo 41 (noted '82-'89).
Lockheed T-33A	E.15-53	(ex 53-5050) ex '41-13' Grupo 41 (noted '84-'88, storage compound 2.89, tail from E.15-56/41-9).
F-104G Starfighter	"C8-15"	"32733/104-15" (c/n 9174, ex WGAF 2623) ex Jbg.34 (noted '85-'89) Spanish colours on starboard side & WGAF c/s on port side.
MS500 Criquet	L.16-23	'96-1' (noted '87-'89).
MS733 Alcyon	F-BMMS	"105" (52S Aeronavale marks) (noted '82-'89).
TB-25N Mitchell	44-29121	"74-17" (ex N86427) ex Malaga (noted '86-'89).
F-86F Sabre	C.5-58	(ex 52-4594, soc 12.71) '102-4' (noted '78-'89).
F-86F Sabre	C.5-71	(ex 52-4718, soc 12.71) '102-8' (noted '78-'87, to Villanueva y la Geltru).
F-86F Sabre	C.5-223	(ex 51-13450, soc 30.6.71) ex '102-32' (noted '78-'89 but as "C.5-104/1-104" by 6.87).
T-6G Texan	E.16-90	ex '793-6' Esc.791 (noted '84-'89, in museum storage compound).
T-6G Texan	E.16-97	ex '793-2' Esc.793 (noted '82-'87, in storage compound).
T-6G Texan	E.16-118	ex '793-3' Esc.793 (noted '83-'89, in storage compound).
SNJ-5 Texan	C.6-125	ex '421-43' Esc.421 (noted '83-'89, in storage compound).
SNJ-5 Texan	C.6-135	(ex Bu90747) ex '421-46' Esc.421 (noted '83-'89, in storage compound).
SNJ-5 Texan	C.6-155	(ex 44-81111, Bu90982) ex '421-35' Esc.421 (noted '80-'89).
SNJ-5 Texan	C.6-159	ex '421-55' Esc.421 (noted '87-'89, storage compound).
T-6D Texan	C.6-168	(ex 49-3305) ex '421-59' Esc.421 (noted '83-'86, in storage compound, sold 8.10.85).
SNJ-6 Texan	C.6-179	(Bu 112067) ex '421-67' Esc.421 (noted '83-'89, storage compound).
T-6G Texan	C.6-188	(ex 49-3056) ex '421-68' Esc.421 (noted '83-'89, storage compund).
T-6G Texan	E.16-200	(ex 53-4568) ex '793-13' Esc.793 (noted '83-'86, sold 8.10.85, to N153NA).
Polikarpov I-16	"CM-260"	replica, also marked as "C8-25" on other side, (noted '87-'89).
Polikarpov I-15	"CA-125"	replica (arrived 6.86, current '89).
Schneider Grunau Baby	EC-MFG	probably in store, not seen at Cuatro Vientos.
Slingsby Sky	EC-RAU	probably in store, not seen at Cuatro Vientos.
Stinson 108-3	-	(bare frame - noted '87-'89).
Vilanova Acedo	-	(first Spanish built a/c, similar to a Bleriot XI) (noted '82-'89).
Vogt Lo 100	EC-OCI	airworthy, stored at Palma del Rio.
Vogt Lo 100	EC-ODK	probably in store, not seen at Cuatro vientos.
WS55 Whirlwind	ZD.1B-22	(c/n WA397) ex '803-4' Esc.803 (noted '78-'89).

The stock of Texans is retained to provide a source of 'currency' for future acquisitions.

In the eighties, lines of Texans and now Cariboux have been seen here and have passed on into the melting pot or into civilian hands. This follows the disposal of the CASA 352 and Dakota fleet in the late Seventies (though a few of the latter have lingered on as will be seen). Recent sightings are detailed below but are by no means claimed to be complete. The T-6 story in particular has many gaps to be filled though it should be borne in mind that not all T-6 disposals were handled by Cuatro Vientos. The T-6 listing below confines itself to those noted in open store at 'CV' awaiting their fate.

DHC C-7A Caribou	T.9-13	(ex 60-3764) ex '353-13' Esc.353 (noted '86, sold to Newcal 27.11.87 as N555NC, departed 11.4.88).
DHC C-7A Caribou	T.9-17	(ex 60-5444) ex '353-17' Esc.353 (noted '86, to N88NC, departed 17.3.87).
DHC C-7A Caribou	T.9-21	(ex 60-5432) ex '353-21' Esc.353 (noted intact '86-'87 and dismantled 7.88-2.89).
DHC C-7A Caribou	T.9-24	(ex 60-5433) ex '371-04' Esc.371 (noted 2.87, to N90NC, departed 6.3.87).
DHC C-7A Caribou	T.9-25	(ex 61-2394) ex '371-05' Esc.371 (noted '86-'87, to museum storage compound by 12.87, current 2.89).
DHC C-7A Caribou	T.9-26	(ex 60-5436) ex '371-06' Esc.371 (noted 5.87, sold 27.11.87, to N666NC, departed 18.4.88).
DHC C-7A Caribou	T.9-27	(ex 61-2390) ex '371-07' Esc.371 (noted 5.87-9.88, engineless 11.88-2.89).
DHC C-7A Caribou	T.9-28	(ex 61-2398) ex '371-08' Esc.371 (noted 5.87, sold 27.11.87, flew to Malta 6.4.88 as N888NC).
DHC C-7A Caribou	T.9-29	(ex 61-2592) ex '371-09' Esc.371 (noted 5.87-2.89).
DHC C-7B Caribou	T.9-30	(ex 62-4191) ex '371-10' Esc.371 (wfu '86, noted as "T-OA" 2.87-5.87, to N95NC, departed 3.8.87).
Douglas C-47B Dakota	T.3-34	(c/n 20721, ex 43-16255, N86440) ex '721-7' Esc.721, (noted '77, departed 20.9.85, to G-BLFK, N952CA).
Douglas C-47B Dakota	T.3-54	(c/n 16954/34214, ex 45-0951, N73856) ex '744-54' Esc.744, (noted '78-'86, to G-BLFL, N951CA).
Douglas C-47B Dakota	T.3-64	(c/n 26342, ex 43-49081, EC-ASF) ex '744-64' Esc.744, (noted '77, allocated N1350M 10.81, dep 27.12.85 as N1350M (G-BMIR allocated but ntu - re-allocated to Wasp XT788) and preserved at Rhein-Main, WG.
Douglas C-47B Dakota	EC-ANV	(c/n 14770/26215, ex 43-48954) ex Navaids Check Service (noted '76-'80, sold 26.9.80).
Douglas C-47B Dakota	EC-ARV	(c/n 16753/33501, ex 44-77278) ex Navaids Check Service (noted '76-'80, sold 26.9.80).
T-6D Texan	C.6-3	ex '421-47' Esc.421 (noted '83).
T-6D Texan	C.6-20	ex '793-102' Esc.793, burnt here 24.5.81.
T-6D Texan	C.6.24	ex '421-66' Esc.421 (noted '83).
T-6D Texan	C.6-30	(ex 42-86142) ex '421-32' Esc.421 (noted '83-'84, to N4996M).
T-6G Texan	E.16-63	ex '793-6' Esc.793 (noted '83, to Luxembourg).
T-6G Texan	E.16-65	ex '793-16' Esc.793 (noted '83).
T-6G Texan	E.16-66	ex '793-10' Esc.793, to N4993A '84.
T-6G Texan	E.16-67	(ex 49-3320) ex '793-21' Esc.793 (noted '82-'83, to N4996H).
T-6G Texan	E.16-69	(ex 49-3326) ex '793-15' Esc.793 (noted '83).
T-6G Texan	E.16-71	(ex 49-3342) ex '793-8' Esc.793 (noted '83-'84, to I-TSEI '84).
T-6G Texan	E.16-72	ex '793-4' Esc.793 (noted '84-'88).
T-6G Texan	E.16-79	(ex 49-3336) ex '793-20' Esc.793 (noted '82-'83, to N4993G).
T-6G Texan	E.16-85	(ex 49-3330) ex '793-23' Esc.793 (noted '83, to N5115D).
T-6G Texan	E.16-86	(ex 49-3337) ex '793-19' Esc.793 (to Luxembourg'83).

T-6G Texan E.16-92 (ex 49-3352) ex '793-31' Esc.793 (to N49939 '84).
T-6G Texan E.16-95 (ex 49-3359) ex '793-1' Esc.793 (noted '82-'84).
T-6G Texan E.16-98 (ex 49-3365) ex '793-18' Esc.793 (noted '84, to N5380X '85).
T-6G Texan C.6-100 (ex 49-3367) ex '793-33' Esc.793 (noted '82, to N4995C).
T-6G Texan E.16-103 (ex 49-3430) ex 793-29' Esc.793 (to Van Nuys, CA).
T-6G Texan E.16-106 ex '793-12' Esc.793 (to Luxembourg '83, to LX-PAE).
T-6G Texan E.16-110 ex '793-6' Esc.793 (to Luxembourg '83).
T-6G Texan E.16-114 ex '793-7' Esc.793 (to Luxembourg '83).
SNJ-5 Texan C.6-121 (ex Bu43767) (to N2960T 8.87).
SNJ-5 Texan C.6-132 (ex Bu91088) ex '421-47' Esc.421 (noted '82, to N29930).
SNJ-5 Texan C.6-134 (ex Bu43942) ex '421-50' Esc.421 (noted '83, to N3931Z).
SNJ-5 Texan C.6-142 (ex Bu51811) ex '421-48' Esc.421 (noted '83, to N3931S).
SNJ-5 Texan C.6-148 (ex Bu 91074) ex '421-51' Esc.421 (noted '83, to N39313).
T-6D Texan C.6-153 (c/n 88-15838) ex '421-40' Esc.421 (noted '83, sold 24.3.83, to N39403).
SNJ-5 Texan C.6-164 (ex Bu84923) ex '421-57' Esc.421 (noted '83, sold 24.3.83, to N3931R).
T-6G Texan C.6-167 (ex 49-3311) ex '421-56' Esc.421 (noted '83, sold 3.9.82, to N3931Y but seen derelict here.
T-6G Texan C.6-170 (ex 49-3269) ex '421-60' Esc.421 (noted '83, sold 3.9.82, to N3931U).
T-6D Texan C.6-174 (c/n 88-16210) ex '421-69' Esc.421 (noted '83, sold 3.9.82, to N393104).
T-6G Texan C.6-186 (ex 49-3003) ex '421-70' Esc.421 (noted '83, to N39311).
T-6G Texan E.16-198 (ex 51-14904) ex '793-25' Esc.793 (noted '84-'85, to EC-DUM).
T-6G Texan E.16-201 (ex 52-8216) ex '793-19' Esc.793 (noted '83-'85, to EC-DUN).

The notes above represent only those details known to the compiler and probably fall far short of the full picture of T-6 storage and disposal here. Note that those Texans which ended up in the museum storage compound are not repeated in the above list.

Stored in one of the Esc.803 hangars in 1987 were Stampe ŜV4C F-BFZJ, AISA I-11B EC-BLD (ex L.8C-74) and the museum's Stinson 108-3 L.2-21/"90-53". They also had a CASA 1131 which was involved in an exchange deal with the French preservation Group Aerien Victor Tatin. Also now stored in here is the now airworthy CASA 352L T.2B-211 (see above). Probably in here but not confirmed are an Me 108 Taifun (from the Group Aerien Victor Tatin), a replica Lilienthal glider, a Zlin Z.326 and a few Texans.

Lying dismantled in a scrap compound adjacent to the dismantled Caribou T.9-21 by 7.88 were Agusta-Bell AB.47G HE.7-14/782-5 and OH-13H HE.7-46/782-27 (both fuselage only) with the tail only of OH-13H HE.7A-55/751-36. Noted here in 11.88 were dismantled T-33A E.15-13/41-7 (ex 53-5380, ex Grupo 41 & Zaragoza store) and a dismantled silver UH-1. It has been suggested that this could be UH-1C HU.8-10 (ex 65-12764) but this is for the moment purely speculation as there are seven other candidates. All these relics were still current during 2.89.

A visit to the field in 4.83 found A75N-1 Stearman EC-AID (c/n 75-6508), ex 05534) and B75N-1 Stearman EC-ATY (c/n 75-6714, ex 07110) derelict and the dumped wreck of PA18-150 EC-AIQ (c/n 18-4615). Derelict by the entrance were four Stinson 108-3 Voyagers of which only EC-AFT, EC-AEY (c/n 5162) and EC-AFG (c/n 4366) were identifiable. All have since departed one way or another.

Preserved near the control tower on the civil side of the field are Dornier Do 28A-1 EC-CPP (c/n 3002 ex D-IHIL) and Agusta-Bell 47J-3B1 EC-AXZ (c/n 2079) (both current '89). Withdrawn from use and stored on the civil side during 1984 (and still current '89) was CASA 1133C Jungmeister EC-ALP (ex ES.1-17, F-BATC). Noted in late '88 were dumped Cessna 180E EC-AXF (c/n 51129) and wfu CASA/SIAT 223.A1 Flamingos EC-CGK (c/n 057), EC-CGL (c/n 058) and EC-CGM (c/n 059). All these were still current 2.89 accompanied by derelict Dornier Do 28A-1 EC-ATZ (c/n 3045, ex EC-WTZ), wfu Do 27B-1 EC-CVO (c/n 151, ex WGAF 5531, D-EKOV, OO-PAN) and derelict IAR Is28M-2A G-BROM.

The hulk of Edgar Percival EP-9 Prospector EC-ASO (c/n 25, ex G-43-4, G-APCT) was here by 1981 and can still be found lying outside the old AISA works.

DOS BARRIOS

Some 80 kms South of Madrid on the NIV/E25, the fuselages of CASA 207 Azors T.7-13/405-13 (ex Esc.405) and T.7-18/405-18 (ex Esc.405) lay dismantled by the side of the main road here by 1985 and were still sitting there side by side in 2.89. They are situated next to a hotel which is itself next to a garage.

DOS HERMANAS

Next to the NIV road, some 10 kilometres South of Sevilla, on the Northern edge of Dos Hermanas is displayed an HA200 Saeta which arrived from Moron some years ago. The aircraft is in silver colour scheme with red trim but no serial or codes and can be found on the roof of 'La Motilla - Oficina de Informacion' which appears to be a property sales office. It was noted here in 5.88 and 11.88. The serial A.10B-53 has been quoted for this machine but is in error as this machine is preserved at Villanubla.

DUENAS

On the E3/620N road between Valladolid and Palencia, reports of a preserved DC-4/DC-6 deserve investigation.

EL COPERO

By late '88 Bell OH-13S HE.7B-28/ET-059-104 (c/n 3904, ex 65-13008) had arrived from Colmenar for display by the gate.

ESCALONA

In 10.84 C-47B Dakota N87805 (c/n 33558, ex 44-77226) was noted on display here (70kms South west of Madrid). It overran the runway at Madrid/Barajas on 28.2.75 and was moved here soon after.

GETAFE

Preserved inside the base behind the main gate here is Douglas C-54E Skymaster T.4-8/352-08 (c/n 27313, ex 44-9087) which was wfu by Esc.352 in 1977 and was still current 2.89, kept a little way inside the base from the main gate. In the intervening years, the engines have been 'robbed' to keep the Caribou fleet flying.

By 5.88 the long serving CASA 207 Azor T.7-1/352-01 (ex Esc.352) had been retired with ex Esc.351 T.7-19/351-02 surviving a while longer as the last active Azor here. By 7.88 both were wfu and certainly they were still parked out on the field in 2.89, reportedly maintained in airworthy condition in case a further need arises for their services. T.7-1 was the first Azor built and will ultimately be preserved in the town.

GIBRALTAR

Included under 'Spain' for the sake of geographical logic rather than due to any unpatriotic leanings, Vulcan B.2K XM571 (8812M, ex 50 Sqn) "City of Gibraltar" flew in on 9.5.84 for preservation at RAF North Front. It was still in immaculate condition in 2.89.

An unidentified Hunter arrived on 12.12.88 as air-freight on an RAF Hercules.

GRANADA/ARMILLA

In 6.87 over 40 CASA 1131Es (licence-built Bucker Jungmann) were still held here in excellent condition in long term hangar storage, the type having been finally withdrawn from Spanish AF service with Esc.781 in 1985 after forty five years service! Most of those involved in the sale are however relative youngsters of about twenty years use. They may well follow many of their fellows on to the civil registers of Europe, indeed several have since been registered in the UK and West Germany. In 9.88 the survivors were offered for sale in three batches, the sale being handled from Albacete (qv).

CASA 1131E	E.3B-143	for sale 16.9.88, to G-JUNG 23.11.88.
CASA 1131E	E.3B-153	ex '781-75' to Albacete and offered for sale 16.9.88.
CASA 1131E	E.3B-312	ex '781-21' for sale 16.9.88.
CASA 1131E	E.3B-340	ex '781-22' for sale 16.9.88.
CASA 1131E	E.3B-367	ex '781-33' for sale 16.9.88.
CASA 1131E	E.3B-369	ex '781-32' for sale 16.9.88, to G-BDPM 24.10.88.
CASA 1131E	E.3B-397	ex '781-1' for sale 16.9.88.
CASA 1131E	E.3B-425	ex '781-81' for sale 16.9.88.
CASA 1131E	E.3B-432	ex '781-35' for sale 16.9.88, to D-ENHD 20.10.88.
CASA 1131E	E.3B-444	ex '781-77' for sale 16.9.88.
CASA 1131E	E.3B-465	ex '781-14' for sale 16.9.88, to D-EFJR 22.11.88.
CASA 1131E	E.3B-466	ex '781-45' for sale 26.9.88.
CASA 1131E	E.3B-475	ex '781-60' for sale 26.9.88.
CASA 1131E	E.3B-484	ex '781-18' for sale 26.9.88.
CASA 1131E	E.3B-487	ex '781-12' for sale 26.9.88.
CASA 1131E	E.3B-489	ex '781-9' for sale 26.9.88.
CASA 1131E	E.3B-501	ex '781-30 for sale 26.9.88.
CASA 1131E	E.3B-508	ex '781-28' for sale 26.9.88.
CASA 1131E	E.3B-509	ex '781-4' for sale 26.9.88.
CASA 1131E	E.3B-520	ex '781-10' for sale 26.9.88.
CASA 1131E	E.3B-522	ex '781-36' for sale 26.9.88.
CASA 1131E	E.3B-528	ex '781-6' flown to WG 16-18.9.87 becoming D-ELEB.
CASA 1131E	E.3B-532	ex '781-13' for sale 26.9.88.
CASA 1131E	E.3B-538	ex '781-83' for sale 26.9.88.
CASA 1131E	E.3B-539	ex '781-16' for sale 26.9.88.
CASA 1131E	E.3B-540	ex '781-25' for sale 26.9.88.
CASA 1131E	E.3B-542	ex '781-51' for sale 30.9.88.
CASA 1131E	E.3B-544	ex '781-37' for sale 30.9.88.
CASA 1131E	E.3B-545	ex '781-24' for sale 30.9.88.
CASA 1131E	E.3B-548	ex '781-5' for sale 30.9.88.
CASA 1131E	E.3B-554	ex '781-31' for sale 30.9.88.
CASA 1131E	E.3B-556	ex '781-11' for sale 30.9.88.
CASA 1131E	E.3B-557	ex '781-59' for sale 30.9.88.
CASA 1131E	E.3B-573	ex '781-20' for sale 30.9.88.
CASA 1131E	E.3B-591	ex '781-2' for sale 30.9.88.
CASA 1131E	E.3B-601	ex '781-17' for sale 30.9.88.
CASA 1131E	E.3B-606	ex '781-73' flown to WG 16-18.9.87.
CASA 1131E	E.3B-610	ex '781-27' for sale 30.9.88.
CASA 1131E	E.3B-612	ex '781-65' for sale 30.9.88.
CASA 1131E	E.3B-615	ex '781-19' flown to WG 16-18.9.87 becoming D-EDNN.
CASA 1131E	E.3B-620	ex '781-26' for sale 30.9.88.
CASA 1131E	E.3B-626	ex '781-29' for sale 30.9.88.

The second batch (for sale 26.9.88) were sold to 'an Arab businessman' whilst the auction of the third batch on 30.9.88 did not go ahead.

GRAN CANARIA

At 'English Beach' on the South of the island an all white AISA I-11B Peque is displayed at the 'Jumbo' shopping centre (noted '88).

JEREZ/LA PARRA

Preserved on the base is former Esc.221 HU-16B(ASW) Albatross AN.1B-13/221-13 (ex 51-5300) (current '87). It has since been painted as "AN.1-13".

LANZAROTE
L1049G Super Constellation F-BHBI (c/n 4626) force landed at Arrecise airport here during the '60s whilst engaged on nefarious business including gun running to Africa. It lay derelict on the field as late as 1984 but was totally destroyed by arson soon after.

LAS BARDENAS
In 1979 it was reported that some thirty F-86F Sabres remained here in use as range targets (still current '88). They include C.5-100 (ex 55-3984, soc 25.3.72), C.5-172 (ex 55-4011, soc 31.12.71), and C.5-239 (ex 51-13454, soc 12.5.67).

On 29.10.86 a USAFE CH-53 airlifted 16 T-33As from storage at Zaragoza to the ranges here. Known serials comprise E.15-1 (ex 51-17537), E.15-12 (ex 52-9947), E.15-31 (ex 57-0645) and E.15-45 (ex 57-0659). By this time eleven Hispano Saetas were also in use here.

Some Spanish AF aircrew were 'interrogated' during 1988 and confirmed that a large number of aircraft are still present on the ranges.

LAS PALMAS/GANDO
Stored at Gando airport on the island of Gran Canaria is/was ex Spantax Douglas DC-7C EC-BSQ (noted '84).

Lying near the end of the runway is the wreck of ex Airtruck Falcon 20C EC-ECB (c/n 210) which ran off the runway here on 30.9.87.

Outside the flying club at Playa del Traja Dillo (across the road from the main airport) PA23 Apache 160 EC-ARH (c/n 23-958) was displayed on a concrete pyramid by '86 but had gone by 11.88. Noted at this time were derelict Cessna F150G EC-BGO (c/n 0105) and a sectioned Cessna 337.

LAS PALMAS/SAN AUGUSTIN
At the Aero Club is ex Spantax Douglas DC-7C EC-BDL (c/n 45230, ex I-DUVI) which arrived during 1976 and was standing engineless by 1984 painted up in garish colours advertising the wares of the Blaupunkt electronics firm.

LEON
The Spanish AF has a technical training school here at Virgen Del Camino aerodrome. On display around the base are the following aircraft.

CASA 2.111 (He 111)	-	possibly ex '271-67'
Hispano HA200D Saeta	C.10B-70	ex '462-70 Esc.462.
Lockheed T-33A	E.15-22	(ex 53-5740)
F-4C Phantom	C.12-01	(ex 64-0884) ex '121-01' Ala.12 (wfu 20.7.78).
F-86F Sabre	C.5-1	(ex 51-13194)
F-86F Sabre	C.5-107	(ex 55-3981, soc 11.10.72) ex '131-8' Esc.131.

Those listed below are in use as ground instructional airframes.

HA220 Super Saeta	A.10-110	ex '214-55' Esc.214.
Lockheed T-33A	E.15-49	(ex 51-9220) ex '41-3' Grupo 41.
Lockheed T-33A	E.15-59	(ex 53-5150) ex '41-12' Grupo 41.
T-6G Texan	E.16-70	ex '793-41' Esc.793.
T-6G Texan	E.16-89	ex '793-32' Esc.793.
T-6G Texan	E.16-107	ex '793-36' Esc.793.
T-6G Texan	E.16-119	ex '793-40' Esc.793.

Also in use here was F-86F Sabre C.5-2 (ex 51-13239) until it moved to Talavera La Real between '83 and '85.

LOGRONO/AGONCILLO
In 4.84 an unidentified AISA I-115 was seen to be preserved by the control tower at the airfield.

Some 4 to 5 kilometres from the city of Logrono on the N111 road to Soria, an AISA I-115 was displayed in a garden some years ago.

MADRID

The Escuela Tecnica Superior de Ingenieros Aeronauticos on the edge of the city has a number of instructional airframes. The school is thought to be within a military reservation, not too far from Cuatro Vientos.

HA200R-1 Saeta	E.14-30	ex '212-60' Esc.212 (noted '75-'81).
HA200D Saeta	A.10B-64	(noted '82-'88).
F-86F Sabre	C.5-235	(ex 51-13417, soc 1.1.69) ex Esc.201, marked "201-12" (starboard) and "201-42" (port) (noted '75-'81, to Mid Atlantic Air Museum, Pennsylvania).
SNJ-5 Texan	C.6-124	(ex Bu90974) ex '421-45' Esc.421 (noted '82-'88).
SNJ-5 Texan	C.6-128	(ex Bu43859) ex '421-45' Esc.421 (noted '82-'88).
WS55 Whirlwind Srs.2	ZD.1B-19	(c/n WA394) ex '803-1' Esc.803 (noted '75-'88.

The Spanish Army train their mechanics at the Instituto Politecnico del Ejercito using Agusta-Bell 47G-2A HE.7A-60/ET-059-110 and an unidentified AB204AS in olive drab colours.

MADRID/BARAJAS

Derelict around the airport in 4.83 were Beagle 206 Srs 2s EC-BES (c/n B027, ex G-ATSD), EC-BFR (c/n B035, ex G-ATVT), and EC-BJF (c/n B043, ex G-ATYX) with ex Aeroflete SA C-47B Dakota EC-ASP (c/n 26980, ex 43-49719, KK202, G-AMZB, OO-SBK). All were still current in 2.89, on the North side near the Iberia maintenance facility.

MAGALLUF/LA PORRASC

Ex TASSA Douglas DC-6 EC-AVA (c/n 43118) was derelict at Palma by 1970, TASSA having gone bankrupt in 1966. By 1975 it had arrived in Magaluf for use as a bar/night club and was still in use as such in an overall blue colour scheme in 7.83. By 2.89 it was repainted in a red/white scheme.

MALAGA

Arriving here in 1979 were ex Moroccan AF Beech 18s N9886A (c/n A932, ex CN-MAL) and N9887A (c/n BA6, ex CN-MAQ) and from the same source DH Dove 7As N9888A (c/n 04534, ex CN-MBA) and N9890A (c/n 04535, ex CN-MBB). All were still present in 1985 though by 5.87 Beech 18 N9887A had moved on and Dove N9890A had progressed to a car scrapyard on the road to Torremolinos. The Beech 18 and two Doves were still current in the yard in 2.89.

Other relics here in 1983 were the semi derelict Scheibe Falke D-KICC (gone by '88), the mortal remains of the unfortunate Spantax DC-10-30 EC-DEG (c/n 46962, overshot and burnt out here 13.9.82, wreck removed by '88) and derelict TB-25N Mitchell N86427 (ex 44-29121). Happily, the Museo del Aire appreciated the importance of the latter and by late '85 it had joined the museum at Cuatro Vientos.

Stored at the airport in 1986 were seven Pyramid Airlines C-47 Dakotas with a eighth arriving late '87. Six were still current during 2.89 minus engines and propellers.

Douglas C-47 Dakota	N330	(c/n 4479, ex 41-18417) Argas titles, to N514GL Global Equipment Leasing, current here as such 2.89, re-activated as EC-EJB.
Douglas C-47A Dakota	N219F	(c/n 9894, ex 42-24032, F-BCYS, ER-AAN, OD-AAN) here since 5.85 at least, current 2.89.
Douglas C-47B Dakota	N925	(c/n 20016, ex 43-15550) here since 5.85 at least, to N512GL Global Equipment Leasing (current 11.88).
Douglas C-47A Dakota	N486F	(c/n 20214, ex 43-15748) arrived 9.87, current 2.89.
Douglas C-47B Dakota	N3161Q	(c/n 15271/26716, ex 43-48915) here since 5.85 at least, to N513GL, still here as such 2.89.
Douglas C-47B Dakota	N3176Q	(c/n 32814, ex 44-76482) to N519GL, returned to active service by 6.88, later to EC-EIS.
Douglas C-47B Dakota	N893	(c/n 16304/33052, ex 44-76720) to N515GL, current as such 2.89.
Douglas C-47B Dakota	N894	(c/n 16455/33203, ex 44-76871) to N516GL, current as such 2.89.

MARIN

The Spanish Navy mechanics school should still have Agusta-Bell AB204AS Z.8-1/003-1 on display.

MERIDA

Some 66 kilometres from Badajoz on the E4NV road towards Madrid (near a Romanian circus) a scrapyard has a heavily doctored light aircraft thought to be a Stinson 108 or a Cherokee.

MORON DE LA FRONTERA

Guarding the gate here is F86F Sabre C.5-231/151-21 (ex 52-5307, soc 4.3.67, ex Esc.151) mounted in flying attitude on a plinth (noted '77-'88). Since 1981 it has shared this task with HA200B Saeta A.10B-52/214-52 (ex Esc.214, current '88).

Inside the Maintenance Hangar on the base are two Northrop (CASA built) SF-5s which are used as a spares source for the active aircraft with Ala.21. They are SF-5A A.9-037 which was written off in a crash-landing at Moron in 1.84 and SRF-5A CR.9-063/211-63 (ex Esc.211) whose flying days ended in a mid-air collision on 18.5.78.

MOTRIL

A radar unit (67 kilometres South of Granada) displays HA200D Saeta A10B-90/"EVA9-1" at the domestic site.

OCANA

Dumped at this glider airfield during '87 was the fuselage of Dornier Do 27A-1 U.9-58/EC-CFL (c/n 120, ex WGAF 5514) which was previously used by the gliding school here. It was not found on a visit in 9.88.

OVIEDO

The wreck of PZL104 Wilga 35 EC-CVU (c/n 86278) was here in 3.83, another victim of the hazardous crop-dusting profession.

ONTUR

Dumped here during 3.85 were AISA I-11Bs EC-BKF, EC-BPN, EC-BTL and EC-BUB. Aircraft wearing these registrations have since been seen flying and it is believed that rather a lot of tail, wing and fuselage swopping has been going on.

PALMA DE MALLORCA/SON SAN JUAN

Stored on the new runway here in 4.83 were ex TAE Douglas DC-8-32s EC-CCN (c/n 45569) and EC-CDC together with seven former Spantax CV990 Coronados. The Spantax Coronado fleet is stored here, mostly in a compound adjacent to Terminal B.

CV990 Coronado	EC-BJC	(c/n 30-10-22, ex N5610) wfu by 3.82, current 2.89.
CV990 Coronado	EC-BJD	(c/n 30-10-23, ex N5611) wfu by 5.83, current 2.89.
CV990 Coronado	EC-BQA	(c/n 30-10-36)
CV990 Coronado	EC-BQQ	(c/n 30-10-34) wfu by 5.87, current on Spantax apron 2.89.
CV990 Coronado	EC-BTE	(c/n 30-10-21, ex N5609) wfu 30.10.81, current 2.89.
CV990 Coronado	EC-BXI	(c/n 30-10-35, ex N5603, OD-AFI, N5603) wfu 29.6.81, current 2.89.
CV990 Coronado	EC-BZO	(c/n 30-10-30, ex N5618, OD-AFG, N6843) noted 2.89.
CV990 Coronado	EC-BZP	(c/n 30-10-18) wfu by 5.87, current 2.89.
CV990 Coronado	EC-CNF	(c/n 30-10-08, ex SE-DAY, HB-ICG) wfu by 5.83.
CV990 Coronado	EC-CNG	(c/n 30-10-07, ex N8497H, HB-ICA) wfu by 6.82, current 2.89.
CV990 Coronado	EC-CNH	(c/n 30-10-17, ex (OY-KVA), SE-DAZ, HS-TGE, SE-DAZ, HB-ICH) wfu by 10.84.
CV990 Coronado	EC-CNJ	(c/n 30-10-14, ex HB-ICE) wfu '81, current 2.89.

Incidentally, the new runway was not usable as such due to sub-standard concrete but nevertheless makes an excellent parking area for tired airliners.

Aero Commander 680T EC-DSA (c/n 1564-20, ex N1199Z, I-ARBO) was lying wfu in the maintenance area to the West of Terminal A by 2.89 minus engines and rudder.

HU-16B Albatross AD.1B-13 (ex 51-7194) can be found near the threshold of runway 24R (still current 2.89).

The field is a former F-86 base and ironically is the only one without a preserved Sabre. This deficiency is expected to be remedied soon.

PLASENCIA

In 5.84 the 'Avion Restaurant' some 17 kms North of here on the N630 had CASA 352L (Ju 52) T.2B-209/742-1 (ex Esc.742) on the roof as an added attraction. By 5.88 the aircraft had gone to West Germany (Sinsheim?).

PLAYA DE ARO/PLATJO D'ARO

Situated 40 kilometres South East of Gerona, an unidentified pink Texan is displayed here as a perfume advert. It was impounded at Barcelona during the sixties after involvement in drug running.

PLAYA DEL PUIG

Ex Trabajos Aereos y Enlaces Douglas DC-7C EC-BEN (c/n 45127) was still here during 1981 serving as the 'Discoteca D-C7' (sic). I have no more recent reports.

PUERTO CHRISTO (MALLORCA)

Ex Trans-Europa Douglas DC-4 EC-BDK (c/n 10373, ex C-54A 42-72268, NI-542, PK-DSC, PH-TSC, F-BELP, EC-WDK, EC-BDK) was by 1976 in use as a bar/restaurant called the 'Bar-D-3'. The restaurant had closed by 1983 but the DC-4 was reportedly still current late in '85 under new management as the 'Sky Club Discoteca'. An alternative source states the aircraft was destroyed by fire during 9.83 when a man boarded the aircraft and set himself alight. I suspect that this is the correct version.

REUS

On the main gate of a military base here is an AISA I-115 marked only with its serial prefix E.9-. On the fuselage it wears the legend "Base - Reus" astride the roundel.

ROTA

Displayed on the base is a Bolkow Helitrainer simulator as used by the helicopter school at Cuatro Vientos until 1966.

SH-3D Sea King Z.9A-4/005-4 of Esc.005 sustained damage here on 14.4.76 and was subsequently withdrawn from use. Does it still survive?

AH-1G Cobra Z.14-7/007-7 (c/n 21126, ex 72-21463) of Esc.007 was withdrawn from use following an accident on 4.5.80 and cannibalised to keep the rest of the fleet airworthy. By 5.85, AH-1Gs HA.14-1/01-701 (c/n 21050, ex 71-15090), HA.14-2/01-702 (c/n 21051, ex 71-15091) and HA.14-8/01-708 (c/n 21127, ex 72-21464) were all in use as ground instructional airframes with Esc.006. Of these, HA.14-1 had progressed to the Mississippi AVCRAD at Gulfport-Biloxi Regional Airport by 6.88 (four AH-1G were sold back to the US Army in 1977 (HA.14-1/2/5 plus one) with a fifth offered for sale later).

SALAMANCA

On the N620, about a kilometre North of the town, PA28 Cherokee EC-CBZ is displayed on a pole at a car dismantler's yard (noted 2.89).

Near the football stadium on the N630 road towards Zamora the former Salamanca/Matacan gate guard C-47A Dakota, T.3-28/744-28 (ex 42-24052), is now on display (current 5.88). It was sold to the owner of a car dismantler's yard at an auction on 3.11.80 but obviously took a long time to leave the base.

SALAMANCA/MATACAN

SNJ-5 Texan C.6-122/793-104 (ex Bu84893) was here by 1979 and due for preservation. It was noted on the gate here with the code "<u>742</u>-104" in 5.87 and was still current in '88.

Already being looked after here was C-47A Dakota T.3-28/744-28 (ex 42-24052) which retired from the based Esc.744 when replaced by the Aviocar (noted '78-'87). This machine was removed during '87 (see under 'Salamanca' above).

By 5.88 Lockheed T-33A E.15-20/41-6 (ex 53-5487, with tail of E.15-15/41-43) had arrived from storage at Zaragoza and was hangared in two sections. The aircraft will eventually be displayed on the gate.

SANCHIDRIAN (WEST)

Noted here in 5.87 were three ex Spanish AF AISA I-115s which appeared to have ground to a standstill in the process of being civilianised. They comprised E.9-156 (in civil colours, but not wearing a registration), E.9-143 (still in military scheme with Academia General del Aire badge) and E.9-166 (civil colours but military serial). All were still current 9.88.

SAN JAVIER

Home of the Spanish AF's Academia General del Aire (Air Academy) CASA 1131L (licence-built Jungmann) E.3B-75/"791-1" (in spurious Esc.791 markings) is preserved on a plinth outside the HQ building (noted '78-'88). In one of the hangars by 5.80 (and still there 9.88) was T-6G Texan E.16-199/793-11 (ex Esc.793).

The Esc.791 Beech T-34A Mentor fleet was withdrawn from use during 1988 and placed in open storage pending disposal, having been superceded by the T-35 Tamiz. It may still be useful to list these though all had disappeared by 3.89 having been moved to Albacete/Los Llanos for storage and disposal.

T-34A Mentor	E.17-03	ex '791-03'	T-34A Mentor	E.17-04	ex '791-04'
T-34A Mentor	E.17-05	ex '791-05	T-34A Mentor	E.17-06	ex '791-06'
T-34A Mentor	E.17-07	ex '791-07'	T-34A Mentor	E.17-09	ex '791-09'
T-34A Mentor	E.17-11	ex '791-11'	T-34A Mentor	E.17-12	ex '791-12'
T-34A Mentor	E.17-15	ex '791-15'	T-34A Mentor	E.17-16	ex '791-16'
T-34A Mentor	E.17-17	ex '791-17'	T-34A Mentor	E.17-18	ex '791-18'
T-34A Mentor	E.17-20	ex '791-20'	T-34A Mentor	E.17-21	ex '791-21'
T-34A Mentor	E.17-22	ex '791-22'	T-34A Mentor	E.17-23	ex '791-23'
T-34A Mentor	E.17-24	ex '791-24'	T-34A Mentor	E.17-25	ex '791-25'

SAN MARTIN DE LA VEGA

Situated some 20 kilometres South East of Madrid, this place seems to be the car scrapping centre for Madrid with dozens of yards. Over the years a number of aircraft have been recorded here including a WS55 Whirlwind (see Benidorm), two AISA I-115s, three Stinson 108-3s and numerous aero engines.

SAN VICENTE DE LA BARQUERA

An Aerotecnica AC-12 was noted in a car scrapyard here (about 35 kilometres West of Santander) during 1985.

SANTA AMALIA

About 25 kilometres from Merida, off the E4NV to Madrid, a Stinson 108-3 was due to be erected on a pole during 1987.

SANTANDER/DE PARAYAS

AT-6D Texan C.6-165/421-54 (ex Bu112200, ex Esc.421) arrived here in 1983 for preservation in front of the control tower (current '88).

SEVILLA

Some 5 kilometres out of the city on the N334 towards Malaga AISA I-115 EC-CSG is on display. It is painted up to advertise 'Foycar/Aviotrans'.

SEVILLA/SAN PABLO

Near the freight area on the civil side, CASA 207 Azors T.7-5/403-02 (ex Esc.403), T.7-8/351-8 and T.7-10/351-10 (both ex Esc.351) were all dumped here by 4.84 and were still current in 12.87. By 5.88 T.7-5 and T.7-8 were in a compound by the road with T.7-10 remaining on the airfield. Ex Spanish AF Convair 440 ECT-024 has been sitting by the hangars here since 1980. All these were current in 2.89.

For the record, an ex Invicta DC-4 was converted to the 'Aerolandia' coffee bar here by 1977. It is no longer current.

SEVILLA/TABLADA

With the withdrawal of the Albatross fleet on 22.12.78, HU-16Bs AN.1A-2/221-2, AN.1A-5/221-5, AN.1B-9/221-9, AN.1B-10/221-10, AN.1B-11/221-11, AN.1B-12/221-12 (all ex Esc.221) were in a dismantled state here by 1980 with HU-16As AD.1-7, AD.1B-10 and AD.1B-12 yet to be attacked.

Stored here in 4.84 were CASA 207 Azors T.7-6/405-15 and T.7-16/405-16 (ex Esc.405). The former had moved to the museum at Cuatro Vientos by 5.87 and the latter remained derelict here in 4.89.

Stored in one of the Esc.407 hangars in 5.87 were HA220 Super Saetas A.10C-91/214-91 and A.10C-111/214-111 (both ex Esc.214). They were still present in 5.88 in a dismantled state and wearing their codes only, no serials. A thorough visit during 3.89 saw no sign of them so they have perhaps moved on.

All CASA 127 (Do 27) reworks are carried out here and several were noted in long term storage during 3.89. Details of which were stored and which were in work are not available but some 25 aircraft were present.

On the dump in 12.87 was an unidentified Bell 47. In 5.87 the fuselage of CASA 127 (Do 27) U.9-47 was reported next to the Ala.52 hangar. It was still to be seen in 12.87 but had gone by 5.88 on which occasion the fuselage of another CASA 127 (coded '781-..' ex Esc.781) was noted in a scrap compound. By 6.88 the wreck of Bonanza F33C E.24A-4/421-44 (ex Esc.421, w/o '78) was here.

The base also hosts a small museum housing the following aircraft.

HA1112M-1L Buchon	C.4K-162	(noted '77-'87) this machine was dumped under a tree in 5.88 awaiting removal to Cuatro Vientos for restoration for the Museo del Aire.
CASA 2.111B (He 111)	"B.2I-25"	(really B.2I-103) (noted outside '77-'89).
HA200 Saeta	E.14A-9	(noted outside '85-'89).

SON BONET (MAJORCA)

At the light aviation field for Palma, AISA I-115s EC-CRA (ex E.9-189) and EC-CQY (ex E.9-150) were both derelict in 8.83 whilst AISA I-11B Peque EC-BUM (ex L.8C-109) was in a dismantled state here in 8.84 and was still current in a hangar during 10.87.

SOTILLO DE LA ADRADA

Ex New York ANG C-97G Stratocruiser 53-0241 (delivered to Albacete as a spares source) moved here when it reached the end of its usefulness. It served as a discotheque until 2.2.85 when it was unfortunately burnt out. Nothing now remains.

TALAVERA DE LA REINA

About 100 kilometres west of Madrid on the E4NV road, a Stinson 108-3 is displayed on a pole. It is used as an eye-catcher and is marked 'Harinera Talaverana'.

TALAVERA LA REAL

Lockheed T-33A E.15-60/41-10 (ex 53-5425, ex Grupo 41) was preserved on the base by 1979. The aircraft has received a new paint job as "E.15-1/73-1" in honour of the resident Ala.73 (now equipped with the F-5) and was still current in 11.88.

F-86F Sabre C.5-2 (ex 51-13239) was in store here by 10.85 for preservation and had taken up its allotted position on the base by 6.87 painted as "C.5-199/732-1" (current 11.88).

TARANCON

Some 80 kms South East of Madrid on the NIII/E101, Boeing KC-97L TK.1-2/123-02 (ex 53-0225, ex Esc.123/Ala.12) lingered here as an attraction at a cafe. The machine had been removed by 1987 and reappeared in 1988 alongside the A7 motorway North West of Barcelona.

TORREJON

Preserved on the Spanish AF (North East) side of the base, in the Ala.12 area, is F-86F Sabre C.5-82/6-082 (ex 55-3966, soc 22.12.71, noted '78-'89) whilst CASA 352L (Ju 52) T.2B-246/792-20 (ex Esc.792) is preserved behind one of the 401 TFW hangars near the AFJROTC buildings. An unidentified T-33A in camouflage colours had appeared near the Ala.12 hangars by 2.89 and has probably arrived from the dump at Zaragoza for battle damage repair training or preservation here.

The Spanish AF's thirty two F-4C Phantoms will have been withdrawn from service with Ala.12 and replaced with the EF-18 by the time this is read. Their fate is uncertain. C.12-01 went to Leon as an instructional airframe some time ago whilst a second airframe is believed to have departed here beneath a Chinook during 1988.

In use for bdr training with the 401st TFW are the following airframes (both the 'chiefs with sharks teeth markings).

F-105 Thunderchief	..-....	"TJ" ex MASDC (noted '87-'89).
F-105G Thunderchief	63-8265	"TJ" ex 128 TFS, Georgia ANG & MASDC (noted '87-'89).
F-4C Phantom	63-7667	ex Arkansas ANG (arr by 5.87, current 11.89).

An ex AdlA T-bird has been residing on the dump on the West side of the field in recent years.

Lockheed T-33A	..-....	ex AdlA, silver c/s coded 'TJ' (noted '87-'89).

Another T-33A (E.15-33/41-31) was in a scrap compound here during 1987 and has since moved to Vicalvaro (qv).

MBB105 HU.15-85/09-113 is reportedly in use by the Civil Guard for ground instruction near the INTA hangars.

Looking back, KC-97L Stratocruiser TK.1-2/123-02 (ex 53-0225) was stored here until 1983 when it moved to Tarancon.

TORREMOLINOS

In 'Pipers' discotheque in Carratera de Cadiz (a street name) is a low wing monoplane (thought to be an AISA I-115) hanging from the ceiling. Further details would be welcome.

VALENCIA

A couple of kilometres from Manises air base in the direction of the city centre is a car breakers yard which has an Aerotecnica AC12 positioned as an 'eye-catcher' in a home grown colour scheme. It was still current in 11.88.

VALENCIA/MANISES

Preserved on the military side of the field are F-86F Sabre C.5-5/1-005 (ex 51-13125, soc 10.4.62) and Mirage IIIEE C.11-7/11-7 (both noted 9.88). The Mirage IIIEE was written off after over-running the runway here on 2.5.77.

On the civil side, ex Aerotransporte de Espana Fairchild F-27 EC-CPO (ex N90713) has been parked by the terminal for several years (current '88).

Dumped here adjacent to the Aero Club area is an ex Spanish AF T-34A Mentor (noted 11.88).

VALLADOLID

A scrapyard adjacent to the Santa Elvira garage between kilometre 194 and kilometre 195 on the N601 (to Villanubla air base) has a Stinson 108 precariously balanced on a pylon. One wing has succumbed to the ravages of time and hangs limply down at a rakish angle to the fuselage. This gives some idea as to how long this particular relic has been in position. This anonymous airframe has been here since at least 1979 and was still current in 11.88.

VICALVARO

Behind some derelict houses on the road to Coslada (South of Torrejon) a T-33A can be found. It was first noted in 5.88 and 9.88 it was mounted on three poles in front of the houses. Although daubed up in a spurious colour scheme, the aircraft comprises the front half of E.15-33/41-31 (ex 57-0647, ex Grupo 41) mated to the rear fuselage and tail of E.15-40/41-27, both from storage at Zaragoza. This machine was held at Torrejon prior to moving here.

Another long-standing relic here is a Stinson 108-3 in the playground of the 'La Jungla' restaurant. Surrounded by trees and very difficult to find, it is painted up in a 'Pepsi' colour scheme.

VILLANUBLA

Noted at the show here in 5.83 were preserved SNJ-5 Texan C.6-152/33-152 (ex Bu90992) and HA200B A.10B-53/203-53. They have since been placed on permanent display on a parade ground just inside the base from the main gate (current 11.88).

Withdrawn from use here by 2.86 were DHC-4 Cariboux T.9-23 (ex '371-03'), T.9-25 (ex '371-05') and T.9-28 (ex '371-08') all ex Ala.37. They soon moved on to Cuatro Vientos for disposal with T.9-25 joining the museum and the other two going to Newcal (see also Cuatro Vientos).

By 9.88 C-7A Caribou T.9-23 (ex '371-03' Esc.371) had joined the Texan and Saeta preserved on the parade ground.

VILLANUEVA Y LA GELTRU

The Sector Museo del Aire Escuela Ocupacional Aeronautica (Catalonia branch of the Spanish AF museum) is situated next to the C246 road between Barcelona and Valls. It was established on 27.6.81 and by 1987 they possessed five airframes.

Aerotechnica AC12	Z.2-11	ex '75-11'
CASA 1131E	-	
HA220B Saeta	A.10B-45	
F-86F Sabre	C.5-71	(ex 52-4718, soc 12.71) ex '102-8', ex Cuatro Vientos.
T-6G Texan	E.16-97	ex '793-2' Esc.793.

Early in 1989 they received from Cuatro Vientos a T-33A comrising the fuselage og E.15-48/41-16 (ex 57-0662) with the tail of E.15-19/41-38. They may be expecting another T-6, Agusta-Bell 47G-3B HE.7B-21 and 47J-3B1 HD.11-2.

VILLANUEVA DEL PARDILLO

Some 25 kilometres North West of Madrid can be found a C-47 and C-54 which have been converted by a Spanish family to form a holiday home. Unfortunately no further details are available but the aircraft were current during 1987. Further investigation required!

VITORIA

In 10.87 the ruined hangars at the old airfield (now replaced by Foronda airport) contained the fuselages of AISA I-115 EC-CTZ (ex E9-116, never converted) and AISA I-11B Peque EC-BTG.

ZARAGOZA

The USAF area here houses F-86F Sabre C.5-143 (ex 55-3971, soc 2.6.72, ex '131-11' Esc.131, noted on a plinth '78-'88). During 1987 it was repainted as "25406/FU-406" in 512 FIS/406 FIW markings. A second F-86F Sabre can be found on the Spanish side of the base in the form of C.5-70/"2-41" (ex 52-4683, soc 31.12.72) (noted 9.87). Note that there has been a lot of confusion as to whether one or two Sabres are preserved here, however, the compiler has received photographs of two aircraft, both taken on the same day.

Lockheed T-33A E.15-50/41-4 (ex 52-9871, ex Grupo 41) is preserved in the Ala.15 area (noted '85-'88).

On the USAFE side of the base, ex AdLA T-33A 53103 (ex 55-3103, ex '314-VP' GE.314) is in use for battle damage repair training together with an F-105 Thunderchief (both noted '87). The T-33A was still current in 7.88 though positioned at the West end of the base for possible fire training. By this time an F-4C Phantom had joined the F-105. All were current in 11.88.

DH Dove 1 G-ARBH (c/n 04196) has been a feature of the landscape here for many years. Her CofA expired on 5.8.75 and the registration was cancelled on 30.5.84. The machine was still derelict here in 11.88. Another old timer is the neglected ex Aertransporte de Espana C-47B Dakota EC-CPO (c/n 34361, ex 45-1091, N86442, T.3-50) (noted '78-'88).

By 1984 the bulk of the Grupo 41 T-bird fleet had been withdrawn from use and were lying in open storage on the field. Most have since been disposed of and it is known that many were moved to the ranges at Las Bardenas for target use (sixteen T-birds were airlifted there by CH-53 on 29.10.86). Confirmed details are listed below. It should be noted that great care should be taken when identifying retired Spanish T-birds since most recipients appear to have collected a front fuselage, rear fuselage and a set of wings from here giving little thought to which aeroplane they came from. Most preserved T-birds in Spain are composite airframes as a result.

Lockheed T-33A	E.15-1	(ex 51-17537) ex '41-42' (noted 4.84, to Las Bardenas ranges 29.10.86).
Lockheed T-33A	E.15-2	(ex 51-17538) ex '41-44' (noted 4.84-4.86).
Lockheed T-33A	E.15-3	(ex 51-17540) ex '41-47' (noted 4.84).
Lockheed T-33A	E.15-4	(ex 51-17543) ex '41-37' (noted 4.84-4.86).
Lockheed T-33A	E.15-6	(ex 51-17554) ex '41-36' (noted 4.84-4.86).
Lockheed T-33A	E.15-7	(ex 52-9934) ex '41-49' (noted 4.84).
Lockheed T-33A	E.15-8	(ex 52-9940) ex '41-50' (noted 4.84).
Lockheed T-33A	E.15-10	(ex 52-9943) ex '41-53' (noted '83-4.84).
Lockheed T-33A	E.15-11	(ex 52-9946) ex '41-2' (noted 4.84-4.86).
Lockheed T-33A	E.15-12	(ex 52-9947) ex '41-35' (noted '83, to Las Bardenas ranges 29.10.86).
Lockheed T-33A	E.15-13	(ex 53-5380) ex '41-7' (noted 4.84-4.86) to Cuatro Vientos (base) by 11.88.
Lockheed T-33A	E.15-15	(ex 53-5382) ex '41-43' (noted 4.84-4.86, tail to Salamanca/Matacan).
Lockheed T-33A	E.15-16	(ex 53-5166) ex '41-52' (noted 4.84).
Lockheed T-33A	E.15-17	(ex 53-5165) ex '41-14' (noted 4.84-4.86) still derelict here 11.88.
Lockheed T-33A	E.15-18	(ex 53-5164) ex '41-1' (noted 4.84).
Lockheed T-33A	E.15-19	(ex 53-5484) ex '41-38' (noted 4.84-4.86, rear fuselage to Cuatro Vientos museum by 2.89 with front of E.15-48).
Lockheed T-33A	E.15-20	(ex 53-5487) ex '41-6' (noted '83-4.86, fuselage to Salamanca/Matacan).
Lockheed T-33A	E.15-21	(ex 53-5555) ex '41-11' (noted 4.84-6.87).
Lockheed T-33A	E.15-24	(ex 53-5762) ex '41-33' (noted 4.84-4.86).
Lockheed T-33A	E.15-26	(ex 53-5759) ex '41-29' (noted 5.85-4.86 on dump).
Lockheed T-33A	E.15-27	(ex 54-1544) ex '41-39' (noted 4.84-4.86, still derelict here 11.88).
Lockheed T-33A	E.15-28	(ex 54-1545) ex '41-41' (noted 4.84-4.86).
Lockheed T-33A	E.15-29	(ex 54-1547) ex '41-34' (noted 4.84-4.86).
Lockheed T-33A	E.15-30	(ex 54-1546) ex '41-40' (noted 4.84-6.87, current on scrap heap 11.88).
Lockheed T-33A	E.15-31	(ex 57-0645) ex '41-20' (noted '84, to Las Bardenas ranges 29.10.86).
Lockheed T-33A	E.15-32	(ex 57-0646) ex '41-19' (noted 4.84-4.86).
Lockheed T-33A	E.15-33	(ex 57-0647) ex '41-31' (noted '83, fuselage to Vicalvaro).
Lockheed T-33A	E.15-35	(ex 57-0649) ex '41-17' (noted 4.84-4.86).
Lockheed T-33A	E.15-37	(ex 57-0651) ex '41-21' (noted 4.84-4.86).
Lockheed T-33A	E.15-38	(ex 57-0652) ex '41-26' (noted on flight line 5.85) to Cuatro Vientos (museum) by 5.88.
Lockheed T-33A	E.15-40	(ex 57-0654) ex '41-27' (noted on dump 4.86, rear fuselage to Vicalvaro).
Lockheed T-33A	E.15-41	(ex 57-0655) ex '41-23' (noted 4.86-6.87, current on scrap heap 11.88).

Lockheed T-33A	E.15-42	(ex 57-0656) ex '41-32' (noted 4.84).
Lockheed T-33A	E.15-43	(ex 57-0657) ex '41-15' (noted 4.86-6.87, current on the scrap heap 11.88).
Lockheed T-33A	E.15-44	(ex 57-0658) ex '41-28' (noted on dump 4.86).
Lockheed T-33A	E.15-45	(ex 57-0659) ex '41-22' (noted 4.84, to Las Bardenas ranges 29.10.86).
Lockheed T-33A	E.15-47	(ex 57-0661) ex '41-18' (noted 4.84-4.86).
Lockheed T-33A	E.15-48	(ex 57-0662) ex '41-16' (noted on flight line 5.85-5.87, on scrap heap 11.88, front fuselage to Cuatro-Vientos by 2.89 with tail of E.15-19).
Lockheed T-33A	E.15-49	(ex 51-9220) ex '41-3' (noted 4.84, to Leon technical school).
Lockheed T-33A	E.15-50	(ex 52-9871) ex '41-4' preserved on base by '85.
Lockheed T-33A	E.15-52	(ex 53-4993) ex '41-5' (noted 4.84).
Lockheed T-33A	E.15-54	(ex 53-5053) ex '41-46' (noted 4.84-4.86).
Lockheed T-33A	E.15-57	(ex 53-5133) ex '41-51' (noted on dump 5.85-4.86).
Lockheed T-33A	E.15-58	(ex 53-5145) ex '41-48' (noted 4.84-4.86).
Lockheed T-33A	E.15-59	(ex 53-5150) ex '41-12' (noted 4.84, to Leon technical school).

SWEDEN

This sprawling country has much to offer the "W&R" enthusiast, albeit mostly in the Southern half of the country. There are many museums around the country displaying a wide range of hardware and a thriving preservation movement exists. Not surprisingly, home produced SAAB products abound.

Most Swedish AF bases are liberally endowed with redundant SAAB fighters for use in various training exercises of a more or less destructive nature. The listings here rely upon 'enthusiast' information rather than official records and are necessarily incomplete. Our Swedish correspondent advises that Satenas alone has consumed the best part of 100 airframes since 1980!

AMAL

The fuselage of Thulin A (a Bleriot XI copy) c/n 18(?) came here (about 180 kms North of Goteborg) for eventual restoration to flying condition by Mikael Carlsson.

ANGELHOLM

Preserved around the base (home of the Draken equipped F 10) in 6.84 were J 29F Tunnans 29248/E (red) ex F 10 (also noted 6.85 displayed by fire section but had gone by 3.86) and 29589/59/F 10 (preserved in a hangar 9.85, on display by 8.88 following restoration by Roy Frojdh). This machine is on the charge of the Flygvapenmuseum.

A 1944 vintage FFVS J 22A 22185/K (red) ex F 10 is under restoration here, also part of the Flygvapenmuseum collection.

Noted on various dumps around the field in recent years have been the following.

AD-4W Skyraider	SE-EBK	(c/n 7946, ex 126867, WV181, G-31-12) ex Svenska Flygjanst (noted '84, to UK 10.85 becoming G-BMFC).
AD-4W Skyraider	SE-EBM	(c/n 7850, ex 127949, WT951, G-31-2) ex Svenska Flygjanst (noted '84, to UK 10.85 becoming G-BMFB).
J 35A Draken	35081	ex '44' F 16 (scrap compound '85-'86).
J 35B Draken	35...	ex '32' F 10 (dumped '86).
J 35B Draken	35248	ex '63' F 10 (stored '84-'86).
J 35B Draken	35264	ex '68' F 10 (stored '84-'86).
J 35D Draken	35354	ex '54' F 4 (stored '85-'86).
J 35D Draken	35391	ex '66' F 4 (stored '85-'86).
J 35D Draken	35...	ex '37' F 21 (stored '86).
J 35D Draken	35...	ex '41' F 21 (stored '86).
J 35D Draken	35...	ex '??' F 4 (stored '86).
J 35D Draken	35...	ex '??' F 4 (stored '86).
S 35E Draken	35918	ex '18' F 11 (scrap compound '84-'86).
S 35E Draken	35948	ex '48(?)' F 11 (scrap compound '86).
J 35F Draken	35431	ex '67' F 16 (scrap compound '85-'86 - rear fuse & fin).
J 35F Draken	35472	ex '21' F 10 (by fire station '85-'88, for rescue training).
J 35F Draken	35513	ex '11' F 18 & Uppsala dump (dumped '87-'88).
J 35 Draken	35...	ex '??' finless (scrap compound '84-'85).

In use for ground instructional purposes is J 35F Draken 35528.

BARKABY

The wreck of Hkp 6B (AB206A Jetranger) 06052 (c/n 8219) was noted here in 10.80, however the helicopter was apparently airworthy again by 1988. In a hangar here in 8.88 was the fuselage of Sk 50 Safir 50057/75 (ex F 21, crashed at Lulea 9.12.74).

In 6.88 the wrecked fuselage of Beagle Pup 2 SE-FOG (c/n 045, crashed at Bromma 13.12.79) was in store here.

ENKOPING

'Rumour has it' that an ex Dutch Navy Lockheed 12 can still be found here (some 50 kms North West of Stockholm).

ESKILSTUNA

Stored in the roof in 6.88 were gliders SE-SHD, and SE-SHE whilst SZD-30 Pirat SE-TGM (c/n W400) was at ground level.

FALKOPING

Nils-Erik Sundblad's Silver Hill car museum here (also known as Klippan and situated about 20 kms South East of Angelholm) should have Caudron Pelican SE-AGA (c/n 7338/45, ex F-AOYC) on display, however the aircraft was to be found at Norrkoping in 6.88.

The Alleberg Segelflygmuseum (Alleberg Gliding Museum, South East of Falkoping off the N47) has the following.

DH82 Tiger Moth	SE-ALM	(c/n 172, ex RNorAF 163)
DH82 Tiger Moth	SE-ATI	(c/n 3113, ex SE-ADF, RSwedAF 5568, later 568)
DFS 108-14 Schulgleiter	138	
DFS 108-30 Kranich	8215	(c/n 076)
DFS 108-30 Kranich	SE-SPK	(c/n 077, ex RSwedAF 8216) on loan from Kontaktgruppen.
DFS 108-70 Olympia	SE-SAE	(c/n 685)
DFS 108-70 Olympia	SE-SDL	(c/n 02) on loan from Flygvapenmuseum.
DFS Weihe	SE-SND	(c/n 219) on loan from Luftfartsmuseet, Arlanda.
Kockum Baby Falk	SE-SGO	(c/n 5)
Scheibe L-Spatz 55	SE-TMY	(c/n E-2)
Schneider ESG-31	SE-ADP	(c/n 84)
Grunau Baby IIB	SE-SAZ	(c/n 001) Schneider-built DFS 108-49.
Schleicher Anfanger II	54	(c/n 1)
S-L Z-12 Zogling	SE-023	on loan from Kontaktgruppen.

GILLSTAD/LIDKOPING

Focke-Wulf Fw 44J Stieglitz SE-BRZ (c/n 1904) is preserved at the Gillstad Bilmuseum (15 kms South West of Lidkoping).

GOTEBORG

The Goteborgs Maritima Centrum (Gothenburg Maritime Museum) displays Sud Alouette II (Hkp 2) 02034 (c/n 1175) ex '2/34' with the Swedish Navy.

The Industrimuseet possesses Albatros B II SE-ACR and an unidentified DFS 108-14 Schulgleiter SG-38.

The Goteborgs Veteranflygsallskap keep their preserved Tiger Moth SE-CHH (c/n 86323, ex NL873, G-ANSH) in the area.

GOTEBORG/ALINGSAS

Gotaverken GV 38 (a 1939 vintage licence built Rearwin 9000 Sportster) SE-AHU (c/n 12) is under restoration at the airfield.

GOTEBORG/SAVE

The airport here (formerly the home of F 9 as an RSwedAF base) has J 35F 35550 in exhibition condition. It belongs to F 10.

GRANNA

On the roof of a motorway service station on the E4 about 40 kms North of Jonkoping is Beech D95A Travel Air SE-EES (c/n TD.539) is displayed (noted '88)

HALMSTAD

Halmstad is the home of the Swedish AF's technical training school (F 14).

Instructional airframes in recent use have included the following.

J 35B Draken	35206	ex '46' F 13 (crash rescue training '84-'88).
J 35B Draken	35253	ex '09' F 10 (noted '84-'88, bdr training airframe).
J 35D Draken	35366	ex '34' F 21 (noted '88, bdr training airframe, Austrian AF marks).
J 35F Draken	35448	ex '43' F 10 (noted '84 -'85, to go to FinnAF).
J 35F Draken	35483	ex '31' F 10 (noted '84-'85, to go to FinnAF).
J 35F Draken	35502	ex '43' F 13 (noted '84-'85, reported as '34' in '85.
J 35F Draken	35512	ex '24' F 13 (noted '84-'85).
J 35F Draken	35521	ex '42' F 13 (noted '84-'85).
J 35F Draken	35545	ex '10' F 1 (noted '84-'85).
J 35F Draken	35546	ex '46' F 1 (noted '84-'85).
J 35F Draken	35609	ex '18' F 17 (noted '84-'88 with skin part removed) .
AJ 37 Viggen	37-3	ex '53', prototype (noted '85-'88, with skin partly removed).
JA 37 Viggen	37323	ex '63' F 13 (noted '85).

The base houses a large number of aircraft on the fire dump.

Pembroke C.52 (Tp 83)	83015	ex '85' F 18 (or F8?) (noted '84-'85).
A 32A Lansen	32286	ex '50' F 6 (noted '84-'85).
J 32B Lansen	32579?	ex '26' F 12 (noted '84-'85, reported as 32526 & 32506 '85!).
J 35A Draken	35046	ex '--' (noted '84-'85, to Ljungbyhed by 6.86).
Sk 35C Draken	35806	ex '51' F 16 (noted '85).
Sk 35C Draken	35808	ex '??' F 16 (fuselage only, crashed 15.3.82, noted '84, to Satenas dump by 1988).
Sk 35C Draken	35813	ex '47' F 16 (noted '85).
J 35D Draken	35308	ex '25' F 4 (noted '84-'85).
S 35E Draken	35939	ex '66' (noted '84).
J 35F Draken	35407	ex '07' F 16 (noted '85).
J 35F Draken	35418	ex '??' F 16 (noted '85).
J 35F Draken	35488	ex '63' F 10 (noted '85).
J 35F Draken	35516	ex '19' F 13 (noted '85).
J 35F Draken	35560	ex '50' F 1 (noted '84-'85).
J 35F Draken	35574	ex '64' F 1 (noted '84).

Two Drakens were noted on the dump in 8.88 of which one was coded '29'.

Kept in the hangar of the Halstad Flygklubb is SG-38 Schulgleiter SE-160 (ex RSwedAF 8033) which belongs to the Halmstad Segelflygklubb (Halmstad Soaring Club).

HELSINGBORG

The prototype BA-4 (Bjorn Andreasson's aerobatic aircraft) SE-ANS is stored here incomplete.

HILLERSTORP

The "High Chapparall" Wild West theme park at Hillerstorp (North West of Varnamo) maintains a small air museum with the following exhibits.

DH60G Moth Major	SE-ADN	(c/n 5018) CofA expired 4.7.68.
PT-19A Cornell	L-AG	(ex RNorAF 115, LN-BFI) RNorAF markings.
AT-16 Harvard IIB	LN-BNN	(c/n 14A-1057, ex 42-12758, FS917, RDAF 31-310) CofA expired 31.12.68, displayed on the roof.
AT-16 Harvard IIB	16030	(c/n 14-299, ex 42-0762, FE565)
Piaggio P.136L	SE-CDE	(c/n 208) ex Bromma.
F-84G Thunderjet	29978	(ex 52-9978) ex RNorAF, dismantled (could be fuselage of 51-9958 with tail from 52-9978).

JONKOPING

In storage here in 6.88 was the wreck of Pik.16C Vasama SE-SZZ (c/n 20) with the wreck of Cessna F150H SE-FBG (c/n 0272, crashed here 10.5.80). A further visit in 8.88 found the wrecks of GY80 Horizon 160s SE-EGK (c/n 52, CofA expired 30.4.79) and SE-EGP (c/n 118, CofA expired 1982).

KALMAR

The former base of the Swedish AF's F 12, an anonymous J 35 Draken is preserved on a pedestal here.

KAREMO

The Karemo Flugmuseum (near Rockneby, about 20 kms North of the town of Kalmar) has the following collection on display.

Aero L-60 Brigadyr	HB-EZE	(c/n 150911)
Aeronca 7EC Champion	SE-CNC	(c/n 718)
AS350B Ecureil	SE-HNS	(c/n 1508, ex D-HLOO)
Antonov An-2	CCCP-70501	(c/n 1421?)
Bell 47G-3B1	SE-HME	(Westland built, c/n WA583, ex South Yemen AF 404, XT404, G-BBZL)
Enstrom F.28A	SE-HHN	(c/n 295, ex OY-HBL) tail-less.
Enstrom F.28C	SE-HHT	(c/n 429) tail only.
Ercoupe 415C	SE-AYS	(c/n 3956)
Fw 44J Stieglitz	SE-CLC	(ex RSwedAF 699?)
Hughes 269C	SE-HCP	(c/n 38-0358)
MFI-9 Junior	SE-CPG	(c/n 02)
MFI-9 Junior	SE-EBP	(c/n 05, ex OH-MFA)
MFI-15-200 Safari	ET-AGB	(c/n 15006, ex LN-BIV, SE-FIM)
MFI-15-200A TS	SE-FIT	(c/n 15832)
MFI-15-200A	-	(c/n 15847) fuselage only.
Mignet Pou-du-Ciel	SE-464	
Noorduyn Norseman IV	LN-BDR	(c/n 92, ex RCAF 492, RNorAF R-AK)
P.31C Proctor	RM169	(c/n H.772, ex RM169, G-ANVY)
PA22 Tri-Pacer	SE-CKM	(c/n 22-6110)
PA22 Colt 108	SE-CZL	(c/n 22-9131)
Rotorway Scorpion	-	(homebuilt)
J 29F Tunnan	29624	ex 'P' (yellow) F 9.
J 32B Lansen	32502	(fuselage only)
Schweizer Teal II	SE-GTO	(c/n 31, ex N2031T)
Sud Alouette II	02042	(c/n 1830, ex Swedish Army 112) ex Swedish Navy.
Taylorcraft BC	SE-ANU	(c/n 1227, ex OH-KLB)
Vertol 44B	01009	(c/n 607) ex Swedish Navy.
-	-	(unknown Finnish Autogyro)

KARLSBORG

A 32A Lansen 32259/43 ex F 6 was noted here in 6.79 for preservation and was still current guarding the gate in '88.

Derelict around the base in 6.79 were A 32A Lansen 32210/39 ex F 6 plus further examples coded '11' and '31' and an ex F 16 J 35 Draken coded '42'. The anonymous Lansen coded '31' was the only occupant reported on the dump in 6.85.

AJ 37 Viggen 37019 (damaged during 1986) was still here in '88. The forward fuselage is expected to be used for training purposes.

LANDSKRONA

Exhibited at the Landskrona Museum is a 1918 vintage Thulin NA biplane (noted '88).

LAXA

Cessna 336 SE-ETZ (c/n 0063, ex OY-TRH, CofA expired 31.12.81) is stored here in non-airworthy condition (noted '88). Laxa is about half way between Goteborg and Stockholm.

LINKOPING

Undergoing restoration at the SAAB factory here (as "31051") is Spitfire PR.19 PM627 (ex Indian AF). This machine went from India to the Canadian Pilots Association but was not restored and was duly obtained by the Swedish AF Museum via an intermediary in the USA. Exchanged in return for the Spitfire were Hunter Mk.50 34006, C-47

SE-IKL (c/n 33154, ex 79008), AD-4W Skyraider SE-EBL (c/n 7937, ex 127922, WT987, G-31-3), A 32A Lansen 32248 (to N4432V and d/d via Lossiemouth 20.6.85) with 'spares ship' 32209 (to N5468X, d/d Malmo-Stansted-Cranfield 20.9.85) and 32120 (ex FC, to Chino via Lossiemouth 19.4.84 as N4767R).

The fifth prototype SAAB 35 Draken, 35-5, is in use as an instructional airframe at the Ljungstedtska Skolan, though it remains on Flygvapenmuseum charge.

To the North of the city, by the E4 motorway, are three aircraft mounted on pedestals:-

J 29F Tunnan	29441	ex '52' F 3 (noted '88, loaned from Flygvapenmuseum).
Sk 50B Safir	50016	ex '81' F 7 (noted '88)
SAAB-Fairchild SF340	-	(noted '88)

LJUNGBYHED

This base houses the Swedish AF's Flying Training School (F 5) equipped with the SAL Bulldog (Sk 61) and SAAB 105 (Sk 60). Preserved at the main gate here is J 29F Tunnan 29666/64 ex F 4 (noted '82-'88).

Crash damaged Sk 61 Bulldog 61044/44 ex F 5 was held on the base during 1988 and is unlikely to be repaired.

Dumped and derelict aircraft noted in recent years have comprised the following.

J 32C Lansen	32932	ex '32' F 11 (fire/rescue training '82-'88).
J 32C Lansen	32934	ex '4' F 11 (fire/rescue training '82-'88).
J 35A Draken	35046	ex '??' (burnt nose, rear fuse & wing on dump '86, ex Halmstad).
J 35A Draken	35059	ex '23' F 16 (dumped '78-'85, on the assault course '86, still present for fire/rescue in '88).
J 35B Draken	35235	ex '??' F 10 (noseless & tail-less, fire/rescue training '82-'88).
J 35D Draken	35307	ex '04' F 4 (stored '85).
J 35D Draken	35312	ex '08' F 4 (tail-less, upside down for fire/rescue training '86-'88).
J 35D Draken	35321	ex '16' F 4 (stored '85, to Satenas dump by '88).
J 35D Draken	35352	ex '45' F 21 (stored '85).
J 35D Draken	35387	ex '38' F 21 (stored '85, to Satenas dump by 4.86).

LJUNGBYHED/HERREDVADSKLOSTER

Kockum Baby Falk SE-SGR (c/n 07) was reported here during '88, status uncertain.

LULEA/KALLAX

Preserved here on poles are S 29C Tunnan 29929/"21" (noted '81-'86) and S 35E Draken 35949/"21" (noted '86-'88), both in spurious F 21 markings. The previous code '65' is visible beneath the Draken's paint scheme.

At the open day in 1981, S 35E Draken 35952/67 ex F 21 was seen to be withdrawn from use and J 35A Draken 35062/26 ex F 16 was derelict on the field. Two Drakens were seen on the dump here during 1987, one of which was coded '32'.

MALMO

Sections of two Hawker B 4/B 4A Harts are here with N Ostergren and will probably be consumed in the restoration of a Hawker Osprey. He also has the fuselage and some other parts of Fw 44 Stieglitz SE-BXL (c/n FW 2825, ex RSwedAF 5782) which he intends to restore to exhibition standard.

The Tekniska Museet (Technical Museum) holds the following:-

Auster J/1	OY-DNU	(c/n 2102)
DH60G Moth Major	OH-VKM	
Klemm K135D (Sk 15)	SE-BHG	(c/n 1806, ex RSwedAF 5010)
Kockum Baby Falk	SE-SHR	
J 35F Draken	35484	
Thulin A	-	(replica forward fuse with original engine)
Thulin B	-	(c/n B2) built 1915, under restoration for Sveriges Tekniska Museum.

Viscount 745	SE-CNK	(c/n 227, ex N7465, VH-TVO, PI-C772) nose section only, remainder dumped at the airport.

MALMO/BULLTOFTA

The nose section of Douglas DC-7B SE-ERK "Boras" (c/n 45451) kept here in poor condition by the Skanes Flyghistoriska Sallskap (The Aviation Historical Society of Skane).

MALMO/STURUP

At the airfield, the firemen use J 32 Lansen 32915/15 ex F 11 to practice their trade, together with the burnt fuselage of an unidentified AD-4W Skyraider (reported as SE-EBK but this was at Angelholm then went to North Weald. I would guess at SE-EBF - can anyone confirm?), the noseless fuselage of Viscount 745 SE-CNK (c/n 227, ex N7465, VH-TVO, PI-C772), and engineless SE210 Caravelle III LN-KLP (c/n 24, arr 30.8.74, TT 29837 hrs). All four were current in '86.

MALMSLATT

On the other side of Linkoping to the SAAB works is the Flygvapenmuseum (Swedish AF Museum). Locations given in this listing are based on where the museum expected to position things when they open another new building in May '89.

Outside

PBY-5A Canso (Tp 47)	47001	(c/n CV-244)
C-47A Dakota (Tp 79)	79007	(c/n 12712, ex 42-92864, LN-IAH, SE-CFR) last mission flown 9.10.81.
Canberra T.11 (Tp 52)	52002	(c/n SH1648, ex WH805)
Pembroke C.52 (Tp 83)	83008	(c/n P66/52)
SAAB J 29A Tunnan	29171	ex 'B'
SAAB J 29F Tunnan	29575	
SAAB A 32A Lansen	32197	
SAAB J 35A Draken	35051	
SAAB AJ 37 Viggen	37-1	'51', first prototype.
Varsity T.1 (Tp 82)	82001	(c/n 622, ex WJ900)

Inside

Albatros/CFM 120 (Sk 1)	04	ex Swedish Army (Hall 1).
B-V V-44 (Hkp 1)	01001	(c/n SW-1-1/497) ex Swedish Navy (Hall 2).
Breguet C.U-1 (B 1)	-	(replica with some original parts) (Hall 1).
Bu 181 Bestmann (Sk 25)	25114	'314' F 5 markings (Hagglund built, c/n 114, ex D-EBIH) (Hall 1).
CFM 01 Tummelisa (O 1)	3656	(c/n 147) (Hall 1).
DH Moth Trainer (Sk 9)	"5558"	(composite a/c, mostly c/n 1720) (Hall 1).
DH Tiger Moth (Sk 11A)	515	(ASJA built, c/n 47, ex SE-BYM) (Hall 1).
DH Vampire F.1 (J 28A)	28001	(c/n EEP42083) (Hall 2).
DH Venom NF.51 (J 33)	33025	(c/n 12374, ex SE-DCD) (Hall 2).
SG-38 Schulgleiter	80	(RSwedAF designation G 101) (Hall 1).
DFS Grunau Baby II	SE-102	(AB Flygplan built, c/n 2152, ex SE-SAP).
DFS 108-30 Kranich II	SE-103	(c/n 072, ex SE-EWN) (Hall 2).
DFS Weihe	SE-104	(AB Flygindustri built, c/n 235, ex RSwedAF 8316) (Hall 2).
Fiat CR 42 (J 11)	2543	F 9 markings (c/n 921) (Hall 1).
Fi 156C Storch (S 14)	3815	'67' F 3 markings (composite a/c) (Hall 1).
FFVS 22 (J 22B)	22280	(Hall 1).
Fw 44J Stieglitz (Sk 12)	670/60	(F 5 markings) (ex SE-EGB) (Hall 1).
Fokker/CVM C.VE (S 6B)	386/3	(c/n 207) (Hall 1).
Gladiator (J 8A)	278/H	(ex Finnish AF, painted in markings of F 19 which served in Finland 1939/40) (Hall 1).
Hawker/ASJA Hart (B 4)	714	(c/n 52, ex Finnish AF) (Hall 1).
Hunter F.50 (J 34)	34016	(Hall 2).
Ju 86K-4 (Tp 9)	155	(c/n 0860412) (Hall 2).
Klemm Kl 35B (Sk 15A)	5081	'116' (c/n 1596, ex SE-AIG) (Hall 1).

Macchi M7	945	ex Swedish Navy (Hall 1).
MFI-9B Militrainer	801-42	(c/n 42, ex SE-EUK) (Hall 1).
MFI-10B Vipan (Fpl 54)	54382	(c/n 10.03, ex 54382, SE-CHI) (Hall 1).
Nieuport 1VG	M-1	ex Swedish Army (c/n 438) (Hall 1).
UC-64A Norseman (Tp 78)	78001	(c/n 492, ex 43-34518, SE-ASC, 78001, SE-CLZ) (Hall 2).
Harvard IIB (Sk 16A)	16109	(c/n 14-366, ex 42-829, FE632) (Hall 2).
P-51D Mustang (J 26)	26020	(c/n 31718, ex 44-63992, 26020, IDFAF 54) (Hall 1).
Phonix 122 DIII (J 1)	947	ex Swedish Army (Hall 1).
L-21B Super Cub (Fpl51)	51256	(c/n 18-6803, ex 51256, SE-CKH, SE-GCT) (Hall 2).
RAAB Katzenstein RK26	536	'101' F 5 markings (RSwedAF designation Sk 10) (c/n 20) (Hall 1).
Reggiane Re.2000 (J 20)	2340	(c/n 405) (Hall 1).
SAAB L-17B (S 17B)	17005	(c/n 17005) (Hall 2).
SAAB B 18B	18172	(c/n 18172) (Hall 2).
SAAB J 21A-3	21364	(c/n 21364) (Hall 1).
SAAB J 29B	29398	("UN" in spurious F 22 markings - Congo campaign 1961/63) (Hall 1).
SAAB 105XT	SE-XBZ	(Hall 2).
SAAB 210 Lilldraken	-	(Hall 2).
SAAB J 35F Draken	35410	(forward fuselage only) (Hall 1).
SAAB 91A Safir (Tp 91)	SE-AYC	(c/n 91-104, ex 91104) (Hall 1).
Seversky EP-106 (J 9)	2134	'53' F 3 markings (c/n 282-19) (Hall 1).
Sparmann S1A (P-1)	814	'61' F 3 markings (c/n 8) (Hall 1).
Sud Alouette II (Hkp 2)	02406	ex '92' F7 (Hall 1).
Spitfire PR.XIX (S 31)	"31051"	(c/n 6S 699626, ex PM627) see Linkoping (Hall 1).

Other aircraft held in the storage and restoration area comprise:-

Beech D-18S (Tp 45)	-	
Bu 181 Bestmann (Sk 25)	25000	(c/n 181-5001, ex D-EXWB)
Vampire FB.50 (J 28B)	28311	(c/n V.0590)
Vampire FB.50 (J 28B)	28317	(c/n V.0604)
DH104 Dove (Tp 46)	G-ANVU	(c/n 04082) arr 18.8.87.
Vampire T.55 (Sk 28C)	28451	
Venom NF.51 (J 33)	33015	(c/n 12364, ex SE-DCA)
DFS Anfanger	-	
DFS108-70 Olympia	SE-SAE	
Donnet-Leveque L-11	10	ex Swedish Navy (belongs to Sveriges Tekniska Museum).
AD-4W Skyraider	SE-EBI	(ex 124777, WV185, G-31-11) soc 3.9.73.
Firefly TT.1	SE-CAW	(c/n F6121, ex PP392)
Meteor T.7	SE-CAS	(c/n G5/1496)
Grumman Goose (Tp 81)	-	collected from Burlington (Vermont, USA) on 15.12.86 by RSwedAF C-130.
George Holmberg Racer	-	1937 homebuilt, on loan.
MFI-15	SE-XCB	(c/n 01) prototype.
Mignet Pou-du-Ciel	-	on loan.
MiG-15bis	-	ex Polish AF.
Nord NC701 Martinet	SE-KAE	(c/n 264)
North American NA16	-	(RSwedAF designation Sk 14) composite of a BT-9 Yale and CA-7 Wirraway, rebuilt at Barkaby.
SAAB L-17A (B 17A)	17329	(c/n 17329, ex SE-BYH)
SAAB J 21A-3	21286	(c/n 21286) to be rebuilt as a J 21R.
SAAB J 21A-3	21311	(c/n 21311)
S 29C Tunnan	29937	ex '09' FC, belongs to Ulf Nylof.
S 29C Tunnan	29970	
J 29F Tunnan	29507	
J 29F Tunnan	29670	ex '20' F 16 (noted '88).
S 32C Lansen	32917	
J 35B Draken	35220	ex '20' F 18 (noted '86).

J 35D Draken	35375	ex '05' F 4 (noted '86).
S 35E Draken	35906	
S 35E Draken	35959	ex '35' (noted '86).
Thulin G	15	ex Swedish Navy (c/n G5), belongs to Sveriges Tekniska Museum.

Noted in a storage facility in 4.86 were the following trio of Lansens which appeared to have moved elsewhere by '88.

J 32D Lansen	32548	ex '32' F13.
J 32E Lansen	32569	ex '08' F13.
J 32E Draken	32530	ex '14'

On the active side of the base in 6.85 was a wfu silver J 35 Draken coded '18'. The fire dump held an A 32A Lansen 32255/25 ex FC (still present '88), J 32C Lansen 32945/45 ex F11 with an unidentified Draken and ex F8 Pembroke. Noted in 8.88 were two Drakens coded '18' (see above) and '28' with J 32C Lansen 32571/851.

MARKARYD

Preserved here (and both current in '88) are Noorduyn built AT-16 Harvard (Sk 16) 16009 and S 29C Tunnan 29945. Markaryd is about 100 kms North of Malmo.

NORRKOPING/KUNGSANGAN

A visit here in 6.88 found PA22 Colts SE-CZO (c/n 22-8953, CofA expired 30.6.80) and SE-EDO (c/n 22-8689, CofA expired 31.1.79) in storage whilst Caudron Pelican SE-AGA (c/n 7338/45, ex F-AOYC, from Klippan) was undergoing rebuild. Also reported in '88 was DH Dove 6 SE-GRA (c/n 04437, ex G-AMZN) though its precise status was not confirmed.

At various private locations around the city three aircraft are under long-term restoration to flying condition.

DH60T Moth Trainer	-	(c/n 1718 or 1720, ex RSwedAF 5110, 560) owned by Kjell Franzen and Ingemar Ehrenstrom.
DH87B Hornet Moth	SE-AGE	(c/n 8136) owned by Foreningen Veteranflyg.
Piper J-3C 40/50S	SE-AHP	(c/n 2371) owned by Kjell Franzen.

The Foreningen Veteranfly Hornet Moth will eventually join the airworthy Chipmunk (SE-BBS) and DH Tiger Moth ("6550", SE-MAG) at the airport.

NYKOPING/OXELOSUND

Noted here in 8.88 (most, if not all, belonging to the resident technical school) were the following. The J 35Fs consisted of fuselages only and were accompanied by a further three unidentified examples:-

S 32C Lansen	32935	ex '35' F 11 derelict.
S 32C Lansen	32940	ex '40' F 11 derelict.
J 35F Draken	35509	
J 35F Draken	35514	
J 35 Draken	35...	ex '16' (fuselage, in Tech School).
J 35 Draken	35...	ex '71' (fuselage, in Tech School).
Sk 61 Bulldog	61071	ex '71' (in Tech School).
Sk 61 Bulldog	61...	ex '??' (in Tech School).
Hkp 2 Alouette II	.....	ex '92' (in Tech School).

A second report lists J 35B Draken 35221 (this is not one of those listed above) and Alouette II c/n 409-92 (both on Flygvapenmuseum charge) with the technical school. The Alouette is presumably the machine listed above.

NYKOPING/NYGE

The wreck of Fpl 61C Bulldog 61062 was noted here 8.79, probably in use for ground instructional purposes. It had moved (with the rest of the Armeflygskolan) to Nykoping/Skavsta by mid '85.

NYKOPING/SKAVSTA

The Armeflygskolan was in residence here mid 1985 having left its old base at Nykoping/Nyge and awaiting a permanent move to Linkoping/Malmen. Noted here in 6.85

was the wreck of Dornier Do 27A-4 (Fpl 53) 53272/82 (c/n 2100, w/o here 13.5.85) whilst Fpl 61C Bulldog 61062/62 was seen to have made the move from Nyge and was probably in use as an instructional airframe. It has since moved on to Malmslatt.

OSTERSUND/FROSON

Preserved on plinths outside the F 4 Head Quarters building are J 29F Tunnan 29401/"29" F-4 marks (ex '21/F 4') with J 35D Draken 35392/"35" F 4 marks (ex '37/F 4').

The front fuselage and cockpit section from J 35D Draken 35345/?? ex F4 was noted at the fire station in 5.86 where it serves for crash rescue instruction.

OSTERSUND/HAMMARNASET

Hilding Andersson keeps his private colloection here which consists of:-

J 29F Tunnan	29373	ex '12' F 4
J 35D Draken	35392	ex '52' F 4
Harvard II (Sk 16)	16145	ex '78' F 4 (Noorduyn built, c/n 75-3497).
Pik.5B	SE-STZ	(c/n 1) Finnish built sailplane.

RONNEBY/KALLINGE

Preserved at the base (the home of F 17) in 6.84 was A 32A Lansen 32151/B (yellow) ex F 17. In 1988 it was reported to be in store for a future base museum.

Derelict airframes seen around the field in recent years (notably the '84 open day) have included the following.

A 32A Lansen	32240	ex F 17, finless (noted 6.84).
S 35E Draken	35901	ex '08' (or '28'?) F 11, at fire station for foam distribution training (noted '84-'88).
J 35B Draken	35241	ex F 12 (finless, amongst the approach lights just off the base for rescue training (noted '84).

The base usually has plenty of hardware for the firemen to play with. In recent years the fire dump has held the following.

A 32A Lansen	32051	ex '61' F 6 (noted '84).
A 32A Lansen	32...	ex '49' F 6 (noted '84).
A 32A Lansen	32258	ex '42' F 6 (noted '84).
A 32A Lansen	32285	ex '27' F 6 (noted '84).
A 32A Lansen	32206	ex '23'(?) F 6 (noted '84).
A 32A Lansen	32268	ex F 11 (noted '84).
A 32A Lansen	32...	ex '38' (burnt out) (noted '84).
Pembroke C.52 (Tp 83)	83015	ex '85' F 8 (c/n P66/65) (noted '84-'88).
Pembroke C.52 (Tp 83)	83012	ex '88' F 8 (c/n P66/61) (noted '84-'88).
J 35A Draken	35060	ex '24' F 16 (noted '84).
J 35B Draken	35225	ex F 18 (noted '84).
J 35B Draken	35271	ex F 10 (noted '84).
J 35B Draken	35272	ex F 18 (noted '84).

SATENAS

A 32A Lansen 32085/33 ex F 7 is normally displayed on the main gate here (noted '82) but was hangared during late '87 for a 'wash and brush up'. It was still hangared in late '88.

Pembroke C.52 (Tp 83) 83016/86 ex F 16 has been in use for crash rescue training here for many years (noted '82-'88) and continues to serve in this role. Other airframes used for rescue training and destructive fire training in recent years are listed below. The Lansens have probably all been consumed by now.

A 32A Lansen	32058	ex '9' F 6 (noted '82).
A 32A Lansen	32100	ex '06' F 6 (noted '82).
A 32A Lansen	32152	ex '44' F 6 (noted '82).
A 32A Lansen	32169	ex '50' F 6 (noted '82).
A 32A Lansen	32202	ex '48' F 6 (noted '82).
A 32A Lansen	32241	ex '09' F 6 (noted '82).
A 32A Lansen	32277	ex '22' F 6 (noted '82).

J 32C Lansen 32903 ex '03' F 11 (noted '82).
J 32C Lansen 32911 ex '1' F 11 (noted '82).
J 32C Lansen 32919 ex '??' F 11 (noted '82).
J 32C Lansen 32923 ex '23' F 11 (noted '82).
J 32C Lansen 32927 ex '27' F 11 (noted '82).
J 32C Lansen 32931 ex '56' F 11 (noted '82).
J 35A Draken 35084 ex '46' (or '47'?) F 16 (noted '82).
J 35A Draken 35085 ex '44' F 16 (noted '82).
S 35E Draken 35907 ex '59' F 21 (noted '82).
S 35E Draken 35928 ex '??' F 21 (noted '82).
S 35E Draken 35960 ex '??' F 21 (noted '82).
J 35F Draken 35438 ex '--' F 13 (noted '82).
A further visit in 4.86 saw almost a complete change with the following being seen.
A 32A Lansen 32223 ex '31' F 6
A 32A Lansen 32277 ex '22' F 6 (also seen in 4.82).
J 35D Draken 35387 ex '38' F 21 & Ljungbyhed.
AJ 37 Viggen 37044 ex '44' F 7 (wreckage of crash, probably on 26.2.86).
The following were recorded during a visit in 1988.
J 35A Draken 35073 ex '37' F 16
J 35D Draken 35321 ex '16' F4 & Ljungbyhed store.
J 35D Draken 35348
J 35F Draken 35463
Sk 35C Draken 35808 crashed 15.3.82, ex F 16 and Halmstad.
Sk 35C Draken 35818

SKOKLOSTERS

The Skoklosters Motormuseum holds a few aeroplanes amongst its earthbound exhibits and can be found a few kms South of Uppsala.
C-47 Dakota (Tp 79) 79002 (c/n 9103, ex 42-32877, 79002, SE-APW).
J 35E Draken 35945 rebuilt from J 35B 35299.
Safir (Sk 50B) 50023 ex '72' F 1 (c/n 91-225).

SODERHAMN

The home of F 15 equipped with the AJ 37 Viggen has A 32A Lansen 32070/H is preserved as a reminder of times gone by. The aircraft was noted in 6.85 and was still current in '88 though repainted as "15" in F 15 markings. Less fortunate was A 32A Lansen 32172/25 ex F 15 which suffered at the hands of the firemen in a fire-fighting demonstration at the open day in 6.85.

J 29F Tunnan 29937/09 was preserved here in 1980 but by 1982 it had moved on to Uppsala for further preservation.

A crash compound on the base held in 6.85 the wrecks of Sk50B Safir 50067/74 ex F15, an unidentified Draken and Viggen.

Dumped around the airfield around this time were.
A-32A Lansen 32127 ex '07' F 15 (noted '85).
A 32A Lansen 32175 ex '27' F 15 (noted '85 - in trees behind fire station).
A 32A Lansen 32... ex '15' (noted '85 on far side, code '15' could be '??' of F 15).
J 32D Lansen 32532 ex '32' F 4 (noted '85 - in trees behind fire station).
J 35A Draken 35053 ex '17' F 16 (noted '85 - by the fire station).

SODERTALJE

Percival Proctor SE-BTR is here (25 kms South West of Stockholm) together with a Cessna Airmaster (either SE-ANO or SE-ANP).

STOCKHOLM

The Sveriges Tekniska Museum (Technical Museum of Sweden) have the following aircraft on display.
Bleriot-Nyrop No.3 3 (hanging from roof 5.87, 1911 vintage Bleriot XI-bis).
Cierva C.30A SE-AEA (c/n 740) (hanging from roof 5.87).

Junkers F.13	S-AAAC	(c/n 715, ex D-343) (hanging from roof 5.87, first aircraft of ABA - AB Aerotransport).
Nyberg Flugan	-	(1902 vintage swedish experimental a/c).
Thulin N	-	(c/n 1.59) (hanging from roof 5.87).

In addition, a DFS 108 Schulgleiter SG-38 is held in store.

Somewhere in the city are BHT-1 Beauty SE-ANX (1944 vintage Swedish single seater, only one built), DH60 Moth SE-BFB and DH Puss Moth SE-AFH.

The KTH (Kungl Tekniska Hogskolan/Royal Institute of Technology) has two airframes serving as ground instructional airframes. They are Hughes 269A (Hkp 5A) 05215 (c/n 220049, belongs to Flygvapenmuseum) and SAAB 37 Viggen 37-61 (ex '37-6', the sixth prototype).

STOCKHOLM/ARLANDA

Suspended inside the airport terminal building is a Bu 181B Bestmann 25056 in F5 markings (noted '88). This replaced Bu 131B-3 Jungmann SE-AGU (see below) which hung in this position in '85).

The Luftfartmuseet aircraft (collected by the Swedish Board of Civil Aviation) are mostly stored around the airfield here though several have turned up in museum collections around the country in recent years. Thought to remain here are:-

Albatros B II	NAB 9	(RSwedAF designation Sk 1, forward fuselage only).
Auster AOP.5	SE-CBT	(c/n 841, ex MS977, G-ANIU, LN-BDU)
Auster AOP.5	SE-BZR	(c/n 1552, ex TJ511) wreckage of crash.
Auster J/5G	SE-CBS	(c/n 3082, ex LN-BDA) wreckage of crash.
Avro Avian IV	SE-ADT	(c/n R3/CN/318, ex G-AAHD)
BEDA Flying Boat	-	
Twin Bonanza	LN-DBE	(c/n GH-98, ex N186AA)
Bell 47D	"SE-HAD"	(composite of several airframes) (noted '88).
Berger Bror	-	(1911 homebuilt, forward fuselage & engine only).
Bleriot XI	-	(belongs to Sveriges Tekniska Museum, good condition).
Bu 131B Jungmann	SE-AGU	(c/n 846) (noted '88).
Cessna F172G	SE-ESL	(c/n 0191)
DH 60G Moth	SE-AGF	(c/n 5132) (noted '88).
DFS 108 Schulgleiter	21	(c/n 210)
DFS108 Schulgleiter	138	
DFS108-70 Olympia	SE-SGF	(c/n 7)
DFS Weihe	SE-SNK	(c/n 237, ex RSwedAF 8318, SE-102)
C-47A Dakota	42-24049	(c/n 9911) ex restaurant at Narrtalje.
AD-4W Skyraider	SE-EBB	(c/n 7962 ex 127947, WT949, G-31-5) (noted '88).
UC-61A Argus	SE-BXE	(c/n 892 ex 43-14898, HB625, LN-MAD) (noted '88).
Firefly TT.1	SE-BRG	(c/n F.6071, ex DT989) to Ska/Edeby by 6.88.
Fw 44J Stieglitz	SE-BWX	(c/n 2816, ex RSwedAF 5773) (noted '88).
Gotaverken GV-38	SE-AHD	(c/n 5, license-built Rearwin 9000 Sportster).
Grunau Baby IIB	SE-SFA	(c/n 098)
Hutter H.17A	LN-GBD	(c/n 1, ex OY-5) (noted '88).
Junkers W 34 (Tp 2A)	SE-BYA	(c/n 2835, ex RSwedAF '71' of F 4) (noted '88).
Junkers Ju 52/3m	SE-ADR	(c/n 4017, ex SE-ADK, SE-ADR, RSwedAF 907) front fuselage section only.
Klemm Kl 34D	SE-BGA	(c/n 1983, ex RSwedAF 5054)
C-60A Lodestar	SE-BZE	(c/n 2593, ex 43-16433, G-AGIJ, SAAF 2593, RNorAF 'T-AE', OH-VKP)
MFI-9B Junior	SE-EFG	(c/n 20) not complete.
MFI-9B Trainer	SE-EFP	(c/n 28) not complete.
MFI-10B Vipan	SE-CFI	(c/n 10.01) no engine (noted '88).
NC701 Martinet	SE-CAL	(licence-built Siebel Si 204D, c/n 159, ex ADLA).
UC-64 Norseman	SE-CPB	(ex RCAF 3538, 42-5050, RNorAF 'RA-Y', LN-AEW)(noted '88).
AT-16 Texan (Sk 16)	16010	ex '71' F 20 (c/n 14-565, ex 42-12318, FE831)(noted '88).
Persson Homebuilt	-	
Rieseler R.III	S-AAR	(1922 vintage Swedish homebuilt).
SAAB 91D Safir	SF-18	(c/n 91-441) ex Finnish AF (noted '88).

J 35E Draken	35937	cockpit section only.
Scheibe Bergfalke II	SE-SUA	(c/n 336)
Scheibe Specht	D-6680	(c/n 808)
SE210 Caravelle III	SE-DAF	(c/n 112, ex HB-ICV) wfu 23.9.74, TT 27321 hrs.
Taylor J.2 Cub	SE-AGL	(c/n 989)
Vertol V.44A (Hkp 1)	01007	(c/n SW7) cockpit section only.

The fire service use SE210 Caravelle III/48T OY-KRC (c/n 29, ex HS-TGH) as a crash rescue training aid here. It was wfu 27.9.74 (TT 34284 hrs) and handed over to the airport fire service in 10.75 (current '88).

STOCKHOLM/BERGASKOLORNA

A Swedish Navy training centre here has a so far unidentified Hkp 2 Alouette II in use as a ground instructional airframe (noted '88).

STOCKHOLM/BROMMA

Convair 440 SE-CCX (c/n 320, ex LN-KLB) was wfu here by 5.87 with props removed. By late '88 the aircraft had been moved to the fire dump, joining an unidentified Lansen which is badly burnt but still on its undercarriage.

STOCKHOLM/SKA-EDEBY

A visit in 6.88 found the fuselage of Cherokee 180 SE-EOO (c/n 28-2185) stored behind a hangar. Also in store are AT-16 Harvard IIs 16029/7 ex F17 and 16112 with the wreck of 16098 in two pieces. 16112 was not recorded on a further visit in 8.88 when 16098 was listed as a forward fuselage only.

The star items here are the two Fairey Firefly TT.1s with Bjorn Lovgren, SE-BRG (c/n F.6071, ex DT989, from Arlanda) and SE-CAU (c/n F.6180, ex PP469), which were being worked on in No.1 Hangar. My suspicion is that one may be a spares source for the other, further details would be most welcome.

Republic RC3 Seabee SE-AXX (c/n 829, ex SE-AXX, LN-TVV) was lying wrecked here in 8.88

SUNDSVALL/ HARNOSAND

In '79 the fire dump here held J 35A Drakens 35049, 35065, 35066 and 35068. At least 35066 escaped a fiery fate as by 6.88 she was preserved here.

TULLINGE

Noted on the fire dump here in 6.85 were J 35A Draken 35047/11 ex F 16 and S 35E Draken 35955/69 ex F 21.

TROLLHATTAN

The fuselages of a PA25 and a Beech 36 were noted in a closed hangar in 6.88 but further identification was not possible.

UGGLARP

Located near Halmstad SwedAF base (Ugglarp is actually West of Sloinge on the E6 road betwen Falkenberg and Halmstad) the Svedinos Bil Och Flygmuseum boasts:-

Auster J/1 Autocrat	SE-CGR	(c/n 2230, ex G-AIZW) (noted '88).
DH60 Moth	"5555"	(c/n 261, ex G-EBNO, S-AABS, SE-ABS) painted to represent a DH 60T (noted '88).
DH82A Tiger Moth	SE-FNA	(c/n 82003, ex D-EMWT) airworthy.
Vampire FB50 (J 28B)	28307	(c/n V.0578) ex 'A' (noted '88).
Vampire T55 (Sk 28C)	28444	ex '74' (noted '88).
DFS 108 Schulgleiter	736	(noted '88).
DFS 108-70 Olympia	SE-SAI	(c/n 210) (noted '88).
AD-4W Skyraider	SE-EBC	(ex USN 127960, WT960, G-31-6) (noted '88).
Canberra T11 (Tp 52)	52001	(c/n 71174, ex WH711) (noted '88).
Ercoupe 415D	SE-BNA	(c/n 4735, ex OY-FAC) (noted '88).
Ercoupe 415D	SE-BFY	(c/n 4409, ex NC3784H) airworthy.
FFVS J 22B	22149	ex 'E' (noted '88).

Fw 44J Stieglitz	5787	(ex SE-BWR) (noted '88).
Fw 44J Stieglitz	SE-BWZ	(c/n CVV.29, ex RSwedAF 647) (noted '88).
Gloster Meteor T.7	SE-DCC	(ex G-AMCJ, G-7-1, G-ANSO) painted as "WS774" (noted'88).
Gotaverken GV-38	SE-AHY	(c/n 15) (noted '88).
Grankvist Autogiro	-	(noted '88).
Hawker Hunter F.50	34070	ex 'P' F 10 (noted '88).
Junkers Ju 52	..+..	ex Luftwaffe, under restoration with F 14 at Halmstad.
Kamov Ka 26	SE-HDM	(c/n 7001307) (noted '88).
Klemm Kl 35D (Sk 15)	5025	(c/n 1899, ex SE-BGF) (noted '88).
M.38 Messenger 2A	SE-BYY	(c/n 6703, ex G-AKAO) (noted '88).
AT-16 Harvard II	16028	ex '92' (c/n 14-725, ex 42-12478, FE991) (noted'75-'88).
AT-16 Harvard II	16033	ex '33' (c/n 14-772, ex 42-12525, FH138) (noted'75-'88).
Pembroke C.52	83007	ex '84' F 8 (c/n P66/51) (noted '75-'88).
J 29A Tunnan	29203	ex 'U' (red) F 16 (noted '88).
J 32B Lansen	32599	ex '59' F 12 (noted '75-'88).
J 35A Draken	35001	(noted '88).
Grunau Baby	SE-SNY	(noted '88).
Tipsy B	SE-AGP	(c/n 504, ex OO-DOT) (noted '88).
Tipsy S.2	SE-AFT	(c/n 30, ex OO-ASC) (noted '88).

UMEA

The unidentifiable wrecks of a Cessna 206 and a Piper Cub were seen here in 6.88.

UPPSALA

Preserved on the gate here is J 35A Draken 35090/52 ex F 16 (noted '83). It would appear to have been replaced during 1988 with J 35F-1 35490/35 ex F 16.

Seen at the 1982 Open Day were preserved J 29F Tunnan 29937/09 in F 16 marks and J 35F Draken 35402/03 ex F 16 which was on trestles and thought to be wfu.

Located on various dumps around the base in recent years have been the following.

J 35A Draken	35056	ex '20' F 16, burnt '82 during fire-fighting display.
J 35B Draken	35269	ex '69' F 18, on an earth mound by the alert area (noted '82-'85).
J 35F Draken	35459	ex '??' F 16, on an earth mound by the alert area (noted '82-'85).
J-35F Draken	35513	ex '11' F 18 (to Angelholm by 8.87).
J 35F-1 Draken	35427	ex '67' F 16 (noted '88, for rescue training).

VASTERAS/JOHNISBURG

The Hasslo Flygteknikcentrum (Aviation College of Sweden) uses the following airframes for ground instructional purposes. A further four airworthy Sk 50 Safirs are on loan from the Swedish AF.

AT-16 Harvard II	16105	ex '18' F 5 (c/n 14-429,ex 42-0892,FE695)(noted'85-'88).
Pembroke C.52 (Tp 83)	83004	ex '84' F 4 (c/n P66/42) (noted '85-'88).
Safir (Sk 50B)	50003	ex '71' F 6 (c/n 91-203) (noted '85-'88).
Safir (Sk 50B)	50012	ex '71' F 4 (c/n 91-212) (noted '85-'88).
Safir (Sk 50B)	50020	ex '71' F 1 (c/n 91-222) (noted '85-'88).
Safir (Sk 50B)	50027	ex '77' F 13 (c/n 91-229) (noted '85-'88).
Safir (Sk 50B)	50055	ex '76' F 4 (c/n 91-264) (noted '85-'88).
S 29C Tunnan	29902	ex '02' F 3 (noted '85-'88).
S 29C Tunnan	29969	ex '16' F 3 (noted '85-'88).
S 29C Tunnan	29974	ex '20' F 3 (noted '85-'88).
J 35F-1 Draken	35496	ex '42' F 10 (noted '88).
J 35F-2 Draken	35555	ex '22' F 10 (noted '88).
J-35F-2 Draken	35582	ex '44' F 1 (noted '88, on a pedestal, belongs to F16).
Alouette II (Hkp 2)	02201	(c/n 1278) ex '01' Swedish Army (noted '88).
Alouette II (Hkp 2)	02204	ex '92' F 6 (c/n 1302, ex 02204, SE-HDI) (noted '88).

The Flygexpo/Flygande Museet also lives here with their airworthy Pembroke C.1 SE-BKH (ex XK884, G-BNPG) and P-51D Mustang (J 26) SE-BKG (ex 44-63864, RSwedAF 26158/K (yellow) F 16, IDFAF .., 4X-AIM, arrived 22.12.86).

SWITZERLAND

Apart from museums and the odd derelict private aircraft, Wrecks and Relics were an extremely scarce commodity in Switzerland ten years ago. Things have changed since then largely due to the Europe-wide growth of interest in aeronautical preservation coupled with the disposal of the Swiss AF P2, Venom and C-3605 fleets, soon to be be followed by the venerable Vampire (replaced by the Hawk) which, incredibly, will have served this air arm for over 40 years! The Swiss have approximately 100 Vampires as I write these words and no doubt within the next 12 months or so the vast majority will enter the preservation scene, or some other less happy area of the "W&R" realm.

ALTENRHEIN

DH Venom FB.50 J-1630 (ex Stans) was stored here in 5.84 for a Swiss collector. In 1988 the registration HB-RVA was allocated and the aircraft is now based at Friedrichshafen in West Germany (some 35 kms North of Altenrhein).

EKW C-3605 Schlepp C-509 had arrived here by late '88 following the sale at Lodrino.

Wrecks recorded here during 9.84 were AS202/15 Bravo HB-HED (c/n V-5) and J-3C-90 Cub HB-OGZ (c/n 12648, ex 44-80352).

BAD-RAGAZ

The wreck of PZL.104 Wilga 35A HB-EZH (c/n 96314) was lingering here during 9.84, the aircraft having crashed here on 28.1.78.

BASLE

Venom FB.50 J-1648 arrived at a military barracks (Zeughaus) in the city by 11.83 for display on the gate.

BASLE/MULHOUSE

In 1976 several ex Ghana AF Cariboux appeared here looking for new owners. Three aircraft were by 1978 refurbished for the Indian AF but continued their stay at Basle for some time after completion due to financial problems. They eventually left around 1979 (certainly between 9.78 and 8.80). The other two aircraft were still in open storage during 9.81 looking very sorry for themselves.

DHC-4 Caribou	N90565	(c/n 28, ex Ghana AF G-400) to Indian AF M-2168.
DHC-4 Caribou	N90567	(c/n 31, ex Ghana AF G-401) to Indian AF M-2169.
DHC-4 Caribou	N90570	(c/n 56, ex Ghana AF G-404) broken up.
DHC-4 Caribou	N90571	(c/n 74, ex Ghana AF G-405) broken up.
DHC-4 Caribou	N90572	(c/n 94, ex Ghana AF G-407) to Indian AF M-2171.

Boeing 707-309C N707ZS (c/n 20261) of Jet Cargo arrived here in 6.83 and was still parked out in open storage 8.87. Surprisingly, she was re-activated by 5.88 as EL-ZGS. Boeing 707-336C N14AZ (c/n 19498) has arrived for storage more recently, still in basic British Airways colours.

Five Crossair Metros are stored outside their hangar area (noted 8.87), three of them unregistered. More details anyone?

On the General Aviation apron, Cessna 310C HB-LCC (c/n 35856) was noted 8.87 and had not flown for over three years. It has since joined a collection at Dulliken.

Span East Douglas DC-6B N617SE (c/n 44088) ceased operations in 6.76 and after some time in open storage here gravitated to the fire dump by 1978 and has since expired at the hands of the firemen.

BERN/BELP

Outside the Heli-Swiss hangar in 7.79 was Sikorsky H-34G 8104 (c/n 58-1671, Bu No 150802, ex 8104 of Mfg.5, WGN). This machine was last noted in 7.84.

In 8.87 the Heli-Swiss hangar held dismantled Bell 206B Jetranger HB-XKN (c/n 1205, ex N18092, G-BBTV) with an anonymous ex Santis example which had been extensively robbed of spare parts and was due for disposal within six months. Alouette III C-GTNI (c/n 2191) was stored pending rebuild for a Spanish customer and Bell 206B Jetranger N604PA (c/n 3091) awaited similar treatment to emerge as HB-XSI.

DH Venom FB.50 J-1649 is to be displayed at the Armee Museum here.

BEROMUNSTER

Partenavia P66B Oscar 150 HB-EMM (c/n 18) was parked out on the field in 8.87 looking neglected.

BEX

DH Venom FB.50 J-1627 flew in on 25.8.85 for preservation with the Aero Club and is now parked out on the airfield (noted '86-'88). The aircraft was offered for disposal in 1988.

EKW C-3605 Schlepp C-539 (ex Lodrino store) was in a yard near the Jordacier factory in Bex town during 9.88.

BIEL

Dornier Do 27H-2 HB-HAK (ex V-602) of the Phantom Para Club was cancelled from the register 15.11.82. It is thought to have gone to West Germany.

BIRRFELD

Bu 133C Jungmeister U-95 (c/n 42, to become HB-MIE) was stored here in the end compartment of one of the lock-up hangars (Noted 8.87). It has since moved to France but retains its Swiss registration.

DUBENDORF

Located on the North East side of Zurich, Dubendorf is the Swiss AF's main base and is well known for the annual 'Flugmeisterschaft' competition and its asssociated open day.

DH Vampire FB.6 J-1049 was preserved on a pole in flying attitude outside the Swiss AF museum here (noted '78-'82). By 1983 the aircraft had been removed from this position and sat on the North side of the field in open storage in the company of J-1070 which had occupied this position since at least 1977. Following use by the fire service its (J-1049's) remains have since been scrapped.

On the fire dump in 1978 was the burnt remains of a Venom FB.54. This may have been J-1586 as the radio call "586" appeared on the instrument panel.

In 8.86 the crash compound held the wreck of Pilatus P3 A-832 and an unknown Vampire T.55. In 8.87 the P3 was still present together with the mortal remains of F-5E Tiger IIs J-3017 (w/o 21.1.87), J-3042 (w/o 10.4.87) and J-3071 (w/o 21.1.87). The compound has since been cleared.

The North West side of the field is often used for storage of aircraft awaiting overhaul or disposal. Few of these merit a mention here as they tend either to return to active service or else pause here only fleetingly before meeting their fate. The Pilatus P-2 merits fuller treatment as the type was almost exclusively disposed of at Dubendorf with 23 aircraft being gathered here for an auction held on 30.5.81:-

Pilatus P2-05	U-103	to HB-RAX 5.8.81 and to Birrfeld.
Pilatus P2-05	U-104	sold at the auction and last reported derelict at Cote 8.82.
Pilatus P2-05	U-107	to HB-RAT at Sion by 8.81.
Pilatus P2-05	U-108	to G-BJAX 15.6.81.
Pilatus P2-05	U-109	to G-BJAT 24.6.81, later N109PL.
Pilatus P2-05	U-115	to HB-RAY 24.9.81 and to Grenchen.
Pilatus P2-05	U-116	to F-AZCD at La Ferte Alais.

Pilatus P2-05	U-117	to F-AZCC at St Rambert d'Albon.
Pilatus P2-05	U-121	to HB-RAU 28.8.81 at Neuchatel/Colombier.
Pilatus P2-05	U-122	reportedly at Stans in '88, to HB-RBC 22.8.88.
Pilatus P2-05	U-125	to Blackbushe, becoming G-BLKZ.
Pilatus P2-05	U-126	to HB-RAZ at Langenthal.
Pilatus P2-05	U-127	to HB-RAS at Sion.
Pilatus P2-05	U-128	to HB-RAV at Birrfeld.
Pilatus P2-06	U-132	to HB-RAW at Yverdon 23.9.81.
Pilatus P2-06	U-136	to HB-RAR 23.7.81 and to 'Oldtimers' at Ecuvillens.
Pilatus P2-06	U-138	to HB-RBA at Bern/Belp, later N138U.
Pilatus P2-06	U-142	to G-BONE 8.7.81.
Pilatus P2-06	U-143	to Blackbushe & became G-CJCI.
Pilatus P2-06	U-144	to HB-RAM 21.9.81 and to Pfaffikon.
Pilatus P2-06	U-147	held for museum at Standort Fruitigen (in store at Dubendorf 8.81).
Pilatus P2-06	U-152	to F-AZCE at La Ferte Alais.
Pilatus P2-06	U-155	to HB-RAP 2.9.82 at Bex.

Outside the above auction, U-105 became D-EMLR, U-106 became F-AZCG with Aero Phoenix, U-110 was sold off to become G-PTWO 26.2.81, U-111 became OO-PTO, U-114 joined the Swiss AF Museum, U-129 became HB-RAW and U-157 was retained at Dubendorf as a spare for the Swiss AF museum but was last noted there 8.81. Three that did not survive were U-145, U-149 and U-153 whose hulks were last noted in the scrap compound at Dubendorf in 1979.

Several Dornier Do 27H-2s had also been stored at Dubendorf since 1980 and were also up for disposal in the sale of 30.5.81. These comprised V-601 (not sold, still in service here 4.89), V-603 (not sold, thought still to be hangared here, perhaps as a spares source), V-604 (to Paraclub Grenchen as HB-HAA,), V-605 (sold to H Dubler as HB-HAB and based at Dubendorf up to 1987, since to Grenchen), V-606 (to HB-HAC with K Zimmermann of Berne) and V-607 (not sold, still in service here 8.88).

The Fliegermuseum Dubendorf (Swiss AF Museum) is housed at Dubendorf with the following collection. The Jungmanns and Jungmeisters described as stored actually hang from the rafters in the Hunter and Mirage hangars on the North side. The Junkers Ju 52s are maintained in airworthy condition (bought second hand prior to the Second World War, they were only retired from Swiss AF service in 1982!) and frequently operate pleasure flights to bring in much neeeded funds for the Museum. On 2.7.88 an expanded museum was opened in new premises at Dubendorf the inmates of which are described as "current '89" in the list below.

Beech G18S	HB-GAC	(c/n 8343, ex 44-87103, NC79848, SE-BTS, HB-GAC, G-8) (current '89).
Bu 131B Jungmann	A-32	(stored Hangar 10 '80-'89).
Bu 131B Jungmann	A-43	(stored Hangar 10 '80-'89).
Bu 131B Jungmann	A-51	(noted '80-'87, current '89).
Bu 181B Bestmann	A-251	(noted '88, current '89)
Bu 133C Jungmeister	U-61	(c/n 8) (noted '80-'87, current '89).
Bu 133C Jungmeister	U-62	(stored '80-'87).
Bu 133C Jungmeister	U-63	(stored '80-'87).
Comte AC-4	HB-USI	(c/n 33, ex CH-249) (noted '88, current '88).
Dassault Mirage IIIC	J-2201	(noted '81, current '89).
DH Vampire FB.6	J-1049	(noted '78-'82).
DH Vampire FB.6	J-1104	preserved on a pole outside museum (noted '87-'89).
DH Vampire FB.6	J-1153	(noted '88, current '89).
DH Vampire T.55	U-1224	(noted '88, current '89).
DH Venom FB.54	J-1642	(open storage 8.82 for museum, noted in museum 8.87, current '89).
DH Venom FB.54	J-1734	fuselage pod (current '88).
DH Venom FB.54	J-1751	(c/n 397) fuselage pod only (noted '81, current '89).
DH Venom FB.54	J-1753	(noted '88, current '89).
Dewoitine D.26	U-288	(c/n 320, HB-RAE) (noted '80-'87, to Luzern).
Dewoitine D.27	257	ex Luzern (noted '88, current '89)

EKW C-35	C-180	ex Luzern (noted '88, current '89).
EKW C-3603-1	C-534	(c/n 54) (noted '80-'81).
EKW C-3605	C-497	(noted '88, current '89).
EKW C-3605	C-534	(noted '88, current '89).
EKW N-20 Aiguillon	-	ex Luzern (noted '88, current '89).
FFA P.16	X-HB-VAD	(noted '80-'81, current as 'J-3004' '89).
Fieseler Fi 156C-3	A-100	(ex RN+VJ) (noted '80-'81, current '89).
Fokker CV.E	C-331	(noted '80-'81, in Hangar 9 '83, to Luzern by 7.88).
Fokker D.VII	"640"	replica with some original parts (noted '81, current '89).
Haefli DH.1	"245"	replica (noted '88, current '89).
Haefli DH.5	"459"	replica (noted '88, current '89).
Hanriot HD.1	653	ex Luzern (noted '88, current '89).
Hiller 360 (UH-12B)	"KAB-202"	(noted '88, current, upstairs, '89).
Junkers Ju 52/3mg4e	A-701	also registered HB-HOS (noted '82-'87).
Junkers Ju 52/3mg4e	A-702	also registered HB-HOT (noted '82-'88).
Junkers Ju 52/3mg4e	A-703	also registered HB-HOP (noted '82-'88).
Messerschmitt Bf 108B	A-209	(noted '81, current '89).
Messerschmitt Bf 109E	J-355	(ex Luzern) (noted '80-'88, current '89).
Morane MS406	J-276	(ex Luzern) (noted '80-'88, current '89).
Nieuport 28C-1 Bebe	607	(noted '80-'81, current '89).
Nord 1203 Norecrin	HB-HOI	(c/n 122) (current '89).
Harvard T.2B	U-328	(ex 42-12298, FE811) (noted '80, in Hangar 9 '81-'83, current '89).
Harvard T.2B	U-332	(ex 42-0664, FE467) (noted '87).
P-51D Mustang	J-2113	(c/n 39808, ex 44-73349) ex Luzern (current '89).
Pilatus P2-06	U-134	(noted '80-'87, current '89).
Pilatus P3-02	A-801	(noted '88, current '89).
Pilatus PC-7	A-901	(noted '88, current '89).
Rech Monoplane	-	(noted '81).
SO1221S Djinn	"V-23"	(really c/n 38/FR56) (noted '80-'87, current, upstairs, '88-'89).

In store for as future exchange material are DH Venom FB.50 J-1557 and FB.54s J-1712, J-1742 and J-1746.

On display outside the 'Hobbyrama' garden centre in Bettlistrasse in the town is Venom FB.50 J-1641 (ex Dubendorf store '82, at the shop '84-'87). To find it, take a left turn from the railway station.

DIEPOLDSAU

DH Venom FB.54 J-1766 had arrived here (on the A14 motorway about 15 kms South of Bregenz) from Neuheim by late '88 for preservation.

DULLIKEN

Preserved here are Cessna 310C HB-LCC (c/n 35856), DH Venom FB.50 J-1624, and fresh from the Lodrino sale EKW C-3605 Schlepp C-533. The C-3605 and Venom were both confirmed in a car park here (to the East of Olten, South East of Basle, near Aarau) during '88.

DUSSNANG

Preserved here (South of Weinfelden) is DH Venom FB.50 J-1639.

EMMEN

DH Venom FB.54 J-1709 (silver colour scheme and spurious serial "J-1700" had been mounted in flying attitude inside the gate of the FFW factory here by 1981 (current '88). Sister aircraft J-1775 has been stored in the open outside Hangar 3 since 1985 (current '88).

DH Vampire FB.6 J-1167 was derelict here in 9.78 whilst J-1163 was in a similar condition in 5.80 (last recorded 5.85). Both appeared to be heading for the local scrap merchant.

FREIENBACH

An industrial estate near the station has EKW C-3605 C-464 on display on the roof of the R Uiker factory (noted 8.88). Freienbach is on the lakeside near Zurich.

GALS

DH Venom FB.50 J-1526 is preserved here (10 kms North East of Neuchatel).

GENEVA

To the East of the terminals, Douglas DC-7C "HB-SSA" (c/n 45187, ex VR-BCW) can be found in use by the fire service as an evacuation trainer (noted '79-'88).

GRANDVILLARD

Displayed on a pole outside the DCA barracks (Flabschiessplatz) here is DH Venom FB.50 J-1544 (noted 8.87). Grandvillard lies between Bulle and Chateau d'Oex.

GRENCHEN

Aircraft in the "W&R" category here during 1984 were Robin DR400/180R Remorquer HB-EZT (c/n 1514), Mooney M20A HB-DUI (c/n 1422) and Cessna 182P HB-CEB (c/n 6263). The latter was still here during 8.87 in use for spares recovery.

Wrecks were plentiful here in 8.87. PA38 Tomahawks in this category were HB-PFN (c/n 38-81A0002, tail-less), HB-PFL (c/n 38-80A0072, damaged beyond repair 11.9.84) and engineless HB-PFI (c/n 38-80A0071). In use as spares sources are Cessna F150J HB-CUV (registration cancelled 6.86) whilst F172M HB-CCV (c/n 1476, ex D-EKOC) is a wreck only. The fuselage of Dewoitine D.26 HB-RAG (c/n 278) is stored in a hangar with the recently restored wings hanging in the Arrow-Tech hangar. L200D Morava HB-LCU (c/n 171401) still squats in one of the hangars, not having moved for some time (it was noted here semi-dismantled in '85).

HERISAU

Preserved here are DH Venom FB.50 J-1559 and FB.54 J-1778.

HOCHSTETTEN

DH Venom FB.54 J-1756 is preserved on a pole in this village (between Kirchberg and Herzogenbuchsee on the N1 from Bern to Zurich).

INTERLAKEN

Through 1978 to 1980 Vampire FB.6s J-1117 and J-1151 (with serial blacked out) were parked out on the field here. By 1987 J-1151 had disappeared whilst J-1117 had progressed to preservation on a pole at the airfield (current '88). This is believed to be the genuine article and should not be confused with J-1051 at Payerne which is painted up as "J-1117".

Over the Summer of 1986 the nose and centre fuselage of a Hunter F.58/F.58A were reported amongst the hangars and buildings on the base. A Hunter nose (probably the same aircraft) was reported in 10.87. No further details are known.

JEGENSDORF

The Zivilschutzzentrum (Civil Defence Centre) here uses Venom FB.54 J-1739. Jegensdorf is some 15 kms West of Burgdorf.

KUSSNACHT

On the North side of Lake Luzern, along the road from Luzern to Weggis, Venom FB.54 J-1564 is preserved in silver colour scheme opposite Herr A Meyer's BP garage. He is also the local Ford dealer (noted '86-'88).

LANGENTHAL

EKW C-3605 Schlepp C-494 had arrived here by late '88, presumably for preservation.

LAUSANNE

One of the La Ferte Alais Yak 11s came here in 1985 for long term restoration to fly with the Foundation pour la Maintien du Patrimonie Aeronautique.

LOCARNO

DH Venom FB.50s J-1539 and J-1611 are thought to have moved here during 1988 from Sion, having failed to take up their allocated marks G-BMOC and G-BMOD respectively.

LODRINO

In the early Summer of 1987 the Swiss AF's ageing EKW C-3605s began to gather here following the decision to withdraw the type due to increasing fatigue problems. Hardly surprising when one considers that these airframes were built before and during the Second World War as C-3603 fighters, then re-engined with turbo-props during the fiftes for further use as target tugs. These superb machines were held in external storage here and auctioned off on 12.12.87. All had departed by late '88.

EKW C-3605	C-464	to Freienbach by 8.88.
EKW C-3605	C-483	(engineless) to Duxford, UK, by 7.88 for Stephen Grey/The Fighter Collection.
EKW C-3605	C-493	to Magadino '88, then to Rennes/St Jaques, France, late '88 becoming F-WZII then F-AZGC.
EKW C-3605	C-494*	to Langenthal.
EKW C-3605	C-495	
EKW C-3605	C-498	not sold at auction.
EKW C-3605	C-499	(engineless) to Booker, UK, by 3.88.
EKW C-3605	C-501	(engineless) to Sinsheim, WG, by 4.88.
EKW C-3605	C-509	to Altenrhein.
EKW C-3605	C-518*	
EKW C-3605	C-523	
EKW C-3605	C-533	(engineless) to Dulliken.
EKW C-3605	C-535	(engineless) to Mannheim, WG, by 8.88.
EKW C-3605	C-539	(engineless) to Bex by 9.88.
EKW C-3605	C-541	(engineless) to Hermeskeil, WG.
EKW C-3605	C-547	(engineless)
EKW C-3605	C-550	to Magadino '88, to F-AZGD.
EKW C-3605	C-551	to Duxford, UK, by 3.88 for Stephen Grey/The Fighter Collection, to Chino (California) by 5.89.
EKW C-3605	C-552	to Magadino '88.
EKW C-3605	C-555	(engineless)
EKW C-3605	C-557*	
EKW C-3605	C-558	to Booker, UK, by 3.88.

The three aircraft marked with an asterisk are included by Swiss sources in the sale though other sources record only nineteen aircraft at the auction. Swiss sources also quote C-518 and C-557 as having gone to Booker where they have most certainly not appeared. As Personal Plane Services at Booker were expected to ship one or two examples to Kermit weeks, perhaps these are they and they went direct to Florida. That is just my best guess - can anyone confirm?

LUGANO

Cessna F150M HB-CXC (c/n 1272) was noted wrecked here during 9.84 when Dornier Do 27 D-EHJG (c/n 470) was seen to be preserved in the clubhouse garden.

LUPSINGEN

Luscombe 8A Silvaire HB-DUX (c/n 2835) is on rebuild at the owner's home here.

LUZERN

The Verkehrshaus der Schweiz (Swiss Transport Museum) is located on the shores of Lake Lucerne and displays the following aeronautical exhibits.

Bell 47G	HB-XAE	(c/n 689) (noted '78-'88).
Bleriot XI-b	23	(noted '78-'88).
Bu 131B Jungmann	A-62	(c/n 75, ex HB-USG, HB-UUG) (noted '85-'87).
Bu 133C Jungmeister	U-60	(c/n 7) (noted '78-'88).
Comte AC.4	HB-KIL	(c/n 35, ex CH-264) (noted '78-'88).
Convair CV990	HB-ICC	(c/n 38) (noted '78-'88).

DH Vampire FB.6	J-1068	(noted '78-'88).
DH Venom FB.54	J-1729	(noted '82-'88).
Dewoitine D.26	U-288	(c/n 320, ex 288, U-288, HB-RAE) (noted '85-'88).
Dewoitine D.27	J-257	(noted '78-'87, to Dubendorf '88).
Douglas DC-3	HB-IRN	(ex 44-77061, KN683) (noted '78-'88).
Dufaux Biplane	-	(noted '85-'88).
EKW N20 Aiguillon	-	Swiss fighter prototype (noted '78, to Dubendorf '88).
EKW Arbalete	-	Swiss fighter prototype (noted '78-'88).
EKW C-35	C-180	(noted '78-'85, to Dubendorf '88).
EKW C-3603-1	C-537	(noted '78-'88).
Farner WF-7	'32'	glider (noted '88).
FFA AS202 Bravo	HB-HFB	(c/n 021, crashed at Altenrhein 5.10.78) front fuselage (noted '83-'85).
Fieseler Fi 156C-3	A-97	(c/n 8063, ex CN+EL) (noted '78-'88).
Fokker C.VE	C-331	ex Dubendorf (noted '88).
Fokker F.VIIA	HB-LBO	(c/n 5005, ex CH-157) (noted '78-'88).
Hanriot HD.1	653	(noted '78-'85, to Dubendorf '88).
Hug Spyr IIIB	HB-112	(noted '78-'85).
Lockheed 9B Orion	"CH-167"	(c/n 180, ex N12222) (noted '78).
Messerschmitt Bf 108	A-210	(noted '78-'88).
Messerschmitt Bf 109E	J-355	(noted '78, to Dubendorf by '80).
Mignet Pou-du-Ciel	HB-MH8	(noted '78-'88).
Morane MS406	J-276	(noted '78, to Dubendorf by '80).
Nieuport 28C-1 Bebe	688	(noted '78-'88).
P-51D Mustang	J-2113	(c/n 39808, ex 44-73349)(noted'78-'87,to Dubendorf'88).
PA18 Super Cub	HB-OPR	(c/n 18-5786) (noted '78-'88).
Rech Monoplane	-	(noted '85-'88).
RRG Zogling	HB-362	(noted '78-'88).
SAL Twin Pioneer	HB-HOX	(c/n 570) (noted '78, to Sion by '88).
Soldenhoff S-5	-	(noted '88).
Spalinger S.21H	HB-305	stored.
Spalinger S.21H	HB-307	(noted '78-'88).
Stierlin Helicopter	X-HB-XVB	(c/n 3) (noted '85).
Sud Alouette III	HB-XDF	(c/n 1216) (noted '83-'88, hanging from roof).
SE210 Caravelle	-	nose section (noted '88).

MAGADINO

Preserved in flying attitude on the gate is DH Venom FB.50 J-1580 (noted '85-'88) whilst preserved on the base is a Pilatus P3 A-858 (noted '87-'88 - ditched in a lake 4.85 but was salvaged reasonably intact).

During 1988 EKW C-3605 Schlepps C-493, C-550, C-552 arrived from the sale at Lodrino and were placed in open storage on the civil side. C-550 has probably since moved on - where to?

The wreck of Cessna F150M HB-CXC (c/n 1271) was noted here in 8.88.

MATRAN

DH Venom FB.50 J-1584 is preserved here (9 kms South West of Fribourg).

MORGES

Preserved at a castle here is DH Vampire FB.6 J-1055 (noted '83-'88).

MUNSINGEN

DH Venom FB.50 J-1646 is preserved here (some 20 kms South of Bern).

NEUHEIM

DH Venom FB.50 J-1545 is stored here (10 kms North East of Zug) pending possible resale. FB.54 J-1766 was in a similar condition but by late '88 had moved to Diepoldsau for preservation.

PAYERNE

By 1980 Vampire FB.6 "J-1117" had appeared on display here at a barracks between the airfield & the town (really J-1051). In 8.86 this machine was seen to have left its perch and was relegated to the dump on the airfield. Mounted on a pole in the viewing enclosure at the base is Vampire FB.6 J-1142 (noted '86-'88).

Anonymity rules here as in 8.80 and 8.81 an unidentified Vampire FB.6 and a Venom were derelict on the field. By 10.82 there were two Venoms here (FB.54 J-1734 plus one other) but by 9.83 only one unmarked example remained.

Noted here during 8.87 were Vampire T.55s U-1201 and U-1202 both wearing the inscription 'AS-11' indicating their use as training airframes in connection with the French AS-11 missile. Whether they were ground instructional airframes or still airworthy is uncertain.

SCHLIERBACH

Preserved here (10 kms North of Sursee) is DH Venom FB.50 J-1578.

SCHOTZ

The Zivilschutzzentrum (Civil Defence Centre) has Venom FB.54 J-1719. Schotz can be found some 15 kms West of Sursee.

SION

Gate guard on the military side of the field is DH Vampire FB.6 J-1190 (noted '78-'88).

Noted in the Farner Air Services hangar on the South side of the field in 6.86 were Pilatus P2-05s U-127/HB-RAS (c/n 47) & U-107/HB-RAT (c/n 27) (both here by '81, current '88) and the wreck of MS883 Rallye 115 HB-ERP (c/n 1364). Both the P2s are owned by members of the Foundation pour le Maintien du Patrimonie Aeronautique who intend to establish a museum at the field. Their Twin Pioneer HB-HOX was here by '85 and Beech D.18S F-BHMM had joined it by 8.88. Dismantled Ryan Navion B HB-ESG (c/n 4-2239, ex N5339K) was also here with the group in '85 but was not recorded in '88. It is probably under restoration somewhere off the field.

In the Air Glaciers hangar, the anonymous Alouette III in use as a source of spares is HB-XCB (c/n 1259) (noted 8.87).

Vampire FB.6 J-1079 sat derelict on the field through 1980-81 finally gravitating to the scrap compound amongst the orchards on the South side. It was recorded here in 8.82 with parts from J-1129 (which was still flying from the base), a set of booms from Venom FB.50 J-1540 and a Hunter centre fuselage. Vampire J-1079 was noted once again in 8.84 when the fuselage pods from J-1169 and J-1178 were also noted. Over the years there have been many exaggerated reports for this dump since many scrap components were junked here and lists of serials quoted emanated from these rather than from whole airframes. An anonymous, boomless, Venom was reported on the dump here in 8.88.

In open store here in 8.85 with Farner Air Services were Venom FB.50s J-1539 (allocated G-BMOD), J-1573 (allocated G-BMOB), J-1611 (allocated G-BMOC) and J-1631. All were still current 8.87 and J-1631 was in the Farner Hangar in 8.88 probably reserved for the museum referred to above. Of the other three, J-1539 and J-1611 are thought to be at Locarno now whilst J-1573 is being restored to flying condition as HB-RVB. It is probably still on the airfield somewhere.

STANDORT FRUITIGEN

Pilatus P2-06 U-147 was auctioned off at Dubendorf 30.5.81 and was reported there in 8.81 stored for a museum at Standort Fruitigen (20 kms South of Spiez). In the absence of any further sightings at Dubendorf the aircraft is assumed to have come here. Further details welcomed.

STANS

The gate at the Pilatus factory is normally guarded by Pilatus P2-05 U-131 (ex HB-GAB, U-101, to A-101, to U-131) in its original markings as "U-101", however this machine was taken indoors during 1987 and remained so in 1988. Having suffered from its spell in the open the Pilatus staff are reluctant to do much with her unless some sort of protective 'bubble' can be provided at the end of it.

DH Venom FB.50 J-1596 is reported to preserved here though its precise location on the airfield (or indeed in the town) remains unknown. It was last recorded in store on the field during 1985.

By 6.88, T-33AN Silver Star 21261 (in USAF marks as "54-21261", ex RCAF 21261, CF-IHB, G-OAHB, G-JETT) had arrived and was stored outside the Pilatus factory. The aircraft was still there in 9.88 and is thought to be destined for the Dubendorf museum.

Stans (or more specifically, the side of the field often referred to as Buochs) was responsible for the disposal of the Swiss Venom fleet. Swiss media sources quote 59 aircraft sold (of which 39 remained in Switzerland) and 200 aircraft scrapped at Buochs. This figure is obviously hopelessly inaccurate since the Swiss AF started with 250 Venoms and lost about 50 during their lengthy flying career. Deducting the 59 healthy aircraft sold off we are left with a maximum of 140 Venoms to meet the scrapman here. This figure is likely to reduce still further taking into account the probability of some disposals from other bases. As you will have realised by now, the author does not have access to any official listing of the Venoms scrapped here and elsewhere, so the following notes represent the details recorded by enthusiasts in recent years.

DH Venom FB.50	J-1503	noted '84, to Wiedlisbach.
DH Venom FB.50	J-1526	noted '84, to Gals
DH Venom FB.50	J-1527	noted 8.83-'85, to USA for spares recovery.
DH Venom FB.54	J-1544	noted '84, to Grandvillard.
DH Venom FB.54	J-1545	noted '84, to Neuheim.
DH Venom FB.50	J-1557	noted 8.83-'85, to Dubendorf.
DH Venom FB.54	J-1559	noted '84, to Herisau.
DH Venom FB.50	J-1564	noted '84-'85, to Kussnacht.
DH Venom FB.50	J-1572	scrapped 8.81.
DH Venom FB.54	J-1578	noted '84, to Schlierbach.
DH Venom FB.50	J-1584	noted '84, to Matran.
DH Venom FB.50	J-1594	noted '84.
DH Venom FB.50	J-1596	noted '85, since preserved here.
DH Venom FB.50	J-1600	scrapped 8.81.
DH Venom FB.50	J-1603	noted '84, to Sinsheim, WG.
DH Venom FB.50	J-1616	to N203DM 3.86.
DH Venom FB.50	J-1624	noted '84, to Dulliken.
DH Venom FB.50	J-1628	noted '84, to Sinsheim, WG.
DH Venom FB.50	J-1630	noted '84, to Altenrhein.
DH Venom FB.50	J-1631	noted 8.83, to Sion.
DH Venom FB.50	J-1636	noted '85, to Le Bourget, France.
DH Venom FB.50	J-1638	noted '84.
DH Venom FB.50	J-1639	noted '84, to Dussnang.
DH Venom FB.50	J-1640	noted 8.83-'84, to Wiedlisbach.
DH Venom FB.50	J-1643	noted 8.83-'84, to Wiedlisbach.
DH Venom FB.50	J-1644	noted 8.83.
DH Venom FB.50	J-1645	fuselage in scrap compound 8.83 (with 7 others).
DH Venom FB.50	J-1646	noted 8.83, to Munsingen.
DH Venom FB.54	J-1712	noted 8.83-'85, to Dubendorf.
DH Venom FB.54	J-1717	noted 8.83-'85.
DH Venom FB.54	J-1721	scrapped 8.81.
DH Venom FB.54	J-1726	scrapped 8.81.
DH Venom FB.54	J-1730	to G-BLIA, to N402DM 10.84.
DH Venom FB.54	J-1739	noted '84, to Jegensdorf.
DH Venom FB.54	J-1742	noted 8.83, to Dubendorf.
DH Venom FB.54	J-1747	to N5471V, to N747J 9.86.
DH Venom FB.54	J-1755	scrapped 8.81.
DH Venom FB.54	J-1758	noted 8.83, to G-BLSD, to N203DM 4.86, to G-BLSD 4.88.
DH Venom FB.54	J-1763	to G-BLSD, to N902DM 7.85.

DH Venom FB.54 J-1765 dumped behind hangar '84.
DH Venom FB.54 J-1766 noted '84, to Neuheim, then Diepoldsau.
DH Venom FB.54 J-1778 noted '84, to Herisau.
DH Venom FB.54 J-1792 dumped behind hangar '84.
DH Venom FB.54 J-1797 noted '84, to Hermeskeil, WG.
DH Venom FB.54 J-1798 noted '84, to Sinsheim, WG.
DH Venom FB.54 J-1799 noted '84, to G-BLIC, to N502DM 6.85.

ULRICHEN

Preserved at the airfield here (10 kms South West of Gletsch) is Venom FB.54 J-1776.

VILLMERGEN

DH Venom FB.50 J-1626 is preserved here (15 kms South East of Lensburg) for possible resale.

WANGEN-LACHEN

The wreck of Cessna F152 HB-CNL (c/n 1465) could be found here during 9.84.

WIEDLISBACH

DH Venom FB.50s J-1503, J-1535, J-1579, J-1640 and J-1643 are stored here (off the E4 motorway North East of Solothurn) for possible resale.

WINTERTHUR

Vickers Viking 1 "D-BABY" (c/n 132, ex G-AHPB) arrived by road in Spring '88 having been displayed at Dusseldorf airport. It is now on show outside the Technorama Museum.

ZURICH/KLOTEN

On display in the main concourse of Terminal B are Bu 131 Jungmann A-67, Messerschmitt Bf 108B Taifun A-201 and Pou-du-Ciel HB-SUR (all noted '78-'88).

Mitsubishi MU-2B-35 9Q-CAA (c/n 618) has spent many years in store ('84-'86 and earlier).

Piaggio P.166 HB-LAY (c/n 359) was in use by the airport fire service for training exercises here in 3.84.

On the dump here by 9.85 were ex Air Afrique DC-8-53 TU-TCP (c/n 45568, arrived from Niamey 6.5.85 for spares recovery) and ex Air France SE210 Caravelle III F-BJTL (c/n 142, arr from Orly 30.7.81 for airport fire service). The DC-8 was inscribed "Training" by 8.87 in recognition of its role with the Fire Section as an evacuation trainer. The Caravelle was used for more destructive training and was destroyed in a fire exercise on 27.9.85 at 14:10 hours!

TURKEY

Turkey is one of very few European countries which are largely virgin territory for British aviation enthusiasts and although a good deal of new information has appeared over the last two years there is obviously much to be discovered here. The growth of tourism in Turkey coupled with the fact that the Turkish authorities are now prepared to sanction the occasional base visit bodes well for the future though it must be stressed that Turkey is a country within which it is not wise to observe military aircraft without prior permission.

ADANA/INCIRLIK

In 6.87 the dump at this erstwhile U-2 base (of Francis Gary Powers fame) was occupied by F-102A Delta Dagger 53426 (ex 55-3426) with an unidentified F-100 Super Sabre and F-4 Phantom. The latter sighting may refer to F-4C Phantom 63-7474 ex 163 TFS/Indiana ANG which arrived by 7.86 for bdr training.

ANKARA/ETIMESGUT

Ex 224 Filo Viscount 794 246 (c/n 246, ex TC-SEC) was withdrawn from use some years ago and remained parked on the airfield in 7.88. By this time C-47 Dakotas 43-6003/12-003 (C-47B c/n 25970, ex 43-48709), 42-6031/12-031 (C-47A c/n 13622, ex 42-93683) and 42-6075/12-075 (C-47A c/n 19357, ex 42-100894) were engineless and probably await scrapping.

BALIKESIR

The base of 9ci AHU equipped with the F-104 Starfighter, Balikesir's gate is guarded by F-84F Thunderstreak 7214/9-214 (ex 53-7214) and F-84G Thunderjet '9-011' (ex 51-10011). Unfortunately the full serials are not worn on these aircraft. Preserved elsewhere on the base is AT-11 Kansan 6865/9-865 (wfu 21.10.83). All three were noted in 4.87 and were confirmed in 10.88. On the fire dump in 4.87 was an anonymous F-84G Thunderjet.

In the process of being scrapped in 10.88 were TF-104G Starfighters 5812/9-812 (c/n 5812, ex KLu D-5812), 5814/9-814 (c/n 5814, ex KLu D-5814) and 12263/9-263 (c/n 5508, ex RNorAF 62-12263).

BANDIRMA

Parked on the field during '87 was an F-84G Thunderjet coded '6-001'. Its status, preserved or derelict, is uncertain.

DIYARBAKIR

The home of 8ci AHU (8th Jet Air Base) possesses two preserved aircraft. They are F-84G Thunderjet 51-11218/8-218 and F-100D Super Sabre 55-2763/8-763 (both noted '87).

Withdrawn from use here is Beech AT-11A Kansan 6923/8-923 (ex Base Flight, noted '88).

ESKISEHIR

Guarding the gate at 1ci AHU (1st Jet Air Base) are F-84F Thunderstreak 7142 (ex 52-7142) (noted '85-'88) in the colours of the USAF's "Thunderbirds" team and an anonymous F-86E Sabre ("7123" noted '85-'88) also in "Thunderbirds" colours.

With 113 Filo, the last RF-84F Thunderflashes were withdrawn from use on 29.8.80 being replaced by the RF-4E Phantom. The surviving RF-84Fs comprised 51-1860, 51-1917, 51-1924, 52-7234, 52-73C1, 52-8722, 52-8733, 52-8758, 52-8759, 52-8764 and 52-8765. Of these, all but 51-1917 (to museum at Istanbul/Yesilkoy) were still derelict on the field in 1987 accompanied by F-84G Thunderjets 51-10987 & 51-11019 and AT-11 Kansan 6933/1-933 (ex 42-37585, wfu 21.10.83). F-84G 10987 and the Kansan were both in excellent condition.

A visit in 7.88 found eight RF-84Fs still on the base, of which 51-1924/1-924 was described as preserved whilst the seven remaining decoys were not identified. By this time an F-100 Super Sabre coded '1-774' was also preserved here.

ISTANBUL/YESILKOY

Now also known as Ataturk airport, C-54D Skymaster ETI-683 was withdrawn from use here in 1975 and stored on the airfield. The Turk Hava Muzesi (Turkish Aviation Museum) was opened on 16.10.85, located on the Southern edge of Ataturk airport and the C-54 has joined the other exhibits on display here:-

Beech AT-11 Kansan	6930	(ex 42-37565) ex '9-930', wfu 21.10.83.
F-102A Delta Dagger	53386	(ex 55-3386)
TF-102A Delta Dagger	62368	(ex 56-2368)
Curtiss CW22R Falcon	TC-TK15	probably ex 2615 (ex 12ci AHU).
DH89A Rapide	TC-ERK	
Dornier Do 27H-2	10293	(c/n 2142, ex D-EFCI) 'KK', arrived by 1988.
Dornier Do 27H-2	10294	(c/n 2114, ex D-ECPI) 'KK', arrived by 1988.
C-47A Dakota	43-6052	(c/n 13877, ex 43-30726) 'YSL-52'.
C-47B Dakota	43-6008	(c/n 26456, ex 43-49195) 'H-008' arrived by 1988.
C-54D Skymaster	ETI-683	(c/n 10788, ex 42-72683)
Grigowicht M5	-	(flying boat captured from Imperial Russia in WW1).
Lockheed T-33A	35744	(ex 53-5744) ex 12ci AHU.
F-104G Starfighter	22344	(c/n 6043, ex 62-12344)
F-104G Starfighter	"12619"	(c/n 8223, ex WGAF 2474) "4-619"
Miles Magister	(TC-KAH)	'77' (probably R1977, c/n 1948)
Miles Magister	TC-KAY	
CL-13 Sabre Mk 2	19207	(c/n 107, ex RCAF) ex 12ci AHU.
CL-13 Sabre Mk 2	19268	(c/n 168, ex RCAF)
T-6G Harvard	04	probably ex 7504.
F-100C Super Sabre	42089	(ex 54-2089) ex '3-089' 3ci AHU.
Piper L-18B Super Cub	10306	
PZL-24C Peteral	2015	
P-47D Thunderbolt	TC-21	probably ex 7121.
F-84G Thunderjet	110572	(ex 51-10572)
F-84G Thunderjet	19953	(ex 51-9953)
F-84F Thunderstreak	28941	(ex 52-8941)
RF-84F Thunderflash	11901	(ex 51-1901)
RF-84F Thunderflash	11917	(ex 51-1917) ex 113 Filo.
UH-19B Chickasaw	52-7577	
Ugur Krus	(TC-KUJ)	(c/n 5144/1957) '44'

IZMIR/CIGLI

Cigli houses the THK's jet flying school (2ci AHU) which operates ageing Cessna T-37s and Northrop T-38s alongside its even older Lockheed T-33s. Second hand T-33s have come from several sources over the years, most recently from France.

A visit here in 4.87 saw a number of T-33As being broken up, .../055, 530../0.., ..3../3.., 17443/443, 17485/485 and 70673/673. A further visit in 10.87 found only 17443 still present but with previously unreported (14153)/153 and T-33AN 21107/107.

IZMIR/GAZIEMIR

The base can be found along the E24 on the Southern outskirts of Izmir just before Cumaovasi and houses a technical training school (whose complement of instructional airframes is unfortunately unknown). In 4.87 an F-84G Thunderjet coded '745' lay on the dump whilst on display inside the base are an F-84F Thunderstreak, F-84G Thunderjet and T-33A.

KAYSERI

Preserved at the base here is C-47A Dakota 43-6025 (c/n 19531, ex 43-15065) ex 'YSL-25' (Noted '88).

KUTAHYA

Located some 80 kms South West of Eskisehir, the base is no longer operational though it still possesses a heliport. Dotted around the base are three F-84F Thunderstreaks two of which are 7007/007 (ex 53-7007) and 7040/040 (ex 53-7040).

MURTED

The home of 4ci AHU equipped with the F-104 Starfighter, the main gate is guarded by CL-13 Sabre Mk 2 19103 in the colours of the 'Flying Swans' aerobatic team. Parked out on the field looking sorry for itself is F-102A Delta Dagger 53392 (ex 55-3392). All these were current during 1986.

SIVRIHISAR

This air base is some 12kms West of the town on road 200 towards Eskisehir. In 4.87 four F-100 Super Sabres were noted at the Western end of the base serving as decoys. Two of them wore the 3ci AHU codes '3-877' and '3-950'. They may be F-100Cs 54-2877 and 54-2950 but are not confired.

TOPEL

Preserved on the gate at the naval air base here by 4.87 was an unidentified S-2 Tracker (current 7.88).

UNKNOWN LOCATIONS

The last ten AT-11 Kansans were withdrawn from use on 21.10.83. Fates are known for only a few and it is likely that several more are still 'alive' and waiting to be discovered.

6815	6833	6840	6865 Balikesir
6867	6880	6904	6923 Diyarbakir
6930 Istanbul	6933 Eskisehir		

It has also been claimed that as late as 1983 the Turkish AF still possessed some 150 F-84F Thunderstreaks in storage somewhere in the country for possible refurbishment (!).

ITALIAN MILITARY TWINS

Piaggio P.136 MM80078 at the Museo Storico in '83; MM80005 behind *(Mike Bursell)*
P.166M MM61874 was resprayed at Guidonia before joining the Museo Storico *(Mike Bursell)*
Beech C-45 MM61762 at Guidonia at the beginning of its storage *(via Fred Martin)*

ITALIAN TWINS

Caravelle VI-N I-DAXT, the Caravelle Ristorante at Breno *(John Wegg)*

S-2A Tracker MM133103/41-42 derelict at Brindisi *(Frank McMeiken)*

The AMI Albatross fleet was initially withdrawn in 1979. HU-16A MM50- 174/15-2 came to Biella for preservation *(Mike Bursell)*

Former Kenyan AF Caribou 5Y-BET stored with Newcal at Luqa, Malta since July '86 *(John Newton)*

Sole Luxembourg entry - ex Spanish AF Texans E.16-106 and E.16-86 in store at Findel 7.84 *(Mike Bursell)*

B-25D Mitchell FR193/NO-L displayed at the Oorlogsmuseum, Overloon in the Netherlands *(Mike Bursell)*

NETHERLANDS

Lockheed 12A L2-38 recovered from Denmark for the MLM, Kamp Zeist *(David Caris)*

Harvard B-103 used by the KLM Apprentice Training School at Schiphol *(Dave Lee)*

The Antony Fokker School at Den Haag - a general view *(Mike Bursell)*

NETHERLANDS

Catalina 16-212 preserved at Kamp Zeist, formerly at Hoeven *(David Caris)*

Gilze-Rijen's Fokker S.14 L-17 on an outing to Deelen 7.88 *(Mike Bursell)*

This HUP-2 Retriever can be found with an Amsterdam car breaker *(Dave Lee)*

DUTCH JETS

T-33A M-54 painted as 'M-52' for the KLu's 75th at Deelen 7.88 *(Mike Bursell)*

F-84F P-170 after a firefighting exercise at Woensdrecht *(Otger v/d Kooij)*

Greek AF RF-84F 1125 on arrival at Volkel on 29.7.88 for restoration *(Otger v/d Kooij)*

NORWAY - THE GARDERMOEN MUSEUM

Northrop N-3PB 320/U recovered from an Icelandic river and rebuilt *(Ian Hogarth)*

Spitfire PR.XI PL979/A-ZB flew until 1954 *(Ian Hogarth)*

Genuine Heinkel 111 (not a CASA 2.111) 1126/5J+CN *(Ian Hogarth)*

NORWAY - THE GARDERMOEN MUSEUM

Ex GE.314 T-33A 117546 painted as 'DP-K' of 718 Skv *(Ian Hogarth)*

Immaculately restored F-86F Sabre 31206/FN-D *(Ian Hogarth)*

F-84G Thunderjet 111209/MU-S in 338 Skv colours *(Ian Hogarth)*

NORWAY - MORE JETS

Vampire F.3 P42408 at Gardermoen painted in 336 Skv marks *(Ian Hogarth)*

Ex WGAF TF-104G 469 served only briefly before retirement to Gardermoen *(Ian Hogarth)*

Ex 334 Skv CF-104D Starfighter 4637 now a decoy at Bodo *(John Slack)*

PORTUGAL

Constellation CS-TLA spent many years as a bar at Faro *(Barry Lewis)*

The fuselage of Chipmunk T.10 1370 lies in a yard at Benedita *(Mike Bursell)*

DH.87B Hornet Moth CR-AAC is stored in the Museo do Ar storage hangar at Sintra *(Phil Stevens)*

PORTUGAL

Douglas C-54A 6606 is in the storage compound at Alverca with the hulk of Super Cub 'CS-207' under the port wing *(Mike Bursell)*

One of several Junkers 52s at Alverca is 6304, fitted with surplus Texan engines *(Mike Bursell)*

Grumman Widgeon 2401 is preserved in Monsanto Park, Lisbon *(Dave Lee)*

PORTUGUESE JETS

G-91R 3065 ex Sintra is derelict at Montijo with other Ginas *(Mike Bursell)*

F-84G Thunderjet 5201 guards the Ota gate in fine style *(Mike Bursell)*

T-33AN Silver Star 1952 is preserved in a park at Chaves *(Dave Lee)*

SPANISH CIVILIANS

Agusta-Bell 47J EC-AXZ preserved at Cuatro-Vientos *(J-C Oge)*

AISA I-115 E.9-156 sits by the roadside at Sanchidrian *(Mike Bursell)*

Ex TASA Dornier 28A EC-CPP preserved at Cuatro-Vientos *(J-C Oge)*

SPANISH MILITARY JETS

F-86F Sabre C.5-70/2-41 preserved on the Spanish side at Zaragoza *(J-C Oge)*

HA200B Saeta A.10B-52/214-52 guards the gate at Moron *(J-C Oge)*

T-bird E.15-51/41-8 is now preserved at Cuatro-Vientos *(Barry Lewis)*

SPAIN - MUSEO DEL AIRE

DH89A Dragon Rapide G-ACYR in the Cuatro-Vientos museum *(Barry Lewis)*

A rarity in the collection is this DH60G Moth Major *(Barry Lewis)*

Cierva C.191VP (Avro 620) EC-AIM, one time G-ABXH *(Barry Lewis)*

SPAIN - MUSEUMS

HA1112M-1L Buchon C.4K-162 at Sevilla/Tablada in May '88 *(Dave Lee)*

CASA Azor T.7-6/405-15 displayed with the Museo del Aire *(Barry Lewis)*

This CASA 2.111B (Heinkel 111) is in the base museum at Tablada *(Dave Lee)*

SPAIN - MUSEO DEL AIRE

Dornier 24T HD.5-2, beautifully presented in its own pond *(Phil Stevens)*

C-7A Caribou T.9-27/371-07 in a sorry state at Cuatro-Vientos 2.89 *(Dave Weinrich)*

Boeing KC-97L TK.1-3/123-03 being reassembled in 2.89 *(Dave Weinrich)*

SWEDEN - MUSEUMS

Junkers F.13 S-AAAC hangs in the Sveriges Tekniska Museum, Stockholm *(John Davis)*
C-47A 79007/797 with the Flygvapenmuseum at Malmslatt *Andy Thompson)*
Also at Malmslatt, Pembroke C.52 83008/85, ex F 13 *(John Davis)*

SWEDEN

Canberra T.11 52002/52 ex F 8 displayed outside at Malmslatt *(John Davis)*

Varsity T.1 82001/80 ex WJ900 also at Malmslatt *(John Davis)*

J 35B Draken 35235 serves at Ljungbyhed with the fire service *(Dave Lee)*

SWEDEN - HOME GROWN JETS

The first prototype Viggen '-1' is now out to grass at Malmslatt *(Andy Thompson)*

The firemen at Ronneby were using J 35A Draken 35060/24 (ex F 16) during 1984 *(Dave Lee)*

J 35D Draken 35321, seen in open store at Ljungbyhed in 1985 has moved to the dump at Satenas *(Andy Thompson)*

SWEDEN - HOME GROWN JETS

J 32C Lansen 32934/34 (ex F 11) is used for rescue training exercises at Ljungbyhed *(Dave Lee)*

J 29F Tunnan 29666/64 (ex F 14) is preserved at Ljungbyhed *(Andy Thompson)*

A 32A Lansen 32285/27 (ex F 6) trains the Ronneby firemen in the deployment of fire appliances *(Dave Lee)*

SWITZERLAND

Dubendorf-based Ju-Air Junkers 52 A-701/HB-HOS *(Eric Gandet)*

Former Swissair Dakota HB-IRN at the Luzern museum *(Eric Gandet)*

Pilatus P2 U-101 within the Pilatus factory at Stans *(Paul Jackson)*

SWISS TRANSPORT MUSEUM

Lockheed 9B Orion CH-167 and other exhibits *(Ken Ellis)*

The N20 Aiguillon prototype at Luzern, now at Dubendorf *(Mike Bursell)*

Largest exhibit at Luzern is ex Swissair Coronado HB-ICC *(Ken Ellis)*

SWISS VAMPIRES AND VENOMS

Vampire FB.6 J-1049 at Dubendorf, now replaced by another *(Mike Bursell)*
The Sion dump 8.82; Vampire FB.6 J-1079 in foreground *(Mike Bursell)*
Venom FB.50 J-1624 immaculately preserved at Dulliken *(Eric Gandet)*

TURKEY

RF-84F Thunderflash 1924 derelict at Eskisehir since wfu 8.80 *(Robbie Shaw)*

Sabre 2 19103 preserved in 'Flying Swans' colours at Murted *(Robbie Shaw)*

Impressive line up of redundant 'Flashes at Eskisehir *(Robbie Shaw)*

TURKEY

P-47D Thunderbolt TC-21 at the Turkish Aviation Museum, Istanbul *(Robbie Shaw)*

A rarity at Istanbul is this PZL-24C Peteral, 2015 *(Robbie Shaw)*

Also with the Turkish Aviation Museum, TF-102A 0-62368 *(Robbie Shaw)*

WEST GERMANY - MILITARY TRANSPORTS

Varsity T.1 WF382, a former Aldergrove hack, at Berlin/Gatow *(Dave Lee)*

Hastings T.5 TG503 at Gatow commemorates the Berlin airlift *(Dave Lee)*

Pembroke C.54 5417 displayed at the Seifertshofen museum *(Dave Lee)*

WEST GERMANY -TRANSPORTS

Super Connie 'D-ALAP' (F-BHML) preserved at Frankfurt *(P J Bish via Ken Ellis)*

Former Nor-Fly Dakota '65371' on the roof at Frankfurt *(Paul Jackson)*

Ex-Polish AF Ilyushin 14 3076 now preserved at Hermeskeil *(Dave Lee)*

WEST GERMANY

Noratlas D-ACUT at Hermeskeil having seen little civil use *(Mike Bursell)*
Dornier 29 'YA-101' with the Dornier museum, Oberpfaffenhofen *(Dave Lee)*
Piaggio P.149D D-ENJX at Offenburg after an accident in 8.83 *(Mike Everton)*

WEST GERMANY

H-34 143 at Seifertshofen. The Dutch Navy have their eyes on it! *(Dave Lee)*

Vertol H-21C 8321 at the Hermeskeil museum entrance *(Mike Bursell)*

Sabre Mk.5 'JB-111' in a barracks at Pinneburg in Hamburg *(Andy Thompson)*

WEST GERMANY - EX-CANADIANS

Ex WGAF F-86E on the Lahr gate in RCAF colours as '23444' *(Andy Thompson)*
A general view of Hermeskeil, CAF T-33 in foreground *(Mike Bursell)*
Avro CF-100 18784 (ex 100784) guards the gate at Sollingen *(via Fred Martin)*

WEST GERMANY - LUFTWAFFE JETS

RF-84F 'BD-119', ex EB-343, at Furstenfeldbruck air base *(Ian Hogarth)*

Dornier-built G-91R/3 3135 in their Oberpfaffenhofen museum *(Dave Lee)*

Derelict at Leck is F-104G Starfighter 2075, as '2476' *(Otger v/d Kooij)*

WEST GERMANY

West Germany is a large country with a very large population of military wrecks and relics, particularly post war jets. In contrast, civilian wrecks are virtually unknown here. Private aircraft seem to be sold abroad as they reach middle age, only a few crash wrecks can be found dumped around the civil fields and these tend to be short term only.

The military scene has been covered in print during 1983 by the excellent 'West German Military Wrecks and Relics' published by the Aviation Society of the Netherlands. In addition, recent Air Britain West German registers have included some Wrecks and Relics details. With this in mind and in order to keep the West German section in this book to manageable proportions I have set out to record only those relics which either still exist, have only recently expired or have some other valid claim for a mention. The reader seeking more dated information is referred to the sources above.

Only the basic details of RAF Germany relics are listed as these are already covered in Ken Ellis's 'Wrecks and Relics' which should already be on your bookshelf.

AACHEN/MERZBRUCK

The frame of PA18-95 Super Cub D-EFTG (c/n 18-1543, ex 51-15543) has been stored here since CofA expiry in '78 (current '85).

AHLHORN

Home of the WGAF's Htg.64 with UH-1Ds and a detachment of A-10A Thunderbolts, Ahlhorn boasts several preserved airframes displayed around the base.

Sycamore Mk.52	7823	(c/n 13481) ex Htg.64 and Braunschweig (noted on the gate '74-'87).
Sycamore Mk.52	7837	(c/n 13503) ex Htg.64 & D-HAHN (ntu). 'SAR' inscription modified to 'BAR' and used as a bar on the base! (noted '79-'85, to Landsberg by '87).
N2501D Noratlas	5356	(c/n 186) ex Ltg.62 (noted '78-'89).
CL-13B Sabre Mk.6	"JA-110"	(c/n S6-1775, ex JB-112) Jg.71 marks (noted '79-'87).

For bdr training purposes, the A-10A Forward Operating Location here have received a Phantom and a Voodoo.

F-4C Phantom	63-7446	ex 171 TFS/Michigan ANG, arr 17.7.86 (current '89).
F-101B Voodoo	58-0265	ex 111 FIS/Texas ANG & MASDC, arr by 4.86 (current '89).

As with most German fire dumps, the situation here changes very slowly. Noted in recent years have been the following.

UH-1D Iroquois	7084	(c/n 8144) ex Htg.64, w/o 28.1.76 (noted '82-'85).
UH-1D Iroquois	7126	(c/n 8186) ex Htg.64, w/o 9.3.74 (noted '75-'82).
UH-1D Iroquois	7150	(c/n 8210) ex Htg.64, w/o 18.12.73 (to Fassberg by '83).
RF-84F Thunderflash	EB-354	(ex 53-7690) ex Est.91 at Meppen (noted '79-'89).

AIR CLASSIK

This seems like a convenient point to refer to Air Classik GmbH (a part of Kurfiss Aviation) who through the seventies and eighties have provided airframes for display at various airports in West Germany and Austria from a central store at Sielmingen near Stuttgart airport. These aircraft have often been displayed at several different airports and some have been passed on to other museums. Air Classik aircraft are dealt with under each location as appropriate.

ALTENSTADT

Displayed at the Luftlande und Lufttransportschule is N2501D Noratlas 5337 (c/n 160) which had previously been preserved at Neubiberg from '75 until airlifted in by CH-53G in '82 (noted '82-'85). The school also has substantial sections of C-160A Transall 5005 (c/n A05, ex YA-053) (noted '84-'85).

Three UH-1D Iroquois hulks were reported here in '86 in use for loading practice. They were 7037 (c/n 4368, ex 64-13661), 7206 (c/n 8326) plus one other.

ARNSBERG

Stored at the airfield (20 kms South of Soest) in 1985 was a PA18 Super Cub with the fuselage frame number 18-1049 (possibly D-EKQH, c/n 18-1017).

AUGSBURG

Preserved outside an MBB (Messerschmitt-Bolkow-Blohm) factory on the Western side of the city by 5.80 was an "Me 109" in the form of an unidentified ex Spanish AF Hispano HA1112K-1L. It is accompanied by ex Swiss AF Messerschmitt Bf 108B A-208 (c/n 2064, painted as "D-IOIO"). Both were current here in '89.

AURICH

Displayed on a pole at the gate of Blucherkaserne in the town (about 75 kms North West of Oldenburg) is F-104F Starfighter 2908 (c/n 5058, ex 59-5005) wearing the false serial "2086" (which is alive at Wittmund). The aircraft had arrived from Jever by '76 and was still current in '89.

BAD GANDERSHEIM

Derelict on the airfield (about 60 kms South of Hanover) in '85 was Dornier Do 27A-5 D-EAWW (c/n 448, ex 5720) whose CofA expired in '79.

BENTLAGE

The gate at the Heer base of Rheine/Bentlage (Theodor Blank kaserne) is guarded by Sikorsky H-34G 8035 (c/n 58-1100) (noted '77-'89).

Derelict behind a building on the far side of the field is the fuselage of Dornier Do 27B-5 5686 (c/n 394) (noted '77-'85).

BERLIN

With the Museum Fur Verkehr Und Technik (Transport & Technology Museum) in the city are the following.

Boeing 707-420	"D-ABOC"	(c/n 18071, ex 4X-ATB, N130KR) presented to Lufthansa by Boeing to mark LH's 200th Boeing purchase. Arr Frankfurt 20.11.86 as 4X-ATB in LH colours, ferried to Berlin/Tegel 21.11.86 as N130KR. Displayed as "D-ABOC" in LH colours.
Schulgleiter SG-38	-	stored
DH U-6A Beaver	58-2020	ex US Army
Dittmar Condor	-	
Douglas C-47B Dakota	A65-69	(c/n 27127, ex 43-49866, ferried in as ZD215 21.6.80) ex RAAF, stored at Gatow.
Eardley Billing	-	replica, stored.
Fi 156 Storch	-	
Fa 330A-1 Bachstelze	-	stored
Fokker DR.1	-	replica
Grob Cirrus	D-3101	
HP Hastings T.5	TG503	(8555M) ex 230 OCU (displayed at Gatow)
Junkers Ju 52/3m	T.2B-108	(c/n 4145) ex Spanish AF, painted as "D-2201" (ex Gatow).
Klemm L.25	F-PCDA	(c/n 138, ex D-1611, TS-AAB, EZ-AAB) stored at Gatow
Lilienthal Gleiter	-	replica
S-D Demoiselle	-	replica

BERLIN/GATOW

Preserved as a memorial to the Berlin Airlift here are ex 230 OCU Hastings T.5 TG503 (8555M) and ex RAAF Dakota III A65-69 (c/n 15686/27127, ex 43-49866) which wore the serial ZD215 for the ferry flight down the corridor to Berlin. Both are with the Museum Fur Verkehr Und Technik (see above).

Vickers Varsity T.1 WF382 (8872M, ex 23 MU 'hack') arrived on 4.7.77 for the fire dump but has since been reprieved and is now preserved on the base.

On the fire dump, the burnt out remains of ex RAE Vickers Valetta C.1 WJ491 were finally scrapped during 1988.

BERLIN/TEGEL

Preserved at Base Aerienne 165 in the French sector of West Berlin is N2501F Noratlas 126 (ex '63-WT' ET.63, AdlA) in camouflage scheme (noted '86).

BERLIN/TEMPELHOF

Preserved as a memorial to the Berlin Airlift are Douglas C-54G Skymaster 45-0557 'Rosinenbomber' (c/n 36010) (noted '72-'88) and C-47B Dakota N951CA (c/n 16954/34214, ex 45-0951, SpanAF T.3-54, G-BLFL, arrived 9.9.86, current '88). The Dak is now painted up as "45-951" of "European Air Transport Services".

BEZGENRIET

Spread around a number of locations, but principally here, is the Sammlung Fritz Ulmer (Fritz Ulmer Collection) which comprises the following.

Arado Ar 79B	D-ECUV	(c/n 0047, ex Luftwaffe, SL-AAP) dismantled.
Bu 131 Jungmann	HB-URP	(c/n 86, ex Swiss AF A-73)
Bu 131B Jungmann	D-EGHC	(c/n 25, ex Swiss AF A-16, HB-USR) stored.
Bu 133C Jungmeister	D-ENOW	(c/n 6, ex Swiss AF U-59, HB-MII) stored.
Bu 180 Student	HB-EFO	(c/n 2106) dismantled.
Bu 181 Bestmann	N9269Z	(c/n FR11, ex 331396, VN174, F-BBMI) stored.
DFS108-30 Kranich II	D-1768	
DFS108-70 Meise	HB-386	
DFS108-70 Meise	HB-514	
DFS Rhonadler	-	replica
Fauvel AV.36	-	
Glasflugel BS.1	-	
Go III Minimoa	OE-0230	(c/n 305)
Go IV Govier	D-8504	
Hirth 'Kria'	-	
Hutter H.17B	D-4703	
Hutter H.17B	D-8045	
Klemm L.25 Ib	D-ENAF	(c/n 277, ex CH-272, HB-EFU) dismantled
Pelzner Gleiter	-	replica
Putzer Doppelraab	-	
Rhonbussard	HB-258	
Rhonsperber	D-6049	
Schneider Grunau 9	-	replica
Grunau Baby IIIB	D-8019	

BIBERACH

Noted at the airfield (about 30 kms South of Ulm) in '85 were the wrecks of Cessna 182F D-EGTE/N3610U (c/n 55010), Cessna F150L D-EEDQ (c/n 0882, crashed 8.82) and Cessna F172H D-ECKX (c/n 0754, CofA expired 4.85).

BIRKENFELD

Displayed inside the Heinrich Herz Kaserne (about 30 kms North West of Ramstein) was ex Pferdsfeld F-84F Thunderstreak DD-339 (ex 52-6746) (noted '66-'83, to Uetersen). It had been replaced by 1987 when F-104G Starfighter 2374 (c/n 8073) ex Jbg.34 was seen to be preserved here (current '89).

BITBURG

Bitburg houses the USAF's 36 TFW with F-15 Eagles. Guarding the gate is a fighter from an earlier era in the form of an F-86E Sabre marked "51-13036/FU-036" (noted '76-'88). The USAF Museum list the aircraft as "FU-036" which indicates a repaint of a so far unidentified airframe.

Six ex AdlA Mystere IVAs arrived in 1982 having been retired from French service and handed back to the US under the terms of Offshore Procurement scheme by which they were procured. They were initially used for bdr training, moving on to other more destructive roles when they were of no further use.

Dassault Mystere IVA	40	ex '8-NH' ET.2/8 (noted '82-'84, to Hahn '85).
Dassault Mystere IVA	54	(noted '82-8.88).
Dassault Mystere IVA	66	(noted '82-8.88).
Dassault Mystere IVA	187	(noted '82-7.86).
Dassault Mystere IVA	194	ex '8-MM' ET.1/8 (noted '82-7.86).
Dassault Mystere IVA	202	(noted '82-'86).

Former AdlA Lockheed T-33A 52-9973 was allocated to Bitburg and following use as a bdr airframe succumbed to the fire dump (noted '83-'84).

In a scrap compound in 6.87 was the fuselage of an F-15 Eagle (the most likely candidate being F-15C 80-0007/BT which bellied in at Soesterburg on 12.9.81) and the very burnt wreck of another fighter.

More up to date bdr fodder has arrived in the form of two F-4Cs which both flew in.

F-4C Phantom	63-7421	ex 'SA' 182 TFS/Texas ANG (arrived 6.6.86).
F-4C Phantom	63-7576	ex 171 TFS/Michigan ANG (arrived 17.7.86).

BOCHUM

Canadair CL-13A Sabre Mk.5 "JA-102" (c/n 931, ex RCAF 23141, BB-131) is preserved along highway 430 (Dortmund-Duisburg) at the Bochum-Wattenscheid exit having moved here from Marl (noted '89).

Some other ex Marl aircraft are now preserved in the Southern part of Bochum. Noted early in '89 were the following.

CASA 352L (Ju 52)	"D-ADAM"	(ex SpanAF T.2B-257, "D-CIAL")
Douglas C-47A Dakota	"N569R"	(c/n 10100, ex 42-24238, FL517, G-AJAZ, EC-ADR, SpanAF T.3-61, N8041B) identity not confirmed.
Gloster Javelin FAW.9	XH768	(7929M) 'E'
F-84F Thunderstreak	"5"	(ex 52-6783, DD-248)

BONN/HANGELAR

In the early eighties, the wrecks of Cessna F172H D-ELNH (c/n 0544, CofA expired 9.78) and Sportavia-Putzer RF-6C D-EHYO (c/n 6001, crashed 5.77) were to be found here. Recorded in 4.87 was the wreck of Cessna 140A D-EKLO (c/n 15436).

BRAUNSCHWEIG

Stored here as a spares source for the DFVLR's flying test-bed D-ADAM is VFW-614 D-BABM (c/n G-013, ex D-BABM, F-GATH) ex Lemwerder (noted '85-'88). Hansa Jet D-CARA (c/n 1021) was wfu here for spares recovery after its arrival on 25.5.84.

BREITSCHEID

Noted here (20 kms North West of Giessen) have been the wrecks of MS Rallye 110ST D-EGRN (c/n 3298, crashed 8.82) and MS894A Minerva D-EDCK (c/n 11975, crashed 9.75).

BREMEN

Used as a training aid by the airport firemen is ex Nora Air Services N2501D Noratlas D-ANAS (c/n 014, ex 5213) (noted '78-'88).

At the Hochschule fur Technik (Technical High School) F-84F Thunderstreak DF-316 (ex 53-7058) may still be present, having come from VFW at Lemwerder (noted '85).

The VFW factory received Fairey Gannet AS.4 UA-112 (c/n F9394) for use as an apprentice training airframe (noted '71-'84). It has since been presented to the museum at Koblenz.

BREMGARTEN

The gate here is guarded by RF-84F Thunderflash EA-101 (ex 53-6719) ex LVR.1, Erding (noted '71-'88). A second 'flash arrived as an underslung CH-53G load on 19.11.85 in the form of EB-341 (ex 52-7377) from Munchen/Allach. It has been preserved by Akg.51.

Three Fiat G-91R/3s arrived for instructional, decoy and bdr use by 8.82 comprising 3058 (c/n 318, ex Lekg.43, bdr behind Building 322 7.84), 3178 (c/n 446, gia in Building 323 7.84) and 3212 (c/n 480, ex Lekg.43) (current '84).

Piaggio P.149D 9186 (c/n 270) has been in use as a ground instructional airframe here (current in Building 323 7.84).

BRUGGEN

Current at this RAFG Tornado base are the following.

BAC Lightning T.4	XM970	(8529M) ex 'T' 19 Sqn, decoy (noted '78-'87).
BAC Lightning T.4	XM973	(8528M) ex 'V' 19 Sqn, decoy (noted '78-'87).
BAC Lightning F.2A	XN783	(8526M) ex 'G' 19 Sqn, decoy (noted '78-'87).
BAC Lightning F.2A	XN789	(8527M) ex 'J' 19 Sqn, decoy (noted '78-'87).
BAC Lightning F.2A	XN792	(8525M) ex 'M' 92 Sqn, decoy (noted '78-'87).
BAC Lightning F.6	XS901	ex 'BK' 11 Sqn, arrived 10.5.88 for bdrt.
Hawker Hunter F.6A	XE608	(8717M) painted in 20 Sqn marks as 'XX' (noted '83-'88). With the departure of 20 Sqn to Laarbruch and the Tornado, the airframe was given a second 'M' serial, 8841M, and allocated for bdr training.
Hawker Hunter T.7	XL566	(8891M) ex '86' 4 FTS & Shawbury, arr 10.86 for bdr.
HS Buccaneer S.2C	XV358	(8658M) ex '035/R' 809 Sqn, for bdrt (noted '84-'88, front fuselage only, rear fuselage at Wildenrath).
Panavia Tornado GR.1	XZ630	(P12) ex BAe Warton, arrived 24.8.88 for weapons loading training.
SEPECAT Jaguar GR.1	XW563	(8563M) 431 MU, preserved outside 14 Sqn block since 23.10.85 as "XX822/AA" (which crashed near Ahlhorn on 2.7.76) in 14 Sqn marks. The aircraft had previously served 431 MU here as a gia.
Whirlwind HAR.10	XP403	(8690M) ex 22 Sqn, departed UK 14.10.81 (noted '83-'87, for bdrt).

BUCHEL

Preserved on the base here are F-104G Starfighter 2058 (c/n 2067) ex Jbg.31 (suffered an accident on 4.12.80) which had been painted as "3033" by 6.87. It joins ex Pferdsfeld F-84F Thunderstreak "DC-211" (ex 52-6707, DD-354) which was in use as a gia here by '73 and was noted on display on the base from '81 to '87. It had moved to Norvenich by 8.88. Former apprentice training Lockheed T-33A JD-395 (ex 58-0688) '3' was noted preserved near the main gate by 6.87 (current '88).

In use as a gia here by 11.86 was F-104G Starfighter 2167 (c/n 7036) which arrived from Jbg.34 on 26.4.85 and was painted in special colours to mark the end of F-104 operations with Jbg.33.

By 9.83, F-104G Starfighter (2444)/"ABDR" (c/n 8187) was parked out on the field by the alert sheds, predictably in use for Aircraft Battle Damage Repair training. It had served on the field as a decoy for at least a couple of years before acquiring the "ABDR" markings. By 5.85 2466 (c/n 8215) sat with (2444)/"ABDR" by the alert sheds.

In July '84 an unidentified Fiat G-91R/3 was reported parked out on the field in use as a surface decoy.

The base hosts a Lehrwerkstatt (technical training school) which has utilised the following ground instructional airframes.

Fiat G-91T/3	3455	(c/n 615) (noted '83).
Lockheed T-33A	9433	(ex 52-9966) ex Jbg.33 (noted '83).
Lockheed T-33A	JD-395	(ex 58-0688) '3' (noted '76-'83, to the gate - see above).
Lockheed T-33A	JD-397	(ex 58-0709, JE-397) '7' (noted '76, to Sinsheim 9.4.84).

F-84F Thunderstreak BF-108 (ex 53-7102) to Norvenich '81.
At Jbg.33's kaserne in Cochem-Brauheck, just off the road between the base and the town of Cochem, F-84F Thunderstreak DC-319 (ex 53-7045) has been preserved by the gate following an accident on 2.5.64 (noted '64-'86). By 1986 it had been joined by ex LVR.1 F-104G Starfighter "2535" (really c/n 8261, ex 2503).

BUCKEBURG

By 1987 an Alouette II had appeared on display at the gate marked as "PQ-131" with the spurious c/n "131".

Alouette II 7623 (c/n 1610) was reported in use as a gia with the Heeresflieger Waffenschule here in 1984 whilst in use as an instructional airframe with the HFWS by 7.87 was Piaggio P.149D D-EBSN (c/n 169, ex 9147). It is certain that 7623 is not the Alouette which now resides on the gate.

In the MBB105 maintenance hangar during 3.88 were the wrecks of MBB105P 8682 plus even smaller remains of a second example.

In the Buckeburg town, the Hubschrauber Museum (Helicopter Museum) is located in Sableplatz (near the town centre).

Air & Space 18A	D-HOBB	(c/n 18-26, ex N6120S) (noted '85-'87).
Bell OH-13H	58-5348	(c/n 2361) ex USAREUR (noted '82-'89).
Bolkow Bo 46	D-9515	(c/n V2) painted as "D-9514/V1" (arr 7.7.72, current '87).
Bolkow Bo 102	-	(c/n 4502) (noted '85-'87).
Bolkow Bo 103	D-9505	(c/n V1, ex D-9505, D-HECA) (noted '78-'89).
Bolkow Bo 105	D-HAJY	(c/n V3) (arr 4.5.70, current '89).
Bolkow Flying Jeep	-	(noted '85-'89).
Sycamore Mk.52	7820	(c/n 13478) ex Htg.64 (noted '70-'89).
Sycamore Mk.52	7833	(c/n 13493) ex Htg.64 (noted '78-'79, to Hermeskeil'82).
Dornier Do 29	"YA-101"	(really c/n 001, ex YD-101) ex Est.64 (noted '78, to Oberpfaffenhofen).
Focke-Achgelis Fa 330	100406	ex Cranfield (noted '82-'89).
Focke-Wulf Fw 61	"D-EBVU"	replica (noted '85-'87).
Georges G1 Papillon	-	(noted '85).
Georges G.2	-	(noted '85).
Gosslich Pedalcopter	-	(noted '85).
Havertz HZ-5	D-HAJU	(c/n 5) (noted '85-'87).
Hiller OH-23C	55-4109	(noted '87-'89).
Kaman HH-43F Huskie	62-4547	(c/n 7608) (Noted '78-'89)
MBB-Kawasaki BK117	D-HBKA	(c/n P2) (noted '88).
Merckle SM.67	"D-9506"	(c/n V3, with parts of D-9506/V2) (noted '85-'89).
Mil Mi-1	CCCP-05712	(noted '85-'89).
Nagler Rolz NR.54	-	(c/n V2) (noted '85).
SARO Skeeter AOP.12	XN348	(c/n S2/7154) 8024M (noted '82-'89).
Siemetzki Asro 4	-	(c/n V1) (stored '85).
Sikorsky H-34G	8109	(c/n 58-1679, ex 150807) (noted '73-'89).
Sikorsky S-64	-	(nose section) (noted '79, to Hermeskeil).
Sud Alouette II	7717	(c/n 1871) (noted '78-'89).
SO1221S Djinn	"7"	(c/n FR8/1109, ex F-BNAY) (noted '82-'89).
Vertol H-21C	8307	(c/n WG7) ex HFB.300 (noted '82-'89).
VFW H2	D-HIBY	(c/n V1) (noted '85-'89).
VFW H2A	-	(noted '85).
VFW H3 Sprinter	D-9543	(c/n E1) (noted '78-'89).
VFW H3 Sprinter	D-9544	(c/n E2) (stored '85).
VFW H3A	-	(c/n V1) (stored '85).
Wagner Rotocar	"TT-046"	(c/n 3) (noted '85).
Zierath Z1	-	(noted '85).

BURGAU

Preserved outside the buildings at the Auto Motor Museum (some 45 kms West of Augsburg) in Bleichstrasse is Fiat G-91R/3 3193 (c/n 461). The aircraft arrived from

Leipheim in the early seventies and is fitted with the tail of c/n 304 (noted '84-'85).

CELLE/ARLOH

Reportedly on display at the airfield by '84 was Piaggio P.149D D-EMEP (c/n 103, ex 9084). It was not seen when the field was visited in 4.84 but could possibly be at the nearby gliding field.

CELLE

MBB105C 9827 (c/n S315, ex D-HDHT) was with the HFVS here by 6.87 as a ground instructional airframe (possibly also used for ground trials). At the same time CL-13B Sabre Mk.6 D-9523 (c/n S6-1784, ex TsLw.3 at Fassberg) was displayed in a hangar at the open day. It was not recorded on a visit to Celle a month later so was presumably only borrowed from Fassberg for the show.

COLEMAN BARRACKS

The scrap compound at this US Army facility near Mannheim usually contains a number of crashed USAREUR helicopters. Noted here in '84 was an ex BelgAF T-33A which was recorded again in a burnt out state during '86. The prime candidate would appear to be FT-3, last recorded on the ranges at Vilseck.

CRAILSHEIN

Noted in 1978 in a playground in the town shopping centre (about 100 kms South of Wurzburg) was Vertol H-21C 8301 (c/n WG1) ex HFB.300. It may well still be present.

DARMSTADT

CM170 Magister AA-162 (c/n 062) was one of several supplied to the Technische Hochschule Darmstadt (Technical University) here in 3.68. It had disappeared by 1977 but turned up again in 5.87 in a state of preservation between two buildings just to the right of the main gate to the US Army airfield here. It was still present in 3.89 but looked ready for the scrap man.

DELMENHORST

Preserved Canadair CL-13B Sabre Mk.5 BB-131 (c/n 931) went to Air Classik at Dusseldorf by 1982.

DETMOLD

A long standing resident with the AAC here is SARO Skeeter AOP.12 XL739 (ex 15/19 Hussars) preserved outside 4 Regiment's HQ. By 5.89 Sioux AH.1 XT550/D had arrived here and was also intended for display.

Current with 71 Aircraft Workshops for battle damage repair training are the following.

Westland Wasp HAS.1	XS571	'614', ex Wroughton(arr 7.84, boom from XT436, noted 5.89).
Westland Wasp HAS.1	XV627	'321', ex Wroughton (arr 7.84, noted 5.89).
Westland Scout AH.1	XW615	ex Wroughton (arr 1.9.87, fuselage pod only).

During 5.89 three Scouts were seen here. Assuming that they were not just visiting, it appears that XW615 has been joined by two other unfortunates.

DIEPHOLZ

Preserved at the WGAF base here was N2501D Noratlas 5284 (c/n 101). She survived until 18.2.81 when she was sold for scrap.

DONAUESCHINGEN

The wreck of Cessna FRA150L D-ECSR (c/n 0140) has languished here (some 50 kms South East of Freiburg) following an accident in 2.85.

DORTMUND

An anonymous Hispano HA1112 Buchon has been reported in store at the airfield here for eventual museum display. More details?

DUSSELDORF

Preserved outside the LTU hangar were Vickers Viking 1 "D-BABY" (really c/n 132, G-AHPB, ex Soesterburg) in full LTU colours with DH Comet 4C G-BDIW (c/n 6470, ex Dan Air) painted in a blue/white scheme with "Flughafen Dusseldorf" titles. Both were still current in '87 but the Viking was roaded to Winterthur, Switzerland, in Spring '88 and the Comet moved to Hermeskeil around the same time. A Fokker DR.1 replica marked "F.102/17" is also on display.

Aero L60 Brigadyr	"OK-LGL"	(c/n 150401, ex OK-LGL, OE-BVL) (noted '82-'87, to Schwenningen by '88).
Bu 181B Bestmann	D-EDIB	(c/n 25039, ex RSwedAF 25039) (noted '85 & wingless '87, gone by '89).
CASA 352L (Ju 52)	"D-CIAK"	(ex Spanish AF T.2B-165) (noted '82-'88, see below)
CASA 1131E (Bu 131)	"D-EBZE"	(ex Spanish AF E.3B-526) (noted '85 & wingless '87, to Schwenningen).
Dornier Do 27B-1	D-EFGG	(c/n 174, ex 5544) ex Marl (noted '87).
Douglas C-47A Dakota	N8041B	(c/n 10100, ex 42-24238, FL517, G-AJAZ, EC-ADR, SpanAF T.3-61) (noted '82-'85, to Marl).
Pembroke C.54	"G-AOJG"	(really c/n 1019, ex 5427) ex Stuttgart (noted '82, nose section to Vienna).
Super Constellation	"D-ADAM"	(c/n 4671, ex F-BHML) (noted '78-'85, to Frankfurt by '88).
Messerschmitt Bf 109E	"6"	replica, ex Frankfurt (noted '82, to Schwenningen by'88).
Me 163B Komet	"54"	replica, (noted '82, to Schwenningen by '88).
CL-13A Sabre Mk.5	"JA-102"	(c/n 931, ex RCAF 23141, BB-131) ex Delmenhorst (noted '82-'84, to Marl by '85).
AT-6A Texan	D-FOBY	(c/n 77-4176, ex PortAF 1608, G-BGGR) (noted '82-'87, to Schwenningen by '88).
Piaggio P.149D	D-EHMG	(c/n 320, ex 9223) (noted '82-'87, to Schwenningen by '88).
F-84F Thunderstreak	"5"	(ex 52-6783, DD-248) (noted '82, to Marl '85).
SARO Skeeter AOP.12	-	(to Schwenningen by '88).
Vickers Viscount 812	G-AVHE	(c/n 363) nose only, ex Southend, UK (noted '85-'87).

By 9.85 the Air Classik area had been transformed into a car park, most of the aircraft moving elsewhere though the smaller exhibits remained at Dusseldorf on the roof of the terminal building. The Dakota and CASA 352 were stored on the apron here by 9.85. The CASA 352 was reportedly the only remaining Air Classik aircraft remaining here in 8.88 and has been purchased by Ju-Air who operate the ex Swiss AF Ju 52s from Dubendorf.

The wreck of T-6J Harvard 4 AA-633 (ex 52-8588, D-FACI ntu) apparently came here from Monchengladbach by the early eighties. What happened to it?

EGELSBACH

Egelsbach is the main West German light civil airfield, a few kms South of Frankfurt. Wrecks reported here have included MS894A Minerva 220 D-EASB (c/n 11066, CofA expired 5.75), Cessna F150L D-EEYR (c/n 0813, crashed 6.84), Cessna FRA150L D-ECUI (c/n 0182, crashed 7.84), Beech 35 Bonanza D-EIOP (c/n D-606, ex NC90569, HB-ECH, CofA expired 7.78), Cessna F150L D-EDAY (c/n 0881, crashed 4.79) and Piaggio P.149D D-EOAL (c/n 047, ex 9033, wfu 4.77).

EGGEBEK

Displayed atop a pole near the main gate is ex Mfg.2 AW Seahawk Mk.101 RB-363 (c/n 6715, current '89) which had arrived here by '82 having previously been displayed at Mfg.2's kaserne in nearby Tarp. A further example of Mfg.2's former equipment is provided by F-104G Starfighter 2309 (c/n 7192) which was hangared here in 5.87 undergoing preparation for display, taking up a position near the tower by 6.87 (current '89).

Mounted on concrete blocks behind the control tower for the benefit of the firemen is the hulk of ex Akg.52 RF-84F Thunderflash EB-322 (ex 53-7661) which arrived here from Est.91 at Meppen many years ago (noted '79-'86).

EGGENFELDEN

Cessna T310P D-IFLB (c/n 0120, ex N5820M) was derelict here (some 90 kms East of Munchen) in the mid eighties following CofA expiry in 4.80.

ERDING

Preserved in flying attitude at the main gate is ex Akg.52 RF-104G Starfighter 2473 (c/n 8222, ex EB-121, painted as "8058" - Erding's post code). The aircraft allegedly suffered an accident at Manching on 15.9.72 and was placed on display here in '74 (still current '87). As this machine still wore the pre 1.1.68 serial EB-121 on its arrival here I suspect it was soc on 15.9.72 following non-flying use at Manching, rather than actually flying up to this date.

An Apprentice Training School here holds the following.

Dornier Do 27A-1	5615	(c/n 283) (serial not worn) (noted '81-'86).
F-104G Starfighter	2468	(c/n 8217) (noted '86).
F-104G Starfighter	"7500"	(really 2507, c/n 8265) painted as "7500" (noted '86).
Lockheed T-33A	9447	(ex 53-5628) (noted '86 - allocated to the Deutches Museum).

On the scrap heap in 8.85 was TF-104G Starfighter 283- (thought to be 2833 ex Jbg.34) though two F-104Fs were reportedly still on the dump here at the same time, (2901, 2920 & 2921 have been quoted, of these 2901 was recorded dumped here between 1.74 through to 8.82).

On the dump in 1986 were ex WS.10 F-104F Starfighter 2921 (c/n 5076, ex 59-5023, - which was painted up as "4711" as long ago as 1974 after a brand of perfume) and Lockheed T-33A 9439 (ex 53-5562). Both aircraft had previously served as instructional airframes with the Lehrwerkstatt.

A number of aircraft were stored on the base for the Deutsches Museum (see under Munchen) until 1981 when the stored aircraft were transferred to Oberschleissheim. Those noted here comprised the following.

AAC.1 Toucan (Ju 52)	363	ex AdlA.
Agusta-Bell 47G-2	AS-058	(c/n 258) (noted '78).
CASA 2.111B	B.2I-177	(c/n 166) ex Spanish AF (noted '78-'80).
Dornier Do 27B-1	5666	(c/n 360, ex 5666, D-EHAV)
Dornier Do 31E	D-9531	(c/n E3)
Douglas C-47B Dakota	1401	(c/n 26989, ex 43-49728, KK209)
ERW VJ101C	D-9518	(c/n X2) (noted '78-'81).
Fi 156C Storch	A-96	(c/n 4299, ex Swiss AF & HB-ARU)
F-104F Starfighter	2903	(c/n 5049, ex 59-4996) ex WS.10.
Lockheed T-33A	9447	(ex 53-5628) to Erding apprentices school.
CL-13B Sabre Mk.6	0105	(c/n S6-1659, ex JD-105) (noted '78-'80).
RF-84F Thunderflash	EB-231	(ex 52-7379) ex Akg.52 (noted '78-'80).
SAAB J 35A Draken	35086	ex '48' F 16, RSwedAF (noted '78-'80).
HH-19B Chickasaw	53-4458	ex USAF
SH-34G Choctaw	8073	(c/n 58-1557) (noted '78).
VAK191B	D-9563	(c/n V1) (noted '78-'81).

ESCHERHAUSEN

Preserved at this small gliding field (some 30 kms South West of Hildesheim) is Vickers Viscount 814 D-ANAB (c/n 369, wfu 4.12.69) (noted '88).

ESSEN/MUHLHEIM

PA24-250 Comanche D-EDYN (c/n 24-2145, ex N7051P) was derelict here in 5.86. PA18-150 D-ENWO (c/n 18-2032, ex 52-2432, KLu R-35) was stored here in recent years.

FASSBERG

Displayed at the main gate by 1987 was Fiat G-91R/3 3105 (c/n 371, crashed 18.7.72) complete with TsLw.3 badge (current '89).

The technical training unit in Hangar 5 here, TsLw.3, trains both Luftwaffe and Heer personnel using airframes usually obtained on long term loan from active units. The following have been recorded.

Alpha Jet	4003	(c/n 0003) (arrived '78, to Jbg.49 by 6.83).
Alpha Jet	4004	(c/n 0004) (to Jbg.43 by 2.82).
Alpha Jet	4075	(c/n 0075) (noted '83).
Alpha Jet	4076	(c/n 0076) (noted '83-'85).
Alpha Jet	4078	(c/n 0078) ex Jbg.43 (noted '85-'88).
UH-1D Iroquois	7047	(c/n 8107) (noted '83).
UH-1D Iroquois	7090	(c/n 8150) (noted '83).
UH-1D Iroquois	7168	(c/n 8228) (noted '83).
MBB105M	8010	(c/n 5010) (noted '85).
MBB105M	8011	(c/n 5011) (noted '83).
MBB105M	8012	(c/n 8012) (noted '83).
MBB105M	8013	(c/n 8013) (noted '83-'85).
MBB105P	8603	(c/n 6003) (noted '85).
MBB105P	8606	(c/n 6006) (noted '85).
MBB105P	8613	(c/n 6013) (noted '83).
MBB105P	8623	(c/n 6023) (noted '83).
MBB105P	8689	(c/n 6089) (noted '83).

The Lehrwerkstatt (Apprentice school) occupy Hangar 6 and have been using the following.

Dornier Do 27A	AC-903	(has been reported as c/n 103 which is unlikely as it was w/o 14.1.57 and has not been seen since) (noted '83-'85).
Dornier Do 27B-1	5556	(c/n 189) (noted '83-'85).
F-104G Starfighter	2245	(7123) ex Jbg.34 (noted '85, see below).
F-104G Starfighter	2327	(c/n 8001) ex TsLw.1 (noted '85, see below).
TF-104G Starfighter	2708	(c/n 5709) ex Jbg.33 (noted '88).
TF-104G Starfighter	2790	(c/n 5920) ex Jbg.33 (noted '85-'88).
CL-13B Sabre Mk.6	D-9523	(c/n S6-1784) (noted '83-'85).
CL-13B Sabre Mk.6	D-9539	(c/n S6-1603) (noted '83-'85).
CL-13B Sabre Mk.6	D-9542	(c/n S6-1740) (noted '83-'85).

At least one of the Sabres (incorrectly quoted as D-9533 - a Dornier DS.10 serial) was still current during '88.

Out on the airfield is a fire training area using mostly life-expired Starfighters and Fiat G-91s.

Fiat G-91R/3	3012	(c/n 0067) ex Jbg.41 (fuselage only) (noted '87).
Fiat G-91R/3	3053	(c/n 310) (noted '72-'83).
Fiat G-91R/3	3090	(c/n 354) no marks (noted '85-6..87).
Fiat G-91R/3	3229	(c/n 498) (noted '85).
F-104F Starfighter	2904	(c/n 5050, ex 59-4997) '3' (noted '76-'83).
F-104F Starfighter	2910	(c/n 5060, ex 59-5007) '2' (noted '83).
F-104F Starfighter	2913	(c/n 5066, ex 59-5013) '1' (noted '83, possibly preserved '88?).
F-104G Starfighter	2007	(c/n 2007) ex Kaufbeuren (noted 3.87-'10.88).
F-104G Starfighter	2160	(c/n 7029) ex LVR.1 (noted '85-10.88).
F-104G Starfighter	2171	(c/n 7040) ex Jbg.34 (noted 5.87).
F-104G Starfighter	2245	(c/n 7123) ex LVR.1 and Apprentice School (noted 5.87-10.88).
F-104G Starfighter	2327	(c/n 8001) ex TsLw.1 and Apprentice School (noted 5.87-10.88).
F-104G Starfighter	2383	(c/n 8086) ex Norvenich gia, no marks, fuselage only (noted '85-10.88).
F-104G Starfighter	2477	(c/n 8226) ex Jbg.31 & Manching (noted '85-10.88).
F-104G Starfighter	2489	(c/n 8239) ex Jbg.31 & Manching (noted '85-10.88).
F-104G Starfighter	(2494)	(c/n 8247) "DA-06" ex Norvenich decoy (noted '85-10.88).
F-104G Starfighter	2529	(c/n 8306) ex Jbg.32 & Manching (noted '85-10.88).
F-104G Starfighter	2540	(c/n 8327) ex Jbg.32 & Manching (noted '85-10.88).
F-104G Starfighter	2581	(c/n 9049) ex Jbg.33 & Manching (noted '85-10.88).
F-104G Starfighter	2583	(c/n 9054) ex Jbg.32 (noted '85-3.87).

TF-104G Starfighter	2719	(c/n 5720) no marks (noted 3.87).
TF-104G Starfighter	2795	(c/n 5925) ex Jbg.34, fuselage only, crash landed 1.84 (noted '85-3.87).
CL-13B Sabre Mk.6	JB-233	(c/n S6-1761) (noted '83).
CL-13B Sabre Mk.6	JB-235	(c/n S6-1745) (noted '83).
RF-84F Thunderflash	EB-113	(ex 51-1923) (noted '83).

Noted behind a hangar during 1985, minus wings and tail was Fiat G-91R/3 3232 (c/n 501).

FINKENWERDER

N2501D Noratlas 5348 (c/n 178) has been preserved at the factory here since the early seventies, a memorial to the many Norries built here by HFB. Former AdlA Noratlas 157/"62-KS" was preserved here by 6.88 on loan from the Musee de l'Air.

FLENSBURG/HARRISLEEFELD

This small civil field had Lockheed T-33A 9459 (ex 54-1523) for non-destructive fire training. It went to Leck in 1980 for preservation.

FLENSBURG/MURWIK

Preserved at the Marineschule is ex Mfg.2 AW Seahawk Mk.100 VB-136 (c/n 6695) which wears the spurious markings "MS-001" (noted '65-'83).

FRANKFURT/RHEIN-MAIN

Air Classik have a large number of aircraft on display in the viewing area on the terminal roof here. The Super Constellation is preserved in a car park outside the airport (too difficult to get it up on the roof!).

Antonov An-2R	HA-MHL	(c/n IG123-02) (arr 22.9.87, current '88).
Bu 181B-1 Bestmann	D-ECES	(c/n 25082, ex Swedish AF 25082, D-ECES, "D-EMIL") (noted '85-'88).
CASA 1131E (Bu 131)	"D-EFEI"	(ex Spanish AF E.3B-506) (noted '85-'88).
CASA 352L (Ju 52)	D-CIAS	(c/n 54, ex T.2B-144, N88927) (noted '80-'88).
CASA 2.111 (He 111)	"G1-FL"	(c/n 535, ex Spanish AF BR.2I-14) (noted '78-'88).
DH82A Tiger Moth	-	(c/n 86618, ex PG732, F-BGEE) (noted '85-'88).
DH89A Dragon Rapide	-	(c/n 6437, ex HB-AME, HB-APE, D-IGUN, "G-RYCR") (noted '85-'88).
DH Venom FB.54	J-1635	ex Swiss AF (arrived 2.8.84, current '88).
Dornier Do 27A-4	D-EDHS	(c/n 371, ex 5671) (noted '80-'84, to Sinsheim by 9.86).
Dornier Do 27B-1	D-EFHO	(c/n 177, ex 5547) (noted '85-'88).
Douglas C-53B	"65371"	(c/n 4828, ex 41-20058, N34989, OY-DCA, OY-KLE, OH-VKA, LN-KLV, OH-VKA, N65371) (noted '85-'88).
Douglas DC-8-21	-	nose section only, quoted as TL-AHI (c/n 45300) but this should have become 5A-GGK then wfu Tripoli '82 (noted '86-'87).
Fiat G-91R/3	3243	(c/n 512) ex Lekg.41 (noted '84-'88).
Fokker D.VII	"5290/18"	replica (noted '88).
Fokker DR.1	-	replica (noted '86-'88).
Hutter H17A	-	(noted '88, on loan from Wasserkruppe).
Junkers Ju 87 Stuka	"T6-KL"	replica, (noted '78-'84).
Klemm K35D	"D-ELLY"	(c/n 1917, ex RSwedAF 5028, SE-BPC, D-EDOD) (noted
Super Constellation	"D-ALAP"	(c/n 4671, ex F-BHML, "D-ADAM") ex Dusseldorf (noted'88).
		'85-'88).
Bf 109E	"6"	replica, (noted '78, to Dusseldorf).
Me 163B Komet	"54"	replica, (noted '78-'88).
Me 262A	"5"	replica, (noted 78-'84).
Morane MS315	F-BBQE	(noted '88).
MS500 (Storch)	"D-EMIL"	(noted '85-'88).
Nord 1002 Pinguin	-	(noted '80) & "D-EMMA" (noted '87), not necessarily the same a/c.

F-84F Thunderstreak "DJ-134" (ex 51-1733, ex DD-374) (noted '82-'88).
Sikorsky S-58C D-HAUD (c/n 58-388, ex OO-SHL, BelgAF B-12) (noted '84-'88).
Stampe SV4 "5-78" (c/n 578, ex F-BDDY) (noted '88).
Lufthansa employ Viscount 814 D-ANAF (c/n 447, wfu 30.1.69, arrived '72) as an instructional airframe, for cabin crew training.

On the other side of the field at the USAF's Rhein-Main air base, Lockheed VC-140B Jetstar 61-2491 ex 58 MAS arrived here from Ramstein on 27.4.87 for bdr training. Ex Spanish AF C-47B Dakota N1350M (c/n 26342, ex 43-49081, EC-ASF, T.3-64) arrived on 25.3.86 and is on display with the Luftbrucke Museum in USAF colours and wearing its US serial. Douglas C-54E EL-AJP (c/n 27289, ex 44-9063, NC88887, N88887, HB-ILU, EI-ARS, LN-TUR, EI-ARS, N88887, FAR-91, N88887) arrived here on 13.10.88 and has since been parked near the gate. It is expected to join the Dak as a memorial to the Berlin airlift.

FRITZLAR

Fieseler Fi 156C-3 Storch D-EKLU (c/n 110061, ex RSwedAF 3809) was under restoration to flying condition at the Heer base (Georg-Friedrichs Kaserne) in 1987 (see also Kassel/Calden).

FROSCHHAUSEN

Bucker Bu 181B Bestmann D-EKOB (c/n 25096, ex RSwedAF 25096) is kept here by private collector C Cichorius.

FURSTENFELDBRUCK

The home of Jbg.49 operating the P.149D (at least, for the time being) and Alpha Jet, Fursty houses several preserved airframes.

Fiat G-91R/3	3252	(c/n 521) ex Jbg.49, displayed on the base, in flying attitude, '81-'88.
Fiat G-91T/3	3402	(c/n 0002) ex Jbg.49, painted in special blue/white "Bavarian AF" colours (noted near the tower '83-'88).
Lockheed T-33A	"AB-773"	(really 9422, ex 52-9930) (noted on base '81-'88).
F-86K Sabre	-	(ex 55-48..) not flown by WGAF, arrived here '66 still in USAF marks and preserved by the tower, to Neuburg by '86.
F-84F Thunderstreak	"DD-244"	"51-1665" (really ex 52-6737, DD-344) ex Pferdsfeld. (noted by Officers' Mess '65-'88).
RF-84F Thunderflash	"BD-119"	(ex 51-17041, EB-343) ex Akg.52, at main gate (noted '70-'88).

The Lehrwerkstatt (Apprentice Training School) are housed in Hangar 6 and in recent years have used the following.

Alpha Jet	4003	(c/n 0003) borrowed from Jbg.49.
Alpha Jet	4020	(c/n 0020) borrowed from Jbg.49 (noted '80).
Dornier Do 27A-1	5619	(c/n 287) ex Marine (noted '80-'85).
Fiat G-91R/3	3073	(c/n 335) ex Jbg.49 (noted '80-'88).
Fiat G-91R/3	3252	(c/n 521) ex Jbg.49 (noted '80, then preserved here).
Fiat G-91R/3	9945	(c/n) ex FDG (noted '88).
Fiat G-91T/3	3450	(c/n 610) (noted '80).
Fiat G-91T/3	3452	(c/n 612) (noted '81, to Uetersen '82).
Lockheed T-33A	9444	(ex 53-5621, EB-399 Akg.52) ex WS.50 (noted '80-'88).

Noted at the show in 10.85 was ex Neubiburg F-104F Starfighter 2918 (c/n 5071, ex 59-5018) wearing a WS.10 badge. Its fate is not known, is it still on the base here?

The wreck of crashed Dornier Do 28D/2 5888 lay in a scrap compound here following an accident on 22.5.80. It was sold for scrap by the mid eighties.

Piaggio P.149D D-EBSN (c/n 169, ex 9147) came here from Neubiburg by 1985 for spares recovery by Jbg.49).

By 8.84 Fiat G-91R/3 3198 (c/n 466) was in use as a decoy here and by 4.88 it was dumped along with 3308 (c/n 579, ex Neubiburg).

GANDERKESEE
Preserved at this civil airfield (South West of Bremen) is Fiat G-91R/3 3120 (c/n 386, noted '86-'88). It is painted in a blue colour scheme.

GEISELWIND
An anonymous ex WGAF Fiat G-91R/3 in "Frecce Tricolori" Italian colours is displayed on a pole in the Freizeitpark here (some 20 kms East of Wurzburg) (noted '82-'85).

GERMERSHEIM
Displayed on the gate at the Hans Graf von Sponeck Kaserne was ex Pferdsfeld F-84F Thunderstreak "BA-102" (ex 52-6816, DD-308, noted '82-'85). The aircraft moved to the museum at Sinsheim by '87.

GOSLAR
At the kaserne of Luftwaffenausbildungsregiment 5 (Fliegerhorst A) in the North part of town (about 75 kms South East of Hanover) on Marienburger Strasse is CL-13B Sabre Mk.6 "GS-338" (c/n S6-1732, ex JB-107) (noted '68-'84). Note that there is a possibility of confusion over the c/n of this airframe. JB-107 was c/n S6-17<u>23</u> in 7.63 when S6-17<u>32</u> was JB-110.

GROSSENBRODE
Lockeed T-33A 9465 (ex 54-1539) came from Erding in 1976 to guard the gate at Fehmarnsund Kaserne, home of Fernmelderegiment 71. It was still current during '84. Grossenbrode is about 60 kms East of Kiel, on the coast).

GUNZBURG
The <u>Sammlung Welzheimer</u> (Welzheimer Collection) keeps the following gliders here (about 20 kms East of Ulm).

Bolkow Phoebus	-	
DFS108-30 Kranich II	D-9019	
Schulgleiter SG-38	-	
Dittmar Condor IV	-	
Go.IV Govier III	-	
Horten 15C	-	
Hutter H.17A	-	
Landsmann Microlight	-	
RRG (Lippisch) Falke	HB-16	painted as "D-FALKE", loaned to Segelflugmuseum Poppenhausen.
RRG Zogling	-	
Schlemp-Hirth Wolf	-	
Rhonbussard	BGA395	(c/n 485, ex BGA395, G-ALKY)
Grunau Baby IIb	-	
Schulz FS.3	-	replica.

GURZENICH WALD
About 20 kms East of Aachen, displayed inside the barracks of VVK.313 (noted '80) is ex WS.10 F-104F Starfighter 2914 (c/n 5066, ex 59-5013). The aircraft is thought to have arrived from a kaserne in Aachen from where an unmarked F-104F disappeared around the same time.

GUTERSLOH
The following W&R airframes should still be current at this RAFG base.

EE Canberra B(I).8	XM244	(8202M) ex 16 Sqn (noted '78-'89, on the fire dump).
Hawker Hunter F.6A	"XF949"	(really XG152, 8843M) ex '20' 1 TWU, arrived 8.2.85, painted in 3 Sqn markings as "XF949/L" for a Families Day in 5.87 and in 4 Sqn markings (as "L" again) for their Families Day in 10.87 (current '89).
HS Harrier GR.1	XV278	arr 3.10.85 on loan from Rolls Royce for weapons load training (current '87).

HS Harrier GR.3	XW917	preserved by the gate from 5.88 wearing both 3 Sqn and 4 Sqn markings.
HS Harrier GR.3	XZ1..	bdr airframe (first noted 1.89).
HS Harrier GR.3	XZ989	(8849M, ex '07' 1 Sqn, crashed Port San Carlos 8.6.82) for bdr (noted '85-'87).
Wessex HU.5	"XR504"	(really XT467/8922M) arrived from Wroughton in 1.86 having been allocated to 18 Sqn for bdr purposes. It was painted up in 18 Sqn markings (as "BF") for the Families Day in 6.87.
Whirlwind HAR.10	XP347	(8688M) for bdr (noted '83-'87).
Whirlwind HAR.10	XP358	ex 'S' 28 Sqn, for bdr, arr from Bruggen by 5.85 (current '87).

HAHN

Former AdlA Lockheed T-33A 41576 (ex '314-WK' GE.314) was returned to USAF charge here for bdr training (noted '83, dumped '86). The following also serve for bdrt.

Dassault Mystere IVA	40	ex Bitburg decoy (noted '85-'88).
F-4C Phantom	64-0879	ex 182 TFS/Texas ANG (arr by 8.86, current '88 coded "HR").
F-101F Voodoo	58-0318	ex ADWC & MASDC FF416 (arr by 4.85, current '89).
F-105F Thunderchief	63-8357	ex 149 TFS/Virginia ANG & MASDC FK055 (arr by 4.85, current '89).

HAMBURG

Retired Lufthansa Boeing 707-430 D-ABOD (c/n 17720) is retained here by the airline for use as a cabin crew trainer (noted '88).

In the Osdorf area of the city (on Osdorfer Landstrasse) is the Reichsprasident Ebert Kaserne which houses the Logistikschule der Bundeswehr. This is reported to use CL-13B Sabre Mk.5 BB-150 (c/n 895, ex RCAF 23105), CL-13B Sabre Mk.6 0107 (c/n S6-1668) and F-84F Thunderstreak DC-233 (ex 53-6977). Nothing was visible from the outside when the facility was checked in 8.84.

HAMM

The wreck of PA22 Colt 108 D-ECCA (c/n 22-8843) lingered here following an accident in 2.78.

HAMMELBURG

Some 20 kms North West of Schweinfurt, preserved at a small civil airfield (off the Arnstein road) in a military training area (housing Kampftruppenschule 1) is ex Jbg.35 F-84F Thunderstreak "DE-175" (ex 51-1724, ex DE-107). This machine arrived on 21.6.64, was restored for further display in 1979/80 and was still current during '85.

HANAU

In 1987 an "Auster" (more likely a Cub or Bird Dog?) marked "64415" was reported here as a gate guard. Further details welcomed.

HEIDE/BUSUM

The wreck of MS893A Commodore 180 D-EGLL (c/n 10936) gravitated here (40 kms South of Husum) following the aircraft's demise in an accident in 4.84.

HERMESKEIL

The Luftfahrtausstellung in Hermeskeil museum was founded in 1973 and has so far accumulated the impressive collection listed below. Hermeskeil is about 30 kms South East of Trier.

Antonov An-2	HA-ANA	(noted '87-'88).
Concorde	"F-WTSA"	replica, (noted '78-'88).
Lightning F.2A	XN782	(8539M) ex 'H' 92 Sqn & Wildenrath decoy (noted 9.86-'88).

PT-18 Stearman	-	(noted '87-'88).
Sycamore HR.52	7813	(c/n 13466, cockpit & tail only) ex Aachen/Burtscheid (noted '81-'88).
Sycamore HR.52	7833	(c/n 13493) painted as "D-HFUM", arr from Buckeburg '82 (noted '87-'88).
CASA 352L (Ju 52)	D-CIAD	(c/n 37, ex Spanish AF T.2B-127) ex Air Classik (arr 23.8.82, current '88).
DH Comet 4C	G-BDIW	(c/n 6470, ex XR398) ex Dusseldorf (noted '88).
DH Venom FB.54	J-1797	ex Swiss AF (noted '85-'88).
Dornier Do 27A-1	5653	(c/n 339, ex D-EFSV) (noted '78-'88).
Douglas C-47A Dakota	111	(c/n 19460, ex 41-100997, RJAF 111, N62443) restored to Royal Jordanian AF markings (noted '80-'88).
EKW C-3605	C-541	ex Swiss AF & Lodrino store (noted '88).
Fiat G-91R/3	3086	(c/n 350) (dismantled in compound '84-'88).
Fiat G-91R/3	3152	(c/n 420) nose only, ex Lekg.43 (noted '78-'88).
Fiat G-91R/3	3170	(c/n 438) painted in ItAF c/s as "5-257" (noted'80-'88).
CM170 Magister	9303	(c/n 080) ex Neubiburg (noted dismantled '84-'88).
Hunting Pembroke C.54	5421	(c/n 1013) ex FvSt & Lechfeld (noted '77-'88).
Hunting Pembroke C.54	5424	(c/n 1016) ex Mfg.5 & Monchengladbach (spurious RAF c/s) (noted '73-'88).
Ilyushin Il-14	3076	(c/n 14.803076) ex Polish AF, flew into Saarbrucken 5.88 (noted '88).
Klemm L25-1B	D-8045	(noted '87-'88).
Super Constellation	D-ALIN	(c/n 4604) ex Lufthansa & Hamburg (noted '80-'88).
F-104G Starfighter	2491	(c/n 8241) (noted '80-'88).
F-104G Starfighter	FX-60	(c/n 9103) ex 23 Esc/10 Wg, BelgAF & Koksijde store (arrived 10.2.89).
Lockheed T-33A	BB-816	(ex 53-5776) nose section only.
Lockheed T-33A	"133393"	(CAF marks, really 9517, ex 58-0681) (noted '80-'88).
Mil Mi-1	031	ex Hungarian AF (noted in compound '88).
Nord 1002 Pingouin	"KG+EM"	(really c/n 91, ex F-BDUP, D-ENHO) (noted '85-'88).
N2501D Noratlas	D-ACUT	(c/n 065, ex 5256) ex Lubeck (noted '74-'88).
AT-6F Texan	D-FDEM	(ex 44-81778, D-IDEM) ex Leutkirch (noted '87-'88).
CL-13B Sabre Mk.6	JA-339	(c/n S6-1651) ex Leipheim (arr 4.2.81, current '88).
F-100F Super Sabre	"63944"	(really ex AdLA 56-4014/11-YR) Arizona ANG marks (noted '80-'88).
Piper J3C-65 Cub	D-EDEW	(c/n 10506, ex 43-29215, D-EDET) (noted '87-'88).
F-84F Thunderstreak	BF-105	(ex 52-6778) ex Niederstetten (noted '81-'88).
Sikorsky S64	-	nose only, ex Buckeburg (noted '82-'88).
Solbr II Glider	D-7160	(noted '87-'88).
Vertol H-21C	8311	(c/n WG11) nose only, ex Niedermendig (noted '73-'88).
Vertol H-21C	8321	(c/n WG21) ex Niedermendig (noted '73-'88).
Vickers Viscount 814D	D-ANAM	(c/n 368) ex Hamburg (arr 14.10,76, current '88).
Vickers VC10	G-ARVF	(c/n 808) (arr 5.81, current '88).
Whirlwind HAR.10	XP352	(8701M, ex Abingdon) (arrived 1.88, in compound '88).

HILDEN

At the private premises of Herr W Toft about 5 kms South of Dusseldorf, Harvard T.2A D-FABY (ex 41-33291, EX318, BelgAF H-40, F-BJBL) is preserved.

HILDESHEIM

Westland Scout AH.1 XP852 arrived at the AAC base here from Wroughton in 9.87 for bdr training. It joined Wasp HAS.1 XT438/465 which arrived from Detmold in 12.85. Both are fuselage pods only.

HOFHEIM

Hunting Pembroke C.54 D-CAKE (c/n 93, ex 5402) was preserved at the Herzog factory here, arriving from storage at Baden-Baden by 1977. It moved on to the museum at Sinsheim circa 1986.

HOHN

At nearby Hugo Junkers Kaserne (formerly Krummenort Kaserne until 9.5.89) Ltg.63 have ex Portugese AF AAC-1 (French built Ju 52/3mg10) c/n 053 preserved within the barracks (noted '76-'89). It is thought to be 6320 but is definitely not either 6300 or 6306 as sometimes quoted. The aircraft is painted in Luftwaffe colours with the code "1Z+IK". They also have ex WS.50 N2501D Noratlas 5355 (c/n 185) (noted '72-'89) which has been repainted as 5255 in order to represent an aircraft which actually served with Ltg.63.

HOPSTEN

Noted in a hangar here in 9.86 were ex Lekg.41 Fiat G-91R/3 3125 (c/n 392) and F-104G Starfighter 2606 (c/n 9134, ex Jbg.33 & Norvenich decoy, derelict here by 10.84). The G-91 was parked out in a dispersal during '85 and has since been displayed on the gate.

An F-104G Starfighter believed to be 2226 (c/n 7101) spent some time parked in a dispersal here in '85 prior to being painted as "DF-101" and installed in Jbg.36's kaserne in Rheine.

On the dump in 10.84 was the wreck of ex Jbg.36 F-4F Phantom 3841 (ex 72-1251) which crashed on 6.12.83.

HUSUM

At Jbg.41's kaserne (on the '200' road into town from the base) two aircraft are displayed. These are Fiat G-91R/4 "3541" (really c/n 0124, ex BR-362) (noted '76-'87) which arrived from Erding and ex Jbg.35 F-84F Thunderstreak DE-121 (ex 52-6752) (noted '76-'84). The F-84F was not recorded on visits in '78 and '87 and is presumably inside the kaserne.

When Jbg.41 re-equipped with the Alpha Jet in '81/'82, half a dozen Ginas were retained for decoy use. Some were relatively short lived in this role and work had started on breaking them up by 8.83.

Fiat G-91R/3	3012	(c/n 0067) ex Lekg.43 (noted '78-'84, to Fassberg).
Fiat G-91R/3	3017	(c/n 0073) ex Lekg.43 (noted '78-'84).
Fiat G-91R/3	3019	(c/n 0075) ex Jbg.41 (noted '78-'86).
Fiat G-91R/3	3025	(c/n 0082) ex Lekg.43 (noted '78-'83, to Leck by 8.84).
Fiat G-91R/3	3033	(c/n 0093) ex Lekg.43 (noted '78-'83, to Pferdsfeld by '84).
Fiat G-91R/3	3125	(c/n 392) ex Jbg.41 (noted '78-'83, to Hopsten by '85).

In use as a gia here by '83 was Fiat G-91R/3 3237 (c/n 506, ex WS.50, noted '83-'84). 3098 (c/n 364) accompanied (with LVR.7) it in a hangar here by 9.84 and an unidentified G-91 and F-104 were still hangared here in '87, the Gina undergoing restoration. This is presumably the Gina recorded as "3541" in a hangar here during 3.88 (the other "3541" was also seen at the kaserne here the same day). The Starfighter is presumably 2505 (c/n 8263) which was in use for bdr training, minus canopy, during 1989.

IMMENSTAAD

Preserved at the Dornier factory here (between Meersburg and Friedrichshafen) in the early eighties were Do 12 Libelle VQ-FAB (c/n 117) and Do 27A-1 "D-ELUT" (c/n 327, ex D-ECAK, YA-912, 5645, D-EIRO). The latter was still current here in '86 whilst the Libelle had gone (on loan) to the Deutches Museum in Munchen.

INGOLSTADT

Between the bases of Manching and Neuburg can be found the Max Immelmann Kaserne at Oberstimm (serving the base at Ingolstadt/Manching). Preserved here is RF-84F Thunderflash "EA-236" (ex 52-7375, EB-336) (noted '72-'85) in Akg.51 marks, commemorating the days when Akg.51 were based at Manching/Ingolstadt.

ISERLOHN

On display with the Truppendienstlichen Fachschule der Luftwaffe at B Hulsman Kaserne here (some 20 kms South East of Dortmund) is ex Jbg.43 Fiat G-91R/3 3139 (c/n 407, noted '83).

JAGEL

Preserved at the base are ex Mfg.2 AW Sea Hawk Mk.100 "VA-229" (c/n 6667, ex VA-234, painted as "VA-007", later "VA-229") which has been here throughout 1970 to '89 and F-104G Starfighter "2381, c/n 6381" (really 2081, c/n 2094) (noted '82-'89). The real 2381 can be found at Beja, Portugal.

JESENWANG

Three relics could be found here in the mid eighties, and perhaps still linger. They are they are Beech 35-833 Debonair D-ECFO (c/n CD-444, crashed 2.80), Cessna 170A D-ELYC (c/n 19537, ex N5303C, CofA expired 9.73), Macchi MB308 D-EJUP (c/n 5844, ex I-NCOM, CofA expired 9.72).

JEVER

Currently the base of Jbg.38 with the Panavia Tornado, preserved on the base are two examples of the former equipment of the previous residents, WS.10.

F-104F Starfighter	2909	(c/n 5059, ex 59-5006) (noted '75-'87).
CL-13B Sabre Mk.6	"BB-103"	(really c/n S6-1730, ex JB-114 of Jbg.43), WS.10 marks, in front of staff building (noted '70-'86).

Three F-104G Starfighters have served here as decoys. Of the two last noted in '83, one was destroyed by the local firemen whilst the other apparently went to Turkey for use as a gate guard.

F-104G Starfighter	2376	(c/n 8075) painted as "BB-371" in WS.10 marks (noted '78-'86)
F-104G Starfighter	2565	(c/n 9011) (noted '78-'83).
F-104G Starfighter	2590	(c/n 9075) (noted '78-'83).

In use for bdr training with LwW.62 (Luftwaffen Werft 62/Luftwaffe Works 62) are:-

Fiat G-91R/3	3258	(c/n 528) ex Jbg.41 (noted '82-'87).
Fiat G-91R/3	3270	(c/n 540) ex Jbg.43 (noted '82-'86).
F-104G Starfighter	2155	(c/n 7024) ex Jbg.32 (noted '85-'87).

KALKAR

At a kaserne occupied by Luftwaffendivision 3 are two preserved aircraft. Long standing resident is an unidentified F-104F Starfighter wearing the spurious marks "4259" (Noted '85-'89). A more recent arrival (circa 1981/82) is Fiat G-91R/3 3310 (c/n 581) from Jbg.43. When visited in 6.85 this machine was not seen from the outside. Kalkar is about 10 kms East of Kleve.

KARLSRUHE

At a kaserne in the North of the city, Luftwaffenunterstutzungsgruppe Sud have F-86K Sabre 55-4881 (one of a batch supplied to the WGAF and not put into service as they had more aircraft than pilots at this time). It is painted in Jg.74 markings as JD-249 (arrived 25.1.62, current '85). A more recent arrival is F-104G Starfighter 2002 (c/n 2002) from LVR.3.

Up to the mid eighties, the fuselage of CM170 Magister AA-206 (c/n 154) in multi-cloured scheme could be found at the Fliegerklause (literally "airmen's refuge") in Erzbergerstrasse in the Northern part of the town. An attempt to search it out in '85 was not successful and it may well have expired.

KASSEL/CALDEN

Stored at the airfield for the Museum Fridericianum is/was Fieseler Fi 156C-3 Storch D-EKLU (c/n 110061, ex RSwedAF 3809). It has also been reported undergoing restoration at Fritzlar during 1987.

On display on the field was Fiat G-91R/3 3147 (c/n 415) which was retired from Lekg.41 circa 1981 and was still current in '85. It had gone by 5.87, probably scrapped.

KAUFBEUREN

Kaufbeuren is the home of the WGAF's TsLw.1 (equivalent to the RAF's 1 SoTT at Halton). The unit uses a selection of dedicated ground instructional airframes and more modern types (eg Tornado) borrowed from active units in order to teach the skills required to service and maintain modern aircraft. The WGAF is unusual in borrowing active aircraft for gia use, most other air arms preferring to use only retired airframes. It may seem strange to include Tornadoes in a book on 'Wrecks and Relics', but remember that we do set out to record those airframes used for ground instructional purposes.

CL-13B Sabre Mk.6 0106 (c/n S6-1664) arrived here from Neubiburg in the mid eighties, probably for preservation?

F-104G Starfighter JA-240 (c/n 8044, 2362 ntu, damaged 16.8.67) was here by 1975 and remained until approximately 1985 when the aircraft moved to Neuburg (qv). RF-84F Thunderflash BD-701 (ex 51-17021) was lying out on the field here in '73 and was still current in '85.

Ground instructional airframes recorded here include the following.

F-104G Starfighter	2006	(c/n 2006) (noted '76-'88).
F-104G Starfighter	2007	(c/n 2007) (noted '76-'86, to Fassberg).
F-104G Starfighter	2136	(c/n 7004) (noted '76).
F-104G Starfighter	2327	(c/n 8001) (noted '75-80, to Fassberg).
F-104G Starfighter	2331	(c/n 8006) (noted '76-'83, to Neuburg).
F-104G Starfighter	2351	(c/n 8030) (to Pferdsfeld '84).
F-104G Starfighter	2586	(c/n 9061) (noted '76).
TF-104G Starfighter	2708	(c/n 5709, ex 61-3038) (to Fassberg).
RF-4E Phantom	3562	(ex 69-7509) (noted '76-'88, Akg.52 badge).
F-4F Phantom	3704	(ex 72-1114) (noted '76-'88).
Panavia Tornado	4322	(noted '82, to Jbg.38 1.2.84).
Panavia Tornado	4341	(noted 7.84, to Jbg.31 by 7.86).
Panavia Tornado	4387	(noted 7.84, to Erding by 7.85).
Panavia Tornado	4395	(noted 7.84).
Panavia Tornado	4439	(noted 7.84, to Jbg.32 11.84).
Panavia Tornado	4465	(noted 5.85-3.88).
Panavia Tornado	4490	(noted 9.85).
Panavia Tornado	4564	(noted 3.88).
Panavia Tornado	4576	(noted 3.88 in Jbg.34 marks).

KERPEN

At Boelcke Kaserne (Jbg.31's barracks a few miles from Norvenich air base) an unidentified F-104F Starfighter marked as "DA-101" is displayed in flying attitude at the main gate (noted '77-'84). By 1983 it had been joined by F-84F Thunderstreak "DA-127" (ex 53-7102, BF-108) from Norvenich.

KIEL/HOLTENAU

Preserved by the secondary gate (since 4.86) is Sikorsky H-34G 8059 which arrived from Westerland having served there as a gia with the MLG (current '88).

KIRCHHEIM-TECK

The wreck of Cessna F152 D-EJJE (c/n 1847) lay here (at Hahnweide airfield) following a crash in 7.85.

KOBLENZ

The Wehrtechnische Studiensammlung was set up here in 1982 and has amassed the following exhibits. Those stored at Manching may by now have made the journey to Koblenz.

Fairey Gannet AS.4 UA-112 (c/n F9394, ex XG852) ex VFW Bremen Apprentice School.

Fiat G-91R/3	3206	(c/n 474) ex Est.61 (noted '85).
Firebird Seeg M1	9856	(c/n 1065108) ex Manching (noted '85).
F-104G (CCV)	9836	(c/n 8100, ex 2391) ex Est.61 (noted '85-'88).
VFW-Fokker VAK-191B	D-9564	(c/n V2) ex Bremen (arr 12.8.82, current '85).

KOLN/BONN

Lodging at the airport is the WGAF's VIP unit the FBS. Guarding the gate to the military part of the field are ex WS.10 F-104F Starfighter 2911 (c/n 5061, ex 59-5008) and ex Jbg.43 Fiat G-91R/3 3129 (c/n 396).

The airport fire brigade were using two Sabres by 1978, one of which is likely to be CL-13B Sabre Mk.5 BB-237 (ex RCAF 23321) which was previously preserved here and the other probably an unidentified Sabre Mk.5 which had languished here since at least 1969.

On the civil side, two long standing wrecks are Beech 95-D55 Baron D-IAVY (c/n TE-537, ex N402Y, OH-BBB) which crashed in 4.76 and Piaggio P.149D D-EKQA (c/n 322, ex AS-473, D-EDYP) whose CofA expired in 9.72.

LAARBRUCH

The following are believed still to be current at this RAFG Tornado base.

Buccaneer S.1	XN956	(8059M, painted as "K" 15 Sqn) ex Lossiemouth, for bdr with 2 Sqn (noted '72-'89).
BAC Lightning F.2A	XN732	(8519M) ex 'R' 92 Sqn (to fire dump 15.3.85 but not burnt. Modified to resemble a MiG-21 and noted as such, in silver c/s and coded "17" in 2.87-'89).
BAC Lightning F.2A	XN788	(8543M) airlifted by Chinook from Bruggen 2.87 for bdr (current 2.89 with 20 Sqn).
BAC Lightning F.6	XR758	ex 'BF' 11 Sqn (arr 10.5.88, with 16 Sqn for bdr 2.89).
EE Canberra B(I).8	XM264	(8227M) ex 16 Sqn, on display outside 16 Sqn hangar (noted '86-'89).
Hawker Hunter F.6A	"XJ673"	(really XE606/8841M) ex '11' 79 Sqn/1 TWU. In 20 Sqn area wearing 20 Sqn marks as "XX" (arrived by road 7.12.84, noted '89).

LAHR

Guarding the gate at this CAF base is CL-13B Sabre Mk.6 JC-373 (c/n S6-1638, last flew 9.5.66) painted up in RCAF marks as "23444" (in honour of the resident 444 Sqn with CH-136 Kiowas, a former Sabre unit at Sollingen). This machine had formerly lain derelict at Neuhausen until 7.81 when it was recovered to Lahr. Following restoration and positioning on a concrete pillar the monument was officially dedicated on 19.6.82. In 1988 it was joined by a CF-104 Starfighter.

Former AdLA F-100D Super Sabre 42239 (ex 54-2239) arrived from Bruntingthorpe, UK, during 10.88 having been re-possessed by the USAF following closure of the museum there. Quite why it should come to Lahr remains to be seen.

There are at least three CF-104 Starfighters serving as decoys here. Further details would be most welcome.

LANDSBERG

Landsberg houses the Transall equipped Ltg.61 together with UH-1D and MBB105 helicopters. The two gate guards reflect an earlier era when Landsberg was the base for the FFS-A flying school.

CM170 Magister	AA-152	(c/n 052) ex FFS-A (noted '78-'87).
T-6J Harvard IV	"AA-666"	"68-4623" (ex 52-8537) ex FFS-A (noted '78-'87).

Ex AdLA Noratlas 128/F-MC (ex '328-EC' CIFAS.328) was ferried in from Chateaudun by EdC.70 in 9.87 and has since been painted in Ltg.61 marks as "GA-125". The unusual code "F-MC" is derived from the delivery call-sign FSDMC. She was parked on the field by 9.88.

Noted at the open day in 9.87 was the front fuselage of Sycamore Mk.52 7837 (c/n 13503) ex Htg.64, inscribed "BAR" - a corruption of the previous "SAR" titles and in recognition of its internal conversion for the alcoholic beverage supply role at Ahlhorn!. This relic was previously preserved at Ahlhorn and it is not yet apparent whether its transfer here is permanent.

LANDSCHUT

Noted here (70 kms North East of Munchen) in 3.86 was the fuselage of a Cessna 401 which appeared to have been G-AWDM. As this aircraft was still flying (as OO-RWG) perhaps some fuselage swopping has taken place.

LET L.200D Morava D-GGDC (c/n 171329) spent several years in open storage here before being resuscitated and despatched to Elstree, UK, on 14.1.87 as G-BNBZ.

LAUDA

In Lauda, about 45 kms South West of Wurzburg, the gate at the Tauberfranken Kaserne (home of Fernmelderegiment 32) is guarded by CL-13B Sabre Mk.6 "371" (c/n S6-1611, ex JB-371) which arrived from Oldenburg many years ago. It was confirmed as current in '85.

LAUPHEIM

Gate guardian at this Heer base was Dornier Do 27B-1 "HF-201" (really c/n 278, ex AS-930 and "PH-437" as a ground instructional airframe, noted '73-'82), the markings being contrived to suit the based HFVS.201. The Dornier was disposed of to Seifertshofen in 1982 in exchange for Sikorsky S-58C "8025" (c/n 58-350, ex N878, OO-SHQ, BelgAF B-14, D-HAUC). This now masquerades as an H-34G, the serial "8025" being derived from the CH-53G equipped Mhftr.25 who are based here.

LECHFELD

Preserved on the gate at Jbg.32's base was F-104G Starfighter 2136 (c/n 7004) ex TsLw.1 which arrived from Kaufbeuren in 1983. The aircraft is painted as "2002" but had moved to the nearby Schwabstadlkaserne (at the Southern end of the base) by '84. (the identity of this aircraft is also quoted as 2579, c/n 9043, ex Jbg.31). At the same kaserne can be found F-84F Thunderstreak "DB-232" (ex 51-1645, ex DD-367, "DB-032") which came from Pferdsfeld (noted '65-'86).

On the base (and visible from the main Augsberg-Landsberg road) is F-84F Thunderstreak "DB-132" (ex 52-6764, BF-104) which came from TsLw.1 at Kaufbeuren (noted '78-'83, current at South gate '87).

Several other airframes are preserved elsewhere on the base. These comprise a third F-84F marked as "DB-32" (its history and continued existence is unconfirmed but one suggestion is that it may be 52-6734 ex DE-254); Lockheed T-33A "DB-396" (ex 57-0681, 9482, "9403") (noted '83-'84); F-104G Starfighter 2100 (c/n 6621) ex Jbg.32 with a second example in the form of 2047 (c/n 2055) ex LVR.1 and a third marked "2004", formerly a decoy on the base (noted '83).

All this seems just a little too good to be true and confirmation of the current situation would be appreciated.

F-104G Starfighter 2525 (c/n 8301) was in use here as a ground instructional airframe in '83 (current '84).

Also part of the Lechfeld base complex is Ulrich Kaserne, home of Fernmelde Lehr und Versuchsregiment 61, which displays Pembroke C.54 5426 (c/n 1018) (noted '85-'88).

Four F-104G Starfighters were put together from various fuselages, wings and rear ends on the Erding dump. They were here by '78 and disappeared in '82. The following details apply to the main fuselages.

F-104G Starfighter	"2004"	(really c/n 6699, ex 2099 Jg.74) (noted '81-'83).
F-104G Starfighter	"2006"	(really c/n 7045, ex 2176) (noted '81-'83, to Messtetten by '85).
F-104G Starfighter	"2104"	(really c/n 8219, ex 2470) (noted '81).
F-104G Starfighter	"2203"	(really c/n 6619, ex 2098) (noted '81-'83, to Sonthofen by '84).

LECK

At the base of Akg.52, operating the RF-4E Phantom, the main gate has been decorated by four examples of the unit's earlier equipment. The T-bird came from the airfield at Flensburg/Harrisleefeld where the firemen used it for rescue training. The Thunderflash was recovered for display purposes following an accident on 6.4.64. The first Starfighter was relegated to bdr training by 1989.

F-104G Starfighter	"2476"	(really 2075, c/n 2088) (arrived 8.83, relegated to bdr training by '89).
F-104G Starfighter	"2477"	(really 2277, c/n 7159) (arrived by '89).
Lockheed T-33A	"EB-397"	(ex 54-1523, 9459) (noted '80-'89).
RF-84F Thunderflash	EB-250	(ex 52-7355) ex Akg.52 (noted '65-'89).

Former Husum decoy Fiat G-91R/3 3025 (c/n 0082, ex Lekg.41) was derelict on the field here by 1984 with "3599" (rear fuselage of 3099 c/n 365, front fuselage of 3299 c/n 570) (noted '84-'89).

LEIPHEIM

Preserved at the main gate here is Fiat G-91R/3 3138 (c/n 406) (noted '80-'85). TF-104G Starfighter 2726 (c/n 5727, ex Jbg.34) was noted here during 6.86 but had progressed to display near the gate by '88.

Several Ginas and T-birds were parked out on the field here, apparently having been discarded from storage. They have since disappeared.

Fiat G-91R/3	3037	(c/n 0097) (noted '80).
Fiat G-91R/3	3102	(c/n 368) (noted '80).
Fiat G-91R/3	3103	(c/n 369) (noted '80).
Fiat G-91R/3	3154	(c/n 422) (noted '80).
Fiat G-91R/3	3188	(c/n 456) (noted '80).
Fiat G-91R/3	3261	(c/n 531) (noted '80-'82).
Lockheed T-33A	9515	(ex 58-0650) (noted '78-'80).
Lockheed T-33A	9518	(ex 58-0682) (noted '78-'80).
Lockheed T-33A	9524	(ex 58-0690) (noted '78-'80).

Derelict near the control tower for many years (noted '73-'80) was CL-13B Sabre Mk.6 JA-339 (c/n S6-1651). By 1980 the aircraft had been removed to Hermeskeil for the museum there.

The A-10A detachment here received F-4C Phantom 63-7467 from 163 TFS/Indiana ANG for bdr training (arrived by 8.86, current 5.87).

LEMWERDER

VFW-614s F-GATI (c/n G-15, ex D-BABN) and OY-TOR (c/n G-04, ex D-BABD) were stored externally at the MBB factory here for several years (F-GATI arrived 2.80). They were finally moved into the factory in 8.88 to serve as training aids for MBB apprentices.

LEUTKIRCH

At a farm near the airfield are Beech D.18S D-INOL (c/n A-471, ex PH-UDS, N9472, CofA expired 3.77) and Cessna 120 D-EJWA (c/n 14962, ex N3686V) which crashed in 8.80.

LOCHAM

A Cessna F150G D-EFMO (c/n 0100) was noted on top of a shop near the railway line here (South West of Munchen) during 1988.

LUDWIGSBURG

The wreck of Gardan Horizon 160 D-ELMP (c/n 79, ex F-BLVZ) appeared here (15 kms North of Stuttgart) following an accident in 1981.

LUTZELLINDEN

The wreck of Cessna F172H D-ECBD (c/n 0680) lay here following an accident in 10.83.

MAINZ/BUDENHEIM

An NBC school here had a Lockheed T-33A for decontamination training until 1981.

MANCHING

Preserved on the main gate of the MBB works is F-104G Starfighter 2104 (c/n 6625, noted '78-'88) marked simply as "MBB". The MBB tech school has two more F-104G Starfighters in use as instructional airframes. These are 2251 (c/n 7131) and 2373 (c/n 8072). Both were noted in '82.

The gate to the WTD.61 (formerly Est.61) area is guarded by VAK191B D-9565 (noted '78-'88).

A Lehrlingwerkstatt (Apprentice School) here possesses a fine collection of instructional airframes.

CL-13B Sabre Mk.6	0101	(c/n S6-1591) ex Est.61, to gia 8.71, allocated N1039B but ntu (current 9.87).
Dornier Do 27A-1	5638	(c/n 318) ex Est.61 (TT 320 hrs) (noted '86).
Fiat G-91R/3	3121	(c/n 388) to gia '79 (current 7.87, see museum below).
Fiat G-91T/3	9957	(c/n 0021, ex 3419) ex Est.61, to gia 1.84 (current '86).
CM170 Magister	(YA-207)	(c/n 071) ex Est.61, to gia 6.67 (current 7.87).
HFB320 Hansa Jet	1608	(c/n 1025, ex D-CARU, D-9537) ex WTD.61 (noted wfu 9.87).
F-104F Starfighter	2917	(c/n 5070, ex 59-5017) painted as "2121", ex MBB, to gia 6.76 (TT 920 hrs).
Lockheed T-33A	9454	(ex 53-5778) ex Est.61, to gia 2.73 (TT 2772 hrs) (Current 9.87).
Lockheed T-33A	9455	(ex 53-5780, painted as "9456") ex Est.61 (TT 2750 hrs) (Current '86).

Other airframes derelict on the field in recent years have comprised the following.

F-104G Starfighter	DA-129	(c/n 9059, crashed 17.5.66) (noted '80-'88).
CL-13B Sabre Mk.6	(0102)	(c/n S6-1593 ex YA-043) (noted '78-'79, to USA).

Several aircraft have been stored here pending their transfer to the Wehrtechnische Studiensammlung museum at Koblenz.

Fiat G-91R/3	3121	(c/n 388) ex Apprentice School (current '88).
Gloster Meteor NF.11	NF11-14	ex 'BV' CEV, AdLA. (noted 7.87).
N2501F Noratlas	199	ex '070-MF' EdC.70, AdLA. (noted 7.87-'88).
Whirlwind HAR.10	XP339	ex Cleethorpes, UK, exchanged for F-104G 2257 (arr 7.87).

A playground in the village of Manching had Dornier Do 27B-1 D-EHAN (c/n 128, ex 55420). The airframe carried no markings and came from Regensburg. It was not found when checked in 1985 and is presumed scrapped.

MANNHEIM

The Bundesakademie fur Wehrtechnik has two ex Manching airframes here. They are Potez-Heinkel CM191B D-9532 (c/n V2) and Fiat G-91T/3 3407 (c/n 0007) ex Est.61 both which was positioned on display outside the college by 9.88.

Ex Swiss AF EKW C-3605 C-535 had arrived at the airfield here by 8.88 from storage at Lodrino, Switzerland.

MARL

Cessna FRA150L D-EDJI (c/n 0242) was dismantled here (30 kms North West of Dortmund) following CofA expiry in 9.81.

The Ikarusflug Museum was set up here in 1985 using mostly ex Air Classik exhibits. Reported here have been the following.

Inside

Convair CV440	-	cockpit section (noted '87).
DH Rapide	D-IGUN	(c/n 6437, ex HB-AME, HB-APE) (noted '87).
Focke-Wulf Fw 190	"1+1>"	replica, (noted '87, to Schwenningen).
Super Constellation	-	cockpit section (noted '87).
Messerschmitt Bf 109	"6+0"	replica, (noted '87, to Schwenningen).

Messerschmitt Me 163	-	replica, (noted '87).
Zlin 526	F-BSEI	(c/n 1051) (noted '87, to Schwenningen).

Outside

CASA 352L (Ju 52)	"D-ADAM"	(ex T.2B-257, "D-CIAL") ex Stuttgart (noted '87-'88).
Cessna 310B	D-IDIX	(c/n 35527) (noted '87-'88).
Dornier Do 27B-1	D-EFGG	(c/n 174, ex 5544) (noted '86, to Dusseldorf).
Douglas C-47A Dakota	"N569R"	(c/n 10100, ex 42-24238, FL517, G-AJAZ, EC-ADR, SpanAF T.3-61, N8041B) (noted '87-'88, identity not certain).
Gloster Javelin FAW.9	XH768	(7929M) ex Air Classik/Monchengladbach (noted '85-'88).
CL-13A Sabre Mk.5	"JA-102"	(c/n 931, ex RCAF 23141, BB-131) ex Dusseldorf (noted '85-'88).
F-84F Thunderstreak	"5"	(ex 52-6783, DD-248) ex Dusseldorf (noted '85-'88).
Klemm Kl.107C	D-EFOH	(c/n 139) (wreck, noted '87).

Of those listed 'Outside', all except the Klemm had disappeared by early '89, some if not all having gone to Bochum (qv).

MEMMINGEN

Preserved at the main entrance to Jbg.34's base is F-84F Thunderstreak "DD-113" (ex 52-6669, DD-320) (noted '67-'88). This aircraft was damaged in a ground accident on 8.6.64 and relegated to display use. By 9.88 it had been joined by an unidentified F-104G Starfighter marked appropriately "2034".

F-104G Starfighter 2460 (c/n 8208) was noted wfu here in 7.85 - any connection with the above?.

A scrapyard on the base has in recent years held the wrecks of F-104G Starfighter 2654 (c/n 7314, ex Jbg.34, crashed 28.1.82) and Piaggio P.149D 9051 (c/n 066) (noted '79-'83).

MENDIG

Preserved near the entrance to this Heer base is former HFB.300 Vertol H-21C 8332 (c/n WG32) (noted '80-'88) which dates from the early seventies when the entire Heer H-21 fleet was stored here pending disposal.

Dumped amongst some trees on the South side of the base is Dornier Do 27A 5678 (c/n 385) (noted '84-'87).

MENGEN

On display with Luftwaffen Ausbildungs regiment 4 at a military base on the South side of the civil airfield (70 kms South West of Ulm) is F-84F Thunderstreak DD-380 (ex 51-1702). Being surrounded by trees it is not visible from outside.

MESSTETTEN

Situated some 80 kms South of Stuttgart, on display at Zollernal Kaserne (which houses Fernmelderegiment 31) is F-84F Thunderstreak DD-306 (ex 52-6639, painted as "DD-113"). The aircraft arrived from Pferdsfeld in 3.71 and was still current in 1988 by when it was accompanied by ex Lechfeld decoy (as "2006") F-104G Starfighter 2176 (c/n 7045) which had arrived by '83.

MINDEN

Preserved at Potts Park (an amusement park in the Dutzen area of town) is N2501D Noratlas D-ACUG (c/n 043, ex 5241) which arrived from Hamburg on 9.6.72 and was still current in 8.88.

The AAC base received Scout AH.1 XP898 from Wroughton in 9.87 for bdr training.

MONCHENGLADBACH

During the mid to late seventies the field was littered with retired Pembrokes, two of which still survive. The Harvard was also a feature of the landscape for many years until moving on to Dusseldorf in the mid eighties.

Hunting Pembroke C.54	5408	(c/n 105) ex Mfg.5 (derelict '76, preserved '81-'88).

Hunting Pembroke C.54	5415	(c/n 1006) ex Mfg.5 (derelict '76, preserved '88 in pink colour scheme!).
T-6J Harvard IV	AA-633	(c/n CCF4-509, ex 52-8588) (derelict '78, to Dusseldorf).

Air Classik have displayed the following aircraft here.

BAC Lightning F.2A	XN784	(8540M) ex 'R' 92 Sqn (arr from Bruggen '85, current by the entrance 5.86).
Fairey Gannet AEW.3	XL450	(8601M) ex 431 MU (arrived from Bruggen '84, current 5.86).
Gloster Javelin FAW.9	XH768	(7929M) 'E' ex Southend (noted '83-'84, to Marl by '85).

Stored here is/was Hunting Provost T.1 G-ASMC (ex XF908, noted 5.86) whilst D55 Baron D-INKY (c/n TE-479) has been reported in use as a children's plaything (obviously the original Dinky toy!).

MOSBACH

FJ Sky-Trac D-HHTF (c/n 14) was stored here for many years following CofA expiry in 6.74.

MUHLDORF

The wreck of PZL Wilga 35 D-ENTT (c/n 86279, ex SP-WRC, D-ELHG ntu) has lingered here (some 80 kms East of Munchen) following its accident in 4.79.

MUNCHEN

In the Allach district of the city, RF-84F Thunderflash EB-341 (ex 52-7377) was resident at the MTU factory here for many years until departure on 19.11.85 slung beneath a CH-53G for preservation with Akg.51 at Bremgarten. Still remaining with MTU is a plinth-mounted F-104G Starfighter comprising the rear of 2054 (crashed 12.10.77) with the front two thirds of a so far unidentified aircraft.

A school in the Bohne district (Munchen-Aubing) has the incomplete airframe of Hagmann EH.102 D-ELHA (c/n V1).

A Dornier factory in Munchen-Neuaubing has a Do 27 on display, possibly c/n 191 (ex D-ENKN, 5558) from Oberpfaffenhofen (noted 10.85). Preserved here in the early eighties were ex Spanish AF Do 24T-3s HD.5-3 (c/n 5344) and HD.5-4 (c/n 5345). The former was converted to the turbo-prop powered Do 24TT whilst the latter was restored using the wings from HD.5-3 and by 1985 was on display at Oberpfaffenhofen.

The BMW Museum in the city has Klemm L.25A-VI "D-1638" (c/n 149, ex D-1638, D-EFAR, HB-...) which arrived from Switzerland on 6.7.79.

In the city centre, by the river Isar, is the Deutsches Museum which houses the national aircraft collection of West Germany together with a vast range of non aeronautical exhibits.

AAC.1 (Ju 52/3m)	363	(noted '80-'88).
Agusta-Bell 47G-2	AS-058	(c/n 258) ex Neubiburg (noted '85-'88).
Airbus A300B	F-OCAZ	(c/n 01) major components (noted '88).
Vampyr	-	built by Akaflieg Hannover (noted '86).
Fs24 Phonix	D-9093	(c/n V1, ex D-8258) built by Akaflieg Stuttgart (noted '86).
Arado Ar 66D	1258	fuselage frame, plus wreckage from another, recovered from the Starnberger See (noted '85-'88).
Bachem Ba 349 Natter	-	(noted '80).
Bleriot XI	-	(noted '88)
Boeing 707-430	D-ABOF	(c/n 17721) cockpit section only, ex Lufthansa (noted '85-'88).
Bolkow Bo 105P	D-HAPE	(c/n V4, ex 9832) (noted '85-'88).
CASA 1131E (Bu 131)	E.3B-555	ex Spanish AF (noted '88).
CASA 2.111B (He 111)	B.2I-177	(c/n 166) ex Spanish AF .
Dornier A Libelle II	VQ-FAB	(c/n 117) (noted '86-'88).
Dornier Do 27B-1	5666	(c/n 360, ex 5666, and display as "D-EHAV") (noted '85-'88).

Dornier Do 31E	D-9531	(c/n E3) (noted '77-'88).
Dornier Do 32E	"D-HOPA"	(c/n "32004") composite of D-HOPF, D-HOPS & D-HOPA c/ns 32001, 32002 & 32003 respectively (noted'86-'88).
Dornier Do 335A-2	240102	'VG+PH' (ex FE-1012) (noted '85-'88, on loan from NASM, Washington DC).
Douglas C-47B Dakota	1401	(c/n 26989, ex 43-49728, KK209) ex Hamburg & Erding.
ERW-Sud VJ101C	D-9518	(c/n X2) (noted '85-'88).
Fieseler Fi 103	478374	(noted '86).
Fieseler Fi 156C	A-96	(c/n 4299, ex Swiss AF & HB-ARU) (noted '80-'88).
Focke Achgelis Fa 330	-	(noted '80-'88).
Fw 44J Stieglitz	D-ENAY	(ex RSwedAF 668, SE-BWH, D-EGAM) (noted '86).
Fokker DR.1	"425/17"	replica (noted '80-'86).
Fokker D.VII	"4408/18"	replica (noted '80-'86).
Grade A Libelle	-	(noted '86).
HAL HF-24 Marut	-	ex Indian AF (stored '86).
HFB320 Hansa Jet	D-CLOU	(c/n 1002, ex D-CLOU, 'D-CASEK') (noted '86-'88).
HKS 3	D-6426	built by Haase Kensche Schmetz (noted '86).
Junkers F13	"D366"	(c/n 2018) (noted '86-'88).
Junkers A 50ci Junior	D-2054	(c/n 3575, ex D-2054, CH-358, HB-UXI) (noted '88).
Klemm L25E	D-EMDU	(c/n 980, ex D-EMDU, SE-ANF) (noted '86-'88).
F-104F Starfighter	2903	(c/n 5049, ex 59-4996) wears WS.10 & Jg.74 badges.
F-104G Starfighter	2153	(c/n 7022) ex Jbg.33 (noted '84-'88).
F-104G Starfighter	-	front fuselage only.
Lockheed T-33A	9447	(ex 53-5628) still with Erding apprentice school 9.86.
Bf 109E-3	"2804"	(really c/n 790, ex SpanAF '6-106') 'AJ+YM' (noted '80-'88).
Me 163B-1A Komet	120370	(ex AM210) (noted '80-'88).
Me 262A-1	500071	'3' (noted '80-'88).
CL-13B Sabre Mk.6	0105	(c/n S6-1659, ex JD-105)
Messerschmitt M 17	D-779	(c/n 25) (noted '86-'88).
Nord 1002 (Me 108)	"D-IBFW"	(c/n 77, ex F-BEAI, OY-AIJ) (noted '86-'88).
Panavia Tornado	9806	(c/n P07) (noted '87).
RF-84F Thunderflash	EB-231	(ex 52-7379) ex Akg.52.
Rumpler Taube	-	(c/n 19) (noted '86).
Rumpler C.IV	-	(c/n 210) (noted '86-'88).
Rutan Quickie Q.2	D-EEWQ	(c/n 1) (noted '86-'88).
SAAB J 35A Draken	35086	ex '48' F 16, RSwedAF.
Schleicher Ka.6	D-9099	(noted '86).
HH-19B Chickasaw	53-4458	ex USAF, 17th AF markings (noted '85-'88).
SH-34G Choctaw	8073	(c/n 58-1557, ex 150808)
Solair 1	D-MXOL	(noted '88).
Sud Alouette II	7584	(c/n 1497)
VAK191B	D-9563	(c/n V1)
Wright Standard Type A	-	replica (noted '88).

MUNCHEN/RIEM

Cessna 182 D-EJOC (c/n 33296, ex N6496A, HB-CPH) has been derelict at the airport since being wfu in 3.80. Cessna 210E D-EMZA (c/n 58579) lay wrecked behind a hangar in 4.85.

Lockheed T-33A 9419 (ex 52-9917) arrived during the seventies for the airport fire service (noted '78). It still clung on to this tenuous existence during '85.

NABERN

The wreck of Bo 209 Monsun 160RV D-EAAX (c/n 182) has been a long term wreck here since suffering an accident in 9.76.

NEUBIBURG

Several airframes continue to inhabit this large base, now the home of several non-flying WGAF units, principally the Fachhochschule (Officers Technical Academy).

Noted in recent years have been the following.

Fiat G-91R/3	3187	(c/n 455) gia with Fachhochschule, gone by '85.
Fiat G-91R/3	3308	(c/n 579) ex Jbg.43 (noted '80-'82, to Furstenfeldbruck by '85).
CM170R Magister	9303	(c/n 080) gia with Fachhochschule '82, to Hermeskeil '84.
F-104F Starfighter	2918	(c/n 5071, ex 59-5018) gia with Fachhochschule by '73 (to Furstenfeldbruck by '85).
N2501D Noratlas	5337	(c/n 160) (arr for Elbeflug '72, displayed here when Elbeflug collapsed, airlifted to Altenstadt '82).
CL-13B Sabre Mk.6	0106	(c/n S6-1664) (noted '78-'85, to Kaufbeuren).
Piaggio P.149D	D-EBSN	(c/n 169, ex 9147) gia with Fachhochschule (noted '80, to Furstenfeldbruck by '85).
F-84F Thunderstreak	DD-302	(ex 52-6601) (arr 22.9.64, scrapped '80).
Sud Alouette II	PP-144	(c/n 1763) crashed 29.4.66, gia with Fachhochschule '80.

The school also use a Dornier Do 27 which was found to be sub-standard whilst still in production and before a c/n had been allocated. It was completed as a ground instructional airframe and presented to the Fachhochschule by the manufacturers, totally devoid of markings. By 1985 it was painted up as "5663" "c/n 357" here.

NEUBURG

Two F-104G Starfighters arrived from instructional use at Kaufbeuren to serve as decoys here. They comprise "JA-240" (really 2362, c/n 8044, noted '85-'88) and 2331 (noted 9.86-8.88). The anonymous F-86K Sabre from Furstenfeldbruck (ex 55-48..) arrived here by '85 and by '86 was installed on the gate in Jg.74 markings as "JD-119" (current '88).

The non-flying functions of Jg.74 are accommodated off the air base at the nearby Wilhelm Frank Kaserne. On the gate are an ex Jg.74 F-104G and an F-86K from the 'unflown' batch.

F-104G Starfighter	2357	(c/n 8037) ex Jg.74 (noted '74-'86).
F-86K Sabre	"JG-74"	(ex 55-4928) (noted '70-'86).

NEUHAUSEN-OB-ECK

Sud Alouette II 7645 (ex instructional at Roth) was noted on a lorry here in 6.87 and was still present in a hangar here in 3.88, a possible candidate for gate-guard duties.

NEU-ULM

Mounted on a pole outside the Konigs Schutzen Scheisshaus is Fiat G-91R/3 3256 (c/n 526, rear fuselage/tail from 3186 c/n 454) which arrived from TsLw.1 at Kaufbeuren by 1978. This location is within sight of the small civil airfield at Neu-Ulm (about 5 kms South of the town on the road to Reutti).

NIEDERSTETTEN

Sud Alouette II 7715 (c/n 1869) was in use as an instructional airframe here with HFS.12 at the Heer base (Hermann Kohl Kaserne) in 6.86. F-84F Thunderstreak BF-105 (ex 52-6778) was here until 1981 when it left for the museum collection at Hermeskeil.

NORDHOLZ

The gate-guard at Mfg.3's base is Fairey Gannet AS.4 UA-113 (c/n F9395, ex XG853) (noted '78-'89).

An ex Marineflieger F-104G Starfighter arrived for the firemen on 20.6.80. The serial has been quoted as 22.. but also reported in 7.84 as ex Jg.71 2462. I believe the former to be correct so we still need the full serial.

NORVENICH

Preserved on the base are F-84F Thunderstreak "DA-232"/"DA-101" (on either side of the fuselage, ex 52-6707) which came from Buchel by 8.88 and F-104G Starfighter 2481 (c/n 8231, ex Jg.74 & decoy "DA-05") painted up as Darryl Greenamyer's N104RB. Both were current 8.88.

F-84F Thunderstreak BF-108 (ex 53-7102) arrived from the Lehrwerkstatt at Buchel in 1981 and following restoration it was installed as a gate guard at Jbg.31's kaserne in Kerpen by 1983.

F-104G Starfighter 2388 (c/n 8095) was serving as a ground instructional airframe here by 3.83.

By 8.85 F-104G Starfighter 2042 (c/n 2049, ex Jbg.31 Weapons Loading Trainer) was parked out by the A-10 shelters here. It was still lurking around the HAS areas in 8.87 when it was accompanied by 2387 (c/n 8094). Both are presumably used either as surface decoys or bdr airframes. Long standing decoys during the F-104 era here were the following.

F-104G Starfighter	2455	(c/n 8203) painted as "DA-03" (current '82).
F-104G Starfighter	2463	(c/n 8212) painted as "DA-04", tail of 2596 (current '82).
F-104G Starfighter	2481	(c/n 8231) painted as "DA-05", tail from 2452, to "N104RB" by '82 (see above).
F-104G Starfighter	2494	(c/n 8247) painted as "DA-06" (current '82, to Fassberg by '85).
F-104G Starfighter	2606	(c/n 9134) broke its back in landing accident at Lossiemouth, UK, 13.8.77, to Hopsten by 9.86.

The A-10A FOL here received F-4C Phantom 63-7536 ex 171 TFS/Michigan ANG on 17.7.86 for bdr training (still current 8.87).

NURNBURG

In storage here by 8.88 was Beech Queen Air 5X-SAM.

OBERPFAFFENHOFEN

A small collection of local products is gathered around the main entrance to the Dornier works here.

Dornier Do 24T-3	HD.5-3	ex Spanish AF and Immenstaad, wings from HD.5-4 which was converted to Do 24TT turbo-prop status (noted '84-'88).
Dornier Do 27A-1	"D-ELUT"	(c/n 327, ex D-ECAK, YA-912, 5645, D-EIRO) (to Immenstaad by '82).
Dornier Do 27J-1	"D-EYLE"	(c/n 2057, ex BLa D-9504, BLa D-01, D-EGVB) (noted '84-'88).
Dornier Do 27	"D-EMMA"	(noted '85-'88).
Dornier Do 27	"D-EMMI"	(noted '85-'88).
Dornier Do 28A-1	"D-IPAT"	(c/n 3010, ex (D-IGES), (D-INLF), D-IATA) (noted'82-'88).
Dornier Do 28D/TNT	D-IFNT	(noted '88).
Dornier Do 29	"YA-101"	(c/n V1, ex YD-101) ex Buckeburg (noted '81-'88).
Dornier Do 31E	D-9530	(c/n E1) (noted '81-'88).
Dornier Do 32 Kiebitz	-	unmanned rotor test vehicle (noted '82-'86).
Dornier Do 335A-2	240102	VG+PH (noted '82 after restoration by Dornier, to Deutsches Museum on loan from NASM Washington DC).
Fiat G-91R/3	3135	(c/n 403) ex Lekg.43 (noted '81-'88).

Note that Do 27 "D-EMMA" is not, as sometimes claimed, a re-paint of "D-EYLE". All three Do 27s were seen together in 10.85 and I suspect the two unknowns could be further ex Belgian Army aircraft. Further information would be appreciated.

OFFENBURG

The wreck of Piaggio P.149D D-ENJX (c/n 044, ex 9030) appeared here following an accident in 8.83. Noted in mid '88 were the hulks of two Bell 47Gs one of which was identified as Sioux AH.1 XT193.

OLDENBURG

Just off the E35 at the Wechloy turn off, N2501D Noratlas D-ACUK (c/n 117, ex 5299)

was preserved at the Familia shopping centre (noted '79-'82). The aircraft has since been scrapped, probably in late '87.
Preserved within the base are/were the following.

Fiat G-91R/3	3087	(c/n 351) ex decoy here, marked "3259" (noted '84-'85 with 432 Staffel).
Fiat G-91R/3	3100	(c/n 366) ex decoy here (noted '84-'85, painted in Tiger stripes).
Fiat G-91R/3	3101	(c/n 367) ex Lekg.43 (noted on a pole '79-'84).
Fiat G-91R/4	BR-361	(c/n 0098) painted as "3336" (noted '82, scrapped by'85).
CL-13B Sabre Mk.6	JB-110	(c/n S6-1734) (crashed 5.12.63, restored for display and placed in front of 431 Staffel HQ building (noted '78-'84).
CL-13B Sabre Mk.6	JB-371	(c/n S6-1813) (crashed 24.9.65, recovered for display purposes, noted on gate '67-'85).

Messerschmitt Me 163 Komet 191904 came here from the museum at RAF St Athan, UK, during 1988.

Following the withdrawal of the 'Gina' Lekg.43, half a dozen aircraft have acted as surface decoys.

Fiat G-91R/3	3048	(c/n 305) (noted '82, scrapped by '84).
Fiat G-91R/3	3060	(c/n 320) (noted '82).
Fiat G-91R/3	3087	(c/n 351) (noted '82, preserved here as "3259" by '84, current '85).
Fiat G-91R/3	3099	(c/n 365) (noted '82, to Leck by '84).
Fiat G-91R/3	3100	(c/n 366) (noted '82, preserved here by '85).

Two more Ginas were noted on the base during an open day in '84, they were 3215 (c/n 483) and 3294 (c/n 565). What happened to these?

OSNABRUCK

RF-84F Thunderflash "ED-119" (ex 51-1869, EB-319), formerly with Akg.52, is preserved with Fernmelderegiment 71 at the General Martini Kaserne (noted '69-'84). The kaserne is in Hauswormannsweg on the South side of the city off the '51' and '68' roads.

PFERDSFELD

Preserved at the main entrance to the air base is Fiat G-91R/3 3303 (c/n 574) (noted '80-'85). It replaced Lockheed T-33A 9426 (ex 52-9935) which after several years of gate guard duties was sold for scrap on 1.6.81 together with 9491 (ex 58-0557), 9500 (ex 58-0600) and 9504 (ex 58-0637) which had served as surface decoys.

The hulk of Fiat G-91R/3 3033 (c/n 0093, ex Husum decoy) was lying derelict out on the airfield (in the Eastern shelter area) by 4.84 (current '85). Ex TsLw.1 F-104G Starfighter 2351 (c/n 8030) was dumped here by 12.84.

A few miles down the road, Jbg.35's kaserne at Sobernheim has CL-13B Sabre Mk.6 "JC-102" preserved within the base (noted '71-'85). The aircraft's true identity is at present unknown.

PFINZTAL-SOLLINGEN

Dismantled in Herr FA Berg's yard, by the side the main road (15 kms East of Karlsruhe), are two N2501D Noratlas hulks which arrived from storage at Basle. They were last recorded by the compiler in '82 but were already long standing relics and may well still be current.

N2501D Noratlas	D-ACUQ	(c/n 130, ex 5312) ex Ltg.61.
N2501D Noratlas	D-ACUH	(c/n 112, ex 5294) ex Ltg.61.

PINNEBERG

In this Hamburg suburb, Luftwaffen Ausbildungsregiment 1 has two aircraft displayed within Eggerstedt Kaserne. The T-bird came here from Aachen and the Sabre from Oldenburg.

Lockheed T-33A	9464	(ex 54-1435) ex Akg.52 (noted '82-'84).
CL-13A Sabre Mk.5	"JB-111"	(c/n 840, ex RCAF 23050, BB-239) (noted '59-'84).

POPPENHAUSEN

The Rhonmuseum (about 15 kms East of Fulda between the 279 and 458 roads) at the Wasserkuppe has the following gliders on display.

Darmstadt D.34C	D-4644	
DFS108-14 Schulgleiter	-	
DFS108-30 Kranich 2B	-	
DFS108-30 Kranich 3	D-7002	
DFS108-70 Meise	D-4679	
DFS Habicht	-	replica.
DFS Rhonbussard	-	painted as "D-HESSELBURG".
Dittmar Condor IV	-	painted as "D-CONDOR".
Greif 1	-	
Putzer-Horten Ho.3V2	-	(c/n 2)
Putzer-Horten III	-	
Hutter H.17A	-	
LET L.13 Blanik	D-1113	
Lilienthal Gleiter	-	replica.
Lippisch Falke	HB-16	painted as "D-FALKE", loan from Segelflugmuseum Gunzburg.
Schleicher Ka.3	-	
Grunau Baby IIB	-	
Grunau Baby III	D-4303	(c/n 05/51)

PREUSSISCH-OLDENDORF

Douglas DC-6 D-ABAH (c/n 42855, ex N90702, JY-ACE, N90702, HP-361, N90702) came here from Frankfurt for display at the 'Mobel-Holstein' furniture store (about 30 kms East of Osnabruck). It was still current in 8.88.

RAMSTEIN

The local Battle Damage Repair Flight have the following airframes, though it is to be hoped that the F-84F, F-101 and F-102 at least end up preserved.

F-84F Thunderstreak	52-6789	ex Greek AF (arr by 10.87).
F-101F Voodoo	57-0386	ex 136 FIS/New York ANG & MASDC FF408 (arr by 4.85, current '88).
F-102A Deta Dagger	56-1125	ex Greek AF & Elefsis decoy (arr by 10.87).
F-105F Thunderchief	63-8362	ex 149 TFS/Virginia ANG and MASDC (arr by 3.86, current 8.87).
F-4C Phantom	64-0917	ex 182 TFS/Texas ANG (arr by 8.86, current 8.88).
F-4E Phantom	74-1641	ex 'RS' 86 TFW, wreck noted 8.87 for bdr with 526 TFS, rear fuselage to Spangdahlem by '89 for bdr.
Lockheed T-33A	FT-38	(ex 55-3044) ex 11 Esc, BelgAF (arr 2.80, current 8.86).
CT-39A Sabreliner	62-4471	ex 58 MAS (noted '85-'87, to Sembach).

RHEINE

At Jbg.36's kaserne in the town (General Wever Kaserne) two aircraft are preserved representing the wing's former equipment. An unidentified F-84F Thunderstreak marked "DF-240" has been here for many years (noted '78-'88). It was joined by F-104G Starfighter 2226 (c/n 7101, ex Mfg.2 - though there is still an element of doubt as to this aircraft's identity) which arrived by road from the air base on 25.7.85 and has been mounted on the gate painted as "DF-101" (noted 6.88). Both are displayed on poles in flying attitude. See also Bentlage and Hopsten.

ROTENBURG/WUMME

Parked out by the control tower at this Heeresflieger airfield (Lent Kaserne) about 60 kms South West of Hamburg is Lockheed T-33A "9520" which crashed 10.4.69. If it was recovered for display purposes and wears its true serial, this makes it ex 58-0684 (noted '83-'89). It has reportedly been joined by a Fiat G-91R/3.

ROTH

Preserved at a WGAF barracks within this Heeresflieger MBB105 base (Otto Lilienthal Kaserne) are the following.

CL-13B Sabre Mk.5	"JA-130"	(c/n 838, ex RCAF 23048, YA-...) ex Oberpfaffenhofen (noted '83-'85)
F-84F Thunderstreak	"DA-379"	(ex 51-1796, DD-379) (noted '65-'85).
RF-84F Thunderflash	"EA-105"	(ex 53-7693, EA-315) (noted '83-'85).

Sud Alouette II 7645 (c/n 1672) was in use as an instructional airframe here in 1980 but was not noted at the '85 open day. At this time an Alouette II wearing the c/n 1194 (which makes it 7506) was used as an underslung load for a CH-53G display (it was back in service with HFS.5 by 5.87).

ROTTENBURG/LAABER

On display at FlaRakRegt 34's kaserne (Generaloberst Weise Kaserne) some 40 kms South of Regensburg is CL-13B Sabre Mk.6 JC-101 (c/n S6-1696) (noted '78-'87).

ROTTWEIL

This civil field has housed several relics though unfortunately there have been no recent reports. Current in the early eighties were the following.

MS894A Minerva	D-EAWL	(c/n 11048) CofA expired 9.83.
Piaggio P.149D	D-EEHG	(c/n 065, ex 9050) stored since 8.85.
Piaggio P.149D	D-EAEG	(c/n 278, ex 9192) CofA expired 7.84.
Piaggio P.149D	D-ELEF	(c/n 307, ex 9211) derelict, wfu 12.83.
Piaggio P.149D	D-EFNP	(c/n 308, ex 9212) CofA expired 6.82.

SAARBRUCKEN

Cessna 310J OE-FAS (c/n 0172) was stored here in 4.87.

ST PETER ORDING

Cessna 150F D-EFRH (c/n 63008, ex N6408F) is used as an attraction here (about 70 kms West of Schleswig), perched on top of a cafeteria.

SCHWELM

The fuselage of N2501D Noratlas 5237 (c/n 39) ex Ltg.61 is preserved here, adjacent to the autobahn about 10 kms South of Dortmund. It was bought for DM 50,000 and arrived from Finkenwerder by 1974 for conversion into a restaurant (current '89).

SCHWENNINGEN

Sometimes referred to as Villingen-Schwenningen, the International Luchtfahrt Museum opened in May '88 and has already gathered a very varied collection. Schwenningen is about 70 kms East of Freiburg.

Aero L60 Brigadyr	"OK-LGL"	(c/n 150401, ex OK-LGL, OE-BVL) ex Air Classik (noted '88).
Antonov An-2	2613	(c/n 1G-2613) ex Polish AF (noted '88).
Bleriot XI	D-EHCI	(c/n 01) flyable replica (noted '88).
Bu 181B Bestmann	D-EDIB	(c/n 25039) (noted '88).
CASA 1131E (Bu 131)	"D-EBZE"	(ex Spanish AF E.3B-526) (noted '88).
Schulgleiter SG-38	D-7033	(noted '88).
Kitten	"D-MZAG"	(noted '88).
Evans VP-2	-	
Fw 44 Stieglitz	-	(noted '88).
Focke Wulf Fw 190	"1-1"	replica (noted '88).
Grade Monoplane	D-EKLB	(noted '88).
Junkers Ju 87 Stuka	"T6-KL"	replica, ex Air Classik/Frankfurt (noted '88).
Klemm Kl.25	D-ENAE	(noted '88).
LIM-2 (MiG-15bis)	1019	(c/n 1B-01019) ex Polish AF, painted in Soviet AF colours (noted '88).
F-104G Starfighter	2043	(c/n 2050) ex Jbg.34 (noted '88)
TF-104G Starfighter	2728	(c/n 5730) ex Seifertshofen (noted '88).

Messerschmitt Me 109 "6"		replica (noted '88).
Messerschmitt Me 262 "5"		replica (noted '88).
AT-6A Texan	D-FOBY	(c/n 77-4176, ex PortAF 1608, G-BGGR) ex Dusseldorf (noted '88).
Piaggio P.149D	D-EHMG	(c/n 320, ex AS471, AC471, 9223) ex Dusseldorf (noted '88).
SARO Skeeter AOP.12	-	(reported as c/n S2-7074 but S2/6920R on plate) (noted '88).
Grunau Baby IIB	D-9209	(noted '88).
Zlin 526	F-BSEI	(noted '88).

SEIFERTSHOFEN

The collection at Eugene Kiemele's scrapyard (about 75 kms North East of Stuttgart) now calls itself the Schwabisches Bauern und Technik Museum. Many of the aircraft are still lying in three compounds around the museum proper.

Beech C-45	44562	ex Aeronavale, Rochefort (noted '80-'87).
Beech 1001A	"KF0090"	(noted '86).
Baron 95-A55	D-IKUC	(c/n TC-194) damaged beyond repair 20.11.81 (noted '86-'88).
Dornier Do 27B-1	"HF-201"	(c/n 278, ex AS-930, "PH-437") ex Laupheim (arr '80, current '87).
Dornier Do 27	AC-930	(noted '88, I suspect this may well be the aircraft noted above with the earlier paintwork visible).
Hunting Pembroke C.54	5417	(c/n 1008) ex FBS (arr 24.2.74, noted '88).
SP-2H Neptune	144685	ex Aeronavale 25F & Rochefort (noted '79-'88).
TF-104G Starfighter	2728	(c/n 5730) ex WS.10 (noted '73-'87, to Schwenningen by '88).
Lockheed T-33A	117487	(ex 51-17487) ex '33-XG' SLVSV/ER.33, AdlA (noted '80-'87).
Lockheed T-33A	FT-09	(ex 51-6663) ex BelgAF (noted '80-'87).
Lockheed T-33A	FT-26	(ex 53-5725) ex BelgAF (noted '80-'87).
Nord 1300	618	(license-built Scheibe Bergfalke) ex AdlA (noted '86).
N2501D Noratlas	5343	(c/n 173) ex Ltg.62 (noted '80-'88).
F-100D Super Sabre	42136	(ex 54-2136) ex '11-EB' EC.1/11, AdlA & Chateaudun (noted '78).
F-100D Super Sabre	42185	(ex 54-2185) ex '11-MO' EC.2/11, AdlA & Chateaudun (noted '78-'87).
F-84F Thunderstreak	FU-160	(ex 53-6899) ex BelgAF (noted '75-'87).
Scheibe Bergfalk	D-5383	(noted '86).
Sikorsky SH-34J	143/D	(ex 147634) ex MLD, soc 4.12.59 (noted '75-'87, planned to go to De Kooy, Netherlands, for gate guard duties).
CH-37B Mojave	50621	(ex 55-0621) ex USAREUR (noted '75-'82).
Vertol H-21C	8310	(c/n WG10) ex HFB.300 & Mendig store (noted '72-'87).
Vertol H-21C	8315	(c/n WG15) ex HFB.300 & Mendig store (noted '72-'87).
Vertol H-21C	8318	(c/n WG18) ex HFB.300 & Mendig store (noted '72-'87).

By 1986 the collection had succeeded in its stated intention of producing a complete H-21C (overall yellow, no marks) from the fuselage of 8318 and the tail of 8310.

SEMBACH

Displayed inside the domestic site on the other side of the road to the base is F-86 Sabre 52-5372 (noted '80-'88).

Battle Damage Repair Training airframes here have comprised the following.

F-4C Phantom	64-0922	ex 163 TFS/Indiana ANG (arr by 8.86, current 8.87).
F-101B Voodoo	58-0267	ex '02' 123 FIS/Oregon ANG & MASDC FF395 (arr by 10.85, current 8.88).
Lockheed T-33A	41581	(ex 54-1581) ex AdlA (noted '80-'82, dumped '84-'86).
CT-39A Sabreliner	62-4471	ex 58 MAS, arrived from Ramstein '88.

SINSHEIM

At the Auto und Technik Museum here (some 30 kms South East of Heidelburg along the A20/E12 autobahn) can be found a vast range of cars, locomotives, engines and the following aircraft.

Antonov An-2	"03"	(ex HA-GEB) Soviet marks (noted '88).
CASA 352L (Ju 52)	"D-2527"	(c/n 148, ex SpanAF T.2B-257, D-CIAL, "D-ADAM", D-CIAL) Lufthansa colours (displayed on poles '85-'88).
CASA 352L (Ju 52)	"RJ+NP"	(noted '87-'88).
CASA 352L (Ju 52)	"5J+CN"	(noted '88).
CASA 352L (Ju 52)	"D-AQUI"	(noted '87-'88).
CASA 2.111 (He 111)	B.2I-82	painted as "5J+GN", ex Spanish AF (stored 10.86, on display '88).
DFS108 Schulgleiter	D-8182	(Hall 1 '86-'88).
DH Dove	-	(noted outside '88).
DH Tiger Moth	DE623	(stored '86, inside '88).
DH Venom FB.50	J-1603	(Hall 1 '86-'88).
DH Venom FB.50	J-1628	(Hall 2 '84-'88).
DH Venom FB.54	J-1798	(Hall 2 '84-'88).
Dornier Do 27A-4	D-EDHS	(c/n 371, ex 5671) ex Frankfurt (stored '86, inside'88).
Douglas C-47A Dakota	N8041A	(c/n 25450, ex 43-48149, KG773, G-AKLL, EC-AEU, T.3-62) ex Spanish AF (noted '86-'88).
EE Canberra B.2	9936	(c/n 6644 but fin from 6651) ex MilGeoAMT (arr 15.9.83, on poles '86-'88).
EKW C-3605	C-501	ex Swiss AF & Lodrino store (noted '88).
Fiat G-91R/3	3264	(c/n 534) ex Lekg.43 (arr 3.9.82, suspended from roof, Hall 1 '86-'88).
Fi 156 Storch	"PT+TP"	(noted '87-'88 - marked "127/H3+BF" in '87).
Fi 156 Storch	"H3+BF"	(c/n "127") (noted '87-'88).
Focke-Wulf Fw 190	"10"	composite airframe using original parts (Hall 2 '86-'88).
Fokker E.III	-	replica.
Glider	D-8055	(noted '88).
Glider	D-9178	(noted '88).
Hispano HA1112-M1L	"4"	(c/n 228, ex C.4K-170, G-AWHS) (noted '85-'88).
Hubner Eindekker	-	(Hall 1 '86-'88).
Hubner Mucke	-	
Hunting Pembroke C.54	D-CAKE	(c/n 92, ex 5402) ex Hofheim (car park '86, inside '88).
Ilyushin Il-14	0833	ex Polish AF, flown to Speyer 4.3.88 (noted outside '88).
Junkers Ju 52	V6+..	stored dismantled '86-'88 with centre fuse of another.
Junkers Ju 88	-	wreckage recovered from Swedish lake (noted '88).
Kamov Ka-26D	D-HBAU	(c/n 7303204) (stored '86-'88, marked CCCP-26001 '88).
Lilienthal Monoplane	-	
LIM-2 (MiG-15bis)	"12"	(ex 1006, c/n 1B01006) ex Polish AF, painted in Soviet marks (noted '88).
F-104G Starfighter	2249	(c/n 7129) (noted '87-'88).
Lockheed T-33A	JD-397	(ex 58-0709) ex '7' Buchel (arr 9.4.84, displayed on a pole, noted '88).
Lockheed T-33A	9401	(ex 51-17471) painted as USAF "63659", ex Stuttgart (noted '86-'88).
Mignet Pou-du-Ciel	"D-EMIL"	(noted '86-'88).
MS500/MS505 Criquet	"H3+BF"	(c/n 127) (noted '88).
Muselkraft	-	man powered aircraft (noted 10.86).
CL-13B Sabre Mk.6	YA-042	(c/n S6-1613, 0104 ntu) (arr 26.7.83, Hall 2 '86-'88).
Harvard T.2B	"FT454"	(c/n 14-555, ex 42-12308, FE821, B-164, 099) (noted '86-'88). See comments under Brasschaat, Belgium.

Raab Krahe II	D-KONY	(noted '86-'88).
F-84F Thunderstreak	BA-102	(ex 52-6816, DD-308) ex Germersheim (noted '87-'88).
SAAB J 29F Tunnan	29392	ex 'I' (yellow) Austrian AF (noted '86, left for Vienna 7.88 in exchange for the MiG-15).
Schleicher Ka-1	D-8117	(Hall 1 '86-'88).
SB-2 Schulgleiter	D-1202	(noted 10.86).
Sikorsky S-58C	D-HAUF	(c/n 58-356, ex OO-SHI, BelgAF B-11) (arr 14.4.82, Hall 1 '86-'88).
Stampe SV4	"1010"	"IF" AdlA markings (noted '87-'88).
Sud Alouette II	-	cockpit section, probably ex BundesGrenzSchutz (noted '87-'88)
Vertol H-21C	8317	(c/n WG17) ex Air Classik (displayed on poles'86-'88)
Vickers Viscount 708	F-BGNU	(c/n 38) ex Air Inter & Mulhouse (displayed on poles '86-'88)

SOEST

The AAC here received Wasp HAS.1 XT436/506 from Detmold by 12.85 and Scout AH.1 XP897 from Wroughton on 1.9.87, both for bdr. Both are fuselage pods only.

SOLLINGEN

Guarding the gate at this Canadian fighter base are the following.

Avro CF-100 Canuck	100784	(noted '83-'88).
CT-133 Silver Star	21417	Canadair built T-33A (noted '85-'88).
CF-104 Starfighter	12785	(noted '85-'88).
CL-13B Sabre Mk.6	23605	(noted '83-'88).

Hidden within the base, a compound still holds a number of CF-104 Starfighters which were retained (with Canadian 'maintenance' serials) for bdr training following their retirement (all noted '88). Strangely, they have been joined by an ex WGAF F-104F.

CF-104 Starfighter	104706	
CF-104 Starfighter	104750	
CF-104 Starfighter	104790	'875C'
CF-104 Starfighter	104799	'861C'
CF-104 Starfighter	104805	'847C'
CF-104 Starfighter	104822	'848C'
CF-104 Starfighter	104835	'849C'
CF-104 Starfighter	104843	'851C'
CF-104 Starfighter	104880	'850C'
CF-104D Starfighter	104634	'821C'
CF-104D Starfighter	104639	'856B'
CF-104D Starfighter	104648	'857C'
CF-104D Starfighter	104653	'822C'
F-104F Starfighter	2921	(c/n 5076, ex 59-5023)

SONTHOFEN

Several airframes have been reported at the Jagerkaserne here which houses a number of non-flying WGAF units. The UH-1D appears to serve as an instructional airframe whilst the others are displayed around the base. The Sabre 5 and F-104F have either moved on or are not easy to see from the outside (there are hangars here.....).

UH-1D Iroquois	7355	(c/n 8475, ex HFR.30 but Htg.64 badge) wfu here by '84 (current '88).
Fiat G-91R/3	3195	(c/n 463 with tail of 3256 c/n 526) ex Decci Base Flt (noted '84-'88).
F-104F Starfighter	2902	(c/n 5048, ex 59-4995) ex WS.10 (noted '73-'84).
F-104G Starfighter	"2203"	(c/n 6619, really 2098 with tail of c/n 6607) ex Lechfeld decoy (noted '84-'88).
CL-13A Sabre Mk.5	"BB-112"	(c/n 819, ex YA-005) (noted '82).

SPANGDAHLEM

Preserved at the main gate, having gained a reprieve from bdr duties, is F-105G

Thunderchief 62-4446 ex 128 TFS/Georgia ANG & MASDC FK088 (arr by 7.86, at the main gate by 7.88).

With 52 TFW for bdrt and systems training (the F-4Es) are the following.

Lockheed T-33A	"52"	(ex AdlA 51-9147) (noted '82-'83).
F-4C Phantom	64-0757	ex 113 TFS/Indiana ANG (arr 8.7.86, current '89).
F-4E Phantom	66-0308	ex 4485 TS (arr 12.2.89 for systems training).
F-4E Phantom	67-0260	ex 4485 TS (arr 12.2.89 for systems training).
F-101B Voodoo	"86-0701"	(arr by 7.86, noted '89).

SPEYER

Auster AOP.5 D-EMAG (c/n 992, ex MT356, HB-EQE) has been in long term storage here since its CofA expired in the mid seventies.

Preserved here by 8.88 were TF-104G Starfighter 2827 (c/n 5957, ex Est.61, positioned by the main gate here) and ex Aeronavale Beech C-45 N61912 (ex SNB-2 134706, Aeronavale 706) which was wfu by Agcat Aviation Mannheim in 1985.

STRAUBING

In the mid eighties, an Army base here (about 110 kms North East of Munchen) had a Lockheed T-33A, probably ex Belgian AF.

STUTTGART

The Daimler-Benz Museum in the Unterturkheim quarter of the city has Halberstadt C.24 D-71 (but it is displayed in Langenburg Castle) and a replica Klemm L.20 marked "D-1433".

STUTTGART/ECHTERDINGEN

Air Classik have displayed the following aircraft on the spectators' terraces at the airport here though all had moved elsewhere by 9.85.

Aero L60 Brigadyr	"OK-LGL"	(c/n 150401, ex OK-LGL, OE-BVL) (noted '78, to Dusseldorf) .
CASA 352L (Ju 52)	D-CIAL	(ex T.2B-257) ex Spanish AF (noted '78-'85, to Marl).
Douglas C-47A Dakota	"D-CORA"	(ex 43-48189, KG773, EC-AEV, SpanAF T.3-62, N8041A) (noted '80-'85, to Sinsheim).
Pembroke C.54	"G-AOJG"	(really c/n 1019, ex WGAF 5427) (noted '78, to Dusseldorf).
Lockheed T-33A	9401	(ex 51-17471) painted as "63659/TR-659/1143" (noted '78-'85, to Sinsheim).
F-84F Thunderstreak	FU-160	(ex 53-6899) ex BelgAF, w/o 5.5.70 (noted '78, to Seifertshofen).
Vertol H-21C	8317	(c/n WG17) (noted '78-'85, to Sinsheim).

UETERSEN

The Luftwaffenmuseum is situated on the non-flying Luftwaffe base on the North side of the airfield. It holds the following airframes.

AW Sea Hawk FGA.6	WV865	(ex A2554) (noted '82-'85).
BAC Lightning F.2A	XN730	ex 'J' 92 Sqn & Gutersloh decoy (noted '83-'88).
Sycamore Mk.52	7804	(c/n 13442) ex Htg.64 (noted '71-'85).
Bucker Bu 181B-1	D-EGUF	(ex RSwedAF 25017) painted as "NF+IR" (noted '82-'85).
CASA 2.111D (He 111)	"GI+AD"	ex Spanish AF (noted '82-'85).
Dornier Do 27A-4	5738	(c/n 467, ex D-EGAQ) (noted '71-'85).
Dornier DS.10	D-9534	(c/n 2) (noted '85).
Fairey Gannet AS.4	UA-110	(c/n F9391 ex XG849) painted as "UA-106" (noted '71-'88).
Fiat G-91R/3	3272	(c/n 542) ex Est.61 (noted '81-'85).
Fiat G-91R/4	BR-239	(c/n 0113) ex (noted '82-'85).
Fiat G-91T/3	3413	(c/n 0015) ex Jbg.41 (forward fuselage only, noted '82-'85).

Fiat G-91T/3	3452	(c/n 0612) ex Jbg.49 (forward fuselage only, noted '82-'85).
CM170 Magister	AA-014	(c/n 229) ex Landsberg (noted '82-'85).
Goppingen GO.3	D-6623	(c/n 410) stored.
Hawker Sea Fury T.20S	D-CACY	(ex WG599, G-9-66, ES3617) (arr 5.6.73, current '85).
HFB320 Hansa Jet	D-CARE	(c/n 1022) (noted '78-'88).
HFB320 Hansa Jet	1606	(c/n 1048, ex D-CISI) ex FBS (noted '88).
Hispano HA1112K	-	ex Spanish AF (noted '82-'85).
Hunting Pembroke C.54	5407	(c/n 102) (arr 10.6.75, current '85).
Lilienthal glider	-	replica (noted '85).
F-104F Starfighter	2906	(c/n 5055, ex 59-5002) ex WS.10 (noted '71-'85).
F-104G Starfighter	2045	(c/n 2053) w/o 30.4.69, ex gia at TsLw.1 (noted '85).
Lockheed T-33A	9469	(ex 54-1568, EB-399) ex Akg.52 & Erding, painted as "EB-399" (noted '69-'85).
N2501D Noratlas	9914	(c/n 152, ex 5330, D-9580) (arrived 16.12.80, current '88).
T-6J Harvard IV	D-FABU	(c/n CCF4-465, ex 52-8544, AA-615) (noted '73-'85).
T-6H Harvard IV	AA-622	(c/n CCF4-491, ex 52-8570) (noted '79-'82, to Oslo/Gardermoen '83).
CL-13A Sabre Mk.5	BB-704	(ex RCAF 23011) ex Oldenburg (noted '73, listed as current '86 but not actually seen for many years).
CL-13B Sabre Mk.6	JB-110	(c/n S6-1643) (noted '82-'85).
F-84F Thunderstreak	BF-106	(ex 52-6804) ex TsLw.1 (noted '66-'85).
F-84F Thunderstreak	DD-339	(ex 52-6746) ex Birkenfeld (noted outside '87).
RF-84F Thunderflash	EB-344	(ex 52-7346) ex Akg.52 (arr 4.7.67, current '85).
Schneider Grunau Baby	D-1979	(stored '85).
H-34G-II Choctaw	8034	(c/n 58-1099) ex FBS (noted '72-'85).
Vertol H-21C	8308	(c/n WG8) ex Niedermendig (noted '73-'85).

One pure guess is that the Hispano Buchon could be C.4K-134, but this remains to be confirmed - any comments?

On the civil side of the field are two derelict Cessna Centurions, both having suffered (related?) accidents in 6.84.

C210J Centurion	D-ECBB	(c/n 59091, ex N6191F)
T210L Centurion	D-EEYW	(c/n 59685, ex (N1185Q))

ULM

Displayed on a pole at the entrance to Boelcke Kaserne (in Romerstrasse) is F-84F Thunderstreak DD-373 (ex 51-1816) which came here from Roth in 1970 (current '85). See also Neu-Ulm.

UNSERE LUFTWAFFE

Not a location, but the title of the WGAF's equivalent to the RAF Exhibition Flight. Airframes used as travelling exhibits since 1980 have comprised the following.

F-104G Starfighter	"3105"	(c/n 8211, ex 2462) Jbg.32 badge (noted '76-'83).
Panavia Tornado	"4888"	(really 9801) (noted '88).
Panavia Tornado	"4300"	(really 9804 c/n P01) last flew 29.3.82, TT 498 hrs (noted '84-'86).

Note that there has been much debate over the identity of Starfighter "3105" above. I believe the above version to be correct but would welcome proof one way or the other. Another (engineless) F-104G Starfighter, 2043 (c/n 2050), was seen at various locations during 1988 and may well have joined 'Unsere Luftwaffe'.

WESTERLAND

Westerland air base on the island of Sylt houses the Marineflieger's technical training school, the Marinefliegerlehrgruppe (MLG) with a variety of Ground Instructional Airframes. The Atlantic here was the first prototype and has now been painted in spurious markings as "6100" to precede the first production WGN aircraft 6101. It wears the fin (and consequently the incorrect c/n) of c/n 03.

The Sea King crashed near Yeovil on whilst on a manufacturer's test flight. It was subsequently replaced by a second 8961 (c/n WA830) to complete the order.

Breguet Atlantic	"6100"	(c/n 01, ex 'A' Aeronavale/Breguet, "UC-301") (noted '82-'85).
F-104G Starfighter	2112	(c/n 6661) (noted '71-'84, to Wilhelmshafen).
F-104G Starfighter	2184	(c/n 7053, parts from 2568) (noted '82).
F-104G Starfighter	2211	(c/n 7081) (arrived '82, to Manching by '85).
F-104G Starfighter	2214	(c/n 7085) (arrived '82).
F-104G Starfighter	2220	(c/n 7093) (arrived '82, to Manching by '85).
F-104G Starfighter	2224	(c/n 7099) (arrived '82, noted '85).
F-104G Starfighter	2324	(c/n 7208) (noted '85).
F-104G Starfighter	2298	(c/n 7181) (noted '85).
F-104G Starfighter	2502	(c/n 8255) (arrived '82, noted '85).
F-104G Starfighter	"6951"	(c/n "1234") composite airframe (noted '82-'85).
Lockheed T-33A	"ME-11"	(ex 51-17480, 9402) ex WS.10 (noted '82, preserved near the hangars '85).
Piaggio P.149D	9181	(c/n 264) (noted '85).
Piper L-18C Super Cub	9620	(ex 54-0743) (noted '82-'85).
Sikorsky H-34G	8059	(c/n 58-1515) ex Mfg.5 (noted '82, to the gate at Kiel).
Sea King Mk.41	8961	(c/n WA765) crashed near Yeovil, UK, 16.1.74 (noted '82-'85).

The fire section were using the hulk of CL-13B Sabre Mk.6 JA-301 (c/n S6-1647) as recently as 1983.

WILDENRATH

W&R airframes at this RAFG Phantom base comprise the following.

BAC Lightning F.2A	XN778	(8537M) ex 'A' 92 Sqn (noted '78-'88).
BAC Lightning T.4	XM995	(8542M) ex 'T' 92 Sqn (noted '78-'88).
BAC Lightning F.6	XR727	(8962M) ex 'BH' 11 Sqn (arrived 10.5.88).
Hawker Hunter F.6A	XF418	(8842M) ex '16' 1 TWU, painted in 92 Sqn 'Blue Diamonds' markings (arrived 15.2.85, noted 7.88).
Hunting Pembroke C.1	WV701	(last flew 3.3.87, 8936M painted on 8.87) ex 60 Sqn. Painted in green/grey camo with black undersides by 4.88).

WILHELMSHAFEN

On display at the Marinearsenal here (Ebke-Riege Kaserne) by 1984 was F-104G Starfighter 2112 (c/n 6661) which last served as a gia at Westerland/Sylt. The kaserne is on the South West side of town and the '104 is not visible from the outside.

Lake LA-4-200 amphibian PH-GUP was stored at the civil field here during 1988.

WITTMUND

Preserved within Jg.71's kaserne in the town of Wittmund are three aircraft.

Bu 181 Bestmann	D-EOYM	(c/n 25105, ex RSwedAF 25105) from Uetersen museum.
F-104G Starfighter	2086	(c/n 6602) ex Jg.71 (noted '74-'89).
CL-13B Sabre Mk.6	JA-112	(c/n S6-....) (noted '69-'89).

WITTMUNDHAFEN

Displayed at the air base, home of Jg.71 with F-4F Phantoms, are an ex Spanish AF Hispano HA.1112M-1L Buchon (licence built Bf 109) and a Sabre.

Hispano HA1112-M1L	"12"	(c/n 194) (noted '78-'82).
CL-13B Sabre Mk.6	JA-111	(c/n S6-....) (noted '79-'89).

In use as decoys here by 7.85 were F-104G Starfighter 2631 (c/n 9183, ex Manching) and Fiat G-91R/3 3268 (c/n 538, ex Lekg.43). Both were still current during 4.89.

The wreck of F-4F Phantom 3787 (ex 72-1197, ex Jg.71) was placed on the dump following its accident on 6.6.77 and lingered into the eighties.

WOLFEGG

A Stark Turbulent D has been reported on display at the Automobilmuseum F Busch here (30 kms North West of Kempten).

WUNSTORF

The gate at this Transall base is guarded by Piaggio P.149D 9035 (c/n 049, painted as "3051" - the local post code) (noted '74-'89).

Under restoration here is an ex Luftwaffe Junkers Ju 52/3M which was recovered from the Hartvigvanzee (near Narvik, Norway) in '86 following an emergency landing with ten other Ju 52s on the frozen lake on 13.4.40 due to a heavy snowstorm.

Ground instructional airframes in Hangar 4 are shared between the technical schools TsLw.3 (actually a detachment known as 4/TsLw.3) and the BAW (<u>BerufsAusbildungsWerkstatt</u> or civilian apprentice school) and have comprised the following.

Dornier Do 27A-1	5616	(c/n 284) 'BAW' (noted '83-'88).
Dornier Do 28D/2	5824	(c/n 4099) (rear fuselage/tail noted '83-'85).
Dornier Do 28D/2	5841	(c/n 4116) (noted '85).
Dornier Do 28D/2	5890	(c/n 4165) ex Jbg.49 (noted '83-'88).
Dornier Do 28D/2	5895	(c/n 4170) (noted '85).
Fiat G-91R/3	3036	(c/n 0096) Ltg.62 badge (noted '83-'88).
Fiat G-91R/3	3245	(c/n 514) ex Lekg.43 (noted '83-'88).
Fiat G-91R/3	3300	(c/n 571, marked "3309") with Ltg.62 badge (noted '83-'88).
Fiat G-91T/3	3447	(c/n 607) ex Lekg.41 (noted '83-'88).
Piaggio P.149D	(9044)	(c/n 058) Ltg.62 badge (noted '83-'88).
Piaggio P.149D	(9056)	(c/n 073) 'BAW' (noted '83-'88).
Transall C-160D	5048	(c/n D70) ex Ltg.62 (noted '83, returned to service).

Standing out near the end of the runway is Fiat G-91R/3 3137 (c/n 405) ex Lekg.43 (noted '82-'89). This replaced F-84F Thunderstreak DE-121 (ex 52-6765, w/o 10.7.63) whose burnt out hulk remained extant on the dump here as late as 1979 (but also quoted as DE-101/52-6687, w/o 15.1.64 - comments?).

Dumped here in early '89 was a Dornier Do 27 ..35, the first two digits of the serial (55 or 56) having been painted over.

WUPPERTAL

Visible from Autobahn 46 (Hagen-Dusseldorf) between the Wuppertal-Varresbeck exit and the Sonnborn autobahn kreuz is a preserved Harvard in overall yellow colours. It is mounted on a pole and had previously been stored for many years with a local farmer. Its identity is not known (noted '85-'89).

ZWEIBRUCKEN

Based here are USAFE's 26 TRW with RF-4C Phantoms and 10 MAS with the C-23A Sherpa. Their engineers now have two airframes with which to practice the art of repairing battle damage.

F-4C Phantom	63-7583	ex 171 FIS/Michigan ANG (first noted '88 but probably arrived mid '86).
F-101B Voodoo	58-0322	ex 123 FIS/Oregon ANG & MASDC FF399, painted as "59-322/ZR" (arr by 10.85, current 9.87).

Type Index

To provide an alternative key to find one's way through the text, entries are listed below in type order by manufacturer. Readers will I trust forgive the few liberties have been taken in order to keep this section within reasonable bounds.

N

O

P

R

Y

Z

Stop Press

A publication such as this can never be fully up to date as the W&R scene is constantly changing and news arrives on the compiler's doorstep almost daily. Strenuous efforts have been made to keep this book as up to the minute as possible and the following notes advise of the latest developments which were either too recent to include in the text or which have hidden beneath the compilers vast piles of notes.

BELGIUM

At Brasschaat former Saffraanberg Do 27J DO-2 is expected to be preserved. Another ex Saffraanberg refugee, Spitfire SM-29, is to be made airworthy at Ludham, UK. Mirages BA-33, BA-46, BA-57 and BD-13 are reprtedly wfu at Bierset now with BA-01, BA-37, BD-14 and BD-15 at Koksijde for storage by 6.89. At Brussels Museum the Aermacchi AL60 is confirmed as I-MACL (marked "89240") and a new arrival is a Sukhoi Su-7BKL which came from Kbely, Czechoslovakia, on 15.4.89. Kleine-Brogel are using their F-104G FX-96 for aircraft towing training and finally Islander B-05/LE has gone to Saffraanberg as a gia following damage sustained in the hangar fire at Butzweilerhof. The Dakota at Westouter is perhaps better listed under Poperinge - it is actually a few kms South of here towards the French border.

DENMARK

Now in use for bdrt at Karup are TF-100F GT-874, RF-84F C-248, C-253, C-281 and C-473. With the fire service here is S 35E Draken 35931 marked "931BOR" (BOR = Brand og Redning/Fire and Rescue). There are plans for a new museum entitled the Nordsjaellands Flyvemuseum at Slangerup. They already have F-84G 22981 and T-33As DT-102 & DT-847 under restoration at Brondby, near Kobenhavn. The museum is also seeking Starfighters RT-667 & R-896 from Alborg, Meteor F.8 B-499 from Karup, a TF-100F from Skrydstrup (either GT-908 or GT-961) together with unknown examples of the F-86D and RF-84F. Alouette III M-388 will replace Sitfire IX 401 on display at Egeskov after the 1989 season.

FRANCE

Tiger Moth F-AZEI and Harvard F-AZDS are now in storage with Mrs Handley at Avignon (ex Montpellier). Preserved at BA274 Limoges by 6.89 were Mirage IIIC 7/2-FD, Magister 477/AJ, Mystere IVA 63 (ex Rochefort) and Super Mystere B.2 158/12-YP. However, the latter was reportedly still current at Taverny (near Paris) during 3.89 in air-superiority blue and presumably not showing her former code '12-YP'. Has she moved or is there some funny painting going on? The SNECMA museum at Melun-Villaroche now have an ex CEV Mirage IIIC from Bretigny. Stored at Montauban in 2.89 were Broussards 23, 102, 127 and 143. Nord 3202 'MDZ' and an anonymous Djinn were preserved. The ex Senegalese Dakotas at Le Bourget were scrapped in early '89, their noses turning up at Cranfield, UK. Magister 135 (ex St Jacques de Grasse) is now at the Musee de Train Miniature at Plan de Grasse. The ALAT museum at Dax has acquired Nord 3400 78 (wreck donated by Amicale des Anciens de l'ALAT), Vertol H-21C FR-69 and Sikorsky H-19 55-864 (both ex Musee de l'Air store at Villacoublay, the latter coming via Le Luc). The storage hangar at Villacoublay is to be cleared soon and the Musee de l'Air are looking for good homes for the contents.

GREECE

One of the last operational F-84s in the world, retired late '88, RF-84F Thunderflash 37050 is now preserved at Larissa.

ITALY

The Fiat G-91PAN at Gallarate is MM6243. G-91R MM6253 is preserved with 33 Gruppo Radar AM at Pescara, MM6267 is with 14 Deposito AM at Modena, MM6282 is at the Scuola Specialist at Capua and MM6391 went to the 11 Deposito Centrale AM at Orte near Viterbo. MM6298 and MM6410 are for the Museo della Scienza e della Tecnica at Milano.

LUXEMBOURG

Cessna F172E D-EMAX (c/n 0055) was stored, unmarked, outside the hangars here during 8.88.

PORTUGAL

Derelict at Funchal throughout 1987 at least was Cessna 172 D-ELEE which appeared to have ground looped. The Noratlas was apparently blown up by revolutionaries in 1975! The compiler has also been advised of a scrapyard between Sintra and Lisbon which contains a substantial number of F-86Fs - more details please Ralph!

SWEDEN

On the dump at Halmstad in 6.89 were J 35Bs 35253/09, 35264/68 (both ex F 10), 35.../09 (ex F 4) and J 35Fs 35418 (ex F 16), 35474, 35516/19 (ex F 13), 35542/46, 35548/05, 35573/32 (all ex F 10). Preserved at Karlsborg in 6.89 were Alouette II (Hkp 2) 02412/91 (ex F 6) and J 29C 29937/09. On the dump were J 35Fs 35504/13 and 35535/01 (both ex F 10).

SWITZERLAND

At Dubendorf the nose of Vampire FB.6 J-1139 is in Hall 5 of the museum. Other notes from 8.89 are that at Beromunster P.66B Oscar HB-EMM was reduced to a dumped fuselage only, at Triengen F150L HB-CDA had a wing missing and at Zurich the DC-8 TU-TCP was still on the dump with another (obscured) aircraft, probably the Twin Otter. Back in 1987 an SA360 Dauphin was reported just on the Swiss side of the French border near Geneva. It was all white with blackened windows and could have been a mock up.

TURKEY

F-104G Starfighter 9082/4-082 (ex BelgAF FX-27) is now preserved at Bandirma. Inside an Army camp by the lake at Egirdir in 5.89 was a Dakota fuselage in yellow, brown and green camouflage. There are now some thirty five F-100 Super Sabres (including F-100Cs 41741, 41782, 41944, 42068, 42115, 42222, 42242, 42276, 42303; F-100Ds 52768, 52769, 53596, 63083, 63355 and F-100F 86976) lying derelict at Konya with another fifty plus in storage to become drones with Flight Systems at Mojave, California.

WEST GERMANY

F-15C Eagle 00007/BT is no longer current at Bitburg. Former Patrouille de France CM170 Magister 545 is now displayed at Berlin/Tegel in the French sector. At Buckeburg P.149D 9147 had been joined in the gia role by ex FDG G-91R 9942 by 5.89. Former Bruntingthorpe F-100D 42239 is expected to guard the gate at Hahn. At Hermeskeil a welcome arrival is MiG-15UTI 301 of the Hungarian AF. The Koblenz museum should by now have ex AdlA Mirage IIIC 10. Zweibrucken also has F-4C 37423 as a gia and there is a third F-4C here in use for bdrt in the shelter area. The mysterious DC-8 nose with Air Classik at Frankfurt Airport is one of the three broken up at Beek (Neths) though I have lost the note which tells me which one.

THE END